Jacques Waardenburg
Muslims and Others

Religion and Reason

Volume 41

Walter de Gruyter · Berlin · New York
2003

Jacques Waardenburg

Muslims and Others

Relations in Context

Walter de Gruyter · Berlin · New York
2003

∞ Printed on acid-free paper which falls within the guidelines of the ANSI
to ensure permanence and durability.

Library of Congress Cataloging-in-Publication Data

Waardenburg, Jacques.
  Muslims and others : relations in context / Jacques Waardenburg.
      p.   cm. − (Religion and reason)
  Includes bibliographical references and indexes.
  ISBN 3-11-017627-0 (hardcover : alk. paper)
    1. Islam − Relations.   2. Muslims − Non-Muslim countries.
  3. Europe − Ethnic relations.   4. Islamic countries − Relations
  − Europe.   5. Europe − Relations − Islamic countries.   I. Title.
  II. Series.

  BP171 .W29   2003
  297.2′8 − dc21

ISBN 3-11-017627-0

Bibliographic information published by Die Deutsche Bibliothek

Die Deutsche Bibliothek lists this publication in the Deutsche Nationalbibliografie; detailed
bibliographic data is available in the Internet at < http://dnb.ddb.de >.

Printed in Germany
Cover design: Christopher Schneider, Berlin
Disk conversion: Readymade, Berlin

Preface

This book starts out from the fact that human beings are different, not only as individual persons but also as groups. People have dealt with this awe-inspiring fact in various ways in the course of history. Often they have closed themselves off from those who are different, or they have tried to dominate and subjugate them. In necessity, people have opened up to exchange with others who could offer what they need. In certain circumstances, some people have become interested in other peoples, have tried to communicate with them, and wanted to know them better. Cultures have had periods of opening up and shutting themselves off in given situations, and there have been reasons for this. They have coped with others in different ways at different times and places.

In Islamic studies, most attention has naturally been given to the study of Islam and Muslim societies as subjects in themselves. This book's interest, however, is in the various openings that Muslims and Muslim societies have shown to the world beyond Islam at given times and places. I am interested in encounters and interactions that have taken place between Muslim and non-Muslim peoples, between the world of Islam and the worlds of other cultures and religions. This also takes into account the imaginary dimension that is so rich in Muslim cultures.

If it is true that at certain times Islam has represented a world more or less closed in on itself, in other periods we find interesting openings, exchanges, and interaction with others, at least in certain regions and among certain groups. Wars have been waged, like everywhere, but Muslims have also pursued economic and cultural exchange with the outside world. Where necessary, Muslims have shown a readiness to learn from others and their culture and to communicate cultural achievements to others who have shown an interest in them. Where and when has this happened? What do we know about Muslim perceptions of the world beyond Islam, not only in the West but also in Asia and Africa? And what do we know about Muslim thought and imagination concerning non-Muslim societies and individuals?

With such questions in mind, the focus of research shifts from Islam to those Muslims who have been actors in such exchanges. How have Muslim societies, groups, and individuals responded to those non-Muslim "others" with whom they have increasingly come into contact? In what

situations and contexts has interaction taken place? What kind of interaction has it been and in which circumstances has it developed into further
communication, cooperation, and dialogue? What has been the role of
experience and that of imagination in Muslim relations with others?

* * *

In the present state of scholarship, we have arrived at a better understanding of the ways in which Islam as a socio-religious system, civilization, and
religion developed in the course of time. We are better informed about the
various contexts in which encounters between Muslims and others have
taken place. There is a rich documentation about the nineteenth and
twentieth centuries, precisely the period in which the Muslim world
became increasingly subjugated to Western nations. This dependence was
most visible during the colonial period; it decreased during the Cold War
but it has increased again since. An important element that has conditioned relations between Muslims and others during the twentieth century
has been the ongoing transformation of Muslim societies. This has entailed processes of modernization and also the emergence of new interpretations of Islam.

We have acquired some insight into the new ways in which Islam and
in particular its sources, the Qur'ān and *Sunna*, have become a new
"resource pool" for Muslims. This has been happening in different ways
in the various parts of the Muslim world, especially since the mid-nineteenth century. "Islam" has always been a resource for maintaining and
articulating Muslim identity through trying historical events and developments. When Muslims defend themselves against pressures, both from
outside and from the powerful in their own societies, Islam represents a
source of resistance. In sometimes seemingly chaotic situations in Muslim
societies, Islam has provided norms, values, and calls to order.

How can we arrive at a better understanding of the relations between
Muslims and others? For a long time, the key to such understanding was
supposed to lie on an intellectual, even a legal and doctrinal level. It
was known that Muslims can interpret, practice, and apply Islam in
various ways. It was then held that the interpretations given to Islam—
the relevant texts of the Qur'ān and *Sunna*, and their applications in the
Sharī'a—would determine the ways in which Muslims relate or at least
should relate to others. Thinking along these lines, a number of experts
hypothesized that relations between Muslims and others would improve
when the former developed a more rational and "enlightened" interpretation of their Islam, a kind of liberal Islam. This may be true for
intellectuals, but it is only one side of the picture. There is another side as
well, that of social practice, and this is what counts for the majority of
people.

The intellectual and ideological articulations of Islam that Muslims have made concerning their relations to others have not developed in a vacuum; rather, they have had much to do with interactions that have affected both parties. On the one hand, a stern, rigid doctrinal fixation of Islam, if it is enforced, can determine views about and also the treatment of non-Muslims. An example is the attitude taken by the Tālibān in Afghanistan, who developed and applied their ideas against a Wahhābī background, in isolation and in a war situation. On the other hand, the presence of intense social contacts between Muslims and others, for instance in common working groups, cannot but influence and "human-ize" the views that people develop of others, warming their practical relations with each other, whatever the doctrines. Unless there is a serious conflict or a situation of oppression that prevents any communication in advance, an existing social interaction may have an important impact on the way Muslims identify what their religion says about attitudes to be taken toward others. If there is no interaction, doctrine will stifle commu-nication.

In the light of this, the study of interactions that have taken place in the past between Muslim and other individuals, groups, societies, and cul-tures obtains a fresh significance. Where have channels of interaction existed between Muslims and others, and where has this involved commu-nication between them?

In treating this subject we should not only take a Western point of view and start out from typically Western (American, French, or other) notions of communication. We should also take into account the point of view and judgment of the Muslims concerned. How have they viewed and judged particular interactions with non-Muslims? Where have they recognized or identified real communication? A scholarly study of interactions and an impartial appreciation of communication has to take into account the views of both sides.

It may very well be that, as a rule, communication between people coming from very different cultures is practically absent. This is not necessarily due to unwillingness, lack of interest, or incapacity on the part of the people concerned. It may very well have its cause in a lack of opportunity, when people live far apart, or unsurmountable cultural differences like language and questions of sensitivity. It may also be due to structural factors such as unfulfilled human needs or unbalanced power relations leading to conflict, oppression, and the will to destruction.

In the shared history of Muslim and other societies and cultures, some periods have been more fertile, witnessing discovery, exchange, and coop-eration, whereas others have been more arid, marked by aloofness, dis-trust, and conflict. The results have varied from creative communication to destructive alienation. Muslim stances toward others must therefore always be seen in their precise historical and social contexts and in the light of prevailing values at the time. As far as possible, one should also take into account the perspectives of the actors themselves and what they have thought is prescribed, allowed, or forbidden.

Muslim attitudes toward others, as they have shown up in actual encounters and relations, have not been as arbitrary, irrational, and negative as may seem at first sight and as many minorities in Muslim territories have believed and sometimes portrayed. As everywhere, abuses of power have occurred, but that in itself has little to do with Islam. Scholarship should try to uncover rationality even where people speak of something irrational, especially when religion or morality is at stake.

I would hope that this book may encourage further precise research on encounters between Muslims and others in the past and at present. In what situations have they taken place? What have the religions or ideologies of the parties concerned taught about meeting others? How have the people themselves in fact acted in such encounters? What can be said about the role not only of practical needs, but also of imagination and broader reflection in these encounters?

* * *

Studying Islam and Muslim societies at the present time, however, forces an author to take note of existing constraints and forms of oppression against which Muslims, like others, cannot but revolt. It seems to me that the time is past when scholars could study Islam only as an ideal or a spirituality, or—for some—as an ideological or political threat. Attention has to be paid to Muslims as they actually live. Research on Muslims and their Islam is not only the study of something foreign, but also something that is part of shared human experience.

Slowly, indeed, a new view of humanity seems to be emerging: as a reality of people who are incredibly diverse, fundamentally different, "others" for each other. In former times, from a Western perspective, humanity was classified according to religions, races, cultures, states. Nowadays we can no longer have such an overall view of humanity from above, so to speak. We have become explorers in a long-term adventure and we can be glad if we can glimpse, from time to time, the contours of that broader humanity of which we are part and which includes Muslims as well as many others.

To be fair, it should be admitted that much misery that has befallen Muslims in many parts of the world during the last two centuries or so has been due less to Islam than to poor leadership unable to respond to a number of forces that have imposed themselves on Muslim societies, often from the West. The other way around, during these two centuries the West in its imperial strivings has been particularly hurt by Muslim resistance. It seems to me that we have here a key to understanding some of the misunderstandings between Muslims and others, especially from the West. The worst for Muslims, perhaps, has been when others have not respected Islam, their religion.

* * *

The seeds of this kind of interest were sown in my parental home and during my education, where one of the rules for learning and understanding was careful reading and listening. When I was eighteen, I went out into the world, that is to say, studying in Amsterdam and later in Leiden, Paris, and further. I slowly became more critical, but I kept on listening and observing.

With my interest in Islam, many of the "others" I happened to meet were Muslims. My research interests developed through encounters with L. Massignon, W. Cantwell Smith, J. Berque, G.E. von Grunebaum, and others between 1956 and 1968. I taught in Los Angeles, Utrecht, and Lausanne between 1964 and 1995; and I put my findings into writing at NIAS in Wassenaar, at the *Wissenschaftskolleg* in Berlin, in Toronto and at Harvard, and last but not least in the hospitable Clubroom of Crêt Bérard near Lausanne. Without mentioning any persons here, I feel grateful for the support I have received from various quarters at often decisive moments, from people letting me do my own work, go my own way, hatch my own texts. Writing this book while using some earlier publications has been a one-man adventure, for whose result I am the only one responsible.

* * *

All the texts in this book were written essentially before September 11, 2001. Yet, the issue of relations between Muslims and others has become still more relevant in the shadow of that day and with the sense of insecurity following it. I have observed Westerners distancing themselves from things Islamic and a certain diffidence toward Muslims who might be on the wrong side.

One may question what consequences violence and the fear of violence may have for relations between Muslims and Westerners in particular. The West bitterly needs several things. First, moral resistance to an atmosphere of threats and fears. Second, continuing education about the Muslim world and the Western world itself, including Western relations with the Muslims and their world in the past and at present. Third, struggle for a healthy and modest mindset when dealing with matters concerning Islam, especially if one knows little about it. Fourth, a sound instinct to let Muslims decide about Islam themselves. And, of course, we should try by all means to distinguish truth from half-truths, moral from immoral action.

When people in the West wonder about their relations with Muslims, it may be relevant to look at the ways in which Muslims have seen and see their relations with others, including Westerners, and why. Ultimately, we all face an ethical problem: how to live with each other without automatically having negative reflexes to things that are Islamic or ... Western.

I may add a few technical remarks. The style of the chapters varies; scholarly papers with many notes and references are found side by side with essays that are primarily reflective, with hardly any notes.

Each chapter has appended a listing of Selected Literature on the main subject(s) discussed in it. A list of these subjects can be found at the end of the book, on pp. 499-501. In this way, the book can be used not only for reading texts, but also for consulting short bibliographies on specific subjects under the general theme "Muslims and Others". Readers interested in Islam itself are referred to my earlier book *Islam: Historical, Social, and Political Perspectives* (Walter de Gruyter: Berlin and New York, 2002).

For the transliteration of Arabic terms, the current simplified English system has been used.

* * *

There is, of course, a certain pretension and generalization in the title of this book. When we speak of "Muslims", we are always dealing concretely with particular ethnic and national groups, with certain movements and institutions, with specific communities and individuals. It will always be possible to find exceptions to generalizing statements about Muslims and those whom they saw as others.

There is also a certain ambiguity in the term "others", used here in the sense of "non-Muslims". Muslims are sensitive to the distinction between those who are part of Islam and those who are not. Sometimes they have been concerned more with themselves and sometimes more with those who were different. As everywhere, there are people who are strongly aware that they themselves are different from others; this leads them to reflect primarily on their own identity. But everywhere, there are also people who are especially aware of the fact that others are quite different from themselves; this leads them to think more about those other people's identity. The notion of "others" is important. Generally speaking, people tend to stress what they consider their own identity if they feel a difference with "others". The others have a positive function: if there are no others, there is no self.

In short, this book deals with Muslims and Others from a Muslim point of view. Here, Westerners are others. From a simplified Western point of view, however, it is Muslims who are others. And "Western Muslims" are a special case to which we are not yet accustomed: they happen to be "other" both to ordinary Muslims and to ordinary Westerners.

At the present time, we are becoming aware that all of us are just others to each other and that we are all different. May this book set its Muslim and other readers to further thinking and contribute in its way to over-coming some misunderstandings between Muslims and at least some others.

The scholarly study of relations between Muslims and others has certain implications for our conceptualization of Islam and for the ways in which we study Muslim culture and societies. This will be the subject of a volume, *Islam, Islamic Studies, and the Study of Religions*, as a sequel to the present one.

Lausanne, December 20, 2002

Content

Section 1: Three Monotheistic Religions

Chapter 1
Christians, Muslims, Jews, and their Religions 39

Chapter 2
Three Monotheistic Religions: Structure and Patterns of Meaning 64

Chapter 6
World Religions Seen in Islamic Light 162

Chapter 7
Twentieth Century Writings about Other Religions:
A Classification 199

Chapter 8
Some Observations on Muslim Studies of Religions 218

Section 4: Muslims and the West, Muslims in the West

Chapter 9
Some Muslim Reflections on the West

Chapter 10
Europe and its Muslim Neighbors: Glimpses of Dialogue

Section 6: Muslims and Others in Processes of Change

Introduction

1. 1950–2000: Contacts with Muslims: Memories in Context

Europe has had nearly fourteen centuries of interaction with Muslim peoples south, southeast, and east of Europe, and further away in Asia and Africa. Since the eighth century C.E., Muslims have been living in regions that later came to be considered part of Europe. Interactions between Europeans and Muslims have become part of a common history of which we are increasingly aware.

Arab, Tatar, and Turkish invasions and conquests from the south, the east, and the southeast of the continent continued to the end of the seventeenth century, leading to a vigorous self-defense and to reconquests. By the end of the eighteenth century, the movement was reversed. It was now Europeans who started to occupy the larger part of the world inhabited by Muslim peoples, and it was now the Muslims who were on the defense. And just as, in the medieval period, Europeans had defended themselves and had pursued their Crusades largely in the name of Christianity, in modern times Muslims took up their own defense while referring to their religion, Islam.

Tensions and conflicts between European and Muslim peoples have often been described as a struggle between two religions, Christianity and Islam, or between two civilizations, a Western and a Muslim one. Such a presentation helped to justify the conflicts, wars, and conquests that took place and the hardships that the winning party imposed on the losing one. Yet, certainly during the colonial period, European decision-makers were well aware that economic and political interests, rather than cultural curiosity or social generosity, were the reasons they occupied Muslim and other foreign territories.

In the colonial period, contacts between Muslims and other people in general became more and more conditioned by the fact of European domination and the rest of the world's dependence. This political context conditioned primarily relationships between Muslims and Europeans, but to some extent also relations between Muslims and other people in the Middle East, Africa, and Asia, including Hindus and Jews. This remained true even if there was no visible European presence.

One of the side effects of colonial relationships was that contacts between Muslims and Europeans were largely restricted to Europeans who had come from the colonizing country and who mostly occupied leading positions in the colonies. Many Muslims were led to identify Europe with the particular "mother country" of these Europeans. The other way around, most Europeans tended to identify "Islam" with the Muslim societies existing in their own respective colonies.

Constructive contacts between Muslims and Europeans at the time were conditioned by the dominant position of the latter and by the economic and political relationships that existed between a given Muslim country and the European one on which it depended. European domination, however, provoked increasing socio-cultural, intellectual, and then political resistance. The first resistance accentuated the distance that Muslim peoples felt existed between themselves and Europeans socially, culturally, and religiously. The second led to the emergence of intellectuals interested in Western culture and prepared to learn from European technology and science while mostly affirming and articulating their own identity and values. The third led to the nationalist ideologies and movements that won nearly everywhere.

* * *

As a somewhat biographical presentation, I would like to recount some memories that indicate how my own interest in research on relations between Muslims and others developed. Born in Haarlem, the Netherlands, in 1930 and growing up there, I myself had no direct experience of the colonial situation. Yet, as a boy I heard stories from and about relatives who lived in "the East Indies" and who often referred to Islam. Immediately after World War Two, there were heated discussions in the country about the future of the colony, that is to say the possible loss of the Indies and its riches.

Indonesia became independent in December 1948, and subsequently many people came to the Netherlands, born Dutchmen, people from mixed marriages, and also persons without Dutch ancestors. They had a difficult time adapting themselves to the Dutch climate, the Dutch ways of life, and the structure of Dutch society at the time. In the Middle East, Israel had been established that same year and enjoyed sympathy after the tragedy of the Jews under the Nazis. A year earlier, in 1947, Pakistan had been created. In all three cases, Indonesia as well as Israel and Pakistan, "Islam" was in the air. Politically, it represented for us the other side, against vested interests. A number of Muslim countries had acquired or were struggling for independence. But more broadly, it represented another world, socially, culturally, and religiously. Islam emerged as something significant, a reality different from European culture and also from India and Israel.

In the early 1950s, in some quarters among the postwar generation in the Netherlands, new questions related to Islam started to arise beside the older, existing ideas. The new presence of Muslim students from various countries contributed to this. I remember a talk by Seyyed Hussein Alatas from Malaysia, who was a student in Amsterdam in the early 1950s, about Islam and democracy. It impressed me not because it was true, but because the speaker believed in what he said; he believed in Islam and he spoke well. I was interested in such things and made it my habit to listen to what Christians, Jews, and Muslims said about themselves. In fact, I was keen on finding out what religions like Islam and Christianity, with their respective messages, represented in the wider world of post-colonial times.

After the experience of an oppressive occupation during World War Two and an exhausting postwar rebuilding of the country, it was a kind of liberation to meet and listen to people for whom the world was larger than the Low Countries. I met Dutchmen who had seen the wider world and students from Asian and African countries who had come to Holland. In that context, "dialogue" was a lived experience. We practiced it out of curiosity and the need for communication, long before dialogue became an ideal and an ideology. A Dutch fellow student who worked in Leiden with Christian and Muslim students from Indonesia had attended dialogue meetings of Christians and Muslims that had been organized in Bhamdoun, Lebanon, in 1954 and 1956. He considered them a major event in the history of Christian-Muslim relations. The Netherlands was a good place to gain first-hand information about international encounters.

After my studies of theology and the science of religion at the University of Amsterdam, I made my internal migration in Holland with an interest in Islam. In 1953, I worked on Arabic grammar on my own and pursued further study at the University. From September 1954 until the end of December 1955, I studied Arabic and Islam in Leiden. I lived then at a newly founded Institute of Social Studies in The Hague, amid graduate students from the Middle East and South and Southeast Asia. This was the beginning of further migration, finding my way by moving abroad, realizing a dream found in books written for Dutch boys in the 1920s and 1930s.

At the outset of 1956, I moved to Paris, with the first drafts of a dissertation in my suitcase. Subsequently, I would live my twenties and thirties largely what was called "abroad", in Paris, the Middle East, Montreal, and Los Angeles. At the time it was not impossible to find a fellowship, funding for a research project, or even a temporary teaching post.

The first Muslim country I visited was Tunisia. I arrived there by the end of March 1956, a few days after the country had gained its independence from France. The boat from Marseille was welcomed with a fanfare on the *quai* of La Marsa, and there was a festive atmosphere in the country, which I traveled from north to south. The enthusiastic expectations for the future expressed by so many Tunisians I met in that spring of 1956 were the finest introduction I could wish to the Muslim world I had been looking for. I could start practicing my Arabic and listened to Tunisians speaking of their country and Islam.

At the time, relations between the older colonizing and colonized countries moved toward economic and social development programs and the recognition of Eastern as different from Western value systems. In the mid–1950s, UNESCO launched its major East-West project to promote educational, cultural, and scholarly exchange between Eastern and Western countries. I was lucky enough to be admitted as a fellow in this scheme in the year 1959–60, to visit Iran and Egypt. I had completed the first draft of my dissertation in Paris and could move eastward. This journey was a decisive experience. Even though I did not attain the fluency in Arabic and Persian I had hoped for, I experienced an open world and certain forms of communication with people in the Muslim world. Since this one-year travel shaped my interest in "Muslims and Others" in a more definite way, it may be useful to recount some memories of it.

Looking back now, more than forty years later, I am amazed to realize that someone just finishing his doctoral dissertation could visit the region and meet people with relatively little trouble in 1959–60. Today it would be impossible. There was an incredible hospitality from all kinds of people, and there were practical facilities at local and Western institutions all over the region.

One needed permission, but could then visit Karbala and Najaf in Iraq, places of Shī'ī learning, then in a still nearly medieval setting. Besides Iraqi, a number of Iranian and some other Shī'ī students and 'ulamā' had settled down here, sometimes for lifelong study. They imposed their authority as the "learned ones" with their archetypal, seemingly stern faces, but were willing to answer questions.

One could travel freely from Iraq to Iran. I had facilities to travel in Iran, see the country, visit monuments, and meet professors, intellectuals, and politicians. People were willing to assist a visitor from abroad and to talk; they were proud to show their places. I met persons on all social levels. I discussed with students for hours over tea while living at a university dormitory. I met erudite scholars and was even admitted to the Shah's summer palace, where I was able to pose a thousand and one questions to the extremely benevolent and polite Minister of Court in August 1959.

After Iran, I made a halt in Lebanon before continuing to Egypt, the next country on my program, where I worked in Cairo from October 1959 until April 1960. The first three months I lived in a dormitory of University City in Guiza, where I caught a bad case of jaundice; a friendly professor had me hospitalized just in time. I remember a festive speech by Nasser at the University on a great day of awarding cultural prizes to Egyptians who had distinguished themselves. Then, staying at the French Archeological Institute, I became more immersed in the French-speaking part of Egyptian society.

Nasser had succeeded in bringing Syria and Egypt and later also Yemen together in the United Arab Republic. He enjoyed fantastic and moving popularity as *the* Arab leader among the students I met at the time. Egypt's economic policy of the late 1950s, however, gave a blow to the wealthier classes, and many Greeks and Italians who had lived here for generations were leaving then.

Moreover, internal security had become a major issue, with much arbitrariness. French diplomats, including the Arabist André Miquel, had simply been put on trial. A Dutch professor in the English Department of the University of Cairo, whom I knew as an exceedingly careful, almost shy man averse to politics, was arrested at night. The embassy was mobilized for his defense and it turned out that, for some reason or other, he had been falsely accused. The state increasingly imposed itself on society, and after a few months I started to sense an atmosphere of suspicion both about what the state was planning to do next and about the willingness of people to follow their leader to the end. Situations and relations are complex in the Middle East, including Egypt, and if it is difficult to know the truth about what happens anywhere, it is even more difficult here.

Beyond the troublesome political scene, however, I remember promising developments in relations between Christians and Muslims in Egypt during the months I spent there in 1959–60. In contrast to the Copts, who kept to themselves, and the Protestants, who had their own programs, the Greek Catholics (called "Melkites") took remarkable initiatives toward dialogue and cooperation with Muslims. The Christian Melkite community consisted largely of descendants of Syrian and Lebanese immigrants who had come to Egypt at the end of the nineteenth century. Under Cromer, officially British "Agent and Consul-General" in Egypt (1883–1907), the country here and there started to prosper, and a number of these Christian immigrants had fared well economically. Mary Kahil, who came from such a family and who had many personal contacts including with some *sheykhs* of al-Azhar, was a central figure in the rapprochement between Christians and Muslims in Egypt.

The Dominican convent in Cairo Abbasiya had established an Institute of Oriental Studies and was focusing on improving relationships with Muslim intellectuals. Georges Chehata Anawati, O.P. (1905–94), of Syrian and Orthodox origin, was a leading figure in these Christian initiatives for dialogue with Muslims. The Institute of Oriental Studies at the time counted some French and other scholars of international reputation.

These initiatives and developments among Uniate Christians in Egypt preceded the Second Vatican Council (1962–5). They played a certain role in inducing the Catholic Church to grant a certain recognition to the Islamic faith, and they spoke out in favor of interreligious dialogue. This meant a breakthrough in the Catholic Church's traditional stance and brought a new outlook, though the Church's fundamental claims did not really change.

Scholars and visitors agree that religion has been and still is a central issue in the Middle East, though they may interpret it differently. Speaking practically, to have any human contact, cooperation, and dialogue in the region, one has to pay attention to the problem of religious diversity, also within the various religions themselves. I had learned this when I studied, and it was amply confirmed during my travel in 1959–60. Religious institutions and dignitaries, priests and 'ulamā' were visibly present in Cairo. Religious communities and religion meant something different here and something more than what we are or were used to calling "religion" in Europe. Religion clearly was an issue, though not necessarily a religious one. Whether it was Muslims or non-Muslims who broached the subject, I was told by certain Westerners at the time that religion, like sex, was no subject of discussion in this part of the world. My experience has been the opposite, but then my curiosity and way of discussing may have been different from theirs.

After Egypt, I spent a short time in Lebanon and sent off the books and documents I had collected. For some two weeks I was then in Jordan, saw the appalling conditions of the refugee camps, and collected documentation. This was in May 1960. The refugees had arrived here from Palestine/Israel in 1948 and 1949. In 1967, many more would follow from the West Bank when it was occupied in the June war.

In Jordan I proceeded to East Jerusalem, which was under Jordanian rule. Mount Scopus was still green; once a week an Israeli bus came to collect books from the Hebrew University Library that had been built there. In East Jerusalem I found accommodation in a Franciscan guest house. In the next days, I saw the holy places for the first time and I visited monuments in the Old City, which was still very lively at the time. I remember the many monks and priests in the streets and also the great number of pilgrims and visitors from the West. There was no sign of disorder, and the place with the Jordanian guards in their typical dress impressed me as a sort of tourist resort with special kinds of facilities. Yet, when speaking casually but attentively with local people, Muslims as well as Christians, they would hint at the catastrophe of 1948. Apparently, as far as I remember, nobody at the time imagined that the situation could become still much worse.

I have an inquisitive nature. After having been in Muslim countries for more than ten months, I wanted to cross another border. One evening, with my Dutch passport, I crossed the Wall through the Mandelbaum Gate, to see the other side, Israel. The first thing that struck me in West Jerusalem when walking around the following morning and entering a Jewish shop was the appearance of Israeli women. They were terribly self-imposing and talkative, and so different from what I had seen of the fair sex in the months before.

Israel was very alive, self-conscious, and proud of being a democratic and open country. I could travel quietly all around from north to south and east to west. Back in Jerusalem and Tel Aviv, I collected documentation, visited Israeli institutions, and saw monuments. I was able to meet a number of personalities, whom I subjected as usual to a crossfire of questions. I listened; most Israelis were rather ignorant about what was going on in the Arab lands, although they often claimed to know about it. Sometimes they wanted to explain it to me.

All of them were proud of the Israeli achievements of the first twelve years (1948–60) and were enthusiastic about telling or showing things to me. I was very well received and with a certain warmth. Holland was known to be pro-Israel, and I met several Dutch immigrants—some from before 1939—who told me a lot about their life and experience. I was impressed by the work of the Israeli Orientalists. The well-known scholar of Turkish, Professor Uriel Heyd, in charge of Oriental Studies at the Hebrew University, kindly received me in his office. He pleaded convincingly that scholars working in this field should see their work as a vocation. Through their work they should build bridges between peoples from different cultures, also in times of tension. I could not agree with him more. That was in 1960.

In West Jerusalem, I had the opportunity to meet Martin Buber (1878–1965). I did not mention this particularly to people at the time. I had simply looked up his number in the West Jerusalem telephone book and called him. I told him who I was and that I had read some of his writings as a student in Amsterdam. He invited me to visit him at his home one morning in May 1960. He had just then finished his monumental innovative translation of the Hebrew Bible into German. Franz Rosenzweig (1886–1929) had undertaken this work together with him after World War One, and he continued it after Rosenzweig's death. Buber had committed himself to the mutual recognition and cooperation of Jews and Arabs inside and outside Israel. He complained to me bitterly—but with complete self-control—about the Zionist pressures to the contrary. He had harsh words for the young Shimon Peres, who wanted Israel to prepare for a nuclear weapons program before engaging in any negotiations with Muslim countries. Together with a medical doctor, Buber edited a journal called *Ner* for cooperation between Jews and Arabs. It was clear to me that, whatever his worldwide fame, the ideas of Buber, as a man of "truth and reconciliation", were rejected outright by the utterly defensive Israeli leadership. I felt that the Israeli state could be hard on its citizens. Buber died two years before the June war of 1967 that would change the Israeli scene completely.

When I recall the standards Buber set at that time, the social ethics of human beings and the special vocation of the Jewish people, then Israeli society is in a moral crisis. Instead of a dialogue with others as "I and Thou", people seem to be living and acting out a monologue among themselves. They are withdrawing into a ghetto, with regard not only to Palestinian and Arab life but also to many thoughtful and reflective people living elsewhere.

The recollection of that conversation with Buber inspires me to raise some essential questions now in his spirit. (1) To what extent can the situation of the country now (Christmas 2002) be considered the direct result of forty years of Israeli and/or Palestinian policies? (2) Ariel Sharon declared war against the Palestinians as "terrorists" in Lebanon in 1982 and in the Occupied Territories in 2001. Can Israel allow itself to continue this war not only militarily, given the sacrifice of Israeli victims and the economic hardship entailed, but also morally, given the way it is conducted and given the norms and values of Judaism? (3) Where do the responsibilities for the conscious destruction of the infrastructure of Palestinian society and humiliation of Palestinian people taken as hostage for suicide bombings against Israelis lie? (4) As the Jews were traumatized in the past, now a traumatizing of the Palestinians is taking place. What are the consequences for all people concerned and their relations with others, now and in the future? (5) Will people on both sides be ready one day to admit that the use of brute force failed as a solution? (6) Can all those who have become guilty of crimes against humanity be judged for them one day when peace has been imposed? In a way, it is good that Buber did not live to see what has happened since 1967.

Looking back on these Middle East experiences more than forty years later, I recall seeing people in great poverty, if not economic and financial despair, but I do not remember any complaint about it. Instead, I remember the great dignity of these people, their respect for each other, and their great openness and hospitality toward visitors. I was spoiled continuously. Societies seemed not to have been organized rationally yet. They consisted of groups and circles leading their own lives with their relatives and friends. The 1950s saw the beginning of development projects that would change these societies. People would be involved in major social processes that they did not imagine but that would overcome them. Thinking it over again, however, I must say that nearly all these societies were under rather strict police control. The people were not free: sometimes they referred to sad political events of the past that should be avoided in the future. When I inquired further, they were sometimes ready to speak. Despite all of this, they seemed not to live in an atmosphere of anxiety and I perceived little nervousness on their part. In fact, I remember quite courageous men and women.

A journey like this, outside the tourist circuit and mostly also outside official circles, belongs to the past. I could still be openly inquisitive in a position of continuously meeting people, without having particular tasks or responsibilities. There was an intense joy in moving from contact to contact, with the possibility of questioning and simply asking people about their life and work. My particular form of communication has always been to pose questions, questions that were often prepared but further improvised during the conversation and then formulated on the spot. I have had this attitude throughout my life, and I am sure that many people resent such a habit. Yet, the people I met during this travel apparently did not.

In a way, this journey was a sort of sensitivity training toward Middle Eastern people in their own contexts. Like other introverts, I have always been rather self-concerned, moving in my own world of experience. Conversations with Louis Massignon between 1956 and 1959 in Paris had certainly been conducive to a certain openness to "the East". Unlike those whom Edward Said calls "Orientalists", I am not aware of having had a particular desire to dominate the East or a delight in taking a hegemonic attitude toward Easterners. The "East" to me was rather a dimension of experiencing things. My journey was indeed toward "the East" and I was taken up by this "East" as a kind of life-world. On my return, I set up an "Eastern room" at home to work in. Yet, during my travel I was not as politically naive as it may seem, and I shunned what is now called "security matters". Instinctively I feel this to be a dirty expression.

I should add one more thing. Before going to the Middle East, I spent more than two years in Paris. Probably it was French culture with its particular ways of thinking and its typical forms of expressing oneself that made the transition to Middle Eastern cultures somewhat easier. If I had been prepared through German, British, or American ways of life, for instance, my ways of communicating would certainly have been different. But given a basic sensitivity, I am sure there would have been communication. And as I remember, I was constantly helped on all sides.

Returning to Europe, I enjoyed seeing and experiencing a softer ambience than the rather harsh, male, tough Middle East. I enjoyed meeting women after having constantly moved within patriarchal structures.

Thanks to the generous help of Gilbert Delanoue, whom I had met in Cairo, my dissertation took a really "French" shape, and in July 1961 I received my doctor's degree at the University of Amsterdam. It concerned scholarly image formation of Islam, a case study of the work of five prominent Western scholars of Islam. It was a rather theoretical subject

suggested by C.A.O. van Nieuwenhuijze when we met at the Institute of
Social Studies in The Hague in 1953. How and why did various recognized and distinguished Islamic scholars from different backgrounds conceptualize Islam the way they did? In an unexpected way, by questioning
the categories with which we conceptualize Islam and through an internal
criticism of current concepts and ideas, such a study can indirectly promote a fresh and better understanding of Islam. Both Orientalists and
Middle Eastern intellectuals showed a certain interest in the subject. The
question of the theoretical framework that underlies and directs our
research is indeed a fundamental one, also in Islamic studies.

I used the year after defending my dissertation to collect documentation
on technical assistance and economic aid given to Muslim countries. But
my further itinerary would be different. At the University of Cairo, I had
become interested in the way a modern university institution functioned
with Arab teaching programs and Arab staff and students in an Arab
society. As I saw it, the formation of a qualified intelligentsia should be
one of the priorities for the development of Arab countries. The quality
and outlook of an Arab intelligentsia in the future would depend very
much on the university education it received.

Encouraged by Jacques Berque, I made a study of universities in the
Arab world, sponsored by the French National Center for Scholarly
Research (CNRS). In the course of 1963–4, I collected on-site documentation about universities in Arab countries and met people able to give
further information.

My study focused on the history and social role of Arab universities.
Like other Third World countries, all Arab countries before and after
independence attributed great importance to offering higher education to
their people, along national lines. But foreign American and French
universities also made important contributions. They offered educational
programs that were open to the West without necessarily surrendering to
Western policies. Indirectly, they could also make a contribution to political independence and social development. At the time of the mandates
between the two World Wars, younger generations of students from
various Arab countries could meet at the American University of Beirut
and discuss the future of their countries, once the French and British
would have left. It is said that more than one movement for national
independence was born or developed at the American University of Beirut. The American University in Cairo made important contributions to
social development in the region. On the other hand, the French University of Algiers was known as a colonial bastion, and the University
Library was sacked by French rightist colonials who did not want it to be
handed over to the Algerians after independence.

The Arab state universities were too politically dependent to offer the
same freedom of socio-political debate as the foreign ones, though these

were not completely free either. In the course of this research, I was impressed by the high ideals and the force with which the founders of the Egyptian University in Cairo, the Syrian University of Damascus, and the University of Baghdad had envisaged the task of these universities for the future of countries on the verge of independence. During this study, a number of people, including officials, showed interest and encouraged me to bring it to a good ending. I was able to prepare the publication of the results, first at the French Archeological Institute in Beirut and then, when I was teaching at the University of California, in Los Angeles, from September 1964 on. In 1968 I returned to Holland.

With the immense increase in the number of students and insufficient financial means at their disposal, Arab universities know difficult times. They have to steer, moreover, between ideological pressures and political surges. More recently, private universities have been founded in several Arab countries, largely for the study of business and public administration.

A singular experience shows how the Arab world can provide a service to Western universities and research, apart from funding endowed chairs. At the end of 1978, I spent two weeks in Kuwait, a city where one could meet interesting people, including expatriate intellectuals, authors, and artists from Egypt, Iraq, and Palestine. It was the first time that I saw an Arab state that was rich, apart from its immigrant workers. People were generous and Kuwait was in a position to assist where Europe failed. Under UNESCO auspices, Jacques Berque had organized a research team to prepare an annotated bibliography on Arab culture. I happened to be responsible for publications in English, German, and Dutch. When the team had finished preparing the text, we discovered that neither UNESCO nor Berque seemed to have considered the costs of publication. An interesting modus operandi! Since the French publishers who had been engaged asked for a substantial subsidy, there was a serious risk that the text would never be published, since bibliographies are a poor market article. Given the immense work that we had done, this was an unbearable thought. So I tried to find on my own a Kuwaiti sponsor for the publication of this bibliography during my stay there. Finally, practically on the last day of my stay, I succeeded in having an audience with a cabinet minister, who promised to support the cause. For once, Arabs proved to be more efficient than Westerners, and UNESCO was quite happy with the solution. The book appeared in 1981.

Kuwait also had other surprises reserved for Westerners. One of them happened at the end of a more formal visit that I paid the Minister of Awqāf (religious foundations) and Religious Affairs. I had carefully prepared my questions and the minister had answered with reasonable precision. Then, at the end of the audience, His Excellency carried out *da'wa*, inviting me personally to accept the Islamic faith. Professional Orientalists may have had such an experience, but I had not. To be sure, Muslim acquaintances had often inquired what I thought of Islam, which I had studied for so long. Maybe they were hoping that I would become a Muslim. A straightforward invitation on this level, however, was unprecedented. I politely declined, saying that I studied Islam but that I was myself a Christian. I could not, however, give a completely reasoned argument for this answer, which, I felt, weighed heavily. Was I indeed a Christian? Was I on the way to becoming a Muslim, too? Would I like to be one, deep inside? Might I renounce my faith under pressure? Was it a personal gesture or a ritual act that the minister had performed toward a visitor whom he absolutely did not know? Questions like these intrigued me.

Twenty years later, I happened to meet again by pure chance the same minister, now retired, and I reminded him of the story. He smiled. We shook hands and a friend took a photo of both of us together. I know now that *da'wa* is an element of Muslim-Christian dialogue.

Meeting Muslims in their countries is different, however, from meeting them in one's own society. In 1968 I had come to the University of Utrecht to teach Islam and the phenomenology of religion. At the time, the first contingents of Muslim "guest workers" had arrived, mainly from Turkey and Morocco. Having been away from the country almost for fourteen years, I kept aloof. However, I was asked to steer a working group on Islam and Muslims in Utrecht in 1974, to consult with people, and to collect data. Afterwards, I went into hiding again, but not for long. In 1982 I had to chair an official working group on the question whether or not the Dutch government could and should pay subsidies in certain cases for religious facilities for Muslims, including prayer halls. The Muslims we met were not students, intellectuals, bankers, or cabinet ministers. We were dealing with the grassroots level, Turks and Moroccans often without much education, with whom we spoke in their cultural centers, prayer halls, or private houses. We listened to what they wanted to tell us about their experiences in the Netherlands and their Islam. In this case, the old roles were reversed. I did not see Muslims as they live in their own country, but now as immigrants to mine.

While doing this work I saw a new aspect of Islamic Studies evolving. It did not concern primarily the founding texts of Islam, Islamic thought, Islamic history, or the situation of Muslim societies outside Europe. Its task would be to follow, from the first generation on, the rise and development of Muslim communities in secular Western contexts and existing forms of interaction between these communities and the societies where they happened to live. It should pay attention to the ways in which Islam as a religion and way of life was interpreted and practiced in these communities, the relations that crystallized between various Muslim groups and organizations themselves, the visions of Islam that arose, and the patterns of interaction and communication that developed between these Muslims and others, that is to say non-Muslims, around them.

This work with Muslim immigrants, in addition to research and teaching, was a time-consuming task, but it opened a more social and human dimension in Islamic studies. I not only had to look at problems and to be in touch with Muslim organizations, but also to inform various Dutch groups about Muslims and Islam and stress the need for acceptance of Muslim "others". For a number of immigrants, Islam was important, and I felt this should be known in Holland where people like to have opinions.

Looking back, after my previous travels in Muslim countries and my work in the USA this work liberated me—at least in part—from certain elements of the collective European memory: the idea that Islam at bottom is a sort of threat, that Muslims are radically different from us because of their Islam, and that we somehow have to give guidance to Muslims. For any problems in this field, the golden rule is and will remain to establish communication and to treat problems as impartially as possible for all parties concerned. For the time being, I had in practice turned from a researcher into a middleman, if not an intercessor.

However, the international scene changed—and an ideological and political resurgence of Islam played a role in this, in part as a cause and in part as an effect. The Middle East has been the pivot of these changes. In 1967 and 1973, two major wars took place between Arab countries and Israel, which has carried out a "classic" colonization policy under military auspices against Palestinian inhabitants of the territories it occupied in 1967. In 1975, a civil war started in Lebanon. In 1979, the Islamic revolution took place in Iran; in 1981 Sadat was assassinated; and in 1982 Israel pushed into Lebanon. In 1987, Intifāda I started, in 2000 Intifāda II. In 1991, the Gulf War was fought; in the same year a civil war started in Algeria. In 1995, Rabin was assassinated by an Israeli. In 2001, the so-called peace process in the Middle East came to an end. In 2002, Israel reoccupied the territories it had left to the Palestine Authority, and the USA made preparations to carry out a war against Iraq. Behind it all there was continuous fighting in Afghanistan since 1979. In 2001, a large-scale terrorist attack took place in New York and Washington, in response to which the USA declared war against international terrorism and routed the Tālibān in Afghanistan.

Whatever the precise long-term and short-term causes of the various forms of Islamic resurgence that became visible in the 1970s, it called for an ideological, social, and political actualization of Islam and directed itself against Israel and the West. After the Cold War was over in 1990, the West, including Israel, in turn started to address what it considered to be the negative sides of Islam, such as fundamentalism, the oppression of minorities, the use of violence, and terrorist action in particular against Israeli civilians. Preparations were made for ideological warfare between

Islam and the West. In Muslim eyes, the USA and Israel represent this West inimical to Islam, Muslim countries, and Muslims generally.

In this political and ideological turmoil, the rising counter-current of dialogue and cooperation between Christians and Muslims demands attention. Following the Bhamdoun conferences of 1954 and 1956, the dialogue programs developed first in the Catholic Church after Vatican II and then at the World Council of Churches in the Unit for Dialogue created for the purpose should be mentioned. Structures for dialogue between Christians and Muslims were created and several dialogue meetings were organized by Muslims in Tripoli (Libya), Tunisia, Amman, Jakarta, and elsewhere. As a result, dialogue meetings have taken place on a local, national, and international level. In the 1980s and 1990s, besides dialogues on squarely religious subjects, other subjects, too, were discussed at such meetings, often including human rights, family planning, and the position of women.

The more spiritual and idealistic trends of the beginnings were encouraged by common declarations of intent and by certain successes, such as were reached against the Apartheid policies in South Africa. They shattered, however, against the walls erected by the wars in Lebanon, Sudan, the Gulf, Bosnia, Kosovo, and Afghanistan. These idealistic efforts revealed themselves to be utterly naive in their estimate of extremist movements, Israeli and US interests, and Iraqi, Iranian, and Pakistani policies. They received a decisive blow from the failure of the so-called peace process.

On looking back, the unconditional US support—or at least laissez-aller—of specific Israeli policies, including the colonization of the Occupied Territories and the annexation of East Jerusalem, with their serious repercussions for the Palestinian population and for the region as a whole, may very well turn out to have been a fundamental political mistake. It was based on an ill-perceived US self-interest and may have bad long-term consequences not only for Israel, but also for the USA. If Israel did not know how to rub shoulders with its neighbors and non-Israeli subjects, America failed in dealing with the world at large, in particular the Middle East. In my view, simple power politics with punitive expeditions has become a formula of the past.

Geopolitical developments as sketched above also have repercussions for Islamic Studies in the wider sense. On the level of academic expertise, these studies concentrate on the study of texts religious or otherwise, history including contemporary history, and Muslim societies at present and in the past. They are carried out in Western as well as Muslim scholarly institutions. On another level, however, research on Islam is carried out in the service of governments (security and defense, policies toward Muslim countries, Muslim immigrants), business corporations and banking (investments, earnings from oil, financial policies), the media (reporting of events, presentations of Islam, general information of the broader public), and what may be called mass-circulation literature (within the parameters of existing market interests, ideological trends, emotional fears and hopes). In this context, just as in colonial days, it is time to plead for a kind of research on Islam and Muslim societies that defends the human dignity of Muslim people against the imposition of foreign interests. Precisely at a time in which Muslims and others tend to be the victims of ideologies, policies, and pressures of their own as well as of Western states, there is reason to sound a human warning supported by reason.

My own itinerary took a new turn in the summer of 1987, when I moved to the University of Lausanne. After years of activity, there was now need and time for thinking and writing. I had enjoyed my contacts with Muslim colleagues like N. Bammate, M. Arkoun, A. Falaturi, S. Balić, and T. Ramadan in Europe. I had met a number of other Muslim scholars on travels or at international conferences, sometimes in connection with particular causes, like human rights (A. A. an-Na'im), dialogue (M. Talbi), feminist theology (Rifaat Hasan), and liberation theology (F. Esack). I had contacts with a few Muslim institutions, like the Islamic Foundation in England, but in such contacts I certainly was no political activist, visiting Libya in 1982 and Saudi Arabia in 1999. Like so many others, I adhere to the value of an independent mind, scholarly critical knowledge, and personal insight and ethics on the basis of truth.

With the freedom granted to Swiss professors, I became more critical about the many misrepresentations and misunderstandings between Westerners and Muslims, on both sides, since the end of the Cold War. On a small scale, we therefore organized scholarly symposia in Lausanne on Muslim perceptions of other religions at present and in the past, and on changes in mutual perceptions between Muslims and Christians. A growing insight into one's own representations of the other and corrections of wrong images of the other lead to a better appreciation of other people's views and their underlying intentions. In this framework, a Jordanian student submitted in Utrecht his doctoral dissertation on the complexities of Muslim Arab views of Judaism during the period 1948–78.

Whereas in the Netherlands I had been dealing mostly with Islam in Arab countries, I now became better informed about work done in and about other Muslim countries, such as Turkey, Pakistan, India, Malaysia, and Indonesia. Attitudes and lifestyle in South and Southeast Asia differ considerably from those in the Middle East, and the articulations of Islam here are different from those in the Arab world, where the past weighs heavily.

In the course of history, there have been problems and abject failures in the relations between Muslims and others, specifically Europeans. They were not the exclusive fault of the Muslims or the Europeans, but were due largely to cultural differences and should be the subject of analysis. On the one hand, Muslims, Europeans, and others have violated norms of human rights in crucial situations, and we should be concerned about the victims on both sides. On the other hand, failures in such relationships are often due to opposed economic and political interests and also to forces and structures of which the people concerned are hardly conscious.

This means that, unlike during the period of the 1960s and 1970s, Christian-Muslim relations nowadays can no longer be seen in terms of two faiths, traditions, or religions that encounter each other. More than a previous generation seems to have thought, relations between Muslims and Westerners, or Muslims and Christians, have depended less on the Muslims and Westerners themselves or on their religions than on the forces of the world in which they lived. If there was confrontation between them, it was largely due to a conflict-laden world context that put them in opposition to each other. States and corporations necessarily follow their own interests, oppressing others or clashing with each other, and there have always been individuals and groups who had an interest in conflicts. Those devoting themselves to justice, reconciliation, and peace have perhaps always been a minority, be it a moral minority. At certain times and places, however, they have been successful. In this connection, too, the kind of relations people entertain with "others" is significant.

So much for my own memories of contacts with Muslims.

2. 1950–2000: Muslims in Contact with Others in Recent History

The book consists of seven sections. They deal with various aspects of the relations that have existed between Muslims and others in the course of time, especially in the second half of the twentieth century. Each section is devoted to a particular subject and this is an introduction to these seven subjects.

How did Muslims view others who were not Muslims? Where and when have Muslims been in closer contact with others? How did they behave and what kinds of relations developed with these other people? Whom did Muslims consider really different from them, really "other"? On what kind of occasions did Muslims open up to others, becoming aware of real differences while entertaining further relations with them? Where did the imagination impose itself on reality, and where did realities correct false images?

My underlying interest is to arrive at some insights into Muslim views of and Muslim contacts with the world and its people outside Islam, in particular situations and contexts. Although adherents and others have both often represented Islam as a more or less closed block with its own particular religion and way of life, it may in fact be much less closed than it seemed to insiders as well as outsiders. In trade, science, and culture generally, Muslims have been more open to contacts with others than is often assumed now, in the aftermath of the colonial period. At the time of the Cold War, these contacts had a particular political character. At the present time, they extend to broader international relations.

Do our ideas about Islam as a world apart still apply, or should they be revised? Are Muslims as different from us as stereotypes on both sides suggest?

2.1. Three Monotheistic Religions: Living with Each Other

Muslims consider themselves part of the three religions that brought the common message of monotheism and three religious scriptures to humankind. Throughout history, how Jews, Christians, and Muslims should live with each other has been a major problem. This was often formulated as the question how their three religions are related in terms of truth. What can be said about these relationships from a scholarly point of view?

The calls of prophets in the course of history to make people turn or return to almighty God were not only incentives to monotheism. They also carried messages about the right way of life to be followed by each person in the community concerned and in society at large. In other words, these calls imposed not only what we would consider a strictly "religious" belief and practice, but also rules of what we would today call social order, law, and ethics or morality, with corresponding prescriptions and prohibitions.

Historically, this led to the growth of different communities aligning themselves with divergent religious traditions. These traditions each led back to a particular prophetic founder followed by a list of successive authorities who followed the message and kept to the tradition established by the founder. We find this in prophetical religions as ancient as Zoroastrianism and also in relatively young religions, like the Bahā'ī.

Historical research has shown that, with the gradual expansion of these religious communities, their religions took on further religious, social, and political shapes that went far beyond their original local forms. This is certainly true for Judaism, Christianity, and Islam. In their new shapes, these religions claimed acceptance of universal validity from their adherents, or at least general recognition of their truth.

Changes could be imposed from outside. The situation of these prophetical religions, like those of other religions, changed, for instance, with the practice of a certain separation between the political and the strictly religious domains. It also changed with the rise and development of what may be called "civil" societies, that is to say societies that, while respecting existing religions, do not identify themselves with one particular religion.

Changes could also occur from inside. Within the communities and societies of the prophetical religions, from time to time movements have arisen that wanted to go back to the scriptural sources of their religion. Sometimes they interpreted and applied these sources in a completely new way, in the context of the time. This could have implications for developing new attitudes toward other religious communities and their traditions.

If people long imagined the existence of one true religion with an array of sects and false religions beside it, present-day experience hints at the presence of a plurality of religious communities, each with its own religion. There also is a plurality of monotheistic religions, even if we confine ourselves to religions that claim to go back to a prophetic founder. Last but not least, there is also a variety of forms that have developed in each prophetic monotheistic religion in the course of time. Although certain forms of Judaism, Christianity, and Islam may claim to represent true Judaism, Christianity, and Islam, in scholarship one has to consider all the forms of a particular religion that have existed in the course of history. I consider such forms particular options within the overall framework of that religion.

Within each religious community, there are differing orientations toward other religions. Most people, of course, are only concerned with their own religion and may be called "isolationists". They are not concerned about "others" at all, and in quite a few cases they are in fact "hegemonists" who want to bring others into their own religion. Most religious communities, however, also include people who have a more universal orientation or who are at least concerned about the existence of others. In quite a few cases, they are prepared to get to know about such others and to make contact with them. Finally, a growing number of people in modern societies are hardly concerned with religion at all.

Islam, Judaism, and Christianity each have certain fundamental views of other religions. Islam, for instance, has the idea of—at least—three privileged monotheistic book religions whose prophets received, by revelation, a scripture that they handed over to their community. It considers the Qur'ān the only scripture that retained its original revealed text and was not corrupted. Judaism has the idea of the covenant of Noah, representing an alliance between God and humankind as a whole, different from the alliance between God and the people of Israel. Some nineteenth- and twentieth-century Jewish thinkers viewed Christianity and Islam as having the special role of bringing the truth of monotheism to the non-Jewish goyim, in the West and in the East respectively.

Christianity knows the idea of grains of religious truth (natural religion, general revelation) spread to humankind outside the Christian

Church, which remains the final truth-holder (revealed religion, special revelation). In the eighteenth century, Enlightenment thinkers like G.E. Lessing and Moses Mendelssohn introduced new visions, based on reason (*Vernunft*), of Christianity and Judaism respectively and of religions in general. More recently, Christian thinkers like Hans Küng (world ethics), Wilfred Cantwell Smith (world theology), John Hick (philosophy of religion), and others developed further views of relations between religions, of a more idealist nature. Several organizations were founded to bring together people from different religious backgrounds for cooperation and dialogue. Recent examples are the "World Conference on Religions for Peace" (WCRP) for religions in general and the "Jews, Christians, Muslims" (JCM) for the three monotheistic religions in particular. At the end of the nineteenth century, a new universalizing monotheistic prophetic religion, the Bahā'ī faith, arose to take up the heritage of the preceding Big Three.

I speak here of "idealist" views insofar as they concentrate on faith and ethics. They do not deal with the social, economic, political, and military realities and forces that block in practice what I would call "normal" relations between people. Here I am thinking for instance of the Middle East conflict around Israel, the North-South opposition with Western domination, the human rights record of many countries, and existing gender discrimination.

Discussions of relations between adherents of the three monotheistic religions already started in medieval times, when in some Muslim cities official debates were held about religious truth not only between various scholars of Islam but also between Muslim, Christian, and Jewish scholars. The discoveries of the existence of other peoples with their religions, the eighteenth-century Enlightenment, and the nineteenth-century missionary movement revived these discussions. They reached new heights with the rise of interreligious dialogue, given the increasing communication in the second half of the twentieth century. Meetings of interreligious dialogue between Christians, Muslims, and Jews have been organized in Europe and North America since the 1970s, if not earlier.

Research on the historical relations between Judaism, Christianity, and Islam has been going on for a long time, but only recently have scholars from these various backgrounds met and discussed their findings. Several scholarly meetings of this kind have taken place, notably in North America.

Empirical scholarly research on the three monotheistic religions deals primarily with textual, historical, and social scientific data. I am thinking for instance of comparisons between religious thinkers of the three traditions; or the study of situations of coexistence, for instance in medieval Spain, in the Ottoman Empire, and in the Arab Middle East. A special field is the study of mutual perceptions, research on various kinds of organized and spontaneous encounters, and inquiries into recent efforts toward cooperation and dialogue. The religious legitimation given to ethnic and other conflicts and the false images presented of other people's religions are drawing broad attention nowadays. Such studies can be deepened by analyzing cultural links between different religions, prevailing concepts and constructs of religion, common efforts and causes pursued by adherents of these different religions, as well as numerous expressions in art and literature that refer to the three religions or their adherents. Comparative studies address what is held in common and what differs in the three respective religions and their presentations by leaders, adherents, and scholars.

Relevant elements for any further analysis of relations between the three religions include the presence and working of symbolisms, the impact of social traditions, and the weight of existing institutions. We also need research on the various forces and contexts that have conditioned mutual religious perceptions and attitudes as well as the behavior of people of these religions toward each other in general or in particular situations. As I see it, for any serious scholarly work in this area, the ways in which people constructed what we nowadays call "religions" should be taken into account. The notion of "God" remains, as a matter of principle, a religious notion.

An important question for further research on relations between adherents of religions is to examine where and in what ways self-criticism is expressed. A realistic view of the empirical reality of religious communities and their religions influences one's view of relations between the adherents of these religions in concrete situations.

The question how such adherents can associate and arrive at cooperation and dialogue has become ever more urgent. People should inform each other about their religions and worldviews. There is need for a moral code of believers living together.

2.2. Encounters between Islam and other Religions in History

Already before his specific call, Muhammad must have met adherents of various religions, such as Christians, Jews, and Zoroastrians, in Mecca or during his business travels throughout the Arabian Peninsula. Probably he sought to obtain information about their religious beliefs and practices, just as he was familiar with current religion in Mecca and with the monotheistic trend of the *Hanifiya* there.

The fact that Christians and Jews had scriptures impressed him and led to the idea that monotheistic religions have a scripture with a divinely revealed contents. These scriptures were not available to non-adherents, but he may have asked for information about them. We do not know whether Muhammad knew liturgical texts used by the Christians or talmudic texts used by the Jews. He may have inquired about them as oral traditions current at the time. After his call, he remained on good terms with Christians in and outside Arabia. The Qur'ān has many references to various kinds of interaction with Jews and Christians on social, religious, and also political issues after the *hijra* (622 C.E.). Muhammad's encounters with adherents of other religions gave a particular direction to the development of Islam during his lifetime.

It was through the great conquests by the caliph ʿUmar ibn al-Khattāb (r. 634–44) and his successors that Muslims came in contact with Christians of various denominations and languages living throughout the Middle East, as well as with Zoroastrians in Iran and Jewish communities spread over the region. The relationship was that of domination by the Arab Muslim conquerors, who in their military camps at first kept separate from the population and did not insist on conversions to Islam. By the end of the seventh century, a conscious effort was made to arabize the administration of the empire, Arabic becoming the official language. During the following centuries, a process of conscious Islamization of the conquered regions took place, especially in the growing towns and cities. From the tenth century on, Islam has spread more through preaching and the example of religious life of holy men than through conquests. The Islamization of large parts of South Asia, Central Asia, Southeast Asia, and also of Africa south of the Sahara took place largely by peaceful means, through preachers and Sūfīs moving along the existing trade routes.

As is well known, the Muslims recognized the religions of the Christians and Jews as well as of the Zoroastrians. The latter three communities enjoyed internal autonomy and applied their own religious law to their members. The Islamic state and society, however, increasingly applied its own, largely Islamic law (*Sharīʿa*). This also regulated relationships between Muslims and the monotheistic non-Muslims living in Muslim territory. Conscious efforts to convert non-Muslims were made under the caliph al-Mutawakkil (r. 847–61), who also established further rules for the place and the behavior of non-Muslims in Muslim society. Formally, they were considered *dhimmīs*, that is as standing under the protection (*dhimma*) of the caliphate.

The situation of *dhimmīs* under Muslim rule has been a subject of much concern in Europe from the sixteenth century on. European Christians had a heart for Christians living under Ottoman, Moroccan, Iranian, and Moghul rule; so did European Jews for Jews living under Islam. The subject took on political relevance when the European powers claimed to represent the interests of particular Christian minorities to the Ottoman government. France, through Francis I, was the first, offering protection to Catholic Christians in the Ottoman Empire; Russia claimed it later for Orthodox Christians, and Britain for Anglicans and Protestants.

As a result, the subject was much discussed at the time and emerged again with the presence of Christians in present-day Islamic states where the *Sharī'a* is applied. It obtained popular attention when Christians and Jews coming from Muslim countries to Europe gave bitter reports about the sad conditions under which Christians and Jews had to live there, especially since the eighteenth century. These reports tended to be critical of Islam, giving information about corruption and misuse of power, the conditions under which *dhimmīs* had to live, and the use of the ideology of *jihād* in wartime.

Scholarly research on the conditions of non-Muslims living under Muslim rule has distinguished between the legal provisions on the subject in Islamic law (*Sharī'a*) as these were elaborated in the various schools of *fiqh*, on the one hand, and the treatment of non-Muslims in the social practice of Muslim societies, on the other. If the legal provisions have a particular common structure that gives recognized non-Muslims the rank of a secondary class of people but protected under Muslim rule, practice has varied immensely in different times and places. The religious leaders of the non-Muslims had to defend their rights continuously and often had to appeal to the highest political Muslim authorities to have these rights recognized and applied. In the absence of rule and order, the situation of non-Muslims could be pitiful; in many cases it was only by paying a certain amount of money to local officials that the wishes and needs of Christians and Jews were taken into account. In the countryside, relations between Muslims and Christians tended to be better than in the towns, where rivalries, intrigues, and a Muslim belief in the superiority of Islam prevailed. A number of studies have been made about this touchy subject of relations between Muslim rulers and non-Muslim subjects. The social history of the groups concerned, the economic context, and the more general political situation should be taken into account to interpret the facts correctly. Reports from travelers as independent witnesses are often sources of precious information. However, the subject has been politicized from different sides, including to show weaknesses of the Islamic social system or the intolerance of Islam. By contrast, Muslims tend to stress the institutional toleration of Islam, compared with intolerant practices of the Christian Churches.

Muslim societies have not been greatly threatened by non-Muslims living under their rule, but rather by non-Muslim invasions and conquests. Paradigmatic in this respect are the Crusades, which are viewed as invasions by barbarian Christians from Western and Southern Europe. Historically speaking, only the first Crusade had clearly religious eschatological as well as other, mundane motivations. Several studies have appeared lately on the ways Muslims at the time viewed and responded to the Crusades, with interesting details about the Franks living in Syria and Palestine. On the occasion of the 900th commemoration of the Pope's call for the Crusades in 1096, the Church expressed its regrets about what had happened.

Another case is the Reconquista of Spain, brought to an end in 1492, which left to Muslims the collective memory of Andalusia as a Muslim Paradise Lost. The responsible Catholic Kings had an outspoken religious ideology addressing Islam as the arch-enemy of Christianity. The Christian "holy war" had to be pursued in North Africa and further.

The most important case, however, of aggression on Muslim territory by Christians from outside, as seen by Muslims, was the colonization of Muslim territories by Britain, France, the Netherlands, Russia, Spain, and Italy. Although it is still a nearly obsessive part of the Muslim collective memory, most Muslims agree nowadays that the European colonization had not so much religious, but rather economic and political motivations, arising also from the competition of European nations in the heyday of European imperialism.

On the other hand, the clearest case of aggression on Muslim territory by Jews from outside, as seen by Muslims, has been the Zionist movement, which resulted in the creation of Israel in 1948 and the expulsion of a great number of Palestinians, as well as the further occupation of Palestinian lands in 1967 and their colonization and further planned appropriation. Most Muslims tend to perceive Zionism as a religiously motivated movement to gain land in the name of God, since some Jews claim to have a divine right to the land. That Zionist Christians support this claim is, in the eyes of many Muslims, the result of Christians having become the victims of Zionist manipulation.

A typical religious attack on Islam and Muslim society, in many Muslims' eyes, has been and is the work of the Christian missions, in particular the Protestant and sectarian ones, but also those of the Catholic Church and its orders. Nineteenth-century French Catholic projects dreamed of a re-Christianization of North Africa; Protestant Evangelicals dreamt of success in their debates with Islamist "fundamentalists"; and American sects launch crusades attacking African Islam. Many Muslims suspect current Christian dialogue efforts of being a new form of imposing Christianity on Muslims, and from time to time rumors emerge of large-scale strategies of converting Muslims into Christians.

Apart from cases of incitement on the part of "fundamentalists" or "militants" on both sides, after World War Two the encounter of Muslims with Christians has been moving toward forms of cooperation and dialogue, in situations of crisis as well as in more peaceful contexts. Relations with Jews and Hindus are more tense, however. In the case of the first, there is the problem of the state of Israel, its appropriation of Arab and Muslim lands, and the threatened position of Muslims in a majority Jewish state. In the case of the Hindus, there is the problem of India, its claims to Kashmir, and the threatened position of Muslims in a

majority Hindu India. Although there have been peaceful relations between Muslims and Jews as well as between Muslims and Hindus, the
state formations of 1947 and 1948 have encouraged conflicts and wars.

2.3. Perception and Categorization of Other Religions

From the beginning of Islam, Muslims tended to consider others, that is
to say non-Muslims, largely in terms of the religions to which these others
belonged. Their religions were categorized as "possessing a revealed
scripture" or "not possessing a revealed scripture", as "monotheistic" or
"non-monotheistic" religions. The relations between Muslims and non-
Muslims as communities depended to a large extent on the category in
which the particular non-Muslim religion was placed.

Of course, there have also been other kinds of religious views of non-
Muslims. One possibility was to rigidly define the term "Muslim" and to
call all non-Muslims simply *kāfirs*, unbelievers. In extreme cases, even
nonconformist Muslims could be considered unbelievers. But we also find,
in a more spiritual orientation, the possibility of recognizing the religious
insight (*ma'rifa*) an individual person can have, not only in Islam but also
in other religious traditions and communities. In early Islam, Muslims and
Christians, often of an ascetic lifestyle, could meet and speak about their
experiences. In the Indian subcontinent, Muslims and Hindus could meet
and speak about the Sūfī and Bhakti path they followed and about
analogous experiences on the way toward the one Absolute Reality.
Throughout Islamic history there have been poets of spiritual inclination,
expressing their love for true believers and their trust in the guidance of
truthful holy men and women. In contrast to such "multi-dimensional"
testimonies, the more rational categorizations of non-Muslim "others", as
carried out by theologians (*mutakallimūn*) and doctors of law (*'ulamā'*
and *fuqahā'*), are rather flat and two-dimensional.

The interesting thing in Muslim categorizations is not only that believers
are categorized according to their particular "religion", but also that the
various religions themselves are described or constructed according to
typically Islamic criteria. Muslims have had an Islamo-centric view of
religions other than Islam.

This tendency was strengthened by accepting Qur'anic data not only
as a basis for morally evaluating other religions, but also as a basis for
empirical knowledge of other religions. Christianity and Judaism are not
so much seen as what particular living Christians and Jews, as adherents
or believers, declare them to be. They are seen primarily as the religions
of Christians and Jews as described and judged in the Qur'ān, with
corrupted scriptures, wrong beliefs, etc. Christians and Jews do not
recognize themselves in this presentation.

This starting point gives a certain schematization to Muslim descriptions and constructions of other religions. It also reinforces the natural tension between empirical research on other religions that employs philological, literary, historical, and social scientific methods, on the one hand, and the judgments given of these religions in the Qur'ān, on the other. This tension is also present in what is considered knowledge of Islam itself: there is a difference between what the Qur'ān says Islam should be and what empirical scholarly research finds Muslims actually doing and believing.

Through its broad expansion and its geographic situation, Islam has been in contact with the other major contemporary religions from the seventh century on. We have texts from the ninth century and later that describe debates on religion between Muslims and others. The knowledge that Muslims like Ibn Hazm, al-Bīrūnī, and al-Shahrastānī had of other religions in the medieval period surpassed the knowledge that Christians and Jews had at the time.

Muslims have always been open to discussions and debates with representatives of other religions.

Such discussions took place not only privately between interested individuals meeting each other at home, in the market, or in other public places. They could also be held at the request of an official, a local governor, or the caliph himself. In the last case, people could be invited to attend the meeting and follow the discussion between various religious leaders and scholars. Each party tried to persuade the others of the rightness, truth, and superiority of one's religion, as if it were a sport event. In such public debates, intelligent argumentation and sharp arguments for or against a particular doctrine were appreciated. In Iran and South Asia, such public debates have been organized up to the twentieth century.

2.4. The Muslim World and the West in Recent Times

Up to World War Two, all European colonial powers except Portugal and Belgium governed Muslim territories or areas in Asia or Africa. Consequently, they had to do with Islam and developed what may be called "Islamic" policies for the administration of these territories. The conduct of these Western policies from a position of domination greatly influenced the image of Islam in European countries even until World War Two.

The stories of colonized Muslim territories after World War One differ considerably. Germany, for instance, lost its colonies after World War One and its Muslim regions were taken over by Britain and France. Sometimes there remained some kind of special relationship with the old colonial power after obtaining independence. This is the case with territories in Africa that had been ruled by France and with older British colonies that now became member countries of the British Commonwealth. In other cases, for instance Algeria, there was a bloody war of independence that ended unhappily. The mandate territory of Palestine did not achieve independence. Part of it became the state of Israel; the other parts came under Jordanian and Egyptian rule until June 1967 and were slated by the United Nations to become a Palestine state. To understand current relationships between the Muslim world and the West, and certainly Europe today, it is important to know about the history of the individual Muslim countries, their relationships to Europe and the West after obtaining independence, and the various factors influencing these relationships during and after the Cold War.

The same rule holds true for those Muslim countries that remained independent. A good example is republican Turkey. It took Europe as a model for its development, which was directed by the state. The state assumed considerable power and distanced itself from Islam, trying to control it as much as possible. Since the 1960s, Turkey has conducted a policy of rapprochement toward Europe, now hoping to join the European Union in the future. Under the Pahlevi regime, Iran followed a similar policy of developing according to Western models. Its switch to become an Islamic state in 1979 brought about a distance to the West, especially when all cultural, social, and economic development was put into a Shīʿī Islamic framework. One should note that Saudi Arabia and several Gulf emirates have also put their cultural and social life in an Islamic, but this time Sunnī framework.

Most people in the Middle East, Africa, and Asia live under poor economic conditions, and their countries are heavily dependent, economically and politically, on the West. Muslim countries, though in varying degrees, share the political condition that their regimes are not democratic in the sense the term is understood in the West. After the honeymoon of independence thanks to national movements, most of these regimes are in tension with a critical opposition calling for justice and the improvement of living conditions. This opposition positioned itself first under the banner of social democracy and/or socialism, but since the late 1970s increasingly under that of Islam. If most regimes have to accommodate to the West for their economic survival, most peoples in fact reject Western domination of their countries.

If people cannot directly express their opposition to the regime in place, they tend to express it toward the West, since in their view the regime is linked, perhaps even subservient, to the West. To most people, the basic difference between the West and themselves is the absence of Islam and presence of secularism in the West, and the presence of Islam and absence of secularism in Muslim countries. Ingeniously, people tend to articulate their opposition to the West in terms of the antagonism between Islam and secularism.

What is generally rejected—given the collective memory of the colonial period—is any Western domination of Muslim countries or societies. For militant Muslims, the expression "Islam versus or against the West" is a key formula, though it may have different meanings for different groups of people. At certain times, the immediate, political meaning overrides the deeper, religious one. But the latter, religious association can resurface unexpectedly. This makes it more difficult to coherently understand Muslim views of the West.

The role of European countries varies and the place of Europe in Muslim-Western relations is complex. One may wonder whether Europe has been able to overcome completely its hegemonic attitudes that were customary in colonial times. European interests seem to have become less political and more economic. Yet, after the oil boycott of October 1973, the European Economic Community became involved in the Palestinian-Israeli debate, which gained in importance. At that time, Islam became a focus of Muslim political activity, leading to the Iranian revolution of 1979 and the rise of Islamist movements elsewhere. Not the West, but the Palestinian problem and the Islamic question may have been at the heart of Muslim concerns in the Middle East during the 1980s.

With the Gulf War of 1991, the situation changed. The USA imposed itself militarily and politically on the Middle East. It also took the initiative for the Middle East "peace process" of the 1990s. The USA had become the world's only superpower, representing the West in military and political terms.

In the course of the 1990s, Muslim countries wondered about their relations with the West and, looking to the USA, there was reason for this. First of all, since the USA sided with Israel, it was felt to be highly partial in the "peace process". Second, the discussion of Huntington's "Clash of Civilizations" showed that a certain trend in the USA assumed a deep conflict between Islam and the West and distrusted things Islamic. Third, the George W. Bush administration, from its very start in January 2000, took a more imperial than collegial stand in international affairs and, with a certain militancy, took American interests as its guideline. In this atmosphere of growing distance between the Western and the Muslim world, the events of September 11, 2001, America's laissez-faire attitude toward Israel's Prime Minister Ariel Sharon, and the declared multifaceted war of the USA against terrorism—ascribed to Muslim terrorists—made Western-Muslim relations more problematic.

Looking back, throughout the twentieth century intense discussions took place among Muslim intellectuals in North Africa, Egypt, and Iran on the subject of the West and on the attitude to be taken toward Western hegemony and its underlying forces. Whatever positions were taken in the second half of the twentieth century, Muslims faced an overpowering force of the West, as in the preceding colonial period but much more visible in economic guise. Those choosing a radical stand first took Marxism and subsequently Islam as an ideology to stand up to undemocratic regimes and the West. Other attitudes were taken by less radical thinkers.

The term "Islam", as it is used by various Muslim groups and persons, can mean very different things. It is a "total" concept for a universe of norms and values, a social, cultural, and religious world. Vis-à-vis the West, it often stands as a symbol for more or less deep differences in views of society and political ideals, in rules of human behavior and religious practice. Muslims are attached to their Islam and believe in it.

In current Western public opinion, the term "Islam" has strong emotional connotations. It was linked to ancient fears of violence, oppression, the abuse of women, and patriarchal authoritarianism. In European cultural circles, medieval Islamic civilization was praised, but no positive follow-up was seen. It was repeatedly said that Islam missed out on the European Enlightenment and the primacy the latter gave to reason, that it lacks the concept of a free, responsible person, and that in the end it contradicts human rights, in particular the rights of women.

Muslims living in the West have made desperate attempts to correct the many wrong presentations of Islam, different from the Islam that is concretely lived by responsible Muslims. Europeans sympathetic to Islam hinted at the spiritual and human values of Islam in its mysticism and poetry. Edward Said and his circle denounced the hegemonic and Eurocentric background of so much Western discourse about Islam and the East, which he saw as leading to serious misunderstandings. A new generation of intellectuals has questioned the very terms "Islam" and "the West" that had been put in a dualistic contrast to each other, as if there were no other terms at play in relations between Muslim and Western people.

2.5. Muslims in Europe at Present

In the twentieth century, Islam became the second religion in Europe in terms of numbers of adherents, and this gives a new urgency here to the theme of "Muslims and Others". How did relations between Muslims and non-Muslim Europeans develop in the course of the century? How did Muslims perceive Europeans? How did Muslim communities develop in Western societies in general?

At the beginning of the twentieth century, the Muslims of Europe, of various ethnic stock, lived primarily in European Russia and in the Balkans. A great number of Russian Tatars and of Bosnians then living under Austrian rule had a modern education and participated in Central and Eastern European economic, social, and also cultural life in St. Petersburg, Moscow, Vienna, and other places. Tatars played a role in the trade with Central Asia and in industrial and financial projects. A number of them lived in the Crimea, and there were also Tatar communities in Finland and Poland under Russian rule. Similarly, educated Bosnians spoke German and had communities living in Vienna and other Austrian cities. Most Muslim communities at the time, however, lived from agriculture and cattle-breeding in Bosnia, Albania, Bulgaria, and in Russia in the Crimea and the Caucasus region. Here, the province of Azerbaijan saw intense industrial development thanks to its oil.

World War One and the Communist Revolution of 1917 would change the rather peaceful coexistence of Muslims and Orthodox Christians in Eastern Europe. Up to 1990, Islam was combated in the USSR but, even under the pressures, survived in terms of private beliefs and traditional customs. In the 1970s and 1980s, a Western scholar of Islam in the USSR, Alexandre Bennigsen, held that, through its resistance to Marxist ideology, Islam would precipitate the end of the Soviet Union.

After the demise of Communism, there has been a resurgence of Islam, connected with ethnic and national self-affirmation, in Russia and the former Muslim USSR Republics that became independent. The recent history of Islam in these areas should be seen in connection with Islamic developments in Iran and Pakistan in the 1980s.

In the Balkans, on the other hand, Muslim communities have had difficulties with governments. The ideological indoctrination opposed any religion, including Islam. In the 1980s, Turkish-speaking Muslims had to leave Bulgaria, and only some of them came back later. In the war of the 1990s, Muslim Bosnians had to defend themselves against attempts by Serbia and Croatia to displace them. The Serbs in particular, applying ethnic "purification", wanted to put an end to vestiges of Muslim religion and culture in Bosnia. Since the late 1980s and especially in the late 1990s, Muslim Albanians in Kosovo lived under Serbian oppression. Whereas Europe was not able to arrive at common action, the USA intervened successfully. The Dayton agreement led to the recognition of Bosnia and the Kosovo war ended with the defeat of Serbia. The Muslims in Albania, who had suffered under the harsh oppression of a ruthless Communist leadership, regained their freedom of religion and have good relationships with the Christians, who constitute a minority in this country.

Relations between Muslims and non-Muslims in Eastern and Southeastern Europe have been intensely conditioned by the fact that Islam is held by ethnic groups, often with Turkic languages, that have been present here through conquests since medieval times. In the twentieth century, political developments have had a decisive impact on these relations.

In Western Europe and North America, on the other hand, Islam as a religion and way of life has established itself simply through economic migration, mostly from outside Europe. This has been a basic factor in the relations here between Muslim immigrants and the non-Muslim Europeans. Later, Muslim refugees and asylum seekers followed.

Looking back, one should note that the Western European populations in the 1960s and 1970s and even later were ill prepared to receive waves of immigrants from outside Europe. Some of them were not used to the presence of "foreigners" at all; contacts were not always easily established with people of other languages, ways of life, and ethnic stock. As a religion, Islam was hardly known and not well received in secular, fundamentalist, and integrist circles. Post-World War Two conflicts in and around the Middle East that had little to do with Islam were easily associated with Islam as a "contentuous" and "violent" element, a kind of threat. Certain media have played on emotions in this sense, for instance around the Gulf War of 1991 and the terrorist attack of September 11, 2001.

In fact, more than in colonial times and in discourses on terrorism, "Islam" has obtained a much more human face for the West through the presence of Muslim residents, neighbors and colleagues here. Muslims are not necessarily a disturbing factor and there are Western converts to Islam. Muslims within Western societies may play a stabilizing role, provided they find employment, enjoy human rights, and can keep to Muslim moral standards while tolerating Western values such as plural societies, democratic procedures, and the recognition that women like men are fully responsible for their own lives. If, on the other hand, future generations of Muslims do not accept this formula and if, moreover, they are not successful in inserting themselves economically and socially in Western societies, they may stay apart while developing critical views of Westerners and of the West as a whole. However, with improved qualifications, the will to learn, and a commitment to civil society and human rights, they have a role to play.

2.6. Muslim-Christian Relationships

Throughout history, conflicting Christian and Muslim parties have used Christianity and Islam to identify and justify themselves as each other's resolute antagonists, especially in times of conflict and political struggle. As a consequence, the articulation of differences between the two religions has had tremendous political consequences. Yet, in times of peace, commercial relations flourished and social and cultural exchange, including translation activities, could take place, for instance around the Mediterranean. Unfortunately, after the Crusades and the reconquest of European territories, the colonial period—with the domination and colonization of the larger part of the Muslim world by European nations and with Western Christian missions being sent to Muslim populations—greatly contributed to re-establishing on both sides the idea of a fundamental antagonism between Christianity and Islam.

Since World War Two, however, this ideological antagonism started to lose some of its edge. The Cold War induced the West as well as the USSR to seek alliances with Muslim countries. The loss of absolute political control, the growth of better knowledge and insight, and increasing communication through the media as well as in more direct ways between groups and persons led to the discovery of the value of dialogue. The West's need for an open world market system, new geopolitical interests, and a growing privatization of religion pushed the Christianity-Islam antagonism somewhat to the background.

Yet, denigration of Islam is not yet over. Defenders of Israel are distrustful of Islam, and Christian Zionists demonize it outright. Some missionary circles depict Islam as the main enemy of Christianity, and certain Western geopolitical interests are intent on predicting, if not a future clash of civilizations in general, then at least one between the West and Islam. The other way around, there are anti-Western Muslims. Certain Islamist movements renew the antagonism between the two religions by refusing dialogue and calling halt to any further growth of Christianity. Others call upon Islam to resist by all means an increasing American or Western imperialism in the Middle East, Africa, and Asia. Each side has an interest in constructing a particular image of "Islam" as an enemy or as a cause demanding absolute loyalty. Both sides, however, are one in constructing "Islam and the West" as a fundamentally given dualism from which there can be no escape. Given this ideological curtain, a number of Muslims and Christians of good will are looking for a realistic dialogue to break the deadlock caused by "dualist" Muslims and Westerners.

On reflection, any anti-Islam campaign or anti-Christianity campaign has weighty long-term negative effects, objectively considered. It awakens collective memories and evokes emotional attitudes, and not only among Muslims. It goes against the clear need for communication and reasoning on the two sides. It has repercussions for Christian and Muslim minorities living as "hostages" on both sides. It neglects the great variety of positions that exist both within the two religions and within the Western and Muslim worlds, which prevent them being accurately presented as two homogeneous blocks. Last but not least, it contradicts the fact that many Muslims and Christians in local situations are living more or less peacefully together, trying to avoid anything that would create painful conflicts. Above all, anti-Islam or for that matter anti-Christianity campaigns do not solve the problem of coexistence of Muslims and Christians—on the contrary.

This does not mean that living together is an easy matter. I would like to make three points in this respect.

First, within Christian and Muslim communities, most people are only concerned with their own religion, their own practice and interpretation of it, and their own communal interests. In this respect, religions function still very much as sovereign states did in the earlier days of nationalism. There is a general lack of elementary education in matters of religious plurality, and many people do not really see a reason why they should want to have to do with people of another religion.

The second point is that of given identity. If the identity of groups or persons is a thing that is given by their religion, contacts with people of another religion or worldview are undesirable, because they might infringe that firm and fixed identity. Even simple changes in organizational structures on the Christian side and of social structures on the Muslim side have been seen as a loss of identity. Maintenance of a given fixed identity of people as well as of institutions has been used as an argument against interreligious communication and dialogue, but also against any change at all.

Third, certain forms and concepts of dialogue lack realism. If dialogue is constructed as an idealistic program only and if no attention is paid to the social, political, and economic realities that have so often blocked normal relations between people, including Muslims and Christians, it remains a private enterprise, a personal happening that does not change given realities. Similarly, if dialogue is constructed as a political program, given ideas, ideals, and norms are imposed in advance on the groups or persons concerned and personal insights or initiatives are neglected or suppressed.

As I see it, most successful dialogues have arisen from common commitments to common human and social causes. The fact that people's religious or other views differ, does not in itself exclude practical cooperation. This implies that, in actual practice, interreligious relations and dialogue may well be served by not putting too much stress on the religions that are unavoidably different and that consequently separate people. Instead, solidarities for just causes bring people together who may discover that they are inspired by common intentions and aspirations.

In the light of Muslim and Christian openings toward dialogue, the current presentation of relations between "Islam" and "Christianity" as two more or less fixed religious systems to which one adheres or social blocs to which one belongs should be abandoned. Such a presentation may be useful for certain purposes, including certain kinds of scholarly research, but it does not do justice to various kinds and forms of interaction between different groups of people and the effects of such interaction.

2.7. Present-day Minorities and Majorities: Christian and Muslim

There have always been minorities, small groups with divergent ways of life and ideas, often of a different ethnic identity and mostly defining themselves differently from the religion of the majority. The reasons for constituting a minority may differ and the existence of minorities is given with the fact of human diversity. From the point of view of the majority, minority groups are hardly noticed unless they can be useful or, for whatever reason, they irritate the majority. From their own point of view, however, such groups defend their way of life, identity, and truth, insisting on having their own human dignity. These groups include Christians living in Muslim societies and Muslims living in secular Western societies.

There is something arbitrary in stressing in Europe the religious aspects of immigrant minorities, as if that were their distinctive mark. Why should we identify, for instance, Turkish immigrants in a country like the Netherlands as "Muslims" rather than as "Turks" or "of Turkish descent"? Why have North Africans in France often been called "les musulmans" ("the Muslims") rather than Algerians, Moroccans, Tunisians, or simply North Africans? Why this stress on religious differences or on the distinction between religious and non-religious people? At present, religious identity is not a public one in Europe and, generally speaking, it is not the most important one in present-day society. And to add to the confusion, for the people concerned, the adjective "Muslim", besides referring to a religious identity, always indicates a social one, too. In contrast to this, the adjective "Christian" suggests more of a religious identity; in Muslim societies it also has the social meaning of being "other", non-Muslim.

There is another problem, too, with these terms. When we speak of "Muslims" and "Christians" as generic terms, we abstract from the considerable variety that exists within each group. Nowadays, the terms are useful mainly as rough indicators of the two large groups that, for nearly fourteen centuries in the Middle East and for some fifty years in the West, have represented an important alternative of religious orientation. However, in the course of time, both groups have greatly diversified and, except for in specific regions, this alternative has lost its nearly absolute "dualist" character. Yet, even though both groups generally have become quite diversified, as minorities they mostly want to remain recognized specifically as Christians and Muslims.

Western Christians tend to worry about the situation of Christian minorities living in Middle Eastern Muslim societies, both the ancient minorities and those resulting from nineteenth- and twentieth-century missions to these ancient Churches. The Christians have often lost social and economic standing since these countries became independent, with Muslim majorities occupying most leading positions and showing little interest in non-Muslim "others".

These worries also concern the future of the Christian faith in the Middle East. In colonial times, Western Christianity kept an open eye on the Christian minority communities. When the Third World countries attained independence, Western Churches prepared and supported good leadership in these communities. An active exchange program, in particular of teachers and students at theological seminaries, was launched and material support was given. At present, Christian minorities in Muslim countries are generally under pressure from Islamists and da'wa work, and sometimes also from governments. They have to withstand both the secularizing tendencies of modernity and the Islamization tendencies of Islamic movements. In regions like Southeastern Turkey, Southern Sudan, and Palestine, they have been exposed to war.

Still broader worries exist among a number of UN Agencies, non-governmental organizations (NGOs), and Western politicians about the human situation in Muslim and other Third World countries generally. There are problems of physical survival but also of human dignity. One path of action is to stress the norms and values of the Universal Declaration of Human Rights of 1947, which was signed by nearly all countries. Unlike some two centuries ago, Western states can no longer explicitly defend the interests of Christians in particular. In 1981, the United Nations has clearly pronounced itself against any form of religious discrimination, and the Committee on Human Rights is attentive to this matter.

Another path of action is the annual reporting by the US Department of State on the situation of religious freedom in a number of countries. In principle, the US then has the possibility of applying sanctions by withholding financial aid from countries with a notably poor record on this issue. But it is not easy to define objective criteria for violations of religious freedom and to apply sanctions without political discrimination.

The present time demands that, in practical matters, Christians in Muslim countries—Catholics, Orthodox, and Protestants—emancipate themselves as much as possible from Western tutelage. In a parallel way, Muslims in Western countries should free themselves from supervision coming from Muslim countries. They all should participate as much as possible as full citizens in the ventures of the societies they live in.

The study of religious as well as other majority-minority relations demands a sensitivity to differences and mutual perceptions but also a realistic assessment of social facts. People act and view their religion differently if they are in a more or less comfortable majority situation than if they constitute a minority that has to struggle for survival. However, in majority-minority relations between Christians and Muslims, the difference in religion is generally overstressed, as if this difference were fundamental for human society and as if there were not other, possibly more important aspects of life in society to be taken into account.

More than one religious community, whether in a majority or in a minority, considers itself superior to other groups, for "religious" reasons perhaps, but with palpable social and often political consequences. Rigid majority-minority relationships tend to rigidify the view and practice both sides have of their own and the other's religion. This not only affects the perception of others, but can also lead to tensions and conflicts, the more so if we are dealing with religions that claim absolute superiority and want to have a complete hold on their adherents. As a result, "others" outside one's own community are viewed not only from outside, but also from above. They are not seen and understood as they identify themselves; something like a foreign scheme and an outside evaluation is imposed on them. If action is taken toward them, it is not so much for their sake, but rather to direct and construct others as an extension of one's own social group.

Minorities usually tend to see the majority religion or a secular major-ity as intolerant or oppressive. Concrete research should disentangle the various aspects of minority-majority relationships in given cases. It is also questionable whether, under specific conditions, a particular religious or secular majority has constituted a real threat for a minority community or if the latter rather lives under the obsession of being oppressed.

Relationships between majority and minority groups are quickly felt and perceived in terms of power, and the presence of power is implicitly or explicitly stressed. But there are different kinds and sorts of power!

Selected Literature

ARKOUN, Mohammed, *Rethinking Islam: Common Questions, Uncommon Answers*, Boulder, Colo.: Westview Press, 1994.

EICKELMAN, Dale F., *The Middle East: An Anthropological Approach*, Englewood Cliffs, N. J.: Prentice Hall, 1981, revised 4th ed. 2001.

FRIEDMANN, Yohanan, *Tolerance and Coercion in Islam: Interfaith Relations in the Muslim Tradition*, Cambridge, U.K.: Cambridge University Press, 2003.

GODDARD, Hugh, *A History of Christian-Muslim Relations* (Islamic Surveys), Edinburgh: Edinburgh University Press, 2000.

HODGSON, Marshall G.S., *The Venture of Islam: Conscience and History in a World Civilization*, 3 Vols., Chicago and London: University of Chicago Press, 1974 (paperback ed. 1977).

Islam and Christianity: Mutual Perceptions since the Mid–20th Century, ed. by Jacques WAARDENBURG, Leuven, etc.: Peeters, 1998.

Islam, Modernism and the West: Cultural and Political Relations at the End of the Millennium, ed. by Gema Martin MUÑOZ, London: I. B. Tauris, 1998.

The Middle East and North Africa (Yearbook), London: Europa Publications, 1950– .

Muslim Perceptions of Other Religions: A Historical Survey, ed. by Jacques
    WAARDENBURG, New York and London: Oxford University Press, 1999.
Muslim-Christian Perceptions of Dialogue Today: Experiences and Expectations,
    ed. by Jacques WAARDENBURG, Leuven, etc.: Peeters, 2000.
The Oxford Encyclopedia of the Modern Islamic World, ed. by John L. ESPOSITO,
    4 Vols., New York and Oxford: Oxford University Press, 1995.
ROBINSON, Francis, *Atlas of the Islamic World since 1500*, New York: Facts on
    File, and Oxford: Phaidon, 1982.
WAARDENBURG, Jacques, *Islam: Historical, Social, and Political Perspectives*, Berlin
    and New York: Walter de Gruyter, 2002.

Section 1

Three Monotheistic Religions

Chapter 1
Christians, Muslims, Jews, and their Religions[1]

I would like to start with some remarks on the relations between Christians, Muslims, and Jews. Given the immensity of the subject, I want to limit myself to relationships between their three religions, but not only as historical traditions. I also want to examine how the people concerned consider and construct their own religion as well as the two other "prophetic" religions. I shall first present some historical and comparative observations on the three religions and then a few recent intellectual voices from the communities concerned that deal with the relationships between these religions. I shall conclude with some observations on much-needed research on relationships between Christians, Muslims, and Jews in history and at the present time. Their own ideas about these religions play a pivotal role in articulating these relationships. I hope that my suggestions will encourage others, too, to explore new paths and find new kinds of minesweepers in the political minefield of Christian-Muslim-Jewish relationships.

1. The Beginnings: New Identities

How did these three communities perceive and judge the arrival of a new religious community that also claimed to have received a divine revelation? Or the other way around, how did a new community perceive and judge the existence of previous religious communities claiming to possess divine revelation?

In a certain way, it was easiest for the *Jews*. Besides the temple cult, they had their religion in its rabbinical form and had preached monotheism in important centers of the Hellenistic world, that is to say the Roman Empire, and this message attracted attention. Then Christianity appeared: first what may be called the Jesus movement, then the preaching of his

---

[1]   This text goes back to a public lecture given at Villanova University, Villanova, Pa., November 2000. It was prepared for publication in a *Festschrift* for Professor Mahmoud Mustafa Ayoub. The author acknowledges with thanks that the editors of the *Festschrift* gave permission for publication of the text in this volume.

resurrection with the communal life of the Jewish Christians in Jerusalem and some other places. The Christians claimed that the Messiah had arrived. However, since, as far as the Jews were concerned, hardly anything had changed and certainly nothing favorable to the Jews, they dismissed the Messianic claim. Christians were considered a sect and were persecuted. In Jewish eyes, the hoped-for Messianic era had not yet arrived.

Some five centuries later, Islam appeared. The Muslim community claimed that a new and final prophet had emerged in Arabia. However, the Jews felt the prophetic age had been closed and that they had no need of a new prophet. Maybe Muhammad was sent as a prophet to the Arabs, but the Jews could not recognize him as the prophet he claimed to be. Moreover, the distance they took to Muhammad also had political implications when fighting broke out between the Muslim community in Medina and the Meccans. The Muslims and Jews living in Medina became estranged and in the end the latter were driven out or killed. However, Muhammad concluded a treaty with the Jews of Khaibar, who from then on were treated as *dhimmīs*, like the Jews in other territories the Arabs conquered.

The Jews remained rather indifferent to the rise of these two later religions and their religious claims. They did not remain indifferent, however, to the rise of Christian communities in the Roman Empire, insofar as these tried to make converts among the Jews, tended to compete with the Jews for positions in society, and especially later increased their anti-Jewish discourse and started persecutions. Historically, Muslims treated Jews less harshly than did the Christians.

Seen from the Jewish tradition, Christianity and Islam are children of Judaism; but the rabbis see them as natural children. They deny the claims of Churches and tend to consider their spiritualization an escape from the realities of life. They reject the claims of Islam even if they appreciate its monotheistic message and its rejection of the human inclination to idolatry. Rabbinical Judaism is seen as the legitimate continuation of the Biblical prophets and what we are used to calling the religion of ancient Israel.

The situation was more complicated in the case of the *Christians*. The first Christians were Jews, and Christianity could very well have remained a Jewish sect. It took a little time before the preaching of Jesus as the Messiah extended to the *goyim* (non-Jews). But this was crowned with success, so that after a century almost all the Christians were "pagan" converts or their descendants. The Christian communities crystallized around the four patriarchal sees of Jerusalem, Antioch, Alexandria, and Rome.

Attitudes to Judaism varied, but on the whole they developed negatively. Many Christians were disappointed and disturbed that only a small number of Jews became Christians. All the Jews should have recognized Jesus as the Messiah, but instead, converted Jews suffered persecution by Jewish authorities, at least in Jerusalem. Even before the destruction of Jerusalem in 70 C.E., the Jewish Christians had left the city, were dispersed, and practically disappeared without leaving a trace. Throughout the Empire rivalries arose between Christians and Jews who had established themselves earlier. The fact that the Christians and not the Jews were persecuted in the Empire added to existing irritations and when Christianity became the state religion in the fourth century C.E., anti-Judaism developed further and led to increasing social and religious discrimination against the Jews.

Attitudes toward Islam also varied. Christians everywhere were much concerned about the Arab conquests of territories where Churches were flourishing. Although Christian communities in the Near East had sometimes welcomed the Arabs as a kind of liberators from the pressures of Greek political and ecclesiastical domination, Islam turned out to be a new weight on them. Christians had rejected the idea that Muhammad could be a prophet; for them there was no need of any revelation after Jesus, once he had been recognized as the Messiah (Christ). Christians outside the Caliphate saw the Arabs and Islam as an aggressive enemy against which all defenses had to be mobilized. Christians living within the Caliphate started to lose their old privileged position by the end of the seventh century C.E., and a slowly growing number of them converted to Islam, especially in the cities. From the mid-ninth century on, Muslims made a concerted effort to bring them to Islam, not without success.

From the outset, Christianity has seen itself as a religion of salvation. In fact, the Christian Church has always proclaimed a particular message of salvation to the world. The Church has always measured and judged other orientations, worldviews, ideologies, and religions according to this particular message, even though its "christocentric" view of religions like Judaism and Islam has undergone theological variations. This self-interpretation and claim of the Church to prescribe the true social order and open access to the eternal destiny and salvation of the whole of humanity could not be accepted by Judaism and Islam.

The case of the *Muslims*, as I see it, was less complex than that of the Jews and the Christians. Islam arose outside the power sphere of the great states of the time, the Christian East Roman Empire and the Zoroastrian Sassanid Persian Empire. It rested on the conviction that, after a range of prophets who had preceded him, Muhammad was the last prophet. He was sent to the Arabs but with a universal message contained in the Qur'ān, which was regarded as God's words, and establishing a social order to be expanded to the conquered and eventually converted territories. Compared with the Jews and the Christians, who had both suffered from foreign domination and various forms of oppression, Muslims seemed to have a "success religion". Their self-confidence was enhanced by the conviction that existing Judaism and Christianity as well as other religions were incomplete if not perverted, whereas Islam, as strict monotheism, was the true religion of the one and only God. And it received an enormous boost through the military successes of the Arabs throughout the Middle East and North Africa, the Mediterranean, Spain, and southern France and Italy—leaving aside the territories east of present-day Iran.

Muslim attitudes toward Jews, after a positive start immediately after the Hijra, had deteriorated soon in Medina, not only because the Jews refused to recognize Muhammad as a prophet and made their own claims, but also because they did not support what may be called the Muslim war against Mecca. Although they were then persecuted in Medina, such persecution stopped when Jews surrendered and entered into a treaty with the conquering Muslims, as happened in Khaibar, and when they behaved according to the rules imposed upon *dhimmīs*. As such, they were in a slightly better position than Christian *dhimmīs*, who were easily suspected of constituting a fifth column in the wars between the Caliphate and the Byzantine Empire and later the crusaders.

Muslim attitudes toward Christians were different. Apparently, during most of his life Muhammad was sensitive to the religious life and practice of Christians as he saw it in Arabia. However, certainly in the war situation against Christian tribes in northwestern Arabia but already from the outset of his preaching and public activity, he clearly rejected all that seemed to contradict strict monotheism as he saw it. As a consequence, the Qur'ān denies such Christian doctrines as the crucifixion and resurrection of Jesus, or the Trinity and the incarnation of God. Christian *dhimmīs* living in Muslim territories, like Jewish ones, enjoyed a protected status as "People of Scripture" (*ahl al-kitāb*). Though not usually persecuted, they lived under pressure and were in fact treated as second-class citizens and distrusted in cases of war with the Byzantines and the Latin Franks.

Seen from a Muslim perspective, Judaism and Christianity were a kind of predecessors of Islam. In the Muslim view, Moses and Jesus had brought fundamentally the same message as Muhammad, that is to say a radical monotheism. However, the Muslim tradition reproaches Judaism and Christianity for not maintaining this postulated monotheistic outlook of their prophets, so that they cannot be called "true" predecessors of Islam. It contrasts a Muslim universalism with Jewish particularism and the self-absolutizations of the Christian Churches. Muslims tend to claim the indisputable absolute character of their own religion. For them it is the absolute religion that has existed since creation, was affirmed by the prophets, and has to be followed by humanity as a sign of submission to God.

2. Distinct Features of the Religions: Further Distinctive Identity Construction

From the outset of their encounters, these communities stressed the originality of their own religions and their own religious identity in contrast to each other. In present-day terms, no syncretism was officially allowed.

Seen in a historical perspective, the three religions have indeed certain distinct features. The communities themselves stress these features as what constitutes their specific identity and as what distinguishes each one fundamentally from the others. The main features are the following.

In *Judaism*, the gift of the Torah as a religious rule of life distinguishes the community from other people(s). It is a sign of election, but conveys in return a specific responsibility. It gives the community a religious status that implies a liberation from the burden of both human tyranny and religious idolatry. The Torah, supplemented by the oral tradition, is recognized as guaranteeing to the community the correct knowledge of the true rules of life. Throughout history, the longing for the Messianic era at the end of time, in the face of the hardships of life, including dispersion (*galūt*), oppression, and persecution, has strengthened communal efforts to endure. The religious ideal is to transform the world in the sense of justice and peace as meant by its Creator. Jewish identity has both ethnic-social and religious aspects.

In *Christianity*, the life, death, and resurrection of Jesus is viewed as the most crucial event of history, inaugurating the arrival of another kind of order (Kingdom). He should be recognized as the Messiah ("Christ") and followed. This leads to a liberation from the forces of the world, a redemption of humankind from evil, and eternal salvation for the faithful. Christians are held to constitute a redeemed community of mutual love, with the task to convey the message of liberation and salvation in word and deed to other people and the world. Salvation implies a liberation both from the burden of the Law in religion and from the oppression of the powers in the world. Christianity sees this world in the light of a new creation to be proclaimed and furthered. The community is organized through the institution of Churches, whose nature, task, and organization have been a long-standing subject of debate. A separation of Church and State, as spiritual and political realms respectively, is accepted. This does not exclude interaction, and the Churches, consequently, have been involved in politics. The Christian identity has strong spiritual as well as social aspects.

In *Islam*, the notion of an absolute monotheism is fundamental; any form of idolatry is rejected. Islam is held to contain the principles of a universally valid social order. The verses of the Qur'ān are considered to have been directly revealed through an intermediate angelic figure. They enjoy absolute authority and are held to constitute a definite and final revelation for humankind. As religious law, the *Sharī'a* contains the rules for communal and personal life to be practiced in Muslim communities. At the end of time, all people will be submitted to a final judgment for their eternal destiny. The Muslim identity has both religious and social aspects.

Much more could be said about what I have described here as the main distinctive features of the three religions. In each one, a number of particular structures developed in the course of history. In this way, the three religions were "constructed".

These communities each developed a particular consciousness of their own history conceived in different ways as valid "tradition". Such a tradition was considered to go back to the earliest beginnings of the community, and a continuity of this tradition was assumed. Besides their various Scriptures, these various traditions have been a source which a community could fall back upon and a means by which it constructed its distinctive identity. In practice, it was not only distinctive features in matters of law and doctrine, religious practice, and life style, but also the canonization of a particular Scripture, the construction of a homogeneous tradition, and the use of certain rules of interpretation that became the backbone of the three communities, giving them their distinctive identity.

3. Historical Variety: Neglected Sub-traditions

Historically speaking, however, the respective traditions, including those about the beginnings of each religion, were not as homogeneous and linear as they were presented within and to the communities themselves. They were in fact constructions made in later times that gave to the adherents the idea of historical continuity and even of linear development. The historical reality of the three religions was far more complex than the later presentation of an unbroken tradition suggests.

In all three cases, almost from the beginning there were different "sub-traditions" resulting from debates between different points of view taken in the community. In a number of cases, such different views led to enduring tensions. Especially when questions of leadership, authority, and power were involved, such tensions contributed to conflicts. These could sometimes be solved through compromise, but in other cases led to separations, or in the worst cases suppression and elimination. The official traditions in all three religions hardly speak of the dissenters who raised their voice but who were marginalized and could be simply forgotten. The fact that they arose and found adherents cannot be denied, however, and shows that the historical reality of the communities of these three religions has been much richer and much more varied than the official tradition could admit. In other words, the construction of what are assumed to be the distinctive features and the authoritative traditions of the three religions does not correspond with the empirical social and historical reality of the religious communities concerned. They are rather normative schemes that were developed in these communities and later imposed on what had been the people's lived reality.

Let me give some examples of the great number of various orientations that developed in the three religions and brought about their astonishing diversity and complexity at the present time.

First, certain new fundamental religious constructions should be mentioned that had a profound impact on the three communities and their further history. In *Judaism*, I note the rise of synagogal communities with what is called rabbinical Judaism devoted to the study of the Torah, and also the development of various kinds of messianism and religious Zionism throughout the history of the diaspora. In *Christianity*, I think of the broad range of interpretations and applications of God's Kingdom, including the idea of the community of saints and the establishment of the monastic orders. I also notice the gradual development of a kind of ecclesiastical order in terms of a spiritual empire—alternative to the political one—but increasingly demanding obedience and claiming to be a guarantee of salvation. Throughout history, there have been a number of chiliastic and spiritualist movements often considered heretical, and in the twentieth century an ecumenical movement has taken off, relativizing existing ecclesiastical structures. *Islam* developed the nostalgia for a pure, paradigmatic religious community that supposedly existed under the first four caliphs. Besides the spirituality of the *turuq* and its various sectarian movements, it developed a variety of ideas about the just society and the ideal Islamic state, with claims of universal validity. Throughout the twentieth century, Islam has been increasingly ideologized in connection with the social and political context in which Muslim communities find themselves.

In all three communities, moreover, there arose a number of religious subcultures, some of which were marginalized or worse, especially when they led to practical separatisms from the mainline communities. *Judaism* had its Samaritans, its Qumran community, its zealots, its followers of Jesus, its Karaites, and a number of sectarian movements of different sorts throughout history. It saw the opposition between Sephardim and Ashkenazim, the Liberals and the Orthodox, but also its Chassidim, its religious Zionists, and its ultra-national activists, with all its consequences for present-day Israel. *Christianity* had its ascetic movements and its communal religious orders, its excommunications after each Ecumenical Council, its East-West schism of 1054, and its sixteenth-century Protestant Reformation. One should mention the Jansenist, Puritan, and Pietist movements in the West, but also the worldwide missionary movement, the rise of the independent Churches in Africa, and of the theology of liberation in Latin America. Different Church models reflect the basic opposition between centralized power in the Roman Catholic Church and autonomous communities in Protestantism. *Islam*, too, has known its separatist and even heretical movements. Right from the beginning there were the Shī'ī, Khārijī, and more ascetically inclined movements. Throughout history, a number of repristination movements have called to go back to Qur'ān and *Sunna* only, whereas the various Mahdist movements announced the end of time. Islam has had its Bābīs, Bahā'īs, and Ahmadīs, its Wahhābīs and Tālibān, but also its Sūfī orders and accommodations to local culture. I should mention the difference between Sunnī and Shī'ī Islam and between the *turuq* as centers of spiritual life and the activist movements aiming at the Islamization of society through political action.

In more recent times, new social constructions were developed in the framework of these religions, sometimes later also taken up by people not belonging to the three religious communities themselves. In *Judaism*, the "ingathering" of diaspora Jews in Israel as well as the continuing debate about the assimilation of Jews in other societies and cultures is to be noted. Great efforts have been made to explain Jewish tradition and life in broader circles. In *Christianity*, the Christian socialist movement, the missionary movement, and the activities for Justice and Peace (*Justitia et Pax*) deserve mention. I am also thinking of current critical movements targeting the present-day economic and political world order, the human rights movements, and movements supporting the poorer Southern as opposed to the richer Northern countries. In *Islam*, a number of movements arose in response first to tradition, then to modernity in the context of changing social and economic conditions. The burden of political power and interests, both national and international, weighs heavily on present-day Muslim societies and the religious communities constituent in them.

In recent times, these three monotheistic religions have known changes and movements in different contexts that would have been difficult to imagine in the nineteenth century. This is an indication that their history is continuing. The ongoing process of the construction of Judaism, Christianity, and Islam is taking place before our eyes.

4. Common Elements and Features of which Adherents are Conscious

Adherents of the three religions have been more or less aware of the fact that Judaism, Christianity, and Islam have elements in common. Best known are elements that can be found in the Scriptures of these religions, directly mentioned or merely alluded to and with which the reader is supposed to be familiar. This is strengthened by the fact that Christianity has also recognized the Hebrew Bible as Scripture. Let me give a few examples.

1. Several figures are common to the Hebrew Bible and the Qur'ān, and also alluded to in the New Testament, for instance Adam (and Eve), Noah, Abraham (willing to sacrifice his son), Joseph, and Moses.
2. In all three Scriptures, we find some basic narratives in common or alluded to, for instance the creation of the world, the creation of man and woman, the mistake of Adam, the deluge and the Ark of Noah, Moses receiving the Tablets of the Law, and the Israelites' veneration of the golden calf.
3. In all three Scriptures, respect is paid to God's powerful reality and to God-given Law. God's generous disposition toward the human being is stressed as is the need for the human disposition of obedience, love, and submission toward God. Several common ethical rules are proclaimed, such as taking care of widows and orphans, the poor, and the strangers.

Looking more closely, however, we see that the presentation of these elements common to the three Scriptures is not the same, but varies. The underlying interpretation sometimes differs considerably, and they are often linked in different ways. This is also true for the Qur'ān, although its often rather allusive style tends to obscure this fact. The more elaborate presentations, for instance, of Abraham's call and wanderings and of Moses' call and his receiving the Law and guiding the Israelites as described in the Hebrew Bible, differ considerably from references to the same material in the Qur'ān and allusions made to it in the New Testament. Historically, such differences can of course be attributed to different sources, but we must also assume that the storytellers and redactors had their own particular intentions when they transmitted or recorded the stories and that they wanted to convey particular messages to their audience or readers. As a consequence, we should read these narratives as already presenting particular interpretations that the storytellers or redactors made out of the materials they had at their disposal, along with their own deeper intentions.

In their attachment to Scripture and tradition, these communities bear a striking similarity. In all three religions we find a canonized Scripture enjoying more or less absolute religious authority and considered to have been revealed. Supplementary to Scripture, there is in all cases a tradition that claims to go back to the founding figures of these religions and that is recognized as authoritative.

In their ways of systematic thinking, once established, the three religions also show remarkable common features. What has been called "natural theology", developed by reason without recourse to revelation, is quite similar in the three religions. The juridical systems of Judaism and Islam are similar in structure. At certain moments during the medieval period, Muslim, Jewish, and Christian thinkers were able to discuss—at least in writing—a number of common philosophical and theological questions. This was because these thinkers shared a common framework of thought based on Aristotelian and Neoplatonic thought.

Even the ways religion was taught to students in the three communities were largely similar, since there existed common traditions of study and teaching.

5. Parallelisms of which Adherents are less Conscious

We are here also concerned, however, with certain features the three religions have in common, but which the adherents themselves are mostly unaware of, since they naturally tend to view things from the perspective of their own particular religion. It is only in a more detached comparative view that such features catch the eye. All three, for instance, have comparable notions of the individual person and stress his or her responsibility.

Parallelisms between these three monotheistic religions are all the clearer if one compares them as a family with other families of religions, such as the Indian religions, the religions of China, or the religions of Antiquity. I would like to give four examples of such parallel features, to which others could be added.

5.1. First of all, common to Judaism, Christianity, and Islam is the idea that something special—a gift implying reciprocal duties—was offered to the community, which it accepted as the foundation for its existence. This kind of communication took place through a particular prophetic figure, and the community accepted the offer subsequently by covenant or alliance, though it did not always live by it. The prophetic figure himself, whether Moses, Jesus, or Muhammad, is held in great honor by the community aligning itself with him.

The communal nature of the deal implies that the gift entails a responsibility of the community as such. At the same time, the members of the community are considered responsible as individual persons. Both communal and individual life is seen as privileged and responsible.

In all three cases, moreover, the community's acceptance of the gift has a wider significance. Christianity and Islam in particular have the whole of humankind and its well-being in view. All three communities consider themselves exempt from a certain disorder or even confusion that is supposed to prevail among people in the "outside" world. They have received a meaningful orientation in the world and this is part of the gift.

From a comparative point of view, this common structure, centered around a gift that was received, seems to me basic to Judaism, Christianity, and Islam, which can be seen as variants. Certain key terms in this respect—God, revelation, alliance or covenant, Law, judgment, paradisiacal situation—have an important place in all three religions. This is also true for certain key intellectual problems; their elaboration—for instance of the relationship between reason and revelation—runs rather parallel.

In all three religions, certain religious elites—scriptural, intellectual, mystical, practical—cultivate a particular expertise in matters related to the gift and claim authority for it. In Orthodox and Catholic Christianity, a highly influential and sometimes powerful hierarchical clergy developed; in Judaism and Islam, rabbis and *'ulamā'* were considered authorities on Law and religion in general. All three religions have also known another kind of authority based on personal religious experience.

Such parallelisms of key terms, of intellectual construction, and of religious elite formation are not merely formal; they can reach substance as well. They are striking from a comparative view, if one considers the three religions as a kind of extended family. But for the people concerned, this family resemblance remained largely hidden behind the religious walls erected and maintained between the religious communities. Even basic knowledge of each other's religion as it is lived in practice has been absent in these communities until very recently.

5.2. A second common feature of the three religions is the claim to possess a *revelation* mediated on divine authority and of absolute validity. All three religions regarded revelation as the highest good. In all three cases, this revelation was somehow linked to a canonized Scripture that became practically the guarantor of revelation. In all three cases, moreover, what was viewed as revelation was considered final and immutable, not only for the community itself, but also fundamentally for the rest of humankind.

As a consequence, in defending the possession of revelation, Scripture has played a pivotal role for these religions. But it could also serve other aims. In the monotheistic religions, Scripture often served to provide access to the ultimate Truth(s) about the community's religion. One could appeal to Scripture against degradations of religion in social life, injustice and immorality in society, misuse of religious law, misconduct by the religious leadership, oppression by the political leadership, and last but not least against false sacralizations of law, tradition, or popular customs. Scripture could also be used, however, to legitimize efforts to "purify" religion. Karaite, Calvinist, and Hanbalī reformers invoked their Scriptures in support of their puritan programs and practices.

The polemics between the three religions often denied and attacked the claims of revelation made by other, that is to say rival religions. The other's Scripture could be viciously attacked at their most sensitive point, that is to say their claimed character of revelation.

As long as the people were not familiar with their own, not to mention other Scriptures, and with the various ways of studying and applying their texts, they were dependent on specialists performing these tasks, "religious *literati*". The latters' authority and even power rested on the fact that Scripture was considered and had even been sacralized as the necessary intermediary to revelation. The specialists had different ways of explaining and applying Scriptural texts and were rivals for the power to control their interpretation and application. In a number of cases in the histories of all three religions, Scripture was simply used to legitimize or support ideas and practices that served other interests.

5.3. A third common feature of the three cases is the nearly absolute value that each religious community and its adherents attributed to its *own religion*. Believers were expected and encouraged to identify unconditionally with their respective religions.

We should see this attitude in its context. For a long time, religions corresponded to autonomous ethnic, national, and other social groups that had to defend themselves to assure their survival or that had to make exorbitant claims to increase their power. Religion was a sensitive spot for every community with common beliefs and religious practices; it was not to be mocked. Throughout history, one of the major tasks of the religious leaders was to support the given community by defending its religion both against disintegration from the inside through heretical movements with a different practice or interpretation of the same religion, and against attacks from the outside by rival communities that followed a different religion. Claims of true revelation, true Scripture and tradition, true beliefs and practices, and true spiritual leadership were not Platonic ideas or exercises in theological thinking. They were intimately linked with political strategies to assure a common ideological mobilization of the faithful and to guarantee control of the community at large. The idea of the absolute self-sufficiency of the religion of the community had a prominent place in this strategy of survival.

Thus, in the course of history the three communities have seen not only each other but also each other's religions as rivals, resulting in an ideological battle. The factual relations between the three religions throughout history can be compared to the rivalries and occasional alliances between tribes or nation-states, empires or power blocs that also use their myths and ideologies to identify and promote themselves while defending themselves against each other. In the case of the three monotheistic religions, however, these religions were absolutized not only by means of intricate ideologies but also through complex forms of spirituality.

5.4. A fourth and last common feature of the three monotheistic religions is the singular but overriding fact that for each of them, all *"others"*, that is to say non-adherents, outsiders, were seen as problematic. From the very beginning, there was a deep concern with one's own religious in-group, of which one was part and parcel. When the community grew and its adherents increased in numbers, there arose a similar concern for its homogeneity, and monolithic views of the religion of the community were useful at the time to strengthen communal awareness. In the case of Christianity, such concerns contributed to the persecution of heretics by the Churches, later softened to their exclusion.

States could later provide passports to their citizens and mutually recognize each other, but religions could not. How could deeper relationships be established between human beings if there were no common views of God, the human being, and the world, no common faith, and no common rule of conduct? How could religions that had erected religious walls between people and that had been absolutized for centuries recognize the rights of other believers?

The late twentieth century witnessed the growth of the notion of a common and broader humanity beyond the differences of religion and of some religious leaders' attempts to give their own community a place within this common broader humanity. One could stress the "special case" of one's own community within this humanity. One could undertake missionary action to bring to others the truth one had been given oneself. One could develop the idea of a religiously-based social order to be extended throughout humanity or imposed on it. One could even launch a worldwide program of practical cooperation and religious dialogue between people of different faiths. In any case, people not belonging to one's own religious community started to be perceived.

It seems to be, however, only with an increase in solid knowledge of processes of modernization, in solid insight into the workings of ideologies, and in solid reflection about humankind's potentialities, that true advancement may be expected. This requires of course a broader responsibility than that for the good of one's own community only. It demands a commitment to norms like human dignity, conditions of life worthy of that dignity, justice, peace, and respect toward every human being.

For people of good will, the centuries-old religious walls erected between Judaism, Christianity, and Islam as rival religious systems seem to become permeable or at least to lose that rigidity that often gave them an inhuman character. People of other religions are no longer fundamentally a religious or ideological problem when we no longer identify them with what we have constructed as their religion. In the end, people should no longer be seen as products of a religion but as responsible agents themselves capable of interpreting and applying their religions the way they see fit.

6. Some New Views Coming from the two Prophetic Religions

6.1. From a Jewish Point of View

An example of a new view from the Jewish side is the book by Ignaz
Maybaum published in 1973 under the significant title *Trialogue between
Jew, Christian and Muslim*. The author, at the time a rabbi of the Liberal
Jewish community in London, presents here his personal "trialogue", his
own effort to grapple with Christianity, Islam and Orthodox Judaism.

Rabbi Maybaum shows himself here a well-schooled theologian who
rejects false romanticism or any idealism that cannot deal with reality. His
interpretation of Judaism appeals to Franz Rosenzweig (1886–1929), but
he does not agree at all with Rosenzweig's rather negative judgment of
Islam during and after World War One. As is well-known, Rosenzweig—
who had thought seriously of converting to Christianity—"converted
back", so to speak, to Judaism. He saw Judaism and Christianity fundamentally as two roads leading to the same God and opened a new kind
of Jewish-Christian dialogue.

Rosenzweig did not see Islam, however, as a full-grown monotheistic
religion. His book *Stern der Erlösung* (1921, 1930²; trans. *The Star of
Redemption*, 1971) contains denigrating remarks about it and he gives
negative judgments about Islam, which, however, he had not studied from
the sources and which he did not really know. As I see it, Rosenzweig,
when he reconverted to Judaism, set himself up against Islam. This has
had more or less catastrophic effects for the image of Islam among those
Jews and Christians who have followed Rosenzweig as their spiritual
leader or model.

Maybaum, however, referring to the Muslim prayer to an Almighty
God—understood and served as both one and unique in Himself—recog-
nizes Islam as a full-grown monotheistic religion. Perhaps Maybaum
could have spoken of not two but three or more possible roads to God—
although he does not use this formula himself. But this is in fact the basis
of the "trialogue" for which he pleads between Jews, Christians and
Muslims as monotheists.

The particular and positive contribution of this author to our subject is
what he calls "prophetic" Judaism. The Jewish Enlightenment (*haskala*)
that started with Moses Mendelssohn at the end of the eighteenth century
was a break in tradition-oriented medieval Judaism, and Maybaum greets
it as a real breakthrough. It led to establishing what was called liberal
Judaism and to the critical historical study of Judaism (*Wissenschaft des
Judentums*). Orthodox Judaism, however, which wanted to give a rational
defense of traditional Judaism, crystallized as a reaction against this
development. It dominated in continental Europe and obtained a veto-
wielding position in present-day Israel. Liberal Judaism, by contrast,

developed in Great Britain and in North America, where it took its own course.

Following Rosenzweig's line, Maybaum accentuates the prophetic character of true Jewish life and thinking. He opposes this to Christian thought, on the one hand, which he reproaches for having made a split between the spiritual and the material aspects of reality, and to Muslim thought, on the other, which he sees as paralyzed through the unconditional submission of the human being to the Almighty God. Maybaum feels that the positive side of prophetic Judaism is due to the immediate link it makes between the human being and God as the divine Being, and to the particular kind of existence that is given to the Jewish believers and that distinguishes them from the *goyim*, the non-Jews.

But such a prophetic Judaism also has its negative sides. Maybaum mentions for instance the marginal character of Jewish existence and the condition of the *galūt* (diaspora), which Maybaum diagnoses for Jewish life inside and outside the state of Israel. What is seen in the "world" (Muslim, Christian, or otherwise) as a way of life set apart or even as a kind of alienation, is for Jewish consciousness in fact the way of being truly human and is characteristic of Jewish individual life and fellowship. The true Jewish believer sees Christianity and Islam as two one-sided fruits of Judaism with which he or she is continuously involved. He or she cannot identify with them, but knows him- or herself as co-responsible for them. Such a deeper consciousness of human responsibility is typical of prophetic Judaism. For this reason, according to Maybaum, it distinguishes itself from Orthodox Judaism, which has become closed within itself.

Looking back on Maybaum's place in the sixties and seventies of the twentieth century, I would say that his thought on the relations between the monotheistic religions is a fruit of the positive dialogue of those years. He does not, however, show a real knowledge of Christianity or Islam as distinct religions that have now become independent from prophetic and rabbinical Judaism. He sometimes passes judgments on them that are in conflict with the facts. His dialogue remains a grappling, an intense spiritual dealing with Christianity and Islam, which he continues to perceive as "children" of Judaism. He does this on the basis of his Jewish identity and self-awareness.

6.2. *From a Muslim Point of View*

In an article from 1989 about Muslim-Christian-Jewish dialogue, Mohammed Arkoun gives his vision of the relationship between Judaism, Christianity and Islam, as well as his thinking on the dialogue to be furthered between the adherents of these religions. Like Maybaum, Arkoun makes an energetic attempt to break out of his own rather closed community, in this case the Muslim one. He appeals to the results of scholarship, in particular the social sciences, and presents some Islamic notions that have universalistic implications, since they transcend the borders of the Muslim community.

To start with the latter, Arkoun views Judaism, Christianity, and Islam in particular as "Scriptural" religions. Jewish, Christian, and Muslim communities constantly refer to their sacred Scriptures, which are subject to a process of constant exegesis and application. The three religions share common problems of text interpretation, that is to say hermeneutics. The societies in which these three religions are alive are marked by the fact that they stand under the authority of a Scripture. The cultural forms and the views of the human being that have been developed by the adherents of these religions and their societies have always borne the mark of their Scripture.

With their essential message of monotheism, Judaism, Christianity, and Islam all call to the service of the one and only God. The fact that there is one and the same God for all three communities guarantees universality. Yet, in the course of their history all three religions have assumed their own social and organizational forms. They have institutionalized themselves, and these forms have subsequently been considered definite and unchangeable. All three religions have developed their own theology, religious law, and ethics in order to fix their own religious system and to protect their own community against the influence of others. They have proclaimed their own character and truth to be exclusive. Arkoun reproaches theologians and jurists for concerning themselves only with developing theology, law, and ethics for their own community alone, without being conscious of wider responsibilities. In other words, he reproaches the monotheistic religions for having closed themselves up within themselves and off from each other.

Arkoun presents a number of critical considerations on the ways in which texts, history, and doctrines in Judaism, Christianity, and Islam have been interpreted and used. In his analysis, he appeals to insights obtained in the humanities, for instance in semiotics and in anthropology. Reality, as it is described in the three religions under consideration, is always an interpreted reality, rich in symbolism, since meanings and significances are expressed in symbolic terms. This kind of interpretation of reality turns out to have serious limitations, however, when we take into account the historical and social contexts of these religions and their history and social reality. The study of symbolism is able to bring to light the meanings these religions, as interpretive systems, have been able to provide in given historical and social contexts.

Arkoun's trust in what scholarship can achieve goes back not only to the Enlightenment tradition but also to his own deeper philosophical premises.

Fundamentally, in this article he speaks about Jewish-Christian-Muslim dialogue as a philosopher.

Mohammed Arkoun stands in the line of humanist thought and he defends the humanist tradition and concept of the human person as a responsible being as they have been articulated in Islamic thought. With this orientation he opposes current ideologizations of Islam in Islamic activism. But he also rejects current Western views that emphasize fatalism and the lack of freedom of the human being in Islam or that see mysticism as the apogee of the human being in Islam. Arkoun has always defended reason. For him, the human being as presented in Islam is a being gifted with reason, that is to say between animal and angel, and this is the basis for human dignity.

Arkoun has taken upon himself a role mediating Islam to the West. He objects to a kind of Western orientalism that is closed in on itself and that is incapable of dialogue with Muslims and of communication with Islam as a living culture and religion. Arkoun has conducted a continuous dialogue with Westerners of all sorts and is guided by the idea of the complementarity of the various cultures and religions. Muslim activists have accused him of letting himself become westernized. Arkoun for his part reproaches the so-called "Islamists" for their poor and one-sided knowledge of the Islam they want to defend. In the final analysis, Arkoun turns out to be a heroic figure combining Islamic and Western values in his own original way.

7. A Historical Point of View

In an important essay published in 1993 under the title "A Dialogue of Creeds", Keith and Kevin Massey investigate the oldest creeds of the three monotheistic religions. Such statements of faith were meant to show the community where it had a common stand distinguishing itself from other communities surrounding it. Instead of tracing historical dependencies, the authors want to show that the monotheistic religions, when formulating their respective statements of faith, had a kind of "dialogical" relationship with each other. Three examples clarify this.

The Jewish creed is contained in the *Shema* of Deuteronomy 6:4 "Hear, O Israel, God our Lord is One" (*ehad*). In contrast to Canaanite culture and religion—with its adoration of El, Athirat, and their children—there is here a clear monotheistic stand. For the redactor of the text there is only one God, the one who liberated the Israelites from slavery in Egypt.

The oldest Christian confession of faith, according to Oscar Cullmann, was formulated in two directions. Towards the Jews it asserted simply that Jesus Christ is Lord; profession of belief in the one and only God was self-evident here and did not need to be expressed in particular. Toward Hellenistic polytheism, however, such a profession needed to be made explicit: in his first Letter to the Corinthians (8:6), Paul formulates the faith both in one God (the Father) and in one Lord (Jesus Christ). He adds that this profession of faith brings salvation (eternal life). Somewhat later, this double profession is formulated in John 17:3: "And this is life eternal: that they might know Thee, the only true God, and Jesus Christ—the anointed one (*christos*)—whom Thou hast sent" (King James translation). With this statement of faith, the community of the Christians distinguished itself from the other religious communities existing at the time: stressing the "unique" character of the God of Israel and the particular importance of the revelation of Jesus (as being sent by God).

The Muslim creed is the *Shahāda*: "I witness that there is no god (or: nothing divine) but God (Allāh) and that Muhammad is his prophet". The authors observe that, curiously enough, this text does not occur as such in the Qur'ān, which demands, in a slightly different formulation, that one should bear witness of one's faith both in God and in his prophet (S. 24:62).

The authors then offer the hypothesis that the formula of the *Shahāda* might go back to the profession of John 17:3. During Muhammad's lifetime this text could have been known in Arabia as the Christian creed. The Muslims would then simply have replaced the name of Jesus by that of Muhammad. The authors submit that this change came around 700 C.E., when a growing number of Christians in the Middle East converted to Islam, creating a need for an Islamic creed that stressed the significance of Muhammad instead of Jesus.

Whereas the *Shema* mentions the unity and uniqueness of God, the Christian creed adds Jesus, while the Muslim creed adds Muhammad replacing Jesus. In each case, the later community situated itself with regard to the preceding one by means of a statement of faith. The three professions of faith of what became the monotheistic religions reflect a debate or dialogue and, consequently, they should be understood in relation to each other.

The three religions themselves, in principle, can resume and continue a dialogue that was stultified after the fixation of their three professions of faith.

8. The Question of Religious Identity

Until now we have taken as our point of departure the idea of religions and religious communities as presented by the latter's religious leaders. Religious identity is then seen as something that is religiously and socially given, primarily by the religious community to which one belongs, with its own tradition and authority.

A very different and more scholarly question, however, is how the people concerned want to identify themselves, religiously or otherwise, together with others or individually. It then becomes clear that, on an empirical level, religious identities vary and that a religious community is not as homogeneous as is often represented or imagined. Someone's religious identity is in fact part of a whole range of identities in daily life, and in most cases it is not as exclusive or dominating as people imagine. This applies particularly to life in modern society, but even in traditional societies the personal "real" identity of people does not coincide with their social role.

It could very well be that the usual definitions of what constitutes a Jew, a Christian, or a Muslim religiously have little to do with the way such people in fact identify themselves or even conceive themselves ideally. This is certainly the case in plural societies, especially in cities where only the individual, not the tradition-bound community, can give explicit information about his or her identity. In the study of religions we should accept the idea that religious communities consist of people with very different motivations and identities and for whom a given religion has a significance that is ever more individualized.

Even in the case of Jews and Muslims, where identity is maintained as strongly as possible by the leaders and in the community, the usual formal criteria are not sufficient to grasp the ways in which people identify themselves. Although religious leaders may try to strengthen the homogeneity of their communities, in practice the "real" identity of persons in modern contexts turns out to be much more fluid than the "official" norms would allow.

Such changes in the contents of identity, largely due to changes in and of societies, unavoidably affect the relationships between Jews, Christians, and Muslims. They may have learned what it is to be a Jew, a Christian, or a Muslim as radically different identities or about Judaism, Christianity, and Islam as rigidly separate religions. These categories were largely developed to underscore one's own truth and to combat syncretism. They stressed the differences more than common ground. In the present-day public sphere, however, these identifications tend to obstruct what I would like to call normal communication between human beings of different backgrounds.

9. Conclusions

The subject of this chapter is what the science of religions can say about relations between Christian, Muslim, and Jewish persons or groups and about the role of their religions in such relations. This contribution does not present new facts, but seeks to put known facts in perspective.

In the preceding pages, I first gave a brief historical view of the three religions and the way in which they saw each other. Once established, they tended to distinguish themselves ever more sharply from each other. One reason was that the communities concerned saw themselves as new and independent entities. They constructed their religions as more or less homogeneous traditions proceeding from revelation, and they constructed the "others" as more or less radically different. I concluded that neither the images that the religions cherished of each other nor the constructions that they presented of themselves conformed to historical and social realities, but had a normative character.

Next I offered a brief comparative view of the three religions. They have a number of elements in common, and adherents have been more or less conscious of this fact, especially with regard to Scripture and systematic thinking. I showed that there are also other common elements and parallelisms that adherents have been hardly conscious of but which become evident in comparative research and research on the interactions that took place between the communities. Such common elements and parallelisms, however, have been interpreted differently in the three religions and again by different trends and schools within these religions. The religious communities themselves have been eager to stress their own distinctive character, notably by indicating the unique character of their religion and its truth and by stressing its historical continuity. I submitted that the religious communities always wanted to prescribe how relations with outsiders ought to be seen. The way in which other religions were constructed from the point of view of one's own religion largely served this purpose. I concluded again that these constructions of relationships between religions are normative and do not correspond to historical and social reality.

I then moved from considering religions and their relationships to the personal voices of two intellectuals from the Jewish and Muslim traditions. I left aside similar voices from the Christian side, such as John Hick and Hans Küng, since I supposed them to be more or less known. The two intellectuals mentioned offer a kind of synthetic unified vision of the three monotheistic religions, in which the specific character of each of them is viewed as its own particular responsibility.

I concluded that the real relationships between people from the three religious communities in given times and places can in fact differ greatly from what has been thought until now about the relationships between their religions. This argument is strengthened by what the science of religions has discovered not only about the empirical and constructed realities of these religions, but also about prevailing constructions and images of "religions" in Western as well as other societies. This means that more research is needed about situations and contexts in which Christians, Muslims, and Jews have been in contact with each other. Christians, Muslims, and Jews live less and less in their familiar traditional societies. Their relationships in "modern", "late modern" and "postmodern" societies inevitably obtain a different character. This increases the priority of the issue of the identity of the persons and groups concerned.

Present-day relations between persons or groups that identify themselves as Christian, Muslim, or Jewish are conditioned by a great number of factors and elements. Religion is one of these elements but not always and not necessarily a decisive one.

The major problem that religions pose, however, is that, in the name of a religion, norms can be proclaimed that have authority for and sometimes even an absolute claim on the adherents, with negative consequences for their relations with non-adherents. I do not mention the possible negative consequences for the adherents themselves, since that remains their own responsibility. Further research on relations between Christian, Muslim, and Jewish persons or groups in given situations and contexts is needed. Only then may we become more able to explain and understand what happens in situations of tension and conflict between groups with different religions. We ought to have more insight into what role lived religions and current representations of those religions play alongside other social forces. The question becomes particularly urgent when people in situations of conflict are willing not only to fight but also to die for their religion.

But a clear distinction must be made between the *people* with their ideas, practices, constructions, and images, on the one hand, and the *religions* and religious leaderships that they claim to adhere to, on the other hand. Close inquiry into the ways people present or represent their own or other peoples' religions and into what such religions mean to them is a key to understanding. Let me suggest three areas in which I think such research is urgently needed.

1) Attention should be paid to the ways people *view their own religion* with the acceptance of differences existing within this religion, *as well as other religions* while accepting that they have a certain validity, at least for the adherents. In Christian, Muslim, and Jewish communities, we observe on the one hand a tendency to take a more objective attitude towards one's own religious tradition and Scripture. On the other hand, there are clear orientations and movements in the three religions that want to fall back on particular elements of the tradition or on particular texts of Scripture and that tend to ideologize them.

Such a rediscovery and reactivation of the sources of one's religion is, in the first place, a personal or communal search. But it has implications for the relations entertained with "others" with whom life has to be shared and for participation in society at large and ideas about how society should be organized.

The far-reaching changes in people's conditions of life and new means of communicating with each other seem to lead necessarily to new orientations toward existing religions. This is particularly true for Christians and Muslims, as adherents of the two largest religions, and for their mutual relations.

2) Attention should be paid to the ways in which people *identify themselves at all*, with or without the help of religion. In many cases people no longer identify themselves primarily through their religion, but rather for instance according to their ethnicity, nationality, social class, profession, or causes to be served, including political adherence. People may identify themselves in different ways in different situations and contexts. Religious identities also have social aspects that vary according to contexts. As a consequence, we should ask what exactly people mean when they identify themselves "religiously" or socially as Christian, Muslim, or Jewish. Do they practice their religion? What does their religion mean to them?

Changes of identity often have to do with experiences that are linked to new and sometimes critical situations, or to contexts in which traditional communal structures are falling apart and in which people have to individualize themselves to survive, as is certainly the case in Western societies. Certain groups discover themselves as being oppressed, and subsequent liberation and emancipatory movements tend to affirm the newly articulated identity of their members. Migrants arriving from outside often redefine their identity in order to survive. Specific crisis situations, but also personal communications can be catalysts in such processes of new self-identification and personalizing or, on the contrary, loss of identity and depersonalization. This certainly holds true for Christian, Muslim, and Jewish communities worldwide and their relations.

3) Attention should also be paid to empirically observable changes in religious communities, the religious leadership, and current changes of orientations in religions like Christianity, Islam, and Judaism. During the last twenty-five years, besides the rise of new religious orientations, a certain "stiffening" in religions seems to have taken place. The last decades of the twentieth century witnessed the rise of a new "fundamentalization" in religions.

Islamic fundamentalism protests against secularization and wants to re-Islamize society, imposing its own version of Islam on all Muslims. Jewish fundamentalism protests against assimilation, wants to Judaize Israeli society, and plays here a political role with religious arguments. Catholic fundamentalism is a protest against the openings offered by Vatican II and plays a political role in affirming and centralizing the Church's power in Rome. Protestant fundamentalism protests against secularization and sees Evangelical Christianity as the remedy for various kinds of evil. Research has been underway for some time to locate, analyze, and explain such "fundamentalisms" in religions and the powers and interests at work in them. Fundamentalist orientations directly affect relations between Christians, Muslims, and Jews.

More promising for the future, however, seems to be the question what happens to religions and to the relations between them in circles that have a "relaxing" and a more "serving" character, opening up to other people, listening to what they have to say, and committing themselves to human causes. Ethics and social concerns may play a primary role here. We ought to know more about orientations and tendencies of this kind among Christians, Muslims, and Jews, without classifying them in advance. So I suggest research should be done among such people about their mutual perceptions, ecumenical activities, cooperation and dialogue even with adherents of other religions, shared ethical concerns, actions of human solidarity, development of self-critical views, and awareness of political and other forms of abuse of religion. My guess is that people of this kind of orientation are willing to cooperate, whatever their Christian, Muslim, or Jewish background.

The question to what extent a self-critical attitude of mind has been cultivated among and by *intellectuals* with a background in one of the three religions under consideration has hardly been asked so far. I am thinking for instance of critical attitudes toward religious, political, and other social institutions and their leaderships. Yet such intellectuals could cooperate.

There was a time in which one placed confidence in the values of world religions as "goods" without further ado. But in practice even world religions have turned out to be highly ambivalent. They can be used for good, but they can also be abused for power and self-interest. A student of religion cannot be unaware of this. Critical scholarship cannot serve idealism, religious or otherwise. It can contribute, however, to a *realistic understanding* of what is happening in the broad field of religions in various contexts. It can discern where religions like Christianity, Islam, and Judaism are used for what is good, and say so. It is, however, up to the adherents to act.

Selected Literature

1. Perspective of the History of Religions

COLPE, Carsten, *Das Siegel der Propheten: Historische Beziehungen zwischen Judentum, Judenchristentum, Heidentum und frühem Islam* (Arbeiten zur neutestamentlichen Theologie und Zeitgeschichte 3), Berlin: Institut Kirche und Judentum, 1990.

2. Scriptures

PETERS, Francis Edward, *Judaism, Christianity and Islam: The Classical Texts and their Interpretation*, 3 Vols., Princeton: Princeton University Press, 1990.

3. Judaism and Christianity in Early Arabia

AHMAD, Barakat, *Muhammad and the Jews: A Re-examination* (Indian Institute of Islamic Studies), New Delhi, etc.: Vikas, 1979.

BOUMAN, Johan, *Der Koran und die Juden: Die Geschichte einer Tragödie*, Darmstadt: Wissenschaftliche Buchgesellschaft, 1990.

HAVENITH, Alfred, *Les Arabes chrétiens nomades au temps de Mohammed* (Collection Cerfaux-Lefort 7), Louvain-la-Neuve: Centre d'Histoire des Religions, 1988.

LECKER, Michael, *Muslims, Jews and Pagans: Studies on Early Islamic Medina* (Islamic History and Civilization, Studies and Texts, 13), Leiden, etc.: E. J. Brill, 1995.

NEWBY, Gordon Darnell, *A History of the Jews of Arabia: From Ancient Times to their Eclipse under Islam*, Columbia, S. C.: University of South Carolina Press, 1988.

RABBATH, Edmond, *Les chrétiens dans l'Islam des premiers temps: L'Orient chrétien à la veille de l'Islam* (Publications de l'Université Libanaise, Section des Etudes Historiques, 23), Beirut: Université Libanaise, 1980.

TRIMINGHAM, J. Spencer, *Christianity among the Arabs in Pre-Islamic Times*, London and New York: Longman, and Beirut: Librairie du Liban, 1979.

4. Judaism in Relation to Islam

DÉCLAIS, Jean-Louis, *David raconté par les musulmans* (Patrimoines: Islam), Paris: Cerf, 1999.

LASSNER, Jacob, *Demonizing the Queen of Sheba: Boundaries of Gender and Culture in Postbiblical Judaism and Medieval Islam*, Chicago and London: University of Chicago Press, 1993.

LEWIS, Bernard, *The Jews of Islam*, Princeton: Princeton University Press, 1984.

Medieval and Modern Perspectives on Muslim-Jewish Relations, ed. by Ronald L. NETTLER, Luxemburg: Harwood Academic Publishers in cooperation with the Oxford Centre for Postgraduate Hebrew Studies, 1995.

Muslim-Jewish Relations: Intellectual Traditions and Modern Politics, ed. by Ronald L. NETTLER and S. TAJI-FAROUKI, Amsterdam: Harwood Academic Publishers in cooperation with the Oxford Centre for Postgraduate Hebrew Studies, 1998.

NEUSNER, Jacob, and Tamara SONN, *Comparing Religions Through Law: Judaism and Islam*, London and New York: Routledge, 1999.

Studies in Islamic and Judaic Traditions, ed. by William M. BRINNER and Stephen D. RICKS (Brown Judaic Studies 110), Atlanta, Ga.: Scholars Press, 1986.

Studies in Muslim-Jewish Relations, Vol. 1, ed. by Ronald L. NETTLER, Chur: Harwood Academic Publishers in cooperation with the Oxford Centre for Postgraduate Hebrew Studies, 1993.

5. Judaism, Christianity and Islam: Historical Relations

ARKOUN, Mohammed, "New Perspectives for a Jewish-Christian-Muslim Dialogue", *Journal of Ecumenical Studies*, 26 (1989), pp. 523–29 (repr. in *Muslims in Dialogue: The Evolution of a Dialogue*, ed. by Leonard SWIDLER, Lewiston, etc.: Edwin Mellen Press, 1992, pp. 343–52).

CRAGG, Kenneth, *The Privilege of Man: A Theme in Judaism, Islam and Christianity*, London: Athlone Press, 1968.

MASSEY, Keith A.J., and Kevin MASSEY-GILLESPIE, "A Dialogue of Creeds", *Islamochristiana*, 19 (1993), pp. 17–28.

PETERS, Francis Edward, *Judaism, Christianity and Islam: The Classical Texts and their Interpretation*, 3 Vols., Princeton: Princeton University Press, 1990.

Religion in the Middle East: Three Religions in Concord and Conflict, ed. by Arthur J. ARBERRY, Vol. 1: *Judaism and Christianity*; Vol. 2: *Islam and The Three Religions in Concord and Conflict*, London: Cambridge University Press, 1969.

Chapter 2
Three Monotheistic Religions:
Structure and Patterns of Meaning

1. Introduction

The religions of ancient Israel, rabbinical Judaism, Christianity, Islam, and lately also Bahā'ī have been the subject of extensive textual and historical studies. Empirical research shows a clear coherent relationship among these religions, not only in their own separate histories, but also in their influences on each other and their interaction. Although some periods of the histories of these religions and certain dark spots, especially in times of oppression, are poorly known, the broad lines of their histories are well-known today. Judaism arose out of the religion of ancient Israel and developed its law and spiritual trends, among them its belief in a coming Messiah. Christianity arose out of the preaching and action of Jesus and the response of his disciples and others who believed in his resurrection. Islam emerged out of the preaching and action of Muhammad, first in Mecca with the group of his followers and later in Medina with an established community. The Bahā'ī religion arose at the end of the nineteenth century around the person of Bahā Ullāh and his preaching. I concentrate here on Judaism, Christianity, and Islam.

Historical research has stressed in particular the way these religions differentiated from each other in the course of history: their separateness. Yet there has been communication between the people concerned. The communities have developed significant relations. Each community thereby made an explicit appeal based on what it considered to be its religion based on revelation.

Further comparative research, however, has also brought to light the presence of certain common currents of thought and practice that can be found in these religions. This is the case even if these religions consider themselves unique and establish barriers between themselves and other religions. Adherents tend to keep a distance from non-adherents. All three religions had their particular scripture to be interpreted; two of them had their own kind of religious law to be spelled out and applied. All three religions had their particular form of piety in the form of the right attitude to be taken or of proper behavior. All three also developed specific forms of spirituality as mysticism based on the authority of experience or as gnosis based on the authority of esoteric insight. All three religions had their demands of reason leading to theology, the study of law, philosophy, and demands of practical life that led to numerous forms of lived religion and in particular of popular religion.

Given their differences in historical development, scholarly research may very well ask what these three religions have in common on a deeper level. That is to say, is there an internal structural coherence which can attribute a role to or a rational relationship with the other religions?

Historically speaking, these three monotheistic religions came from the Semitic world of the Middle East. There were other monotheistic religious communities, but the number of their adherents declined severely in the course of time. There are also other monotheistic religions that arose in the region in modern times. I restrict myself here, however, to the three religions that have for centuries been in interaction, including long-lasting conflicts that did not remain limited to the Middle East. The history of religions shows an open-ended variety of trends, options, and ways of living in each religion in the past and at present. In fact we can speak of various communities living side by side with their own traditions within each religion. Only some of these survived to the present day, considering themselves the right or true community.

Comparative research has tried to show differences and common features of these religions as they have developed in history. Social science research has paid attention to the functions these religions fulfilled in their social and historical contexts and to the social functions of the various elements of these religions.

2. Adherents' Perspectives on what these Religions have in Common

The question of a commonality between the three religions is far from new. From the beginning, some adherents have been interested less in where the religions differed than in a search for what is common to them and distinct from other religions or worldviews. In the adherents' attempts to find what they have in common, I distinguish at least four perspectives.

1) One can look from within a particular tradition of faith at the truths of the other two traditions, judging them in terms of one's own truth.

2) One can search for a religious truth that transcends the three distinct religions. A number of people see, for instance, the typical exclusive belief in one God as the unifying bond. This may be called a theological construction. Those who consider the three a unity of "Abrahamic"

religions make what I call a mythical construction. Mohammed Arkoun constructs unity around all three religions' belief in one original divine Word or in one original Scripture as the source of the three scriptures these religions consider to have been revealed. Evidently, all these constructs of the unity of the three religions are based on a particular religious faith. Even Lessing's ingenious attempt to recognize Revelation as the final truth to which the religions should be subjected was limited by the fact that, although all three claim to be the result of Revelation, the human being is not able to prove the presence of Revelation. In the end, the content of Revelation is not known.

3) The proponents of a trialogue between these three monotheistic religions assume some kind of family relationship, but centered on one religion in particular. Ignaz Maybaum, for instance, one of the first who used the term, saw Judaism as the "prophetic" religion that outshines the other less or non-prophetic ones. Ismāʿīl Rāji al-Fārūqī, who also used the term, saw Islam as the "reasonable" religion that supersedes the two others. Mohammed Arkoun simply keeps to the authoritative Muslim expression of "the three heavenly religions". He considers them all "heavenly" because he considers their three Scriptures to be based on Revelation. In all three cases, the Scripture concerned has had an immense impact on the society and culture concerned. Kenneth Cragg, for his part, sees the fundamental commonality of the three religions in their recognition of "the privilege of man". In a study on the subject, he offered a penetrating analysis of the interpretation the three religions give to the human person.

4) Marshall Hodgson and Wilfred Cantwell Smith looked for the ways Christianity and Islam have developed as historical religions, trying to identify their historical structures and to designate the way they present themselves nowadays.

What kind of solution can a more critical scholarship propose?

3. The Three Religions as a Critical Scholarly Problem: The Science of Religion

What do the three religions have in common from a critical scholarly point of view? We have to distinguish several levels of research:

1. The first and basic level is that of outward behavior, specifically ritual and social behavior found in all three religions. This is open to far-reaching empirical research.

2. The second level is that of sensitive and esthetic expression and reception, specifically in the domain of the arts and of literature. Certain forms are appreciated in certain religions, whereas other forms are not and may even be prohibited.

3. The third level is that of moral and ethical decision-making and action. Here we are dealing with norms and values promoted in a particular religious tradition, in particular circles, or in a particular movement.

4. The fourth level is that of conscious spirituality as opposed to purely material orientations or teachings followed without full consciousness of their consequences and implications.

Although the justifications and interpretations of particular religious data may differ, many elements of a religious way of life and of life as such, as viewed in the three religions, can show striking similarities.

3.1. Historical Problems of the Three Religions

In speaking of the three monotheistic religions, we are dealing not only with ideas, but also with a variety of historical and social data. This is especially true for Christianity, which can be called the most "organized" of the religions considered.

There have been and are many different *Christian* communities, traditions, institutions, and movements. They grew out of Jesus' messianic preaching, the Jesus movement proclaiming his resurrection, a growing number of local communities, the rise of the patriarchates, the growing organization of the Church, and the domination of the bishop of imperial Rome. Official recognition by the state was followed by the development of an imperial Church claiming to be infallible and disparaging those not recognizing its authority. After the Enlightenment, the nineteenth and twentieth centuries witnessed, on the one hand, an enormous plurality of Christians of very different adherences and local Churches in global expansion, in particular through the missions. On the other hand, we see at present an ecumenical outreach and a growing concern with the life and survival of people, but also a more defensive attitude of the Churches toward the impact of economic and political forces on them. Christianity cannot be viewed as a historical or social unity; different Christian institutions and religious authorities have divergent views and interests.

Similar remarks can be made about *Islam*. It started with the preaching of Muhammad, the prophetic movement led by him, and the ensuing socio-political forms that the community subsequently took. Here too, a number of movements have arisen and traditions been established, mostly linked with current socio-political interests. The result has been an immense historical and social variety in what may be called the Muslim commonwealth. The variety here is even clearer than in Christianity, because Islam has no institution or leadership claiming to give authoritative judgments. The twentieth century in particular shows many orientations and movements in view of existing historical, social, and political forces within and having an impact from outside the community. The impact of the West, the spread of Muslim minorities throughout the world, and the increasing politicization of Islam have shown new aspects of it in the twentieth century. This has been due largely to the challenge of and response to twentieth-century economic and political interests.

Judaism, too, though by far the smallest of these three religions, is characterized by historical and social variety. The ideas of an alliance between God and the people and of a religious law of divine origin and authority given to the people go back to the story of Moses receiving the law at Mount Sinai. The development of synagogical and rabbinical Judaism may have started during the Babylonian exile. It implied basic reorientations of religious life. The period in which Christianity arose and split off from Judaism was one of upheaval for the Jewish community inside and outside Palestine, with various responses given to historical events, including Roman rule and the life in diaspora outside Palestine. Most of the time, Jewish communities lived in diaspora under Muslim and Christian rulers. After the emancipation during the nineteenth century and with the participation in secular Western society and culture, the twentieth century gave a new turn to Jewish history. The growth of a richly varied Judaism in North America, the rise and success of the Zionist movement with its "ingathering" of the diaspora, and the establishment of Israel after the genocide suffered in Europe showed new aspects of Judaism. Orthodox Judaism established itself powerfully in Israel, where the national interest and religious legitimization were interwoven. I submit that Judaism in and around Israel has become politicized in ways comparable to the politicization of Islam in most Muslim countries. Judaism is being mobilized in Israel and beyond to safeguard and defend not only the survival of the Jewish people, but also the interests of a particular state. Like Christianity and Islam at an earlier stage, Judaism has become subjected to national interests and military power. As I see it, this puts a question mark behind claims of universality.

This quick survey shows that, from a scholarly point of view, it is no longer possible to envisage these three religions as separate historical and social entities. The question of what they have in common can no longer be answered naively and becomes all the more interesting. What can be said, for instance, about the historical and social nature of these three religions?

3.2. The Nature of the Three Religions

In ordinary discourse as well as in Muslim discourse and current "trialogue" discourse, Judaism, Islam, and Christianity are mostly subsumed in the concept of monotheistic religions. This is an oversimplification, whatever the good intentions. Empirically speaking, we confront manifest differences and even oppositions.

Judaism, for instance, is fundamentally linked to the Jewish people in their particularity, comparable in this respect to Shintō, which is linked to the Japanese people. In both cases, ethnic, social, and religious aspects are closely interwoven. From a Jewish perspective, Christianity and Islam are, at best, seen as being historically indebted to Judaism, which is seen as their paternal religion that gave them the task to spread monotheism among the non-Jews. The Christian and Muslim perspectives are completely different. The history and social role of Judaism has been closely linked to the survival of the Jewish people. This has now been concretized and largely identified with the survival of the state of Israel, to the point where the claim of carrying universal ethical values, as maintained in liberal Judaism in Europe and North America, has been deflated. Even for diaspora Jews who do not practice religion, Israel represents a focus of loyalty and unity. In this light, criticism of the state of Israel is easily seen as a form of antisemitism. Other monotheistic religions are, at most, seen in the framework of the Noachite alliance; Jewish orthodoxy hardly participates in interreligious dialogue. A Jew retains his or her Jewish identity as a quality given by birth, even if he or she abandons religion and secularizes. Judaism, then, may be called an exclusivist religion; it accepts converts but does not proselytize. Lately there has been a growing tendency to view Christianity in the line of Judaic aims and purposes.

Christianity, whatever may have been its historical roots in Judaism, is a fundamentally different kind of thing. It can be viewed as a messianic, future-oriented movement that distanced itself from the Judaism of historical tradition and law, which could not recognize Jesus' messianic character. It can also be viewed as an emancipatory movement that detached itself from Judaism and spread into the wider Hellenistic world. Arguments can be made to deny that Christianity is a truly monotheistic religion. As it understands itself through its scripture, it proclaims a kind of universal salvation. It seeks to realize a new kind of order in persons and the world. Christianity typically crystallized as a religion, essentially different from the world, and organized in its own way in the numerous Churches as Christ-like communities. In the nineteenth century, Christianity developed worldwide missionary work. In the twentieth century it started its ecumenical movement. After World War Two, with the end of the missionary era, a concern with interreligious cooperation and dialogue has evolved. According to its self-understanding, Christianity is completely different from Judaism and Islam.

Islam, whatever its historical roots in Judaism and Christianity, is again very different from these two religions. It is a kind of universally oriented monotheism and sees Judaism and Christianity as former stages in the history of Revelation, with a deformation of true monotheism. It calls for human abandonment to God as the supreme form of monotheism, with the religious law prescribing the right way of living. Islam also offers the outlines of a socio-religious system. It sees this as a new social order of absolute justice, of universal validity. A Muslim remains a Muslim in a social sense if he or she does not practice religion. Islam is open to interreligious cooperation and dialogue within the parameters set out in the Qur'ān. Other religions are categorized according to whether or not they have a scripture and whether or not they are monotheistic.

From an empirical point of view, it is legitimate to ask whether the three entities are comparable and whether they constitute one category or group of religions at all. We call them "religions", but this term is derived from an ordinary, common discourse and has been applied to the three entities as a common predicate. Our search for structure in Judaism, Christianity, and Islam, however, has to take a different and more critical starting point.

4. The Conceptualization of the Three Entities as "Religions"

4.1. Conceptualization by Adherents

Practically, the conceptualization of the three religions was developed from within the framework offered by one of them. In the West, this was mostly Christianity. It was the work of thinkers oriented either more institutionally and professionally or more independently and freely.

The professional thinkers were theologians and jurists. They articulated religion so as to serve communal and individual life. In Christianity, clergy and monks paid much attention to doctrine, morality, and ethics. In Judaism and Islam, rabbis and *'ulamā'* devoted themselves to the study of Torah and *Sharī'a*. In the course of history, those articulations that were not supported by a community mostly disappeared.

The thinkers who were more independent did not have a specific official responsibility to a community. They could be philosophers and historians, social and political thinkers, authors and artists, or just persons who were spiritually moved or inspired. In modern times, they would probably be thinkers and also ideologists developing new ways of describing their religion.

All conceptualizations of the three religions were of course constructed from given traditions and developed in particular historical and social situations. Concepts in general use could take on particular meanings in a given religion, corresponding to particular needs of its community existing at a particular time and place.

The concepts used may be of a general nature, but specific spokesmen of particular religious communities could use them with a particular meaning in specific situations. We should be careful about blanket attributions of such concepts to a particular religion as such without asking what meaning it could have had in its time. The history of thinking in these three religions is indeed largely the history of the interpretations and applications that particular spokesmen of the three religions gave of elements of their tradition or of their tradition as a whole. Important in this context is that they conceptualized or "constructed" their religion in the process. We should see traditions as processes of ongoing interpretations. From time to time, there were then new conceptualizations and constructs or significant changes in the meaning of existing ones.

4.2. Conceptualization by Scholars

Not only adherents but also scholars who were not committed to the religions studied have conceptualized the three entities in their own ways in the course of their studies. Historians of religions considered them "religion". In doing so, though working historically, they were often indebted to the ways theologians and jurists conceptualized their religions. They were also indebted to the common discourse about Judaism, Christianity, and Islam as three different and separate "religions". But in this discourse, each party underscored that its own religion was different from the two others and that each religion constituted an autonomous entity, a "unit" separate from other "units".

A scholarly conceptualization, however, does not necessarily follow the categories of adherents or of common discourse. Whereas that discourse stressed differences between the communities with their religions, one could just as well stress areas of common concern. I am thinking of human problems that have to be solved, of popular religion and the practical needs of life underlying it. One may think as well of mystical religion and the authority of experience underlying it, and of putting religion in abstract terms with the underlying demands of reason, or of gnostic esotericism and the underlying formation of spiritual elites.

Scholars of religions have often been prone to accept the views of established religious leadership as authoritative. Such scholarship, however, has not been critical enough to see the bias of existing religious authorities. The latter, of course, see it as their task to support their communities and to defend the identity and truth of these communities against the claims of other communities. For other communities could offer possible solutions for specific problems of life, solutions that, taken in themselves, might be no less and sometimes perhaps even more reasonable. A scholarly study of religions should not be made subservient to apologetic concerns of whatever kind or of whatever leadership.

More refined and detailed comparative studies of relevant data show the shallow character of establishing definite and permanent similarities and differences between Judaism, Christianity, and Islam as such. Scholars cannot conceptualize these three entities in any definite and fixed way. Within each religious community, and also in scholarship, different conceptualizations and constructs of religion made by different persons, including scholars, exist side by side. On closer analysis, different interests and intentions underlie such different conceptualizations. It is naive, at least in the field of culture and religion, to believe that definitions and conceptualizations can be valid once and for all for everyone on earth.

5. Elements and Values Held in Common in the Three Religions

Let us come back to the question what these three religions have in common and in what sense each of them may be called unique. They clearly have at least four elements in common, though these elements can also be found elsewhere.

1. The human being is held to be a person responsible for his/her actions.
   Notwithstanding existing differences of opinion about the degree and kind of freedom of human beings, all three religions accept (a) that there are certain norms and rules that have to be obeyed and (b) that the basic norms for human behavior are based on revelation about "God" (the origin of the rules and the aim of life).

2. In contrast to existing forms of mischief (harm, *Unheil*), some kind of grace (salvation, *Heil*) is offered that the human being should accept.
   There are very different views of this grace, of the way in which it is offered (for instance as commandments and prohibitions), and of the way in which it should be accepted (for instance by obedience and submission), with different effects (for instance for the relationship between the human being and "God").

3. There is a distinct community that lives in accordance with the prescribed lines.
   There are different views about the nature of this community.

4. Reference is made to "God" and "Revelation".
   The three religions and each religion separately includes different notions and different concepts about God and Revelation. All three religions believe that there is ultimately only one God and that God is not an object of ordinary knowledge. They hold that God is fundamentally unknown, but that He makes Himself known in some way at His initiative and in His way, that is by Revelation. The notion of revelation has very different contents in different circles.

In actual fact, the three religions have many more common elements. They affirm, for instance, the creation of the world, a particular view of linear history going toward a good ending, a certain view of the cosmos and the wider world, etc.

Moreover, the three religions clearly recognize a number of norms and values, though these are not limited to these religions only. Their pursuit is prescribed:

God—service to God—faith—relations to God resulting from faith;

Human dignity—attention given to the other—relations resulting from this;

Justice—peace—human life—compassion—repentance—pursuit of these norms and values.

6. Proposed Approach in the Study of Religions in General

I submit three points of my own approach in the study of religions. On the basis of this approach, I shall deal with the question of a common kind of structure that would link the three monotheistic religions.

1. Religions consist of a number of elements that we can study as data or facts but that adherents in individual and social life take to be more than facts. As a surplus, and in certain connections, they are meaningful and convey meanings. I call such elements "signs" suggesting or conveying meanings and meaning patterns. They can become "symbols" through a process of interiorization. Symbols distinguish themselves from signs in that they can lead to experiences felt to be deeply meaningful and possibly leading to personal insights and transformations.

For adherents, religions constitute a kind of world or system of meanings, or at least a reservoir of meanings somehow stored in the signs and symbols.

Consequently, religions like Judaism, Christianity, and Islam can be characterized as signification systems, specifically as sign and symbol systems. This is the "objective" side of religions. It presupposes the existence of a "subjective" side for people who regard them as meaningful.

2. The subjective side of religions is the way people interpret and apply their religions, what they themselves make of their religions, and what makes them see certain elements of these religions as particularly meaningful, that is as signs or symbols. Elementary experiences, upbringing, education, and religious instruction play a preparatory role. But it seems to me that it is a particular intention or problematic of a person or a group that makes a specific element appear particularly meaningful.

I assume that ordinary intentions of human life can be "loaded" in some kind of absolute way. As a result, they can take on a religious meaning or refer to data that a person or group holds to have an absolute value. In that case, the people concerned will tend to read a kind of spiritual meaning or simply a "religious" meaning into those particular data. Such data then not only become significant phenomena to them, but may also become religiously significant, that is to say religious phenomena. Constellations of religious phenomena may develop particular connections and condense into systems that people are accustomed to call religions.

Religious meanings may present themselves and may be experienced as being beyond space and time. In fact, however, they occur to persons and groups in particular situations and contexts. At a given moment, a particular person or group may experience a specific text, doctrine, or ritual as highly significant and may subsequently objectify and "eternalize" this subjective significance into a spiritual meaning or value that is true and exists beyond time and space.

The relevant research question here is, why, in a given situation, particular people experience, apply, and develop a specific subjective reading of religious phenomena that touch them. This reading is highly relevant to them. In general terms, why and how do people spiritualize religious phenomena for themselves, and do they give spiritual or religious readings of ordinary phenomena?

3. Under the impact of the rationalization of life and modernization of society, the existing religions have undergone significant transformations, in particular in the nineteenth and twentieth centuries. One trend has been an effort to give rationalizing interpretations of religions, that is say to rationalize them to make them viable for the challenges of modernity. In Christianity first, but then also in Judaism and Islam, intense intellectual efforts have been made to "reconstruct" the religion in accordance with the demands of the time. One way of doing this was to go back to scripture and tradition, to select particular elements of them, and to construct with the help of reason and modern scholarship a kind of synthesis enabling people to respond to the new challenges of life. I leave aside other kinds of "constructs" that resisted changes to existing religions, clinging for instance to the fundamental texts and to ritual precision.

As a result, more rational constructs of Judaism, Christianity, and Islam have been developed, and not without success. These religions could fulfill new functions on a social and collective level; they conveyed new kinds of meaning to adherents, and they could also be used or instrumentalized for broader social and political purposes. Precisely in the twentieth century, a great number of new, mobilizing ideological constructs of these and other religions have been developed under the powerful impact of economic, political, and technological forces. Young people, of course, are more prepared than older people to accept new versions of religious traditions from pre-modern times that had long been accepted as self-evident. New conceptualizations of Christianity, Islam, and Judaism respond to similar challenges. The responses may be different, but they show certain common trends, such as a trend toward liberation theology and the pursuit of justice and peace.

7. Signs and Symbols Held in Common in the Three Religions

Each one of the three religions has a wide range of signs and symbols, especially in their scriptures and their religious practices. Signs and symbols that are connected with the basic truths and ritual practices of the community have a "strong" meaning for adherents. In modernizing contexts, there is increased variation in the way different individuals and groups draw on particular signs and symbols in view of specific meanings. On the other hand, certain symbols lose their symbolic power and others take on completely new meanings. People may show an increased sensitivity to particular symbols in particular situations and contexts.

The scriptures and traditions of the three monotheistic religions have a number of religious signs and symbols in common. Of course, their meanings may show differences and other meanings may overlap them in particular times and places. Notwithstanding profound differences between the various monotheistic traditions, one can speak of a common reservoir of certain core signs and symbols in these three religions. It would certainly be possible to catalogue them.

At the present time, two important developments should be noticed. First, new signs and symbols have emerged to which adherents of these religions apparently are sensitive, but they may awaken sensitivity among other people as well. Religious and social aspects seem to be closely linked here.

Second, through increased communication, attention is awakening for what is meaningful to people from another religious tradition. For instance, in former times Orthodox icons or Islamic Qur'ān calligraphy could evoke instinctive reflexes of rejection in Western Europe, but now they seem to be more accepted, even if their meanings are not well understood. What is relevant here is that signs and symbols of other people are recognized at all and are supposed to be at least meaningful for others.

8. New Constructs of the Religions

In the past, most constructs of Christianity, Islam, and Judaism were made by authoritative community leaders assisted by theologians and jurists (experts of religious law), emphasizing the differences between the communities with their religions. Most new constructs of these religions, however, have been made by non-established religious leaders and thinkers. That is to say, the "constructors" nowadays come from groupings that had no voice in more traditional societies. Differentiation is increasing in religious communities. Especially in Islam and in Protestant Christianity, the basis of the construction of religion has enlarged considerably. Parallel to this broader basis, the impact of ideological currents on reformulations of the three religions is significant, although the established leadership takes a defensive attitude.

Another, opposite process has led to new thinking about conceptualization in religion. At least in Christianity and in certain quarters of Islam, "ecumenically" oriented movements have brought about new constructs that various groups in the religion share. In most cases, there are new common concerns about liberalization and fundamentalization, feminist theology and the theology of liberation, with relevant social and political commitments connected with them. Movements toward more openness, ecumenical movements, and movements to combine forces in pursuit of relevant causes provide impetus to modify and change current constructs, to add new elements, or to make new constructs altogether.

9. The Three Monotheistic Religions Seen as "Subsystems" of one Religious Core System

The problem formulated at the beginning of this chapter was that of a possible structural or rational coherence between Judaism, Christianity, and Islam. In other words: can we discover a structure in which these religions participate or of which they are part? In search of an answer, we listened to what adherents and critical scholarship have to say. Thus far, we did not find a satisfactory answer.

We then turned to the role of symbolism in religions, which we viewed as signification systems, that is to say as sign and symbol systems. We found that the three religions have a core of symbols held in common, though interpreted in very different ways. Moreover, we saw in more recent developments of these religions not only parallel responses to challenges of the present time, but also the rise of new and partly common symbols, as well as a growing recognition of others' symbolic expressions. At this point we can tackle the problem of a structural coherence of the three religions.

If we can see the three religions as three separate sign and symbol systems with certain symbols held in common, and if we can speak of certain shared signs and symbols as constituting a core system, then the three religions can be logically viewed as subsystems of that core system. This core system consists of elements and values held in common.

Certain founding patriarchal figures, certain basic moral and legal prescripts, certain views of the responsibility of the human person, certain views of justice and peace, certain views of history and expectations for the future have major significance for more than one system and sometimes for all three of them. Logically, such elements and values, as well as the signs and symbols representing them, constitute a core system in which the religions participate and of which these religions are in fact subsystems.

Consequently, the three religions can be seen in two ways:
1) as three separate systems each consisting of symbolic elements that partly overlap;
2) as three subsystems of one core-system consisting of symbolic elements, some of which have significance for two or even all three religions.

I submit that Judaism, Christianity, and Islam are linked not only through historical and social ties and direct interactions. They are also linked through a symbolic core system that consists of common and other important symbolic elements. As a consequence, they can be considered subsystems of this core system.

In the course of history, the three subsystems have become historically linked to religious communities that have gained and defended their own independence, socially and historically. They have also become independent systems, ideologically and theologically.

They considered themselves self-sufficient, and they mostly developed the idea of a fundamental otherness, incompatibility and even conflict among themselves. In some cases, this has led to the idea of a radical exclusivity.

When the three communities had won their independence, they wanted to maintain and defend it. Indeed, they declared new revelation impossible, they closed and canonized their scriptures and early traditions, and they created systems of religious law and doctrine that tended to mark them off from others. In other words, it is the very nature of the three religions as religious systems to consider themselves self-sufficient and closed. As a consequence, all three were liable to become fixed, reified, ideologized, and politicized. The efforts made by the communities to construct their religions as nearly absolute entities have led to making them socio-religious bastions comparable to socio-political states.

Conflicts that occurred between the three religions should be attributed not only to political and economic forces and interests. They are also due to the religions' forgetting their links with the core system and abandoning the notion of a common symbolic reservoir. Certain "extreme" currents in these religions contributed to the process by advancing claims of religious exclusiveness and uniqueness in contrast to empirical observation and rational deduction.

In the course of history, the constructs that certain religious leaders in particular made of their three religions—legitimized through the claim of revelation, that is divine origin, and carrying the weight of religious authority—have been held to be incompatible. The idea of incompatibility and conflict among these religions was substantiated by a number of real conflicts and has also been followed by critical intellectuals and scholars of religions. To defend the idea of a symbolic core system of the three religions against accusations that it is illusory or gnostic, I contend that it is a scholarly view based on empirical evidence and held for the sake of scholarly truth.

10. Scholarly Consequences

From the moment that we study Judaism, Christianity, and Islam as not a priori separate and even confrontational entities, research can take new directions. We do not have to study common phenomena in a theoretical framework of three separate traditions. Indeed, the recognition of the constructive nature of the traditions and of the very concepts of religion concerned enables a better understanding of the variety of meanings of phenomena that are common to the three religions. Let me give two examples of such research.

1. In the study of the scriptures—Hebrew Bible, New Testament, Qur'ān— we should pay attention to figures that have had a symbolic value. We can see how a figure like Adam—including the story of him and Eve—is presented in the three scriptures and commented upon in the commentaries. One must refer to *midrash* literature and Talmud, to Paul and successive exegetes, and to *tafsīr* literature. Comparisons with earlier stories about primordial man in the Mesopotamian and Iranian traditions may usefully be added. We can even follow this up in later spiritual and present-day feminist interpretations.

The leading question is what kind of meaning the fundamental texts and their readers have seen in the figure of Adam and his story with Eve. Similar research can be done on the meanings of other highly symbolic figures like Abraham and his sons, Joseph, Moses, Solomon, John the Baptist, Jesus. This presupposes solid textual, historical, and comparative research, but is animated by the question what such figures have meant to different groups of people and what the latter have made of them.

One can also address symbolic models of religious behavior as presented in the three scriptures. I am thinking of human repentance before God or other human beings, human heeding what is felt to be God's will, human urge toward liberation, and God's assistance implored in it. Models like these have had a symbolic power with an impact of adherents' kind of behavior.

One can even address the three scriptures themselves and the symbolic power of having God's word in human writing. How did generations in the Jewish, Christian, and Muslim traditions express what they saw as the profound meaning of the presence of these scriptures? If we consider a scripture—like a religion—as a signification and symbol system in itself, what kind of meanings did the adherents find in them and attribute to them? It was through such meanings that believers were attached to these religions.

2. In the study of communal life in Judaism, Christianity, and Islam, we can discern what can be called symbolic models of human communities. These models represent symbolically how community life should be. I am thinking of the twelve tribes of Israel, named after the sons of Jacob and brought by Moses into an alliance implying special duties and privileges; the earliest Christian community, which considered itself to be participating in the body of the resurrected Christ; and the early Muslim community living under Muhammad's guidance with prophetic words and deeds. These models of communal living have had immense symbolic value for the communities concerned. Closer study is needed of the empirical realities of Jewish, Christian, and Muslim social life, including their tensions and conflicts, and of the means to resolve those tensions and conflicts. One can also pay attention to symbolic representations that made these communities survive: as elected people apart from other peoples, as a Church realizing God's kingdom, as the community (*umma*) of all those who have abandoned themselves to God.

The very meaning of communal life according to such models becomes apparent in the moral or legal rules of behavior prescribed for the members of the community. Like the symbolic model of the community, the moral and legal rules have a normative character and should be followed. There are also rules of behavior toward "outsiders", specifically people belonging to other monotheistic religions.

Adherents consider the symbolic models of communal life and the rules of behavior indispensable. Their meaning is expressed in what is seen as fundamental values preserved by the models and rules, such as justice to all members, brotherly love, equality before God, and privileged human communication within the community.

This investigation presupposes solid sociological, socio-historical, and anthropological research. It is then concerned, however, with the normative symbolisms recognized in the life of the communities studied.

3. Especially in the second half of the twentieth century, powerful voices have been raised to defend and promote on a worldwide scale particular norms and values, on the basis of certain symbols, doctrines, practices, and community models presented in world religions. The three monotheistic religions had thereby a place of choice. Given the signs and symbols

of the three religions, one may indeed hold that they designate—in present-day terms—norms and values of human life that emerge in all religions. Certain human rights can be found as values proclaimed in the religions, and common struggles to realize these values, such as the dignity of women, are in fact found in all religions or at least their basic myths and scriptures. Besides defending a certain order, all religions have hammered on improving the situation of humankind in human societies and privately.

Especially in the monotheistic religions, innumerable efforts have been made in many sectors of society for justice, social development, improving the situation of women, education, health care, and last but not least stimulating the search for knowledge and insight. In religions like the monotheistic ones, it is not market value or increasing power that count, but moral values and the responsibilities of persons and groups. The common struggle for these values is probably a fundamental part of interreligious cooperation and dialogue. In fact, the people dedicated to this struggle do not ask about each other's religion or denomination. Adherents of monotheistic religions cooperating in this way are neither religious extremists nor secularist diehards, but belong to what is probably the majority of believers, that is to say moderate and in some sense progressive.

Until now, I have not mentioned a common argument generally advanced in favor of the deeper unity of the monotheistic religions: the fact that all three religions believe in one God. I did not mention and use this commonly held argument for several reasons. For a number of believers, it is of course an argument and will strengthen their awareness of unity and scholarly arguments for it. For other groups of believers—Jews, Christians, Muslims—however, it is not such an argument, because they consider themselves to be the only true monotheists. In fact, monotheists have often battled each other about questions relating to the one God. The various ideologizations of monotheism have been anything but tolerant to non-adherents. Moreover, claiming unity among monotheists because they are not dualists, polytheists, or atheists is only a negative, not a positive argument. Most important, the contents of various forms of monotheism are different. "Extreme" monotheists will deny that Christianity's doctrines and practice make it a monotheistic religion at all. So I do not think that the fact of monotheism as such is a valid scholarly argument for a convergent structure of the three monotheistic religions. At most, it is an extra argument for the existence of a broader, empirically proved structure. On the other hand, the fact that adherents all consider themselves monotheists, enables discussion among them about God. I submit that monotheism gives a common rational coherence, but is not as such a structural coherence of these three religions.

Until now, nearly all conceptualizations of the three religions have been developed on the basis of normative categories current in one specific religion. Muslims have always viewed Judaism and Christianity in terms of their own typically Islamic concepts, like that of religions of *ahl al-kitāb* (people of revealed Scripture) that have been superseded by Islam. Jews have viewed Islam and Christianity from a Judeocentric view, at best as two monotheistic religions that had to be preached to pagan peoples in the East and in the West, in the framework of the Noachite alliance with humankind as a whole. Christians have viewed Judaism on the basis of their own "New Alliance" (New Testament) replacing the "Old Alliance" with the Jewish people. And they have viewed Islam on the basis of their refusal to accept Muhammad as a prophet, if they accepted post-Christian revelation at all. In the three cases, we are dealing with typically Islamic, Jewish, and Christian normative categories, not with descriptive categories that are generally valid.

It is true that openness towards dialogue on the part of Christians has made it possible for Jews and Muslims to define themselves and their own religion in their own terms. Yet it also remains true for many Christians that dialogue remains bound within a theological framework of Christian making. Very few scholars are equally familiar with all three religions on the basis of an adequate knowledge of the four basic languages of Hebrew, Arabic, Greek, and Latin. Few scholars are equally familiar with Jewish, Christian, and Muslim theological thinking, or with Jewish, Islamic, and Christian religious or Church law. And those who might be are theologians, rabbis, and *'ulamā'* or *fuqahā'*, irrevocably thinking from one particular theological or other tradition. How then can we arrive at least at the widest horizon and the least biased approach?

To come to a more adequate conceptualization that does justice to the other's point of view, one needs impartial, truly scholarly work. The key, I suggest, is to be attentive to and to do justice to what is meaningful to people in the three religious traditions, without speaking from an a priori position. Such research should be based on factual knowledge on a textual, historical, and sociological level, but it should then also search for the meaning of these facts for the people concerned. Moreover, such research should also inquire about the assumptions of various religious traditions and religious constructs, and it should be able to question the nature of current conceptualizations of the three religions.

I suggest that research should focus on a few core questions that have been tackled in all three religions. Besides the norms and values of human life to which I referred earlier, they have wrestled with many common problems concerning God, revelation, individual and communal life, a person's responsibility, justice and order in society, choosing good over evil, etc. Such core questions have been treated by different thinkers and schools of thought, cutting through the three traditions and communities.

One cannot but hope that such research will concentrate in particular on the meanings that these religions, or parts of them, have for people at the present time. Without communication on a human level, however, it will be almost impossible to grasp what is meaningful, not for the researcher him- or herself, but precisely to "others".

Such research of course can also go beyond the three monotheistic religions and search for wider patterns and structures of meanings. It may also be able to identify universal aspirations that may have emerged in local contexts but that deal with problems inherent to humankind.

In our approach, the exploration of meanings—and of patterns and structures of meaning—in Judaism, Christianity, and Islam is based on empirical materials, but it is more than purely factual research, more than establishing facts and their connections. It is concerned with meanings and meaningful connections and poses questions about the logic of such meanings. In short, this approach demands thinking, questioning, and hypothesizing. The study of religious data is carried out not only on the basis of empirical facts but also on the basis of reason.

This research does not assume in advance that there are absolute oppositions between the religious communities concerned, nor that such communities can come to cooperation and dialogue on the basis of their religions alone. Religions have strengthened conflicts, but they have also initiated peace efforts. Fundamentally, there are highly problematic differences between religions as they have been constituted and, unfortunately, the people concerned do not know how to live with such differences very well.

Perhaps more than in former times, present-day research is aware of poly-interpretability and the polyvalent use of all religions. Both universalistic and highly particularistic interpretations can be given to them; this depends not only on the people, but also on situations and contexts.

The important question, it seems to me, is which of the many elements of a particular religion by specific groups or persons are selected and considered particularly relevant in a specific situation or context. What are the criteria of selection? And once such a selection has been made and a certain interpretation been given, what kind of behavior or action is promoted or legitimated by it? Each selection, interpretation, and application should be studied in depth without being schematized in advance. Applying general normative categories like "fundamentalist" and "liberal" block rather than promote true understanding of what people do with their religion.

It is probably needless to say that scholarly research on meanings is not carried out in the service of particular ideas that are dear to us. Critical scholarship also implies a self-critical attitude toward our own position. And where we inquire about other people's interpretations or about meanings by which other people live, certainly in other societies or cultures than our own, we need the right hermeneutical tools. For those others are different from us. The problem is then to grasp how the other identified or identifies him- or herself, and what this identification actually meant or means to him or her in a given context.

Selected Literature

1. Visions of Structure

ARNALDEZ, Roger, *Trois messagers pour un seul Dieu*, Paris: Albin Michel, 1983.

BUSOOL, Assad Nimer, *Islam's Relationship to Christianity and Judaism*, Chicago: American Islamic Educational Foundation, 1994.

EPALZA, Mikel de, *Jesus zwischen Juden, Christen und Muslimen: Interreligiöses Zusammenleben auf der iberischen Halbinsel (6.–17. Jahrhundert)*, ed. by Reinhard KISTE, Frankfurt on Main: Otto Lembeck, 2002 (French edition: *Jésus otage: Juifs, chrétiens et musulmans en Espagne [VIe–XVIIe s.]* [Series "Jésus depuis Jésus"], Paris: Cerf, 1987).

FĀRŪQĪ, Ismāʿīl Rāji al-, *Islam and Other Faiths*, ed. by Ataullah SIDDIQUI, Markfield, U. K.: The Islamic Foundation, and Herndon, Va.: The International Institute of Islamic Thought, 1998/1419.

KRITZECK, James, *Sons of Abraham: Jews, Christians and Moslems*, Baltimore and Dublin: Helicon, 1965.

MAYBAUM, Ignaz, *Trialogue between Jew, Christian and Muslim* (The Littman Library of Jewish Civilization), London: Routledge & Kegan Paul, 1973.

PETERS, Francis Edwards, *Children of Abraham: Judaism / Christianity / Islam*, Princeton: Princeton University Press, 1982.

ROSENZWEIG, Franz, *Der Stern der Erlösung*, Frankfurt on Main: Kauffmann, 1921; English translation: *The Star of Redemption*, trans. from the 2nd edition of 1930 by William W. HALLO, London: Routledge & Kegan Paul, 1971.

SHARON, Moshe, *Judaism, Christianity and Islam: Interaction and Conflict*, Johannesburg: Sacks, 1989.

2. Trialogue: Study and Action

The Abraham Connection: A Jew, Christian, and Muslim in Dialogue, ed. by George B. GROSE and Benjamin J. HUBBARD, Notre Dame, Ind.: Cross Cultural Publications, 1994.

ARKOUN, Mohammed, "New Perspectives for a Jewish-Christian-Muslim Dialogue", *Journal of Ecumenical Studies*, 26 (1989), pp. 523–9 (repr. in *Muslims in Dialogue: The Evolution of a Dialogue*, ed. by Leonard SWIDLER, Lewiston, etc.: Edwin Mellen, 1992, pp. 343–52).

ARNALDEZ, Roger, *A la croisée des trois monothéismes: Une communauté de pensée au Moyen Age*, Paris: Albin Michel, 1993.

BAUSCHKE, Martin, *Trialog und Zivilgesellschaft*. Band I: *Internationale Recherche von Institutionen zum trilateralen Dialog von Juden, Christen und Muslimen*; Band II: *Berichte und Texte* (Schriftenreihe der Karl-Konrad-und-Ria-Groeben-Stiftung), Berlin: Maecenata Verlag, 2001.

BURRELL, David B., *Freedom and Creation in Three Traditions*, Notre Dame, Ind.: University of Notre Dame Press, 1993.

CRAGG, Kenneth, *The Privilege of Man: A Theme in Judaism, Islam and Christianity*, London: Athlone Press, 1968.

Drei Wege zu dem Einen Gott: Glaubenserfahrung in den monotheistischen Religionen, ed. by Abdoldjavad FALATURI, Jakob J. PETUCHOWSKI, Walter STROLZ (Veröffentlichungen der Stiftung Oratio Dominica), Freiburg, etc.: Herder, 1976.

Juifs, Chrétiens, Musulmans en dialogue, by Astérios ARGYRIOU et al. (Collection Histoires Religieuses), Paris: Ed. du Signe, 2002.

KUSCHEL, Karl-Josef, *Abraham: A Symbol of Hope for Jews, Christians and Muslims*, London: SCM Press, 1995.

Lexikon religiöser Grundbegriffe: Judentum, Christentum, Islam, ed. by Adel Theodor KHOURY, Graz, etc.: Styria, 1987.

OSMAN, Fathi, et al., "Jesus in Jewish-Christian-Muslim Dialogue", *Journal of Ecumenical Studies*, 14 (1977), pp. 448–65.

Religionsgespräche im Mittelalter, ed. by Bernard LEWIS and Friedrich NIEWÖHNER (Wolfenbütteler Mittelalterliche Studien 4), Wiesbaden 1992.

SACHEDINA, Abdulaziz, "Jews, Christians, and Muslims according to the Quran", *Greek Orthodox Theological Review*, 31 (1986), pp. 105–20.

SHAFIQ, Muhammad, "Trilogue of the Abrahamic Faiths: Guidelines for Jewish, Christian and Muslim Dialogue", *Hamdard Islamicus*, 15 (1992), pp. 59–74.

Theoria – Praxis: How Jews, Christians, and Muslims Can Together Move from Theory to Practice, ed. by Leonard SWIDLER, Leuven: Peeters, 1998.

Three Faiths—One God, ed. by John HICK and Edmund S. MELTZER, Albany, N. Y.: SUNY Press, 1989.

Trialogue of the Abrahamic Faiths: Papers Presented to the Islamic Studies Group of the American Academy of Religion, ed. by Ismā'īl Rāji al-FĀRŪQĪ (Issues in Islamic Thought 1), Alexandria, Va.: Al Sa'dāwī Publications, and Herndon, Va.: International Institute of Islamic Thought, 1982 (repr. 1991/1411).

Universale Vaterschaft Gottes: Begegnung der Religionen: Christlich-islamisch-jüdisches Symposium, Freiburg 1986, ed. by Abdoldjavad FALATURI, Jakob J. PETUCHOWSKI, Walter STROLZ, Freiburg, etc.: Herder, 1987.

WAARDENBURG, Jacques, art. "Religionsgespräche I. Allgemein", in *Theologische Realenzyklopädie*, Vol. 28 (Berlin and New York: Walter de Gruyter, 1997), pp. 631–40.

Zukunftshoffnung und Heilserwartung in den monotheistischen Religionen: Christlich-islamisch-jüdisches Symposium, Morschach/Schweiz, 1982, ed. by A. FALATURI, W. STROLZ, S. TALMON, Freiburg, etc.: Herder, 1983.

3. Social Scientific and Psychoanalytical Research on Monotheisms

LAMBERT, Jean, *Le Dieu distribué: Une anthropologie comparée des monothéismes* (Series "Patrimoines"), Paris: Cerf, 1995.

SIBONY, Daniel, *Les trois monothéismes: Juifs, chrétiens, musulmans entre leurs sources et leurs destins*, Paris: Seuil, 1992.

Section 2

Muslim Encounters with Other Religions in History

Chapter 3
The Earliest Relations of Islam with other Religions[1]

Is it possible to distinguish phases in the early growth of the new religious movement founded by Muhammad that correspond to its successive interactions with existing religious communities? The problem is an old one and well-known. In his dissertation of 1880, for instance, C. Snouck Hurgronje connected the occurrence of the Ibrāhīm cycle in the Qur'ān with Muhammad's conflict with the Jews in Medina.[2] Moreover, numerous studies have been made over the last hundred and fifty years of Jewish, Christian, and other influences on Muhammad's preaching and practice[3] and on the insti-

---

[1] This is a revised version of a paper titled "Towards a Periodization of Earliest Islam According to its Relations with Other Religions". The paper was published in *Proceedings of the Ninth Congress of the Union Européenne des Arabisants et Islamisants. Amsterdam, 1st to 7th Sept. 1978* (Publications of the Netherlands Institute of Archaeology and Arabic Studies 4), ed. by Rudolph PETERS, Leiden: E. J. Brill, 1981, pp. 304–26.

[2] Christiaan SNOUCK HURGRONJE, *Het Mekkaansche Feest*, Leiden: E. J. Brill, 1880 (repr. in his *Verspreide Geschriften*, Vol. I [Bonn & Leipzig: Kurt Schroeder, 1923], pp. 1–124, especially pp. 23–7). Partial French translation of this book as "Le pèlerinage à la Mekke" by BOUSQUET in *Oeuvres Choisis—Selected Works de C. Snouck Hurgronje, présentées en français et en anglais* par Georges-Henri BOUSQUET et Josef SCHACHT (Leiden: E. J. Brill, 1957, pp. 171–213; see especially pp. 186–90). Cf. also SNOUCK HURGRONJE, "Une nouvelle biographie de Mohammed" (first published in *RHR*, 15e année, t. 30, 1894), repr. in ID., *Verspreide Geschriften*, Vol. I, pp. 319–62 (especially pp. 334–6) and in his *Oeuvres Choisis—Selected Works*, pp. 109–49 (especially pp. 122–5). It becomes clear here that Snouck Hurgronje, in his interpretation of the Ibrāhīm story, wanted to refute the idea that the *millat Ibrāhīm* was the religion of the ancient *ḥanīfs* before Muhammad's public activity. Snouck Hurgronje's theory was influenced by Aloys SPRENGER; see his *Das Leben und die Lehre des Mohammad* (3 Vols., Berlin: Nicolai, 1861–5), Vol. 2, pp. 276ff.

[3] For the literature on the various kinds of historical influences on Muhammad, see Maxime RODINSON, "Bilan des études mohammadiennes", *Revue historique*, 229, fasc. 465 (January-March 1963), pp. 169–220. Studies on such influences continue to appear; see for instance Erwin GRÄF, "Zu den christlichen Einflüssen im Koran", in *Al-Bahit: Festschrift Joseph Henninger* (Studia Instituti Anthropos 28), St. Augustin bei Bonn: Anthropos Institut, 1976, pp. 111–44; lately Christoph LUXENBURG, *Die syroaramäische Lesart des Korans: Ein Beitrag zur Entschlüsselung der Koransprache*, Berlin: Das Arabische Buch, 2000. Attention is given here to the liturgical use of the Qur'ān in relation to Christian Syriac liturgical sources. The present approach presupposes such studies of historical influences but also assumes that Muhammad was not

tutional development of early Islam.[4] In the 1950s, however, Snouck Hur-gronje's theory was duly criticized.[5] New biographical studies of Muhammad have been made that place him in the social and political situation of his time[6], and considerable progress has been made in Qur'anic studies.[7] As a consequence, it seems appropriate to look again into the problem of the rise of Islam as a historical religion and the different phases of that rise from the point of view of the history of religions.[8]

Even if one assumes that certain ideas and practices of the new religious movement had been in the air and that certain social, economic, and political needs and expectations of the time made the Arabs sensitive to Muhammad's preaching, the problem remains. How did all of this lead to a particular religious movement with an autonomous set of ideas and practices and constituting an independent community? And how, subse-

---

a passive receptacle of them. Just like the authors of the first chapters of Genesis, the Hebrew prophets, Jesus, and Paul, Muhammad too should be seen primarily according to his response to and "digestion" of the values, norms, and rules he encountered or was confronted with. This, of course, is also part of historical research. An analysis of the different roles taken by Muhammad throughout his career after the model of earlier prophets is given in Jan HJÄRPE, "Rollernas Muhammad", *Religion och Bibel* (Uppsala), 36 (1977), pp. 63–72.

[4]   "Institutional development" means here largely the development of institutionalization, "institutions" being taken in the broader sense of the word. See for instance Shelomo Dov GOITEIN, *Studies in Islamic History and Institutions* (Leiden: E. J. Brill, 1966), pp. 73–134.

[5]   So Youakim MOUBARAC, *Abraham dans le Coran: L'histoire d'Abraham dans le Coran et la naissance de l'Islām: Etude critique des textes coraniques suivie d'un essai sur la représentation qu'ils donnent de la religion et de l'histoire* (Etudes musulmanes 5), Paris: Vrin, 1958, especially pp. 51–95. Also Willem Abraham BIJLEFELD, *De Islam als na-christelijke religie: Een onderzoek naar de theologische beoordeling van de Islam, in het bijzonder in de twintigste eeuw* (with a summary in English), Den Haag: Van Keulen, 1959, especially pp. 124–36.

[6]   We are thinking here in the first place of the two studies by W. M. WATT, *Muhammad at Mecca* (1953) and *Muhammad at Medina* (1956). We used these studies for the factual data of this paper, as well as Rudi PARET, *Mohammed und der Koran: Geschichte und Verkündigung des arabischen Propheten* (Stuttgart: Kohlhammer, 1957, 1966[2]). Cf. also Maxime RODINSON, *Mahomet*, Paris: Club français du livre, 1961; revised edition, Paris: Seuil, 1968 (English translation: Penguin Press, 1971 [Pelican Book 1973]).

[7]   One may think of the semantic studies carried out on the Qur'ān, for instance by IZUTSU, *God and Man in the Koran* and *Ethico-Religious Concepts in the Qur'ān*. On the progress in research on the Qur'ān see for instance Rudi PARET (ed.), *Der Koran* (Wege der Forschung 326), Darmstadt: Wissenschaftliche Buchgesellschaft, 1975, who also provided a precise translation of the Qur'ān with commentary (Stuttgart: Kohlhammer, 1961 and 1971).

[8]   On this approach, see the Conclusion of this chapter (pp. 105–7), which, while not claiming originality in the facts brought together here, seeks to offer a new formulation and treatment of the problem of the gradual growth of a religious purification movement into a reform movement and then into a religion and its connection and interaction with the religious communities it met in the course of its development.

quently, did this religious movement become a religion on a par with the great religions that existed in the Middle East at the time?

The keys to solving this problem lie in the interactions that took place between the prophetic leader with his community, on the one hand, and with other existing religious communities, on the other hand. These interactions took place in specific historical and social contexts. It is especially the second kind of interaction, between Muhammad and existing religious communities, that is relevant for a periodization of earliest Islam. Attention is paid here to Muhammad's relations with the polytheists in Mecca, the Jews in Medina, and the Christians in Northern Arabia.

1. The Meccan Polytheists

The sheer fact that Muhammad started preaching in Mecca implies that he explicitly set himself apart from the world in which he had grown up and with whose assumptions and rules he had been familiar. His message was directed primarily to the *mushrikūn* (polytheists), in particular the Meccans whom he identified as such. Even apart from the further political consequences, his interaction with the Meccan milieu was extremely important from the point of view of the history of religions.[9]

As W. Montgomery Watt demonstrated[10], Allāh was a god recognized by the Meccans as *rabb al-bayt* and lord of the town, but not as the only divine being. To Muhammad, Allāh became instead *rabb al-'ālamīn*, a universal god—creator, sustainer and judge—outside whom there was nothing divine. This message, together with the theme of resurrection, judgment, and afterlife, led to violent debates between Muhammad and the Meccans. He reproached them for not being able to recognize the oneness and uniqueness of God and to draw the logical consequences of such a recognition. Instead of powers like Fate and Time, it was this almighty *al-ilāhu* who decided on the major determinants of life. In contrast to a current confidence in a good life on earth and material well-being, Muhammad preached a human being's status as a creature and any creature's dependence on God as Creator. He preached a morality of divine commandments instead of tribal tradition, a sanction of eschatological reward and punishment instead of tribal honor, and religion as a basis for human solidarity instead of tribal and other factional interests.

---

[9]   See for instance WAARDENBURG, "Un débat coranique contre les polythéistes". This is an abridged form of an originally more extensive paper. The author is indebted to Dr. G. H. A. Juynboll for kindly drawing attention to a few mistakes that occurred in this paper. The historical facts of Muhammad's interaction with the Meccans have received much attention already. Cf. also WENDELL, "The pre-Islamic period of *Sīrat al-Nabī*".

[10]   WATT, *Muhammad at Mecca*, especially pp. 23–9; ID., "Belief in a 'High God' in pre-Islāmic Mecca"; ID., "The Qur'ān and Belief in a 'High God'".

These notions of divine commandments and judgment and of religious community were probably not completely new to the Meccans. But ideas and practices that may have been half-known from other religions were presented now in a new, "Arabicized" form.

In response to disbelief in his prophethood, Muhammad elaborated a more historical dimension of his activity, in fact of a rather legendary nature. He did this by means of stories about prophets of the East, which contained both Arabic elements like the seven *mathānī* and patriarchal figures from the Judeo-Christian tradition. Such prophets of the past, in whose line Muhammad put himself, could serve as an argument in sermon and debate, and they also linked the prophet with both the Arab and the patriarchal past.

The religious basis of the new movement, and in particular the authority of its prophet, was elaborated in different terms. Most important perhaps was the claim that Muhammad's "recitations" or *qur'āns* were due to revelation through an angel. They were held to be prophetic words. Although there was a link with the past through the notion that earlier prophets like Mūsā (Moses) and ʿĪsā (Jesus) had brought revelation by means of a revealed scripture, the Qur'ān stresses the fact of Muhammad's own revelation. This consisted of Arabic verses (*āyāt*) that he received and recited.

There are many aspects to this particular belief in this kind of revelation, with regard to its form, content, roots, and so on.[11] The most important element as far as our theme is concerned is that Muhammad assumed prophetic authority not only in his words, like the typical Old Testament prophets, but also in his deeds, like Moses and the patriarchs. Characteristically, in his case prophetic words were directly followed by action. I submit that their recitation as such should be considered a particular kind of "oral action" that could be followed by visible action.

His claim that his message was basically the same as that of the prophets before him, in particular Ibrāhīm (Abraham), had many implications. It gave his activity a supplementary authority and charismatic quality, it provided a link with the Judeo-Christian religious tradition, and it gave his message a kind of universality. Those who joined the movement entered the group of the believers of the primordial universal monotheistic religion, so to speak in its Arab branch. The Arabs would have their own religion while sharing in the universal one that started with Ibrāhīm (Abraham).

---

[11] On Muhammad's concept of revelation the classical study is Otto Pautz, *Muhammeds Lehre von der Offenbarung, quellenmäßig untersucht*, Leipzig: Hinrich, 1898. Tor Andrae hinted at Manichaean influences in his *Mohammed: Sein Leben und sein Glaube* (Göttingen: Vandenhoeck & Ruprecht, 1932), pp. 77–92 (English translation *Mohammed, the Man and his Faith*, New York: Harper Torchbook TB 62, 1960, pp. 94–113). Cf. also Thomas O'Shaughnessy, *The Koranic Concept of the Word of God* (Biblica et Orientalia 11), Rome: Pontificio Istituto Biblico, 1948.

The refusal of the majority of the Meccans, and certainly their leaders, to drop their religious tradition and abjure divine powers besides Allāh, whose veneration was part of the tradition, led to intense debates with the prophet, who raised his demands on this point. He finally rejected any compromise, arrived at a position of absolute monotheism, and separated his movement rigorously from the *mushrikūn* ("associationists", polytheists) with their basic sin of *shirk* or *ishrāk* ("associationism", polytheism: giving God "associates"), from which they had to be purified. At this point, significantly, the earlier openness and receptivity on the part of the prophet stopped, and the fight against idolatry in any form became one of the striking features of the religion that developed. Paradoxically, the Meccan opposition caused the new religion to develop the stories of the prophets and to stress the continuity of the prophetic monotheistic message and the claim of divine revelation and absolute truth. This religion insisted on the need for repentance with a view to the Judgment to come, and if needed to fight for recognition of the unity of God as a defense of God's honor. To summarize, the Meccan resistance forced Muhammad to give the necessary historical, theological, and social weight to the message he conveyed in word and action.

When Mecca finally fell in 629 C.E./7 A.H., once it had been purified of traces of idolatry, a number of ancient practices and ideas were retained, provided they did not constitute *shirk*. The religious purification movement of the beginning became a reform movement in the footsteps of the prophets. And it became a "complete" religion when the ancient Meccan ritual of *'umra* and *hajj*, slightly modified, was incorporated in it. The transfer of certain traditional Arab Meccan practices, though with a change of meaning, into the new setting made the movement into a religion that Muhammad held to be complete. The acceptance of the *hajj* as a ritual duty in Islam was the last important contribution that Meccan polytheism, or rather polydaimonism, made, in a singular kind of interaction, to the formation of Islam. In various ways, the interaction between Muhammad and the Meccan polytheists contributed to shape the new religion.[12]

2. The Jews in Medina

Although hardly any Jews appear to have been living permanently in Mecca itself, certain elements of Jewish religious ideas and practices apparently were known and must have reached Muhammad both before and after the beginning of his prophetic activity. Well-known elements are

---

[12] Muhammad's interaction with Bedouin *mushrikūn* played a role too, but this has been left out of account here.

the worship of one god only, the connection between divine revelation and scripture, and the existence of scriptures in languages other than Arabic. Already in the early *sūras* of the Qur'ān we find eschatological representations, certain cult practices, and references to biblical stories. The latter contained Judaic elements that may have reached Muhammad directly or via Christian channels.

Since the prophet was convinced that his inspirations had the same origin as those of former prophets, there was no harm in looking for further information, as is referred to in S. 25:4–6 and S. 16:103. As W. Montgomery Watt observes[13], the existence of Jewish and Christian informants does not detract from the fact that it was Muhammad who gave a new and definite Arabic formulation to truths held in Christian and Judaic religion. With their new formulation, these truths obtained a new meaning within the whole of the message conveyed by the prophet in word and deed.[14]

Precisely his notions of the universality of prophetic revelation and of the unity of all revealed religion made it possible and legitimate for Muhammad to adjust his cultic regulations in certain respects to Judaic ones. This happened when the prospect of going to Yathrib presented itself, where some Jewish tribes were living alongside Arab ones. One could speak of an "ecumenical" effort in matters of ritual: Friday (the preparatory day for Shabbāt) was accepted as the day for public worship, Jerusalem as the *qibla* for prayers, the fast of ʿĀshūrā on 10 Muharram was made parallel to the Jewish one of 10 Tishrī. A midday *salāt* was added to the two existing ones, so that there would be three daily prayers in Islam as in Judaism. Last but not least, Muslims were allowed to eat the food of the people of Scripture and to marry their women.

Muhammad must have implicitly hoped that he would be recognized by the Jews as a prophet, if not for them, then at least for the Arabs. His open attitude to them can be seen, however, as more than tactical policy-making. It was also a logical consequence of the universalist assumptions underlying his own religious preaching. In this light, we have to see Muhammad's appeal to the Jews for reconciliation as based on the common faith in one God.[15]

---

[13] WATT, *Muhammad at Mecca*, pp. 80–5. The originality of the Qur'ān, strictly speaking, is given precisely with its Arabic presentation.

[14] In the history of religions, attention should be given both to establishing historical facts and to discerning the meaning of these facts for particular groups and persons in the given historical and social context. In the absorption of facts within a particular religious tradition, there nearly always occurs a change of meaning that needs careful analysis. Even the most direct factual influences often imply considerable changes in meaning and interpretation.

[15] S. 29:46: ... *wa-ilāhunā wa-ilāhukum wāhidun* ... The nature of this appeal and its later interpretation deserve further study as well as the responses to it from Jews and Christians then and in later times.

It was through his contact with Medinan Jews, some of whom converted, that Muhammad received further religious information. So he learned, for instance, that the Jews had their *tawrāt* and the Christians their *injīl*, that Mūsā had been the founder of Judaism and had preceded 'Īsā who, as the last prophet until now, came from the Jews, and that Ibrāhīm had preceded both of them. Apparently, Muhammad held that the Jews and Christians of his time were two branches of the ancient Banū Isrā'īl. Learning more about Judaism, he must have become more aware of the weight of religious tradition and history and the importance of historical action.

The Jews, however, did not follow this line and were in fact able to undermine his authority by denying the divine origin of his revelations. This was possible precisely because Muhammad held that his inspiration was in essence identical with the revelation given to the Jews, something the latter denied. Muhammad then reoriented himself completely and appealed to the religion of Ibrāhīm as he saw it. He made some changes in ritual practice away from that of Judaism, taking for instance Mecca instead of Jerusalem as the *qibla* for prayers. The introduction and use of Ibrāhīm materials clearly made Muhammad's movement more acceptable to the Arabs for whom Ibrāhīm was a well-known figure, while retaining a monotheistic framework. The results, in debate and action, of the confrontation between the Jewish claim to be God's chosen people and Muhammad's claim to be God's chosen prophet are well-known.[16] In the end, the Jews of Medina fell victim to the war between the Muslims of Medina and the Meccan leadership.

Muhammad's interaction with the Jewish tribes in Medina had profound consequences for the further development of his religious movement. Besides the halachic-biblical elements that he had absorbed earlier in Mecca, certain Jewish ritual regulations provided a model for ritual innovations made by Muhammad in the period of rapprochement that started shortly before the Hijra. In the period of opposition, however, starting about a year and a half after the Hijra, the Jewish model was abandoned. His negative experience with the Jews caused Muhammad to be disillusioned in his assumption of the unity of the "revealed religions". As a consequence, he seems to have maintained, instead of the idea of the unity of "revealed religions", that of the unity of "revelations" proceeding from one and the same God. In this view, the revelations given to Moses and Jesus in the form of scriptures were distorted subsequently by the Jews and the Christians respectively.

This conclusion could not but result in Muhammad distancing himself from the existing religion of the Jews, and all the arguments which could

---

[16] See for instance WAARDENBURG, "Koranisches Religionsgespräch".

be brought against it and all possible evidence for Jewish sins were hammered out in *qur'āns*. Apart from what he had learned from Judaism and partly incorporated into his own religious movement, Muhammad's "Jewish experience" must have reinforced his prophetic self-consciousness considerably. It forced him to reconsider the meaning of his preaching and acting and to consider the significance of his movement not only in terms of history but also for the future.

He now moved toward identifying his movement completely with the religion of Ibrāhīm, the *millat Ibrāhīm*, the monotheistic *hanīfiya*. Through the acceptance of the figure of Ismāʿīl and the idea of the *millat Ibrāhīm* something of the notion of a chosen people and its historical role was transferred and applied to the Arabs. However, paradoxically enough, it was precisely the experience of the particularism of Judaism that appears to have stimulated Muhammad's elaboration of a more universalistic orientation. Significantly, the movement took the name of the Hanīfiya now, before becoming known as "Islam". Just as the resistance of the Meccans had enriched the new religion with Arab elements and induced a strict monotheistic stand, so the resistance of the Jews in Medina brought not only a greater precision to the new religion but also a universalization of its monotheistic stand.

3. The Christians in Northern Arabia

Certain elements of Christianity must have been in the air in the Mecca where Muhammad grew up and along the caravan routes where he traveled. Besides the notion of one almighty God and certain biblical stories, there were the ideas of Judgment and the Day of Judgment, representations of the Hereafter, certain practices of worship and various religious-ethical values and virtues. Materials of this kind can be found in the Qur'ān already in the early Meccan periods, with patriarchal figures from the Old Testament, apocryphal stories about Mary and Jesus, and the notion of angels and of more abstract spiritual entities. As later in the case of Judaism and as a matter of principle, Muhammad could assimilate data from Christian communities on the assumption of the unity of revealed religions and later that of revelations.

Probably Muhammad already made open or implied statements against Christianity in the Meccan period, when he saw here infringements of his strictly monotheistic stand. But on the whole the attitude of the prophet was open and favorable with regard to the devotional attitudes and moral virtues that struck him among the Christians, as expressed for instance in S. 57:27, 5:82–4. Before the Hijra, for security reasons, adherents of the community moved to Christian Ethiopia, and apparently Muhammad made approaches to Christian tribes before he decided to go to Yathrib (Medina).

In the first Medinan years Muhammad compared the Christians most favorably with the Jews during his conflict with the latter and used stories about 'Īsā as part of his ideological attack on the Jews. After his victory, however, first over the Jews and then over the Meccans in 629 C.E./7 H., there came a remarkable change in his attitude toward the Christians and Christianity. This ended in the command to wage war against them in the well-known passage of S. 9:29–33.[17] How is this change to be explained?

A first explanation of this change in the prophet's attitude to Christians is that Muhammad, when expanding to the north, was confronted with tribes that were mostly Christian and linked to what may be called the Byzantine defense system. Muhammad's attack on certain Christian doctrines may have been primarily of a political nature, so as to loosen these tribes from their Christian overlords by making an ideological attack on their religion. It is questionable, however, whether there may not have been better political means to get these tribes on the prophet's side than by attacking their religion. So we have to look for another explanation, without denying that Muhammad made political use of his religion in his fight against the Christian tribes. This had happened already in his dealings with the Meccans, the Jews in Medina, and also some Bedouin tribes.

A singular aspect of the Qur'anic texts directed against the Christians and Christianity is their doctrinal interest. This had hardly been present in Muhammad's refutations of the polytheists and the Jews. Another particularity is that only certain Christian doctrines are mentioned to be refuted, so that the question may be raised whether and why Muhammad was so badly informed about Christianity.[18] A third striking fact is that the Qur'anic texts directed against the polytheists and the Jews seem to reflect real debates in which Muhammad used any argument he could find in the arsenal of the beliefs of the other party. The Qur'anic texts against the Christians, however, are rather wishy-washy and give the impression of a man shouting at an enemy who is far away.

The new attitude the prophet was taking against the Christians must have been due to several factors. He must have been disillusioned with the

---

[17] For the Qur'anic views and judgments of the Christians and their beliefs and practices as well as the polemic against them, see McAuliffe, Qur'ānic Christians. Cf. W.M. Watt, "The Christianity criticized in the Qur'ān", The Muslim World, 57 (1967), pp. 197–201. Cf. my article mentioned above in note 16. For the historical facts, see the studies by Watt and Paret (quoted above in note 6).

[18] The lapidary information given in the Qur'ān about Christianity and Judaism is not only a scholarly problem but has also caused religious concern among Christians and Jews, especially when they set out to pursue dialogue with Muslims. The Qur'anic view of other religions and other scriptures needs further analysis. Cf. "The Qur'ānic View of other Scriptures: A Translation of Sections from Writings by 'Afīf 'Abd al-Fattāh Tabbāra and al-Ustādh al-Haddād", trans. A. J. Powell, The Muslim World, 59/2 (1969), pp. 95–105.

idea of the unity of the revealed religions through his experience with the Jews in Medina. But it was also the immediate consequence of his new conceptualization of what his religion was like, as expressed and elaborated in the *millat Ibrāhīm* idea. The old name of the movement, the *hanīfīya*, suggests, besides the originally Meccan religious "purification movement" against polytheism, a kind of "reform movement" with regard to the *ahl al-kitāb*. Once this monotheistic religious reform movement had become "established" after the victories over the Jews and the Meccans, Muhammad simply drew the consequences. When he attacked what he held to be the false doctrines of the Christians, it was not because he had studied Christianity. It must rather have been because he had been struck by those Christian doctrines that were contrary to his own message and to what was called now "the true religion" (*dīn al-haqq*, S. 61:9, 48:28, 9:33), the *millat Ibrāhīm*, the *hanīfīya*, *islām* as he conceived it.

In Medina, Muhammad had got to know the Jews in close proximity, just as he had known the Meccans from his childhood. We must assume that he was less immediately familiar with the life of the Christians. He seems to have seen their religion always from a distance, first respecting and even admiring what he saw of their devotions and virtues, later combating what he thought to be their doctrinal errors.

The explanation offered here of the change in Muhammad's vision of the religion of the Christians does not preclude the view that he used the term "the true religion" against the Christians in warfare, just as he used the Ibrāhīm story against the Jews in political conflict. Our contention, however, is that Muhammad's view of Ibrāhīm and "the true religion" represents an autonomous religious structure beyond the political use made of it, and that it logically precedes this use.

The key to the other problem, of why Muhammad provides so little information about Christianity, and information which does not represent orthodox Christianity at that, is simply that he saw no need for it. He had already constructed his own religion first as a religious purification movement (*hanīfīya*), then as a religious reform movement (*millat Ibrāhīm*), and finally as the completed "true religion" (*dīn al-haqq*). Muhammad was not a scholar of religion or a theologian but a prophetical reformer. As a reformer, all he saw of the religion of the Christians was what was objectionable in his monotheistic view and what should be reformed, and in the case of the Christians this concerned doctrine. In a similar way, he had been struck by the idolatry of the Meccans and the religious pretenses of the Jews. He directed his reform activities against those elements he found objectionable in the religions he had met.

Muhammad's change of policy in his actual dealings with Christian tribes in the North can be interpreted along these lines. The earlier treaty with

Judhām suggests that the prophet was initially prepared to enter into alliances with Christian tribes. He had made them from time to time also with other tribes and groups without making specific religious demands. Then, between the defeat at Mu'tah (September 629) and the expedition to Tabūk (starting in October 630), he changed his policy, at least in the North. Alliances were concluded now only on the basis of acceptance of Islam, so that the Christian tribes, if they wanted to avoid war, had only the alternative to accept Islam and enter into alliance or to settle with a treaty imposing the payment of an annual tribute.

Whereas in the South, Christian tribes who refused to become Muslims preferred a treaty settlement like the Christians of Najrān, in the North such tribes opposed Muhammad's troops with armed resistance. It is important to keep in mind that the commandment of war as contained in the Qur'ān (S. 9:1–37) was almost certainly not directed against the Christians as Christians but against political enemies who happened to be Christians. In this war, Muhammad used the religious structure at the basis of his monotheistic purification and reform movement as a war ideology, just as he had used the idea of the Ibrāhīm religion against the Medinan Jews a few years earlier. But the monotheistic idea itself and the idea of Ibrāhīm's religion as such had already been conceived before the political and military conflicts with the Jews and the Christians arose.

It should be noticed in this connection that the commandment of war against the Christians as contained in S. 9:1–37 does not stand in isolation. It is linked immediately with a similar commandment against the Jews, with the argument that neither Christians nor Jews are true monotheists. And it is also linked with the general commandment of war that Muhammad proclaimed in March 631 against all Arabs who had remained pagan. The unbelief of the *ahl al-kitāb* is practically equated here with the unbelief of the pagan Arabs, which seems to be an obvious conclusion from the standpoint of a reform movement in wartime.

In other words, the new attitude that Muhammad took toward the Christian tribes was also a consequence of his general decision to impose the *dīn* that had been destined for the Arabs in effect on all Arabs without exception, including the Christian and Jewish Arabs. Christians and Jews were not forced to adopt Islam themselves, but they had to recognize the dominance of this *dīn* as the religious basis of society, and they had to pay tribute accordingly. The religious movement that had started in Mecca as a purification movement and that had become a religious reform movement in Medina had now become a religion in the full sense of the word, implying a new social order of Arab society.

Let us sum up the consequences of the interaction between Muhammad and his movement, on the one hand, and the Christians in Arabia, on the other hand. The first thing to be noticed is that the Christians whom

Muhammad had to deal with were not a given community with which the prophet lived, like the polytheists in Mecca and the Jewish tribes in Medina. They were scattered, they had varying political allegiances, they belonged to different groupings and sects, and they had different forms of piety, including ascetic ones. Partly as a consequence of this state of affairs, there was much less real interaction possible between Muhammad and the Christians than with the polytheists in Mecca or the Jews in Medina.

The new religious movement owed in particular to the Christians the elaboration of the idea of a creating, sustaining, and judging God, as well as a large part of its eschatology and certain devotional practices. A particular ascetic lifestyle current among Christians could provide a model for pious Muslims. It has been observed that such elements were "in the air" in Mecca and in other places in Arabia at the time and that this made for an open attitude on Muhammad's part toward the way of life and religious practice of the Christians. During the Medinan conflict, Muhammad compared the Christians favorably with the Jews, notwithstanding the fact that neither group recognized him as a prophet. But the Christians were less dangerous politically in the struggle between Medina and Mecca, and Muhammad may have been attracted by their virtuous life.

The situation changed when Muhammad had to confront Arab tribes in the North who were Christians. His religious movement presented itself at this time not only as a religious reform movement of polytheism, Judaism, and Christianity, but also as the monotheistic religion destined for the Arabs.

The prophet now refuted Christian doctrines about God's essence and the relationship between God and humans. This was in itself a logical consequence of the absolute monotheism that he preached. It resulted historically from the way in which his religious movement had developed into "the true religion" that reinstated the *millat Ibrāhīm* from which the Jews and the Christians had departed. The religious movement had established itself and was becoming a religion in its own right.

Politically, Christian tribes had to choose now between adopting the new religion or accepting a treaty with payment of tribute, if they wanted to avoid war. The resistance of the Christian Arab tribes in the North against Muhammad's expansion there may have accelerated the ideological use of his monotheistic doctrine against them. His refuting all that seemed to be contrary to strict monotheism and his imposing the Islamic social order on all Arabs including the Christian and Jewish ones was in the last analysis a consequence of Muhammad's desire to realize the monotheistic *millat Ibrāhīm* with which he had increasingly identified his religious movement.

The resistance of the Christian tribes had other consequences as well. It must have been one of the many factors that, in the end, contributed to the transition of Islam from a religious purification and reform movement and a religion destined specifically for the Arabs to a truly universal religion. This was called the *dīn al-ḥaqq*, opposed to existing Judaism and Christianity, not restricted to the Arabs but claiming universal validity. The Christianity of the northern Arab tribes, paradoxically, may thus indirectly have contributed to the full development of the new religion of Arabs and others and to the sense of competition with Christianity that this religion developed in general.

Looking back at the interaction of the new Islamic religious movement with the existing religious communities, we are struck by the importance of sociopolitical factors. Much research has been devoted to their study. Yet on closer analysis, one has to recognize another dimension as well, and here the interactions just described take on all their significance and weight. Muhammad acted on earth and at the same time recited verses (*āyāt*) held to be inspired by an angel and having religious authority. In his actions he behaved as a leader and statesman; because of his inspirations he was considered a prophet.

Each encounter with another socio-religious community, consequently, took place on two levels: a settling of affairs in the realm of sociopolitical action, and an interaction of religious ideas and practices due to and leading to particular religious inspirations. If Muhammad had not considered himself to be a prophet nor been considered one by his followers, he would have been obliged to deal with the Meccans, the people of Yathrib, and the various Bedouin tribes simply as a politician, without this second—religious—dimension. It was precisely his prophethood and its recognition by his community that made his interactions take place on two levels at the same time.

In the preceding, a rough sketch has been given of the main phases of the development of the new religious movement, through successive interactions with existing religious communities, into an established religion. Now it is worthwhile to pay attention for a moment to an aspect of its internal development and to the links that exist between the attitudes taken by Muhammad toward other religions and the progressive self-definition of Islam as a religion. What does the Qur'ān say about the religion Muhammad brought, defined as *millat Ibrāhīm* and as *dīn*?

4. *Millat Ibrāhīm* in the Qur'ān

After the studies by C. Snouck Hurgronje and A. J. Wensinck on the patriarchal figure of Ibrāhīm and his religion in the Qur'ān, further inquiries by Y. Moubarac and W. A. Bijlefeld have brought some corrections to Snouck Hurgronje's stress on the political aspects of the Ibrāhīm story.[19] They have also given a more precise dating of some verses of the Qur'ān that Snouck Hurgronje held to be Medinan.[20] It has become clear that, already in the Meccan period of the Qur'ān, Ibrāhīm had a special link with the Ka'ba and the Meccans, even though Muhammad apparently did not know in this Meccan period that Ismā'īl was a son of Ibrāhīm. These inquiries demonstrated that there is a continuous development in the Qur'ān of the Ibrāhīm concept, whose basic notions were already present in the third Meccan period.

R. Paret summarized the significance of Ibrāhīm in the Qur'ān as:[21]
(1) the founder or purifier of the Ka'ba;
(2) the prototype of all *muslimūn* as his spiritual descendants;
(3) a patriarchal figure who preceded Mūsā and 'Īsā with their revelations, and to whom Muhammad could appeal as a *hanīf* (monotheist) and not a *mushrik* (polytheist), without him being a Jew or a Christian.

In the Qur'anic Ibrāhīm story, the latter is in fact the prototype of Muhammad. All spiritual descendants of Ibrāhīm are true monotheists and participate in the privileges of the *millat Ibrāhīm*. Through the Qur'ān, the community of Muslims has received the definitive revelation and has become *ahl al-kitāb*. As true monotheists, the Muslim community is part of the *millat Ibrāhīm* in a purer sense than the Jews and Christians, who deviated.

I would like to contend that this appeal to the *millat Ibrāhīm* gave to Muhammad's movement a new, more universal dimension. The claim could now be made that the movement was not only a purification of polytheism and a reform of existing Judaism and Christianity, but that it was also a religion in its own right. With its universalist outlook beyond existing Judaism and Christianity, it could envisage a *Pax Islamica* throughout the Arabian peninsula if not beyond.

On the one hand, by recognizing the value of the revelation given to Jews and Christians, Islamic religion has a particular relationship to Judaism and Christianity beyond the existing forms of these religions. It can accept, for instance, on the basis of its particular assumptions, the presence of spiritual *hanīf* monotheists within the Jewish and Christian com-

---

[19] On the Ibrāhīm problem, see besides the literature quoted above in notes 2 and 5 also Arent Jan WENSINCK, *Mohammed en de Joden te Medina* (Leiden: E. J. Brill, 1908), pp. 131–3; ID., art. "Ibrahim", in *EI¹*, Vol. 2 (1920), pp. 431–2, and E. BECK, "Die Gestalt des Abraham am Wendepunkt der Entwicklung Muhammeds: Analyse von S. 2.118 (124)–135 (141)", *Le Muséon*, 65 (1952), pp. 73–94.

[20] S. 14:39 should be considered a Medinan interpolation within a Meccan text S. 14:35–41. S. 2:126 is a later Medinan elaboration of the Meccan S. 14:35–40, and verse 127a may be a later interpolation in the whole of v. 125–9. See BIJLEFELD, *De Islam als na-christelijke religie* (see above note 5), pp. 127–32.

[21] PARET, *Mohammed und der Koran* (1966², see above note 6), pp. 108–10.

munities. In this way, the idea of a *millat Ibrāhīm* is of paramount importance for the relations between Islam and other religions.

On the other hand, by claiming to offer a universal monotheism as *millat Ibrāhīm*, Islamic religion would in the course of its history develop a certain dialectic between its universal prototype, the *millat Ibrāhīm*, and its particularistic tendencies linked to historical developments. So the idea of the *millat Ibrāhīm* is also of major importance for the self-view of Islam. The *hanīfīya* of Ibrāhīm, as an interior spiritual experience that demands a break with manifest as well as hidden forms of idolatry—as dependence on false absolutes—has played a major role in the history of Muslim spirituality.

The fact that Muhammad had a model of his religion in the *millat Ibrāhīm* as an ideal and pure religion—the absolute religion—is highly significant. It must have been a major incentive to construct and develop a religion with its own kind of monotheistic faith in contrast to other forms of monotheism and with its own kind of social order in contrast to other sociopolitical structures. A number of sayings and actions of Muhammad become more understandable against the background of this notion of a primordial universal religion that he formulated, in good Semitic tradition, in terms of a patriarchal genealogy.

Was there not in the back of Muhammad's mind from the very beginning the notion of a kind of *ur-religion*, the primordial religion given to Adam? Did this notion perhaps crystallize at the end of the Meccan period into the conception of the *millat Ibrāhīm* that received its definite shape in Medina?

This leads to a key question that must be left open here. What kind of relationship may Muhammad have envisaged between the empirical *dīn al-islām* (Islam), that he brought to earth and that would have its history here, and the universal *ur-religion* of the *millat Ibrāhīm*, that provided a normative model for it?

5. *Dīn* in the Qur'ān

If we leave aside the use of *dīn* in the sense of "judgment" as being less relevant for the present inquiry, a survey of the use of the concept of *dīn* in its meaning of "religion" in chronological order in the Qur'ān leads to the following result:[22]

---

[22] On the concept of *dīn*, see for instance Josef HOROVITZ, *Koranische Untersuchungen* (Berlin & Leipzig: Walter de Gruyter, 1926), p. 62 (also compared with *milla*); IZUTSU, *God and Man in the Koran*, pp. 228–9; Louis GARDET, art. "dīn", pp. 293f. (also compared with *milla*); BRAVMANN, *The Spiritual Background of Early Islam*, pp. 1–6, 34. See also HADDAD, "The Conception of the Term *dīn* in the Qur'ān", which analyzes the term *dīn* basically in terms of "God's Action" and "Man's Action".

In the Meccan period, *dīn* appears as the religion of an individual (S. 109:6; 10:104) or a people—including a people of unbelievers, though their religion can in fact be changed (40:26). There should be no factions and divisions within the *dīn* (30:32; 42:13). *Dīn* implies possession of religious prescriptions, right ones (42:13) or wrong ones (42:21); it is the right monotheistic worship of God (*lahu al-dīnu wāsiban*, 16:52) for which the human being has been created and to which he or she is called as a *hanīf* (10:105; 12:40; 30:30 and 43). The worship (*dīn*) should be directed to God alone and completely (7:29; 10:22; 29:65; 31:32; 39:11 and 14; 40:14 and 65); the pure worship (*al-dīnu'l-khālisu*) is toward God (39:3). The right *dīn* is the *milla* of Ibrāhīm the *hanīf* (6:161). Unbelievers have *milla*s that are bad (14:13, 38:7), as opposed to the good *milla* of Ibrāhīm, Ishāq, and Ya'qūb (12:37 and 38).

In the Medinan period, *dīn* is used much more often and in many more different contexts. It is illuminating to observe a clear development in its use, according to the chronological order of Medinan Suras as proposed by Th. Nöldeke. At the beginning of the Medinan period, for instance, a well-known text (S. 2:256) affirms that there is no enforcement (*ikrāh*) in religion (*dīn*).[23] A text from the historically following Sura (98:5) summarizes the right religion (*dīn al-qayyimati*) as consisting of monotheistic worship (as performed by *hanīf*s), *salāt* and *zakāt*. S. 8:39 then commands fighting until there is no more *fitna* and until the religion or worship is monotheistic only (… *hattā lā takūna fitnatun wayakūna al-dīnu kulluhu li-'llāhi* …). The commandment to fight for the right religion will come back repeatedly from now on.

Next, in Sura 3, three verses speak of *dīn*. For the first time *islām*—presumably the *masdar* aspect is here predominant—is connected with *dīn* in the famous saying *Al-dīn 'inda 'llāh al-islām* (3:19). Verses 83 and 85 reject any other religion than the *dīn Allāh* and *islām* as *dīn* (… *a-fa-ghaira dīni 'llāhi yabghūna* … (83), … *wa-man yabtaghi ghaira 'l-islāmi dīnan* … (85). Like verse 19, these verses 83 and 85 imply that, in terms of true religion, there is no alternative for the human being but "to surrender" (*islām*), verse 83 adding that, in its being, the whole creation has "surrendered" (*aslama*) already.

Subsequently, in S. 61:9 for the first time, the expression *dīn al-haqq* is used to mean the religion that will be made triumphant over every religion (… *'alā 'l-dīni kullihi* …), a statement repeated in S. 48:28 with a slight nuance, and also in S. 9:33 (*Huwa 'llādhī arsala rasūlahu bi-'l-hudā wa-dīni'l-haqqi li-yuzhirahu 'alā 'l-dīni kullihi* …). *Dīn al-haqq*, "the true, real religion", is a stronger expression than *al-dīn al-qayyim*, literally "the immutable, stable religion". Although Islam is not identified explicitly with

---

[23]   Cf. R. PARET, "Sure 2, 256: *lā ikrāha fī d-dīni*. Toleranz oder Resignation", *Der Islam*, 45 (1969), pp. 299–300.

the *dīn al-ḥaqq*, such an identification is implied. There is here not only a commandment to fight, but also a promise of victory over all other religions, in other words an ascertainment of the worldly superiority of Islam.

After a text with a monotheistic tendency as had appeared already in the Meccan period with regard to *dīn* (4:146), S. 24 contains some interesting statements. In verse 2 it is said that the *dīn Allāh* has no place for pity if a major offense has been committed, which suggests a certain rigidity. In verse 24 it is said that on Judgment Day Allāh will requite the people according to … *dīnahum al-ḥaqqa* …, while Allāh himself will be recognized as the clear truth (… *huwa al-ḥaqqu 'l-mubīnu* …). These two verses having referred to an ethical commandment and to the conscience of the human being, verse 55 again promises that Allāh will make powerful the religion that He has thought right for His believers (… *wa-la-yumakkinanna lahum dīnahum* …), a well-known theme.

S. 60:8–9, next in chronological order, refers to a rule of war. When people did not fight "in religion" (*qātala fī 'l-dīn*) against the faithful they should be treated kindly, for instance by treaty, but as soon as there has been such "fighting in religion" a treaty is impossible. After a text in which an allusion is made to the powerlessness of unbelievers seeking to justify their religion before Allāh (49:16), we arrive at the well-known last two *sūras* in chronological order.

S. 9 has four verses in which *dīn* occurs. In case of conversion, the people become "brethren in religion" (… *fa-ikhwānukum fī 'l-dīn* …, verse 11), if they also perform *ṣalāt* and pay *zakāt*. Verse 29 is the famous commandment to make war against: (a) unbelievers; (b) those who do what is forbidden; and (c) those among the people who received Scripture and who do not adhere to the true religion: … *wa-lā yadīnūna dīna 'l-ḥaqqi mina 'lladhīna ūtū 'l-kitāba* … In all three cases the war should continue until they pay tribute. According to verse 36, the *ḥarām* character of four months in a year is right religion (*al-dīn al-qayyim*). And verse 122 exhorts people from each army group to receive instruction in religion (… *li-yatafaqqahū fī 'l-dīni* …), in order to "warn" the others when they return home.

An important verse occurs in the chronologically last *sūra* (5:3, 5): "… *al yawma ya'isa 'lladhīna kafarū min dīnikum fa-lā takhshawhum wa-'khshawnī 'l-yawma akmaltu lakum dīnakum wa-atmamtu ʿalaikum niʿmatī wa-raḍītu lakumu 'l-islāma dīnan* …". The unbelievers are radically separated from "your" religion and have nothing to hope for; God has perfected His grace toward the community; He is satisfied that the faithful have *islām* as religion. Whether *islām* is used here as a proper name remains open to discussion. Verse 57 of the same S. 5 forbids making a treaty with those among the people who had received the Scripture but who made a mockery of the new religion: "… *lā tattakhidū 'lladhīna 'ttakhadhū dīnakum huzuwan wa-laʿiban mina 'lladhīna ūtū 'l-kitāba min qablikum wa-'l-kuffāra awliyāʾa*."

Some texts of the Medinan period that use *dīn* in connection with the *millat Ibrāhīm* are particularly interesting in the context of our inquiry. Thus, the early text S. 2:130–2 states that only a fool can reject the *millat Ibrāhīm*, that Ibrāhīm surrendered (*aslama*) to God, and that Ibrāhīm like Ya'qūb said to his sons: ... *inna 'llāha 'stafā lakumu 'l-dīn* ... ("... Allah has chosen your religion for you ..."), and that they should not die without being *muslim* (with a strong verbal aspect: "surrendering to God"). The key words *millat Ibrāhīm*, *aslama* and *dīn* that occur in these three verses are united here in one whole.

S. 22:78 likewise combines a statement about *al-dīn* (namely, that there is nothing in it that "burdens you": ... *wa-mā ja'ala 'alaikum fī 'l-dīn min harajin millata abīkum Ibrāhīma* ...) with the expression *millat Ibrāhīm*, "your father", indicating the nature of this religion. Here again, as a third term, *muslim* is added as the name that Ibrāhīm gave to the faithful of his *milla*: "... He called you *muslims (huwa sammākumu 'l-muslimīna)* ...". *Millat Ibrāhīm*, *aslama*, and *dīn* apparently belong together.

The development of the use of *dīn* as a concept in the Qur'ān apparently reflects the development of earliest Islam from a purifying religious movement to a reform movement and then to a new independent religion. Corresponding with the latter phase, we find *dīn* in a reified sense, for instance in S. 3:73, and as synonymous with *millat Ibrāhīm*, in S. 6:161; we find it used as a kind of "war ideology" in the commandments to war, for instance in S. 8:39, and as indicating an all encompassing religious, social, and political system in S. 5:3. The *dīn* of Muhammad's movement is opposed to the *dīn* of the unbelieving polytheists. In contrast to the Jews and Christians, the adherents of *dīn al-islām* are part of the *millat Ibrāhīm*. The relationship between these two appears to be of crucial importance.

The connections between the use in the Qur'ān of *dīn*, on the one hand, and *islām*[24] and *imān*[25], on the other, demand further attention. A few

---

[24] On the concepts of *islām*, *aslama* etc., see for instance Dawid KÜNSTLINGER, "'Islām', 'muslim', 'aslama' im Ḳurān", *Rocznik Orientalistyczny*, 11 (1935), pp. 128–37; RINGGREN, *Islām, 'aslama, and Muslim*; BANETH, "What did Muhammad mean when he called his Religion 'Islam'? The Original Meaning of *aslama* and its Derivatives"; Abdul Khaliq KAZI, "The Meaning of Īmān and Islām in the Qur'ān", *Islamic Studies*, 5 (1966), pp. 227–37; IZUTSU, *Ethico-Religious Concepts in the Qur'ān*, pp. 189–91; Muhammad Abdul RAUF, "Some Notes on the Qur'anic Use of the Terms Islām and Imān", *The Muslim World*, 57 (1967), pp. 94–102; S. McDONOUGH, "Imān and Islām in the Qur'ān", *Iqbal Review*, 12/1 (1971), pp. 81–8; BRAVMANN, *The Spiritual Background of Early Islam*, pp. 7–26.

[25] On the concept of *imān*, see, besides the articles by KAZI, RAUF, and McDONOUGH mentioned in the previous note, for instance Helmer RINGGREN, "The Conception of Faith in the Koran", *Oriens*, 4 (1951), pp. 1–20; IZUTSU, *The Structure of the Ethical Terms in the Koran*, pp. 118–22, 173–5; ID., *God and Man in the Koran*, pp. 198–204, 216–9; ID., *Ethico-Religious Concepts in the Qur'ān*, pp. 184–8; BRAVMANN, *The*

remarks must suffice here. For a long time, deep into the Medinan period, *islām* is the act of self-surrender to the divine will, stepping out of the status of a *jāhil* into that of a *muslim*, which remains for a long time an active participle before being used as a noun. According to S. 51:36, there were also *muslimūn* before the emergence of the historical religion of Islam.

Only much later does *islām* become a full noun and the name for the new religion, but even then it retains to some extent its *masdar* aspect. Later *aslama*, too, acquires the technical meaning of joining the community in an external way (S. 49:14) without certainty about the inner conviction of the convert. This is indicated by *imān*, the inner religious attitude before God. Just as, in Mecca, *dīn* stands for religious attitude and worship, so *imān* stands for the pure, monotheistic faith in God. *Mu'min* at the beginning of the Medinan period can still be used for the faithful among the *ahl al-kitāb*, too. The opposite of *islām* (and *imān*) is *kufr*.[26]

Aslama ("to surrender oneself") is near to *'abada* ("to serve") and *akhlasa*[27] ("to make pure, to free from admixture"), all being part of the good *dīn* according to the Qur'ān.

Conclusion: Toward an Archeology of Religions and Islam

This chapter has traced the way in which, in the course of Muhammad's public activity, his prophetic message developed and crystallized into a fully-fledged religion, both as a social and historical reality and according to the inspirations of its prophet. In treating this problem, we have distinguished several phases in the development of earliest Islam, basing our argument on two assumptions.

The first assumption has been that the interactions that took place between the new religious movement with its prophetic leader and the three major existing religious communities were of paramount importance for this process. We attempted to establish a certain periodization of earliest Islam accordingly. Our second assumption has been that the two main conceptualizations of the notion of religion in the Qur'ān, *millat Ibrāhīm* and *dīn*, as they developed in successive Qur'anic revelations, furnish a key to understanding. The development of these two notions

Spiritual Background of Early Islam, pp. 26–31. Cf. Robert Caspar, "La foi selon le Coran: Étude de thèmes et perspectives théologiques", *Proche Orient Chrétien*, 18 (1968), pp. 7–28, 140–66, and 19 (1969), pp. 162–93.

[26]   Cf. Waldman, "The Development of the Concept of *kufr* in the Qur'ān".

[27]   Cf. Ringgren, "The Pure Religion". The concept of *akhlasa* needs further investigation, as do other Qur'anic terms used in connection with *dīn* and left aside here (see for instance Paret, *Mohammed und der Koran* [see above note 6], pp. 72–4).

refers not only to the external forms this religion took in combining worldly action with religious inspiration and thought. It also suggests a particular notion that Muhammad himself had of what his religion, as true religion, should be.

What was *"islām"* with a small "i" before it became "Islam" with a capital "I", that is to say as a religion in history? This is in fact a search, beyond written history, for the beginnings of historical Islam. The very fact that "Islam" has become the name of a historical religion makes it difficult to unearth what *islām* in the course of Muhammad's lifetime meant and implied. At present, the term "Islam" refers to something that is now largely a norm and ideal of Muslims and a subject of research of Islamicists. The first tend to interpret "Islam" mostly in terms of their own commitment, the latter, unfortunately, have tended to interpret this "Islam" in terms of Western ideas of religion. Notwithstanding the difficulties of the enterprise, scholarly research tries to push backward into history beyond the moment at which Islam became a more or less fixed and "established" religion. Like archeologists wanting to reach the earliest stage of a culture, we do our best to reach an earlier stage of Islam in which it was still a "religion" in becoming. This is a serious question for a "history" of religions that might even be called an "archeology" of religions.

We saw that the *millat Ibrāhīm* represented for Muhammad the *ur-religion*, some kind of primordial monotheistic religion of universal validity. A problem that deserves further research is the extent to which Muhammad continued to recognize the priority of this primordial religion over the empirical religion that he established in Medina. Or did he finally arrive at a straight identification of his own "Islamic" religion with the primordial religion of Abraham and finally Adam?

In the last analysis, this problem touches the claim of the universality of Islam. Whereas "universality" for us is mostly expressed in terms of an idea that is generally valid, in Muhammad's time it was first of all expressed in terms of a common origin. Ibrāhīm being the *hanīf* or monotheist par excellence, he is considered to be the "father" of all monotheistic "surrenderers" to God. He is the father of a postulated universal and eternal monotheistic religion, proper to humankind, that started with Adam. While Ibrāhīm had instituted monotheism in contrast to idolatry, Muhammad "rediscovered" it. He proclaimed its essential truth, first, in contrast to the Arab idolaters of his time and, second, to the Jews and Christians of his time. Muslims as "surrendered ones" are supposed to follow the religion of Ibrāhīm, which remains the model and norm for their own religion.

I have often wondered whether, in the course of the history of Islam, Muslims have always seen Islamic religion as *the only* or merely as *one possible* realization of the primordial religion, the *ḥanīfīya*, on earth. In this "archeological" kind of research, the question of what constituted "primordial religion" and "universal religion" for Muhammad and how he saw his own religion in relation to it is essential. It should be treated, however, independently of what happened after his death. As a consequence, our "archeological" research of the development of Muhammad's vision of "religion" is less concerned about what has been understood by "Islam"[28] in later times. This includes its precise religious beliefs, prescriptions, and practices, as well as its doctrinal developments and the idea of a "natural monotheism" given as *fiṭra* within each human being.

Many interpretations have already been given of these delicate but decisive years of the beginnings of Islam, and none of them has proved to be exhaustive.[29] An impartial history—or even archeology—of religions can make a contribution by throwing more light on what I see as crucial phases of earliest Islam: those of religious purification, of religious reform, and of constitution as a religion (*dīn*).

---

[28] For the later use of this term, see for instance SMITH, *An Historical and Semantic Study of the Term Islam as seen in a Sequence of Quran Commentaries*; cf. ID., "Continuity and Change in the Understanding of 'Islam'", pp. 121–39.

The underlying assumption that the Qur'anic texts date from Muhammad's lifetime has been fundamentally questioned by John WANSBROUGH, *Quranic Studies: Sources and Methods of Scriptural Interpretation* (London Oriental Series 31), Oxford etc.: Oxford University Press, 1977; and his *The Sectarian Milieu: Content and Composition of Islamic Salvation History* (London Oriental Series 34), Oxford etc.: Oxford University Press, 1978. Discussion of Wansbrough's work should take into account Angelika NEUWIRTH, *Studien zur Komposition der mekkanischen Suren* (Studien zur Sprache, Geschichte und Kultur des Islamischen Orients, N.F. 10), Berlin and New York: Walter de Gruyter, 1981.

[29] A history of "religions" also needs to take into account data that had a religious connotation or significance at the time in which they occurred. In Islamic studies, social and political realities, for instance, should always be considered. With regard to our theme the observation of Tor Andrae on the connection of the development of Islam and the growing awareness of Arab identity within the framework of a universal monotheistic religion deserves attention: "Hence we must assume that the struggle for religious independence, and the belief in a general monotheistic religion, revealed to all peoples, which came from the Manichaean and Syrian *hanpe*, did not, in Mohammed's time, so far as he was aware, originate in direct connection with these sects, but rather as a feeling after a new independent religion, free from the idol-worship of heathenism, and not bound by any Jewish or Christian rites or laws—and thus a religion to which one could swear allegiance without having to sacrifice national distinctiveness and independence, such as one would have to do on joining a foreign religious community (*umma*)" (Tor ANDRAE, *Mohammed, the Man and his Faith* [see note 11 above], p. 110).

Selected Literature

ASSIOUTY, Sarwat Anis al-, *Révolutionnaires parmi les Disciples de Jésus et les Compagnons de Muhammad* (Recherches comparées sur le Christianisme Primitif et l'Islam Premier 4), Paris: Letouzey et Ané, 1994.

BANETH, David H., "What did Muhammad mean when he called his Religion 'Islam'? The Original Meaning of *aslama* and its Derivatives", *Israel Oriental Studies*, 1 (1971), pp. 183–90.

BRAVMANN, Meir M., *The Spiritual Background of Early Islam: Studies in Ancient Arab Concepts*, Leiden: E. J. Brill, 1972.

GARDET, Louis, art "*dīn*", in *EI²*, Vol. 2 (1965), pp. 293–6.

GOITEIN, Shelomo Dov, *Studies in Islamic History and Institutions*, Leiden: E. J. Brill, 1966.

HADDAD, Yvonne Y., "The Conception of the Term *dīn* in the Qur'ān", *The Muslim World*, 64 (1974), pp. 114–23.

HAWTING, Gerald R., *The Idea of Idolatry and the Emergence of Islam: From Polemic to History* (Cambridge Studies in Islamic Civilization), Cambridge: Cambridge University Press, 1999.

HOYLAND, Robert G., *Seeing Islam as Others saw It: A Survey and Evaluation of Christian, Jewish and Zoroastrian Writings on Early Islam* (Studies in Late Antiquity and Early Islam 13), Princeton, N. J.: Darwin Press, 1997.

IZUTSU, Toshihiko, *The Structure of the Ethical Terms in the Koran: A Study in Semantics*, Tokyo: The Keio Institute of Philological Studies, 1959.

—, *God and Man in the Koran: Semantics of the Koranic Weltanschauung*, Tokyo: The Keio Institute of Cultural and Linguistic Studies, 1964.

—, *Ethico-Religious Concepts in the Qur'ān*, Montreal: McGill University Institute of Islamic Studies, McGill University Press, 1966.

The Life of Muhammad, ed. by Uri RUBIN (The Formation of the Classical Islamic World), Aldershot: Ashgate, 1998.

MCAULIFFE, Jane Dammen, *Qur'ānic Christians: An Analysis of Classical and Modern Exegesis*, New York: Cambridge University Press, 1991.

RINGGREN, Helmer, *Islām, 'aslama, and muslim*, Uppsala: Gleerup, 1949.

—, "The Pure Religion", *Oriens*, 15 (1962), pp. 93–6.

ROBINSON, Neal, *Christ in Islam and Christianity: The Representations of Jésus in the Qur'ān and the Classical Muslim Commentaries*, London: Macmillan, 1991.

SMITH, Jane I., *An Historical and Semantic Study of the Term Islam as Seen in a Sequence of Quran Commentaries* (Harvard Dissertations in Religion 1), Missoula, Mt.: Scholars Press, 1975.

—, "Continuity and Change in the Understanding of 'Islam'", *The Islamic Quarterly*, 16, Nr. 3/4 (1973), pp. 121–39, and *Islam and the Modern Age*, 4, Nr. 2 (1973), pp. 42–66.

WAARDENBURG, Jacques, "Koranisches Religionsgespräch", in *Liber Amicorum: Studies in Honour of Prof. Dr. C. J. Bleeker*, Leiden: E. J. Brill, 1969, pp. 208–53.

—, "Un débat coranique contre les polythéistes", in *Ex Orbe Religionum: Studia Geo Widengren ... dedicata*, Vol. 2, Leiden: E. J. Brill, 1972, pp. 143–54.

WALDMAN, Marilyn A., "The Development of the Concept of *kufr* in the Qur'ān", *Journal of the American Oriental Society*, 88 (1968), pp. 442–55.

WATT, William Montgomery, *Muhammad at Mecca*, Oxford: Clarendon Press, 1953, etc.

—, *Muhammad at Medina*, Oxford: Clarendon Press, 1956, etc.

—, "Belief in a 'High God' in pre-Islāmic Mecca", *Journal of Semitic Studies*, 16 (1971), pp. 35–40.

—, "The Qur'ān and Belief in a 'High God'", *Der Islam*, 56/2 (1979), pp. 205–11.

WENDELL, Charles, "The pre-Islamic period of *Sīrat al-Nabī*", *The Muslim World*, 62/1 (1972), pp. 12–41.

Chapter 4
Cases of Interreligious Dialogue under Muslim Rule[1]

This chapter explores some Muslim notions of religion that have manifested themselves in encounters with adherents of other religions. The interest of such notions is that they underlie the way Muslims have interpreted other religions, as well as Islam, when discussing with non-Muslims.

I am concerned here only with Islam's historical encounters with three religions, or rather religio-cultural worlds, that have enriched an intellectual and spiritual Muslim elite at different moments in history. These are the world of Eastern Christianity, conveying the Greek and Hellenistic heritage, that of Hindu thinkers with the classical Indian heritage, and that of nineteenth-century Western Christianity, conveying the European heritage. Muslims have often been more interested in the cultural contribution of others, their knowledge, and its practical applicability than in a possible religious contribution. But still, beyond the basic texts of Qur'ān and *Sunna* various other concepts and notions of religion could, and did, emerge in these encounters. This fact is worth considering more closely.

1. Eastern Christianity in Early ʿAbbāsid Times (ca. 750–833 C.E.)[2]

The claim of the new ʿAbbāsid dynasty around 750 C.E. to establish a truly Islamic state distinct from the preceding Umayyad "kingdom" meant

---

[1]   Revised and enlarged version of the shorter text "Muslim Notions of Religion as Manifested in Interreligious Discourse", in *Selected Proceedings: XVIth Congress of the International Association for the History of Religions. Rome, September 3–8, 1990*, ed. by Ugo BIANCHI, with the cooperation of Fabio MORA and Lorenzo BIANCHI, Rome: 'L'Erma' di Bretschneider, 1994, pp. 531–40. See for the larger original text "Cultural Contact and Concepts of Religion. Three Examples from Islamic History", in *Proceedings: 15th Congress of the Union Européenne d'Arabisants et d'Islamisants, Utrecht, September 14–19*, ed. by Frederick de JONG in *Miscellanea Arabica et Islamica: Dissertationes in Academia Ultrajectina prolatae anno MCMXC* (Orientalia Lovaniensia Analecta 52), Leuven: Peeters and Departement Oriëntalistiek, 1993, pp. 293–325.

[2]   See in particular Hans PUTMAN, *L'Eglise et l'Islam sous Timothée I (780–828)*, Beirut: Dar El Machreq, 1975. The text of Timothy I was first studied by Alphonse MINGANA

that from now on society and state were to be based on one official religion, as had been the case in Sassanian Iran, the Eastern Roman Empire, and earlier states in the Middle East. This would further a markedly legalistic notion of religion connected with political objectives.

This project encouraged the development of *fiqh* and *'ilm al-hadīth* in order to critically formulate what should be considered *Sharī'a* (law) for the Muslim community and society at large. The Muslim *umma* distinguished itself from other religious communities that had their own prescriptive systems partly by its particular religious law (*Sharī'a*), which was equally valid for all its members, and partly by its specific doctrines. Central among these was the acceptance of the Qur'ān, not only as one prophetic utterance alongside others, but as the final divine Revelation, considered the definitive Word of God itself. The Qur'ān was supplemented by the prophetic tradition (*Sunna*).

Just as the jurists (*fuqahā'*) developed the prescriptive system of the *Sharī'a* with which they easily identified Islam as a religion, the theologians (*mutakallimūn*) elaborated a doctrinal system with which they tended to identify Islam. Their theology (*kalām*) allowed for a theological discussion between Muslims and non-Muslims, provided that basic Islamic tenets like the Qur'ān and Muhammad were respected. We have several reports about such discussions between Muslims and Christians.

One text from early 'Abbāsid times, studied by A. Mingana in the original Syriac text and by Louis Cheikho and more recently Hans Putman in the later Arabic version, describes a "dialogue" between the Nestorian Catholicos (equivalent to Patriarch) Timothy I (728–823) and the Caliph al-Mahdī (r. 775–85). The dialogue is described in a letter from Timothy I to his friend the learned priest Sarjis, both of the "Church of the East", that is to say the Nestorian Church. What does this text tell us about Muslim concepts and notions of religion?

As a recognized official, the Catholicos apparently had regular contact with al-Mahdī, as he did later with Hārūn al-Rashīd (r. 786–809), but there also seems to have been something like a mutual personal liking between the two men. If we take it that Timothy I is indeed the author of the text, we have before us an interesting account of the questions posed by the highest Muslim political officeholder to the highest Christian

who published the Syriac text with translation and introduction in his *Woodbrooke Studies: Christian Documents in Syriac, Arabic, and Garshuni*, Vol. II (Cambridge: Heffer, 1928), pp. 1–162. He published a study about it under the title of "The Apology of Timothy the Patriarch before the Caliph Mahdi" in *Bulletin of the John Rylands Library*, 12 (1928), pp. 137–298. Robert CASPAR published a critical edition of the Arabic text under the title of "Les versions arabes du Dialogue entre le Catholicos Timothée I et le calife al-Mahdī (IIe–VIIIe siècle)" in *Islamochristiana*, 3 (1977), pp. 107–75.

spiritual officeholder. It is the Caliph who, according to etiquette, asks the questions and the Catholicos who answers, committed to the creed (*i'tiqād*) of his Church. This kind of questioning enables Timothy to give a quiet, considered, and precise exposition of the Christian faith, and there is reason to suppose that this text served as the basis of further statements by Eastern Christians on their own religion while facing a Muslim presence that made itself ever more palpable. It is important to note that there is no polemical tone and no desire to refute Islam, but only to answer clearly all the questions posed by the Caliph.

There were eight questions for Timothy to answer and he sometimes did this in an original, even ingenious way. They concerned the nature of Christ, the three persons (*aqānīm*) of God, circumcision, the *qibla* of Jerusalem for prayers, the testimony of the Bible on Muhammad, the judgment given by Christians about Muhammad, the death of Christ (was it by his free will, if it happened on the cross?), Muhammad's appearance as a prophet after Christ (in the Christian view, the only prophet after Jesus was to be Elijah), and the accusation of the corruption (*tahrīf*) of the Bible (refuted with rather ingenious arguments). This allows us to identify the main contours of the notion of religion that al-Mahdī propounds, clad in the concepts and literary style of a Christian author around the end of the eighth century.

Religion, in the Caliph's view, is first of all something "given", rather than a matter of personal commitment. This is probably a common way for political and Church leaders to look at religion, because for Timothy, too, religion is a given thing. For him, it is a doctrine or creed (*i'tiqād*) accepted by people who acknowledge it as true.

Second, religion goes beyond concepts; it has as its core notion a profound awareness of God as unique and one. All the questions posed about "one and three", "one and two", seem to poke fun at numerical or logical contradictions of Christian doctrines. They seek to demonstrate the mental confusion resulting from any loosening of the basic truth of *tawhīd* and speculating about God's nature or essence.

Third, the discussion about Scriptural proofs, prophetic announcements of Muhammad, and verification of a prophet's mission dominate the whole discussion. For both parties, Scriptural texts are true, unconditionally true, imposed from Beyond, and anything but human writing. Beyond the concept of sacred Scripture, there is a deeper notion of "Divine" words that are true in themselves and are recited or read with awe. Both al-Mahdī and Timothy have this awareness of absolute Truth with regard to their Scriptures.

The Christian author depicts al-Mahdī as a wise man, as a man who knows to ask essential questions about the Christian faith, and as someone who listens to the answers. Timothy sees him as open-minded, notwithstanding his evident disbelief in typically Christian doctrines that go beyond clear rationality. He lacks the bitterness of an Ibn Hazm or the haughtiness of an Ibn Taymīya. In a similar vein, Timothy's patient explanations have nothing of the polemical spirit of the Byzantine theologians or the pretense of the Latin authors. Within this courtly style of exchange, reason prevails and good manners count.

The broader context of this Muslim-Christian dialogue on religious matters is the breakthrough of a Muslim elite toward the Greek-Hellenistic cultural heritage. This is testified to by an increasing number of translations made of Greek and Syriac texts into Arabic. In fact, the Muslim encounter with Eastern Christianity and the discovery of the Greek-Hellenistic cultural heritage are intimately related, for it was the Christians who were culture bearers and started the translation work. The role of Christian secretaries, medical doctors, and translators in and around the court was considerable, and Timothy I represented this Christian, cultivated community better than anyone else could have done, as Head of the Church of the East. He was a man of learning and a participant in the affairs of the country. He also was consistently loyal to ʿAbbāsid interests.

It appears that, until the reversal brought about by al-Mutawakkil (r. 847–61), the accepted concept of religion, whatever the shadow cast by its legal and doctrinal interpretation, was still general enough to allow openness to other faiths and admit a search for knowledge and culture beyond denominational differences. On the highest level, it did not obstruct an interreligious discourse that, as such, tended to broaden the notion of religion. With al-Mutawakkil, such a relatively open interreligious dialogue was finished, at least for a time, except privately and among friends.

2. Hindu India in Early Moghul Times (1556–1605 C.E.)[3]

With the conquest of a large part of northern India in 1535, Bābur (r. 1494–1530) laid the foundations of the Moghul empire, in which a Muslim government was to rule a majority Hindu population for more than three centuries. Bābur, himself a man of culture and a writer[4], brought with him Turkic cultural traditions that became part of the court culture and left their mark on the social structure of the leading classes.

---

[3] See in particular RIZVI, *Religious and Intellectual History in Akbar's Reign* (see literature under 6.).

[4] Bābur is best known as an author for his *Bābur-nāma*, his autobiography written in Chagatāy Turkish (English translation by ANNETTE S. BEVERIDGE, *The Bābur-nāma in English*, 2 Vols., London 1921–2). He was, however, also an important poet (his *Dīwān* contains besides Turkish also some Persian poems) and wrote several prose works. Bābur wrote mostly in Chagatāy Turkish and was proud of being of Turkish descent.

After his death in 1530, his son Humāyūn ruled for ten years but then was defeated by Shīr Khān Sūnī, the Afghan ruler of Bihar, and had to go then into exile. For some time he found refuge at the court of Shah Tahmāsp in Isfahan, where culture flourished. In 1555, he succeeded in taking Delhi again and in his turn introduced the court and Muslim nobility to Persian culture, which was to leave its mark on Moghul culture in its Indian surroundings.[5] But he died suddenly by accident in January 1556, and his then fourteen-year-old son Akbar (1542–1605) took over. He not only re-established the empire in precarious circumstances, but also became one of the greatest emperors India has known.[6]

Akbar ruled from 1556 until 1605. Though not a man of great culture himself, he continued the tradition of enlightened Muslim rulers in organizing public debates on religious issues in Islam. This was part of courtly culture, putting the participants' intellectual capacities to the test in discussions about legal and theological problems. The audience must have attended such discussions as a kind of intellectual sporting event, while at the same time becoming more aware of the religion they had in common. Akbar organized such discussions from early on, probably not only as a contest between religious thinkers for spectators to enjoy, but also to learn from them himself. In his thirties, he already showed religious inclinations, being keen on meditation and prayer, interested in philosophical questions and religious law, and continuously in touch with Muslim Sūfīs and Hindu ascetics. During the religious debates, he may also have been interested in judging the capacities of 'ulamā' and sheykhs, measuring their limitations, and drawing conclusions for his future course of action.[7] All of this, together with political considerations and personal ambitions, was to produce a religious breakthrough rarely found in

---

5 Humāyūn wrote Persian verse and was a patron of mathematics and astronomy. During his stay at the Persian court of Shah Tahmāsp, he was under pressure to become Shīʿī, and at the Moghul court there would be an important Shīʿī group.

6 There is not yet a definitive biography of Akbar. Most important for our purposes is RIZVI's study on *Religious and Intellectual History in Akbar's Reign*. Cf. SRIVASTAVA, *Akbar the Great*; see also IKRAM, *Muslim Civilization in India*, pp.143–65, and MUJEEB, *The Indian Muslims*, pp. 238–44 and 254–64 (for all these see literature under 6.). Cf. C. Collin DAVIES, art. "Akbar", *EI*², Vol. 1, pp. 316–7, and F. LEHMANN, art. "Akbar", *Encyclopedia Iranica*, Vol. 1, pp. 707–11. For historical sources, see MUKHIA, *Historians and Historiography during Akbar's Reign* (see literature under 6.). The two most important sources are the chronicles written by Abu'l-Fadl 'Allāmī and 'Abd al-Qādir Bādā'ūnī, both translated into English. Akbar's son Jahāngīr left an interesting description of his father in his *Tūzuk-i Djahāgīrī* (English translation by Alexander ROGERS, ed. by Henry BEVERIDGE, Vol. 1, London: Royal Asiatic Society, 1909 [repr. New Delhi: Munshiram Manoharlal, 1978], pp. 33–45).

7 Besides possible religious motivations and general political motivations in favor of cooperation with other religious communities (in particular Hindus), Akbar must have had internal political motivations in organizing these religious discussions. He must have been searching how to control the dominating court 'ulamā'.

Islamic history and certainly in the history of Muslim rulers.[8] It led to a new notion and concept of religion, different from that of the *fuqahā'* and *mutakallimūn*, that allowed discussions with non-Muslims in a new openness.

The main phases of this development were as follows: In February-March 1575, at the age of thirty-three, Akbar ordered an *'Ibādāt-Khāna* (House of Worship)[9] to be erected quite near to his palace (*Dawlat-Khāna*) in Fathpūr Sīkrī, the new capital he had built. Here Muslim scholars carefully chosen by the emperor himself, first Sunnīs and later also Shī'īs, held discussions about religious and philosophical subjects. The participants were seated in the four *īwāns* (vaulted halls) around the courtyard: the nobles on the east side, and the *'ulamā'* and philosophers on the north side. Akbar used to attend the meetings held on Thursday night, which could sometimes continue on Friday afternoon, after the *jum'a* prayer in the mosque of Fathpūr Sīkrī and after Akbar's regular visit to the *khānqāh* (Sūfī center) of *sheykh* Salīm Chistī, who was already living at the site before Fathpūr Sīkrī was built.[10]

Apparently irritated by the *'ulamā'*'s technical and also personal quarrels and their lack of vision on matters of general concern, Akbar encouraged new scholars to be invited so as to broaden the horizon of these discussions. In this way he also constituted a more critical and logically oriented opposition to the established Sunnī court *'ulamā'*, who apparently were keener to serve their self-interest and please the emperor to obtain favors than to face problems of general importance squarely.

A second phase started in 1578. Historians mention a religious inspiration through an ecstatic experience, that Akbar had during a hunting party on April 22 of that year.[11] As a result, he apparently thought of retiring and adopting an ascetic way of life. This did not happen, but just as he had invited Shī'ī *'ulamā'* to the meetings in the *'Ibādat-Khāna* at the end of 1575, he allowed non-Muslims, too, to participate in the discussions in the fall of 1578. At first only Hindus (except yogis) were involved, the best known of them being Bīrbal, apparently a close friend of Akbar and a sun worshipper whose example he followed. It may be

---

[8] For the description of this religious breakthrough, I refer to Rizvi's study (see literature under 6.), in particular Chapter 3, with its critical use of the historical data given by Abu'l-Fadl. I would like to stress, however, the gradual nature of the breakthrough as a "process" to be divided into several phases.

[9] On the *'Ibādat-Khāna*, see for instance Rizvi's study (see literature under 6.), pp. 107–27.

[10] Akbar had close relationships with the Chistī *tarīqa* (Ikram's study [see literature under 6.], p. 156).

[11] A poetic description of what happened is given by Abu'l-Fadl. See his *Akbar-nāma*, trans. by Henry Beveridge, Vol. III (Calcutta: Asiatic Society, 1921), Ch. 43 (pp. 345–8 in the edition of Ess Ess Publications, New Delhi 1973).

recalled that the Hindus now enjoyed a *dhimmī* status without paying *jizya* and Akbar's Hindu wives celebrated their own rituals as a matter of course.

The arrival, in the same year, of a Parsee priest with a group of *mobeds* led not only to a new kind of discussion bearing on the principle of light (*nūr*) and on *ishrāq* (illumination) philosophy, which had also developed in Iran, but also to the ritual practice of continuous fire burning.

Five years later, in 1583, a Swetambara Jain leader arrived with 67 monks at Fathpūr Sīkrī. They stayed for no less than two years and other Jain visits followed.

The first Christians, a Jesuit mission headed by Robert Acquaviva, arrived on February 28, 1580. Antony Monserrate has left an interesting historical account of it.[12] Two other Jesuit missions followed during Akbar's reign. The last one, headed by Francis Xavier, arrived in 1594 and left only after Akbar's death in 1605.[13]

The presence of Jesuit missionaries at Akbar's court has given rise to various scholarly interpretations. What seems sure is that as soon as he had discovered that his visitors were keen on converting him, Akbar seized the occasion to inform himself about the Christian religion and Christian lands in Europe. He enticed them into discussion by asking them many questions, though being less inclined to answer theirs. The Jesuits probably did not know quite what to make of an emperor blessed with so much intellectual curiosity and spiritual mobility, which accorded neither with the teachings of the Church and still less with those of the Counter-Reformation. Nor had they experienced such an attitude elsewhere.

As Sayyid Athar Abbas Rizvi has formulated it, the results of such religious discussions, which were held not only in the *'Ibādat-Khāna*, but also privately in the palace itself, were threefold.[14] First, the ignorance of many *'ulamā'* and the extent to which not only various schools in Islam but also various religions differed came to light. Second, it became clear that wise men could be found in all religions and that, as Rizvi expresses it, "truth is nowhere absent". Last but not least, Akbar himself was encouraged to reflect and transform his own thinking. Whereas at the beginning of his reign he had, according to his own words reported by contemporary historians, tried to convert Hindus forcibly to Islam, he accepted them now as partners and was more open to the values of wisdom (*ḥikma*) and reason (*'aql*), self-criticism and spiritual growth.

---

[12]   HOYLAND and BANERJEE, *The Commentary of Father Monserrate, S.J. on his Journey to the Court of Akbar* (see literature under 6.).

[13]   CAMPS, *Jerome Xavier S.J. and the Muslims of the Moghul Empire* (see literature under 6.).

[14]   See the end of Chapter 3 of RIZVI's study (see literature under 6.).

There is reason, indeed, to assume that both his own experience and the religious and interreligious discussions he had initiated changed the concept and notion of religion with which Akbar must have been brought up. This was the legal conception of Islam, upheld by the *ulamā'*, as a body of rational knowledge. Based on revelation and reason, it had been formulated in its definitive form in the first centuries of Islam and was then transmitted on authority to subsequent generations. It claimed that to know the *Sharī'a* was to know religion.

It must be assumed that Akbar did not arrive at this religious break-through only because of political motivations to get rid of the control of the dominating *ulamā'*. It was also a completely new notion of what religion itself is and does that made Akbar support *ijtihādī* or *taḥqīqī* Islam, based on individual reasoning and personal asserting of truth. This was in contrast to *taqlīdī* Islam, based on imitation of the legal and doctrinal model of Islam formulated by the *ulamā'* and *mutakallimūn* and ever more reified.[15]

A new phase started in 1579, when a new religious policy took shape. On Friday, June 26 of that year (1 Jumādā 987 H.) the emperor person-ally read the *khutba* in his own name, assuming the classical title of *khalīfa*. In August-September of the same year (Rajab 987 H.) a *maḥdar* titled "the Infallible Decree" and signed by the court *ulamā'* themselves after they were subjected to calculated pressure, gave the emperor author-ity to make his own decision in matters of *Sharī'a* whenever the leading *ulamā'* differed in their opinions on a question.[16] In this way, Akbar was enabled to choose from among the divergent opinions of the *ulamā'* the one that conformed best with his policies and administrative needs. After having put down a rebellion against his new policy, inevitably instigated by some *ulamā'*, he succeeded in freeing himself of his two leading opponents at court, the *ulamā'* Makhdūm al-Mulk and Sheykh 'Abd al-Nabī. He then could pursue his own path.[17]

Rizvi has summarized Akbar's own religious beliefs and practices as far as they are known to us.[18] Together with his religious policy sketched above, this summary gives some idea of Akbar's own expressed concep-tion and underlying notion of religion. On a religious level, distinct from

---

[15] The opposition of *ijtihād* to *taqlīd* was to become an important theme in the writings of nineteenth- and twentieth-century Muslim Reformers.

[16] A poetic description is given by Abu'l-Fadl in Chapter 47 of his *Akbar-nāma* (see above note 11), pp. 390–400. Compare the critical account by Bādā'ūnī in his *Muntakhabu 't-tawārīkh*, English translation by William Henry Lowe, Vol. II (Patna: Edition Academica Asiatica, 1973), pp. 276–81.

[17] See Rizvi's study (se literature under 6.), Chapter 4, "The End of the Old Order".

[18] See Rizvi, Chapter 10. On Akbar's hospitality to non-Muslims, their beliefs, and practices, see the critical remarks by Bādā'ūnī in his chronicle mentioned above in note 16, for instance, pp. 263–72, 331–6.

the political one, Akbar rejected attitudes of dogmatism and persecution, considering the use of reason as primary in approaching one's own religion and those of others. In his opinion, however, reason alone is not sufficient for a true religious and spiritual life; it should be supplemented by a spiritual guide, a *sāhib-i dil* ("one who has a heart", that is understanding). Religious discourse should not limit itself to *'ilm*, knowledge of religion as handed down by tradition, but should rather concentrate on *hikma* (wisdom). After his *mahdar* of 1579, Akbar started urging, though not obliging, his courtiers to renounce *taqlīdī* Islam and to opt for *ijtihādī* or *tahqīqī* Islam. Consequently, two major orientations in Islam came to exist at court that might be called a traditional and a more rational one. Akbar did not, however, force either Muslims or Hindus to adopt particular religious convictions or devotions or move away from Islam or Hinduism.

Rizvi mentions some idiosyncratic beliefs and practices that Akbar adopted after 1580, during the last twenty-five years of his life. Compared to his younger years he showed certain ascetic tendencies in his own lifestyle. He put restrictions on the killing of animals in his realm and developed certain vegetarian ideas and practices himself. He believed firmly in *tanāsukh*, the transmigration of souls, and had his head tonsured in accordance with this belief and in conformity with local practice. Most astonishing, perhaps, was his practice of adoring the sun while bearing a Hindu mark on his forehead and his accommodating himself to different ways of praying according to different rituals that existed. In all of this, however, Akbar remained a monotheist.

The final phase of Akbar's religious policy was his creation of the so-called *dīn ilāhi* at the beginning of the 1580's.[19] There has been much discussion about this since, besides his religious policies just described and his personal beliefs and practices, the *dīn ilāhī* might perhaps give a clue to Akbar's deepest notion of religion. All scholars agree that one of the main functions of the *dīn ilāhī* was to bring Muslims and Hindus together, religiously and in practical life. But beyond that, opinions differ greatly. Was the *dīn ilāhī* a new syncretistic religion? Did Akbar consider himself a prophet and the center of this new religion? Were there particular doctrines and rules of life imposed on the *dīn ilāhī*? Little is in fact known of it, and it has been the object of much speculation, even during Akbar's

---

[19]   About the *Dīn ilāhī*, see Aziz AHMAD, art. "Dīn-i ilāhī", *EI²*, Vol. 2, pp. 296–7, and the same author's study "Akbar: Heretic or Apostate", published as Chapter 6 of his *Studies in Islamic Culture in the Indian Environment* (see literature under 6.), pp. 167–81. See also Chapter 10, "The Dīn Ilāhī", of RIZVI's book (see literature under 6.). Cf. ROY CHOUDHURY, *The Din Ilahi of the Religion of Akbar*; see also SHARMA, *The Religious Policy of the Mughal Emperors* (for both see literature under 6.), and his article "Akbar's Religious Policy", *The Indian Historical Quarterly*, 13 (1937), pp. 302–22 and 448–81.

own lifetime, among the established Muslim and Hindu religious leader-ships.

Unless new, convincing evidence to the contrary can be adduced, I am inclined to follow Rizvi's critical and realistic assessment of the *dīn ilāhi*. According to him, it consisted of a small group of prominent Muslims and some Hindus who had sworn full allegiance to the emperor and the empire and were ready to sacrifice life, property, honor, and if necessary religion for its sake. Like Ismāʿīl Safavī (1487–1524), the founder of the Safavid dynasty in Iran, but without *tarīqa* connections, Akbar demanded complete devotion from his highest dignitaries for the sake of the dynasty and the empire. They, indeed, considered themselves to be *murīds* of their emperor and continued to do so up to the reign of Awrangzīb (1658–1707). This put the seal on full cooperation between Hindu *rajputs* and Muslim grandees during this period.

According to this critical view, the *dīn ilāhi* had no religious signifi-cance in itself, but was a necessary means to a political end, that is, absolute loyalty to the Moghul throne and total devotion to the empire, the declared policy of which was *sulh-i kull* (universal toleration). Full Muslim-Hindu cooperation was a conditio sine qua non for the survival of the Moghul empire, and the *dīn ilāhi* encouraged this, without replac-ing the individual members' own beliefs and opinions. The outside world, however, and certainly the established Muslim and Hindu religious lead-erships that had their own vested interests, considered the *dīn ilāhi* to be a new and rival religion, or at least a new *tarīqa*. It was neither. Akbar's marked tendency to glorify sovereignty and the state may go back to the ancient Iranian ideology of kingship, revived by the Safavids.[20] In any case, it confirms that, to survive, the empire had to transcend the partisan interests of the religious communities it comprised, whether they were Muslim or Hindu.

What can we say about Akbar's concept and underlying notion of reli-gion? It was certainly not a legal or doctrinal one as developed by the *ʿulamāʾ*, but went back to a completely different notion of what religion is. In fact, it was based on personal search in the Sūfī and Hindu tradition and can be called "mystical" in that the individual's own religious experience is fundamental. Instead of calling Akbar's concept of religion syncretistic—nearly all religions are in one respect or another syncretistic—I would prefer to call Akbar's concept of religion a personal monotheism. It is an adoration and veneration of the Divinity, arising out of a personal

---

[20]   At the 16th IAHR Congress in Rome in September 1990, Dr. Gudmar E.E. Aᴎᴇᴇʀ read a paper "Kingship Ideology and Muslim Law at the Court of Akbar the Great Mogul". He treated the question of the nature of the growing claims of authority, both mundane and spiritual, by Akbar. A kingship ideology was implied in this. Did it derive from Persian or Indian sources and was it compatible with Islam, be it Sunnī or be it Shīʿī?

search starting from within the religious tradition in which a person is born and then reaching out beyond it.

As a consequence, Akbar's concept of religion has little to do with the clearly defined concepts of the Greek and Hellenistic philosophical tradition of thinking. The latter led to the formation not only of Christian and Jewish theology and philosophy but also of the Islamic system of the religious sciences (*'ulūm al-dīn*) as developed, transmitted, and safeguarded by the *'ulamā'*. In short, Akbar's concept of religion must be seen not in a Middle Eastern, but in an Indian cultural tradition and context. Akbar himself, through his upbringing and early experience as a ruler, may be called a unique combination of Islamic faith and Indian cultural and religious tradition. He then proposed a unique solution for overcoming the danger of a dichotomy between them. He did this in large part through the force of his exceptional personality.

The broader context of this Muslim-Hindu dialogue is that of the break-through of a Muslim elite toward the Indian cultural heritage. Akbar should be understood as one of the bridges between the Islamic faith and Indian civilization. For Akbar as a Muslim, as for al-Bīrūnī[21] before him and Dārā Shukōh[22] after him, Hindu religion and culture represented a new and foreign world, a world apart. Instead of closing themselves off from it or limiting themselves to an exclusively religious Sūfī and Hindu realm, these persons tried to understand this world and make it under-stood. At Akbar's translation bureau of the sixteenth century, the *Maktab-Khāna*[23], the *Mahābhārata* and other great Sanskrit texts, as well as relevant Arabic, Turkish, and even Latin Christian texts, were translated into Persian. It may very well be compared to al-Ma'mūn's *Bayt al-ḥikma* of the ninth century, where the great texts of Greek philosophy and science were translated from Syriac and Greek into Arabic. Akbar wanted the Indian cultural heritage to be known to the Muslim elite in the Moghul empire and beyond, so that Muslim culture would be enriched by it.

---

[21] On al-Bīrūnī (973–after 1050), see, for instance, D.J. BOILOT's article "al-Bīrūnī", *EI*², Vol. 1 (1960), pp. 1236–8. The description al-Bīrūnī gives of Hindu religion and culture in his *Kitāb ta'rīkh al-Hind* (trans. E. SACHAU; see literature under 6.) is a monument of Muslim science of religion in the medieval period.

[22] On Dārā Shukōh (1615–59), see, for instance, Satish CHANDRA's article "Dārā Shukōh", *EI*², Vol. 2, pp. 134–5. Dārā Shukōh, the eldest son of Shah Jahān and considered the heir apparent to the throne, was brushed aside by his brother Awrangzīb. Having become a spiritual mediator between Muslim and Hindu spirituality, he was finally accused of heresy and executed. See Aziz AHMAD, "Dārā Shikōh and Aurangzeb", Chapter 8 of his *Studies in Islamic Culture in the Indian Environment* (see literature under 6.), pp. 191–200.

[23] On Akbar's translation program, see Chapter 6, "Translation bureau of Akbar (*The Maktab Khana*)" of RIZVI's study (see literature under 6.), pp. 203–23.

Akbar's concept of religion is that of a personal monotheism stretching beyond Islam and encompassing all who are involved in a personal search for the Divinity. His underlying notion seems to have embraced both the individual's own religious realization and the effort to transcend earthly religious differences and dichotomies in the common adoration of the absolute One. It opened a new path for interreligious dialogue.

3. Western Christianity in Colonial Times (Egypt ca. 1850–1905)[24]

After these two instances of the Muslim discoveries of the Greek-Hellenistic and the Indian cultural heritage, my third example concerns the Muslim discovery of the nineteenth-century European cultural heritage. At the time, Muslim elites came to know European culture and religion and responded to certain judgments of Islam that were current in Europe at the time.

Muhammad 'Abduh (1849–1905) played an important role in this possibly first longer modern Muslim-Christian, or perhaps Euro-Arab, dialogue. He had studied at al-Azhar, but he came to know European society and culture during his stay in Paris and his travels in various European countries. After his return to Egypt from exile in 1889, 'Abduh abstained from politics, occupied several important positions, and dedicated himself to educational, social, and religious reforms. We have a unique presentation of Islam and Christianity from his pen in the six articles *Al-islām wa'l-nasrāniyya ma'a 'al-'ilm wa'l-madanīya* ("Islam and Christianity together with science and civilization"), which he published in *al-Manār* from August 20, 1902 on. They are a lengthy response to an article that the Syrian Greek Catholic journalist Farah Antūn (1861–1922), living in Cairo, had written on Ibn Rushd and published in his journal *Al-jāmi'a al-'uthmānīya* in 1900. Antūn's thesis was that Christianity has been more tolerant than Islam toward science and civilization. 'Abduh defended the opposite thesis. His six articles were published immediately afterwards in book form, and in 1905 a second edition appeared.

This book is often considered a specimen of modern Muslim apologetics, but I think there is more to it. It is relevant to the encounter of Islam with Western Christianity in colonial times, particularly because the author wants to compare the principles of both religions and in fact

---

[24] See in particular Gunnar HASSELBLATT, *Herkunft und Auswirkungen der Apologetik Muhammad 'Abduh's (1849–1905): Untersucht an seiner Schrift: Islam und Christentum im Verhältnis zu Wissenschaft und Zivilisation*, Diss. Göttingen, 1968.

proposes a new concept of religion that he may have developed precisely thanks to his interest in religion and culture as it existed in Europe. Its true intention appears in the last section, which does not concern Christianity at all, but seeks to mobilize Muslims in general, and Egyptians in particular, to apply their intelligence in the search for knowledge. Thus at one and the same time, they are called upon to revitalize science and religion, true religion being intimately linked to reason for ʿAbduh. Since ʿAbduh had to write his articles quickly, without the leisure to consult the existing relevant texts and literature, this book has a spontaneity and directness that derive from his deepest convictions.

When comparing the principles of Islam with those of Christianity, ʿAbduh concludes that, in contrast to Christianity, the principles of Islam favor the development of science and philosophy. Islam's call to belief in God's existence is also a call to the intelligence—that nature has given to the human being—to follow its own necessary course. The call to belief in Muhammad's mission is based on the Qurʾān's invitation to follow something that is evident in itself. It is not to obey a religious authority that contradicts the demands of reason, as he sees happening in Christianity. ʿAbduh's presentation of Islam implies a concept of religion as something thoroughly conform to reason.

What can be said about ʿAbduh's concept and underlying notion of religion? It differs from the concept of religion held in medieval *fiqh* and *kalām* as well as that held by the Sūfis. ʿAbduh relates his concept here to the actual history of Islam and Christianity and to the realities of Islam and Muslim society in Egypt and the Muslim world at the beginning of the twentieth century. He appropriates for Islam the concept of reason as it was current in nineteenth-century European philosophy and science, with the powerful impulse which the faith in reason gave to the development of the sciences in Europe and North America. This perspective elevates ʿAbduh's discourse far above simple apologetics. His concept of religion linked to a faith in reason becomes a means of mobilizing the minds of people. This is clearly shown in the third part of his book.

"Most of what you see of what people call 'Islam' is no Islam at all!" is ʿAbduh's verdict; knowledge of true religion and ethics does not exist among Muslims any longer, he maintains. In the course of time, religion has become petrified here and, as a consequence, science has stagnated and come to a halt in Muslim lands. This stagnation has had pernicious effects on all sectors of social and religious life. The petrification of religion is symbolized by the immobility of the ʿulamāʾ. They have long resisted anything new and have not asked about the principles and laws of the world, since, according to ʿAbduh, they are no friends of science and civilization.

One of the main remedies against this current illness is for science and religion to fraternize again, as at the beginning of Islamic history and as prescribed by the Qur'ān. For, unlike in other religions, in Islam there is in principle no conflict between science and religion. This is the heart of 'Abduh's message. The more scholars study their own religion again, the more they will study the worldly sciences too. 'Abduh's intent here is programmatic and educational. People should use the gift of reason and intelligence with regard both to religion (acquiring true knowledge of it) and to civilization (obtaining scientific knowledge useful to it). This is no less than a religious duty. Evidently, 'Abduh himself experienced the enthusiasm of discovering and acquiring knowledge and the enrichment it brings.

The broader context of this effort to present religion as the mobilizing force for science and civilization is that of the breakthrough of a Muslim elite to the European cultural heritage. This goes beyond the mere introduction of Western technology and applied sciences. Numerous translations of books from Western languages, including Russian, into Arabic, Persian, Turkish, and Urdu made their way throughout the Muslim world from the mid-nineteenth century on. Western schools in Muslim countries stimulated new kinds of thinking for generations of Muslim youth. In this open intellectual and cultural climate, a new kind of intercultural and interreligious dialogue could start. It would go far beyond the limitations of religious polemics expressed in missionary tracts and in the Muslim apologetic responses to what was felt to be a Western attack on Islam. However, during the twentieth century, this tide of cultural exchange and dialogue with Europe and North America remained limited to certain elites. It took place, but keeping a distance from the storms of ideological agitation and political confrontation, with much misery on the ground.

4. Conclusion

In the foregoing pages, I showed three moments of encounter: between Islam and the Greek-Hellenistic heritage, the Indian heritage, and the European cultural heritage. They led to ensuing situations of dialogue between Islam and Eastern Christianity, Hinduism, and Western Christianity. Some conclusions about our subject, Muslim notions of religion as manifested in interreligious discourse, impose themselves as a result.

Various concepts and underlying notions of religion had already developed earlier in the course of Islamic history. During Muhammad's lifetime, there was a shift from the call to recognize, worship, and serve God in his uniqueness and unity (*tawhīd*) to the constitution of a community living under God's command. It was supposed to follow precise prescriptions, first under the direct authority of the Prophet and, after his death, according to his tradition (*Sunna*). Soon after Muhammad's death, different concepts of the nature of the religious community arose, and Shī'īs and Khārijīs parted from what were later to be called the Sunnīs. On the subject of religious life, puritanical attitudes met opposition, whereas the tendency to interiorize religion would lead to mystical notions of religion. In the field of religious knowledge, various schools of *tafsīr* and '*ilm al-hadīth*, *fiqh*, and *kalām* developed, with different concepts and notions of Islam as a religion. Besides the various directions in which mystical experience evolved, the concept also developed of a more esoteric kind of religion, beyond the external forms, into which adepts had to be initiated. This trend continued certain gnostic traditions that had existed in the Middle East long before the rise of Islam. These various concepts and notions of religion that developed within the Muslim community during the first centuries of Islam have been studied and are more or less known. Our search here has been rather for concepts and notions of religion that were held by Muslims, but that manifested themselves, not in intra-Muslim, but in interreligious discourse.

The interreligious discourses of al-Mahdī, Akbar, and Muhammad 'Abduh show a noteworthy openness toward the cultural heritage of the Greeks, the Indians, and the Europeans, an openness expressed in translation movements. Those involved in the discussions exploited the knowledge of other religions and cultures available at the time. After the death of the proponents of these discussions, however, powerful reactions occurred against such openness and receptivity. They were fueled by tough '*ulamā*' defending the particularities and exclusivity of the Islamic faith.

There are some significant differences between the three Muslim discourses discussed above. Akbar's policy and attitude were essentially an Indian affair; Christians were hardly involved, and Western political interests were still largely absent. In 'Abbāsid times and later, the scene in the Middle East was dominated by Muslims, and the discussions in which Christians were involved could have repercussions for the Christian minorities living under Muslim rule. As for Muhammad 'Abduh, his ideas fit into a context in which religious conflict between Muslims and Christians was taken for granted. In its relations with Europe, the Muslim world was the dominated party and the Europeans made them feel it. The social and political context of the three discourses, as well as their ideological implications, have been left aside in this presentation.

Our main finding is that the three Muslim discourses treated here worked with concepts and notions of religion that, without being in contradiction with the basic Qur'anic data, were developed in consonance with new cultural surroundings. These concepts and notions of religion not only led to new knowledge and views of other religions and cultures. They also made discourse with non-Muslims possible. The very fact of cultural and religious interaction tends to bring about developments, adaptations, and changes in the concepts and notions with which people of different cultural and religious traditions view each other and interpret each other's religions. Under the impact of experiences of interaction, people can learn new things. They may adapt and change their basic notions of what religion is, see their own religion in a new way, and see the other people's religion with new eyes.

Our starting hypothesis was that Muslims have had several concepts and underlying notions of religion and that they have interpreted other religions in terms of these concepts and notions. This chapter appears to have confirmed this hypothesis. Furthermore, we assumed that new concepts of religion tend to be developed during intercultural encounters and in interreligious discourse. We have proved this to be the case in the three instances studied. Our third and concluding hypothesis is that intercultural encounters and interreligious discourse developing into dialogue cannot help but lead to a further development of current notions and concepts of religion. Although definite proof can only be furnished by further research, the data of this chapter provide at least some evidence for this last hypothesis.

Selected Literature

1. Expansion of Islam

ARNOLD, T.W., *The Preaching of Islam: A History of the Propagation of the Muslim Faith*, Lahore: Sh. Muhammad Ashraf, 1914 (repr. 1961, 1965, 1968).

BULLIET, Richard W., *Conversion to Islam in the Medieval Period: An Essay in Quantitative History*, Cambridge, Mass., and London: Harvard University Press, 1979.

Conversion to Islam, ed. by Nehemia LEVTZION, New York and London: Holmes and Meier, 1979.

2. Jews and Christians as dhimmīs in Muslim Territory

COURBAGE, Youssef, and Philippe FARGUES, *Chrétiens et Juifs dans l'Islam arabe et turc*, Paris: Fayard, 1992.

FATTAL, Antoine, *Le statut légal des non-musulmans en pays d'Islam* (Recherches 10), Beirut: Imprimerie Catholique, 1958, etc.

MASTERS, Bruce, *Christians and Jews in the Ottoman Arab World: The Roots of Sectarianism* (Cambridge Studies in Islamic Civilization), Cambridge, U. K.: Cambridge University Press, 2001.

TRITTON, Arthur S., *The Caliphs and their non-Muslim Subjects: A Critical Study of the Covenant of 'Umar*, London: Oxford University Press, 1930 (repr. London: Cass, 1970).

YE'OR, Bat (ps.), *The Dhimmi: Jews and Christians under Islam*, trans. from the French, rev. and enlarged English edition, Rutherford, N. J.: Fairleigh Dickinson University Press, 1985.

—, *Les chrétientés d'Orient entre jihād et dhimmitude VIIe–XXe siècle*, Paris: Cerf, 1991; English edition: *The Decline of Eastern Christianity under Islam: From Jihad to Dhimmitude. Seventh-Twentieth Century*, Madison, etc.: Fairleigh Dickinson, 1996.

3. Jewish Communities in Muslim Territory

3.1. General

Lewis, Bernard, *The Jews of Islam*, Princeton, N. J.: Princeton University Press, 1984.

Medieval and Modern Perspectives on Muslim-Jewish Relations, ed. by Ronald L. Nettler, Luxemburg: Harwood Academic Publishers, 1995.

Studies in Muslim-Jewish Relations, Vol. 1, ed. by Ronald L. Nettler, Zug: Harwood Academic Publishers, 1993.

3.2. Medieval Period

Fischel, Walter J., *Jews in the Economic and Political Life of Mediaeval Islam* (1937). Enlarged edition New York: Ktav, 1969.

Goitein, Solomon Dob, *A Mediterranean Society: The Jewish Communities of the Arab World as Portrayed in the Documents of the Cairo Geniza*, 6 Vols., Berkeley and Los Angeles: University of Califonia Press, 1967–93.

Hirschberg, Haim Zeev (J. W.), *A History of the Jews in North Africa*, 2nd, revised edition, trans. from the Hebrew, Vol. I: *From Antiquity to the Sixteenth Century*, Leiden: E. J. Brill, 1974.

Stillman, Norman A., *The Jews of Arab Lands: A History and Source Book*, Philadelphia: The Jewish Publication Society of America, 1979/5739.

Wasserstrom, Steven M., *Between Muslim and Jew: The Problem of Symbiosis under Early Islam*, Princeton, N. J.: Princeton University Press, 1995.

3.3. Modern History

Baron, Salo Wittmayer, *A Social and Religious History of the Jews*, Vol. 18: *Late Middle Ages and Era of European Expansion (1200–1650): The Ottoman Empire, Persia, Ethiopia, India and China*. Second edition revised and enlarged, New York: Columbia University Press, and Philadelphia: The Jewish Publication Society of America, 1983/5743.

Bensimon-Donath, Doris, *Evolution du judaïsme marocain sous le Protectorat français 1912–1956* (Ecole Pratique des Hautes Etudes, 6e Section, Etudes juives 12), The Hague: Mouton, 1968.

Cohen, Amnon, *Jewish Life under Islam: Jerusalem in the Sixteenth Century*, Cambridge, Mass., and London: Harvard University Press, 1984.

Epstein, Mark Alan, *The Ottoman Jewish Communities and their Role in the Fifteenth and Sixteenth Centuries* (Islamkundliche Untersuchungen 56), Freiburg: Klaus Schwarz Verlag, 1980.

Hirschberg, Haim Zeev (J. W.), *A History of the Jews in North Africa*, 2nd, revised edition, trans. from the Hebrew, Vol. II: *From the Ottoman Conquests to the Present Time*, ed. by Eliezer Bashan and Robert Attal, Leiden: E. J. Brill, 1981.

Kenbib, Mohammed, *Juifs et musulmans au Maroc 1859–1948: Contribution à l'histoire des relations inter-communautaires en terre d'Islam* (Thèses et

Mémoires No. 21, Université Mohammed V, Publications de la Faculté des Lettres et des Sciences Humaines), Rabat: Université Mohammed V.

KRÄMER, Gudrun, *The Jews in Modern Egypt 1914–1952*, Seattle: University of Washington Press, 1989.

LANDAU, Jacob M., *Jews in Nineteenth Century Egypt* (New York University Studies in Near Eastern Civilization 2), New York: New York University Press, and London: University of London Press, 1969.

LANDSHUT, Siegfried, *Jewish Communities in the Muslim Countries of the Middle East: A Survey ... for the American-Jewish Committee and the Anglo-Jewish Association*, London: The Jewish Chronicle Ltd., 1950.

REJWAN, Nissim, *The Jews of Iraq: 3000 Years of History and Culture*, London: Weidenfeld and Nicolson, 1985.

STILLMAN, Norman A., *The Jews of Arab Lands: A History and Source Book*, Philadelphia: The Jewish Publication Society of America, 1979/5739.

—, *The Jews of Arab Lands in Modern Times*, Philadelphia and New York: The Jewish Publication Society, 1991/5751.

TOLÉDANO, Joseph, *Les Juifs marocains* (series Fils d'Abraham), Turnhout: Brepols, 1989.

4. Christian Communities in Muslim Territory

4.1. Medieval Period

Communautés chrétiennes en pays d'islam du début du VIIe siècle au milieu du XIe siècle, par Anne-Marie EDDÉ, Françoise MICHEAU and Christophe PICARD, Paris: Sedes, 1997.

Conversion and Continuity: Indigenous Christian Communities in Islamic Lands, Eighth to Eighteenth Centuries, ed. by Michael GERVERS and Ramzi Jibran BIKHAZI (Papers in Medieval Studies 9), Toronto: Pontifical Institute of Medieval Studies, 1990.

DUCELLIER, Alain, *Chrétiens d'Orient et Islam au Moyen Age, VIIe–XVe siècle*, Paris: Armand Colin, 1996.

LE COZ, Raymond, *L'Eglise d'Orient: Chrétiens d'Irak, d'Iran et de Turquie*, Paris: Cerf, 1995.

4.2. Modern Times

DADRIAN, Vahakn, *Histoire du génocide arménien: Conflits nationaux des Balkans au Caucase*, Paris: Stock, 1996.

HAJJAR, Joseph, *Les chrétiens uniates du Proche-Orient*, Paris: Seuil, 1962.

HEYBERGER, Bernard, *Les chrétiens du Proche-Orient au temps de la Réforme Catholique (Syrie, Liban, Palestine, XVIIe–XVIIIe siècles)* (Bibliothèque des Ecoles Françaises d'Athènes et de Rome, 284), Rome: Ecole Française de Rome, 1994.

JOSEPH, John, *The Nestorians and their Muslim Neighbors: A Study of Western Influences on their Relations*, Princeton, N. J.: Princeton University Press, 1961.

—, *Muslim-Christian Relations and Inter-Christian Rivalries in the Middle East: The Case of the Jacobites in an Age of Transition*, Albany, N. Y.: SUNY Press, 1983.

LE COZ, Raymond, *L'Eglise d'Orient* (see under 4.1.).

PANZER, Regina, *Identität und Geschichtsbewusstsein: Griechisch-orthodoxe Christen im Vorderen Orient zwischen Byzanz und Arabertum* (Studien zur Zeitgeschichte des Nahen Ostens und Nordafrikas 3), Hamburg: Lit Verlag, 1997.

SCHLICHT, Alfred, *Frankreich und die syrischen Christen 1799–1861: Minoritäten und europäischer Imperialismus im Vorderen Orient* (Islamkundliche Untersuchungen 61), Berlin: Klaus Schwarz Verlag, 1981.

WATERFIELD, Robin E., *Christians in Persia: Assyrians, Armenians, Roman Catholics and Protestants*, London: Allen & Unwin, 1973.

4.3. Palestine

The Christian Heritage in the Holy Land, ed. by Anthony O'MAHONY, Göran GUNNER and Kevork HINTLIAN, London: Scorpion Cavendish, 1995.

5. Zoroastrian Communities in Muslim Territory

SPULER, Berthold, *Iran in frühislamischer Zeit*, Wiesbaden: Franz Steiner, 1952.

6. Muslims in India

AHMAD, Aziz, *Studies in Islamic Culture in the Indian Environment*, Oxford: Clarendon Press, 1964.

AZIZ, Khursheed Kamal, *Muslim India 1800–1947: A Descriptive and Annotated Bibliography*, Vol. 1, Rawalpindi, etc.: Ferozsons, and Islamabad: National Documentation Centre, 2001.

BĪRŪNĪ, al-, *Kitāb ta'rīkh al-Hind*, trans., with notes and indices, by C. Edward SACHAU, *Alberuni's India: An Account of the Religion, Philosophy, Literature, Geography, Chronology, Astronomy, Customs, Laws and Astrology of India about 1030*, 2 Vols., London: Trübner, 1888, 1910[2] (repr. New Delhi: Munshiram Manoharlal, 2001).

CAMPS, Arnulf, *Jerome Xavier S.J. and the Muslims of the Moghul Empire: Controversial Works and Missionary Activity* (Supplementa. Neue Zeitschrift für Missionswissenschaft, VI), Fribourg: St. Paul's Press, 1957.

FRIEDMANN, Yohanan, "Medieval Muslim Views of Indian Religions", *Journal of the American Oriental Society*, 95/2 (April-June 1975), pp. 214–21.

—, "Islamic Thought in Relation to the Indian Context", *Parusārtha*, 9 (1986), pp. 79–91.

HABIBULLAH, A.B.M., "Medieval Indo-Persian Literatures relating to Hindu Science and Philosophy, 1000–1800 A.D.: A Bibliographical Survey", *Indian Historical Quarterly*, 14 (1938), pp. 167–81.

HOYLAND, John Somervell, and S.N. BANERJEE, *The Commentary of Father Monserrate, S.J. on his Journey to the Court of Akbar*, London: Oxford University Press, 1922.

HUART, Clément, and Louis MASSIGNON, "Les entretiens de Lahore (entre le prince impérial Dārā Shokūh et l'ascète hindou Baba La'l Das): Persian Text with Translation", *Journal Asiatique*, 209 (1926), pp. 285–334.

IKRAM, Sheikh M., *Muslim Civilization in India*, New York and London: Columbia University Press, 1964.

KHAN, Rasheeduddin, *Bewildered India: Identity, Pluralism, Discord*, New Delhi: Har-Anand Publications, 1995.

MUJEEB, Muhammad, *The Indian Muslims*, Montreal: McGill University Press, 1967.

MUKHIA, Harbans, *Historians and Historiography during Akbar's Reign*, New Delhi: Vikas, 1977.

RIZVI, Sayyid Athar Abbas, *Religious and Intellectual History in Akbar's Reign, 1556–1605, with special reference to Abu'l-Fazl*, New Delhi: Munshiram Manoharlal Publishers, 1975.

ROY CHOUDHURY, Makhan Lal, *The Din Ilahi of the Religion of Akbar*, Calcutta: Das Gupta & Co., 1941, 1952[2] (repr. = 4th ed. New Delhi: Munshiram Manoharlal, 1997).

SHARMA, Sri Ram, *The Religious Policy of the Mughal Emperors*, London, etc.: Oxford University Press, 1940 (repr. New Delhi: Munshiram Manoharlal, 1988).

SHAYEGAN, Daryush, *Les relations de l'hindouisme et du soufisme d'après le Majma' al-bahrayn de Dārā Shukōh*, Paris: Ed. de la Différence, 1979.

SRIVASTAVA, Ashirbadi Lal, *Akbar the Great*, 2 Vols., Agra: Shiva Lal Agarwala, 1962–7.

Section 3

Muslim Perceptions of Other Religions

Chapter 5

Two Shining Lights:
Medieval Islam and Christianity[1]

If in the medieval period the faith and moral life of the best of Muslims and Christians radiated something of the light given in their respective religions on an intellectual level, the broader masses, baptized or circumcised, testified to the existence and powerful impact of Islam and Christianity on a social level. This may still hold true, but what was unique for that medieval period, which we define here for our purposes as extending from 622 to 1453, was the link between these two religions and the two political colossi of the time. These were the Byzantine Empire, on the one hand, with collateral states in Southern Europe, and the Caliphate, on the other hand, with the main successive dynasties in the Middle East: Umayyads (661–750), Abbāsids (750–1258), Fātimids (in Egypt 969–1171), Ayyūbids (in Egypt 1171–1261), Mamlūks (in Egypt 1261–1517), Rūm Seljuks (in Anatolia 1077–1307), and Osmanlis (ca. 1281–1924).

A vicious struggle between the East and the West of the time had started long before: Greeks and Persians, Romans and Parthians, East Roman Empire and Sassanid Empire. With the Arab Muslim conquests, the ideology changed but the antagonism continued and, most remarkably, the people also. Christians and Muslims continued to think in terms of an ideological and religious conflict, and their imagination worked accordingly. After all, it was not the Persians but the Christian Byzantines who had been able to resist the victorious Arabs, even though they had to cede their southern and eastern Mediterranean territories and fell back as far as the mountainous border of East Anatolia. On the Muslim side, very soon the dream developed of taking Constantinople, the Empire's capital.

---

[1]   Revised and enlarged text of a lecture given at the Eleventh Spring Symposium of the University of Birmingham on *The Two Shining Lights: Islam and Christendom: Empire, Caliphate und Crusades*, March 19–22, 1977. A first version was published under the title "Two Lights Perceived: Medieval Islam and Christianity" in *Nederlands Theologisch Tijdschrift*, 31, Nr. 4 (October 1977), pp. 267–89. References only indicate the most important sources, available in Western languages.

The basic fact, however, remains that, notwithstanding several severe threats during the first three centuries of Islam, Constantinople and Rome were not occupied. The Muslim capital moved from Damascus to Baghdad (founded in 762) and then to Cairo; the Arab hegemony on the Muslim side gave way to that of the Persians and later the Turks. The medieval East-West struggle alluded to began to wind down precisely because these Turks launched their drive westward through Anatolia in 1071. But even then, it still took nearly four centuries before Constantinople fell, after the Ottoman occupation of the larger part of the Balkans. The symbolic importance of this event is such that several historians mark it as the end of the Middle Ages.

We mentioned the different ideologies: Byzantium standing for the Christian cause and Christian truth; the Caliphate and its successors standing for the Muslim cause and Islamic truth. Muhammad was seen as the restorer of true religion on the one side and as the perfidious rebel on the other. Popular imagination depicted him accordingly. Jesus was regarded by Byzantine Christians as largely divine, but by Muslims as a prophet and never as more than a privileged man. Here, too, the popular imagination did its work, but the reverence for Jesus on the Muslim side contrasts glaringly with the calumnies heaped upon Muhammad on the Christian side. Revelation was seen as God's communicating to humankind through his word. On the one side this was held to be identical to one particular human being, on the other side to be identical with specific and fixed wordings brought together in one particular Scripture. The ensuing debate was reinforced by an inborn polemical bent and lust for dispute among people at the time, as we can see it directly in the Qur'ān and in texts reporting intellectual controversies between Muslims and Christians as well as among Christians themselves. Very quickly the Muslim-Christian debate itself became absolutized, representing a kind of supreme effort ("holy war") for the Muslims and a sanctifying spiritual testimony for the Christians.

1. Christians in Muslim Territory

Between the two political colossi, there were Christians living within Muslim territory, at the beginning still writing Greek. Many of them had welcomed the Arab conquerors as liberators, since Orthodox patriarchal and Byzantine imperial power had weighed heavily on the dissident monophysite Jacobites and Copts and other non-Chalcedonians like the Armenians. They did not greatly care about Constantinople, under which they had in fact suffered; they were more or less sick of disputes with the Greeks and the semi-inquisition by the official Church about the right Christian doctrine. Within five centuries, the great majority of the Near

Eastern and all North African Christians had converted. Among those who retained their religion were Syrian, Coptic, and Armenian Monophysites, Mesopotamian and Persian Nestorians, and Greek Orthodox Christians, mostly in greater Syria. The Christians lived in what may be called an "antipathetic symbiosis" with the Muslim environment, alternating between sufferings and hope, due to their uncertain position as a minority and the changing fortunes of the Muslim-Byzantine war. Their Muslim Arab overlords suspected them of being a potential fifth column. In their isolated situation, their culture survived, but without undergoing radical reorientations or achieving substantial discoveries; instead, it became increasingly tradition-bound. In their struggle for survival, their imagination played an important role. Their lurid stories about Muhammad and Islam—which they did not really know but experienced mainly as oppressive—found their way to Byzantium and later to Western Europe. Here they formed part of an overall sinister image of Islam held by people who had never seen a Muslim. This image was consciously encouraged by the Church, whether Eastern or Western.[2]

The way Christians and Muslims viewed each other without actually meeting was very much determined by the situation of permanent warfare. In particular the great war constitutes the historical background of the polemical religious writings of both Byzantines and Arabs, apart from the epic war poetry in which both boasted of their bravery.[3]

In Muslim territory, the situation developed. While the Arab and Byzantine armies kept each other in check or went into combat on the border, an intellectual struggle started after the conquest of Syria and the establishment of the Umayyad dynasty in Damascus (661–750). It seems that the Christians started to question the Muslims. From a threatened position and feeling oppressed, they could in this way offer resistance, expressing themselves in a fundamental attack by the mind on Islam at those points where the bases of their own existence, that is to say of their Christian identity, were at stake. Both within Muslim territory and in Byzantium, Christians viewed Islam in these first centuries as a heresy of the one great and true Christian religion. But precisely as a heresy, it meant a threat to that true religion, and the tactics were the same as in the case of the Christian heresies. The polemicists refuted Islam point for point on those issues where it clashed with elements of the firm construct of Christian theology, law, and ethics, as had been elaborated during the fifth to seventh centuries.

---

[2]   See DANIEL, *Islam and the West*. For the historical setting see SOUTHERN, *Western Views of Islam in the Middle Ages*.

[3]   For the role of religion in Arab-Byzantine relations see, for instance, CANARD, *Byzance et les musulmans du Proche Orient*.

1.1. First Period

In this first period, until the beginning of the ninth century and within Muslim territory, Christianity exerted socio-political, cultural, and religious pressure on Islam. The socio-political pressure consisted in a whole-hearted defense of the privileges the conquerors had given to various Christian communities within Muslim territory. This had happened in the form of treaties concluded between the conquerors and the Christian towns and regions that surrendered rather than going to battle. The cultural pressure consisted of the use of the full cultural heritage, including a glorious history, broad knowledge, and brilliant scholarship, against what were felt to be desert nomads without much education.

The religious pressure, however, was the most important in the context of our theme. The Christians raised questions about Islam to which the Muslims had to find an answer. This forced the latter to determine their attitude, not only on a socio-political level as victorious Muslims toward subdued Christians, but also on a religious level. This implied the relationship of Islam as a new religion to Christianity as an established one. As a result, the main issues of the Muslim-Christian debate were already formulated in this Umayyad period. From the beginning, the Muslims formulated and maintained their position against the Christians. In regard to the doctrine of God, this meant that only His will is the source of all human action, and that God is to be considered as One—a frank denial of the Trinity. In regard to the doctrine of Christ, this meant that the Christian Christology should be replaced by the Qur'anic Christology that denies the crucifixion of Jesus and resolutely denies any divine nature in Christ. And in regard to the doctrine of revelation it meant acceptance of the doctrine of prophecy, rather than incarnation and the doctrine of divine Words brought together in a Scripture identical with God's Word, rather than the doctrine of the divine Word incarnated in a human person. This led to the accusation, based on the Qur'ān, that the pure revealed Scriptures brought by Moses and Jesus had been falsified, resulting in the Biblical Old and New Testament, which thus cannot be held to have been revealed as scriptures. The victories of the Arab Muslim armies were interpreted as a sign of God's predilection for Islam.

In the debate, attention is drawn again and again to what the Qur'ān has to say about the Jews and the Christians, their scriptures, the claimed "announcement (*a'lām*) texts" in the Bible referring to Muhammad's coming, the constant accusation of *shirk* ("polytheism") directed specifically at the idolatrous Arabs before Islam and the Christians, etc.[4]

---

[4]   For a survey of the Muslim polemical literature against Christianity see STEINSCHNEIDER, *Polemische und apologetische Literatur in arabischer Sprache* (including references to Christian authors); GOLDZIHER, "Ueber muhamedanische Polemik gegen Ahl al-kitāb";

On the Christian side, we have from this Umayyad period St. John of Damascus' treatment of Islam in Chapter 101 of his book on the heresies, which is part of his great work *Pēgē tēs gnōseōs*.[5] Other pieces on Islam have been attributed to him, but their authenticity is doubtful. St. John considered Islam to be a forerunner of the Antichrist: *Prodromos tou Antichristou*. The encounter between Muslims and Christian theologians in Syria in this period was a powerful incentive to Muslims to develop theological thought, with an apologetic tendency.[6]

1.2. Second Period

It was, however, under the Abbāsid dynasty (750–1258) and especially in the middle part of the ninth century under caliphs like al-Ma'mūn (r. 813–33) and al-Mutawakkil (r. 847–61) that a wave of polemics arose, encouraged by the rulers' stressing of Islam as the official religion and religious ideology, by the state's growing interest in existing religious differences and disputes, and by an increasing Islamization of society. State interference extended beyond Muslim doctrinal expression such as the status of the Qur'ān. It also led to a stricter formulation of the rules according to which— and the limits within which—non-Muslim minorities such as Jews or Christians could enjoy the protection (*dhimma*) of the state.[7]

In the polemical writings of this period, we find on both sides the use of philosophy, in particular Aristotelian logic and metaphysics. Christians had known and developed it for centuries in their theological thought. Theodore Abū Qurra (c. 740–c. 826) applied it in his refutation of Judaism and Islam.[8] Muslims had learned it through translations from

---

Erdmann FRITSCH, *Islam und Christentum im Mittelalter: Beiträge zur Geschichte der muslimischen Polemik gegen das Christentum in arabischer Sprache*, Breslau: Müller & Seiffert, 1930; ANAWATI, "Polémique, apologie et dialogue islamo-chrétiens: Positions classiques médiévales et positions contemporaines". A chronologically arranged bibliography of Muslim-Christian dialogue (taken in the broadest sense) during the medieval period and later was published in the first issues of *Islamochristiana*, from 1975 on.

[5] *Patrologia Graeca (PG)*, ed. Jacques-Paul MIGNE, Vol. 94, cols. 764–73 (*Peri haireseōn*). The *Dialexis Sarrakenou kai Christianou* attributed to St John (*PG*, Vol. 106, cols. 1335–48; shorter version *PG*, Vol. 104, cols. 1585–96) was written by Abū Qurra (*PG*, Vol. 97, col. 1543).

[6] BECKER ("Christliche Polemik und islamische Dogmenbildung") was one of the first scholars who drew attention to the fact that Islamic theology in its early development was very much conditioned by questions raised by Christian theologians. This has led to numerous investigations of the origin and early development of Islamic *kalām*, which we cannot go into here.

[7] Two classical studies on the situation of religious protected minorities (*dhimmīs*) in Muslim territory are those written by TRITTON, *The Caliphs and their non-Muslim Subjects*, and by FATTAL, *Le statut légal des non-musulmans en pays d'Islam.*

[8] *Contra haereticos, Judaeos et Saracenos varia* of Abū Qurra in *PG*, Vol. 97, cols. 1461–1609. His Arabic texts were edited by Louis CHEIKHO and by Paul SBATH. See Georg GRAF, *Die arabischen Schriften des Theodor Abu Qurra, Bischofs von Harran (ca. 740–*

Syriac and directly from Greek and—thanks to the effort of the Muʿta-zilites—had applied it in the formulation and reasoned defense of Islamic religious doctrines. Sects within Islam and Christianity also used philosophy for their debates and mutual refutations.

In this period, the initiative shifted to the Muslim side, again on different levels. On the socio-political level, pressure was exerted first against Iranian cultural and political hegemony, which led to the downfall of the influential Barmecid family under Hārūn al-Rashīd in 803. More than half a century later, similar pressure was exerted against the Christians, who roused hostility through their prosperity and their social and cultural influence. Under al-Mutawakkil, Christianity came under severe attack, for instance in the "Edict of ʿUmar", which regulated the position of the Jews and Christians as religious minorities. It also found expression in al-Jāhiz's (d. 869) vehement reply to a Christian tract. He demonstrated here the vices of the Christians with unambiguous invectives and attacked the social position of Christians.[9]

On a cultural level, the Christians within Muslim territory still dominated the Muslims who remained the learners—and were willing to learn—in the fields of philosophy, medicine, and sciences, in which the Christians excelled, the Arabs priding themselves on their ethnic and linguistic superiority and on their religion: Islam. Indeed, this ninth century saw a growth and flowering of Arabic literature together with a decisive development and formulation of the religious sciences of Islam: *tafsīr* (Qur'ān exegesis) and *hadīth* (science of tradition), *fiqh* (jurisprudence) and *kalām* (philosophical theology).

Muslims now took initiatives on a religious level, too. I have already mentioned al-Jāhiz, who wrote at the request of the caliph al-Mutawakkil. We know refutations of Christianity written in the same period around 850 by the convert ʿAlī al-Tabarī (d. 855) and by Abū ʿĪsā al-Warrāq (d. around 861).[10] Besides philosophical arguments, scriptural arguments

---

820): *Literarhistorische Untersuchungen und Übersetzung* (Forschungen zur christlichen Literatur- und Dogmengeschichte X/3–4), Paderborn: Schöningh, 1910.

[9]   The text of al-Jāhiz, *Risāla fi'l-radd ʿalā'l-nasārā*, was edited by Y. FINKEL in his *Three Essays of Abū Othmān Amr ibn Bahr al-Jāhiz* (Cairo: Salafiyya Press, 1926) and translated by him into English in *Journal of the American Oriental Society*, 47 (1927), pp. 311–34. See also Ch. PELLAT, "Christologie Ğāhizienne", *Studia Islamica*, 31 (1970), pp. 219–32.

[10] The polemical text of ʿAlī al-Tabarī, *Al-radd ʿalā'l-nasārā*, was edited by I. A. KHALIFÉ and W. KUTSCH in *Mélanges de l'Université Saint-Joseph*, 36/4 (1959), pp. 115–48. An apologetic text by the same author, *Kitāb al-dīn wa'l-dawla*, was edited by Alphonse MINGANA (Manchester: Manchester University Press, 1923, and Cairo: Muqtataf, 1342) and translated by him as *The Book of Religion and Empire* (Manchester: Manchester University Press, 1922).

For the polemical text of al-Warrāq, *Kitāb al-maqālāt*, see THOMAS, *Anti-Christian Polemic in Early Islam*.

were now used, too, for instance by Muhammad ibn Jarīr al-Tabarī, which testifies to an increasing Muslim acquaintance with the Bible through information obtained primarily from converts.

There were Christian initiatives too. Seventeen polemical treatises against Islam were written by Theodore Abū Qurra, mentioned above, who saw Muhammad as an Arianizing false prophet. Besides the polemical literature written by Christian Arabs[11], there are also reports on discussions, real or fictitious, between Christians and Muslims.[12] We have for instance in a Syriac source a report of a debate that a certain patriarch John, probably a Jacobite, is said to have held with an "emir of the Agarenes". Another Syriac source reports on a discussion of the Nestorian Catholicos (patriarch) Timothy I (728–823) with the Abbāsid caliph al-Mahdī (r. 775–85).[13] This text has been influential among the Christians. It was probably from within territory acquired by the Byzantines by conquest at the beginning of the tenth century that a famous but fictitious religious discussion between two friends, the Christian al-Kindī and the Muslim al-Hāshimī, was described, possibly in terms tinged with Nestorianism. As a literary work, it sets the discussion at the court of al-Mutawakkil and it shows sophistication in reasoning as well as frankness in expression.[14]

---

[11] For Christian polemical literature in Arabic against Islam, see the bibliography of STEINSCHNEIDER, *Polemische und apologetische Literatur in arabischer Sprache*, and Georg GRAF, *Geschichte der christlichen arabischen Literatur*, 5 Vols. (Studi e Testi 118, 133, 146, 147, 172), Città del Vaticano: Biblioteca Apostolica Vaticana), 1944–53.

[12] On religious disputations between Muslims and Christians in early Islam, cf. the address of Jan BRUGMAN, *Godsdienstgesprekken tussen Christenen en Moslims in de vroege Islam*, Leiden: E. J. Brill, 1970.

[13] See above Chapter 4 on "Cases of Interreligious Dialogue under Muslim Rule" under section 1.

[14] For the disputation of the patriarch John, see F. NAU, "Un colloque du patriarche Jean avec l'émir des Agaréens", *Journal Asiatique (JA)*, Série 11, no. 5 (1915), pp. 226–79. Cf. Henri LAMMENS, "A propos d'un colloque entre le patriarche Jean et ʿAmr b. al-Ās", *JA*, Série 11, no. 13 (1919), pp. 97–110.

For Timothy I, see Alphonse MINGANA, "Timothy's Apology for Christianity", in his (ed. and trans.) *Woodbrooke Studies: Christian Documents in Syriac, Arabic, and Garshuni*, Vol. II (Cambridge: Heffer, 1928), pp. 1–162 (Syriac text with translation and introduction), and ID., "The Apology of Timothy the Patriarch before the Caliph Mahdi". A critical edition of the Arabic text was published by Robert CASPAR in *Islamochristiana*, 3 (1977), pp. 107–75. See also PUTMAN, *L'Eglise et l'Islam sous Timothée I (780–823)*.

The text of the discussion between al-Hāshimī and al-Kindī was edited by Anton TIEN, *Risālat ʿAbd Allāh b. Ismāʿīl al-Hāshimī ilā ʿAbd al-Masīh ibn Ishāq al-Kindī, wa-risālat al-Kindī ilā 'l-Hāshimī*, London, 1880 and 1885, and Cairo, 1895 and 1912. A description and partial translation was given by Sir William MUIR, *The Apology of al Kindy, written at the Court of al Maʾmūn (circa A.H. 215; A.D. 830), in Defense of Christianity against Islam*, London: SPCK, 1882, 1887[2].

Within Muslim territory, however, Christianity's earlier pressure on Islam is now replaced by Islam's increasing pressure on Christianity. Some major theological Muslim refutations of Christianity have been preserved, like those by the Zaidī Shī'ī al-Qāsim b. Ibrāhīm[15] (785–860), by the Ash'arite theologian al-Bāqillānī[16] (d. 1013), and by the Mu'tazilite theologian 'Abd al-Jabbār[17] (d. 1025).

2. Byzantium and Islam

Apart from such exchanges and polemics between Muslims and Christians within Muslim territory, there were embassies and letters exchanged between Arab Muslims and Byzantine Christians, and there were polemical writings between them as well.[18] The Greek theologian Photios (c. 820–91), for example, was attached to a Byzantine embassy to the caliph al-Mutawakkil in 855–6, and a fictitious correspondence is known between the caliph Umar II (r. 717–20) and the emperor Leo III.[19]

---

[15] Al-Qāsim b. Ibrāhīm's refutation of Christianity, *Kitāb al-radd 'alā 'l-nasārā*, was edited and translated by I. DI MATTEO, "Confutazione contre i cristiani dello Zaydita al-Qāsim b. Ibrāhīm", *Rivista degli Studi Orientali*, 9 (1922), pp. 301–64. Cf. Wilferd MADELUNG, *Der Imām al-Qāsim ibn Ibrāhīm und die Glaubenslehre der Zaiditen*, Berlin: Walter de Gruyter, 1965.

[16] For al-Bāqillānī's refutation of Christianity, see ABEL, "Le chapitre sur le Christianisme dans le 'Tamhīd' d'al-Bāqillānī".

[17] For 'Abd al-Jabbār's refutation of Christianity, see his *Al-mughnī fī abwāb al-tawhīd wa'l-'adl*, Vol. V: *Al-firaq ghair al-islāmiyya*, ed. by M. M. al-KHODEIRI (Cairo: Academy, 1965), pp. 80–151. See also his *Tathbīt dalā'il nubuwwat sayyidna Muhammad*, ed. by 'Abd al-Karīm 'UTHMĀN (Beirut: Dār al-'arabiyya, 1966/1386, 2 Vols.), pp. 198ff. Cf. PINES, *The Jewish Christians of the Early Centuries of Christianity*, and STERN contesting the conclusions of S. Pines in his "Quotations from the Apocryphal Gospel in 'Abdeljabbār" and "'Abdeljabbār's Account of how Christ's Religion was Falsified by the Adoption of Roman Customs".

[18] A survey of Byzantine views of Islam is given by TRAPP in his *Manuel II. Palaiologos*, pp. 13*–48*, and by John MEYENDORFF, "Byzantine Views of Islam", *Dumbarton Oak Papers*, 18 (1964), pp. 115–32. A survey of Byzantine polemical literature is given by A.-Th. KHOURY, *Les théologiens byzantins et l'Islam, textes et auteurs (VIIIe–XIIIe s.)*. Cf. his *Polémique byzantine contre l'Islam*, Leiden: E. J. Brill, 1972². See also Wolfgang EICHNER, "Die Nachrichten über den Islam bei den Byzantinern", *Der Islam*, 23 (1936), pp. 133–62 and 197–244.

[19] On the embassy of Photios, see Francis DVORNIK, "The Embassies of Constantine-Cyril and Photius to the Arabs", in *To honor Roman Jakobson: Essays on the Occasion of his Seventieth Birthday, October 11, 1966*, Vol. I (The Hague: Mouton, 1967), pp. 569–76. The letter to 'Umar is supposed to be Emperor Leo III's answer to the caliph 'Umar II (r. 717–20), who inquired about the Christian faith. An Armenian version of this letter has been preserved and was translated by A. JEFFERY, "Ghevond's Text of the Correspondence between 'Umar II and Leo III", *Harvard Theological Review*, 37 (1944), pp. 269–332. A shorter Latin version of the letter is to be found in *PG*, Vol. 107, cols. 315–24. The authorship has not been established with absolute certainty.

There is a famous quotation from the first letter that Nicholas I Mystikos, Patriarch of Constantinople (901–7, 912–25), sent around 913 to the Abbāsid caliph al-Muqtadir (r. 908–32) in Baghdad:

> "Two sovereignties—that of the Arabs and that of the Byzantines—surpass all sovereignty on earth, like the two shining lights in the firmament. For this one reason, if for no other, they ought to be partners and brethren. We ought not, because we are separated in our ways of life, our customs, and our worship, to be altogether divided; nor ought we to deprive ourselves of communication with one another by writing in default of meeting personally. This is the way we ought to think and act, even if no necessity of our affairs compelled us to it."[20]

The emperor Michael III (842–67) received at least one letter from a caliph inquiring about his faith and summoning him to accept Islam. He left the answer to Nicetas of Byzantium "the Philosopher", who lived between 842 and 912 and who wrote two answering letters in the 860s. Nicetas also wrote a defense of the doctrine of the Trinity, followed by a lengthy refutation of the Qur'ān.[21]

Nicetas, who had studied the Qur'ān in Greek translation, refuted the first eighteen Sūras plus the ending of S. 36. In this work, he used philosophy to arrive at a rational theology; in contrast to his predecessors, he considered Islam not a Christian heresy, but a real, though false religion. So he refused to accept, for instance, an appeal made in the Qur'ān to both Christians and Muslims to pray together to the same, one God. Instead, he concluded that Muslims and Christians do not pray to the same God. He reproached Islam for holding an idea of God that is corporeal and consequently not elevated enough. This reproach was often made by Byzantine polemicists, on the basis of a faulty translation of shamad in S. 112:2. Of a much lower and in fact insulting level is a pamphlet written against Islam in Constantinople around 905 and wrongly ascribed to a bishop Arethas.[22]

A new wave of Byzantine Christian-Muslim polemics arose in the tenth century. By that time, Byzantine armies had reconquered Calabria, Crete, and Cyprus, and during the reign of Romanos I Lepapenos (r. 919–44), they moved via Cilicia to Syria. In Byzantium and Syria, some larger treatises in Greek were written against Islam, and a more popular Byzan-

---

[20]   *PG*, Vol. 111, col. 28B.
[21]   For the letters, see *PG*, Vol. 105, cols. 807–21 and 821–41. The larger work *Anatropē tēs tou Arabos Mōamet plastographētheisēs Biblou* (Nicetae Byzantini *Refutatio Mohamedis*), was written during the reign of Basil I (867–86). For this text, see *PG*, Vol. 105, cols. 669–805; the refutation of the Qur'ān is to be found in cols. 701–805.
[22]   The author of this letter would have been Leo Choirosphactes, identified as such by R. J. H. Jenkins. See Meyendorff's article (mentioned above in note 18), p. 128–9. Cf. the translation and analysis by Armand Abel, "La lettre polémique 'd'Aréthas' à l'émir de Damas", *Byzantion*, 24 (1954), pp. 343–70.

tine literature on the subject also flourished, probably designed to bring the population of the reconquered territories back to Christianity. This must have been an era of hope also for Christians living deeper in Muslim territory and praying for a final victory of the Byzantines over the Muslims. Quite a number of polemical treatises were written by Christians within Muslim territory during this period, including the refutations of the works of two Muslim polemicists by two Jacobite theologians, Yaḥyā b. ʿAdī[23] (893–974) and Ibn Zurʿa[24] (943–1008).

History, however, took another course. Not only was a Muslim collapse prevented, but the Byzantines were pushed further and further back. This took a most serious turn with the arrival of the Seljuk Turks in the later eleventh century, their subsequent penetration deep into Anatolia, and their harassment of pilgrims going overland to the Holy Land. The stream of polemical pamphlets subsided now.

The scene changed again significantly with the Crusaders. They arrived shortly before 1100, reinforced themselves in successive waves, and disappeared a century and a half later. The Crusades were essentially a Latin affair, but they had their repercussions on the re-emerging polemical literature in the Middle East itself. Christian Arabs like Bartholomew of Edessa[25] (twelfth century?), Elias of Nisibis[26] (975–1046), the Nestorian ʿAbdallāh b. al-Tayyib[27] (d. 1043), and Paul al-Rāhib[28] ("the Monk") of Antioch (twelfth century) could afford now to start writing lengthy treatises against Islam.

---

[23] Yaḥyā b. ʿAdī refuted the *Kitāb al-maqālāt* of al-Warrāq. On this author, see Augustin PÉRIER, *Petits traités apologétiques de Yaḥyā Ben ʿAdī*, and *Yaḥyā Ben ʿAdī: Un philosophe chrétien du Xe siècle*, both Paris: Gabalda, 1920. Cf. Georg GRAF, *Die Philosophie und Gotteslehre des Jaḥjā ibn ʿAdī und späterer Autoren*, Münster: Aschendorff, 1910.

[24] Ibn Zurʿa refuted the *Awāʾil al-adillat* of al-Balkhī (d. 931) who was dependent on al-Warrāq. On Ibn Zurʿa see Cyrille HADDAD, *ʿĪsā Ibn Zurʿa, philosophe arabe et apologiste chrétien*, Beirut: Dār al-kalima, 1971.

[25] Bartholomaei Edesseni *Elenchus aut Confutatio Agareni (Elenchos Agarēnou)*, see PG, Vol. 104, cols. 1383–1448. Although the author's lifetime is not known, it has been submitted that this text was written between 1129 and 1146, when Edessa was in Frankish hands.

[26] Elias of Nisibis was a Nestorian metropolite. His main work was translated into German by Louis HORST, *Des Metropoliten Elias von Nisibis Buch vom Beweis der Wahrheit des Glaubens*, Colmar: E. Barth, 1886.

[27] ʿAbdallāh b. al-Tayyib was a well-known philosopher and physician in the first half of the eleventh century, and author of several theological treatises.

[28] P. KHOURY published a study on a treatise by Paul al-Rāhib, that is *Paul d'Antioche, évêque melkite de Sidon (XIIe s.)*. Of major interest is his "Letter to the Muslims" (text pp. 59–83, trans. pp. 169–87), to which Ibn Taymīya answers in his *Al-jawāb al-saḥīḥ*. See M.H. SIDDIQI, "Muslim and Byzantine Christian Relations: Letter of Paul of Antioch and Ibn Taymīyah's response", *Greek Orthodox Theological Review*, 31 (1986), pp. 33–45.

The other way round, Muslims like al-Ghazzālī[29] (1058–1111), al-Qarāfī[30] (d. 1285), Saʿīd b. Hasan al-Iskandarānī[31] (d. 1320), Ibn Taymīya[32] (d. 1328), and Ibn Qayyim al-Jawzīya[33] (d. 1350) produced lengthy refutations of Christianity. Their treatises show all the features that pervade Islamic polemical literature against Christianity: the denial of the Trinity and of the divinity of Jesus, proofs of the prophetic quality and mission of Muhammad including "announcement (aʿlām) texts" drawn from the Bible, contradictions and inconsistencies in the Old and the New Testament, proofs of Muhammad's prophecies and miracles, evidence of the dignity and superiority of Islam, and the condemnation of the liturgical and ethical practices of the Christians on the grounds that they are as wrong as the Christian beliefs.

On the Byzantine side, knowledge about Islam increased markedly after the eleventh century. The polemical tradition continued in theological treatises such as Ch. 28 of the *Panhoplia dogmatikē* (c. 1100) of Euthymios Zigabenos and Ch. 20 of the *Thēsauros orthodoxias* (c. 1200) of Nicetas Choniates. Under the dynasty of the Paleologi (1261–1453), some fresher accounts and more original treatises appeared. We have for instance the Greek translation by Demetrios Kydones[34] (c. 1350) of a refutation of the Qurʾān and Islam written by the Dominican Ricoldus de Monte Crucis around 1310. The four *Apologiai* and four *Logoi* refuting the Qurʾān that were written by the emperor John VI Cantacuzenos[35] (r. 1341–54) under the name of the monk Joasaph (d. 1383), who used the Kydones translation, also come to mind. Of greater interest still is the

---

[29] Al-Ghazzālī, *Réfutation excellente de la divinité de Jésus-Christ d'après les Evangiles: Texte établi, traduit et commenté* par Robert CHIDIAC, Paris: Ernest Leroux, 1939. See also WILMS, *Al-Ghazzālīs Schrift wider die Gottheit Jesu*. Ghazzālī's authorship for this *Al-radd al-jamīl* was convincingly denied by Hava LAZARUS-YAFEH in her article "Etude sur la polémique islamo-chrétienne: Qui était l'auteur de *al-Radd al-jamīl li-Ilāhiyyat ʿĪsā bi-sarīh al-Injīl* attribué à al-Ghazzālī?", *Revue des Etudes Islamiques*, 37, no. 2 (1969), pp. 219–38.

[30] Al-Qarāfī, *Kitāb al-ajwiba ʾl-fāhira*, Cairo, 1904/1322.

[31] Saʿīd b. Hasan al-Iskandarānī, *Masālik al-nazar fi nubuwwat sayyid al-bashar*, ed. and trans. with introduction and notes by Sidney Adams WESTON, *Journal of the American Oriental Society*, 24/2 (1903), pp. 312–83.

[32] Ibn Taymīya, *Al-jawāb al-sahīh li-man baddala dīn al-masīh*, 4 Vols., Cairo 1322/1905. See Thomas MICHEL, *A Muslim Theologian's Response to Christianity: Ibn Taymiyya's Al-Jawab al-Sahih*, Delmar, N. Y.: Caravan Books, 1984.

[33] Ibn Qayyim al-Jawzīya, *Hidāyat al-hayāra min al-yahūd wa ʾl-nasārā*, Cairo 1322/1904.

[34] Demetrii Cydonii translatio libri fratris Richardi, ordinis praedicatorum, *Contra Mahometi Asseclas*, in *PG*, Vol. 154, cols. 1037–1152. Demetrios Kydones translated the book into Greek probably between 1354 and 1360. It has been supposed that the *Christianae fidei confessio, facta Saracenis* of Kydones (*PG*, Vol. 154, cols. 1151–70) might also go back on an original text of Ricoldus de Monte Crucis.

[35] Joannis Cantacuzeni *Contra Mahometem Apologiae et Orationes (Apologiai kai Logoi)*, in *PG*, Vol. 154, cols. 373–692. These texts were probably written in 1360.

work written by the emperor Manuel II Paleologos (d. 1425) on his discussions with a Turkish (abusively called "Persian") "partner in dialogue", which has been considered the greatest Byzantine apology of Christianity against Islam.[36] From the same time are a debate between Joseph Bryennios (d. 1430) with a Muslim[37] and a refutation of Islam by the theologian Symeon of Thessalonike (d. 1429) in his fragment *Kata ethnōn.*[38]

In these polemical writings, the Christians (Byzantines and Arabs) and the Muslims (mainly Arabs and Persians; there was not yet a polemical literature by Turks against Christianity in the medieval period) saw each other as radical antagonists regarding religious truth. Mainly theologians and jurists spoke here, together with two emperors who reached the same results in a slightly milder tone. They all were moved and wrote against a background of war and political tensions.

But such polemics should not blind us to the existence of wide areas of peaceful culture shared by Muslims and Byzantine and Arab Christians. These areas comprise philosophy and science, trade and travel, and certain ways of life, though each within his own society, in matters of authority, behavior, and social order.

There is even more than that. The theologian Gregory Palamas (1296–1359), a friend of the emperor John VI Cantacuzenos, wrote an account of his travel (probably as a prisoner) to Asia Minor in 1354.[39] A constant stream of pilgrims from Byzantium and the Latin West made their way overland through Muslim territory to the Holy Land and back. In various regions, Muslims and Christians shared a number of beliefs and practices in popular religion, in particular saint veneration and forms of adoration. One community could borrow such practices from the other without any official authority being involved. In real life, religion can be borrowed on a popular level just as well as this is possible on a higher social and cultural level for more refined culture, for instance through translations. This happened with the translation of Greek philosophy and science from Syriac and Greek to Arabic in ninth-century Mesopotamia and from Arabic to Hebrew and Latin in twelfth-century Spain.

---

[36] The conversations took place in Ankara in December 1391. See TRAPP, *Manuel II. Palaiologos.* This study contains a survey of Byzantine views of Islam, a text edition with an introduction and a summary of the text. The seventh dialogue was translated by A.-Th. KHOURY, *Manuel II Paléologue.*

[37] Asterios Argyriou, *Iōsēph tou Bryenniou: Meta tinos Ismaēlitou dialexis*, Athens, 1967.

[38] See *PG*, Vol. 155, pp. 77–81.

[39] The account is followed by a refutation of Islam. The text was published in *Neos Hellēnomnēmōn* (Athens), 16 (1922), pp. 7–21.

3. The Latin West and Islam

It is useful to cast light from a different direction on the Arab-Byzantine relations just described, on the views that these Muslims and Christians had of each other and each other's religion, and on the social and historical scene in which those views arose. This light is provided by a comparison of the relations between the Arabs and the Byzantines with the relations between the Arabs and the Latin West, and these two pairs' views of each other. The relations and views of the Latins were quite distinct from those of the Byzantines.

The incursion of Arab armies into West Roman territories was no less violent than into the East Roman ones: North Africa, Spain, Southern France, Southern Italy, and most Mediterranean islands were occupied in the eighth and part of the ninth century, often almost completely. For centuries to come, there would be a kind of water curtain through the Mediterranean.

As in the East, the Arab conquests caused panic in the West. Here, however, it took nearly three centuries before we can find a clear religious and ideological antagonism expressed in thought and literature. But then, from the end of the eleventh century on, the Muslim Saracens were viewed as the arch-antagonists of the Latin West and of Christianity. A negative image of Islam developed everywhere, varying according to region from completely black to dark grey.[40]

Byzantium as an empire waged in fact one continuous war, although with changing fronts at land and on the sea, and suffered under a growing spiritual pressure from Islam from the latter's beginning on. The Latin West received its blow, however, right at the beginning of the eighth century and again in the ninth. Then it started to awaken, fighting various separate wars in various countries. Southern France was reconquered in the ninth century, as was most of Southern Italy. Sicily was conquered by the Normans between 1061 and 1072.

The Reconquista of Spain started in 1062, the crusading drive of the popes in 1095. As a result, Western Europe became involved with Asia Minor, Syria, and Palestine, then with Egypt and Tunisia and later with the Balkans. The crusading drive revealed an aggressive Europe, but it brought this still largely barbarious region into contact with the outside world, including Islam and its superior civilization. Byzantium and especially Italy, France, and Spain, after an initial break of relations with the lost shores of the southern Mediterranean, resumed and intensified their commercial relations with the Muslim side of the sea. For Western Europe

---

[40] A bibliography of medieval and also later Western literature about Islam can be found in DANIEL, *Islam and the West*, pp. 395–408.

this holds true especially from the thirteenth century on; the rise of the Italian city-states was due in large part to these commercial links.

Byzantium had produced a range of polemical writings against Islam already from the ninth and perhaps even from the eighth century on. This corresponded with the ongoing war, but people had little information about the great adversary. The Latin West started its polemics later in waves corresponding to the ups and downs of the crusading drive. Up to the twelfth century the Latin West was certainly no better informed about Islam than Byzantium was. The apology for Christianity needed for such polemics did not begin until the work of Peter Damian (1007–72) and Guitmond of Aversa, and it took some time before the Latins became aware that Islam denied the trinity of God and the crucifixion of Christ. It must have been the eleventh-century situation, when Christian armies reconquered territories in Spain that had been conquered by Arabs and Berbers in the eighth century, that brought about a certain interest in Islamic matters. This led to intellectual efforts of study and refutation, as a trend quite distinct from the violent crusading impulse.

In the Latin tradition, Islam was seen mostly as a heresy of Christianity and not as a false religion. Pope Gregory VII (r. 1073–85) affirmed that the Jewish-Christian and the Islamic God of creation are one and the same and that according to all three religions He wants to provide salvation to a rational creature.[41] Interestingly enough, changes in awareness and views of Islam started with theological reconsiderations. Derived from philosophical theology rather than scripture, theological handbooks appeared for the refutation of Islam that were based on reason. Anselm's *Cur deus homo?*, completed in 1098, which the author dedicated and handed over personally to Pope Urban II (r. 1088–99) that summer near the battlefield before Capua, draws much of its inspiration from the refutation of views concerning God that could well be held by Islam.[42] Peter the Venerable (1092–1156), abbot of Cluny, visited Spain in 1142–3. He organized the work of the *Corpus cluniacense* containing translations from the Arabic, including the first Latin translation of the Qur'ān, by Robert of Ketton.[43] The thirteenth century saw some remarkable theologians who paid attention to Islam. Thomas Aquinas (1225–74) wrote his *De rationibus fidei contra Saracenos Graecos et Armenos* of 1270, and his *Summa contra gentiles* of uncertain date. Raymond Marti

---

[41] See DANIEL, *Islam and the West*, p. 43.
[42] See Julia GAUSZ, "Anselm von Canterbury und die Islamfrage", *Theologische Zeitschrift* (Basel), 19 (1963), pp. 250–72. For Anselm's "theology of religions", see GAUSZ, "Anselm von Canterbury: Zur Begegnung und Auseinandersetzung der Religionen".
[43] Petrus Venerabilis, *Tractatus adversus nefandam sectam Saracenorum libri 13*. See *Patrologia Latina* (PL), Vol. 189, cols. 659–720. For the *Corpus cluniacense*, the classical study is that of KRITZECK, *Peter the Venerable and Islam*.

(c. 1215/20–92) who knew Arabic, wrote his *Summa* against the errors of the Qur'ān in 1260 and his *Pugio fidei adversus Mauros et Iudaeos* in 1278. Roger Bacon (c. 1214–94), aware of the plurality of religions, wrote his *Moralis philosophia* and *Opus tertium*.

Besides their socio-political significance and their religious aspects, the relations between the Latin West and the Muslim world were especially important on a cultural level.[44] True, Europe borrowed most of its legends and stories about Muhammad and Islam from the Byzantines and from the Arab Christians at the time of the Crusades, adding its own fantasies to them. But if Islam was seen as a negative entity as a religion, as a culture and civilization it was not. Extending even to regions like Spain and Sicily, it was a kind of wonderland to which Western imagination could easily add supplementary miracles. Most important, however, was that in matters of philosophy and science, medicine and technology, the Latin West was prepared to learn from the Arabs in Sicily and Spain. For centuries it respected Arab learning. The knowledge gained by means of the immense volume of translation work done from Arabic, often via Hebrew, into Latin was an impetus to the first Renaissance of the twelfth century.[45] The Arab culture had a palpable influence on learning everywhere in Europe in the thirteenth century. Together with the Greco-Latin world, it provided a powerful stimulus to early Renaissance figures such as Dante (1265–1321) and Petrarch (1304–74). The cultural relations between Islam and Byzantium differed greatly from those between Islam and the Latin West precisely because of the latter's cultural lag and its efforts to catch up.

4. Christian Attitudes: East and West

It is worthwhile to look at some other aspects of Byzantine society that had implications for religious attitudes toward Islam and to compare them with parallel ones in Western Europe.

4.1. If Byzantium was one strongly centralized state that was theocratically linked to the Orthodox Church, in the Latin West several countries, of which only a few were part of the Holy Roman Empire, found themselves in rivalry. The only central authority in the West was the Pope, whose ecclesiastical and political power had been increasing since the Cluniac

---

[44]   For the civilizing influence of Islam on medieval Western Europe cf. the inaugural address of Fokke SIERKSMA, in Dutch, *Een en ander over de moslemse bijdrage aan de westerse beschaving*, Leiden: Universitaire Pers (Publishers), 1974.

[45]   For a survey of the translations carried out, see, e.g., MYERS, *Arabic Thought and the Western World in the Golden Age of Islam*, especially Ch. 7: "The impact of translations on the West" (pp. 78–131).

movement (tenth to twelfth centuries) and the Gregorian reforms of 1074. In 1053, the schism with Orthodoxy was sealed.

Papal initiatives were essential for all matters concerning Islam, such as the expansion of the Latin rather than Orthodox ecclesiastical jurisdiction to Southern Italy and Sicily after the Arabs' defeat, the reconquest of Spain, and the crusading drive. This entailed support for Barbastro's expedition in 1064, the visit of Urban II to Toledo in 1088 and his call to convert the conquered territories, and the stimulation of interest in Islam in Europe. In 1094, when the Byzantine emperor Alexis appealed for help against the Rūm Seljuks in Anatolia, the Papal response was prompt: a call for a crusade to the Holy Land. It is difficult to underestimate the role of the Popes in Europe's relations with Islam. This is still clear in 1455, when Pius II (r. 1458–64) wrote to Mehmet II, the conqueror of Constantinople in 1453, a letter in which he offered him the succession to the Byzantine emperors and temporal leadership of the Christian Orient, if he converted.[46] One can hardly imagine the Patriarch of Constantinople taking such initiatives.

4.2. Since the second half of the eleventh century, Byzantium had been continuously under threat and the object of relentless Turkish pressure. Precisely during this time, the Latin West liberated itself from the Arab grasp in Italy, parts of Spain, and the Mediterranean islands. For Byzantium, the only possible attitudes toward Muslims and Islam were war and polemics, though these might be softened in the case of certain emperors and their writings. The Latin West, however, could adopt a wider spectrum of attitudes and admit different currents in its stand toward Muslims and Islam.

This included a fresh theological and cultural orientation. Men like William of Tyre (ca. 1130–86) (*Historia rerum in partibus transmarinis gestarum*), William of Tripoli (12th c.) (*Tractatus de statu Saracenorum*) and Ricoldus de Monte Crucis (c. 1243–1320), with his *Confutatio* (or *Improbatio*) *alchorani* and *Itinerarium* written around 1310[47] had lived in a close acquaintance with Muslims in the Middle East. Thomas Aquinas

---

[46]   Pius II, *Lettera a Maometto II*, a cura di Giuseppe TOFFANIN, Naples: Pironti, 1953. Since the letter has not been found in the Ottoman archives, it is highly doubtful that this letter was in fact sent off.

[47]   Ricoldus had written this important work around 1310, taking into account his observations and the knowldge he had acquired in Mesopotamia at the end of the thirteenth century. For his *Itinerarium* see the study of Ugo MONNERET DE VILLARD, *Il Libro della peregrinazione nelle parti d'Oriente di frate Ricoldo da Montecroce*, Rome: Ad S. Sabinae, 1948. The *Improbatio* (or *Confutatio*) *alcorani* (PG, Vol. 104), retranslated from the Greek, was printed in Sevilla in 1500 and translated into German by Martin Luther under the title *Verlegung des Alcoran, Bruder Richardi Prediger Ordense*, Wittenberg, 1542. Cf. above note 34.

and Roger Bacon worked in their theological centers paying attention to Islam. Raymond Lull (1235–1315) combined scholarly with theological qualities and was driven by missionary zeal. He urged the Latin Church Council of Vienne in France (1311–2) to create schools for Arabic (and other eastern languages) for missionary work especially among Muslims. As a result, the Council decided to establish Oriental Studies at five universities.

Nicolas of Cusa (1401–64) revealed perhaps the broadest culture and most spiritual view of them all in his *Learned Ignorance* (*De docta ignorantia*, 1440) and his "philosophical dialogue" *The Peace of Faith* (*De pace fidei*, written in or after 1453). In his *Sifting the Qur'ān* (*Cribratio alchorani*, c. 1461), he attempts to sift out what he considers to be the Christian and the non-Christian elements of the Qur'ān, offering a detailed critique, on internal evidence, of those places where the Qur'ān departs from Christian teachings. His view is that of a philosophical mind: if Islam is a corrupt form of Christianity, and if Christianity is the real starting point of Islam, then Islam's return to Christianity—for him the Church—should be a real possibility. In his *De pace fidei*, Cusanus expresses himself, in prayer, in more universal terms. If God does not hide Himself, since He wants to be understood, then people will not defect.[48]

4.3. In the late medieval West, the mendicant orders played an important role in missionary work to Muslims and in supporting Christians living in Muslim territory. In 1219, during the fifth crusade, Francis of Assisi

---

[48] "... *Nam nemoa te recedit, nisi quia te ignorat. Si sic facere dignaberis, cessabit gladius et odii livor, et quaeque mala; et cognoscent omnes quomodo non est nisi religio una in rituum varietate* ...". The texts of Cusanus' *De pace fidei* and of his *Epistula ad Ioannem de Segobia* were edited and commented upon by Raymundus KLIBANSKY and Hildebrandus BASCOUR, *Nicolai de Cusa De Pace Fidei* (Mediaeval and Renaissance Studies, Supplement III), London: The Warburg Institute, University of London, 1956. The quotation is from p. 7 of this edition. The first complete German translation was made by Ludwig MOHLER and published in *Schriften des Nikolaus von Cues*, ed. Ernst HOFFMANN, Vol. 8: *Über den Frieden im Glauben – De pace fidei* (Philosophische Bibliothek 223), Leipzig: Meiner, 1943. See now the Latin text and German translation by Dietlind and Wilhelm DUPRÉ as *De pace fidei – Der Friede im Glauben*, in Nikolaus von Kues, Philosophisch-theologische Schriften, ed. by Leo GABRIEL, Vol. III (Vienna: Herder, 1967), pp. 705–97.

The *Cribratio alchorani* was translated and commented upon by Paul NAUMANN and Gustav HÖLSCHER and published in *Schriften des Nikolaus von Cues*, ed. by Ernst HOFFMANN, Vols. 6 and 7: *Sichtung des Alkorans – Cribratio Alcorani*, Leipzig and Hamburg: Meiner, 1943, 1948[2] and 1946 respectively. The introduction of this book (*Prologus, Alius prologus*, and *Contents*) was given in its Latin text and translated by Dietlind and Wilhelm DUPRÉ as *Cribratio alchorani – Prüfung des Korans*, in Nikolaus von Kues, *Philosophisch-theologische Schriften*, ed. by Leo GABRIEL, Vol. III (Vienna: Herder, 1967), pp. 799–817. Cf. also the article by RESCHER quoted in note 50 below.

On Nicolas of Cusa, see for instance Pauline M. WATT, *Nicolaus Cusanus: A Fifteenth-Century Vision of Man*, Leiden: E. J. Brill, 1982.

(1181/2–1226) visited Egypt, where he was received by the Ayyūbid Sultan al-Kāmil. He established the Franciscan order, of which Raymond Lull and Robert Bacon were tertiaries. The Dominican order, founded by Dominic (1170–1221), included scholarly figures like Raymond of Peñafort (c. 1185–1275), Raymond Marti and Ricoldus de Monte Crucis who visited Baghdad around 1291. The Dominicans devoted themselves to missionary work among Jews and Muslims, in particular in Spain, where they were also instrumental for the Inquisition. The role of the monasteries in the Byzantine Empire in relation to Islam was much less knowledgeable and active.

4.4. Especially in the thirteenth and fourteenth centuries, apocalyptic visions of Islam and its ending were alive even in the higher ecclesiastical hierarchy of the Latin West. The Mongols who had taken Baghdad in 1258 were thought to play a role in this; the Popes contacted them on several occasions. The impending end of Islam and the forthcoming conversion of all Muslims was euphorically expected.[49] This idea was sometimes linked to the legendary Christian king "Prester John", who with his Christian empire was thought to be threatening Islam from the rear, and with whom the Western Christians would unite for the final defeat or conversion of Islam.

One of the projects of Columbus' voyage was to contact the Christians supposed to live in East Asia, so that they would attack the Muslims from the rear.

To summarize, in Byzantium after 1100, almost the only attitude toward Islam was that of defensive war and polemics, while in the same period in the West, a variety of attitudes crystallized. From 1100 to 1250, a real discovery and assimilation of the Arab cultural heritage took place in Western Europe. From 1250 to 1400, this was followed by a period of quite wild fantasies about Muhammad and Islam. Then interest in Islam declined.[50] With the Ottoman conquests and after the fall of Constantinople in 1453 Christian polemics against Islam revived.[51] For two and a half centuries, Europe was then to face imposing Turkish military power.

---

[49]   On the intellectual activity of the Christians and their euphoria in thirteenth-century Spain, see Robert I. BURNS, "Christian-Islamic Confrontation in the West: The Thirteenth-Century Dream of Conversion", *The American Historical Review*, 76/5 (December 1971), pp. 1386–1434. See by the same author *Muslims, Christians and Jews in the Crusader Kingdom of Valencia: Societies in Symbiosis*, New York and Cambridge: Cambridge University Press, 1984.

[50]   See Nicolas RESCHER, "Nicholas of Cusa on the Qur'ān: A Fifteenth-Century Encounter with Islam", *The Muslim World*, 55/3 (July 1965), pp. 195–202. The periodization is given on pp. 195–6.

[51]   Just as in the West after the Reformation and Counter-Reformation, in Muslim territory too, Christian polemical writing against Islam continued. I think for instance of

5. Some Special Subjects

5.1. Spain

Like the Christian minorities in the Arab East until the eleventh century, the Christian Mozarabes in Spain seem to have played a constructive role in the cultural life of Muslim Spain from the eighth until the eleventh century. The relationships which existed between Muslims, Jews, and Christians in the Cordoban emirate and later caliphate (756–1031) were fundamentally positive.[52] This situation, which is comparable to that of tenth and eleventh century Sicily under Muslim rule (902–1091), came to an end with the politicization of religion when the reconquest started in 1062. The Christians in the North became part of the expanding Catholic Church, and the Muslims in the South became more and more narrowly Islamized with the rule of the Almoravids (1086–1130) and the Almohads (1130–1269) from North Africa in Spain. The reconquest was encouraged by the popes and led to the arrival of the North African dynasties in support of the Muslims who had been defeated by the Christians in the battle of Zallaka in 1086. There are deeper links between the papal policies towards Muslims and Islam from the mid-eleventh century on and the more aggressive relations that developed between Christians and Muslims in Spain in the following years.

Spain also had some outstanding Muslim thinkers who polemicized against Christianity.[53] The most famous among them is Ibn Hazm (994–1064), who wrote his *Fisal*[54] as an apologetic treatise of "comparative religion" with an incisive refutation of the Jewish and Christian scriptures, employing great erudition and refined critical acumen. Worth mention in this

---

Anastasios Gordios (c. 1655–1729), on whom Asterios Argyrios wrote an unpublished dissertation *"Sur Mahomet et contre les Latins": Une oeuvre inédite d'Anastasios Gordios, religieux et professeur grec (XVIIe–XVIIIe s.). Edition critique*, etc., 2 Vols., Strasbourg, 1967. Cf. Id., "Anastasios Gordios et la polémique anti-islamique post-byzantine", *Revue des Sciences Religieuses*, 43 (1969), pp. 58–87.

[52]   A first positive appreciation of this period of Spanish history, formerly called "black", was given by Castro, *The Structure of Spanish History*.

[53]   We are indebted here to Miguel de Epalza, "Notes pour une histoire des polémiques anti-chrétiennes dans l'Occident musulman", *Arabica*, 18 (1971), pp. 99–106.

[54]   *Kitāb al-fisal fī'l-milal wa'l-ahwā' wa'l-nihal*, 5 books in two Vols., Cairo, 1899/1317–1903/1321. Cf. Miguel Asín Palacios' succinct translation with introduction, *Abenházam de Cordoba, y su historia crítica de las ideas religiosas*, 5 Vols., Madrid: Real Academia de la Historia, 1927–32. On Ibn Hazm's polemic against Christianity and its further influence, see Behloul, *Ibn Hazms Evangelienkritik*. See also Abdelilah Ljamai, *Ibn Hazm et la polémique islamo-chrétienne dans l'histoire de l'Islam*, Diss. Tilburg, Netherlands, 2001. On Ibn Hazm's polemic and earlier polemics against Judaism cf. Camilla Adang, *Muslim Writers on Judaism and the Hebrew Bible: From Ibn Rabban to Ibn Hazm*, Leiden etc.: E. J. Brill, 1996.

respect are also Abū'l-Walīd al-Bājī (d. 1081)[55] and Ibn Sab'īn (d. 1271), who even maintained correspondence with Frederick II (1194–1250).[56] The converted Franciscan ʿAbdallāh al-Tarjumān wrote a refutation of Christianity in his *Tuḥfa* in 1420.[57]

On the other hand, we see in the Christian North during the twelfth century an intellectual and cultural thirst for knowledge, of which the translation enterprise was an essential part. In this a noteworthy contribution was made by Peter the Venerable and his Benedictine men through the *Corpus cluniacense*, established to obtain knowledge of Islam through the translation of important primary sources. The political successes of the Christians stimulated further cultural efforts in the thirteenth century, with practical language training. The development of philosophical analysis and theological argumentation was supported by a faith in reason and in human intellectual capacities. This period testifies to a spirit of enlightenment in which Islam in the last analysis could be viewed as a kind of ignorance to be overcome by means of enlightened thought and persuasion. It came to an end with the militant ideology of the Church and the Catholic kings in the fourteenth century, with intolerance practiced first against the Jews and then against the Muslims. The inquisition to which the Christians were subjected was now extended to the non-Christians. Unless they converted to Christianity, Jews were expelled from Spain and Portugal in 1492 and Muslims in 1502. Nearly all Moriscos, the descendants of those Muslims who had then converted to Christianity, were expelled in 1609–10.

5.2. Muslim Interest in Europe

Looking for a moment at the Muslim side, we see a striking difference between the interest given to Byzantium and to the Latin West during the medieval period. Whereas Byzantium was fairly well known to the Muslims and was considered as a kind of equal partner with parallel cultural expressions and comparable loyalties to religion and culture, Muslims had

---

[55] See D. M. DUNLOP, "A Christian Mission to Muslim Spain in the XIth century", *Al-Andalus*, 17 (1952), pp. 259–310, and Abdelmağid TURKI, "La lettre du 'moine de France' à al-Muqtadir billāh, roi de Saragosse et la réponse d'al-Bāğī, le faqīh andalou", *Al-Andalus*, 31 (1966), pp. 73–153. Cf. Alan CUTLER, "Who was the 'Monk of France' and when did he write?", *Al-Andalus*, 28 (1963), pp. 249–69.

[56] See M. A. F. MEHREN, "Correspondance du philosophe soufi Ibn Sab'īn Abdoul-Haqq avec l'empereur Frédéric II de Hohenstaufen", *Journal Asiatique*, 7e Série, XIV (1879), pp. 341–454.

[57] *Tuḥfat al-arīb fī'l-radd ʿalā ahl al-salīb*, Cairo, 1895. French translation by Jean SPIRO "Le présent de l'homme lettré pour réfuter les partisans de la Croix. Par ʿAbd-Allāh ibn ʿAbd-Allāh, le Drogman. Traduction française inédite", *Revue de l'Histoire des Religions*, 12 (6e Année) (1885), pp. 68–9, 179–201 and 278–301. See EPALZA, *La Tuḥfa*.

a virtually total lack of interest in Western Europe, apart from the city of Rome. In Arabic texts we find little intellectual attention to and even no imagination about this part of the world. Its people were probably considered uneducated barbarians from whom nothing could be learned. The information obtained from traveling merchants apparently evoked no further curiosity, and even the Crusades originating in the Latin West were viewed as invasions without cultural relevance. On the contrary, we may suppose that, from the eleventh century on, this Europe came to be seen as representing first annoyance, then an increasing physical threat to life in what was felt to be the civilized world of Islam. It may correspond to the way the Byzantines viewed the Arab invasions of the seventh century, aggressive peoples in the Balkans or, for that matter, the Latin barbarians who destroyed Constantinople in 1204.

5.3. Latins and Byzantines

I spoke of the different relations between Islam and the Latin West, on the one hand, and between Islam and Byzantium, on the other hand, and I looked at the different views about Muslims and Islam that existed in medieval Byzantine and Latin Christianity and that resulted at least in part from these relationships. I should say a few words now about the relations between Eastern and Western Christendom and the resultant different attitudes toward Muslims and Islam. Byzantine and Latin Christianity both underwent a similar challenge by the Arabs (or later the Turks against Byzantium) and Islam, but practically in isolation from each other.

If Western Europe borrowed part of its intellectual armory of arguments against and most of its legends about Islam from or through the Byzantines, Byzantium received hardly anything from Europe. The distance between Western and Eastern Christendom paralleled their different political interests. In both cases Western Europe and Western Christendom imposed themselves.

The Crusades, although responding to a call for help sent out by the emperor, were a Western affair, and they greatly increased the tensions between Byzantium and Rome. In 1204, in fact, Byzantium received its mortal wound not from Islam, but from the Latin West, and it was thus largely paralyzed in its defense and resistance against the Turks. There is reason to assume that Rome viewed with mixed feelings the subsequent struggle to the death that the Byzantines had to wage. In any case, Rome could not mobilize Europe subsequently to major offensives against the Turks and offered hardly any direct and badly needed assistance to Constantinople.

Our fancy may be caught by thinking what course the history of Islamic expansion would have taken if the schisms of 1054 and earlier between East and West had not occurred, how Muslim-Christian relations would have developed, and what kind of views Muslims and Christians around the Mediterranean might have had of each other in that case. On the other hand, precisely because Christianity was not homogeneous, response to the presence of Muslims and Islam could differ. Further reflection could develop later in Western Europe, which escaped Ottoman occupation.

6. Medieval Muslims and Christians: Common Structures

Until now I have traced in broad outlines the origins and contents of the different views that Muslims and Christians held of each other at various times and places in the medieval period. There is need to correct the one-sidedness of this approach. For on closer analysis, what the conflicting parties themselves felt to be an absolute antagonism seems to have been embedded in certain assumptions and presuppositions that Muslims and Eastern, Byzantine, and Western Christians shared.[58] There is reason to look for possible common structures underlying the positions of the parties that seem on first sight to be so antagonistic to each other. This would require further inquiry, but I would like to submit some hypotheses in a more comprehensive perspective.

6.1. In the first place, there was a common religious structure with at least four basic elements: (1) faith in one God; (2) a belief that this God manifests his will through nature, his acting in history, and precisely known revelations; (3) the notion of one true religion rising above existing false religions and heresies; and (4) the acceptance of various religious communities or rather "nations" considering themselves as living under God's more or less exclusive protection. The elements of this religious structure and their connections were articulated in different ways by means of different theological views. Yet, in the last analysis, a certain mutual understanding of the differences remained possible, it seems to me, because there was a common religious structure, a common philosophical framework, and a common appeal to nature and historical events as evidence for the existing order.

---

[58] Attention to such common assumptions and presuppositions has been drawn, for instance, by VON GRUNEBAUM in his "Parallelism, Convergence, and Influence in the Relations of Arab and Byzantine Philosophy, Literature, and Piety". Such an approach could also be applied to medieval Spain and Southern Italy with Sicily and to medieval philosophical and theological thought as carried out by Muslims and Eastern, Byzantine, and Western Christians. It would also be fruitful to analyze certain common social structures and cultural patterns.

The people concerned were sometimes conscious of the fact that they held much in common. The Christians, on the one hand, tried to clarify and expound revelation by means of philosophical reason along the lines of Aristotle and Plotinus; faith to them had its own specific *ratio*, so that they were looking for the *ratio fidei*. Besides that, they appealed to the authority of the Church, its tradition, and its power—visible like that of the state—as an argument for their particular truth.

The Muslims, on the other hand, defended with the help of reason God's oneness and uniqueness against any possible infringement. So they carried out rationalistic attacks both on the existing texts of the Bible and on the mysteries of faith the Christians believed in. Their general stand in religious matters was to take the Qur'ān as their starting point and last recourse, and to accept arguments based only on reason.

But whatever the difference between the positions taken by various Muslims and Christians about the elements of this common religious structure, they all affirmed as self-evident the truth of the beliefs that they held about these elements. Looking from a distance and from a philosophical point of view, we may say that it was their particular view of truth that made them choose and interpret these elements in various ways and made them see each other in various ways as well.

6.2. The assumption of the presence of such a common structure does not alter—and actually rather elucidates—the fact that there was at the same time in their own consciousness a serious, definite, and "total" opposition between the causes held and defended by Muslims and Christians. The continuous military struggle, interrupted by incidental truces, should be seen not only in the light of the two conflicting religious ideologies but also in terms of the political relationship of two powerful colossi, as a struggle for power. In a similar vein, many of the actual struggles can be interpreted in terms of the natural envy of barbarians for the riches of higher civilizations, both Muslims and Christians being sometimes in the "barbarian" position. Military history weighs heavily on the relationship between the two religions. One should keep in mind that Byzantine Christianity, until the tenth and after the thirteenth century, and Latin Christianity, until the mid-eleventh century, found themselves fighting on the defensive against Islam. The political antagonism between Christian and Muslim countries was seen as the more absolute, probably, since there was hardly a third party of significance in the political field until the Mongol conquests.

The basic military and political opposition then derived support from the different religious beliefs and practices as well as the different social norms of the two systems. Such norms, practices, and beliefs had by then come to be—not only the expression but also—the legitimization of the social systems in question. Each society was organized within the framework of a religion; each one was a nation defining itself according to its religion. Life, thought, and society were identified in religious terms that were more or less definite, and this gave a permanency to their existing differences and contrasts. Psychologically speaking, both camps projected each other's religion as their ideological antagonist.

A study of Muslims' and Christians' views of each other is in many respects a study of mutual misunderstandings. Many factors played a role in this, including emotional ones such as the fear of a superior power imposing itself with a foreign religion and ideology. Misunderstandings also arose from the fact that both sides interpreted the other religion in terms of their own, without relativizing it. Islam saw Christianity as believers gone astray but to be respected as people of Scripture; medieval Christianity saw Muslims largely as believers misled by ignorance and evil. Neither party could adequately place the other's claim to absolute truth, for reasons that deserve further analysis.

On the level of apologetic method, both Muslims and Christians had recourse to scripture and reason to convince each other and themselves. But they did this in different ways.

Each party used its own scripture to affirm itself against the other. The Muslims here had a definite advantage, since Muhammad had lived later than Jesus and since he and not Jesus had left a scripture. Also, the Qur'ān, as the word of God itself, was weightier than the Bible, since for the Christians the Word of God was Christ and not the Bible.

The Muslims recognized that things religious transcend reason, but they also held that religion should not contradict reason. By subjecting Christianity to a simple rational criticism in their polemics, they adduced devastating arguments against it. The Christians, on the other hand, believed in religious mysteries that were not only inaccessible to reason but could in fact contradict it. So they could certainly develop rational arguments against Islam, but they could not press as hard against it rationally as the Muslims could against Christianity. Rather than being combative against the other, they tried to explain their faith. In fact, according to Christian doctrine, reason could not force the human mind to see the truth of the Christian faith; it needed God's grace to do so.

There were nuances, of course. Both Orthodox and Latin Christian theologians could be terribly rationalistic in their refutations of the Muslim faith. In Islam, there were different theological schools, and the Muʿtazilites were in the vanguard of Muslim polemics against Christianity. We still need a careful investigation of the precise implications of Muʿtazilite, Ashʿarite, and Maturīdite theology for the interpretation of non-Muslims. In fact, we still need a critical analysis of the implications of Qur'anic theology—and of certain theological lines in the *hadīth* literature—for the interpretation of non-Muslims. On the whole, Islam, claiming to be the religion of the golden mean, tended to view other religions, including Christianity, as "exaggerations" of Islam on certain given points.

There were supplementary problems in the relation between Christianity and Islam, as well. One problem was that Muslims often supposed that the Qur'ān contained everything that needed to be known about Christianity, both facts and judgments, so that further study of Christianity was hardly necessary. Christians, for their part, could not consult their scripture to know about Islam: they were simply obliged to study it from the sources, with the means at their disposal.

On an intellectual level, there was a certain inequality. Later powerful thinkers like Ibn Sīnā (980–1037) and al-Ghazzālī could not be matched by Byzantine theologians at the time. And it took time for the Latins to produce thinkers able to digest the critical thought of an Ibn Bājja (d. 1138) or Ibn Rushd (1126–98).

Both sides had a structural intolerance toward religious minority groups. This does not exclude acknowledging toleration of certain groups combined with indifference on the Muslim side and a certain toleration in individual cases on the Christian side, for example under the Norman kings of Sicily or by an exceptional figure like Frederick II. In both cases, the prevailing attitude of the religious majority, however, was to feign not to see the minority and its religion and to avoid any intense contact.

On the Muslim side, in the medieval period there were no massacres of civilians of another religion, no persecutions by the state, and there was no violent repression of Christians within Muslim territory, except in some cases under the Fātimid caliph al-Hākim (r. 985–1021) who was considered insane by his immediate surroundings. On the Christian side, there was a more aggressive attitude, and Muslims tried to avoid being a minority. Most Muslims at the time left their territory once it had been conquered by Christians. Only in the sixteenth century did it come to a persecution of Muslims in Spain.

The prevailing structural intolerance implied that nobody tried to reformulate on reflection questions of truth in the light of the other's existence or claims. But everyone's right to be judged according to his or her own religious law was acknowledged, even if the Christians did not recognize the revelation of the Muslims and if the Muslims gave their own interpretation of the revelation of the Christians. On the whole, in practice Muslims could put Christian minorities under social pressure, whereas Christians developed a missionary approach to Muslim minorities. Each religion could exert particular pressures on adherents of the other. Both considered this largely unavoidable, and the dominant considered it just.

These structures are fundamental to understand the relations and mutual views of Christians and Muslims, Christianity and Islam, in the medieval period. Wilhelm Dilthey stated that the starting point for the intellectual work of this period is constituted by the problems of the three monotheistic religions.[59] Medieval thought cannot be understood unless one takes into account not only the problems it tried to find an answer to, but also the problems with which the existence of these two religions confronted thinkers. That there were common deeper structures also appears from the fact that such problems were recognized by both sides, Christian and Muslim. The other party was partly viewed according to the answer it was able to give to common problems.

Moreover, both were confronted with the other's existence and had to find a solution for it. Islam did this by calling the Christians *ahl al-kitāb*, "people of Scripture", implying partial recognition. The Christians hesitated between calling Islam a heresy and a false religion. For Christian consciousness, a kind of dialogue might be possible with the first, whereas the second had to be denounced and refuted.[60]

Strikingly medieval, to our sense, was the religiocentric, centripetal, and nearly solipsistic worldview, religiously fixed, of both civilizations. Strikingly medieval too was the idea that adherence to a faith other than one's own implies a fundamental separation. In fact, it was religion that provided the area of deeper human, social, and cultural contact between these civilizations, although to the people concerned, the two religions were inextricably linked to the two civilizations in question and separated them.

Baghdad and Byzantium, Cordoba and Rome, Islam and Christianity: two "shining lights", as the title of this chapter suggests? They were so in that they could not look into each other's light, blinded as they were by each other's claims, unable to perceive each other as they were. So their views of each other became distorted and at least some of their adherents projected at given times and places the other religion as the enemy. In the end, no new light was shed any more and the radiance disappeared.

Apparently, wars are not conducive to perception of the other's light. This, in a way, is the tragic history of Latin/Byzantine-Muslim relations and of Christian-Muslim relations in general: that both were too caught up in the conflict and too prone to identify truth with their own cause to be able to take distance from themselves and a good look at each other. Theologians, both Muslim and Christian, were the chief servants of the conflict, rationalizing its religious side from the assumptions and presuppositions

[59] Wilhelm DILTHEY, *Einleitung in die Geisteswissenschaften* (*Gesammelte Schriften I*), Leipzig and Berlin: Teubner, 1923, p. 273.
[60] *Muslim Perceptions of Other Religions: A Historical Survey*, ed. by Jacques WAARDENBURG, New York and Oxford: Oxford University Press, 1999. Cf. GODDARD, *A History of Christian-Muslim Relations*. A survey of Christian attitudes toward Islam is given by MOUBARAC, *La pensée chrétienne et l'Islam*.

of their respective religious views. But in broader circles, too, people deeply felt that the two religions were mutually exclusive, not only because of the education received from the religious leaders but also because of deeper loyalties toward their respective communities. Looking from a distance, we can now better perceive the true proportions of these two "shining lights". As a matter of fact, we can see that both lights illuminated each other, although their adherents could hardly be aware of it.

Selected Literature

ABEL, Armand, "Le chapitre sur le Christianisme dans le 'Tamhīd' d'al-Bāqillānī", in *Etudes d'Orientalisme dédiées à la mémoire de Lévi-Provençal*, Vol. 1, Paris: Maisonneuve & Larose, 1962, pp. 1–11.

ANAWATI, Georges C., "Polémique, apologie et dialogue islamo-chrétiens: Positions classiques médiévales et positions contemporaines", in *Euntes Docete: Commentaria Urbaniana* (Rome: Pontificia Universitas Urbaniana), 22 (1969), pp. 375–452.

BECKER, Carl Heinrich, "Christliche Polemik und islamische Dogmenbildung", in his *Islamstudien*, Vol. 1, Leipzig: Quelle & Meyer, 1924, pp. 432–49.

BEHLOUL, Samuel-Martin, *Ibn Hazms Evangelienkritik: Eine methodische Untersuchung* (Islamic Philosophy and Science. Texts and Studies, 50), Leiden, etc.: E. J. Brill, 2002.

BOUAMAMA, Ali, *La littérature polémique musulmane contre le christianisme, depuis les origines jusqu'au XIIIe siècle*, Alger: Entreprise Nationale du Livre, 1988.

BURNS, Robert I., *Moors and Crusaders in Mediterranean Spain: Collected Studies*, London: Variorum Reprints, 1978.

—, *Muslims, Christians and Jews in the Crusader Kingdom of Valencia: Societies in Symbiosis*, New York and Oxford: Oxford University Press, 1984.

CANARD, Marius, *Byzance et les musulmans du Proche Orient* (Variorum Collected Studies Series), London: Variorum Reprints, 1973.

CASTRO, Américo, *The Structure of Spanish History*, Princeton, N. J.: Princeton University Press, 1954.

DANIEL, Norman, *Islam and the West: The Making of an Image*, Edinburgh: Edinburgh University Press, 1960; new, revised edition Oxford: Oneworld, 1980.

EPALZA, Miguel de, *La Tuhfa, autobiografía y polémica islámica contra el Christianismo de ʿAbdallāh al-Taryūmān (fray Anselmo Turmedo)*, Rome: Accademia Nazionale dei Lincei, 1971.

FATTAL, Antoine, *Le statut légal des non-musulmans en pays d'Islam* (Recherches 10), Beirut: Imprimerie Catholique, 1958, etc.

GAUDEUL, Jean-Marie, *Encounters and Clashes: Islam and Christianity in History*, 2 Vols., Vol. 1: *A Survey*; Vol. 2: *Texts*, Rome: PISAI, 1984.

GAUSZ, Julia, "Anselm von Canterbury: Zur Begegnung und Auseinandersetzung der Religionen", *Saeculum*, 17 (1966), pp. 277–363.

GODDARD, Hugh, *A History of Christian-Muslim Relations* (Islamic Surveys), Edinburgh: Edinburgh University Press, 2000.

GOLDZIHER, Ignaz, "Ueber muhammedanische Polemik gegen Ahl al-kitāb", *Zeitschrift der Deutschen Morgenländischen Gesellschaft*, 32 (1878), pp. 341–87 (repr. in his *Gesammelte Schriften – Collected Works*, Vol. II, Hildesheim: G. Olms, 1970, pp. 1–47).

GRUNEBAUM, Gustav E. von, "Parallelism, Convergence, and Influence in the Relations of Arab and Byzantine Philosophy, Literature, and Piety", *Dumbarton Oak Papers*, 18 (1964), pp. 89–112.

HAGEMANN, Ludwig, *Christentum contra Islam: Eine Geschichte gescheiterter Beziehungen*, Darmstadt: Primus Verlag, 1999.

Islamic Interpretations of Christianity, ed. by Lloyd RIDGEON, Richmond, U. K.: Curzon, 2001.

KHOURY, Adel-Théodore, *Les théologiens byzantins et l'Islam, textes et auteurs (VIIIe–XIIIe s.)*, Louvain, etc.: Nauwelaerts, 1966, 1969[2].

—, *Manuel II Paléologue: Entretiens avec un musulman, 7e Controverse. Introduction, texte critique, traduction et notes* (Sources Chrétiennes 115), Paris: Cerf, 1966.

KHOURY, Paul, *Paul d'Antioche, évêque melkite de Sidon (XIIe s.)* (Recherches 24), Beirut: Imprimerie Catholique, n.d. (1965).

KRITZECK, James, *Peter the Venerable and Islam*, Princeton: Princeton University Press, 1964.

LEIRVIK, Oddbjörn, *Images of Jesus Christ in Islam: Introduction, Survey of Research, Issues of Dialogue*, Uppsala: Swedish Institute of Missionary Research, 1999.

MASSON, Denise, *Monothéisme coranique et monothéisme biblique: Doctrines comparées*, Paris: Desclée de Brouwer, 1976.

MINGANA, Alphonse, "The Apology of Timothy the Patriarch before the Caliph Mahdi", *Bulletin of the John Rylands Library*, 12 (1928), pp. 137–298.

MOUBARAC, Youakim, *La pensée chrétienne et l'Islam: Bilan des recherches.* (I) *Des origines à la chute de Constantinople* (Unpublished Thèse d'Etat, Paris 1969); (II) *Recherches sur la pensée chrétienne et l'islam: Dans les temps modernes et à l'époque contemporaine* (Publications de l'Université Libanaise, Section des Etudes Historiques, 22), Beirut: Université Libanaise, 1977.

MYERS, Eugene A., *Arabic Thought and the Western World in the Golden Age of Islam*, New York: Frederick Ungar, 1964.

PINES, Shlomo, *The Jewish Christians of the Early Centuries of Christianity, according to a New Source*, Jerusalem: Israel Academy of Science and Humanities, 1966.

PUTMAN, Hans, *L'Eglise et l'Islam sous Timothée I (780–823)*, Beirut: Dar El Machreq, 1975.

RISSANEN, Seppo, *Theological Encounter of Oriental Christians with Islam During Early Abbasid Rule*, Abo: Abo Akademi University Press, 1993.

SOUTHERN, Richard W., *Western Views of Islam in the Middle Ages*, Cambridge, Mass.: Harvard University Press, 1962, 1978[2].

STEINSCHNEIDER, Moritz, *Polemische und apologetische Literatur in arabischer Sprache, zwischen Muslimen, Christen und Juden* (Abhandlungen für die Kunde des Morgenlandes 6,3), Leipzig: Brockhaus, 1877 (repr. Hildesheim: Georg Olms, 1966).

STERN, Samuel M., "Quotations from the Apocryphal Gospel in ʿAbdeljabbār", *Journal of Theological Studies* (Oxford), 18 (1967), pp. 34–57.

—, "'Abdeljabbār's Account of how Christ's Religion was Falsified by the Adoption of Roman Customs", *Journal of Theological Studies* (Oxford), 19 (1968), pp. 128–85.

SWEETMAN, J. Windrow, *Islam and Christian Theology*, Two Parts, London: Lutterworth Press, 1954–7.

THOMAS, David, *Anti-Christian Polemic in Early Islam: Abū 'Īsā al-Warrāq's 'Against the Trinity'*, New York and Cambridge: Cambridge University Press, 1992.

TRAPP, Erich, *Manuel II. Palaiologos: Dialoge mit einem 'Perser'* (Wiener Byzantinistische Studien II), Vienna: Böhlau, 1966.

TRITTON, Arthur S., *The Caliphs and their non-Muslim Subjects: A Critical Study of the Covenant of 'Umar*, London: Oxford University Press, 1930 (repr. London: Cass, 1970).

WAARDENBURG, Jacques, "Selected Bibliography", in *Muslim-Christian Perceptions of Dialogue Today: Experiences and Expectations*, ed. by Jacques WAARDENBURG, Leuven, etc.: Peeters, 2000, pp. 305–23.

WATT, W. Montgomery, "The Christianity criticized in the Qur'ān", *The Muslim World*, 57, Nr. 3 (1967), pp. 197–201.

WILMS, Franz-Elmar, *Al-Ghazālīs Schrift wider die Gottheit Jesu*, Leiden: E. J. Brill, 1966.

Chapter 6
World Religions Seen in Islamic Light*

1. Nature and Relevance of the Inquiry

Since the beginning of Islam, Muslims have been aware of the existence of other religions. At its height, between the eighth and fourteenth centuries C.E., Islamic civilization collected much information about these religions, more than was known in other civilizations at the time.[1] They also had to be evaluated, not only according to the points of view given in Qur'ān and *hadīth*, and the more abstract norms worked out in *kalām* and *fiqh*. Muslims based their opinions also on the knowledge they had acquired of these religions and on their observation of the actual behavior of their adherents. Their knowledge was closely linked to the relations they maintained or wanted to maintain with other people, taking into account the norms and values current in their own societies.

The study of Muslim perceptions of other religions and of Muslim views about their value or lack of value is still in its beginnings.[2] The same

---

*   This is a revised version of a paper published in the *Festschrift* for W. Montgomery Watt, *Islam: Past Influence and Present Challenge*, ed. by Alford T. WELCH and Pierre CACHIA, Edinburgh: Edinburgh University Press, 1979, pp. 245–75. For a broader treatment of the subject, see *Muslim Perceptions of Other Religions*.

[1] After the *Fihrist* of Ibn al-Nadīm (written 987/377), the work of scholars like Ibn-Hazm and al-Bīrūnī, al-Shahrastānī and Rashīd-al-Dīn provides evidence of the relatively advanced state of knowledge about other religions available in medieval Islamic civilization. Then, from the fourteenth century on, there was a sharp decline of interest in them, and it is only after World War Two that Muslim authors have again written books of 'comparative religion'.

[2] Descriptions and judgments given by Muslim thinkers can be analyzed separately, but they are closely related, and one and the same work may have descriptive as well as appreciative aspects. Cf. J. WAARDENBURG, "Tendances d'histoire des religions dans l'Islam médiéval", in *Akten des VII. Kongresses für Arabistik und Islamwissenschaft (Göttingen, August 15–22,1974)* (Abhandlungen der Akademie der Wissenschaften in Göttingen, Phil.-Hist. Klasse, Dritte Folge Nr. 98), Göttingen: Vandenhoeck & Ruprecht, 1976, pp. 372–84; ID., *Zien met anderman's ogen* (Looking through another's eyes), The Hague – Paris: Mouton, 1975 (inaugural address Utrecht); ID., "Jugements musulmans sur les religions non-islamiques à l'époque médiévale", in *La signification du bas moyen âge dans l'histoire et la culture du monde musulman: Actes du 8me Congrès de l'Union européenne des arabisants et islamisants, Aix-en-Provence, septembre 1976*, Aix-en-Provence: EDISUD, 1978, pp. 323–41. See also MONNOT, *Penseurs*

holds true for the scholarly study of the social relationships that have existed between societies, groups, and persons who identify themselves as 'Muslim', on the one hand, and other people who do not, on the other hand.[3]

To what extent and in which cases did and do those Islamic values and norms that are considered to be religiously true and legally valid have immediate practical effects on the communication between Muslims and others? It is of interest to ask how certain situations of life that Muslims shared with non-Muslims in different times and places, and that in themselves had little to do with religion, influenced their mutual perception and appreciation.

Can we speak of certain structural rules in the ways in which Muslims, as Muslims, have tended to relate to non-Muslims in specific social and institutional settings and that have given certain kinds of Muslim self-identification with certain ideological and other claims with reference to Islam? Each religion allows for a range of different attitudes toward outsiders and it is of interest to know what is possible and not possible in given cases. Or is it difficult to speak of "general rules" in a world religion like Islam, with adherents living in widely different social and cultural contexts? Yet there apparently are certain prescriptions of behavior that show up with some regularity among Muslims of different cultural areas.

There are also certain patterns of argumentation and certain standard reproaches made to other religions and there are certain proofs constantly given of the preeminence of Islam. The judgments passed do not need to be based on a real knowledge or understanding of other religious views. They seem to be simply a logical consequence of given assumptions and of the kind of truth in which people put their faith. In the medieval period, and later, too, people simply judged other religions on the basis of their own ideas and experiences.

---

musulmans et religions iraniennes; ID., "L'histoire des religions en Islam, Ibn al-Kalbi et Razi", *Revue de l'histoire des religions*, 188 (1975), pp. 23–34; ID., "L'écho musulman aux religions d'Iran", *Islamochristiana*, 3 (1977), pp. 85–98. Cf. Seyyed Hossein NASR, "Islam and the Encounter of Religions", in *Proceedings of the XIth Congress of the International Association for the History of Religions*, Leiden: E. J. Brill, Vol. III, 1968, pp. 23–47.

3 There are of course a number of studies on the relationships which have existed between Muslim and other communities and societies, but they have very different starting points and the analysis of the various aspects of these relationships is rarely carried out in depth. Some of these studies want to prove a particular point for or against Islam and lack an objective, nonpartisan approach. The simple fact that the Muslim self-identification always carries some religious meaning does not imply that religion is the determining factor in the relationships and views concerned. But it is possible to concentrate on the religious aspect without closing one's eyes to the many other aspects inherent in all views and relationships.

A scholarly and impartial study born out of a desire for understanding rather than out of a spirit of controversy in these matters also has a practical relevance. Relations between Muslims and non-Muslims have been very much impoverished and hurt by misunderstandings and wrong judgments on both sides.

2. Interest of Islam

Of the world religions, Christianity and Islam are interesting in terms of the kind of distinction made between those who do and who do not belong to the community of believers. Both religions are exclusive in their claims to truth based on revelation and both maintain the universal validity of these claims. Christianity and Islam welcome people as adherents. They conduct missionary activity and have developed certain views about other religions and certain guidelines and codes about how to respond to outsiders. In Islam the underlying norms have been systematized to some extent and have become a subject of discussion in recent years. The actual practice has varied according to cultural settings, social conditions, economic relations, and political circumstances.

Islam distinguishes itself among the many religions, ideologies, and worldviews by an extraordinary consciousness of norms it holds to have been revealed. These norms are considered to be absolute and of universal validity, providing human thought and action with an unconditional regulator.

Islam is unique, too, in its conception of religion, just as Judaism and Christianity have their own distinct ways of conceiving of religion. In the Muslim vision there is one primordial religion of absolute monotheism that has existed from the beginnings of humanity and is given with the human innate nature. It could be called the natural religion of humankind, corresponding with the order of creation. This primordial religion, moreover, was revealed at the beginning and at regular intervals in history through the intermediary of prophets. The "history of religions" is basically, then, the history of this primordial religion, revealed through the prophets from Adam to Muhammad, with the responses of the various communities to their prophets' preachings and prescriptions. The differences between the various religions are due not so much to different contents of their revelations as to specific historical contexts in which the prophets worked and to peoples' general laxity in keeping to the standards of the religion given to them. Moreover, people distorted their prophets' fundamentally identical teachings. These distortions are palpable in the differences between the scriptures that the major prophets are held to have brought to them and that are considered to go back to one heavenly model.

This is what may be called an Islamic 'theological' vision of religion itself, which contains the principal elements of an Islamic 'theology of religions'. There is one God, whom human beings have to become conscious of, to whom they should surrender, and whose will is that they obey the religious prescriptions. There is one fundamental Revelation that is contained in its linguistically pure form in the Qur'ān. And there is one monotheistic Religion that is, beyond empirical Islam, the primordial and eternal Islam, radically opposed to all forms of idolatry or 'associationism' and to all forms of disobedience to the basic rules of religion.

This vision of humankind's religious history underlies the judgments given by the Muslim *mutakallimūn* (theologians) and *fuqahā'* (jurists) on the religions outside Islam. These judgments concern the religious systems—doctrines, prescriptions, and rites—rather than the individual people adhering to them. Yet, as elaborated by the *'ulamā' and fuqahā'*, these judgments imply certain rules of behavior toward the adherents of these religions. We can lay bare at least the most important norms underlying Muslim judgments of other religions or religious systems. To a large extent, foreign doctrines and practices were perceived, evaluated, and judged in terms of the internal discussions taking place within the Muslim community and in particular among the *mutakallimūn*. Certain religions were thought to correspond to certain sects in Islam. In the nineteenth and twentieth century, non-religious ideological and political systems were also discussed and largely refuted by Muslim authors. This falls, however, outside the scope of this chapter.

3. Particular and Universal Norms

It is important to make a clear distinction between two kinds of norms that are recognized by Muslims. First, there are those norms and values that are considered to be valid only within the Muslim community or within a given Muslim society, even if a Muslim may hope that all humankind will turn to Islam one day. Then there are those norms and values that, in the Islamic religious view, have been proclaimed explicitly to all humankind and are considered valid for each human being. The former, more particular ones were developed largely once the community had come into existence; they address the Muslim community and tend to have a specific and particular nature. The latter, more universal ones were part of Muhammad's preaching to the Meccan and other 'non-Muslim' Arabs of the Jāhilīya, they are of a much more general nature. The universal notions of Muhammad's preaching to the 'non-Muslims' as they can be found in the Qur'ān, should be studied as having been considered valid at the time they were proclaimed, independently of the ways in which Islam developed later as a historical religion.

In the course of time, historical Islam further developed specific doctrines, norms, and values that members of the Muslim community are
expected to adhere to. They superimposed themselves on the universal
norms of the order of creation, primordial religion, and revelation, valid
for all humankind. Most Islamic views and norms on other religions were
formulated and elaborated after the Hijra and up to the tenth century
C.E. They had important consequences as long as circumstances allowed
at least a partial application within Muslim territory. As long as the
balance of power in Muslim relations with the outside world favored the
Muslim side, the Islamic rules could be applied in Muslim territory, at
least in principle. People identified themselves with religious communities
considered largely autonomous social units.

In modern times the more universal norms mostly contained in the
Meccan parts of the Qur'ān and supposed to be valid for all humankind
have been increasingly stressed, for instance in debates on human rights.
However, for a long time the more specific and particularistic Islamic
norms, mostly bound to tradition-oriented societies, have been dominant.
The question is legitimate whether those norms that are of a typically
Islamic nature will be stressed again in the current trend toward Islamic
revitalization or whether they may tend to recede with increasing international, intercultural, and inter-religious communication. In stress-situ-
ations, when a Muslim community is or feels threatened, the particularist
norms regain their importance in comparison with the more universal
ones. Islamists, moreover, will call to implement as much as possible the
specifically Islamic prescriptions in Muslim societies.

4. Historical Meetings with other Religions: Social and Political Factors

It is useful to distinguish several phases of the encounters of Islam with
a great number of other religions in the course of history.

1) Muhammad himself grew up within the Jāhilīya religious institutions
of Mecca. In and outside the town he must have met Christians and Jews,
Zoroastrians and perhaps also Manicheans, and there he must have heard
of the Sabians. After the Hijra in 622 C.E., he had further dealings with
the Jews in Yathrib and also elsewhere, with Christians of various backgrounds, lifestyles, and persuasions, and with many Arab tribes who had
their own Jāhilīya customs. He probably also met representatives of
Zoroastrian, Sabean, and perhaps other religious communities living in
Arabia.

2) During their first conquests outside Arabia in the seventh and eighth
centuries C.E., Muslims encountered a number of religious communities:

a) Zoroastrians in Mesopotamia, Iran, and Transoxania;

b) Christians of various persuasion: Nestorians in Mesopotamia, Iran, and Central Asia; Monophysites in greater Syria, Egypt, and Armenia, but also further eastward; Orthodox Melkite Byzantine Christians in greater Syria; Orthodox Latins in North Africa; Arians in Spain and dispersed elsewhere;

c) Jews in Mesopotamia and Iran, greater Syria, Egypt, North Africa, and Spain;

d) Samaritans in Palestine;

e) Mandeans in south Mesopotamia (calling themselves Sabians);

f) Harrānians in northern Mesopotamia (calling themselves Sabians);

g) Manicheans in Mesopotamia, Egypt, Iran, and Central Asia;

h) Buddhists in Sind and Central Asia;

i) Hindus in Sind;

j) Other smaller religious communities in eastern Africa and spread throughout the Middle East and North Africa.

3) Between the ninth and thirteenth centuries C.E armed confrontations often brought Muslims in longer contact with:

a) Orthodox Melkite Byzantine Christians in Anatolia and on Mediterranean islands;

b) Latin Christians in Spain, southern France, southern Italy with Sicily, and on Mediterranean islands;

c) Latin Crusaders in greater Syria;

d) Monophysite Armenians living between the Muslim and Byzantine empires;

e) Slavs in southeastern Russia;

f) Turkic tribes, who were at first non-Muslims in central Asia before their conversion and arrival in Muslim territory;

g) Buddhists in Sind, the Panjab, and Central Asia;

h) Hindus in the Panjab;

i) Other smaller religious communities in East and West Africa and spread through the Middle East and North Africa.

During this period there were peaceful relations with the recognized non-Muslim minorities (Christians, Jews, Zoroastrians, Harrānians) living within Muslim territory. There were also peaceful contacts where Muslim traders established themselves: on the west coast of India with the Hindus, in Burma with Buddhists, in China with adherents of Chinese religions, etc.

4) Between the thirteenth and the sixteenth centuries, the peaceful encounters increased between Muslims (traders and especially Sūfīs) and adherents of local beliefs in India, Burma, Malaysia, Sumatra, Java, and China, leading to an expansion of Islam in these regions. There were armed confrontations with the Mongol invaders, which led to an encounter with

their religion and to further contacts of Muslims with Nestorians and Buddhists in Central Asia. There was the confrontation with the Turkic invaders under Timurlan. The increasing conquest of North India brought about further contacts with Hindus, while the further extension of Muslim territories in East and West Africa led to further meetings with African religions. The Ottoman conquest of the Balkans brought further encounters with Orthodox Christianity. When the Byzantine Empire collapsed in 1453 and when Spain was conquered by the Christians in 1492, relations with Latin Christianity took new forms.

5) From the sixteenth to the nineteenth century there was a heightened confrontation between the Muslim world and the Latin Catholic, Anglican, and Protestant (Lutheran, Reformed) West. The latter now started dominating the sea routes and implanting commercial posts, mostly peacefully, in Muslim territories along the sea route to Southeast Asia and China. The Ottoman Empire dominated the Balkans with its mostly Orthodox Christian population and the Arab world with important Christian minorities. The Moghul Empire dominated the greater part of India and entailed Muslim interactions with the majority Hindu population. The expansion of Islam into Africa, Malaysia, Indonesia, and Central Asia proceeded with numerous encounters with the religions in those regions.

6) The nineteenth until the mid-twentieth century was another period of confrontation, now mostly political, between Muslim states and the quickly expanding West, heir to Christian tradition. Christian missionaries started to work in Muslim territories. In this time we witness the growth of Islamic polemics, at first linked with the national movements, against religions like Christianity, Hinduism, and Judaism and against non-religious ideologies that began to dominate the world scene. Since World War Two, there have been at least two major armed conflict areas where Islam played a role, if not as a religion then as an ideological instrument of political action, that between Pakistan and India and that between the Arab countries and the state of Israel.

Whatever may have been the different attitudes taken by different people in different situations, it is fair to say that throughout the nineteenth and twentieth centuries there have been situations of tension and conflict between certain parts of the Muslim world and certain nations of Europe, much more than with any other non-Muslim region except Israel. The judgments made by Muslims about Christianity cannot be considered separately from these political and military confrontations, and the same holds true for Muslim judgments about Judaism and Hinduism during the second half of the twentieth century.

One of the most important elements in the historical encounters of Muslims with people of other religions has been *power* of various kinds:

military, political, economic, demographic, and legal. Islamic law, for instance, as long as its rules on *dhimmīs* were applied, implied that within a territory governed by Muslims the power of non-Muslims remained restricted to their own religious communities. It is significant that when various Muslim factions struggled for power, alignments with non-Muslims within Muslim territory hardly ever took place, with the exception of certain alliances at the time of the Crusades. When Jews or Christians, because of their personal or professional qualities, took part in the conduct of the state or could improve their economic position considerably, voices were quickly raised calling for humiliation. Religious minority groups regarded their exclusion from the exercise of power easily as religious discrimination. A number of other factors have also played an important role in the relations between Muslims and others. In the relations with the outside world, wars, in particular with Christian states, were a means of measuring power and a way of increasing it. With the expansion of Europe, the role of the Muslims in these wars became increasingly defensive.

An important social factor molding Muslim attitudes toward other people in specific situations has always been the example or opinion of the religious leaders and the ruler. As experts in religious law and as charismatic individuals, *'ulamā'* and Sūfī *sheykhs* especially have had great influence on the mostly illiterate faithful by letting them know the religiously prescribed or recommended attitude toward *kuffār* (infidels) in general and specific groups of non-Muslims in particular. The personal stance of the ruler and the attitude of the ruling group on this issue have been especially important, since in the absence of a clergy or Church organization, the will of the political ruler tended to be decisive in determining popular attitudes or curbing extreme positions. Popular exactions of non-Muslims sometimes served the rulers' interests.

In recent times, modern *education* has proved to be increasingly important for the development of more tolerant attitudes among people. Even providing a small amount of good information about the faith of other people opens things up and may then encourage the further step of acquiring some basic knowledge about their religion. With such knowledge, new attitudes can replace traditional ones and an established religious legitimation of a social prejudice can be revised, at least in principle. The number of stereotypes about non-Muslims, and vice versa, is still enormous.

The very fact of constituting a majority or not has important consequences for the attitudes Muslims take toward non-Muslim minorities living in the country. Discrimination may take place without the majority group being fully conscious of it or able to regret it. Muslims in a minority position obviously develop different attitudes toward non-Muslims than those who are a majority.[4] In most cases, their first care is to preserve their identity as Muslims, that is to say their particular religion, culture, and way of life. Like other minorities, they will often avoid attracting attention and disturbing the non-Muslim majority unless they feel that their religion is at stake.

Many factors work independently of any specific religious adherence. An important geographical factor has always been the opposition between nomads and sedentary people and that between townspeople and people in the countryside. Important at present is the ability to migrate. Political factors can divide people with different religious adherence on concrete political and economic issues, but the religious difference may very well be used politically to reinforce the division. An important factor is the social stratification when certain classes or professions have a high percentage of adherents of a particular religion. Sociologically speaking, social or economic tensions may reinforce religious ones and vice versa. In the cultural field, people of different religious adherence may cooperate as well as be divided. Coming from different religious traditions, they may stress their own particular identity as distinct from others. This does not exclude cooperation with others, however. It may be an incentive to cooperate with others.

The most important factor, however, remains the *kind of Islam* that predominates in a given Muslim community, how the latter has been Islamized, and whether or not such a community feels threatened—with or without reason—by another religious group or community. An Islamist movement, party, or majority may be zealous to Islamize a country in direct or indirect ways. Normally this leads to tensions and conflicts with non-Muslim communities that want to retain their faith, identity, and dignity.

5. Variations of Judgments in History[5]

5.1. Buddhism

It has become clear from relatively recent studies[6] that only a few authors in medieval Islam knew about Buddhist doctrines, and then only in bits

---

[4] There is need for studies in depth on attitudes Muslims living temporarily or permanently in Europe and North America take toward various subjects. In a country like the Netherlands, Islam is now the second religion but little research on Muslim views and attitudes has been carried out.

[5] For bibliographical data, see for instance MONNOT, "Les écrits musulmans sur les religions non-bibliques" et ses "Addenda et corrigenda". See also STEINSCHNEIDER, *Polemische und apologetische Literatur in arabischer Sprache*. For the Muslim-Christian writings, see the "Bibliographie du dialogue islamo-chrétien", *Islamochristiana*, 1 (1975), pp. 125–76; 2 (1976), pp. 187–249; 3 (1977), pp. 255–86; 4 (1978), pp. 247–67; etc.

[6] Daniel GIMARET, "Bouddha et les Bouddhistes dans la tradition musulmane", *Journal Asiatique*, 257, Nrs. 3–4 (1969), pp. 273–316. Cf. LAWRENCE, *Shahrastānī on the Indian Religions*, pp. 100–14.

and pieces. Buddhism as such has on the whole remained outside the horizon of Islam, since there were only a few direct contacts. Ibn al-Nadīm in his *Fihrist* (written in 377/987) deals with the person of the Buddha and some of his teachings.[7] Al-Shahrastānī (d. 1153/548) knows of a distinction between the Buddha (*al-Budd*), whom he compares with the figure of Eliyah/*al-Khidr*, and a Bodhisattva (*Būdhāsf*). He notes the appearance of the Buddhists (*ashāb al-bidada*) in India and pays attention to their appearance in India and their ethical doctrines.[8] Al-ʿĪrānshahrī (end ninth/third century) must have given details of Buddhist cosmology that have been lost but some of which were used by al-Bīrūnī[9] (d. after 1050/442). The author of the *Kitāb al-bad' wa-'l-ta'rīkh* (written around 966/355) deals with the Buddhist doctrine of transmigration.[10] It is only Kamāla Shrī's account of Buddhism, which forms part of the end of the *Jāmiʿ al-tawārīkh* or World History of Rashīd al-Dīn (d. 1318/718), that presents an overall view, and this was written by a Buddhist and shows many legendary features.[11] It is striking that al-Bīrūnī does not pay much attention to Buddhism in his extensive description of Indian religion and philosophy.

Ibn al-Nadīm calls *Būdhāsf* the prophet of the *Sumaniyya*, a word derived from the Sanskrit *śramana* meaning "Buddhist monks".[12] These *Sumaniyya* are described by Muslim authors as the religious people who had lived in the East before the coming of the "revealed" prophetical religions, that is to say in ancient Iran before Zarathustra's appearance, as well as in ancient India and China. As a parallel to this, the Chaldeans—from whom the Harrānians would be the last descendants—are described as the religious people who lived in West Asia before the coming of the revealed religions there. This is for instance reported by al-Khwārizmī (d. 997/387) and al-Bīrūnī. In other words, the *Sumaniyyūn* and the *Khaldāniyyūn* were held to have been the ancient idolaters in the East and

[7]   *Fihrist*, ch. 9, sec. 2 (ed. and trans. by Bayard DODGE, 2 Vols., New York: Columbia University Press, 1970, pp. 831–2).

[8]   *Kitāb al-milal wa-n-nihal*, ed. William CURETON (2 Vols. in 1, London: Printed for the Society for the Publication of Oriental Texts, 1842–6), and ed. by Muhammad Abu-'l-Fadl BADRĀN (Cairo: Matbaʿat al-Azhar, 1947/1366).

[9]   *Tahqīq mā li-l-Hind min maqūla maqbūla fī al-ʿaql aw mardhūla*, ed. in the Arabic original by Edward C. SACHAU, London: Trübner, 1887 (repr. Frankfurt on Main: Institute for the History of Arabic-Islamic Science at the Johann Wolfgang Goethe University, 1993), pp. 4 and 166.

[10] *Kitāb al-bad' wa-al-ta'rīkh* (Le livre de la création et de l'histoire d'Abou-Zeïd Ahmed ben Sahl el-Balkhī), ed. and trans. by Clément HUART, 6 Vols., Paris: Leroux, 1899–1919, Vol. I, pp. 187–8.

[11] Karl JAHN, "Kāmalashrī-Rashīd al-Dīn's 'Life and Teaching of Buddha': A Source for the Buddhism of the Mongol Period", in his *Rashīd al-Dīn's History of India*, pp. xxi-lxxvii, with Facsimile Mss.

[12] On the Sumaniyya, see GIMARET's article (see above note 6), pp. 288–306.

the West respectively before the appearance of the prophets. Buddhism, as *Sumaniyya*, was considered to have been the ancient idolatrous religion of the 'eastern' people. How did medieval Muslim authors represent these *Sumaniyya*?

The main doctrines of the *Sumaniyya* as reported in medieval Islam were the worship of idols, the belief in the eternity of the world, a particular cosmology (implying, for instance, that the earth is falling into a void and that the world periodically goes under and is reborn), and the doctrine of transmigration of souls (*tanāsukh al-arwāh*). Most interesting in this connection, however, was the idea that the *Sumaniyya* were skeptics who denied the validity of reasoning (*nazar*) and logical inference (*istidlāl*).Since the real Buddhists, as is well known, did not reject reasoning at all, we have here an example of a basic mechanism we meet in other cases too. In *kalām*, a particular theoretical position is refuted and may then be attributed to a specific group of poorly-known non-Muslims. This is done not because it was known that they held this doctrine in reality but simply in order to predicate a hypothetical heretical doctrine to a little-known group of outsiders. This implies a particular way of 'judging' non-Muslims as representing known heretical positions in historical Islam, that is to say in view of the one primordial monotheistic religion of "eternal" Islam. In this vision, there is ultimately no plurality of religions. There is one religion with its various dissident orientations, one religious community with its various dissident groups.

5.2. Hinduism

Medieval Islam was somewhat better informed about Hinduism than about Buddhism. This is clear from the often still largely imaginary way in which India is treated in travel accounts, historical works, geographical and general encyclopedic works, and works of *kalām* insofar as they have reached us.[13] The main issues discussed in connection with religion in India were the doctrine of transmigration of souls (*tanāsukh al-arwāh*), idol worship (the famous statue in Multān was a case in point), the caste system, and some peculiar doctrines and practices that struck the Muslims, such as extreme asceticism and the burning of widows and slaves at the death of the husband. Only in a few cases, however, can we speak of an appreciation of or judgment on Indian religion based on actual study.

The celebrations of the millenary of al-Bīrūnī's birth in 973/362 have drawn new attention to his work, including his famous book on India

---

[13]   For a survey of the channels through which information on India reached the medieval Muslims, see LAWRENCE, *Shahrastānī on the Indian Religions*, pp. 17–29, 267–77.

Tahqīq mā li'l-Hind min maqūla maqbūla fī 'l-'aql aw mardhūla.[14] This is an important primary source. Not only the excellent information it offers, especially in view of the time in which it was written, but also some implied judgments are of interest here. First of all, though for al-Bīrūnī Indian civilization is different from ancient Greek civilization, he thought them to be comparable and even to have been in agreement in a distant past. He believed that there is a basic 'original unity of higher civilization'[15] between them, and he opened the eyes of educated Muslims to Indian as well as Greek science and philosophy, so that both could be integrated into one intellectual world view. Second, al-Bīrūnī held that in both India and in Greece there had been and still were philosophers who, through their power of thought, had arrived at the truth of the one God, corresponding with the message that had been revealed to the prophets. Third, this kind of universal religious thought developed by Indian and Greek philosophers was only the possession of a literate elite, the *khawāss*, anywhere. In contrast to this, the illiterate masses, the *'awāmm*, both within Islam and outside, tend to give way to the innate human disposition to idolatry. Fourth, al-Bīrūnī extended his affirmation of God's universality to the point that he contended that God was not only known through prophetic revelation and abstract philosophy. Greeks and Hindus, too, knew of him as the One and sought spiritual unification (*ittihād*) with him, leading to a deeper insight of the mind.[16]

It is interesting to compare the results of the more empirical approach of al-Bīrūnī with the view and appreciation of Indian religions given by the theologian al-Shahrastānī a hundred years later. Al-Shahrastānī treats Hinduism in his *Kitāb al-milal wa'l-nihal* in the chapter on the *Ārā' al-Hind*. Its six sections deal successively with the Sabians, the *Barāhima*, the three groups of *ashāb al-ruhāniyyāt* (proponents of spiritual beings), the *'abadat al-kawākib* (star-worshippers), the *'abadat al-asnām* (idol-worshippers), and finally the Indian philosophers. Whereas al-Bīrūnī divides the Hindus into the literate and the illiterate, al-Shahrastānī grades them according to degrees of idol worship. Bruce Lawrence demonstrates con-

---

[14]   Ed. by Edward C. Sachau (see above note 9); English translation by the same (London 1888, 1910²). Important is also AL-BĪRŪNĪ's *Al-āthār al-bāqiya 'an al-qurūn al-khāliya*, dealing with other religions, too (ed. by E.C. Sachau, Leipzig 1887 [repr. 1958]; English translation by the same under the title *The Chronology of Ancient Nations*, London 1879).

[15]   Franz ROSENTHAL, "Al-Biruni between Greece and India", *Biruni Symposium* (Persian Studies Series 7), ed. by Ehsan YARSHATER (New York: Iran Center, Columbia University, 1976), p. 12.

[16]   See for these issues Bruce B. LAWRENCE, "Al-Biruni's Approach to the Comparative Study of Indian Culture", *Biruni Symposium* (see previous note), pp. 24–47, and ID., "Al-Bīrūnī and Islamic Mysticism" (mimeographed text of a paper read at the Biruni Conference held in Pakistan in 1973).

vincingly that al-Shahrastānī used the model of Sabianism to describe different forms of Hindu worship.[17] His judgment of the Hindus is differentiated in the same way as his judgment of the Sabians. There are gradations in idolatry. The Vaiṣṇavas and Shaivas are like the Sabian *ashāb al-rūhāniyyāt*: they venerate Viṣṇu and Śiva as spiritual beings or mediators who were incarnated and brought laws albeit without a scripture. Consequently, they cannot be called idolaters in the real sense of the word. Those adoring Āditya and Chandra (sun and moon considered as deities) are star worshippers (*'abadat al-kawākib*) which is a grade lower but still not idolatry. Only those who adore and prostrate themselves before idols they made themselves are real idolaters (*'abadat al-asnām*) of the lowest rank, comparable with the Arabs of the Jāhilīya.

Sabianism, for al-Shahrastānī, serves as a kind of model to describe a sort of religion that is situated between monotheism and polytheism. In the same way, dualism and Christianity can serve as models to describe particular types of religion. In his view, there have been varieties of Sabianism: the ancient Sabians, the Greek Sabians, the Indian Sabians, and the later Sabians in Harrān. Al-Shahrastānī considers the Sabians as followers of the ancient 'prophet' Hermes ('Ādhīmūn), a Hellenistic figure later identified with the Qur'anic Idrīs (Enoch). These Sabians had abandoned the true prophetic teaching of Idrīs and constituted a particular kind of deviation from true monotheism. This deviation was comparable with but distinct from the deviations of the Zoroastrians, Jews, and Christians from the monotheism preached by Zarathustra, Moses, and Jesus respectively. The Qur'ān mentions the Sabians (S. 2:59; 5:73; 22:17) indeed in a positive sense beside Christians, Jews, and Zoroastrians. Bruce Lawrence submits that al-Shahrastānī tried to rehabilitate a great deal of Hindu religiosity by presenting it as forms of Sabianism considered to be more or less lawful.

Whereas the *Sumaniyya* were described in *kalām* as thinkers rejecting reason and in fact as agnostics (*mu 'attila*), the *Barāhima* were described as thinkers accepting reason and believing in one God (*muwahhida*) but rejecting prophecy.[18] This too was a philosophical position unacceptable in Islam and projected upon a particular group of non-Muslims, the *Barāhima*. Again, no inquiry was made about the doctrines really held by that group, whose name recalls the Brahmins. Categories like *Sumaniyya*, *Barāhima*, and *Sābi'a* are technical terms designed within *kalām* as names for positions rejected by *kalām*. They do not give information about what the "real" Buddhists, Brahmins, and Sabians thought. They are just theological predicates to which the reality of the religions concerned is simply subordinated.

---

[17]   LAWRENCE, *Shahrastānī on the Indian Religions*. Cf. ID., "Sharastānī on Indian Idol Worship", *Studia Islamica*, 37 (1973), pp. 61–73.

[18]   On the Barāhima, see LAWRENCE, *Shahrastānī on the Indian Religions*, pp. 75–100.

The ideas on Indian religion held by al-Bīrūnī and al-Shahrastānī can be supplemented by elements of Rashīd al-Dīn's view of India.[19] They show flexibility in Muslim interpretations of Hinduism and a disinclination to reject the whole religion outright.

This conclusion is supplemented in two publications by Yohanan Friedmann. First, he shows that the Hanafī and Mālikī schools of law were willing to include Hindus within the category of *ahl al-dhimma*.[20] Even when they went on worshipping their gods side by side with the monotheistic Muslims, they could enjoy the latter's protection on condition that they paid *jizya*. In other words, Hindus were not considered categorically as *mushrikūn* (polytheists) strictly speaking, and they were not treated according to the *Sharīʿa's* prescriptions for the *mushrikūn*: conversion, departure, or death.

Second, Friedmann describes six Muslim thinkers other than al-Bīrūnī, al-Shahrastānī, and Rashīd al-Dīn, whose views on Hindu religion were not simply negative either.[21] Al-Gardīzī (d. ca. 1060/452) describes two of the four basic divisions of Hindu religion in monotheistic terms. The *Kitāb al-badʾ waʾl-taʾrīkh* (written ca. 966/355) suggests that the monotheistic *Barāhima* revere Allāh who sent an angel to them in human form. Amīr Khusraw Dihlawī (1253–1325/651–727) holds that the Hindus are better than the dualists and the Christians.

Two later figures are even more remarkable. The first is the prince Dārā Shukōh (1615–59/1024–69). He looks for a rapprochement between Hinduism and Islam. He holds that all scriptures of humankind, including the Vedas, stem from one and the same source and that they constitute a sort of commentary on each other. He even contends that the advent of Islam did not abrogate the religious truth contained in the Vedas or supersede the religious achievements of the Hindus. The Sūfī Jān-i-Janān (d. 1781/1195) makes a distinction between those Hindus who lived prior to Muhammad's mission with a religion that pleased God and those Hindus who lived later and who are mistaken by not converting to Islam once it is preached to them. The special position of the emperor Akbar (1542–1605/949–1014), with his positive appreciation of Hinduism and other religions outside Islam, and the *dīn ilāhī* which he advocated have been subject of various studies.[22]

All of this shows that there has been a wide range of Muslim perceptions, appreciations, and judgments of Hinduism. Examples from the nineteenth and twentieth centuries could easily be added.

---

[19]   Facsimile in K. JAHN, *Rashīd al-Dīn's History of India*.
[20]   Yohanan FRIEDMANN, "The Temple of Multān: A Note on Early Muslim Attitudes to Idolatry", *Israel Oriental Studies*, 2 (1972), pp. 176–82.
[21]   FRIEDMANN, "Medieval Muslim Views of Indian Religions".
[22]   See above Chapter 4 on "Cases of Interreligious Dialogue under Muslim Rule" under section 2.

5.3. Judaism[23]

As Moshe Perlmann observed some sixty years ago[24], although there was bitter Muslim-Jewish strife in the early Medinan stage of Islam, of which the Qur'ān bears evidence, classical Islam directed its polemics mainly against Christianity. Whereas the Christians had a powerful Byzantine state behind them and, in the lands conquered by Muslims, defended themselves intellectually against the new religion, the Jewish communities kept to their own communal life, did not discuss their religion with outsiders, and seldom attacked Islam. So the number of polemical treatises directed exclusively against Judaism is relatively small and not of early date.

Although critical statements and polemical utterances occur already in the Qur'ān and in the *hadīth* literature[25], proper information about Judaism as a religion and way of life was only later supplied by converts. As Perlmann observed, some of the old arguments already used in pre-Islamic times by Christians against Judaism found their way, again through converts, into Muslim circles and were then used in the Muslim-Jewish polemic. Descriptions of Judaism were given in historical works[26], in encyclopedic works like the *Kitāb al-bad' wa'l-ta'rīkh* attributed to al-Mutahhar al-Maqdisī (d. ca. 985/375), and in the *milal* literature, in particular the books of Ibn Hazm and al-Shahrastānī.

The best known polemical treatises of Muslim authors against Judaism are the following. Ibn Hazm (994–1064/384–456) wrote three such treatises[27], one of them against the Jewish *wazīr* Ismā'īl b. Yūsuf ibn al-

---

[23] M. PERLMANN, *Moslem Polemics directed against Jews* (unpubl. PhD. Thesis, London 1941, 159 pp.). Cf. ID., "The Medieval Polemics between Islam and Judaism". See also GOLDZIHER, "Ueber muhammedanische Polemik gegen Ahl al-kitāb", and SCHREINER, "Zur Geschichte der Polemik zwischen Juden und Muhammedanern".

[24] PERLMANN, *Moslem Polemics* (see previous note), ch. I 'Introduction'.

[25] WAARDENBURG, "Koranisches Religionsgespräch"; VAJDA, "Juifs et Musulmans selon le *Hadīt*".

[26] See for instance Karl JAHN, *Die Geschichte der Kinder Israels des Rashīd ad-Dīn* (see Selected Literature under Rashīd al-Dīn, *World History*).

[27] *Kitāb al-fisal fī 'l-milal wa-l-ahwā' wa-n-nihal*, five books in two Vols. (Cairo 1899–1903/1317–21). Cf. PALACIOS' succinct translation with introduction, *Abenhāzam de Córdoba y su Historia crítica de las ideas religiosas*. According to I. Friedländer (see below), 130 pages containing the polemical treatise *Izhār tabdīl al Yahūd wa-n-Nasārā li-t-tawrāt wa-l-injīl* have been inserted into the *Kitāb al-fisal* (I, 216–II, 91), adding to the treatment of the Jews in I, 98–116 that in I, 116–224.

 On Muslim polemics against Judaism up to Ibn Hazm, see ADANG, *Muslim Writers on Judaism and the Hebrew Bible*. On Ibn Hazm's polemic against Judaism, see I. FRIEDLÄNDER, "Zur Komposition von Ibn Hazm's Milal wa-n-Nihal", in *Orientalische Studien: Theodor Nöldeke zum siebzigsten Geburtstag ... gewidmet ...*, ed. by Carl BEZOLD, 2 Vols. (Gießen: A. Töpelmann, 1906), Vol. I, pp. 267–77. The third polemical treatise against Judaism is *Ar-radd 'alā Ibn-an-Naghrīla al-yahūdī*. On this polemic, see

Naghrīla (993–1056/383–448). Samaw'al al-Maghribī (ca. 1125–75/ 519–70) wrote the *Ifḥām al-Yahūd* after his conversion in 1163/558[28], Saʿīd b. Hasan al-Iskandarānī (d. 1320/720) converted from Judaism in 1298/697 and wrote a treatise against Judaism and Christianity[29]. Well-known are al-Qarāfī (d. 1285/684)[30] and Ibn Qayyim al-Jawzīya (d. 1350/751); the latter also wrote a treatise against both Judaism and Christianity[31]. In 1360/761 Abū Zakarīyā Yaḥyā ar-Rāqilī[32] wrote a tract against Judaism while living in Christian Spain. Somewhat later the con-vert ʿAbd al-Haqq al-Islāmī, who must have lived in Morocco at the end of the fourteenth/eighth century, wrote a refutation of Judaism.[33] There are, moreover, refutations of Judaism within the general *kalām* works, for instance in the *Kitāb al-tamhīd* of al-Bāqillānī, written around 980/369.[34]

Muslim authors' principal argument specifically against Judaism was the doctrine of *naskh* (abrogation), the idea that a revelation occurring later in time abrogated an earlier one, and also that a revealed religious law of a later date replaced an earlier one. In the Muslim view, God could

---

M. PERLMANN in his "Eleventh Century Andalusian Authors on the Jews of Granada", *Proceedings of the American Academy of Jewish Research*, 18 (1949), pp. 269–90. See also E. GARCÍA GÓMEZ, "Polémica religiosa entre Ibn Hazm e Ibn al-Nagrīla", *Al-Andalus*, 4 (1936), pp. 1–28. Cf. Ignaz GOLDZIHER, "Proben muhammedanischer Polemik gegen den Talmud, I: Ibn Hazm, Zeitgenosse Samuel Naghrīlā's (al-Bāramikī)", *Jeschurun*, 8 (1872), pp. 76–104 (repr. ID., *Gesammelte Schriften* ed. by Joseph DESO-MOGYI, Vol. 1, Hildesheim: G. Olms, 1967, pp. 136–64).

28 Samaw'al al-Maghribī, *Ifḥām al Yahūd* ('Silencing the Jews'), ed. and trans. Moshe PERLMANN (Proceedings of the American Academy of Jewish Research 32), New York: American Academy for Jewish Research, 1964.

29 Saʿīd b. Hasan al-Iskandarāni, *Masālik an-nazar fī nubuwwat sayyid al-bashar*, ed. and trans. with introduction and notes by Sidney Adams WESTON, *Journal of the American Oriental Society*, 24, Nr. 2 (1903), pp. 312–83. Cf. I. GOLDZIHER, "Saʿīd b. Hasan d'Alexandrie", *Revue des Études juives*, 30 (1895), pp. 1–23 (repr. ID., *Gesammelte Schriften* [see above note 27], Vol. III, pp. 397–419).

30 Ibn Idrīs al-Qarāfī as-Sanhājī, *Kitāb al-ajwiba l-fākhira ʿan al-as'ila al-fājira*, in the margin of ʿAbd-al-Rahmān BAÈEGIZĀDE, *Al-fāriq bayna 'l-makhlūq wa-l-khāliq*, Vol. I (Cairo 1904/1322), pp. 2–265.

31 Ibn Qayyim al-Jawziyya, *Kitāb hidāyat al-hayārā min al-Yahūd wa-n-Nasārā* (Cairo 1905/1323). See I. GOLDZIHER, "Proben muhammedanischer Polemik gegen den Tal-mud, II: Ibn Kajjim al-Ğauzija", *Jeschurun*, 9 (1873), pp. 18–47 (repr. ID., *Gesammelte Schriften* [see above note 27], Vol. I, pp. 229–58).

32 Abū Zakariyyā Yaḥyā al-Rāqilī, *Ta'yīd al-milla*. See M. Asín PALACIOS, "Un tratado morisco de polémica contra los judios", in *Mélanges Hartwig Derenbourg (1844–1908): Recueil de travaux d'érudition. Dédiés à la mémoire d'Hartwig Derenbourg par ses amis et ses élèves* (Paris: Leroux, 1909), pp. 343–66.

33 ʿAbd al-Haqq al-Islāmī, *Al-husām al-majrūd fī r-radd ʿalā l-Yahūd* (or alternatively: *As-sayf al-mamdūd fī r-radd ʿalā [akhbār] al-Yahūd*). See M. PERLMANN, "ʿAbd al-Hakk al-Islāmī, a Jewish Convert", *Jewish Quarterly Review*, 31, Nr. 2 (Oct. 1940), pp. 171–91.

34 Ed. by Richard J. MCCARTHY (Beirut: Librairie Orientale, 1957), pp. 122–31. See BRUNSCHVIG, "L'argumentation d'un théologien musulman du xe siècle contre le Ju-daïsme". See also below note 53.

reveal his will successively in different ways, and this implied that a series of revelations was possible. Jewish thinkers, on the other hand, held that God does not change his decree and dispensation and that it is impossible for him to change his mind. They therefore rejected *naskh*, had little interest in what happened outside their own community or in further religious history, and did not recognize the Qur'ān any more than they had the New Testament.

In response to this position, Muslims like Ibn Hazm declared it an error to think that God was not able to change his mind or that there could be only one fixed revelation given by God, the Torah. Muslim polemicists made much effort to convince the Jews of the necessity of *naskh*. They tried to demonstrate that abrogation was already present in the Torah itself, for instance where the law of Jacob had clearly been superseded by the later and different one of Moses. The discussion among scholars like Ibn Hazm, al-Juwaynī, and Fakhr al-Dīn al-Rāzī about a "revealed text" led to a debate on revelation, and this led to a further questioning about what God had intended with his revelations. This also meant a further elaboration and refinement of the doctrine of *naskh* within Islam itself, with its repercussions for the Muslim polemic against Judaism. Various positions were possible about the relationship between the Qur'ān and the earlier scriptures, between the *Sharī'a* and preceding religious laws.

Ignaz Goldziher gave the general historical framework of Muslim polemics against *ahl al-kitāb* in general and Judaism in particular in a publication of 1878.[35] He considers the Qur'ān itself the oldest document for this polemic, in which the three main themes of the polemic are already outlined. These are the accusation that the *ahl al-kitāb* changed and corrupted their scriptures (*tahrīf* 2:73; *tabdīl* 4:48, 5:16, 45, 52; *taghyīr* 3:72), the refutation of particular doctrines, and the rejection of certain of their rites and customs. It is worthwhile to recall the main points that Goldziher makes on the accusation of *tabdīl*.[36]

The Qur'ān had stated in so many words that Jews and Christians had corrupted their scriptures, and this was to remain the main accusation against the *ahl al-kitāb*. Different arguments could be used as proof of the corruption of a hypothetically perfect text imagined the original *tawrāt* and *injīl* brought by Moses and Jesus respectively. One of these arguments was that of *tajsīm* or 'anthropomorphism' in the broadest sense of the word. There were unworthy passages about patriarchs, prophets, and

---

[35] GOLDZIHER, "Ueber muhammedanische Polemik gegen Ahl al-kitāb".

[36] Cf. Ignazio DI MATTEO, "Il tahrīf od alterazione della Bibbia secondo i Musulmani", *Bessarione*, 38 (1922), pp. 64–111 and 223–60; 39 (1923), pp. 77–127. See also Hartwig HIRSCHFELD, "'Muhammedan Criticism of the Bible", *Jewish Quarterly Review*, 13 (1901), pp. 222–40.

leaders, their lineage, words, and deeds, and scandalous stories that should not occur in a sacred text and that thus indicated unworthy authorship. There were also obvious textual contradictions. There were certain 'mistakes' like the substitution of the name of Isaac for Ishmael as the son whom Abraham had to sacrifice. Moreover, certain texts that ought to figure within the scripture were lacking and it was to be assumed that these texts had been suppressed from the original and pure *tawrāt*. These texts included the tenet of the resurrection at the end of time with the following reward and punishment and the mention and recognition of prophets outside Israel. Finally, the prophecies of those biblical prophets who were not mentioned in the Qur'ān were held to be altogether super-fluous.

Muslims agreed that the Torah was apparently not identical with the pure *tawrāt* given as a revealed scripture to Moses, but there was considerable variation in opinion on the extent to which earlier scriptures like the *tawrāt* were corrupted. On the one hand, Ibn Hazm, who was the first thinker to consider the problem of *tabdīl* systematically, contended, like the later al-Qarāfī, Ibn Qayyim al-Jawzīya, and al-Tarjumān, that the text itself had been changed or forged (*taghyīr*). To support this position, he drew attention to immoral stories that had found a place within the corpus and to particular contradictions within the text itself.

On the other hand, al-Qāsim b. Ibrāhīm, al-Tabarī, Fakhr al-Dīn al-Rāzī, and Ibn Khaldūn held that the text itself had not been forged but that Jews and Christians had misinterpreted their scriptures (faulty *ta'wīl*). This was especially the case with those texts that predicted or announced the mission of Muhammad and the coming of Islam, the so-called *a'lām* texts. Others again contended that certain texts, in particular the *a'lām* texts, to whose existence the Qur'ān already made reference but which were not easy to find, had apparently been omitted by the Jews and Christians, but that they had added or forged nothing of the original pure text. It depended then very much on a Muslim scholar's particular inter-pretation of the meaning of *tabdīl* whether he would show more or less respect for the Bible, and whether and how he would quote from it. But there could also be contradictions. Ibn Hazm, for instance, rejects nearly the whole Hebrew Bible as a forgery but cheerfully quotes the *tawrāt* when bad reports are given of the faith and behavior of the *Banū Isrā'īl* as proofs against the Jews and their religion.

Another argument of Muslim polemicists, connected with that on forgery of the text, was the proof of Muhammad's prophethood. The Qur'ān had stated that the mission of Muhammad and the coming of Islam had been announced in the earlier scriptures. When such announcement (*a'lām*) texts could not easily be found, Jews and Christians were accused of hiding them. A number of Muslim polemicists now read through the Bible looking for them. They interpreted certain texts in often ingenious ways in what may be called a 'Muhammadan' Bible exegesis. There were variations in the number of Bible passages considered a 'lām texts, and not everyone agreed that Jews and Christians had actually omitted a 'lām texts from their scriptures. Goldziher's article treats the fifty-one Bible passages that al-Qarāfī refers to as a 'lām texts announcing the mission of Muhammad and the coming of Islam.

Closely connected with the accusation of *tahrīf* or *tabdīl* of the text of the scriptures is the reproach that the historical transmission (*tawātur*) of the text of the *tawrāt* had not been reliable through the course of time. As a consequence, *tahrīf* (change of the original text) could have occurred since the life of Moses. In opposition to the claims of the Jews, the Muslims held that the transmission of the Judaic tradition had been no more reliable than that of other spurious traditions. There were no lists (*isnāds*) of transmitters of the texts. Some authors, for instance, used Biblical stories about the untrustworthiness, lack of faith, and changeability of the Israelites as polemical arguments. Such stories not only prove that the Israelites could not be God's chosen people and children, but they also give plausibility to the view that the Israelites were not able to faithfully transmit the *tawrāt* given by Moses. Muslim polemicists held Ezra in particular responsible for having made impermissible innovations.

The issue of *tawātur* has been an important one in Muslim polemics. Good *tawātur* not only guarantees the authenticity of an ancient text, but can also serve as a guarantee and proof for miracles witnessed by people who subsequently testify to them. This issue as well as that of *tahrīf* and of a 'lām texts were also important in the Muslim polemic against Christianity.

Other arguments too could be used in the Muslim-Judaic polemic. For instance, Samaw'al al-Maghribī, a Jew converted to Islam, uses the nearly Christian argument that the Talmud makes life a burden impossible to bear. He also uses the fundamental difference between Rabbinites and Karaites within Judaism as an argument to show its weakness.[37]

Some authors cited the dispersion and the humiliation (*dhull*) of the Jews to prove the truth of Islam, to which God had given victories on earth. This could provide an opening for conversions to Islam.

Other arguments concerned Jewish rites and customs.

---

[37] See above note 28. A later Maghribī polemic by al-Maghīlī (d. between 1503 and 1505/ 909 or 910) was analyzed by G. VAJDA, "Un traité maghrébin 'Adversus Judaeos': 'Aḥkām ahl al-dimma' du shaykh Muhammad b. 'Abd al-Karīm al-Maghīlī", in *Études d'Orientalisme dédiées à la mémoire de Lévi-Provençal* (Paris: Maisonneuve et Larose, 1962), Vol. II, pp. 805–13.

It is interesting to see how in these polemics between representatives of Islam and Judaism a certain common understanding developed about what should be considered as valid scriptural and rational arguments and proofs. Such proofs had to be based on scriptural revelation, prophethood, miracles, and sound historical transmission, because these were considered the constitutive elements of a valid religious tradition. Each author could stress one or more elements in particular.

As a general rule, influenced as they were by what they typically expected from divine revelation, sacred scripture, and prophethood, Muslims had great reservations about the analogous claims, scriptures, and prophetical qualities upheld in Judaism. Their expectations were in fact derived from their own kind of belief in scripture and their own view of Muhammad's preaching and work. Muslim reservations were reinforced by the fact that the Jewish community did not recognize Muhammad as a prophet or the Qur'ān as revelation and that it rejected abrogation (*naskh*).

5.4. Christianity[38]

5.4.1. Historical Development of Muslim Polemics: There is an abundant polemical literature in Islam against Christianity and many of the existing texts have not yet been edited. The Qur'ān contains some statements from the Meccan period against polytheism that may have been addressed against Christians as well. After more favorable judgments about Christians given in the Qur'ān earlier in the Medinan period, a wave of polemic starts at the end of that period. At that time, Muhammad was confronted with Christian Arab tribes opposing his expansion to the North.

---

[38] See besides STEINSCHNEIDER and *Islamochristiana* (mentioned above in note 5) also Ali BOUAMAMA, *La littérature polémique musulmane contre le Christianisme, depuis les origines jusqu'au XIIIe siècle* (Thèse de doctorat d'Etat, Université des Sciences humaines de Strasbourg, 1976 [492pp.]); Erdmann FRITSCH, *Islam und Christentum im Mittelalter: Beiträge zur Geschichte der muslimischen Polemik gegen das Christentum in arabischer Sprache* (Breslau: Müller & Seiffert, 1930); I. DI MATTEO, *La divinità di Cristo e la dottrina della Trinità in Maometto e nei polemisti musulmani* (Rome: Pontificium Institutum Biblicum, 1938). Important are bibliographies on "Muslim-Christian dialogue", e.g. Georges C. ANAWATI, "Bibliographie islamo-arabe ... Dialogue islamo-chrétien", *Mélanges de l'Institut Dominicain d'Études Orientales du Caire*, 9 (1967), pp. 200–2; ID., "Polémique, apologie et dialogue islamo-chrétien: Positions classiques et positions contemporaines", *Euntes Docete: Commentaria Urbaniana* (Rome: Pontificia Universitas Urbaniana), 22 (1969), pp. 375–452; ID., "Vers un dialogue islamo-chrétien", *Revue Thomiste*, 64 (1974), pp. 280–306, 585–650. Robert CASPAR, "Le dialogue islamo-chrétien: Bibliographie", *Parole et Mission*, 33 (1966), pp. 313–22; 34 (1966), pp. 475–81; ID. and J. DEJEUX, "Bibliographie sur le dialogue islamo-chrétien", *Proche-Orient Chrétien*, 16 (1966), pp. 174–82. See also J. WAARDENBURG, "Selected Bibliography", in *Muslim-Christian Perceptions of Dialogue Today: Experiences and Expectations*, ed. by Jacques WAARDENBURG, Leuven, etc.: Peeters, 2000, pp. 305–23.

The main Qur'anic accusations against the Christians are that they attribute a son to God, that they envisage a trinity, that they believe that Jesus was crucified, that their Scripture is corrupted, and that they venerate priests and other people besides God. In short, they commit *shirk* and are to be considered *kuffār*, unbelievers or infidels.[39]

A first real confrontation with articulate Orthodox Christians who were theologically schooled took place in Damascus in the time of the Umayyad dynasty.[40] The initiative here was apparently taken by the Christians who, partly spurred on by a superior culture and partly out of self-defense, posed questions to the Muslims. They were newcomers who had to open up their resources in order to respond. Their answer concerned primarily ideas about the word of God, the nature of prophecy and revelation, the unity and uniqueness of God, the destiny of humankind, the Day of Judgment, and salvation. These issues constituted some of the roots of the rise and further development of *kalām*. In the beginning of these debates, the Christians with their theological reasoning were in a superior position.

In the first half of the ninth century, this situation changed. Thanks to the translations of Greek philosophical texts and assimilation of Aristotelian logic, rhetoric, and metaphysics and in particular the intellectual efforts of the Muʿtazila, Muslim theologians began to confront Christian theologians as equals. Both parties often dealt with structurally parallel or even identical theological problems. The strength of Muslim thought in the middle of the ninth century C.E is clear in, for instance, Abū ʿĪsā al-Warrāq's refutation of Christian doctrines.[41] The Muslim-Christian polemic was then carried out mainly with philosophical-dialectical arguments and in particular by Muʿtazilite *mutakallimūn* whose writings, unfortunately, have nearly all been lost. There was a close connection between the intra-Muslim polemic and the polemic against outsiders such as Dualists and Jews. The Christians were often compared with particular heretics like Murji'ites, Zindīqs, and Rāfidites, just as these groups could be attacked for having 'Christianizing' tendencies.

---

[39] On the Qur'anic views and judgments of Christians, see McAuliffe, *Qur'ānic Christians*. Cf. W. Montgomery Watt, "The Christianity criticized in the Qur'ān", *The Muslim World*, 57, Nr. 3 (1967), pp. 197–201. Cf. Waardenburg, "Koranisches Religionsgespräch".

[40] For the historical background of the medieval Muslim polemics against Christianity, see Chapter 5 on "Two Shining Lights: Medieval Islam and Christianity". Cf. the first version under the title "Two Lights Perceived: Medieval Islam and Christianity" in *Nederlands Theologisch Tijdschrift*, 31, Nr. 4 (October 1977), pp. 267–89.

[41] David Thomas, *Anti-Christian Polemic in Early Islam: Abū ʿĪsā al-Warrāq's 'Against the Trinity'*, New York and Cambridge: Cambridge University Press, 1992.

The Mu'tazilites themselves, however, who led this intellectual combat for Islam, were in an ambivalent position. Having assimilated the Greek art of reasoning, they could successfully combat the Christians and refute with Aristotelian logic their doctrines of the trinitarian divine substance and the divine nature of Jesus. They had to pay their own price, however, for having arrived at the formulation of doctrines that practically denied the eternal attributes of God and the eternal character or uncreatedness of the Qur'ān. Such doctrines were not accepted in the Muslim community. Like the philosophers, the Mu'tazilite theologians were more and more threatened by the rising Ash'arite school of *kalām*, which respected "irrational" sides of the Islamic faith.

From the middle of the ninth century on, Muslim polemics against Christianity combined the use of logical arguments in the Greek philosophical tradition and a more frequent use of scriptural arguments based on the Old and New Testaments. This presupposed a better knowledge of the Bible, thanks to translations and information passed on by converts.[42] In the debate with the Christians about scripture, the question of *naskh* arose as in the polemic with the Jews. The Christians, however, took a more lenient attitude on this issue, since they themselves believed in the 'abrogation' of the Old Covenant by the New one.

The principal point of attack against Christianity with regard to scripture, consequently, is not *naskh* as in the case of Judaism but rather the accusation of *tahrīf*, corruption of the text both of the Old and of the New Testament.[43] Various positions could be held with regard to the New Testament, each with its own consequences for the arguments used against the Christians.

Closely connected with the *tahrīf* argument for the Qur'ān and against the Bible are the arguments derived from the doctrine of prophecy and prophethood. Just as the Qur'ān had been declared the uncreated Word of God by the mid-ninth century C.E., so Muhammad's status as the prophet proclaiming definite truth now became fixed. The argument of a wrong *tawātur* of an original pure *injīl* given by Jesus was reinforced by contradictions between the gospels, which Muslim polemicists were glad to demonstrate. The four issues of *naskh* (abrogation), *tahrīf* (corruption of text), *nubūwa* (prophecy), and *tawātur* (transmission) were the basis of

---

[42]   For instance, 'Alī al-Tabarī, a convert from Christianity (d. 855 C.E.), cites a great number of Biblical passages in which the mission of Muhammad and the coming of Islam were allegedly announced. The text of his *Ar-radd 'alā 'l-nasārā* was edited by Ignace-Abdo KHALIFÉ and W. KUTSCH in *Mélanges de l'Université Saint-Joseph*, 36, Nr. 4 (1959), pp. 115–48. The text of his *Kitāb ad-dīn wa-d-dawla* was edited by Alphonse MINGANA (Manchester: Manchester University Press, 1923; Cairo: Muqtataf, 1342 H.).

[43]   See above note 36. What has been said of *tahrīf* (*tabdīl*) of Jewish scriptures holds equally true for Christian scriptures.

the polemics of the *mutakallimūn* against Christianity, as they had been against Judaism. But here too, there were considerable variations in interpretation.

The Muslim polemics against Christianity, however, went beyond the typical *kalām* works and struck other cords too. The Qur'ān *tafsīrs* of the ninth and tenth centuries C.E. show increasingly polemical tendencies against Christianity. They can now quote texts from the New Testament and other Christian sources in support of certain views of the Qur'ān and its commentator against Christianity.

Armand Abel has suggested that stories of figures like Dhū 'l-Qarnayn in the Qur'ān and stories like the *Qisas al-anbiyā'* of al-Tha'ālibī about prophets from the past who are mentioned in the Qur'ān show on closer analysis certain polemical tendencies against Christianity or the *ahl al-kitāb*. Abel proposed that more popular poetry and folk literature, like the story of 'Antar or the *Alf layla wa-layla*, should also be investigated on this issue. The Muslim controversy with Christianity has found expression in many ways.

Another important problem that demands further inquiry is whether and where the literature of religious controversy also denotes social controversies. The refutation of Christianity as a religion implied a humiliation of the Christians as a community living in Muslim territory. Al-Jāhiz did this consciously, not only refuting Christian doctrines but also describing the Christian people as a kind of social evil.[44] In such cases, controversial literature becomes a function of a more general social pressure exerted for particular reasons at particular times and places on particular non-Muslim minorities in Muslim societies. This holds true for such literature addressed not only against the Christians but also against Jews, Manicheans, Zoroastrians, and Hindus. Such questioning also gives social and political contours to the many variations that can be found in Muslim writings on other religions.

Among the polemicists against Christianity, Ibn Hazm has a place apart. He treats Christianity twice, first among the polytheists (*Fisal* I, 48–65) and then, in the probably inserted *Izhār tabdīl al Yahūd wa-n-Nasārā li-t-tawrāt wa-l-injīl* (see above note 27), among the *ahl al-kitāb* (*Fisal* II, 2–75). Just as on the Jewish Scriptures (Hebrew Bible or Old Testament, *Fisal* I, 98–224), he makes an extremely severe attack on the Christian Scriptures (New Testament, *Fisal* II, 2–75). Here he denounces the contradictions between different texts and absurdities in certain texts, which

---

[44] Al-Jāhiz, *Risāla fī r-radd 'alā n-Nasārā*, ed. by Jusa FINKEL in his *Three Essays of Abū Othmān Amr ibn Bahr al-Jāhiz* (Cairo: Salafiyya Press, 1926) and translated by him into English in *Journal of the American Oriental Society*, 47 (1927), pp. 311–34.

he lays at the door of the Evangelists in the case of the Gospels. The textual mistakes he uncovers furnish him as many arguments against the Christian doctrine of the literal inspiration of the Bible.[45]

A few decades later, however, at the end of the eleventh century C.E., the author of *Al-radd al-jamīl* (al-Ghazzālī?) follows the same track when refuting Christian doctrines. He takes the New Testament text at its face value and argues precisely on the basis of this text against the doctrine of the divine nature of Jesus.[46] There is an immense difference in organization and execution between the two refutations of Ibn Hazm and al-Ghazzālī if indeed he was the author.

Some major refutations of Christianity of the thirteenth and fourteenth centuries are more compilations of the current arguments against Christianity than original work. One example is the *Kitāb al-ajwiba 'l-fākhira*[47] by al-Qarāfī, who held that Christians are not *mushrikūn* (polytheists) but simply *kuffār* (unbelievers or infidels, that is, non-Muslims).

Ibn Taymīya (d. 1328/728), in his *Al-jawāb as-sahīh li-man baddala dīn al-masīh*[48], holds that the textual forgery of the Bible is restricted to the historical parts only. With regard to the legislative parts of the Bible, not the text but the Christian exegesis is at fault.

---

[45] An English summary of Ibn-Hazm's criticism of Old and New Testaments (*Fisal* I, 116–II, 91) is given by J. Windrow Sweetman, *Islam and Christian Theology*, Part One, Vol. II (London: Lutterworth Press, 1955), pp. 178–262. On Ibn Hazm's polemic against the New Testament, see Samuel-Martin Behloul, *Ibn Hazms Evangelienkritik: Eine methodische Untersuchung* (Islamic Philosophy, Theology, and Science 50), Leiden, etc.: E. J. Brill, 2002. See also Abdelilah Ljamai, *Ibn Hazm et la polémique islamo-chrétienne dans l'histoire de l'islam*, Diss. Tilburg, The Netherlands, 2001. See also above note 27.

[46] The complete title is *Al-radd al-jamīl li-ilāhiyyat ʿĪsā bi-sarīh al-injīl*. The text was edited, translated, and commented upon by Robert Chidiac, S.J., *Al Ghazali, Réfutation excellente de la divinité de Jésus-Christ d'après les Evangiles*, Paris: Ernest Leroux, 1938. A German translation and commentary was given by Franz-Elmar Wilms, *Al Ghazālīs Schrift wider die Gottheit Jesu*, Leiden: E. J. Brill, 1966. On the authorship, see also Hava Lazarus-Yafeh, "Etude sur la polémique islamo-chrétienne: Qui était l'auteur de al-Radd al-jamīl li-Ilāhiyyat ʿĪsā bi-sarīh al-Injīl attribué à al-Ghazzali", *Revue des Etudes Islamiques*, 37, Nr. 2 (1969), pp. 219–38. Cf. also the summary given by Sweetman in the study cited in the previous note, on pp. 262ff.

[47] See above note 30.

[48] Edition in four Vols. (Cairo 1905/1322). Ibn Taymīya is also the author of *As-sārim al-maslūl ʿalā shātim ar-rasūl* (Hyderabad 1905/1322) and of *Ar-risāla al-qubrūsiyya* (Cairo 1919). On his "Letter to Cyprus", see Thomas Raff, *Das Sendschreiben nach Zypern, Ar-risāla al-qubrusīya, von Taqī ad-Dīn Ahmad Ibn Taimīya (661–728 A.H./ 1263–1328 A.D.): Edition, Übersetzung und Kommentar*, Diss. Bonn, 1971. Ibn Taymīya's *Takhjīl ahl al-injīl* is still in manuscript (Ms. Bodl. II 45, according to Fritsch, *Islam und Christentum im Mittelalter* [see above note 38], p. 25). See Thomas F. Michel, *Ibn Taimiyya: A Muslim Theologian's Response to Christianity*, Delmar, N. Y.: Caravan Books, 1984.

The latter two authors, together with the more Sūfī-minded Muhammad Ibn Abī Tālib (d. 1327/727)[49], were responding to a polemical treatise directed by Paul al-Rāhib (Paul of Antioch, twelfth century) against Islam.[50]

Most of the existing polemical arguments are assembled in the refutations given by al-Qarāfī and Ibn Taymīya, so that one can find here nearly all the components of the previous polemics.

As mentioned earlier, in the section on "Judaism", Saʿīd b. Hasan al-Iskandarānī and Ibn Qayyim al-Jawzīya wrote combined refutations of Judaism and Christianity.[51] An important refutation of Christianity was the *Tuhfa*[52] written in 1420 C.E. by the converted Franciscan ʿAbdallāh al-Tarjumān in Tunisia.

There are, moreover, refutations of Christianity within the general works of *kalām*, for instance in the *Kitāb al-tamhīd* of al-Bāqillānī, written around 980 C.E.[53], and in volume 5 of the massive *Mughnī* of the Muʿtazilite theologian ʿAbd al-Jabbār (d. 1025/415).

5.4.2. Muslim Objections against Christianity: The charges and accusations made in Muslim polemical writings against Christianity may be summarized in the following scheme.[54] I neglect here the numerous variations and various accents that show up in the work of the individual authors.

1) *There has been a change and forgery of textual divine revelation.*

This objection against the biblical text falls under the headings of *tahrīf* and faulty *tawātur*, dealt with earlier. The forgery has allegedly borne fruit not only in a falsification of Christianity when measured against the

---

[49] Author of the *Jawāb risālat ahl jazīrat Qubrus*, Ms. Utrecht, Cod. ms. or. no. 40 (according to FRITSCH, *Islam und Christentum im Mittelalter* [see above note 38], pp. 33–4).

[50] On Paul al-Rāhib, see Paul KHOURY, *Paul d'Antioche, évêque melkite de Sidon (XIIe s.): Texte établi, traduit et introduit* (Recherches XXIV), Beyrouth: Imprimerie Catholique, n.d. [1965]. Of special interest is his *Letter to the Muslims* (text pp. 59–83, trans. pp. 169–87), which Ibn Taymīya and the others answered. See also above n. 48.

[51] See above notes 29 and 31.

[52] *Tuhfat al-arīb fī r-radd ʿalā ahl as-salīb* (Cairo 1895). French translation "Le présent de l'homme lettré pour réfuter les partisans de la Croix', par ʿAbd Allāh ibn ʿAbd Allāh, le Drogman: Traduction française inédite", *Revue de l'histoire des religions*, 12 (6e Année) (1885), pp. 68–9, 179–201, and 278–301. See the study by Miguel DE EPALZA, *La Tuhfa, autobiografía y polémica islámica contra el Christianismo de ʿAbdallah al-Taryūmān (fray Anselmo Turmedo)*, Rome: Accademia Nazionale dei Lincei, 1971.

[53] Ed. by MCCARTHY (see above note 34), pp. 75–104. See A. ABEL, "Le chapitre sur le christianisme dans le 'Tamhīd' d'al-Bāqillānī (mort en 1013)", in *Études d'Orientalisme dédiées à la mémoire de Lévi-Provençal* (see above note 37), Vol. I, pp. 1–11.

[54] For this scheme, cf. FRITSCH, *Islam und Christentum im Mittelalter* (see above note 38), pp. 39–150, and WILMS (see above note 46), pp. 223–43.

original monotheistic teachings of Jesus. It also led to the Christians' refusal to accept Muhammad as a prophet. This was due to their neglecting the announcements (a 'lām texts) contained in their own scriptures and the rational and scriptural proofs of Muhammad's prophethood given by his miracles and in particular by his transmission of the Qur'ān to humanity.

2) *There have been doctrinal mistakes, in particular about things divine.*
This is largely due to the change and forgery of textual revelation and involves three main issues:

a) The Christian belief in the *incarnation*, that Jesus had a divine nature and was the son of God, is thoroughly rejected. The Qur'ān denies that Jesus was more than a prophet and the *mutakallimūn* tried to prove this by means of reason. They refused on logical grounds to make a distinction between Jesus' human nature, able to suffer, and his divine nature, unable to do so. The *mutakallimūn* pointed to the differences between the christologies of different Christian Churches and groups. They argued that the unsoundness of the doctrine of hypostatical union between God and man was already proved by the confusions and contradictions resulting from it. The *mutakallimūn* also refuted the doctrine of the incarnation because it implied that God was drawn into a range of physico-physiological happenings. Ibn Taymīya and al-Qarāfī as well as the author of *Al-radd al-jamīl* noticed that the human weakness of Jesus, as stressed in parts of the Gospels, and certain words of Jesus and his disciples implied that he had no divine nature at all. In the Gospels, Jesus never claimed to be God.

b) The *trinitarian* doctrine held by the Christians that God consists of one substance and three persons is rejected outright on the basis of the Qur'ān, which denies anything that might infringe on the oneness of God. The *mutakallimūn* further refuted the idea by means of reason: they developed a logical argumentation against it and refuted attempts by Christians to construct analogies of the Trinity in its defense. Arguments also were drawn from the New Testament itself, which nowhere mentions the trinity as such. In particular the idea of a father-son relationship within God was revolting to Muslim thought. It would imply that the one and only God would become contingent by the concept of *tawallud* (procreation).

c) The *soteriological* doctrines held by the Christians also met a frank rejection. The doctrine of original sin goes against the Qur'ān and is contrary to divine justice. The belief that the sins of individually responsible people could be remitted by someone else through atonement goes against the Qur'anic ideas of justice and human obedience to divine commands. Moreover, it conflicts with reason. The Christian idea of a redemption of the faithful from their sufferings and sins, from the burden of the law and the demands of the world, is in clear conflict with the daily experience of the Christians themselves.

There are two reasons for nearly all Christians' doctrinal mistakes. First, they affront the fundamental truth of *tawhīd* through their inclination to *shirk*. Second, these formulations are felt to be logical impossibilities. Just as there cannot be two eternal principles, so there can be no mingling of God and the human being, and there cannot be three eternal principles within one. The consequence of these doctrinal mistakes is that the Christians hold beliefs that are in direct conflict with reason. Their lack of sound reasoning leads them into a maze of philosophical and theological confusion and into contradictions that they themselves abusively call 'mysteries'.

3) *There have been mistakes in religious practice.*

These are a consequence of not adhering to a true account of revelation and not fulfilling the demands of sound reason:

a) In matters of liturgy, the reproach generally made to Christians is that they indulge in *idol worship* when adoring Jesus or venerating Mary, the saints, images, and other objects held to be sacred.

b) In ritual practice, Christians are reproached for *laxity*, such as the abandoning of circumcision and the neglect of ritual purity as prescribed by Mosaic law.

c) The Christians introduced inadmissible *novelties* after the lifetime of Jesus. Al-Qarāfī and Ibn Taymīya point out the different liturgical and popular religious celebrations and feasts, the sacraments (eucharist, baptism, confession), the veneration of Mary, church laws (marriage, celibacy, excommunication), and mistaken customs like the veneration of saints.

Other kinds of arguments were also used. Christian ethics, for instance, were judged to be extravagant in their demands; asceticism was rejected. The human free will toward God, as accepted in Christianity, was largely denied. Attention was drawn to the divisions among the Christians themselves and to a certain intellectual blindness in their religion that could lead to stupidities in practice. The defeat of the Christian armies and the concomitant victory of Islam were seen as a sign of God's providence.

On the other hand, arguments were coined to counter Christian attacks on Islam and to work out a convincing apology for Islam. The Christian objections to the Qur'ān, for instance, had to be met; the Christian rejection of Muhammad's prophethood had to be refuted; the unity of the prophetic revelations from Adam to Muhammad had to be proved. And it had to be proved both from the scriptures and by means of reasoning, first, that Muhammad was the seal of the prophets and, second, that Islam was the final universal message for all humankind. Polemics against non-Muslims ended in an apology for Islam.

The most tragic consequence of all these scriptural, doctrinal, and practical errors, in the Muslim view, was not only that the Christians were alienated from the true message of Jesus. They also could not listen to the message preached by Muhammad and thus remained closed to the concluding revelation that he brought.

5.4.3. Some Assumptions of these Objections: Further analysis tries to lay bare the norms and criteria underlying these arguments. The accusation of literary and historical forgery of scriptures held to be "revealed", as leveled in the Qur'ān, presupposes the model of revelation as conceived in Islam, that is to say a literal text brought by a prophet. As a result, however, the critical Qur'anic texts concerning the forgery of Christian and Jewish scriptures unknown to Muhammad were applied to the Bible in a search for what the Qur'ān said should be there, that is to say announcements of Muhammad's coming. The Qur'ān prescribes what should have been in the Hebrew and the Christian Bible. In other words, the idea of literal scriptural revelation tended towards literal interpretations of scriptures and of what such scriptures say about previous scriptures.

The accusation of wrong transmission is one way of explaining what was seen as the "mistakes" of the Bible: why it does not say what it is supposed to say. The accusation emerged from a kind of commonsense idea of good literary and historical transmission of a given text through reliable transmitters, applied to sacred texts.

Norms and criteria underlying the accusations against the Christians about their doctrinal mistakes include the following:

1) the assumption that the statements relating to the one and only God, as they are found in the Qur'ān, are the last word on the subject;

2) the assumption that the Qur'ān provides not only true but also sufficient knowledge of God;

3) the assumption that the Islamic model of revelation is the only possible one; and finally

4) the assumption that the categories of Aristotelian philosophy are adequate for reflection on this kind of religious problems.

Looking back, there has been a kind of Qur'anic "imperialism" toward preceding scriptures and religions.

On closer consideration of these objections against Christianity, one cannot but conclude that the Muslim vision was touched painfully by the Christian one on several sensitive points:

1) Making a distinction between different persons within the divine substance implies relativizing or even denying God's absolute unity. For Muslim feeling, God is one and unique and cannot be divided within himself.

2) The notion of a fall of creation, an original sin by human beings and the concomitant necessity for atonement through a self-sacrifice of the Creator is contrary to an assumed palpable, revealed and reasonable harmony within creation. It implies a denial of an assumed harmonious relationship between creation and Creator and a limitation of the human ability to carry out the positive tasks and responsibilities assigned to human beings.

3) The idea of a mixture of human and divine in one person held to be God's incarnation as the Son of God is not only a logical impossibility and an affront to clear thinking. It is also blasphemous insofar as it basically infringes upon and attacks the honor of God.

4) Reports on events as presented in religious scriptures cannot be true if they conflict with Qur'anic statements that apparently deny the possibility of such events. For Muslim feeling, Qur'anic statements are unconditionally true and take precedence over other sources of true knowledge.

In its refutation of Manicheism, *kalām* had to work out the implications of *tawhīd* and in its refutation of Judaism, it had to work out the implications of *naskh*. The refutation of Christianity led to further elaborations in *kalām*. Two issues dominated here: the implications of the doctrine that the Qur'ān is to be considered as God's word, and the nature of the relationship between God's substance and his attributes.

Although in more recent times[55] a new polemical literature can be found against religions like Judaism and also Hinduism, Muslim polemics and apologetics against Christianity have by and large taken the lead. From Rahmatullāh al-Hindī's *Izhār al-Haqq* (1867) to the present day, a stream of pamphlets and books addressed against Christianity or taking an apologetic stand for Islam against the claims of Christianity has been published. Generally speaking, they are a response to the impact of the West. More particularly, they respond to a wave of anti-Islamic literature produced in various circles, religious and otherwise, in the West in the course of the nineteenth and twentieth centuries. On the whole, the arguments of this response are the same as those advanced in the classical apologetic and polemical texts mentioned above, as far as theology is concerned. These latter texts, moreover, have been reprinted in the course of the twentieth century.

---

[55] Anawati, "Polémique" (see above note 38), esp. pp. 416–50. A survey of apologetic literature up to 1946 is given by Dorman, *Toward Understanding Islam*. Useful accounts were given by the late Arthur Jeffery, "New Trends in Moslem Apologetic", in *The Moslem World To-Day*, ed. by John R. Mott (London: Hodder and Stoughton, 1925), ch. xx, pp. 305–21; Id., "A Collection of anti-Christian Books and Pamphlets found in Actual Use among the Mohammedans of Cairo", *The Muslim World*, 15 (1925), pp. 26–37; Id., "Anti-Christian Literature", *The Muslim World*, 17 (1927), pp. 216–19.

Without considering extremes here, it is worth noting that in apologetic and polemical texts of the second half of the twentieth century certain old arguments have been presented in new forms. Moreover, arguments have been added that are not of a theological but more of an ideological or political nature and defend more general human causes:

1) A general reproach is that the Christians do not live up to their religion in which the Sermon on the Mount is the norm.

2) Missionaries and their work and literature are seen as the agents of Western imperialism against which a battle has been launched.

3) Literary and historical criticism of the Bible is used to confirm the Muslim doctrine of Christian corruption and wrong interpretation of the Bible, implying that the Bible cannot be considered literal divine revelation.

4) Non-Muslim Western writings and philosophical thought expressing criticism of Christianity are quoted to attack Christianity and to defend Islam.

5) The basic tenets of Islam are assiduously defended, such as absolute monotheism, the position of the Qur'ān as divine revelation, Muhammad's prophethood, the trustworthiness of the greater part of the *hadīth* literature, and the claimed announcements of Muhammad's mission in the Bible with proofs of his prophethood, miracles, and freedom from sin.

6) There is a rich apologetic literature about social facts connected with Islam that have been attacked in the West: patriarchal structures and the inferior position of women, the political instrumentalization of religion, authoritarianism, religious legitimation of violence (*jihād*), and so on.

7) Social facts in the West that suggest immorality and degeneration are brought out into the open and seen as signs of the inadequacy and poor state of the Christian religion that is victim of secularism.

8) Islam is often presented ideally as a moral force and as the religion of the golden mean and of reasonableness, as opposed to Christianity's incomprehensible mysteries of faith.

This apologetic literature may be of an elementary nature. Yet it deserves to be studied carefully not only in its rise and function within specific socio-political contexts, but also in connection with opposite trends in the Muslim community, such as the existing reverence for Jesus, the search for cooperation and dialogue with Christians, and more widely the collaboration of believers of different faiths[56] facing common worldwide or regional problems.

---

[56] See for instance, the positive texts about other religions which are treated by Abdelmajid CHARFI, "L'Islam et les religions non musulmanes: Quelques textes positifs", *Islamochristiana*, 3 (1977) 39–63.

6. Some Reflections on Muslim Views and Judgments

It has become clear from the foregoing that the names under which religions other than Islam have been described and refuted, like *Sumaniyya*, *Sābi'a*, *Barāhima*, *Zandaqa*, *Thānawiyya*, and to some extent also the Judaism of *tawrāt* and the Christianity of *injīl*, are not so much descriptive but basically value concepts. They serve primarily as normative predicates for doctrinal positions as identified, debated, and refuted in *tafsīr*, *kalām*, and *fiqh*. The same holds true for the basic concepts under which these religions are classified, like *ahl al-kitāb*, *ahl al-dhimma*, *mushrikūn*, *kuffār*. Some of these concepts have been taken from the Qur'ān, especially those referring to Jews and Christians. They all served to qualify, appreciate, and judge the reality, foreign to Muslim feeling, of non-Muslim religions. Fundamentally, they reflect the basic Muslim view of other religions as deviations from the one primordial religion, due to certain "exaggerations" and logical errors.

The living actual reality of other religious beliefs is subordinated a priori to some primary value categories. Buddhists are skeptics who deny reason, Brahmins are rationalists who reject prophecy, the Jāhilīya was pure idolatry, Christians are tritheists, Manicheans are dualists. These names and concepts qualify reality so that the reality of the religions concerned is predicated before being investigated. Only when something more became known about them could the meaning of the names and concepts be better defined and variations in judgment arise.

Often parallels are drawn between certain groups of non-Muslims and certain heretical groups in Islam. This implies not only that heretical opinions could be attributed to influences from outside. We may also infer from the parallelism between heresiography and the study of other religions that there was a deeper interest in and search for the basic structures lying behind all deviations from true Islam, whether inside or outside the Muslim community and its common religion. The idea was that such parallel mistaken groups were at fault because they made the same kind of 'exaggeration' or doctrinal error, either within the Muslim community or outside it. Even idol-worshippers could be seen, basically, as Muslims by origin who deviated, like later the Sabians, dualists, Jews, and Christians. Heretics and non-Muslims could be grouped according to certain basic theological 'sins': *shirk*, *thānawiyya*, *ta'tīl*, *dahriyya*, *tanāsukh*. In this framework, the doctrine of incarnation could be viewed as a form of *shirk*, associationism, polytheism, or even idolatry. All those not adhering to true primordial monotheistic Islam share the common designation: *kuffār* (infidels).

In the course of history, when Muslims came into contact with peoples unknown previously, the tendency developed to subsume religions like

Zoroastrianism, official Hinduism, and official Buddhism under the heading of the "people of Scripture" or rather (the people) "of a semblance of Scripture" (*shibh kitāb*). Another tendency has been to distinguish, among the adherents of religions like Judaism, Christianity, and also Hinduism, certain people who are nearest to Islam since they clearly believe in one God, possibly because they follow their innate *fitra* (monotheistic religious disposition). In later times, on the whole, a somewhat less unfavorable judgment of non-monotheistic religions has developed than had prevailed in the first centuries of Islam.

The relatively favorable judgment that Judaism and Christianity enjoyed from the beginning, at least with regard to the teachings of their founders, is due mainly to the distinction the Qur'ān makes between *ahl al-kitāb*[57] (people of Scripture) and *mushrikūn* (polytheists). Jews and Christians are counted among the former. They are *kuffār*[58] (unbelievers, infidels) nevertheless, and judgments of Jews and Christians made by *mutakallimūn* (Muslim theologians) never denied this. Yet distinctions could be made between different kinds of Jews and Christians, when better information about the 'real' Jews and Christians became available in the course of time and when Muslim thinking developed and became more refined.

Muslims have mostly interpreted Qur'anic statements about Jews and Christians as straightforward statements of facts that had to be accepted on religious authority. This applied for instance to the Qur'anic accusation that the Jews venerated Ezra, to the Qur'anic denial of the crucifixion of Jesus, to the Qur'anic claim that the Jewish and Christian scriptures are a falsification of the true books brought by Moses and Jesus, and to the Qur'anic hint at the presence of *a'lām* (annunciation) texts in the Jewish and Christian scriptures. The testimonies of the Old and New Testaments about these and other issues and their significance and what particular Jewish and Christian exegetes said about these Bible texts were secondary on every score.

It was not necessarily any lack of natural curiosity that kept Muslims from delving into these literary expressions of religious experience of Jews and Christians. It was rather because they held that the Qur'ān contained everything worth knowing in matters of religion and even in other domains. After all, the Qur'ān gave some negative judgments about the religions of the Jews and Christians, including their scriptures. This is probably why Muslims hardly ever paid attention to elements of these religions that were not mentioned in the Qur'ān. I am thinking for instance of most Hebrew prophets in the Old Testament, the nature of the Messianic expectations held by the Jews, or the idea of salvation bound

---

[57]   See G. Vajda, art. "Ahl al-Kitāb", in *EI²*, Vol. 4, pp. 264–6.
[58]   See W. Björkman, art. "Kāfir", in *EI²*, Vol. 4, pp. 407–9.

up for the Christians with the life and work of Jesus on earth, their calling
him "Christ" in connection with the "Kingdom of God" and its manifes-
tation on earth. Muslims may have been curious about such beliefs different from their own, but studying them had no religious relevance. On the
contrary, from a religious point of view, these beliefs were erroneous and
should not be heeded.

When Muslim theologians and jurists spoke about 'Jews' and 'Christians', they meant in the first place those people who adhere to the
particular doctrines known as the tenets of Judaism and Christianity as
they are described, evaluated, and judged in the Qur'ān. They spoke in
fact not about Judaism and Christianity as religions for their own sake,
but rather about the implications of the Qur'anic views and concepts of
Judaism and Christianity. The information that reached them about the
'empirical' Jews and Christians and their "real" scriptures was interpreted and judged on the basis of the Qur'anic statements. At most this
empirical information could be used to 'illustrate' and elaborate statements found in the Qur'ān.

Only in the most recent times have Muslims inquired from Jews and
Christians what these people themselves believe. One of the first impres-
sions a reading of traditional Muslim accounts of other religions arouses
in a present-day scholar is: 'but this is not what those people in fact
believed or believe, this does not take into account what their doctrines
and practices actually meant or mean to them!'

One of the tasks of the *mutakallimūn* was to refute false doctrines.
Judging other religions, their doctrines, ethics, and rituals, mainly falls
under the heading of *kalām*. Judgments are given here according to the
rules prescribed by the science of *'usūl al-dīn* and within the framework
of the particular theological and juridical schools to which the scholar
belongs or whose arguments he uses.

Muslim views on the subject of a 'theology of religions' are attracting
some attention now in the West, but hardly for their own sake, that is to
say out of a genuine interest in these views themselves. They are mostly
seen in connection with one religion only, Christianity, without taking
into account broader Muslim theological and juridical issues involved.[59]
For a proper study of what may be called the growth of an Islamic
'theology of religions', we first need detailed studies of the theological
views of thinkers like al-Baghdādī, al-Bāqillānī, al-Māturīdī, 'Abd al-

---

[59]   The relations between Islam and Christianity should be seen as part of the relations
between Islam and the other religions in general. Similarly, the attitudes taken by
Muslims toward Christians are part of overall attitudes taken by Muslims toward
different kinds of other believers. For Muslims the legal and ethical aspects of such
relations and attitudes are not less important than the doctrinal aspects.

Jabbār, al-Juwaynī, and others to understand the method they followed when judging particular types of religions in their refutations. It would then be possible to distinguish certain Muʿtazilite, Ashʿarite, and Mātu-rīdite, and other variations of an Islamic 'theology of religions' and their interpretations of basic notions given in the Qur'ān.[60] We would then also be in a better position to see to what extent Muslim discussions about other religions in *kalām* run parallel to issues of theological and juridical debate in Islam itself. In such a debate, one Muslim party could try to defeat another Muslim party, for instance by reproaching it with holding a Manichean-dualistic or a Christian-associationist doctrine or position within Islam.

There are a number of technical questions in this kind of research. Since theological judgments always imply the use of certain core concepts that occur in the Qur'ān and the *hadīth* literature and in technical *kalām* vocabulary, it is important to see what variations existed in the interpretation of these concepts. In the *tafsīr* literature for instance it is important whether a broader or a more narrow interpretation is given of Qur'anic verses, which then may become 'harsher' or 'milder' for certain groups of non-Muslims. Concepts like *fitra* and *dīn*, *tawhīd* and *shirk*, *īmān*, *islām* and *kufr*, *wahy* and *kashf*, *ʿaql* and *naql* come back again and again with different nuances of meaning.

There are also certain background questions. All judgments on other religions imply certain implicit or explicit views and assumptions of a more general nature that have consequences for the way in which non-Muslims are envisaged. Such underlying views and assumptions should be brought to light. In Islam, the concept of religion (*dīn*) itself and the relations between revelation and reason, between revelation and religion, and between religion and other domains of life have been interpreted differently. The same holds true for basic views of the human being, human nature, human rights, and humanity as a whole, with implications for possible communication and dialogue, understanding, and cooperation with other people. These issues caused some Muslim travelers and historians, philosophers and mystics to take more lenient attitudes toward people of other faiths than the professional theologians and jurists.

In the study of Muslim views of other religions, we have to be aware indeed that theological and juridical views and judgments constitute only one, albeit an important, factor in the attitudes taken toward people of other faiths. Personal sympathies, practical interests, social necessities,

---

[60] See, for instance, Peter ANTES, "Das Verhältnis zu den Ungläubigen in der islamischen Theologie", in *Glauben an den einen Gott: Menschliche Gotteserfahrung im Christentum und im Islam*, ed. by Abdoldjavad FALATURI and Walter STROLZ (Freiburg, etc.: Herder, 1975), pp. 117–29. See also Mahmūd b. ASH-SHARIF, *Al adyān fī l-Qur'ān*, Cairo 1970.

and unavoidable political factors play an increasingly important role in choosing a position for or against a rapprochement. There may be particular reasons to stress or veil what a Muslim sees as the 'lesser' sides of the other faith, to play down or to emphasize loyalty toward one's own community, and to use or leave out Islam as a symbol of this solidarity. An important factor too, of course, is the stand someone takes toward what he or she considers to be "true" Islam and its relation to society and empirical reality at large. This implies the way in which someone considers Islam to be the absolute religion as well as the way in which someone defines him- or herself as a Muslim. Important, too, is whether one prefers to apply typically "Islamic" norms and criteria or more universally oriented ones, as discussed in section 3 at the beginning of this chapter.

Elements like these account for a certain flexibility in Muslim judgments about other religions, including the properly theological and juridical ones given by *mutakallimūn* and *'ulamā'* in general. It is, consequently, not possible to say that Islam as such leads to specific views, judgments, and actions, or to explain the latter by a reified entity 'Islam'. What counts is the particular interpretation and application chosen. We should pay attention instead to ideas formulated and practices carried out in the different schools and trends, the different cultural and political contexts that have existed within the Muslim community. Our sources allow us to say only what Muslims thought other religions and their own religion were, not what Islam itself and what its relationships with other religions are.

In summarizing our findings, I would say that there is no evidence that Muslims saw either Buddhist and Hindu or Jewish and Christian people and faiths at all. What they saw in fact were images developed within their own cultural and religious orbit. They had their own ideas about non-Muslims, developed on the basis of some Qur'anic and *hadīth* texts, some knowledge of the Bible and other texts, and a growing number of empirical observations. This was a collection of Islamocentric materials. Up to the European Renaissance, however, the Muslim scholars mentioned had a broader knowledge about the religions of the world than their Latin and Byzantine, Indian and Chinese colleagues. What was lacking was a proper notion of the other's religious existence, an ideal of understanding the other in terms of his or her own social setting, history, and culture, and the effort to see the other in terms of universal rather than specifically Islamic rules and problems. This gives many Muslim judgments the same provincial character that is also striking in so many Christian opinions about other religions. On this score, both religions seem to be on the same footing.

Selected Literature

ADANG, Camilla, *Muslim Writers on Judaism and the Hebrew Bible: From Ibn Rabban to Ibn Hazm*, Leiden, etc.: E. J. Brill, 1996.

BĪRŪNĪ, al-, *Kitāb ta'rīkh al-Hind*, trans., with notes and indices, by C. Edward SACHAU, *Alberuni's India: An Account of the Religion, Philosophy, Literature, Geography, Chronology, Astronomy, Customs, Laws and Astrology of India about 1030*, 2 Vols., London: Trübner, 1888, 1910² (repr. New Delhi: Munshiram Manoharlal, 2001).

—, *The Chronology of Ancient Nations: An English Version of the Arabic Text of the Āthār-ul-Bākiya of Albiruni, or "Vestiges of the Past"*, trans. and ed., with notes and index, by Edward SACHAU, London: Allen, 1879 (repr. Frankfurt on Main: Minerva, 1969).

BRUNSCHVIG, Robert, "L'argumentation d'un théologien musulman du Xe siècle contre le Judaïsme", in *Homenaje a Millás-Vallicrosa* (Barcelona: Consejo Superior de Investigaciones Científicas, 2 Vols., 1954–6), Vol. 1, 1954, pp. 225–41.

DORMAN, Jr., Harry Gaylord, *Toward Understanding Islam: Contemporary Apologetic of Islam and Missionary Policy*, New York: Columbia University Press, 1948.

FRIEDMANN, Yohanan, "Medieval Muslim Views of Indian Religions", *Journal of the American Oriental Society*, 95, Nr. 2 (April-June 1975), pp. 214–21.

—, "Islamic Thought in Relation to the Indian Context", *Parusārtha*, 9 (1986), pp. 79–91.

GOLDZIHER, Ignaz, "Ueber muhammedanische Polemik gegen Ahl al-kitāb", *Zeitschrift der Deutschen Morgenländischen Gesellschaft*, 32 (1878), pp. 341–87 (repr. in his *Gesammelte Schriften*, ed. by Joseph DESOMOGYI, Vol. 2, Hildesheim: G. Olms, 1967, pp. 1–47).

IBN AL-NADĪM, *The Fihrist of al-Nadīm: A Tenth-Century Survey of Muslim Culture*, trans. by Bayard DODGE, 2 Vols., New York and London: Columbia University Press, 1970.

JAHN, Karl, *Rashīd al-Dīn's History of India: Collected Essays with Facsimiles and Indices* (Central Asiatic Studies 10), The Hague, etc.: Mouton, 1965.

LAWRENCE, Bruce B., *Shahrastānī on the Indian Religions* (Religion and Society 4), The Hague and Paris: Mouton, 1976.

LAZARUS-YAFEH, Hava, *Intertwined Worlds: Medieval Islam and Bible Criticism*, Princeton, N. J.: Princeton University Press, 1992.

MCAULIFFE, Jane Damman, *Qur'ānic Christians: An Analysis of Classical and Modern Exegesis*, New York and Cambridge: Cambridge University Press, 1991.

MONNOT, Guy, *Penseurs musulmans et religions iraniennes: 'Abd al-Jabbār et ses devanciers* (Etudes musulmanes 16), Paris: J. Vrin, 1974.

—, *Islam et religions* (Islam d'hier et d'aujourd'hui 27), Paris: Maisonneuve et Larose, 1986.

—, "Les écrits musulmans sur les religions non-bibliques", *Mélanges de l'Institut Dominicain d'Études Orientales du Caire*, 11 (1972), pp. 5–48, and "Addenda et corrigenda à la liste des écrits musulmans sur les religions non-bibliques", *ibid.*, 12 (1974), pp. 44–7; also in the author's *Islam et religions* (see above), pp. 39–82.

Muslim Perceptions of Other Religions: A Historical Survey, ed. by Jacques WAARDENBURG, New York and London: Oxford University Press, 1999.

PALACIOS, Miguel Asín, *Abenházam de Córdoba y su Historia crítica de las ideas religiosas*, 5 Vols., Madrid: Academia de la Historia, 1927–32.

PERLMANN, Moshe, "The Medieval Polemics between Islam and Judaism", in *Religion in a Religious Age* (see below), pp. 103–38.

RASHĪD AL-DĪN, *World History*; German translations with commentaries by Karl JAHN: *Die Geschichte der Oğuzen* (Vienna, etc.: Böhlau, 1969), *Die China-geschichte* (Vienna, etc.: Böhlau, 1971), *Die Geschichte der Kinder Israels* (Vienna: Verlag der Österreichischen Akademie der Wissenschaften, 1973), *Die Frankengeschichte* (Vienna: Verlag der Österreichischen Akademie der Wissenschaften, 1977), *Die Indiengeschichte* (Vienna: Verlag der Öster-reichischen Akademie der Wissenschaften, 1980).

Religion in a Religious Age, ed. by Solomon Dob GOITEIN, Cambridge, Mass.: Association for Jewish Studies, 1974.

ROBINSON, Neal, *Christ in Islam and Christianity: The Representations of Jesus in the Qur'ān and the Classical Muslim Commentaries*, Basingstoke: Macmillan, 1991.

SCHREINER, Martin, "Zur Geschichte der Polemik zwischen Juden und Muham-medanern", *Zeitschrift der Deutschen Morgenländischen Gesellschaft*, 42 (1888), pp. 591–675.

SHAHRASTĀNĪ, *Livre des religions et des sectes*. French translation of the author's *Kitāb al-milal wa'l-nihal*, with introduction, notes, and bibliography. Pre-pared under the auspices of UNESCO by Daniel GIMARET, Guy MONNOT, and Jean JOLIVET (Collection UNESCO d'Oeuvres représentatives, Série arabe), 2 Vols., Leuven: Peeters, and Paris: UNESCO, 1986 and 1993.

STEINSCHNEIDER, Moritz, *Polemische und apologetische Literatur in arabischer Sprache, zwischen Muslimen, Christen und Juden* (Abhandlungen für die Kunde des Morgenlandes 6,3), Leipzig: Brockhaus, 1877 (repr. Hildesheim: Georg Olms, 1966).

TAHMI, Mahmoud, *L'Encyclopédisme musulman à l'âge classique: Le livre de la création et de l'histoire de Maqdisī*, Paris: Maisonneuve et Larose, 1998.

VAJDA, G., "Juifs et musulmans selon le Ḥadīṯ", *Journal Asiatique*, 209 (1937), pp. 57–127.

WAARDENBURG, Jacques, "Koranisches Religionsgespräch", in *Liber Amicorum presented to Prof. Dr. C. J. Bleeker*, Leiden: E. J. Brill, 1969, pp. 208–53.

—, "Muslim Studies of Other Religions", in *Muslim Perceptions of Other Religions: A Historical Survey*, ed. by Jacques WAARDENBURG, New York and London: Oxford University Press, 1999, pp. 1–101.

Chapter 7
Twentieth Century Writings about Other Religions: A Classification[1]

In the course of the twentieth century, a great number of books, articles, and pamphlets written by Muslims in different parts of the world and in various languages and bearing on religions other than Islam, have seen the light. Although no exhaustive bibliography of these publications is available, the present chapter attempts at least to sketch a typology of such writings according to their general character and orientation. This typological sketch is based on publications that have appeared since World War Two and that can claim to be of a certain intellectual level. Besides publications in English, some publications in Arabic have been taken as examples, as long as they do not deal specifically with Arab Christians, but either with Christianity in general or with Western Christianity in particular. Besides some books dealing with religions in general, books dealing with Christianity have been of particular interest for this research. Roughly speaking, the latter may be characterized as an exercise in trying to see through the eyes of others.

1. Informative Literature of a More General Nature

Some time ago, I found by chance in a London bookshop a copy of Ahmad Abdullah al-Masdoosi's *Living Religions of the World*, with the subtitle *A Socio-Political Study*.

---

[1] Revised and extended version of a paper presented at the 10th Congress of the *Union Européenne des Arabisants et Islamisants* in Edinburgh, September 1980. The first version was published in *Proceedings: 10th Congress, Union Européenne des Arabisants et Islamisants, Edinburgh, September 9–16, 1980*, ed. by Robert HILLENBRAND, Edinburgh: Edinburgh University, 1982, pp. 107–15.

For bibliographical details of some titles I have drawn on the valuable bibliography of Arabic publications on the subject compiled by Patrice Claude BRODEUR in his Ph.D. thesis in the study of religion *From an Islamic Heresiography to an Islamic History of Religions* (see Selected Literature under section 1.), pp. 297–319. He is preparing a book on present-day Arab Muslim scholarship in the field of Religious Studies.

It had appeared in 1962[2]. In his Preface, the author hints at the present significant period of human history, in which Muslims are in danger but also have possibilities undreamed of before. Because of the need for reflection on the international situation, the author plans a further study entitled "Islam and Contemporary World Conflict"[3]. In this book he would want to pay attention to the attitude that the Eastern and Western powers take toward Muslims and the present dilemma for Muslims either to adopt a policy of alliance or to keep a neutralist policy.

This dilemma led the author to study in the present book first the relative numerical, territorial, and political strength of the various religions of the world, including Islam. He gives estimates of the numbers of adherents and information about the spiritual and religious aspects of these religions, so as to contribute to a better understanding of them. He also offers material for a comparative study of the social and political aspects both of the living religions and of what the author calls the "rising Imperialist Powers of the East", that is to say China, Japan, India, and the USSR, against which he warns the reader. Information about "declining Western imperialism" is given through data about the period of colonization.

The result is a readable book of a certain standard, though more assertions are made than questions asked. One feature is the presence of not less than 75 tables with data on the Muslims in all their aspects, including economic ones such as the oil reserves, as well as about the numbers of other believers. They also offer the dates of imperialism, about which there is an attractive map, "Rise and Fall of Imperialism" from 1920 until 1962. There is also a chart of the political strength of the various religions in the United Nations.

The introductory Chapter I, "What is religion?", treats the subject from various angles. It makes a distinction between revealed and non-revealed religions and treats not only religious but also political developments in the twentieth century. Chapters II and III provide data on Islam and Muslims under headings like "social conditions", the "geographical importance" of the Muslim world, and the "ideological strength" of Islam. The subsequent chapters treat the various religions, each chapter ending with the heading "Political Power". There is a clear bias against Hinduism, and under Judaism most attention is paid to Zionism. There are two further chapters, a shorter one on "Points of concord and conflict between Islam and Christianity", and a longer one on the "Rise and fall of colonialism".

---

[2]   This book (see Selected Literature under section 1.) is an English rendering and elaboration by Dr. Zafar Ishaq ANSARI of the original Urdu edition *Mazāhib-i-Ālam*, Karachi: Maktaba-i-Khuddam-i-Millat, 1958.

[3]   I do not know if this book, to be written in Urdu, actually appeared.

Though based on existing sources, it is a new kind of book, presenting religions as ideological strongholds with underlying economic and political power. Religions are not seen as ideational systems but as power blocks or parts of existing power blocks. Islam as a power occupies the center of interest. After reading this political Muslim account of the religions of the world, the reader remains somehow in the dark about what is exactly understood by "religion".

Another English book by a Pakistani author, but of a much lower standard, is Mahmud Brelvi's *Islam and Its Contemporary Faiths*, which appeared in 1965.[4] The author starts the book by presenting "A summary of universal religious ideals" held in the great religions (pp. VI–VII). In his Preface, he presents some thought on religious subjects and expresses the hope that this book will offer answers to the attacks on Islam missionaries have made. He shows concern with the ways in which Islam is described in Western studies and gives an apologetic response: "This book has been compiled as objectively as humanly possible, without condemning any faith or any people for that matter. But, the author will not offer any apologies if the chapter on Islam may be tempting enough for any discerning and intelligent reader to accept the faith of Islam" (p. 38). The pages that follow briefly describe the nine great religions of the world, each chapter having a short bibliography. In his Conclusion, the author takes issue with the treatment given to Islam in John B. Noss' well-known book *Man's Religions* in the revised edition of 1956.

A somewhat older historical view of religions is ʿAbbās Mahmūd al-ʿAqqād's book *Allāh* of 1947.[5] As the author puts it in his Introduction, this is a book about "the evolution of faith in God up to pure monotheism", and he describes the stages of this "hunger for belief" in the course of the history of humankind. The first part treats the ancient religions. The second part deals with the Banū Isrāʾīl, philosophy, Christianity, and Islam. The third part, interestingly, treats later religions, the main philosophers in the various religious traditions, philosophy as it further developed, mysticism, the natural sciences, and other subjects. The religions are viewed here within the evolution of humankind.

In this category of general informative literature about the various religions, in which explicit criticism or apologetics is largely absent, Muhammad Abū Zahra's *Al-diyānāt al-qadīma* of ca. 1940[6] may also be included.

---

[4] Publications in Western languages are quoted in the "Selected Literature" section at the end of this chapter. The same author also wrote in English a substantial book on *Islam in Africa*.

[5] A. M. AL-ʿAQQĀD, *Allāh: Kitāb fiʾ nashʾat al-ʿaqīda al-ilāhīya*, Cairo: Dār al-maʿārif bi-misr, 1947, 1976[7].

[6] M. ABŪ ZAHRA, *Al-diyānāt al-qadīma*, Cairo: Matbaʿat Yusuf, ca. 1940; new edition Cairo: Dār al-fikr al-ʿarabī, 1965.

This book treats ancient Egyptian religion, Hinduism, Buddhism, Confucianism, and Greek and Roman paganism (*wathanīya*). These "ancient religions", well described with their ethics, are the opposite of the "heavenly (revealed) religions" (*al-diyānāt al-samāwīya*). The historical data were taken from Western books.

The more rationally constructed book *Al-dīn* by Muhammad ʿAbdallāh Dirāz, of 1952[7], is a plea for the empirical, rational study of the history of religions as a scholarly discipline. It consists of four essays that are presented as "preparatory investigations" for the study of the history of religions.

2. Critical Accounts of Other Religions or Parts of Them

These books are based on literary and historical materials to which the authors apply internal criticism dealing with contradictions in the material itself or external criticism consisting in this case not only of scholarly arguments but also of references to the Qur'ān, considered as normative. These accounts cannot be called apologetic, however, since their focus is on the material under study and the right of existence of the other party is recognized. But the accounts are presented in conformity with a clear norm of revelation.

The clearest example here is Ismāʿīl Rāji al-Fārūqī, *Christian Ethics: A Historical and Systematic Analysis of its Dominant Ideas*, of 1967. The author, who participated in seminars on theological subjects at McGill University, Montreal, in order to familiarize himself with Christian thought, treats the New Testament and Patristic literature at length and discusses them critically. His book is a kind of Muslim history-of-religions approach to Christianity and its ethics in particular, but of a critical nature.

As the author had argued in an article published in *Numen* two years earlier[8], the study of another religion does not consist simply of collecting data and systematizing them into what he calls the "construction of meaning-wholes". It also implies an evaluation or judgment of such meaning-wholes.

---

[7]   M. A. Dirāz, *Al-dīn: Buhūth mumahhida li-dirāsat taʾrīkh al-adyān*, Cairo: al-Matbaʿa al-ʿālamīya, 1952. A new edition appeared in Cairo: Matbaʿat al-saʿāda, 1969. See also his English article, "Islam's Attitude towards and Relations with other Faiths", *The Islamic Literature* (Lahore: Shaikh Muhammad Ashraf), 10, Nr. 2 (February 1958), pp. 9–16.

[8]   al-Fārūqī, "History of Religions: Its Nature and Significance for Christian Education and the Muslim-Christian Dialogue" (see Selected Literature under section 2.).

When al-Fārūqī speaks of the necessity, the desirability, and the possibility of such an evaluation in terms of what he calls a "critical meta-religion", he formulates on a more sophisticated level an assumption made by most Muslims writing on religions other than Islam. This assumption is that, for the sake of truth, they should pass judgment on "outside" religion, if not at the beginning, then at the end of the investigation. Here lies the major distinction, as far as I can see, between a study of religions that is intent on explaining and understanding, on the one hand, and this approach to Christianity, which reminds one of similar ideological approaches by Christian missionaries and theologians to Islam.

Muslim studies of Christianity and Judaism falling within this category of critical accounts inevitably contain criticism of their Scriptures and their reports about prophets. The pre-eminence of the prophets themselves remains respected beyond doubt. They are, so to speak, to be restored as carriers of revelation. In this respect, it is revealing to see, for instance, how individual authors, varying from al-ʿAqqād to Kāmil Husayn, Khālid Muhammad Khālid to Ghūdah al-Sahhār, Fathī ʿUthmān to al-Muhāmī[9], construct what may be called the essential meaning of Jesus in their biographies of Jesus written as variations on a basic Qur'anic christology.

A special case is the book by Muhammad ʿAtā al-Rahīm that was published in England under the title *Jesus Prophet of Islam* in 1977. It supplements a biography of Jesus based on the Qur'anic pattern while using New Testament data with the teaching of Unitarians. The latter are considered to represent the true Christian religion in the course of the history of Christianity.

Other Biblical figures also received attention. ʿAbd al-Razzāq Nawfal in his *Yūhannā al-maʿmadān, al-nabī Yahyā*[10] stresses the prophethood of John the Baptist.

---

[9]   ʿAbbās Mahmūd AL-ʿAQQĀD, *ʿAbqarīyat al-masīh*, Cairo: Dār al-hilāl, 1952; new edition with an additional chapter under the title *Hayāt al-masīh fī 'l-ta'rīkh wa-kushūf al-ʿasr al-hadīth*, Cairo: Dār al-hilāl, 1958 (repr. 1986).

   Muhammad Kāmil HUSAYN, *Qarya zālima*, Cairo: Maktabat al-nahda al-misrīya, 1954 (repr. 1974).

   Khālid Muhammad KHĀLID, *Maʿan ʿalā al-tarīq: Muhammad wa'l-masīh*, Cairo: Dār al-kutub al-hadītha, 1958.

   ʿAbd al-Hamīd Ghūdah AL-SAHHĀR, *Al-masīh ʿĪsā b. Maryam* (series "al-Kitāb al-fiddi"), Cairo: Al-sharīka al-ʿarabīya li'l-tibāʿa, 1959.

   Muhammad Fathī ʿUTHMĀN, *Maʿa 'l-masīh fī'l-anājīl al-arbaʿa*, Cairo: Dār al-qawmīya, 1961 (repr. 1966).

   Muhammad ʿAbdu 'l-Rahīm ʿANBAR AL-MUHĀMĪ, *Baina ʿĪsā wa-Muhammad*, Cairo: Dār al-Gami Eiyin li't-Tab wa'n-Nasr, 1966 (repr. 1967).

   See also SCHUMANN, *Der Christus der Muslime*, especially pp. 86–111.

[10] ʿAbd al-Razzāq NAWFAL, *Yūhannā al-mamadān, al-nabī Yahyā* (ʿalaihi al-salāt wa'l-salām), Cairo: Dār al-shaʿb, n.d.

'Abbās Mahmūd al-'Aqqād treats Abraham as a prophet in his *Ibrāhīm Abū'l-anbiyā'*.[11] The author argues that Abraham was a prophet and the "father" of all prophets. He thus denies the exclusively Jewish interpretation of Abraham as the father of Isaac and the Israelites. He brings about a typical "Islamic" universalizing of the particularistic interpretation of Abraham in the Jewish tradition. This goes back to the data contained in the Qur'ān. On the other hand, al-'Aqqād himself is particularistic when he claims that the message of the Qur'ān is the same as that of Abraham and that Islam is the result of the right interpretation of the Qur'ān.

Muslim authors have severely criticized the traditions handed down after the prophets and the further history of the religions after their prophets' death generally. This history is seen fundamentally as a betrayal of the message, norms, and prescriptions given by the founding prophets. Besides the direct experiences of imperialism by particular groups of Muslims, Muslims see a Qur'anic basis in their view of Christian history, including the Crusades, as one of decline and betrayal of the message of Jesus.

Authors like Muhammad Husayn Haikal and Seyyed Hossein Nasr could speak of a betrayal of Christianity, which turned from a religion of love into a religion of fighting, both internecine of Christians against each other and in aggression against and conquests of the outside world. Others again describe without much regret what they see as the sad fate of Christianity in a secularizing Western society that is in moral decline.

3. Apologetic and Polemical Writings

Although apologetic and especially polemical writings are critical by their very nature, the kind of criticism they contain differs from that of the critical accounts just treated. These are oriented towards a specific subject study and recognize the right of existence of the other party, taking note of differences. Their views can be shared to a greater or lesser extent by critical scholarship in the West, too.

But in the apologetic and polemical writings of any religion, including Islam, all stress is laid on the truth of one's own religion as opposed to outsiders, the defense of one's religion against intellectual attacks made from outside, and if needed counterattacks on particularly aggressive religions and ideologies. In this kind of writings, religions tend to be treated as more or less reified entities, almost as ideological blocks, and

---

[11] 'Abbās Mahmūd AL-'AQQĀD, *Ibrāhīm Abū'l-anbiyā'*, Cairo: Dār al-hilāl, n.d. (repr. Beirut: Maktabat al-'asrīya, 1981).

when the authors are Muslims, it is Islam that is constantly proved superior to the others. Islam is simply held to be always right.

The category of apologetic and polemical writings contains publications of all sorts but primarily of a more popular character, in the twentieth century directed especially against Christianity at first, against Judaism and Hinduism later. They mostly repeat particular motifs ad nauseam, their standard arguments being drawn from criticism of the biblical text, church history, political confrontations in the period of colonial imperialism, and, lately, evidence of the wrong picture that stupid missionaries and shrewd orientalists have presented of Islam. Although this popular variety has long had an impact on people in Muslim societies, we leave it aside since it is not up to the level under discussion here. It deserves to be studied, however, just as much as certain popular missionary tracts that have been distributed in Muslim countries until recently.

What I have in mind here are twentieth-century writings on the pattern of Muhammad 'Abduh's *Al-islām wa'l-nasrānīya ma'a 'l-'ilm wa'l-madanīya* of 1902, Muhammad Rashīd Ridā's *'Aqīdat al-salb wa'l-fidā*, and Muhammad al-Ghazālī's *Al-ta'assub wa'l-tasāmub baina 'l-islām wa'l-masīhīya.*[12]

Three major varieties of this category can be distinguished.

1) First, there are books that offer informative material as a kind of history of religions or comparative religion. However, because of the kind of criticism they contain, these books fit into the category of apologetics, rather than into that of critical studies. Representative in this respect is the four-volume work by Ahmad Shalabī, *Muqāranat al-adyān* ("Comparative Religion"). In their order of appearance, these are: *al-Masīhīya* ("Christianity", 1960), *al-Islām* ("Islam", 1961), *Adyān al-Hind al-kubrā: al-Hindawīya, al-Jaynīya, al-Būdhīya* ("The great religions of India: Hinduism, Jainism, Buddhism", 1964), and *al-Yahūdīya* ("Judaism", 1965).[13]

What is new in Ahmad Shalabī's approach is not so much the description of the historical development of individual religions, but the plain use

---

[12]   Muhammad 'ABDUH, *Al-islām wa'l-nasrānīya ma'a 'l-'ilm wa'l-madanīya*, Cairo: al-Manār, 1902. It first appeared as articles in six issues of *al-Manār* in 1902 and then as a separate publication of Maktabat al-Manār the same year.
    Muhammad RASHĪD RIDĀ, *'Aqīdat al-salb wa'l-fidā*, Cairo: Maktabat al-Manār, 1934[3]. It first appeared in his *Tafsīr al-Qur'ān al-hakīm* (12 Vols., Cairo: al-Manār, 1906–34; Vol. VI, 1911, pp. 18–59) and then as a separate publication.
    Muhammad AL-GHAZĀLĪ, *Al-ta'assub wa'l-tasāmuh baina 'l-islām wa'l-masīhīya*, Cairo: Dār al-tawzī' wa'l-nashr al-islāmī, 1989.
[13]   Ahmad SHALABĪ, *Muqāranat al-adyān*, Cairo: Maktabat al-nahda al-handītha, 1960–65. The four volumes have been reprinted in successively enlarged editions. Vol. 1: *al-Masīhīya*, 1960, 1977[5]; Vol. 2: *al-Islām*, 1961, 1977[5]; Vol. 3: *Adyān al-Hind al-kubrā*, 1964, 1976[4]; Vol. 4: *al-Yahūdīya*, 1965, 1974[4].
    These four volumes also appeared in Indonesian.

of comparisons between details of the four religions. The author presents in this way parallels for particular religious phenomena, establishing in this way their human, rather than revelatory character. From the parallel, for instance, between the Christian trinity and the Hindu triad, the author concludes that the Christian idea of trinity is not due to revelation. Earlier, the results of historical-critical research had been used to demonstrate the human character of the gospels and deny their revelation. As in Christian apologetic literature, here too the claim of revelation is at stake and any revelation claimed by "others" is denied or at least reduced to a minimum.

Because of the bulk of information presented, it could be argued that Ahmad Shalabī's work deserves to be placed in category (2), that of "Critical accounts". The nature of the Prefaces to the various volumes, however, justifies placing the work in the category of a particular kind of apologetics and even polemics. In the Preface to the volume on Christianity, for instance, the author reports on various books written by Christians on Islam. He takes a militant stand against missionaries and Western imperialism with its agents. In contrast to pure Christianity as a religion, Shalabī denounces political Christianity, which served to bring Asian and African countries under the sway of the West. Moreover, this political Christianity created a state of mind among the Christians in which they came to categorically oppose Islam, Islamic thought, and Muslims generally in all fields. In his conclusion to this volume, Shalabī offers what he calls a scientific criticism of Christianity.

2) The second variety of apologetic and polemical writings is represented, for instance, by Mansūr Husayn ʿAbd al-ʿAzīz, *Da ʿwatu ʾl-haqq aw al-haqīqa baina ʾl-masīhīya waʾl-islām*, of 1972.[14] It offers a thorough internal criticism of the New Testament, which taken in itself could be classified as a reasonable critical study. But then, according to the same criteria but colored by a religious evaluation, the author presents Islam as the right alternative and the better religion. This is polemics combined with apologetics in the full sense of the word.

3) The third variety consists of bitter, straightforward, fully-fledged denunciations, in particular of Christianity, Judaism, and Hinduism. A low-key example is Alhaj A. D. Ajijola's *The Myth of the Cross* of 1975, with its particular dedication[15]. The author is clearly Nigerian, and some inquiry on the social and historical context of the book would not be out of place. Another publication belonging to this variety is Abdus-Samad

---

14 Mansūr Husayn ʿABD AL-ʿAZĪZ, *Da ʿwatu ʾl-haqq aw al-haqīqa baina ʾl-masīhīya waʾl-islām*, Cairo: Maktabat ʿalāʾ ʾl-dīn, 1972.

15 The book is "… dedicated to the Nigerian Muslim youths who attended Christian missionary schools and were subjected to vigorous propaganda by the Christian missionaries".

Sharafuddin, *About "The Myth of God Incarnate"*, of 1978.[16] This takes up the theme of a book published a few years earlier, whose authors are the well-known British theologian Maurice Wiles and the philosopher John Hick. This book discusses the myth-character of the dogma of the incarnation. Just as Muhammad ʿAtā al-Rahīm sides with the Unitarians, so Sharafuddin congratulates the authors of the book, whom he sees in the line of true Christianity.

4. Writings in the Tradition of *Kalām* and *Fiqh*

This category includes what may be called the more scholastic type of Muslim writing on other religions. It is heavily dependent on Qur'ān and *Sunna*, but makes use of empirical data to substantiate the Qur'anic normative pattern. One example is Muhammad Abū Zahra's book *Muhādarāt fi'l-nasrānīya* ("Lectures on Christianity", 1942).[17] Comparing the New Testament with the Qur'ān, the author chooses from the New Testament data that do not conflict with, but rather supplement the Qur'ān. He also indicates the points at which historical Christianity has deviated from the original pure religion. Christianity at present has little to do with the message of the prophet ʿĪsā (Jesus).

An example of a more systematic theological nature seems to be Mahmūd Abū Rayya, *Dīn Allāh wāhid ʿalā alsinat jamīʿ al-rusul*, of 1963.[18] The key of the book is the concept of the "one religion of God" beyond all empirical religions.

5. Writings with a more Philosophical Concept of Religion

Books written by Muslim authors about religion outside Islam, about religion in general, or about other religions in particular can be divided

---

[16] The author expresses the wish "… to strengthen the hands of their (i.e., the Muslims') Christian brothers, and support their basic argument in the light of the Holy Qur'ān", intending his booklet as "… a genuine bond between true Christianity and Islam" (p. ii).

[17] M. Abū Zahra, *Muhādarāt fi'l-nasrānīya: Tabhathu fi'l-adwār allatī marrat ʿalaiha ʿaqāʾidu 'l-nasārā wa-fī kutubihim wa-fī majāmiʿihim al-muqaddasati wa-firaqihim*, Cairo: Dār al-fikr al-ʿarabī, 1942/1361 (repr. 1949/1368; new repr. Cairo: Dār al-kitāb al-ʿarabī, 1961/1381). The book was reprinted several times.

[18] Mahmūd Abū Rayya, *Dīn Allāh wāhid ʿalā alsinat jamīʿ al-rusul*, Cairo: ʿĀlam al-kutub, 1963; second, revised and enlarged edition, 1970. Cf. Ali Merad, "Un penseur musulman à l'heure de l'oecuménisme: Mahmūd Abū Rayya (1889–1970)", *Islamochristiana*, 4 (1978), pp. 151–63. I have not seen this book, which apparently takes the "one religion of God" as its theological starting-point. It then considers not only empirical Islam, but also empirical Christianity and possibly other religions, against a norm that is beyond these historical religions and to which the Qur'ān refers.

into two groups. On the one hand, there are those that make clear, direct references to the Qur'ān and *Sunna*. On the other hand, a small number of books are written within a certain philosophical or theological framework, and it is possible to find a kind of intrinsic rational structure in their argumentation. Generally speaking, there is a certain relationship between the concept of religion used in the description of other religions and a particular normative view of religion in general that takes up certain lines given in the Qur'ān. Whereas in most Western studies of religions a sharp distinction is made between "science" of religion that is empirical and rational and a "philosophy" of religion that is rational and normative, in most Muslim studies the boundary between these is rather fluid. This makes it difficult in Muslim countries to speak of "history of religions" or "science of religion" as an autonomous discipline, although at present increasingly trends toward the development of such a discipline as a scholarly study of religion can be noted.

There are indeed quite a few books about religions that would be classified as "philosophy" of religion in Western countries. The ideas developed in them have important consequences for the way in which not only religion itself, but also the nature of the different religions is viewed. And this has repercussions for the way in which the relations between different religions are envisaged. I give here three examples of writings by Muslim scholars who approach other religions from such a "philosophical" angle that are available in Western languages.

Al-Fārūqī's concept of a "critical meta-religion" is a good example. He proposes the concept as being of such a general nature as to enable a comparison and evaluation of systematized "meaning-wholes" between religious data. Phenomenology as a descriptive approach to religion would be followed by an evaluative one.[19] Mahmūd Abū Rayya may have had a similar idea in mind when speaking of "one religion of God".[20] In his later work, however, al-Fārūqī tends to identify this "meta-religion" in fact with Islam, so that its critical function toward Islam is sacrificed.

A second example is the work of Seyyed Hossein Nasr. In his "Islam and the Encounter of Religions" of 1968[21], he makes a distinction between Islamic views of other religions on the level of *Sharī'a* and on the level of esotericism (*haqīqa*). In the first case, religions are seen and interpreted as divine Laws; in the second case they are viewed from the perspective of Sūfism. Whereas empirical scholarship works on textual and historical data, accepting Muslim Sūfī insight could provide a metaphysical back-

---

[19]   AL-FĀRŪQĪ, "History of Religions: Its Nature and Significance for Christian Education and the Muslim-Christian Dialogue" (see Selected Literature under section 2.).

[20]   Cf. above note 18.

[21]   This text was later reprinted and also translated on various occasions. See for instance the author's *Sufi Essays*, pp. 123–51.

ground not only for Islam, but for all religions, through its concept of the unity of revelation. For this author, the Sūfīs are "guardians of Islam and of all traditions".

A third example of books with a philosophical concept of religion is Kāmil Husayn's book *Al-wādi al-muqaddas*, of 1968[22]. It reflects upon the encounter of religions on the basis of deeper human intentions and motivations.

Further study of this category of Muslim writings on religions and religion with a philosophical concept of religion is needed.

6. References to Other Religions in *Adab*

This category is clear enough. It comprises views on religions other than Islam as well as their adherents that are expressed in Muslim works of literature, *adab*. In contrast to the preceding categories of reasoned writing, these views have a literary character. I abstain from giving examples here.

7. Writings Calling for Practical Cooperation and Joint Action

This category and the next one are not necessarily uncritical toward other religions and in some cases they do not lack apologetic and even polemical elements. Criticism and the claims of truth, however, are subordinated here on a practical level to a more open attitude toward beliefs held in other religions, Christianity in particular. A willingness to learn can be sensed here. There is a certain "common sense", a feeling for reality, an awareness of the best interests of humanity as a whole. In Muslim eyes, the difference between this category and the next one is probably more one of accent than of principle.

Writings in this category call for practical cooperation and joint action in fields that are not of a religious nature, for instance a common struggle, nation-building, social development, economic independence, social justice, and peace. Differences are acknowledged, but they are not stressed, since other interests are at play and other causes have priority. On a popular level, the virtues and potentialities of cooperation with the others may be stressed, and their religion may be painted in a rosy light, also for practical purposes. Religion may also not be mentioned at all, and only those qualities that all people have or ought to have in common are

---

[22]   K. HUSAYN, *Al-wādi al-muqaddas*, Cairo: Dār al-maʿārif, 1968. For the English translation under the title *The Hallowed Valley* see Selected Literature under section 6.

stressed. Whereas in apologetic and polemical writings all differences tend to be reduced to religious ones, in this category the religious factor is played down for the sake of unity and common action.

8. Writings Directed Towards a Positive Religious Dialogue

This category consists of writings directed toward a positive religious dialogue, in the light of which other religions are viewed. Such an attitude is not necessarily that of modernist "Westernizers". It does not imply a lack of understanding of the differences either between religions or between religious communities. Muslim authors falling within this category are not prone to make concessions. They stress, however, a common spiritual cause shared by Muslims and other believers. Consequently, a new kind of interest may be awakened, though perhaps less in the other religions taken as such than in how their adherents interpret them and what they do with them. Several variations are possible.

The common cause may consist in a joint witness of all believers and a defense against atheism, secularism, or unbelievers as the case may be. This variety seems to have a more political importance.

It is more interesting to examine some instances when the common cause is that of study. Particular aspects of other religions or of one other religion may become the subject of interest and be studied in view of their ethical or religious significance. The background of these writings is a dialogical intention. Several of the biographies of Jesus mentioned earlier would fall under this heading. One may think, for instance, of Fathī 'Uthmān's *Ma 'a 'l-masīh fī'l-anājīl al-arba 'a* of 1961, mentioned earlier.[23] It makes an effort to understand Jesus through the Christian interpretation and takes the community of Muslims and Christians for granted. His question, for instance, is not how to refute the doctrine of redemption but to see to what extent the doctrine of redemption is a determining factor in the separation of Muslims and Christians. He hints at common tasks in the field of ethics.

In this connection, Muhammad Kāmil Husayn's *Qarya zālima* of 1954[24] deserves mention. This study looks beyond literary and historical criticism and beyond the "official" Christian and Muslim interpretations of "Good Friday" for the deeper roots of the religious emotions and intentions involved. The learned author tries to find an explanation for the sensitivity to evil and for the obsession with the notion of sin which

---

[23] Cf. above note 9.
[24] Cf. above note 9. For the English translation under the title *City of Wrong* see Selected Literature under section 2.

he senses in the Christian consciousness. He alludes to it when putting his finger in this book on the disciples' traumatic experience of Jesus' death. They felt responsible and guilty for it and consequently developed a great fear of committing sins again.

These two books on issues that are highly sensitive not only for Muslims, but also for Christians, could hardly have been written if the authors had not had personal friendships crossing religious frontiers and an open attitude to common religious problems.

Dialogue, however, is not the same as studying other religions. No less a critical mind than Sādiq al-ʿAzm writes that dialogue without knowledge is nonsensical, implying that dialogue requires study and thought.[25] On such a basis, certain kinds of dialogue may lead to new views of other religions and better perceptions of the people adhering to them.

First, there are more or less official dialogues organized both by the World Council of Churches and by the Pontifical Council on Religious Dialogue of the Vatican. Meetings were organized also by Amistad in Cordoba (1974 and 1977), by Qadhdhāfī in Tripoli (February 1–6, 1976), and at the CERES in Tunis between 1974 and 1991. I leave aside other fruitful meetings both in Muslim countries and in Europe and North America and their resulting publications.

Second, there are many "unofficial" dialogues that sometimes leave their mark, for example the answers to a questionnaire handed out by Youakim Moubarac to Muslim intellectuals around 1970.[26]

Third, there are now several writings by Muslim authors stressing the need for dialogue. In this context the name of al-Fārūqī returns. In 1968, he designed a kind of dialogue between Muslims and Christians on the basis of a "reconstruction of religious thought" that would be "compatible with both Islam and Christianity". In the article he wrote on this subject in 1968[27], he does not take Christianity and Islam as two separate historical traditions, but speaks of a "Western understanding of Jesus" and a "Western figuration of Christianity" beside which others exist as well, for instance in Islam. The relationship between the monotheistic religions has been a matter of spiritual and intellectual concern for this author.

---

[25] Quoted in *Christentum im Spiegel der Weltreligionen: Kritische Texte und Kommentare*, ed. by Heinz-Jürgen Loth, Michael Mildenberger, Udo Tworuschka, Stuttgart: Quell Verlag, 1978, 1979², pp. 302–3.

[26] The results were published in *Les musulmans: Consultation islamo-chrétienne* (see Selected Literature under section 2.). This is Vol. 14 of the series "Verse et controverse: Le chrétien en dialogue avec le monde". More or less elaborate and highly interesting answers were given in writing by Muhammad Arkoun, Hassan Askari, Muhammad Hamidullah, Hassan Hanafī, Muhammad Kāmil Husayn, Ibrahim Madkour, and Seyyed Hossein Nasr. They figure as such on the title page of the book.

[27] Ismāʿīl Rāji al-Fārūqī, "Islam and Christianity: Diatribe or Dialogue?", *Journal of Ecumenical Studies*, 5 (1968), pp. 45–77.

Other Muslim intellectuals who have written positively about dialogue with other believers, including Christians, are Hasan Saʿab, Hasan Hanafī, and Mohammed Talbi. Hasan Saʿab worked on legal and moral aspects. Hasan Hanafī, who has done research on Christian theology, advances Feuerbach's thesis that theology is in essence anthropology. Mohammed Talbi's position is most philosophical in terms of human communication and reasonable in his judgments.[28]

9. Other Writings

An argument can be made to add a "dust-bin" category of writings on subjects related to Islam, in which other religions are dealt with only incidentally. It would also include historical and social scientific writings, including about religious minorities in Muslim territories and Muslim minorities outside the Muslim countries.

10. Conclusion

The criteria for our typology are—with the exception of the categories (6) and (9)—the more or less normative nature of the publications, on the one hand, and the degree of willingness to take cognizance of faiths and religions outside Islam, on the other hand. In category (4), the norms applied are drawn mainly, but not exclusively, from revelation (Qurʾān) and reason. In all other cases, human experience and common sense seem to provide most of the criteria and norms that play a role. It should be admitted that the types I distinguished are approximate and that many publications can easily be placed in more than one category. This, however, would also be the case with other typologies. A typology is devised in the first place to put some order into what seems to be a more or less chaotic mass of material.

Some remarks are in place about the kind of literature mentioned here and the way to study it. Its full significance can hardly be understood by a mere reading of the texts. These should be seen against the background of a whole history of this kind of writing in Islam, even if we focused on the period since World War Two, the "terminus a quo" of the examples in this chapter. Recent history has not been without consequence for the

---

[28] Saʿab, "Zum islamisch-christlichen Dialog" (see Selected Literature under section 2.). Hanafī, *Religious Dialogue and Revolution*; Id., "Théologie ou anthropologie". Talbi, *Islam et dialogue* (for all three see Selected Literature under section 1.).

possible ways of viewing Christianity, Judaism, and Hinduism during the twentieth century.

A further important factor in this period is the development of ideologies of various kinds that, to the extent that they have led to new interpretations of Islam, may also have affected Muslim views of other religious systems. Even purely nationalist ideologies without making any appeal to Islam have also touched upon other religions, for instance through their invectives against missionaries and their encroachments on the life of Muslim society, which they have seen as testifying to an aggressive Christianity. One should here clearly distinguish between what has been written about Christian and Jewish minorities inside Muslim countries, on the one hand, and what has been written on Christianity and Judaism outside Muslim territory and perceived as a threat, on the other.

When the assessment of certain other religions is negative in these writings, as it frequently is, this goes back in the first place to negative social experiences inflicted by what are felt to be "foreigners". These experiences are then often related to what is held to be the religion of the other party. A variety of views of this religion are then developed in which Qur'anic statements, however interpreted, may play a more or less important role. Often the non-religious and non-ideological factors that have made the others behave as they did or do are hardly seen, unless pertinent ideologies (nationalist, socialist, "Islamist") function as eye-openers.

In societies and cultures where Islam is the main religion, it is only natural that emphasis should be placed on the ideal character of Islam and often its absolute character as the religion of God. We should also not be surprised that other religions, as well as the empirical aspects of Islam, are seen very much within the domain and inside the limits set by normative patterns read from the Qur'ān—except by those who have a scholarly or ideological training. Let us not forget that the scholarly study of religions only made significant progress in the West when it arrived at insights that touched Western religion itself. It is only recently that the concept of "religion" itself has come under scrutiny in the Western study of things religious. One cannot demand that these things happen in the Muslim world in the same way.

An interesting correlation must be noticed between views held about religions outside Islam, on the one hand, and views held about Islam itself, on the other hand. Whenever the "self-view" of Islam has become such that the existence of other religions and faiths is hardly acknowledged and a religious plurality only grudgingly admitted, there arises a profound misunderstanding of other cultures and religions, such as Europe knew perhaps in its imperial heyday. It finally may lead perhaps to some kind of alienation when Islam is fully absolutized ideologically.

Selected Literature (in Western languages)

1. On Religions and Religion in General

BRELVI, Mahmud, *Islam and Its Contemporary Faiths*, Karachi, 1965.

BRODEUR, Patrice Claude, *From an Islamic Heresiography to an Islamic History of Religions: Modern Arab Muslim Literature on 'Religious Others' with Special Reference to Three Egyptian Authors*, Ph.D. Thesis, Harvard University, 1999.

HANAFĪ, Hasan, "Théologie ou anthropologie?", in *Renaissance du monde arabe: Colloque interarabe de Louvain*, sous la direction de MM. Anouar ABDEL-MALEK, Abdel-Aziz BELAL et Hassan HANAFĪ, Gembloux: Ed. Duculot, 1972, pp. 23–47.

—, *Religious Dialogue and Revolution: Essays on Judaism, Christianity and Islam*, Cairo: The Anglo-Egyptian Bookshop, 1977.

HUSAYN (HUSSEIN), Muhammad Kāmil, *The Hallowed Valley* (Arabic 1968), trans. by Kenneth CRAGG, Cairo: American University Press, 1977.

MASDOOSI, Ahmad Abdullah al-, *Living Religions of the World: A Socio-Political Study* (Urdu 1958), trans. and ed. by Zafar Ishaq ANSARI, Karachi: Begum Aisha Bawany Wakf, 1962.

NASR, Seyyed Hossein, "Islam and the Encounter of Religions" (1968), repr. in the author's *Sufi Essays* (Albany, N. Y.: SUNY Press, 1973), pp. 123–51.

TALBI, Mohamed, *Islam et dialogue: Réflexions sur un thème d'actualité*, Tunis: Maison Tunisienne de l'Edition, 1972; English translation by L. MARCHANT: "Islam and Dialogue: Some Reflections on a Current Topic", *Encounter* (Rome), Nrs. 11–12 (1975), repr. in *Christianity and Islam: The Struggling Dialogue*, ed. by Richard W. ROUSSEAU (Scranton, Pa.: Ridge Row Press, 1985), pp. 53–73.

2. On Christianity

AJIJOLA, Alhaj A.D., *The Myth of the Cross*, Lahore: Islamic Publications, 1975.

BORRMANS, Maurice, *Jésus et les musulmans d'aujourd'hui* (Jésus et Jésus-Christ 69), Paris: Desclée, 1996.

FARŪQĪ, Ismāʿīl Rāji al-, "History of Religions: Its Nature and Significance for Christian Education and the Muslim-Christian Dialogue", *Numen*, 12, Nrs. 1–2 (1965), pp. 35–95.

—, *Christian Ethics: A Historical and Systematic Analysis of its Dominant Ideas*, Montreal: McGill University Press, 1967.

GODDARD, Hugh P., *Muslim Perceptions of Christianity*, London: Grey Seal, 1996.

—, "Christianity from the Muslim Perspective: Varieties and Changes", in *Islam and Christianity: Mutual Perceptions since the mid–20th Century*, ed. by Jacques WAARDENBURG, Leuven and Paris: Peeters, 1998, pp. 213–55.

HASSABALLA, Waheed, "Le christianisme et les chrétiens vus par deux auteurs arabes" (Fadlallāh and Hudaybī), in *Islam and Christianity: Mutual Perceptions since the mid–20th Century*, ed. Jacques WAARDENBURG, Leuven and Paris: Peeters, 1998, pp. 159–211.

HUSAYN, Muhammad Kāmil, *City of Wrong* (Arabic 1954), trans. Kenneth CRAGG, Amsterdam: Djambatan, 1959; New York: Seabury Press, 1966; Oxford: Oneworld, 1994.

Les musulmans: Consultation islamo-chrétienne (Verse et Controverse 14), ed. by Youakim MOUBARAC, Paris: Beauchesne, 1971.

SAʿAB, Hasan, "Zum islamisch-christlichen Dialog", Kairos, N.F. 10 (1968), pp. 29–52.

SCHUMANN, Olaf H., "Das Christentum im Lichte der heutigen arabisch-islamischen Literatur", Zeitschrift für Religions- und Geistesgeschichte, 21 (1969), pp. 307–29.

—, Der Christus der Muslime: Christologische Aspekte in der arabisch-islamischen Literatur, Gütersloh: Gerd Mohn, 1975.

SHARAFUDDIN, Abdus-Samad, About 'The Myth of God Incarnate', being A Unique Collection of Theological Essays: An Impartial Survey of its Main Topics, Jeddah: King Abdul-Aziz University Press, 1978 (Arabic and English text).

STÜMPEL-HATAMI, Isabel, Das Christentum aus der Sicht zeitgenössischer iranischer Autoren: Eine Untersuchung religionskundlicher Publikationen in persischer Sprache (Islamkundliche Untersuchungen 195), Berlin: Klaus Schwarz, 1996.

WISMER, Don, The Islamic Jesus: An Annotated Bibliography of Sources in English and French, New York: Garland, 1977.

3. On Judaism

COHEN, Mark R., "Islam and the Jews: Myth, Countermyth, History", Jerusalem Quarterly, 38 (1986), pp. 125–37.

HADDAD, Mohanna Y.S., Arab Perspectives of Judaism: A Study of Image Formation in the Writings of Muslim Arab Authors 1948–1978, Doctoral Dissertation University of Utrecht, 1984; Arabic edition Kuwait: Dār al-silsil, 1989.

Israeli Judaism: The Sociology of Religion in Israel, ed. by Shlomo DESHEN, Charles S. LIEBMAN, Moshe SHOKEID (Studies of Israeli Society, VII), New Brunswick and London: Transaction Publishers, 1995.

JOHNS, Anthony H., "Let my People go! Sayyid Qutb and the Vocation of Moses", Islam and Christian-Muslim Relations, 1 (1990), pp. 143–70.

KLEIN, Menachem, "Religious Pragmatism and Political Violence in Jewish and Islamic Fundamentalism", in Studies in Muslim-Jewish Relations, Vol. 1, ed. by Ronald L. NETTLER (Chur: Harwood Academic Publishers, 1993), pp. 37–58.

NETTLER, Ronald L., Past Trials and Present Tribulations: A Muslim Fundamentalist's View of the Jews, Published for the Vidal Sassoon International Center for the Study of Antisemitism, The Hebrew University of Jerusalem, Oxford, etc.: Pergamon Press, 1987 (Sayyid QUTB's Our Struggle with the Jews).

—, "A Post-colonial Encounter of Traditions: Muhammad Saʿīd al-ʿAshmāwī on Islam and Judaism", in: Medieval and Modern Perspectives on Muslim-Jewish Relations, ed. by Ronald L. NETTLER (Luxembourg: Harwood Academic Publishers, 1995), pp. 175–84.

RAHMAN, Fazlur, "Islamic Attitudes towards Judaism", The Muslim World, 72 (1982), pp. 1–13.

ROSEN, Lawrence, "Muslim-Jewish Relations in a Moroccan City", International Journal of Middle Eastern Studies, 3 (1972), pp. 435–49.

SCHONEVELD, J., The Bible in Israeli Education: A Study of Approaches to the Hebrew Bible and its Teaching in Israeli Educational Literature, Assen/Amsterdam: Van Gorcum, 1976.

4. On Hinduism

ALI, Javed, "Understanding the Hindu Phenomenon", *Muslim and Arab Perspectives*, 7 (1995), pp. 31–40, 195–204.

AZIZ, Khursheed Kamal, *Muslim India 1800–1947: A Descriptive and Annotated Bibliography*, Vol. 1, Lahore: Ferozsos, 2001.

Communalism in India: History, Politics and Culture, ed. by Kandiyur N. PANIKKAR, New Delhi: Manohar, 1991.

DURRANY, Muhammad Khan, *The Gītā and the Qur'ān: An Approach to National Integration*, Delhi: Nag Publishers, 1982.

ENGINEER, Asghar Ali, "The Hindu-Muslim Problem: A Cooperative Approach", *Islam and Christian-Muslim Relations*, 1 (1990), pp. 89–105.

GANDHI, Rajmohan, *Eight Lives: A Study of the Hindu-Muslim Encounter*, Albany, N. Y.: SUNY Press, 1986.

HASSAN, Riffat, "The Basis for a Hindu-Muslim Dialogue and Steps in that Direction from a Muslim Perspective", in *Religious Liberty and Human Rights*, ed. by Leonard SWIDLER, Philadelphia: Ecumenical Press, 1986, pp. 125–42.

Inter-Religious Perceptions of Hindus and Muslims: Papers Presented to the All India Seminar in New Delhi, compiled with an Introduction by Khurram Shah DURRANY, New Delhi: The Department of Comparative Religion, Indian Institute of Islamic Studies, New Delhi, 1982.

KHAN, Rasheeduddin, "Towards Understanding Hinduism: Reflections of Some Eminent Muslims", in the author's book *Bewildered India: Identity, Pluralism, Discord*, New Delhi: Har-Anand Publications, 1995, Chapter 8 (pp. 153–92).

MAHMUD, Syed, *Hindu-Muslim Cultural Accord*, Bombay: Vora, 1949.

McDONOUGH, Sheila, *Gandhi's Responses to Islam* (Islamic Heritage in Cross-Cultural Perspectives 1). New Delhi: D. K. Printworld, 1994.

MILLER, Roland E., "The Dynamics of Religious Coexistence in Kerala: Muslims, Christians, and Hindus", in *Christian-Muslim Encounters*, ed. by Yvonne Yazbeck HADDAD and Wadi Z. HADDAD (Gainesville: University Press of Florida, 1995), pp. 263–84.

NARAIN, Harsh, "The Concept of Revelation in Hinduism and Islam", *Islam and the Modern Age*, 6, Nr. 1 (1975), pp. 32–64.

—, "Feasibility of a Dialogue between Hinduism and Islam", *Islam and the Modern Age*, 6, Nr. 4 (1975), pp. 57–85.

SIDDIQUI, Mohammed Khalil Abbas, *Hindu-Muslim Relations*, Calcutta: Abadi Publications, 1993.

SMITH, Wilfred Cantwell, *Modern Islam in India: A Social Analysis*, Lahore: Minerva Bookshop, 1943; revised edition London: Victor Gollancz, 1946 (reprint Lahore: Ashraf, 1963); revised edition Lahore: Ripon Printing Press, 1947.

TROLL, Christian W., "Sharing Islamically in the Pluralistic Nation-state of India: The Views of Some Contemporary Indian Muslim Leaders and Thinkers", in *Christian-Muslim Encounters*, ed. by Yvonne Yazbeck HADDAD and Wadi Z. HADDAD (Gainesville: University Press of Florida, 1995), pp. 245–62.

5. On Buddhism

Scott, David, "Buddhism and Islam: Past to Present Encounters and Interfaith Lessons", *Religion*, 42 (1995), pp. 141–71.

6. On Confucianism

Islam and Confucianism: A Civilizational Dialogue, ed. by Osman Bakar and Cheng Gek Nai (University of Malaya Civilizational Dialogue Series), Kuala Lumpur: University of Malaya Press, 1997.

7. On Islam and Religious Plurality

Arkoun, Mohammed, "The Notion of Revelation: From *ahl al-kitāb* to the Societies of the Book", *Welt des Islams*, 28 (1988), pp. 62–89.

Ayoub, Mahmoud, "The Word of God and the Voices of Humanity", in *The Experience of Religious Diversity*, ed. by John Hick and Hasan Askari (London: Gower, 1985), pp. 53–65.

Charfi, Abdelmajid, "L'Islam et les religions non musulmanes: Quelques textes positifs", *Islamochristiana*, 3 (1977), pp. 39–63.

Expert-Bezançon, Hélène, "Regard d'un humaniste égyptien, le Dr Kāmil Husayn, sur les religions non-musulmanes", *Islamochristiana* 14 (1988), pp. 17–49.

Farūqī, Ismā'īl Rāji al-, "The Role of Islam in Global Interreligious Dependence", in *Towards a Global Congress of the World's Religions*, ed. by Warren Lewis (New York: Rose of Sharon Press, 1980), pp. 19–53.

Husayn (Hussein), Muhammad Kāmil, *The Hallowed Valley* (Arabic 1968), trans. by Kenneth Cragg, Cairo: American University of Cairo Press, 1977.

Moussalli, Ahmad S., "Islamic Fundamentalist Perceptions of Other Monotheistic Religions", in *Islam and Christianity: Mutual Perceptions since the mid–20th Century*, ed. by Jacques Waardenburg (Leuven: Peeters, 1998), pp. 121–57.

Shepard, William, "A Modernist View of Islam and Other Religions (Ahmad Amīn)", *The Muslim World*, 65 (1975), pp. 79–92.

—, "Conversations in Cairo: Some Contemporary Muslim Views of Other Religions", *The Muslim World*, 70 (1980), pp. 171–95.

Troll, Christian W., "Salvation of non-Muslims: Views of Some Eminent Muslim Religious Thinkers", *Islam and the Modern Age*, 14 (1983), pp. 104–14.

Vogelaar, Harold S., "Religious Pluralism in the Thought of Muhammad Kāmil Hussein", in *Christian-Muslim Encounters*, ed. by Yvonne Yazbeck Haddad and Wadi Z. Haddad (Gainesville: University Press of Florida, 1995), pp. 411–25.

Zebiri, Kate, "Relations between Muslims and non-Muslims in the Thought of Western-educated Muslim Intellectuals", *Islam and Christian-Muslim Relations*, 6 (1995), pp. 255–77.

Chapter 8
Some Observations on Muslim Studies of Religions[1]

In June 1988, the International Association for the History of Religions organized a small conference in Marburg on the development and institutional setting of the discipline in different areas of the world.[2] Papers were read about the study of religions in African and Asian countries, in a Catholic and a Jewish environment, and also in a Muslim context. A Muslim speaker remarked that, fundamentally, Islam as a religion does not object to this kind of studies.[3]

The present chapter is meant as a contribution to the same subject, leaving aside the history of Muslim views of other religions.[4] I confine myself to making a preliminary exploration of the present-day setting of the scholarly study of religion as it exists in Muslim countries around 2000.[5] I take here the scholarly study of religions in its broadest sense:

---

[1]   A first draft of this paper was read at the 17th Congress of the International Association for the History of Religions held in Mexico City, August 1995. This is a revised version of an earlier text published in *Numen*, 45 (1998), pp. 235–57, and in *Perspectives on Method and Theory in the Study of Religion: Adjunct Proceedings of the XVIIth Congress of the International Association for the History of Religions, Mexico City, 1995*, ed. by Armin W. GEERTZ and Russell T. McCUTCHEON, with the assistance of Scott S. ELLIOTT, Leiden, etc.: E. J. Brill, 2000, pp. 91–109.

[2]   The conference was titled "The Institutional Environment of the Study of Religion". The papers under discussion were contained in the Conference Guide. Most of them were published in *Marburg Revisited: Institutions and Strategies in the Study of Religion*.

[3]   This observation was made by Prof. Mahmoud ZAKZOUK from al-Azhar University (later Minister of Waqfs and Islamic Affairs). He added, with reference to S. 109:6, that there is a Qur'anic basis for studying not only the "celestial religions" of the *ahl al-kitāb* (Judaism and Christianity), but other religions as well. See *Marburg Revisited*, pp. 144–7. Prof. Azim A. NANJI from the Institute of Ismaili Studies in London also spoke positively about the study of religions other than Islam and referred to S. 5:48, postulating a multifaith world. See *Marburg Revisited*, pp. 147–9. In the broader discussion that followed, the need for personal and institutional cooperation between scholars inside and outside the Muslim world was stressed. See *Marburg Revisited*, pp. 153–6.

[4]   See *Muslim Perceptions of Other Religions: A Historical Survey*. Cf. WAARDENBURG, *Islam et Sciences des Religions* (in particular Part Two: "Approches musulmanes d'autres religions").

[5]   This article is based on a few books written in "Islamic" languages, some books and articles in "Western" languages, and oral information acquired at random. It is a continuation of my contribution to the Marburg conference of 1988, "Religious Studies

textual studies, the history of religions, comparative studies, social scientific studies, and what I call "research on meaning" including phenomenological, hermeneutical, and semiotic approaches.[6]

I shall here very succinctly survey the scholarly study of Islam, of other religions, and of religion in the perspective of the social sciences as it has been pursued in at least some Muslim countries.[7] I leave aside philosophically oriented work in which other religions are referred to but not closely studied. In conclusion, I shall mention some incentives for the study of religions that can be found in the Islamic cultural tradition. In a time of encounter—rather than clash—of civilizations, this tradition should be continued to the benefit of scholarship in our field, carried out by Muslims and non-Muslims alike.

1. Islamic Studies

Throughout history and in the various regions of Muslim civilization, Islamic institutions of learning have always given much attention to Islamic thought and its history, mainly through the study of relevant Arabic texts.[8] The Islamic thought studied here is primarily religious thought, such as the study of the Qur'ān and its commentaries (*tafsīr*), the study of Tradition (*'ilm al-hadīth*), the study of Islamic Law or *Sharī'a* (*fiqh*), scholastic theology (*kalām*), and also mystical thought (*tasawwuf*). But it can also include philosophical and scientific thought within the framework of Islamic civilization, such as Aristotelian *falsafa*, Iranian *ishrāq* philosophy, and cosmological doctrine.[9]

---

in the Muslim World". Cf. Peter ANTES, "Religious Studies in the context of Islamic culture", in *Marburg Revisited*, pp. 143–56. No bibliography exists of nineteenth- and twentieth-century Muslim studies of other religions. It would be worth tracing doctoral dissertations in Western languages written by Muslim authors concerning religions other than Islam.

[6]   For this division, see WAARDENBURG, *Des dieux qui se rapprochent*; ID., *Perspektiven der Religionswissenschaft*.

[7]   More detailed research on publications in Arabic, Persian, Turkish, and other "Islamic" languages is needed to cast light on relevant new findings by Muslim scholars. Apart from more scholarly work, a mass of more popular religious writings on Islam and also more popular writings on other religions exists in all Muslim countries.

[8]   These institutions have a long history. By way of introduction, see WAARDENBURG, "Some Institutional Aspects of Muslim Higher Education and their Relation to Islam". On the history of Islamic education, see e.g. SHALABĪ, *History of Muslim Education*. Cf. ASHRAF, *New Horizons in Muslim Education*.

[9]   A comprehensive view of the history of Islamic thought in the broader sense by a number of Muslim authors is given, for instance, in *A History of Islamic Philosophy*. On *ishrāq* philosophy, see the works of Henry CORBIN as discussed in *Henry Corbin*, ed. by Christian JAMBET, Paris: Les Cahiers de l'Herne, 1981. On cosmological doctrine, see Seyyed Hossein NASR, *An Introduction to Islamic Cosmological Doctrines*, Cambridge: Harvard University Press, 1964.

The textual study of religious thought has always been at the center of study in mosques and in the traditional Islamic educational institutions (*madāris*). The latter generally disappeared when university institutions were established.[10] Within modern universities, this study is concentrated in the Faculties of *Sharī'a*.[11] Although these faculties concentrate on the study of religious Law and its sources, such as Qur'ān and *hadīths*, they also address disciplines like *'usūl al-dīn* (principles, i.e., methodology of religious studies) and *kalām* (scholastic theology). Islamic thought can also be studied in a more detached way in the Arts Faculties, for instance in Departments of Arabic Language and Literature, Philosophy, or History.[12] Since World War Two, besides the regular universities, some new institutions have been founded to promote scholarly research on the history of Islamic thought. Examples are the Research Institute of the Turkish Encyclopedia of Islam in Istanbul[13], the Institute of Islamic Studies at the Hamdard University in New Delhi[14], and the Royal Academy of Islamic Research in Amman.[15]

For the last half-century, the study of Islamic thought has become increasingly relevant for present-day Muslim orientations toward Islam, including what is called re-Islamization. Institutions of a new kind have been established with the explicit aim of training students in the spirit of Islam,

---

[10] Traditional Islamic education had its own system of schooling and preparing future *imāms* of greater mosques, teachers of religion, judges, Islamic scholars, etc. Most famous is probably al-Azhar in Cairo, which became a state university with faculties other than the "Islamic" ones in 1961. On al-Azhar, see ECCEL, *Egypt, Islam, and Social Change.*

[11] In Turkey these faculties are called Faculties of Theology. Seven of them have chairs of history of religions at present.

[12] Departments of Arabic can include the study of the Qur'ān text. Departments of Philosophy may give attention to the history of Islamic thought, schools of Western thought, and sometimes also doctrines of other religions such as Christianity. Departments of History can treat the history of Islamic civilization, but sometimes also ancient civilizations and religions. This is the case, for instance, at the University of Cairo, where critical scholarship on the Qur'ān text developed from Muhammad Khalafallah in the late 1940s up to Nasr Abu Zayd, who is now working at the University of Leiden.

[13] When the new Turkish Encyclopedia of Islam (*İslâm Ansiklopedisi*) was planned in the early 1980s, a Research Institute (*Türkiye Diyanet Vakfı İslâm Araştırmaları Merkezi, İSAM*) was established in Istanbul to prepare it. Junior researchers attached to this Institute are encouraged to pursue doctoral and post-doctoral research, if necessary abroad. It has some 150 researchers on its staff and the *İslâm Ansiklopedisi* has about 2000 collaborators, also outside Turkey. The first volume appeared in 1988; Vol. 24 appeared in 2001. In the meantime, a gigantic library is being built up. This is one of the largest projects of Islamic studies known to me; it has been carefully planned and is executed with discipline.

[14] Hamdard University in New Delhi started as a private university, but later became a state university. Its Institute of Islamic Studies has a rich collection of manuscripts, most of them waiting to be studied.

[15] This is the *Āl al-bayt* Foundation, devoted to research on Islamic civilization.

more specifically with an Islamic worldview. This happened first on a national level.[16] Then, several "international Islamic universities" were created, for instance in Islamabad, Kuala Lumpur, and Khartoum, which attract students from many Muslim countries. These "Islamic" universities base themselves on religious principles and seek to integrate the various disciplines within an Islamic worldview, comparable with Catholic or Protestant universities that aim at such an integration within a Catholic or Protestant worldview.[17] An American institution working in this sense is the International Institute of Islamic Thought, established in 1981 at Herndon, Virginia, near Washington, D.C. It was followed by the School of Islamic and Social Sciences, established in Leesburg, Virginia, in 1996.[18] A fourth example is the International Institute of Islamic Thought and Civilization, established in Kuala Lumpur.

Although studies based on an Islamic worldview may take ideological forms, there are deeper motivations, too. Religious studies nowadays, in particular in Asian, African, and Latin American countries, are often motivated by the desire to rediscover and appropriate one's own religious and cultural heritage. Such studies are then fundamentally studies of one's religion, culture, and civilization, of which one may also bear witness to others. Religious studies can then lead to a new kind of knowledge and understanding of one's own roots. They often foster a better knowledge of the values of one's own religion and possibly a new understanding and better practice of it.[19] This is also increasingly the case with religious studies in Western countries.

---

[16]   Several institutions of Islamic studies have been established on a national level. Saudi Arabia established several new institutions; Iran modernized existing institutions in Qom. In Pakistan, the Institute of Islamic Research was founded at the beginning of the 1960s, with Fazlur Rahman as its first Director. It was originally meant to function as an advisory body to the government; at present it is part of the International Islamic University in Islamabad. In Indonesia, the first State Institute for Islamic Studies (IAIN) was founded in 1960; in 1985 there were 14 such Institutes with 84 Faculties altogether. A number of Indonesian graduate students have been sent to the University of Leiden, to McGill University in Montreal and elsewhere for further training.

[17]   On the International Islamic University in Islamabad, see MALIK, "Islamic Mission and Call". The Islamic worldview is promoted by what is called the "Islamization of knowledge". This program, launched by Ismāʿīl Rāji al-Fārūqī in the USA, strives to develop a specifically Islamic epistemology and to study economics, anthropology, education, and social sciences in general on the basis of Islamic premises. See *Islamization of Knowledge: General Principles and Work Plan*. See also AHMED, art. "Education: The Islamization of Knowledge". For a thorough study, see STENBERG, *The Islamization of Science*.

[18]   The institution at Herndon was founded by Ismāʿīl Rāji al-Fārūqī with funding from Saudi Arabia.

[19]   For examples of religious studies to rediscover one's own religious heritage in Africa and China, see *Marburg Revisited*, pp. 99–141. The remark is valid not only for quantitatively small religions such as the traditional African religions, but also for the larger religions. History of religions in China is largely the study of Chinese religions,

This orientation has always existed in Jewish studies. It is also obvious in Islamic studies, where Islam may be presented as the best of all religions and ideological systems. Ideological orientations can mobilize students and people in general to acquire a knowledge that is socially and religiously relevant. But they may also lead to intellectual subservience when certain issues cannot be questioned and discussed. In Muslim countries, Islamic studies function in a Muslim context, in Western countries in a mostly secular one.[20]

Most Muslim countries at present assign Islam a specific place in society, often with a kind of "official" or "officialized" version of Islam presented in the public sphere. Islamic education in state institutions will be in the spirit of that version of Islam. The variety of existing traditions, forms of modernization, and kinds of political organization accounts largely for the variety of ways in which Islam is presented in Muslim educational institutions. This is even the case in "Islamic" states, such as Saudi Arabia, Iran, Pakistan, and Sudan, which claim to be based on the *Sharī'a*, though they interpret it differently. This situation also explains the various ways in which Islamic studies are organized in present-day Muslim countries.[21] It affects the ways in which other religions are presented and studied. Notwithstanding various pressures to which Islamic and religious studies have been exposed in a number of Muslim countries, there are always scholars, teachers, and students who are concerned with the search for true knowledge, both of their own and of other religions.

---

in Japan largely that of Buddhism, etc. In many countries—including for many people in the West today—the ideal of studying far-away "foreign" religions now takes second place to that of studying one's own "religious system" in which one can become more or less involved. This was evident at the IAHR Congresses held in Mexico City (1995) and Durban (2000).

[20] Throughout history, Islamic educational institutions have upheld the tradition of keeping a certain aloofness from immediate political interests. This was possible because of their financial independence as *waqf* institutions. In Iran, the traditional Shī'ī religious institutions, for instance in Qom, still retain this financial independence. This allowed them, for instance, to take a critical attitude to the secularizing policies of the Shah, which contributed to the revolution of 1979. The Shī'ī institutions in Najaf and Karbala (Iraq) enjoyed independence until the 1970s.

[21] In the past, teachers and students throughout the Muslim world were very mobile; students used to travel to study with reputed scholars. This pattern has been revived in a new way with the possibility for Muslim students to obtain scholarships to study at national and international Islamic universities. The Azhar University in Cairo and the Universities of Riyadh, Mecca, and Medina in Saudi Arabia, as well as the International Islamic Universities mentioned above, offer scholarships to thousands of students from many countries.

2. The Study of Religions Other than Islam

Medieval Islamic civilization could be proud of scholars like al-Bīrūnī (973–after 1050)[22] and al-Shahrastānī (1086–1153)[23], who were "medieval" scholars of religions, but eminent ones and in the case of al-Bīrūnī, of recognized genius. The following centuries, however, show a lack of interest in the study of other religions than Islam. What is the present situation?[24]

2.1. Books on Other Religions

At present there is a certain renewal of interest in this field. People with a university education, students, and also a broader public ask for information about other religions. In a number of Muslim countries, popular books on other religions, especially the monotheistic ones, are on sale in Arabic, Turkish, Indonesian, and other languages. They are sometimes translated from Western languages, sometimes directly written in the language concerned; nearly all of them pass judgment on other religions.[25]

---

[22] Abū 'l-Rayhān al-BīRŪNī is especially known for his *Kitāb ta'rīkh al-hind* ("The history of India") or *Kitāb tahqīq mā li'l-hind min maqūla maqbūla fī'l-'aql aw mardhūla* ("Ascertaining of statements to be accorded intellectual acceptance or to be rejected concerning India"), translated under the title of *Alberuni's India: An account of the Religion, Philosophy, Literature, Geography, Chronology, Astronomy, Customs, Laws and Astrology of India about A.D. 1030*. He wrote a number of scientific works, innovative at the time, some of which testify to his precise knowledge of the religious calendars, festivals, etc. of various peoples and religious communities, including Christians.

[23] Abū'l-Fath al-SHAHRASTĀNī is especially known for his *Kitāb al-milal wa'l-nihal* (Book of religions and systems of belief), translated into French under the title *Livre des religions et des sectes* by Daniel GIMARET, Jean JOLIVET and Guy MONNOT, 2 Vols., Leuven and Paris: Peeters and Unesco, 1986 and 1993. He also wrote on the Islamic religious sciences, in particular *kalām*.

[24] See above Chapter 7 on "Twentieth Century Writings about Other Religions: A Classification". Cf. WAARDENBURG, "Religious Studies in the Muslim World"; ID., "Muslimisches Interesse an anderen Religionen im soziopolitischen Kontext des 20. Jahrhunderts". See also the publications mentioned above in note 4.

[25] A few examples of books written by Muslim authors may be given:
In Arabic: Muhammad ABŪ ZAHRA, *Muhādarāt fī'l-nasrāniyya: Tabhathu fī'l-adwār allatī marrat 'alaihā 'aqā'id al-nasārā wa-fī kutubihim wa-fī majāmi'ihim al-muqaddasa wa-firaqihim* ("Lectures on Christianity, treating the stages through which the dogmas of Christianity have passed, their Books, their Ecumenical Councils and their divisions"), Cairo: Dār al-kitāb al-'arabī, 1942), and *Al-diyānāt al-qadīma* ("The ancient religions"), Cairo: Dār al-fikr al-'arabī, ca. 1940. The first book seeks to be informative, but it represents the traditional Islamic view of Christianity and is still authoritative. Muhsin AL-'ABID, *Madkhal fī ta'rīkh al-adyān* ("Introduction to the history of religions"), Sousse: Dār al-kitāb, 1973. A large work that discusses the value of other beliefs and practices is Hasan KHĀLID, *Mawqif al-islām min al-wathaniyya wa'l-*

As far as I could ascertain, most of these books directly or indirectly make it clear to the reader in often blunt terms that Islam is the only true religion and the true alternative to the other religions that are described.

This is the general starting point from which the religions are approached, but a distinction should be made. On the one hand, there are what may be called apologetic, polemical, and ideological accounts.[26] On the other hand, books also exist on religions other than Islam that are more descriptive and pass judgment only at the end and in a rational way. Some informative books breathing an atmosphere and style of tolerance have seen the light, for instance in Indonesia and Turkey.[27]

2.2. Teaching and Research

Although teaching and research on religions other than Islam must be called modest in scope, some interesting initiatives have been taken. The Research Institute of the Turkish Encyclopedia of Islam in Istanbul pays attention to the history of religions. At the beginning of 1998, a chair for the study of the three monotheistic religions was established at the University of Rabat, with the cooperation of UNESCO. Research on ancient religions of the Near East is being planned by Prof. ʿAbd al-Majīd al-Charfī (Arabic: al-Sharfī) in the Faculty of Arts in Manouba, at the University of Tunis. In Lebanon, several universities, Christian, Muslim, or otherwise, now offer courses in the field of history of religions. In

---

yahūdiyya waʾl-nasrāniyya ("Islam's attitude to paganism, Judaism and Christianity"), Beirut: Maʿhad al-inmaʾ al-ʿarabī, 1986.

In Turkish: Günay TÜMER and Abdurrahman KÜÇÜK, *Dinler Tarihi* ("The history of religions"), Ankara: Eylül, 1997[3], and Hilmi YAVUZ, *Dinler Tarihi Ansiklopedisi* ("Encyclopedia of the History of Religions"), Istanbul, 1976. In libraries one can still find the "classical" work of the German (non-Muslim) scholar Annemarie SCHIMMEL, *Dinler Tarihine Giriş* ("Introduction to the history of religions"), Ankara, 1955.

In Persian: Muhammad Javād MASHKŪR, *Khulāsa-i adyān dar tarīkh-i dīnhā-i buzurg*, Teheran: Intishārāt-i sharq, 1989[3]/1368.

In Indonesian: H. ABU AHMADI, *Perbandingan agama* ("The study of religions"), Jakarta: Rineka Cipta, 1970 with several reprints, and A. MUKTI ALI, *Ilmu perbandingan agama* ("The scholarly study of religions"), Yogyakarta: Yayasan Nida, 1975.

26 Ahmad SHALABĪ, *Muqāranat al-adyān* ("The comparison of religions"), Cairo: Maktabat al-nahda al-hadītha, 1960–5. It contains four volumes: *al-Masīhīya* ("Christianity") (1960), *al-Islām* ("Islam") (1961), *Adyān al-hind al-kubrā: Al-hindawīya, al-jaynīya, al-būdhīya* ("The great religions of India: Hinduism, Jainism and Buddhism") (1964), and *al-Yahūdīya* ("Judaism") (1965). It has been reprinted several times and translated into Indonesian, Urdu, and Turkish.

27 Such studies have been made especially by students of Prof. Mukti Ali in Yogyakarta. I have not yet found similar empirical descriptive "phenomenological" accounts of religious phenomena in other Muslim countries. In Turkey, Hikmet TANYU and his disciples established history of religions as a discipline.

countries like Turkey[28] and Indonesia[29], universities have teaching positions in the history of religions. In Malaysia and Pakistan, there is some
teaching of comparative religion at universities. Some universities in
Muslim sub-Saharan African countries have Departments of Religion
where Christianity, Islam, and local traditional religions are taught.

In most Muslim countries, however, as in many other Asian and African
countries, the field of Religious Studies or History of Religions has not yet
been institutionalized. This happens earlier in countries that have multifaith
societies than in countries with homogeneous Muslim societies.

2.3. Library Resources

The library facilities in these countries are under great financial pressure,
so that books on other religions are often dispensed with. It is painful to
see that libraries that were reasonably well equipped throughout the
1950s and 1960s deteriorated sharply in the 1970s.[30] At present, hardly
any good books in English, not to speak of other Western languages, on
the history of religions are available in the bookshops and libraries of
these countries, simply because of lack of hard currency.[31] One could
think of offering a gift of scholarly books in the field. Another initiative
would be to make available translations of some important religious texts
of other religions into the language of the country, possibly with comments by an adherent of the religion concerned.[32] One can also think of

---

[28]   When the Faculty of Theology was established at the University of Ankara in 1949, it
      comprised a chair of history of religions. Professor Annemarie Schimmel taught there
      from 1954 until 1959. On the development of history of religions in Turkey, see Hikmet
      TANYU, "Türkiye' de dinler tarihi'nin tarihçesi", in *Ankara Üniversitesi Ilāhiyat Fakültesi
      Dergisi*, 8 (1961), pp. 109–24. For present-day research and publications, see Mustafa
      ERDEM, "Türkiye' de dinler tarihi sahasinda yapılmıs lisansüstü tezler üzerine düşün-
      celer", in *Türkiye I: Dinler Tarihi Arastýrmalan Semposyumum (24–25 Eylül 1992)*,
      Samsun, 1992, pp. 83–95.
[29]   The State Institutes for Islamic Studies (IAIN) have Departments of Comparative
      Religion in their Faculty of *Ushuluddin* (Principles of religion). At the IAIN in
      Yogyakarta, Mukti Ali initiated such a program. Cf. below notes 40 and 52, also on
      the development of comparative religion in Indonesia.
[30]   The Library of the Institute of Islamic Research in Pakistan, now attached to the
      International Islamic University in Islamabad, for example acquired many books on
      comparative religion in its first decade, during the 1960s. After the departure of Fazlur
      Rahman, acquisitions in this field virtually stopped.
[31]   There are exceptions, however, such as the Library of the Research Institute of the
      Turkish Encyclopedia of Islam in Istanbul. The library of the International Institute of
      Islamic Thought and Civilization (ISTAC) in Kuala Lumpur has a good collection of
      books on the various world religions. It succeeded in acquiring part of Bertold Spuler's
      personal library. The Library of the Abd al-Aziz Foundation in Casablanca has a
      splendid collection of Arabic and Western books.
[32]   One might also think of translating some of the volumes of the series "Spirituality of
      Mankind" into at least one oriental language, retaining some of the texts in the original
      language.

adapting a Western introduction to the study of religions. In this way, a
new kind of "textbooks" of history of religions could be designed.

2.4. Teaching of Languages

Ancient Indian languages like Sanskrit or Pali are of course taught in a
number of universities in India. It would be of interest to know whether
they are also taught in some Muslim universities in the Indian subcontinent. There is instruction in ancient Egyptian at the University of Cairo,
and in Accadian at the University of Baghdad, but it is difficult to know
to what extent ancient religious texts are studied there. Biblical Hebrew
is taught at several universities, for instance at those of Cairo and Rabat.
It used to be possible to study ancient and middle Persian texts—besides
Arabic ones—of religions like Mazdaism and also Manicheism[33] at the
University of Teheran.[34] It would be important to know where in Muslim
countries Syriac, Greek, and Latin are taught.

2.5. The Study of Christianity, Judaism, and Hinduism

The "heavenly" religions, which are considered to have been revealed,
receive particular attention in Muslim writings; this is especially true of
Christianity. In Egypt, for instance, a number of books have been published in Arabic on Jesus, the Gospels, and especially the early history of
Christianity. These subjects are nearly always presented within the parameters of the Qur'anic data on them, but sometimes Qur'anic and
Biblical data are compared.[35] In Iran from the 1870s on, however, there
has been a tradition of more independent writing on Christianity, largely
in response to the Christian missions, to which several outstanding authors have contributed.[36]

Recently some studies have appeared in Arabic, Turkish, and French
on medieval Islamic polemical literature against Christianity.[37] Such works

---

[33] See for instance the monumental collection of Arabic texts on Manicheism, edited and
    studied by S. Hasan TAQĪZĀDEH and Ahmad Ashgār AL-SHĪRĀZĪ, *Mānī va dīn-i ū* ("Mani
    and his religion"), Teheran, 1956/1335.
[34] The religion of Zarathustra has always aroused curiosity and interest among Iranian
    intellectuals as part of the national heritage.
[35] See GODDARD, *Muslim Perceptions of Christianity*. See also his bibliography "Works
    about Christianity by Egyptian Muslim Authors, 1940–1980".
[36] See STÜMPEL-HATAMI, *Das Christentum aus der Sicht zeitgenössischer iranischer Autoren*.
[37] In Arabic: 'Abd al-Majīd al-SHARFĪ, *Al-fikr al-islāmī fī'l-radd 'alā 'l-naṣārā ilā nihāyat
    al-qarn al-rābi'/al-'āshir* ("Islamic thought in its refutation of Christians up to the end
    of the fourth/tenth century"), Tunis: Al-dār al-tūnisiyya li'l-nashr, and Algers: Al-
    mu'assasa al-waṭaniyya li'l-kitāb, 1986. The conclusion was translated into French by
    Robert CASPAR, "Pour une nouvelle approche du christianisme par la pensée musul-
    mane", *Islamochristiana* 13 (1987), pp. 61–77. Compare, by the same author, "Polé-

may serve new polemical purposes, but they may also offer a reassessment of the medieval positions and a fresh consideration of the relationship between the two religions.[38]

Besides studies like those mentioned, addressed to readers with a more open mind, a widespread popular and often rather cheap kind of polemical literature against Christianity continues to exist. Since they are written in Arabic, Turkish, Persian, and Urdu, these writings are not well known in the West.[39] They fall outside our subject. Muslims who simply want to obtain information about Christianity and do not know foreign languages must be rather at a loss with only the available literature to go on. Contacts with adherents of other faiths, of course without aiming at conversion, may lead to better information and may encourage the study of other religions, including Christianity. Studying religions does not necessarily mean adhering to them.[40]

Present-day books about Judaism and Hinduism, as far as I have been able to verify, are almost exclusively polemical, especially regarding the

---

miques islamo-chrétiennes à l'époque médiévale", *Studia Religiosa Helvetica*, Jahrbuch Vol. 1, Bern, etc.: Peter Lang, 1995, pp. 261–74.

In Turkish: Mehmet AYDIN, *Müslümanların hıristiyanlığa karşı yazdığı reddiyeler ve tartışma konuları* ("The refutations written by Muslims against Christians and the subjects of their disputes"), Konya: Selçuk Üniversitesi basımevi, 1989.

In French: BOUAMAMA, *La littérature polémique musulmane contre le christianisme depuis ses origines jusqu'au XIIIe siècle*.

[38] A contribution in this sense is the Ph.D. Dissertation by AASI, *Muslim Understanding of Other Religions*, submitted at Temple University in 1986 and later published by the Institute of Islamic Research in Islamabad. Dr. Aasi prepared his dissertation under Ismāʿīl R. al-Fārūqī, one of the first Muslim scholars to develop the project of an "Islamic" science of religion which he wanted to be able to contribute to interreligious dialogue. See his article "History of Religions: Its Nature and Significance for Christian Education and the Muslim-Christian Dialogue", *Numen*, 12 (1965), pp. 35–95. Al-Fārūqī wrote a long study *Christian Ethics* (Montreal: McGill University Press, 1967). Here he studies New Testament and patristic data in detail, to judge these according to Islamic criteria. Apart from the fact that the author neglects for instance twentieth-century Christian ethical thinking, his study is an evaluative, not an empirical one. Given this orientation, it is regrettable that he does not go into the ethical dimension of Muslim-Christian cooperation and dialogue. Fundamentally, the book asserts confrontation between Islam and Christianity, also in matters of ethics. Cf. the collection of essays of al-FĀRŪQĪ (*Islam and Other Faiths*, ed. by Ataullah SIDDIQI, Markfield, U. K.: The Islamic Foundation, and Herndon, Va.: The International Institute of Islamic Thought, 1998/1419). A scholarly monograph on al-Fārūqī's work in its context is needed.

[39] The other way round, one must add that the presentation of Christianity by Westerners in these languages has often been of a rather cheap apologetic nature, too. Christian polemical literature against Islam has mostly been rather narrow.

[40] This is certainly the case in Indonesia, where interfaith dialogue has been officially encouraged, if not prescribed for the last thirty years. An "Institute for the Study of Religious Harmony" was founded in Yogyakarta in 1993. In 1995, a new periodical saw the light, *Religiosa: Indonesian Journal on Indonesian Harmony*, published by the State Institute of Islamic Studies (IAIN) in Yogyakarta. Cf. below note 52.

political use of these religions after World War Two. Zionism, for instance, is considered as a political outgrowth of Judaism and viewed as a religious phenomenon.[41] By comparison, Muslim refutations of Hinduism are less extreme.[42] There are instances, on the other hand, of Muslim researchers willing to learn either Hebrew or Sanskrit in order to study Judaism or Indian religions. To what extent the results of their work have been published or disseminated in other ways is difficult to know.

2.6. Study in the West

Given the overall situation in Muslim countries in the field, students wanting to study other religions and cultures may be advised to enroll in Western universities. They require, however, besides substantial financial means, a capacity for intellectual adaptation and the courage to pursue studies in a secular climate. Everywhere religious studies is now a recognized discipline. Well-known study programs in religion operate at present, for instance, at the School of Oriental and African Studies in London; at Harvard University in Cambridge, Massachusetts; and at the 5th Section of the École Pratique des Hautes Études in Paris.

Christianity and Muslim-Christian relations can be studied at a specialized institution connected for instance with Georgetown University in Washington, D.C., and with the University of Birmingham, which offers instruction up to the Ph.D. level, with the participation of both Muslim and Christian teaching staff.[43] A well-known institution exists at Hartford, Connecticut, which cooperates with the Department of Religious Studies at Temple University in Philadelphia, Pennsylvania.[44]

In Lebanon, an Institut d'Etudes Islamo-Chrétiennes is attached to the (Catholic) St. Joseph University in Beirut, and a Center for Christian Muslim Studies (Centre d'Etudes Christiano-Islamiques) has been established at the (Orthodox) University of Balamand near Tripoli, also with the participation of both Muslim and Christian teaching staff. Such courses are not meant to win adherents or to mobilize enemies, but to offer

---

[41] HADDAD, *Arab Perspectives of Judaism*. This study makes clear how much the interest in other religions is conditioned by contextual factors. In case of political conflict, a distorted view of the religion of the other party arises, especially if this religion plays a role in the conflict.

[42] For positive Muslim statements about Hinduism, see for instance KHAN, "Towards Understanding Hinduism: Reflections of Some Eminent Muslims".

[43] Centre for the Study of Islam and Christian-Muslim Relations in Birmingham, U.K. The Centre was founded in 1976. It was first part of Selly Oak Colleges and became part of the University of Birmingham in 1999. See Chapter 17 on "Between Baghdad and Birmingham: Opportunities of Minorities".

[44] The Duncan Black Macdonald Center for the Study of Islam and Christian-Muslim Relations at Hartford Seminary, Hartford, Connecticut, USA.

reliable and solid knowledge. Interest among Muslim students in the study of Christianity and other religions has been growing over the last decades under the impact of growing communication (Internet!), sheer curiosity, and the search for information, as well as the context of Muslim-Christian cooperation and dialogue.[45]

3. The Study of Religions in the Social Sciences

A promising perspective for Muslim studies of present-day religions is that offered in sociological and anthropological research. Research on contemporary Muslim societies started in the colonial period and was then largely conditioned by colonial needs and political interests, although there have always been independent scholars. French ethnographers and sociologists, for instance, did fieldwork in French territories in North and Subsaharan Africa[46], while English-speaking anthropologists tended to do their research in those countries that were part of the British Empire[47]. Since independence, this research tradition has been taken up critically, and research was then further developed both by Western and by Muslim researchers of the countries concerned. When studying their societies, they have not necessarily taken religion as their main focus, but several of them have been interested in Islam's role in society.

The development of the social sciences in African and Asian countries has been encouraged in many ways by scholarly institutions from France, Britain, and the USA. Several research institutions were created, such as the Centre d'Etudes et de Recherches Economiques et Sociales (CERES) in Tunis, which organized numerous international colloquia and published a number of studies on Tunisian, North African, and Mediterranean subjects. Recently, however, it closed down. Associations for the study of sociology have been founded in the Maghreb. At the conferences organized every two years by the International Society for the Sociology of Religion, several North African sociologists have contributed papers on Islam as a social factor in North African societies and in the Arab world in general.

Sociological research that takes into account Islamic structures, life styles, and customs is also carried out in Egypt. The Social Studies Research Center at the American University of Cairo, for instance, has produced interesting publications on women and family life in the country that have been relevant to issues like family planning. For a number of

---

[45] See for instance Muslim contributions in journals like *The Muslim World* (since 1910), *Islamochristiana* (since 1975), and *Islam and Christian-Muslim Relations* (since 1990).

[46] For instance Octave DEPONT and Xavier COPPOLANI, *Les confréries religieuses musulmanes*, Algiers: A. Jourdain, 1897.

[47] One thinks of the many studies by John Spencer TRIMINGHAM about Islam in Africa.

years, UNESCO has had a Social Science Research Office in Cairo. In Lebanon, the social sciences have been developed first at the American University of Beirut.

The social sciences are still somewhat sparsely represented at universities in Muslim countries, perhaps with the exception of Southeast Asia. Governments have been supporting research projects that corresponded with the needs of government administration. Sociological studies that were critical of a given society, including its religion, were little encouraged. Interest in the study of social change and of social development, including the role of religion, touches sensitive issues and has often wanted or unwanted political implications. As a rule, social scientists in Muslim countries have been cautious when religious issues are at stake. The example of two important Egyptian studies on the religious situation in the country needs to be followed in other Muslim countries as well.[48]

The conditions seem to be somewhat easier in historical research. Current research on the social history of Muslim countries also pays attention to the role that religion played in Muslim societies of the past and to the relationships that existed between Muslim and other communities.

Typically, social scientific research that pays attention to religion seems to have developed in particular in countries like Egypt, Lebanon, and India. These are countries with different religious communities with their own religious and cultural traditions. This could stimulate interest in comparison and encourage more objective observation. The study of the social history of such countries is also rewarding, not only for the study of the religions in themselves, but also of their interaction in specific historical and social contexts. A whole range of studies has been carried out, for instance, on the history of Islam and society in the Indian context, where the history of the relations between Muslim and Hindu communities, including communal strife, has attracted the attention of Indian Muslim scholars. The combination of historical and social scientific research has been particularly fruitful for the study of the role of religious institutions and movements in precise contexts in the course of time. In studies on the Middle East, increasing attention is being paid to the role of minority groups, including the various Christian communities in relation to their Muslim environment.[49]

---

[48] There are exceptions, too. The Center of Political and Strategic Studies of the Egyptian journal *al-Ahrām* published in 1995 a large Report on the religious situation in Egypt (*Taqrīr al-hāla 'l-dīniyya fī Misr*) of some 389 pages, with precious details of official and unofficial religious institutions, movements, and groups. A second volume with the same title but updated appeared in 1998. This is an example of what I mean by the social sciences contribution of Muslim researchers on religion.

[49] There is a trend among present-day Muslim Arab historians to see and describe the history of the Arab Christian communities within the broader Arab history. This is in sharp contrast to an earlier "denominational" historiography.

The impact of the study of religion in the social sciences may even be more fundamental. Muslim social historians, sociologists, and anthropologists could very well address certain problems that have been neglected by mainstream Western scholarship on religion.

The West itself seems to have had a nearly innate tendency either to idealize and spiritualize religion and religious concerns or, contrarily, to take an overall critical attitude towards them, an attitude sometimes ideologically inspired.

A certain suspicion of the West and Western Christianity that has grown in Muslim countries in the course of the twentieth century if not earlier may perhaps now bear scholarly fruits. Muslim scholarly research on Western Christianity and Judaism in their various social contexts, based on the sources, could perhaps throw some new light (1) on the intricate relationships between religious and social aspects of Western societies and (2) on the various social roles of the Christian and Jewish religions in the West.[50]

4. Furthering Muslim Interest in the Scholarly Study of Religions

4.1. Awakening Interest

Wider circles of people of different backgrounds and cultures increasingly ask for reliable information about religions, in particular the living ones. The question is how to provide this information. The media and Internet undoubtedly awaken interest in other cultures, but lack the means to respond to this interest adequately. Needed are, first, good general books on the various religions and, second, good teaching of the subject at schools and in universities.

Increasing contacts with people of other faiths have already done much to correct old images and stereotypes. Reading what the Qur'ān says about Christians and Jews and developing one's ideas on the basis of those texts is one thing. Inquiring among people how they live and what they

---

[50] Muslim researchers, perhaps less distracted by excessive specialization and what may be called scientific precision engineering, may display a capacity to put forward a more comprehensive view of the roles of particular religious groups and their religions in specific situations. This could enhance the study of the role of religions as potential motivating forces of people and groups of people, apt to bring about certain transformations. It could also enhance the study of the social and political strategies in which a particular religion is used for purposes other than religious ones. This social science perspective can of course be taken by any scholar, but it seems to me that Muslim scholars can make a special contribution, since they are more familiar with linkages between socio-political and religious action. They may also be more sensitive to the positive fruits of such linkages.

have to say about life and their beliefs is another matter: a kind of knowledge that can be empirically reviewed and extended.[51]

Interest and research in other societies and cultures can be enhanced on a scholarly level by workshops, symposia, and colloquies. The themes of "Mediterranean culture" and "Euro-Arab dialogue", for instance, have brought together European and Muslim researchers at a number of meetings. Such was the case with a conference organized by the European Science Foundation on the subject of "Individual and Society around the Mediterranean". It took place in Istanbul in July 1998, and the issue of religion popped up in various sections.

But in Muslim culture there are specific, more abstract concepts that can awaken interest in other religions. An idea like that of the "heavenly religions" suggests a kind of communality between Muslims, Christians, and Jews on a spiritual level, and it could encourage further study of Christianity and, probably at some later time, Judaism. And the idea of "revealed scriptures" draws attention to the notion that the study of each other's Scriptures can be beneficial and that it could be done in common.

More generally, the notion of a plurality of religions in the world and the growing awareness of plural societies is gaining ground. It implies the need for adherents of the various religions to live and work together. This is particularly the case in those countries that have always had a variety of religions, like Indonesia or Lebanon, or where cooperation between Muslims and Christians has been at the basis of the country's creation, like Nigeria, Malaysia, or Sudan. Such countries may see an interest in developing scholarly-based information about religions for practical and pragmatic reasons.[52]

4.2. European and Muslim Cultural Traditions

There is a certain analogy between European and Muslim civilization in the way in which certain scholarly interests in this field developed. Europe had cultural traditions like the Renaissance, Humanism, and Enlighten-

---

[51] The two can also be combined. One example is the work of the Muslim-Christian Research Group GRIC (Groupe de Recherches Islamo-Chrétien), a team of Muslim and Christian scholars working together. Thanks to their efforts, four substantial publications have seen the light: *The Challenge of the Scriptures* (1989), the original French edition of which appeared in 1987; *Foi et justice: Un défi pour le christianisme et l'islam* (1993); *Pluralisme et laïcité, Chrétiens et musulmans proposent* (1996); and *Péché et responsabilité éthique dans le monde contemporain* (2000).

[52] On the study of religions in Indonesia, see STEENBRINK, "The Study of Comparative Religion by Indonesian Muslims". Cf. above notes 29 and 40. Could a country like Indonesia, or Turkey for that matter, not organize, in cooperation with the IAHR, a workshop or conference of Muslim scholars working in the field of the scholarly study of religions?

ment, from which this interest could further develop in the eighteenth century. The Muslim civilization has a similar cultural tradition even earlier, in the medieval period. In Europe, textual and historical studies brought new knowledge and insights about the Bible and the world in which it originated, including Near Eastern religions and cultures, Judaism, and early Christianity. The Muslim civilization not only has many texts that are waiting to be edited and studied, but also a great number of societies in which the role of religion can be studied. If European interest in other cultures and religions was enhanced by the voyages of discovery and further intercultural contacts, Muslim countries have been experiencing even more thoroughgoing intercultural contacts since the nineteenth century. The question has been raised about the beginnings and early development of "religious studies". Could reputed medieval scholars like al-Bīrūnī and al-Shahrastānī not be a source of inspiration for further scholarship in this field by researchers from a Muslim background?[53]

4.3. Scholarship

The study of religions, Islam as well as others, however, demands considerable effort, whether such a study is textual, historical, or social scientific. Technical training and mental discipline are essential for anyone seriously investigating languages, texts, historical facts, and social structures of whatever religion. But scholarly rigor can be learned.

I would like to point out, however, two deeper problems for the development of the study of religions in the Muslim world.

The first problem is the adage that Islam is the final and true religion. Whether this is true or not cannot be decided by empirical scholarship. In fact, the study of religions as developed in the West modestly puts the question of the ultimate truth of these religions between brackets (*epochè*).

---

[53] This does not imply that the present-day European or North American study of religions should be considered the only model possible. The birth of the study of religions in Europe was linked closely to nineteenth-century cultural and social conditions and nineteenth-century forms of religion in Europe. And the situation was different in different countries, for instance France, Britain, Germany, Switzerland, and the Netherlands. For a general overview, see SHARPE, *Comparative Religion*. For the beginnings of the history of religions, see Hans G. KIPPENBERG, *Discovering Religious History in the Modern Age*, trans. from German by Barbara HARSHAW, Princeton and Oxford: Princeton University Press, 2002. For relations with German Protestant theology, see Sigurd HJELDE, *Die Religionswissenschaft und das Christentum: Eine historische Untersuchung über das Verhältnis von Religionswissenschaft & Theologie*, Leiden: E. J. Brill, 1994. For relations with French Catholic theology, see Henry PINARD DE LA BOULLAYE, *L'Etude comparée des religions: Essai critique*, 2 Vols., Paris: Beauchesne, 1922 and 1925. For relations with Orthodox Judaism, see *Wissenschaft des Judentums: Anfänge der Judaistik in Europa*, ed. by Julius CARLEBACH, Darmstadt: Wissenschaftliche Buchgesellschaft, 1992.

It assumes that science cannot answer the question, but can put it in perspective. I imagine a kind of *Religionswissenschaft* leading to a philosophical questioning. However, various religions claim for themselves the same thing, and that in good faith. The claim as such, whether applied to Buddhism, Christianity, or Islam, has an unfortunate impact.[54] It distracts attention from the obvious fact that there are other people than Muslims, Christians, or Buddhists and other religions than Islam, Christianity, or Buddhism and that we may want to know these people and their religions.

But the claim also poses serious questions to professional scholars beyond Islam. Why do they bother to study other cultures and religions? What can be the relevance of knowing cultures and religions other and perhaps earlier than one's own? Is this not simply a private interest of a few people? Why should such research and teaching be funded by public money? And if one attaches oneself to the truth proclaimed in one particular religion—Islam or another one—, is scholarly research about others then not a loss of time and effort? Anyone teaching "other" religions can be asked to answer such questions.

The second problem is the fact that Islam has become increasingly ideologized and politicized during the last decades, probably more so than Christianity or Buddhism. This stands in the way of scholarly observation and study. Just as Christian churches and groupings have their own more or less "official" interpretations of Christianity, so numerous Muslim groupings, movements, and even countries have their own interpretation and practice of Islam. In both cases, it is difficult to make a fair, unprejudiced study of different orientations within one's culture and religion. But one is submitted to ideological pressures that may have political implications, if only for one's public career. One is asked to take sides. And if a fair study of different orientations within Islam is already a problem, it is even more the case for the study of other religions than Islam. A scholarly interest in Christianity may be perceived and judged as a Christian influence on someone having too little faith in Islam. And conflict-ridden relations with present-day Judaism and Hinduism do not facilitate their impartial study in a Muslim context.[55]

---

54   The same remark should be made about similar claims by other religions and ideologies. Whether such claims are right or wrong is a different matter; what I want to argue is that they stand in the way of careful empirical and rational research and are a burden on scholars. Researchers have their own approaches to their subject of inquiry. Yet they have to work in a cultural and social (and sometimes religious) climate that does not always appreciate innovative knowledge. This is particularly true for the study of religions or ideologies "other" than those current in society. Absolutizing discourses in one's own society are a burden on a scholar's mind, certainly when he or she studies religions!

55   Just as in Muslim studies of Judaism and Christianity a problem is presented by the fact that the Qur'ān makes value judgments that are positive though not empirical, in the

We know better than before that the ideological and broader political context is not without relevance for intercultural studies. The last fifty years, for instance, have been much more favorable for Muslim studies of Christianity than for such studies of Judaism. The effort of Muslim-Christian dialogue has had beneficial effects for cooperation between Western and Muslim researchers. I am convinced that peace in the Middle East, apart from its beneficial human effects, would facilitate the study of Muslim-Jewish relations in history. It would also enhance comparative studies, for instance, of religious Law or of the Scriptures and their interpretations. This in turn would have a beneficial effect on mutual understanding between Muslims and Jews who are of good will.

There is a real need for in-depth studies not only of relationships between the three monotheistic *religions* throughout history, but also of relationships between Muslim, Christian, and Jewish *communities*, especially their religious aspects in history and at the present time. Given the nature and magnitude of the task, such studies should be made in cooperation between researchers of different backgrounds.

5. Conclusion

The study of religions is a demanding field of research in its own right. Where living religions are concerned, it requires an openness to scholarly contact and encounter, discussion and debate. As a consequence, it requires freedom of research, thought, and expression. Such attitudes, needed for any cultural effort, should be promoted institutionally and should be defended by scholars in whatever part of the world.

It is too soon to assess the extent to which Muslim students in Western countries use the opportunity to familiarize themselves with the study of Islam as well as of religions in general, as these studies are practiced there. The same holds true for the way in which they will convey the knowledge they obtained to their own circles, possibly in their countries of origin. Much depends on whether and how Muslim students have access to the facilities existing at Western universities and how they use them. Much, too, depends on whom they happen to meet and whether they are encouraged to see in our studies a scholarly way to truth and experience them as a human enrichment.[56]

---

study of Asian religions like Buddhism or Hinduism, the problem is reversed. The Islamic tradition has given a very negative judgment, accusing their adherents of atheism or polytheism. Neither positive nor negative general evaluations from whatever source should impinge on the empirical study of religions as they are constructed and lived.

[56]   One must make a distinction between the situation of Muslim researchers working in the contexts of the various Muslim countries and that of those working in the contexts of various Western countries. Certainly in the case of the latter, there is no a priori

Selected Literature

AASI, Ghulam Haider, *Muslim Understanding of Other Religions: An Analytical Study of Ibn Hazm's* Kitāb al-fasl fī al-milal wa-al-ahwā' wa al-nihal, Ph.D. Diss., Temple University, Philadelphia, Pa. 1986.

AHMED, Akbar S., art. "Education: The Islamization of Knowledge", in *The Oxford Encyclopedia of the Modern Islamic World*, John L. ESPOSITO (Editor in Chief), New York and Oxford: Oxford University Press, 1995, Vol. 1, pp. 425–8.

AL-AHRĀM, *Taqrīr al-hāla 'l-dīniyya fī Misr* (Report on the religious situation in Egypt), 2 Vols., Cairo: Center of Political and Strategic Studies of al-Ahrām, 1995 and 1998.

ASHRAF, Syed Ali, *New Horizons in Muslim Education* (Introductory Monographs on Islamic Education 1), Cambridge and London: Hodder and Stoughton, 1985.

—, and Syed Sajjad HUSAIN, *Crisis in Muslim Education* (Islamic Education Series), London: Hodder and Stoughton, 1979.

BECK, Herman L., "A Pillar of Social Harmony: The Study of Comparative Religion in Contemporary Indonesia", in *Modern Societies and the Science of Religions: Studies in Honour of Lammert Leertouwer*, ed. by Gerard WIEGERS in association with Jan PLATVOET, Leiden, etc.: E. J. Brill, 2002, pp. 331–49.

BĪRŪNĪ, *Alberuni's India: An Account of the Religion, Philosophy, Literature, Geography, Chronology, Astronomy, Customs, Laws and Astrology of India about A.D. 1030*, trans. by Edward Carl SACHAU, 2 Vols., London: Trübner, 1888, 1910[2] (repr. New Delhi: Munshiram Manoharlal, 2001).

BOUAMAMA, Ali, *La littérature polémique musulmane contre le christianisme depuis ses origines jusqu'au XIIIe siècle*, Alger: Entreprise nationale du Livre, 1988.

DANGOR, Suleman, "The Attitude of Muslim Scholars towards New Approaches in Religious Studies", *The American Journal of Islamic Social Sciences*, 10 (1993), pp. 280–6.

ECCEL, A. Chris, *Egypt, Islam, and Social Change: Al-Azhar in Conflict and Accommodation* (Islamkundliche Untersuchungen 81), Berlin: Klaus Schwarz, 1984.

FĀRŪQĪ, Ismāʿīl R. al-, *Christian Ethics: A Historical and Systematic Analysis of Its Dominant Ideas*, Montreal: McGill University Press, 1967.

GODDARD, Hugh P., *Muslim Perceptions of Christianity*, London: Grey Seale Books, 1996.

—, "Works about Christianity by Egyptian Muslim Authors, 1940–1980", *The Muslim World*, 80 (1990), pp. 251–77.

HADDAD, Mohanna Y.S., *Arab Perspectives of Judaism: A Study of Image Formation in the Writings of Muslim Arab Authors, 1948–1978*, Doctoral dissertation, University of Utrecht, 1984.

---

reason why researchers of a Muslim background should not work alongside researchers of a non-Muslim, including Christian, background, also in the field of religious studies. It seems to me that the proof of true scholarship lies in its empirical and rational findings that have general validity, and not in its adherence to particularly Western norms and values or a particular Western academic style. The scholarly study of religions is not a "Western" discipline.

A History of Muslim Philosophy: With Short Accounts of Other Disciplines and the Modern Renaissance in Muslim Lands, ed. by Mian Mohammad SHARIF, 2 Vols., Wiesbaden: Harrassowitz, 1963 and 1966.

Islamic Interpretations of Christianity, ed. by Lloyd RIDGEON, Richmond, U. K.: Curzon, 2001.

Islamization of Knowledge: General Principles and Work Plan, ed. by ABŪ SULAY-MĀN and ʿABDUL HAMID, Herndon, Va.: International Institute of Islamic Thought, 1989².

KHAN, Ibrahim H., "The Academic Study of Religion with Reference to Islam", *Scottish Journal of Religious Studies*, 11 (1990), pp. 37–46.

KHAN, Rasheeduddin, "Towards Understanding Hinduism: Reflections of Some Eminent Muslims", in the author's book *Bewildered India: Identity, Pluralism, Discord*, New Delhi: Har-Anand Publications, 1995, Chapter 8 (pp. 153–92).

MALIK, Jamal, "Islamic Mission and Call: The Case of the International Islamic University, Islamabad", *Islam and Christian-Muslim Relations*, 9 (1998), pp. 31–45.

Marburg Revisited: Institutions and Strategies in the Study of Religion, ed. by Michael PYE, Marburg: Diagonal-Verlag, 1989.

MUSLIM-CHRISTIAN RESEARCH GROUP (GRIC), *The Challenge of the Scriptures: Bible and Qur'ān*, Maryknoll, N. Y.: Orbis, 1989.

—, *Foi et justice: Un défi pour le christianisme et l'islam*, Paris: Centurion, 1993.

—, *Pluralisme et laïcité, Chrétiens et musulmans proposent*, Paris: Bayard/Centurion, 1996.

—, *Péché et responsabilité éthique dans le monde contemporain*, Paris: Bayard, 2000.

Muslim Perceptions of Other Religions: A Historical Survey, ed. by Jacques WAARDENBURG, New York and London: Oxford University Press, 1999.

NASR, Seyyed Hossein, "Islam and the Encounter of Religions", in *Proceedings of the XIth International Congress of the International Association for the History of Religions*, Vol. 3, Leiden: E. J. Brill, 1968, pp. 23–47 (repr. in the author's *Sufi Essays*, Albany, N. Y.: SUNY Press, 1973, pp. 123–51).

Religiosa: Indonesian Journal on Indonesian Harmony (since 1995). Published by the State Institute of Islamic Studies (IAIN) in Yogyakarta.

SHAHRASTĀNĪ, *Kitāb al-milal wa'l-nihal*, trans. into French under the title *Livre des religions et des sectes* by Daniel GIMARET, Jean JOLIVET and Guy MONNOT (Collection UNESCO d'oeuvres représentatives. Série arabe), 2 Vols., Leuven: Peeters, and Paris: UNESCO, 1986 and 1993.

SHALABĪ, Ahmad, *History of Muslim Education*, Beirut: Dar al-kashshaf, 1954.

SHARPE, Eric J., *Comparative Religion: A History*, La Salle, Ill.: Open Court, 1986².

SIDDIQI, Nazeer, *Iqbal and Radhakrishnan: A Comparative Study*, Rawalpindi, etc.: PAK, 1989.

STEENBRINK, Karel A., "The Study of Comparative Religion by Indonesian Muslims", *Numen*, 37 (1990), pp. 141–67.

STENBERG, Leif, *The Islamization of Science: Four Muslim Positions Developing an Islamic Modernity* (Lund Studies in History of Religions 6), Lund: University of Lund, 1996.

STÜMPEL-HATAMI, Isabel, *Das Christentum aus der Sicht zeitgenössischer iranischer*

Autoren: Eine Untersuchung religionskundlicher Publikationen in persischer Sprache (Islamkundliche Untersuchungen), Berlin: Klaus Schwarz, 1996.

TAQĪZĀDEH, S. Hasan, and Ahmad Ashgār AL-SHĪRĀZĪ, *Mānī va dinī ū* ("Mani and his religion"), Teheran, 1956/1335.

WAARDENBURG, Jacques, "Some Institutional Aspects of Muslim Higher Education and their Relation to Islam", *Numen*, 12 (1964), pp. 96–138.

—, "Religious Studies in the Muslim World", *Conference Guide, Marburg Conference, June 1988*, pp. 49–66.

—, "Muslimisches Interesse an anderen Religionen im soziopolitischen Kontext des 20. Jahrhunderts", in *Loyalitätskonflikte in der Religionsgeschichte: Festschrift für Carsten Colpe*, Würzburg: Königshausen & Neumann, 1990, pp. 140–52.

—, *Des dieux qui se rapprochent: Introduction systématique à la science des religions*, Geneva: Labor et Fides, 1993.

—, *Perspektiven der Religionswissenschaft* (Religionswissenschaftliche Studien 25), Würzburg: Echter, and Altenberge: Oros, 1993.

—, *Islam et Sciences des Religions: Huit leçons au Collège de France*, Paris: Les Belles Lettres, 1998.

—, "Muslim Studies of Other Religions", in *Muslim Perceptions of Other Religions* (see above), pp. 1–101.

Section 4

Muslims and the West, Muslims in the West

Chapter 9
Some Muslim Reflections on the West[1]

1. Introduction

If the East has enjoyed a symbolic value in European culture, the West has had intense symbolic meanings in the Muslim world. The associations accompanying these terms have differed, however. From the eighteenth century on (and deep into the twentieth century), the East tended to evoke for Europeans the land of the rising sun with a piercing light, access to the sources of life and the universe, and enhanced spirituality. With the exoticism of mystical poetry and wisdom, the East represented for a European cultural public the region of soft souls.

In contrast, the West traditionally suggested to Muslims the land of the setting sun (if not death). While for a younger generation it raised the hope of a new kind of life and future, during the nineteenth and twentieth centuries it became increasingly associated with power and riches and with the corresponding aggression and greed. The Western mind had developed rationality, resulting in scientific knowledge and technology, material empiricism, and a critical attitude toward metaphysics and reli-

[1] This text is a reworked version of the text "Muslim Reflections on the West" in *Islamic Thought in the 20th Century: Thematic Essays*, ed. by Suha TAJI-FAROUKI and Basheer M. NAFI, London and New York: I. B. Tauris, 2003. Thanks are due to the editors and publisher for permission to publish it here. I want to thank Dr. Taji-Farouki for her careful and accurate editorial work on this text.

I am here concerned with writings by Muslim authors about the West, first Europe and then also North America, both in "Islamic" and Western languages, constantly increasing since the mid-nineteenth century. It gives information about Western societies and countries. The more reflective literature is concerned with historical relations between Muslim countries and the West, contemporary relations (including Western influences on contemporary Muslim societies), and attitudes that should be adopted toward the West as power. Other genres are travelogues, literary texts, and personal memoirs. Much of the more popular literature concerns attitudes or actions that Muslims are encouraged to adopt, giving moral and religious directives. The texts explored here have their origin in very different groups, varying from typically "Islamic" circles that refer directly to Islam as their norm, "Muslim" circles that combine cooperation with non-Muslims with Islam as their religion, and "modernist" circles of what may be called "social" Muslims.

gion. With its destructive powers and desire to dominate, the West represented for a more informed Muslim public the region of tough minds.

If these are some symbolic meanings of East and West, what have been the actual historical, socio-cultural relations between the West and the Muslim world?[2] And what has been the Muslim discourse on the West in this context? For analytical purposes I distinguish four kinds of discourse: political, socio-economic, cultural, and spiritual. They are mostly closely related.

Until World War Two, the Muslim discovery of the West was largely a discovery of Europe, or at least of certain European countries and cities.[3] In the course of the nineteenth century, Europe was gradually discovered as a civilization, not only as a power that made itself felt through the occupation of Muslim land. Students traveled to study and be trained in Europe, specifically France and Britain.[4] Works from the main European languages, including Russian, were translated into Arabic, Ottoman Turkish, and Persian. In the opposite direction, European writers and scholars visited Muslim countries; quite a few of them were genuinely interested in archeology and history, but also in the present-day living conditions of the people. Some of them devoted themselves to academic studies as "Orientalists". Some taught at educational institutions in centers of Muslim culture such as Cairo and Lahore. Others lived and worked in places of Muslim-European encounter, like Paris or St. Petersburg. Muslim authors wrote about various aspects of European culture during the nineteenth century, generally with admiration, upholding some of its elements as an example to be followed in their own countries. Other views and judgments also developed, however.

An important example of more critical Muslim views of the West is the periodical *al-Manār* (The Lighthouse), a monthly edited in Cairo by Muhammad Rashīd Ridā from 1898 until his death in 1935. This gives interesting accounts of the ways in which the encounter between Islam and the West took place in the heyday of European colonial rule from a Salafī point of view.[5]

"The West" was, and remains, an idea subject to discourse. The first kind of discourse, conducted by Westerners (especially those representing the West to non-Westerners elsewhere), describes it with pride. This imagined

---

[2] LEWIS, *Islam and the West*.

[3] LEWIS, *The Muslim Discovery of Europe*. Cf. ABU-LUGHOD, *Arab Rediscovery of Europe*. See also Ami AYALON, "The Arab Discovery of America in the Nineteenth Century", *Middle Eastern Studies*, 20, Nr. 4 (1984), pp. 5–17.

[4] YARED, *Arab Travellers and Western Civilization*. Cf. Anouar LOUCA, *Voyageurs et écrivains égyptiens en France au XIXe siècle*, Paris: Didier, 1970.

[5] SHAHIN, *Through Muslim Eyes*. An in-depth study of *al-Manār's* views of the world at large at the time of its writing is needed.

West, with its civilization, is held up as an example to non-Westerners (or at least it was in the colonial period).

The second kind of discourse about the West (generally conducted by non-Westerners among themselves) is charged with a range of emotional responses. Most of those subscribing to this discourse had never been to the West. They felt its power directly or indirectly and allowed their imagination to develop concerning it. Their discourse was linked to certain reported experiences and offered an interpretation of these. The imagination it encapsulated was the result of the feelings and emotions evoked by such experiences.

The same remark applies to specifically Muslim discourses about the West. Around the Mediterranean and in the Middle East, Muslims knew about Christians. They had their own history and experience with them, as subjected populations within and as enemies outside their borders.

After the expulsion of the Moriscos from Spain (and with the exception of the Ottoman conquerors on their way to Vienna in 1529 and 1683), up until the 1820s, Europe did not hold any particular attraction for Muslims. It was a region peripheral to what in their view was the central band of the world, stretching from Morocco to Indonesia. The Muslim discourse about the West (which began in the nineteenth century) was concerned mainly with Europe up until World War Two.[6]

2. The Problem under Study

The following discussion explores some major orientations developed by Muslim intellectuals toward "the West" as an idea (and as a reality) during the twentieth century. Whether appreciative or critical of the West, these orientations implied (and sometimes explicitly developed) articulations both of their own identity and of Islam as their specific cultural legacy and normative system. Whereas Westerners mostly ask "how does Islam relate to the West?", the interest here is how Muslim intellectuals (in the broader sense of the word) perceived, digested, and constructed "the West". There is also a consideration of whether there were certain links between their constructions of the West and the ways they identified with Islam.

It is taken for granted that Muslim views and judgments of the West developed largely in terms of internal exchanges and debates in Muslim

---

[6]   For a succinct history of successive images of the West including Europe, see Gerhard HÖPP, "Feindbild 'Westen': Zur Rolle historischer Zäsuren im 20. Jahrhundert", in *Wessen Geschichte? Muslimische Erfahrungen historischer Zäsuren im 20. Jahrhundert*, ed. by Henner FÜRTIG and Gerhard HÖPP (Zentrum Moderner Orient, Berlin, Arbeitshefte Nr. 16), Berlin: Das Arabische Buch, 1998, pp. 11–26.

countries. The Muslim discourse about the West has been fundamentally a discourse among Muslims and is part of the social and intellectual history of Muslim societies. Yet the West itself had a direct impact on this discourse in colonial times. The debate at that time concerned the direct military and political power of the (European) West and how to remove it. Following decolonization and during the Cold War, Western power in Muslim countries has been indirect and exercised largely through economic processes. Since the end of the Cold War, however, the (American) West has been exercising more direct power, with a corresponding impact on the Muslim discourse about the West. This has been the case especially since the Gulf War of 1991, the Afghan war of 2001, and the "War on Terror" declared after September 11, 2001.[7]

Perceptions (certainly those of other cultures) are rarely immediately given. Instead, they are embedded in discourses of a cultural and ideological, but also of a socio-economic and political nature. Muslim discourses about the West developed in particular historical contexts and situations, in which certain Muslims and certain Westerners encountered each other.[8] While the resulting Western views and practices are more or less known, what were the Muslim perceptions, seen not from a Western but from their own point of view and according to their own intentions? The following exploration, which concentrates especially on the Middle East, addresses this question.

3. Different "Wests" Experienced and Perceived by Different Muslim Groups

Of course, not only one and the same "West" existed for all Muslims, just as there was not one and the same "Islam" for all Westerners.[9] At

---

[7]   The role of the factor and use of power in relations between Western and Muslim countries cannot be overestimated. Subjugation has been and remains a determinant factor in Muslim perceptions of the West. The experience of various forms of Western domination has given rise to negative attitudes. This experience, which has become part of Muslim collective memory, comprises: expropriations of Muslims' lands; humiliation of Muslim populations; alienation of Muslims from their culture; imposition of a Western economic system; destruction of potential bases of Muslim power; creation of "bridgeheads" for the West in the Muslim world, and the frustration of expectations awakened through Euro-Arab and other dialogues between Westerners and Muslims. The Gulf War (1990–1), the Bosnian War (1992–5), and the USA support of Israeli policies against Palestinians and the Palestinian cause have enraged a number of Muslim political and other thinkers. See for instance KORESHI, New World Order.

[8]   The mutuality of perceptions is important. See Gegenseitige Wahrnehmungen – Orient und Okzident seit dem 18. Jahrhundert. In this volume, see especially Henner FÜRTIG, "Āyatollāh Chomeinīs Bild vom Westen" (pp. 355–75).

[9]   The expression "Islam and the West" is conceptually problematic, since it suggests the existence of two definable entities. However, it has caught much public attention. On

different times and in different places there were different "Wests", with different connotations, for different Muslim societies and groups. Moreover, the historical context in which encounters between Muslims and Westerners have taken place has undergone immense changes during the nineteenth and twentieth centuries. Muslim discourses on the West have changed accordingly in the course of time.

In the *pre-colonial* period, the West did not pose an immediate danger to Muslims, except for incidental wars and conquests, as in the Balkans and earlier in Russia, Spain, and Italy.

In the *colonial* period, which extended for different lengths and with different impact for different Muslim countries, "the West" (identified with Europe) was the place of origin of foreign occupants and colonizers. When Muslims wrote about the West or Europe at that time, they meant in particular the country that ruled them and with which they had some direct experience. Between the two World Wars, Europe as a whole might be seen as an aggressive military and political entity (with the exception of Germany, Scandinavia, and most of Eastern Europe).

In the *post-colonial* period, Europe lost its power over most Muslim territories, while the USA was able to impose its growing hegemony over the Muslim part of the world. It appears that in the 1960s, the expression "the West" in Muslim countries began to refer primarily to the USA. Like World War Two, the Cold War gave the West a new meaning as the "Free World", while the presence of the USSR helped to keep the West's power within certain limits.[10]

October 27, 1993 Prince CHARLES delivered a much-cited speech "Islam and the West" in Oxford (Text in *Islam and Christian-Muslim Relations*, 5, Nr. 1 [1994], pp. 67–74). See also the statement paper by Khurshid AHMAD (Pakistan), "Islam and the West: Confrontation or Cooperation?" (Text in *The Muslim World*, 85, Nrs. 1–2 [1995], pp. 63–81). See also Annemarie SCHIMMEL's speech on receiving the 1995 Peace Prize of the German Book Trade Association (Text in *CSIC Papers* [Birmingham], Nr. 6 [July 1996], pp. 7–13). Compare also with Seyyed Hossein NASR, "Islam and the West: Yesterday and Today", in *The American Journal of Islamic Social Sciences*, 13, Nr. 4 (1996), pp. 551–62; Ali A. MAZRUI, "Islamic and Western Values", in *Foreign Affairs*, 76, Nr. 5 (1997), pp. 118–32. The expression "Islam and the West" seems to have become especially current since the Gulf War of 1991.

[10]   The Cold War prevented relations between the West and Islam from becoming dualistic; there was always the third factor of the Eastern Bloc countries. For the impact of the Cold War on Western and Eastern Bloc attitudes toward and views of Islam, see Jacques WAARDENBURG, "The Study of Religion during the Cold War: Views of Islam", in *The Academic Study of Religion during the Cold War*, ed. by Iva DOLEŽALOVÁ, Luther H. MARTIN, and Dalibor PAPOUŠEK (Toronto Studies in Religion 27), New York, etc.: Peter Lang, 2001, pp. 291–311.

The end of the Cold War implied re-orientations on the past of Muslim countries, too. See Ellinor SCHÖNE, "Die islamische Staatengruppe und das Ende des Ost-West-Konflikts – die Sicht der Organisation der Islamischen Konferenz", in *Wessen Geschichte?*, pp. 97–115. See also Henner FÜRTIG, "Die islamische Republik Iran und das Ende des Ost-West-Konflikts", in the same volume, pp. 73–95.

This period ended with the demise of the USSR, especially when a New World Order was imposed with the Gulf War of 1991. "The West", as military and political power, was now practically identified with the USA. The capital of the West became Washington, D.C., and the American war against the *Tālibān* in Afghanistan (October-December 2001) accentuated this fact.

Muslim discourses on the West also vary from country to country and in accordance with their experiences with the West. The geographical area of the Muslim world is vast, and there are great differences between countries. In the Middle East, for instance, the Iranian revolution changed the official pro-Western discourse at the time of the last Shah into a virulent anti-Western and especially anti-American discourse (from 1979 on). The growing Islamization of Pakistan, especially after Zia ul-Haqq's rise to power in 1977, could have led to a growing distance from the West, were it not for the fact that Pakistan and the USA needed each other during the first Afghan war against the Soviet invasion (1979–89). Similarly, Turkey, which had been indispensable for the West during the Cold War, enjoyed broad NATO support. For its part, it has felt itself to be part of the West, to the extent that it has sought acceptance in Europe as a potential member state of the European Union (EU). Its alignment with the West has increasingly become a subject of debate in Turkey.

Discourses on the West in the Arab countries of the Middle East have depended to a large extent on a series of issues. These include commercial ties with or financial backing from the USA; open or tacit support from the West (i.e., the USA) for Israeli policies; and the strategies of particular Arab rulers (those of Nāsir [Nasser] or Sadat, for example). In general, Middle Eastern Muslim discourse on the West is critical, especially of the USA for its backing of Israel. However, public statements naturally follow the official political guidelines of the countries concerned. Since its attack on Kuwait in 1990, Iraq has been practically ostracized by the West, as was Libya after the Lockerbie episode.

Outside the Middle East, Muslim encounters with the West have been varied. Muslims in India (a secular state) live under pressures magnified by tensions with Pakistan; they are very much involved in their own minority problems, and may look with certain hopes to the West. In Indonesia, where *Pancasila* is the official state ideology, there is an official Islam regulated by the state, and direct political expressions of Islam have been suppressed for decades. A democratization movement started in the 1990s and led to the ousting of Suharto in 1998. Defenders of civil society and democracy look to the West for moral and practical support (as is also the case in other Muslim countries with undemocratic regimes). Economically, Indonesia is very dependent on the USA (and on Australia). Malaysia, with its Tiger ambitions of becoming a major economic power, has its own internal problems. Islamist pressure there seeks increasing Islamization and an orientation toward other Islamic countries, rather than the West. The Central Asian republics still stand very much under Russian influence, and they look for economic support from the West.

In North Africa, Libya has never had a very positive experience with the West; under Qadhdhāfī, it became for a time a proponent of resistance against American influence. Its relations with the West, like those of other oil-producing Muslim countries that do not want Western ideological influence, seem to remain restricted to economic and financial spheres.

For the other three Maghreb countries, France represented "the West" for a long time; this has now broadened to Southern Europe and the European Union. After a promising start and notwithstanding great potential, Tunisian social and cultural openness to European values has been blocked by the current regime. Algeria has become submerged in its internal problems since the repression of Islamist advances in 1990. Only Morocco, since the death of Hasan II, seems to be opening up to more constructive relations with the West, while adapting its cultural heritage along more liberal lines. For the last few years it has implemented policies in favor of human rights. It also participates actively in international efforts to improve the situation of the countries of the South.

Muslim countries further south see the West primarily from an African context. In West Africa, Islamist pressures (apparently supported by Saudi Arabia and Libya) seek to create a greater distance to the West. However, all these countries (as most countries elsewhere) are economically dependent on the West. During the last thirty years of turbulence, in spite of being repeatedly called to order by the West on issues of human rights and democracy, Nigeria has chosen its own path. Several northern provinces have declared themselves "Islamic" and have adopted the *Sharī'a*. In 1999, a more democratic regime came to power; it is renewing older links with the West and trying to revive democracy and the country's older, more liberal cultural and political tradition.

In contrast, the current regime in Sudan resists all Western influence, including efforts to help end the civil war. Its official line is Islamist, and constant reference is made to the *Sharī'a*, which has been imposed on the whole country, including the South. Muslim East Africa has not experienced the West as directly as North or West Africa. Islamist pressures there (apparently supported by Saudi Arabia and Pakistan) call for a greater distance to the West.

Evidently, Muslims perceive many "Wests". The term itself requires some delineation.

4. The Term "the West" in Muslim Discourse

Muslim intellectuals (rather than political or religious leaders) are the focus of interest here. This is because, among them, a kind of critical reflection about the West and Islam has been taking place. In addition, it is among the intellectuals that one finds a number of individuals who know more about the West than others, thanks to their education (often at Western institutions).

That said, just as Rashīd Riḍā wrote much about the West without any knowledge of European languages, we also find in the later twentieth century individuals who offer their ideas about the West without any detailed knowledge of it. What presents itself is thus more of an ideological discourse about relations between the West and Islam than a precise study of the human realities indicated by the two terms (particular Western and Muslim peoples and groups, with their specific societies and histories). In short, in most Muslim discourse, the West is a construct, just as the East is a construct in most Western discourse.

In Muslim usage in the second half of the twentieth century, the term "the West" appears to have acquired a greater importance than earlier terms used to indicate non-Muslim blocs, like "Christianity", "Franks", or "Europe". The West suggests a geographical area, but the term has been used with meanings that are loaded with value and emotion.

1) One meaning, current for a long time, was that of the opposition Orient—Occident, as East—West. The "Orient" represents the lands of the rising sun, to which "Eastern spirituality" and life are ascribed, whereas the "Occident" stands for the lands of the setting sun, with the suggestion of a fatal materialism and death. The fallacy of this essentialist scheme of interpretation has been exposed in a range of critical publications already in the early 1960s, for instance by the German scholar Kurt Goldammer in 1962.[11]

2) A second (and currently more important) meaning of "the West" is political. It is a political concept in which the aspect of power typically predominates. In contrast, Christianity indicates more the aspect of religion and Europe nowadays more that of culture. The old colonial powers (in particular Britain and France, but also Russia and the Netherlands) represented "the West" during the colonial period. The Pan-Islamic movement arose as a resistance to the West's advance. In the context of the Cold War, "the West" stood for North America and Western Europe, combined as a power bloc in the "East-West" conflict. It held negative connotations for those who declared themselves "progressive". This

---

[11] GOLDAMMER, *Der Mythus von Ost und West.*

"West" was seen as the political force supporting Israel, without which the latter would have succumbed. In this sense, the West, as a power, is a potential enemy.

3) A third meaning of "the West" is linked to modernity. Some have seen Europe as a modern civilization; on this basis it has been an object of admiration. By definition, the West is "modern", i.e., endowed with technological progress, economic development, scholarly knowledge, and the use of reason. This evidently also represents power, but not in the brutal sense. In this meaning, the West has positive connotations for those who want to develop society along "modern" (and mostly "Western") lines, but negative connotations for those who want to adhere to tradition and older ways of life. The direct link between modernity and the West is severed by those who make a clear distinction between modernization in general and Western models of modernization in particular, and between the use of reason in general and its use in the service of specific Western interests.

4) A fourth meaning of "the West" indicates a particular "way of life" in its ordinary external aspects, without showing much concern for its traditions, lasting values, or more fundamental problems (in contrast to more complex ways of life that do carry such a burden).

5) A fifth and final meaning has a much more symbolic and radically normative character. Here, "the West" represents a world that may best be described as barbarian (a modern *jāhilīya*, from an Islamist viewpoint). In this meaning, the West stands for a disintegrating society in which egoism and human solitude prevail. It is the land of loss of mind, where materialism reigns and where people are imprisoned by their desire for goods and money. It is the land of loss of soul, where secularity dominates and people drift without deeper norms and higher values. It is the land of loss of true feelings, where changing appetites are the norm and people fall victim to desire and lust. It is the land of loss of human dignity, with a value system based on economics, and where people aggressively exploit each other. Finally, it is the land of metaphysical alienation and loss of God, with human-made idols and people who have no relationship to Being, nature, history, or each other.

This barbarian West is seen not only as destructive to itself, with violence flaring in bitter economic, social, and political conflicts, but also as a real danger for the rest of the world and especially the Muslim part of it. Its deep aggression has been demonstrated in its policies of colonialism, economic exploitation, and political domination over the rest of the world. At the same time, it seduces people to imitate it and to be utterly dependent on it. Once seduced by the system or forced to surrender to it, they gradually lose their identity and authenticity. In contrast with the image of the West as exemplary in nineteenth-century modernizing circles or in twentieth-century republican Turkey and Pahlevi Iran, this image of the West (as presented by Abū 'l-ʿAlā' al-Mawdūdī and Sayyid Qutb, for example) is utterly grim, inhuman, and repulsive.

These disparate images of the West appear in Muslim writings in the second half of the twentieth century. They convey messages—mostly warnings—to the reader. Of course, large parts of "Western" reality fall outside the scope of Muslim observers. Countries like Greece, Austria, Switzerland, Belgium, or the Scandinavian countries are rarely discussed or even mentioned. Continental European art, literature, and cultural history (perhaps with the partial exception of France) appear to be poorly known. Discussions between European thinkers and changes in the self-view and self-evaluation of Europeans that occurred before, during, and after the period of the Iron Curtain are rarely taken into account. Those currents in European countries that argue against Western domination and that show solidarity with "Third World" countries are mostly unknown or neglected. There is hardly any understanding of the reasons behind the various, at times ambiguous attitudes toward Islam that have prevailed in European societies and that cannot be reduced to willful distortions. In brief, the factual knowledge in Muslim countries about Europe and the West in general is still rather poor, and insight in Western civilization and religion is largely lacking.

For Muslims, the impact of this West, both as a reality and as an idea has been tremendous during the twentieth century. Muslims thus feel that "the West" has imposed itself forcefully on their societies, just as non-Muslim minorities in the Muslim world feel that "Islam" has imposed itself forcefully on them. Apparently, both the West and Islam represent oppression for those who do not belong to them.

One should note that a number of intellectuals who studied in the West in the course of the twentieth century overcame the enthusiasm of their youth for French, British, German, or American culture and later reverted to a more distanced attitude, sometimes stressing their Islamic identity. Muhammad Husayn Haikal (1888–1956)[12], who had put his hope on Europe, was disillusioned. Taha Hussein (1889–1971)[13], who once had pleaded for Egypt's Greek heritage and its belonging to Europe, later saw it primarily as part of the Muslim world. Others opted for a Muslim-Western dialogue. The more personal the responses to the West, the more striking they are. Fazlur Rahman (1919–88)[14] analyzed the transformation of Islam's intellectual tradition. ʿAlī Sharīʿatī (1933–77)[15] articulated the social and political message of Islam, specifically in the Iranian context

---

[12] JOHANSEN, *Muhammad Husain Haikal.*
[13] HUSSEIN, *The Future of Culture in Egypt.*
[14] RAHMAN, *Islam and Modernity.*
[15] SHARĪʿATI, *On the Sociology of Islam*; ID., *Marxism and Other Western Fallacies.*

before 1979. Mohammed Arkoun[16] stresses the need to learn from critical Western science and culture. Abdallah Laroui[17] notes the complementarity of Islam and Europe. Mohammed Talbi[18] insists on the necessity of dialogue across the Mediterranean and within societies on both sides. Tariq Ramadan[19] defends the good right of Muslims to pursue modernity to a certain extent and inquires about a contribution by Muslims from the West to the future of Islam itself. Farid Esack[20] calls for a theology of liberation and a common effort toward it. Nasr Abu Zayd[21] develops a criticism of current religious discourse.

A number of intellectuals have begun to take active part in Euro-Arab, Christian-Muslim, and other inter-cultural and inter-religious dialogues with Westerners and others, pleading for more communication, cooperation, and dialogue beyond political or ideological barriers.[22] All of them stress their Muslim identity and emphasize their intention to sustain it, if not always religiously, then at least socially, based on moral standards largely derived from Islam. These intellectuals advocate "modernizing" society but object to being labeled "Westernized". Iranian intellectuals in particular have been alert to the danger of being "contaminated" by Westernization and defend Iranian culture and Islam.[23]

5. Islamist Views of the West and Secularity

Among the many responses of Muslim thinkers to Western influences on Muslim societies, the "Islamist" ones distinguish themselves through an ideological militancy, constructed on the basis of Islam. In Egypt and Pakistan, Sayyid Qutb[24] and Abū'l-ʿAlā' al-Mawdūdī[25] generated a specific image of the West as an enemy and danger.

---

[16] ARKOUN, *Pour une critique de la raison islamique*. On Arkoun, see Jacques WAARDENBURG, *Islam: Historical, Social, and Political Perspectives* (Religion and Reason 40), Berlin, etc.: Walter de Gruyter, 2002, pp. 147–51, 153–59.

[17] LAROUI, *Islam et modernité*; ID., *Islamisme, modernisme, libéralisme*. On Laroui, see my *Islam* (see above note 16), pp. 145–8.

[18] TALBI, "Possibilities and Conditions for a better Understanding between Islam and the West". On Talbi, see my *Islam* (see above note 16), p. 144.

[19] RAMADAN, *Islam*; ID., *Les musulmans d'Occident et l'avenir de l'islam*.

[20] ESACK, *On Being a Muslim Finding a Religious Path in the World Today*.

[21] ABOU ZEID, *Critique du discours religieux*.

[22] *Muslims and the West: Encounter and Dialogue*. Cf. *Euro-Arab Dialogue: The Relations Between the Two Cultures*.

[23] NARAGHI, *L'Orient et la crise de l'Occident*. Cf. ĀL-I AHMAD, *Occidentosis*. See also MUSAWI LARI, *Western Civilisation through Muslim Eyes*.

[24] On Sayyid Qutb (1906–66), see for instance MOUSSALLI, *Radical Islamic Fundamentalism*.

[25] On Abu'l-ʿAlā al-Mawdūdī (1903–79), see Seyyed Vali Reza NASR, "Mawdudi and the Jamaʿat-i Islami: The Origins, Theory and Practice of Islamic Revivalism", in *Pioneers of Islamic Revival*, ed. by Ali RAHNEMA (London: Zed Books, 1994), pp. 98–124, and my *Islam* (see above note 16), pp. 347–8.

Especially since the 1970s, Muslims joining Islamist groups have affirmed anew their Islamic identity, largely rejecting Western criticisms of Islam or of particular situations in Muslim countries and passing judgment on values and practices in Western countries. In contrast to what is perceived (particularly since the end of the Cold War) as the prevailing hegemonic "Western" model of society, Islamist authors claim that Islam offers a viable and superior alternative model. They contend that Islam itself is able to provide the true solution to the problems of the modern world.[26]

Islamist critics see both Western political and economic liberalism and Marx-inspired socialism and communism as variants of one Western "secular" model of society. They perceive this secular model as a conscious project on the part of the West to "Westernize" the world by means of a total "secular" colonization of all aspects of society. The creation of Israel is seen as a tool in this larger project, putting a foreign and inimical entity in the heart of the Arab-Muslim East in order to divide and subdue it.

Such Islamist literature is conflict-oriented and stresses the persistence of a continuous ideological conflict that has existed between Islam and the West throughout history. On the part of the West, it perceives from the very beginning a project to "westernize" the world, whether via a more religious "Christianization" or by a more cultural "assimilation". In the latter case, they attribute to the West an image of the East and Islam constructed specifically to serve Western political interests, while the West has presented itself as promoting human values and cultural progress.

This literature sees in Islam, from its beginnings, a project to "Islamize" the world. It holds that this should now be brought to fruition, in opposition to "Westernization". Muslims who happen to be fascinated by the West should be "de-westernized" and Muslims in general should be defended against the temptations of Christianization. On the other hand, wherever possible, Christians should be de-Christianized and Islamized. Western civilization should be demystified and its negative effects exposed, while the truth of Islam should be continuously demonstrated. In this great ideological conflict, the West has tried to understand Islam already since the medieval period, whereas Islam developed an interest in knowing the West only much later.

For Islamists, the opposition between Islam and the West essentially goes back to the conflict between Islam and secularity. Islamists interpret the secular order, and particularly the ideology of secularism arising from the West, as the real enemy of Islam.

---

[26] The phenomenon of Islamism itself (and what are at times ideologically oriented interpretations of it) would require separate treatment.

In Paul Khoury's view[27], Islamism started to develop as a mode of self-defense against the activities of Christian missions and the encroachment of the West in general on the Muslim world. It then became highly critical of the claims of Western modernity and especially the imputed project of "westernizing" Islam and Muslim societies. Finally, it took the shape of an active project to Islamize the world. This conflict-ridden process took off at the very same time that Western societies began to question their own philosophical foundations.

Islamism itself constitutes an internal movement within Muslim societies. It has to do with a broader process of redefining what it means to be a Muslim; as a movement, it is part of the recent social history of Muslim societies. In the Arab-Muslim world, Islamism manifests itself in an increasing attachment both to the Islamic religion as an all-encompassing normative system and to the Arab-Muslim cultural heritage. Whereas Western colonization is categorically rejected and fought against, modernization as such is not rejected. On the contrary, Islamists call on Muslim societies to adopt from Western civilization its science, technology, and organization of public services. However, they reject the West's ideology and its basis: secular materialism. Indeed, they insist that Muslim individual and social life should be ever more (re-)Islamized.

Within the Islamist trend, some thinkers made a conscious effort to develop an Islamic epistemology distinct from the epistemology of typically Western scholarship.[28] In nineteenth- and early twentieth-century Europe, some Catholic and Protestant thinkers developed a Catholic or Protestant worldview on the basis of the data of faith. They established denominational universities to apply such worldviews in teaching and scholarship. In a similar vein, in the 1970s some Muslim thinkers sought to apply an Islamic epistemology in various disciplines, producing Islamic social sciences, Islamic economics, etc. Together with the system itself, these disciplines would be taught at the new International "Islamic" Universities founded in Islamabad, Kuala Lumpur, and elsewhere. The final aim of these efforts was to carry out an "Islamization of knowledge", a term coined by Ismāʿīl Rāji al-Fārūqī[29] and worked out by a group of Muslim thinkers since the beginning of the 1980s.

This project also implies a critical view of the West, as well as efforts to arrive at a new kind of knowledge. It imputes false claims of universality and materialist presuppositions to Western scholarship and seeks to maintain a distance to this. However, just as with denominational teaching and scholarship claiming to be "Catholic" or "Protestant", an "Is-

---

[27] KHOURY, *L'Islam critique de l'Occident dans la pensée arabe actuelle*.
[28] See STENBERG, *The Islamization of Science*.
[29] AL-FĀRŪQĪ, *Islamization of Knowledge*. Cf. ID., "Islamizing the Social Sciences".

lamic" epistemology turns out to be acceptable only to its own adherents. It runs the risk of becoming simply a "sectarian" way of obtaining knowledge, outside of the general criteria for ascertaining whether a given claim of knowledge is viable or not. The price of Islamism is that it develops its own ideological discourse not only in Islamic religious, social, and political matters, but also in its perception, interpretation, and study of reality outside Islam. It cannot be described as research scholarship; it rather becomes *Weltanschauung*, ideological worldview affirmation.

6. Political Discourse on the West and its Impact

The Muslim political discourse on the West is based on the experience of the West as a power, and its main concern is how to respond to that power. In its critical form, it perceives the West as the origin of forces destructive of the Muslim world. In the past, colonialism was the most obvious form of the imperialist policies of the West. Nowadays, the latter imposes itself through economic, political, and cultural imperialism. It supports regimes that act in conformity with its interests and opposes those that do not recognize a Western-centered world order. It continues to support Israel and its policies. It imposes an economic open-market system that is regarded as catastrophic for most developing countries. This critical political discourse against the West focuses on the hegemonic behavior and claims of the USA. It often takes ideological forms with recourse to Islamic legal rules. In extreme cases, a *jihād* (supreme effort, also war) has been proclaimed.

A milder strain of this political discourse does recognize the value of certain Western democratic institutions and of efforts to sustain social and economic development, especially those undertaken by non-governmental organizations (NGOs). It appreciates initiatives taken by the Red Cross/Red Crescent, Amnesty International, and human rights organizations to combat abuses. Certain norms and values formulated in the West but deemed to be universal in nature have also been accepted in Muslim countries. These include freedom of conscience and religious freedom (although the claim is retained that Islam is the absolute religion, from which no departure is allowed).

There is a general view that norms and values that are valid in themselves can be (and are) politically misused and that the application of accepted rules is not always guaranteed in Western countries either. It is often said that democracy in practice has certain drawbacks and that Muslim states are not bound to follow Western models. Islamist activists want to replace Muslim states by Islamic states based on the *Sharī'a*.

Current Muslim discourses on the political impact of the West are replete with remnants of traumatic experiences from the past. Examples are experiences of colonial wars and oppression, forced labor and migration, the direct and indirect effects of the Cold War, oppression and conscious destruction in occupied territories, and discrimination in Western societies. There is a revolt against the Western tendency to regard any Muslim or Palestinian resistance to American or Israeli abuse of power as "terrorism". At the same time, the "state terrorism" of Israel, of undemocratic regimes in Muslim countries, and of the USA after September 11, 2001 are denounced.

Samuel P. Huntington's theory of a pending clash of civilizations is utterly rejected in Muslim quarters[30], while initiatives for Euro-Arab and Euro-Muslim dialogues are welcomed. A number of dialogue meetings between Muslims and Christians have also been organized in Muslim, as well as in Western countries.[31]

If it is not possible in most Muslim countries to openly state matters of political protest against the government or against the practices of state officials, such matters can be formulated in terms of norms imposed by Islam. The attentive listener (or reader) can recognize political messages in what appear to be purely religious discourses on first sight.

7. Socio-economic Discourse on the West and its Impact

Given the imperative of development in Muslim societies, one of the main subjects of debate is the form that a just society should take in a Muslim context. During the Cold War, the ideological, economic, and political confrontation between capitalist "liberal" and socialist "guided state" models of development were much discussed. Most current socio-economic Muslim discourse stresses the need to realize social justice, but

---

[30] HUNTINGTON, "The Clash of Civilizations?". Responses to this article by F. AJAMI, K. MAHBUBANI, R.L. BARTLEY, L. BINYAN, and J.J. KIRKPATRICK in *Foreign Affairs*, 72, Nr. 4 (Fall 1993), pp. 2–26. See especially Roy P. MOTTAHEDEH, "The Clash of Civilizations: An Islamicist's Critique", *Harvard Middle Eastern and Islamic Review*, 2, Nr. 2 (Autumn 1995), pp. 1–26.

A year later appeared HUNTINGTON's *The Clash of Civilizations and the Remaking of World Order*. Among the many reactions to this book, see for instance Roman HERZOG, *Preventing the Clash of Civilizations: A Peace Strategy for the Twenty-first Century*. With comments by Amitai Etzioni, Hans Küng, Bassam Tibi, and Masakazu Yamazaki, ed. by Henrik SCHMIEGELOW, New York: St. Martin's Press, 1999. For a different kind of reasoning, see TIBI, *Krieg der Zivilisationen*.

[31] Regular meetings have been organized by the CERES in Tunisia and the "Āl al-Bayt Foundation" and the "Institute for Interfaith Relations" in Jordan. Dialogue conferences have been organized, for instance in Indonesia, Iran, Malaysia, Pakistan, and Turkey. Many meetings have been held in Europe. For example, at one such meeting in the Netherlands in October 1994, genuine dialogue appears to have been achieved. See *Islamic Revival and the West: Common Values, Common Goals*.

rejects materialist assumptions and practices as violating Islamic norms. Certain authors reject in principle the idea of orienting oneself toward foreign models, while some claim that the *Sharī'a* contains all the elements necessary to realize a just socio-economic order.

In its critical forms, the current Muslim socio-economic discourse denounces and rejects poverty, injustice, oppression, and corruption. It defends the rights of the poorer nations of the South against the self-enriching practices of those of the North. It can extend to broader discussions about human rights, democracy, and civil society, and it may support the emancipation of women in, for example, the right to work.[32] Criticism is directed against lack of control over transnational corporations and against the effects of economic globalization on the weaker nations in the South.[33] What is subject to attack is not only the West, but also the current economic world order supported by the West.

There is also a more moderate variety of this socio-economic discourse on the West. One finds, for example, a clear appreciation of some NGOs that assist needy Muslim populations and countries. These work on a grass-roots level and their fruits are readily visible. They tend to be appreciative of agriculture, small enterprises, handicrafts, and the contribution of peasants, entrepreneurs, and craftsmen (who are often looked down upon in society).

The impact of the West on socio-economic realities in Muslim countries is seen in terms of a necessary modernization process. Accordingly, the question is raised as to what models are followed and to whose advantage the process works. Some of the discourses discuss bitterly the exploitation of oil, water, and other natural resources without adequate distribution of the benefits. (Besides their economic benefits, nationalizations also have great symbolic value for the populations concerned.)

Most economic discourses are concerned with the increased poverty of large parts of the population, the increased indebtedness of the countries concerned, and the growing dependence on foreign banks and investors to extricate economies from financial crisis. Surprisingly, the immense costs involved in government armaments' procurement are rarely mentioned.

---

[32] As a consequence, the socio-economic discourse touches issues that are sensitive to traditional societies as well as to political regimes: it spreads critical thought. See, for example, AN-NA'IM, *Toward an Islamic Reformation.*

[33] As such, its position is oriented more broadly toward the West, especially in current debates on North-South relations and globalization.

8. Cultural Discourse on the West and its Impact

Practically all Muslim discourse about the West has a cultural dimension, since it deals specifically with human and moral issues that result from the cultural encounter between Muslim societies that have their own cultures, on the one hand, and a technologically superior West with its own civilization, on the other.[34] The West is perceived here first of all as representing "modernity", as a rationalist force exercising an onslaught against existing forms and ways of human life that do not conform to rational demands.[35] The problem is then how to preserve fundamental Islamic values and culture against the devastation wreaked by those who might be considered technological or economic "barbarians" from the West.

Whereas early enthusiasts endeavored to imitate Western ways of life as much as possible, later (and especially after independence), a more self-assertive trend has insisted on the need to adopt from the West only what is of real use to Muslim societies. According to this, Muslims can and should adopt technology and science from the West, but they should not adopt those Western (i.e., non-Muslim) norms and values that contradict fundamental teachings of Islam. The existence of certain positive cultural forces and achievements in the West that are of general validity is recognized, however, and Muslims are encouraged to discover and study these for their own benefit.

A critical version of such a cultural discourse maintains that the West has fundamentally surrendered itself to material gain and rational modernity, implying secularity and the loss of norms and values.[36] This has been to the detriment not only of Westerners themselves (and their culture); it also represents a real danger for Muslims, inasmuch as the West is spreading and propagating its secular program to the whole world (and, moreover, is acquiring substantial economic and political benefits from this). Con-

---

[34] In the last quarter of the nineteenth century, the Egyptian periodical *Al-Muqtataf* regularly published pieces concerning relations between East and West. See L.M. KENNY, "East versus West in Al-Muqtataf, 1875–1900", in *Essays on Islamic Civilization: Presented to Niyazi Berkes*, ed. by D. P. LITTLE, Leiden: E. J. Brill, 1976, pp. 140–54. Just after World War Two, a prominent Egyptian intellectual wondered why there was so much misunderstanding between Europe and Muslims and what could be done about it. See M.H. HAEKAL (HAIKAL), "Les causes de l'incompréhension entre l'Europe et les musulmans et les moyens d'y remédier", in *L'Islam et l'Occident* (Paris: Les Cahiers du Sud, 1947), pp. 52–8.

[35] The debate on Western culture is then part of the broader debate on Islam and modernity.

[36] This position is forcefully presented by Seyyed Hossein NASR. See, for example, his books *Islam and the Plight of Modern Man*; *Knowledge and the Sacred*; *Traditional Islam in the Modern World*.

sequently, Muslims should protect themselves against this program and outlook. One way of doing this is by passing on a good Islamic education to children and youngsters and providing good instruction to adults. When Muslims adopt cultural achievements from the West, these have to be measured and purified according to Islamic standards. In this critical view, there is a certain diffidence about non-Islamic cultural expressions in the West.

In a more positive view of Western culture, however, its expressions of full humanity and its search for beauty, goodness, and truth are recognized, although Muslims should not study its literature, art, and thought without a critical sense. Here we find a positive appreciation of efforts certain circles in the West are making toward cooperation and dialogue. In this kind of discourse, it is precisely obscurantism, isolationism, and an incapacity to cooperate and engage in dialogue with others that are seen as major handicaps for a common future.

Muslim discourses on the impact of Western culture on Muslim societies have been complex. Once this impact is acknowledged, the foremost problem is how to distinguish its good from its undesirable aspects. Education is a good example; it also shows the relevance of what people do with it.

During the colonial period, several Western countries attached much importance to educating sectors of the younger population in various Muslim countries in accordance with a particular model of French, British, or American training.[37] At private schools (Christian or otherwise) and at public schools, teachers from abroad went to great pains to conduct classes as they would have done back home. Some countries established research institutes that allowed Western scholars to acquire knowledge of the country on site and provided local scholars access to Western publications. These institutes also spread knowledge of the language, history, and culture of these countries to a prospective elite. Study fellowships, practical training courses, and cultural exchange programs brought promising young people from these countries to the West. From a Western point of view, the resulting cultural impact of the West on the Muslim world through education, study, and training was beneficial. Cultural distances were bridged and people of different cultures could meet and cooperate.

The post-colonial Muslim cultural discourse on the West has seen this spread of Western (mainly European but also American) culture as a mixed blessing. Besides the older Western countries with their national interests in the region, international bodies began to play an increasingly

---

[37] There is an urgent need for a comparative study of these as well as various Muslim educational models.

important role: a lot of cultural exchange and assistance currently takes place through international channels. However, certain problems generated by the educational system have persisted. On the one hand, Muslim students became familiar with a Western language and certain aspects of European culture. On the other, during the colonial period, schools implemented a Western-type program and paid relatively little attention to the Muslim people's own language and literature, history, and culture. These subjects, moreover, were mostly taught from a "colonial" perspective. After independence, most of the cultural and educational institutions came under government auspices and were re-oriented along more national and also Islamic lines. Questions arose concerning how the curriculum should be organized and in which language it should be taught. Debates on the "Arabization" of education and culture that began in postcolonial North Africa continue to this day. With less knowledge of English, the cultural distance to the West can only grow. Indeed, the notion of culture itself has become a subject of debate.

It seems to be indeed in the fields of school education, higher education, and research (and the broader area of the arts and sciences) that the debate on the impact of Western culture has had the most immediate consequences. Without access to educational technology such as computers, students will remain far behind their Western counterparts. Without an adequate knowledge of English and access to materials in English, future generations will be isolated from the international arena. Muslim countries need experts in all fields, but also qualified leadership, to represent them on an intellectual level. On the other hand, pupils and students should be familiar with (and remain loyal to) their own cultural heritage, including Islam. They should not become alienated from their own country, risking disappearance in the "brain drain" to the West.[38]

Whatever the points of view taken, however, education and culture are first and foremost a practical problem in Muslim countries and "Third World" countries generally. There is a lack of good libraries and Western books; books from abroad are terribly expensive, and only a few of them have been translated into Arabic, Turkish, Persian, or Urdu. Intellectuals (including teachers) have to live under financial and other stress. Their wives have to take jobs and they often have to accept a second job if they want their children to study. For intellectuals and those who aspire to become intellectuals, the West represents a paradise primarily because of its schools, universities, bookshops, and libraries. In the long run, this may remain—besides a more comfortable way of life—the real attraction of the West for Muslim elites. The debate on education in Muslim coun-

---

[38] Some observations made at the time remain valuable. See WAARDENBURG, *Les universités dans le monde arabe actuel*, Vol. 1.

tries is in fact a debate about the future of culture there. This cannot be well envisaged in separation from the West. When there is no knowledge of a Western language, when ideological barriers narrow people's horizon, when the conditions of living do not permit minds to develop, and when there are serious economic constraints, a particular cultural tradition is likely to disappear.

Some countries and international organizations and foundations offer grants to students to study in the West. Some Near Eastern intellectuals suggested developing a discipline called "Occidentalism", to provide students with critical knowledge of the West.[39] This has led to debates, but, as far as I know, not to visible results.

Curiously, the West (or in this case Europe) has not yet stepped in. Various measures could be suggested, including the creation of "Euro Fellowships" by the European Union to allow creative minds (especially from the southern and eastern shore of the Mediterranean) to study or carry out research in member countries of the European Union. The European Union might establish chairs of European studies at universities in chosen Arab countries around the Mediterranean. A further initiative would be to inaugurate courses at universities in Muslim countries on relations between Western and Islamic civilization. There should also be more regular cultural exchanges between Europe and the Muslim world. Such projects would all require political will and sizeable support from the European Union or other European institutions and foundations.

In the Muslim world and specifically the Middle East, there have been many internal debates on subjects of immediate interest to the encounter of Western and Muslim cultures. One, for example, concerns the possibility (and desirability) of cultural exchange and dialogue of Muslims with representatives of other civilizations, including the Western one.[40]

Another concerns the relationship between what is deemed universally valid and what is held to be typically Islamic. Must cultural affairs necessarily always be cast in an Islamic perspective? There are now "Islamic" declarations of human rights, "Islamic" universities, and a program for the "Islamization" of knowledge. The discussion here addresses the place of typically Islamic institutions in the broader international cultural world.[41]

---

[39]   See, for example, Hasan HANAFI, *Muqaddima fī 'ilm al-istighrāb* (Introduction to the Study of "Occidentalism"), Cairo: Dār Fannīya, 1991. "Occidentalism" as a critical study of the West would be the counterpart of "Orientalism" as the critical study of the East.

[40]   As I see it, such exchanges should be promoted on various levels, have different kinds of private and public funding, and be open to local initiatives.

[41]   One thinks here of the academic status of the international Islamic universities in Islamabad, Kuala Lumpur, and Khartoum.

A third topic is the realization of rights and duties of persons and groups in Muslim societies. To what extent, in a given Muslim country, can a civil society be realized; to what degree can human rights be applied; and in what ways can legal protection be effectively guaranteed to women? There have been intense debates on these matters in several Muslim countries, all incorporating references to the West, and it is important to detail their concrete results.[42]

The fourth topic, that of the ideal Islamic state based on the *Sharīʿa*, might be considered an internal Muslim affair.[43] However, the results of the vigorous debates on this subject do touch Muslim relations with the West. For example, the *Tālibān* experiment was hardly condemned by Muslim religious authorities. What are the limits of claims to establish an Islamic order that potentially violates fundamental human rights? This question is practically relevant in the case of minorities that have special links with the West. In an era of globalization, states can no longer permit themselves to retreat fully from the rest of the world and to neglect its judgments.

These four topics (and many others in the cultural sphere) have been discussed intensely in Muslim societies in recent decades. This discussion has taken place more or less in the West's shadow, or at least with the West ever on the horizon, even if the debate has not always referred consciously to the West. If there is no reference to the West, does this indicate the narrow horizon or the provincial character of the debate? If the West is referred to, in what sense is this done? If a specific Islamic orientation is sought, what does this imply not only for future relations with the West, but also for participation in the broader international debate on the issues in question?

All in all, the impact of Western culture did not end with independence and it does not restrict itself to information technology or abstract science. It is no longer primarily transmitted through foreign schools and foreign language books, but through the media, the internet, and socially. Turkish students discuss religious taboos with German counterparts, Iranian researchers discuss Heidegger in the Islamic Republic, Pakistani intellectuals discuss postmodernism in an Islamic state, and many Muslim critical minds practice a Marxist analysis of society. Current Western

---

[42] Examples arise in the calls of the Sudanese scholar Abdullahi Ahmed an-Naʿim concerning human rights and the work of the Egyptian scholar Saʿad ad-Din Ibrahim on civil society, to mention two well-known names. Throughout the Muslim world, independent activists are working for human rights, including women's rights, without paying lip-service to Western interests.

[43] For the development of ideas on the Islamic state, see, for example, ENAYAT, *Modern Islamic Political Thought*.

philosophies touching upon text interpretation, dialogue, social justice, and human rights are far from unknown in Muslim intellectual quarters. Indeed, the Western impact on thought throughout the Muslim world is ongoing, not only in the case of so-called liberal but also in so-called fundamentalist and other forms of thought. With a healthy natural curiosity, Muslim students are interested in history, literature, sociology, and recently also the history of religions as practiced in the West. Even Western "Orientalism" attracts those interested in "other" points of view. In cultural matters, "Islamic" and "Western" are stamps rather than identities.

It is fair to say that, after the ideological opposition proclaimed between Islamism and the secular order (with the West represented as hell and Islam represented as heaven on earth), the tendency is now towards a more intellectual stand. For reflecting Muslim intellectuals, the very reality of "the West" has become an intellectual problem. How did the West become what it is now, in its many European and North American varieties? What have been the forces at work in Western civilization, strengthening or weakening it? Do a certain individualism, social disintegration, and secularization visible in the contemporary West constitute a unique Western case or are they part of more general processes that occur in all "modernizing" societies? How can the impact of faith and religion in Western and Muslim societies be assessed? On this level, the very relationship between "Islam" and "the West" and between Muslims and Westerners can be discussed as an intellectual and ethical problem for both sides. In fact, a number of Iranian intellectuals have wrestled with such problems for half a century.[44] Their debates cannot be seen independently of their views of the West, its civilization, and also its religion.[45]

9. The Spiritual Discourse on the West's Religion and its Impact

A more "spiritual" Muslim discourse on the West concerns the foundations of contemporary Western life and culture, i.e., its ontological basis and metaphysical assumptions.[46]

---

[44] See BOROUJERDI, *Iranian Intellectuals and the West*. This provides ample details about the life and work of intellectuals like Āl-e Ahmad, Makarem-Shirazi, ʿAlī Sharīʿatī, Abolhasan Jalili, Ehsan Naraghi, Hamid Enayat, Daryush Shayegan, Seyyed Hossein Nasr, Abdolkarim Sorush, and others. See Chapter 19 on "Muslims and Westerners: Changing Attitudes".

[45] It is noteworthy that interesting studies of Christianity have emerged in Iran. See STÜMPEL-HATAMI, *Das Christentum aus der Sicht zeitgenössischer iranischer Autoren*.

[46] This is evident in the numerous publications of Seyyed Hossein NASR. See "Selected Literature".

In its critical, pessimistic form, such discourse holds that the West has paid too high a price for the particular development of thought that gave rise to its technology and scientific thought. This price was the severing of its civilization from its very source: from Being. Floating mainly on rational, material, and secular interests, Western society is doomed to collapse. In the course of the twentieth century its internal tensions and conflicts became manifest in the rivalries of imperialism and colonialism, most notably in the two World Wars and the following Cold War. They are indications that Western civilization is falling apart.

In its positive variant, however, this philosophical discourse admits that, although weak, spiritual forces are present in the West and resisting the downward movement. The final outcome of the battle of these positive forces with those of materialism and secularity is uncertain, however.

In fact, this metaphysical discourse about the West tends to assume a basic dualism between an Islam connected with a particular metaphysics, on the one hand, and a West lacking such a metaphysics, on the other.

Until the mid-twentieth century, Muslim discourses on Western religion were preoccupied with the presence of Christian missions in Muslim territory; they were intent on refuting Christianity. This trend is weaker now, and Christianity is seen less as an aggressive enemy. Muslim reports on and from Europe indeed mention the fact that religion is weakening there and even disappearing from public life.[47]

Muslim discourse has critically described the rise of a secular view of life, first originating in Western Europe, then spreading all over the West and finally extending to the East, including Muslim countries. Subsequently, this discourse focused on the struggle against secularism (the doctrine bringing about a secular order), including in Muslim societies, considering it an all-pervading subversive influence from the West. A huge corpus of Muslim religious writings has been devoted to the task of combating secularism as an ideology and to re-instilling religious faith and practice in Muslim societies. This discourse implies a certain willingness to recognize the positive role of Christianity in the battle against the demon of secularity which threatens Western society and people as well.

In its critical view, this discourse affirms (as indicated) that the West is losing its religious and moral foundations. Secularity is taking the place of religion and secularism, as a negative ideological force, is spreading from the West to Muslim countries like a kind of disease. By implication, it is the West that is finally responsible for any secularization that may take place in Muslim societies. For the West itself, this negative course furnishes proof that Christianity is not the right religion.

---

[47] The idea prevails that in the West religion has made way for secularity. See KHOURY, *L'Islam critique de l'Occident.*

In contrast, the more moderate Muslim discourse on Western religion in decline tends to recognize the persistence of a basic theism and morality in the West. This is then viewed as a step toward the Muslim demand to recognize Islam as a valid faith and religion and ultimately as religious truth. The Islamic recognition of Jesus as a prophet and of Christianity as a revealed religion is then used as an argument for the mutual recognition of Islam and Christianity and their communities as valid religions and religious communities.

There is a remarkable alertness on the part of Muslim intellectuals to denounce influences from Western secular philosophies as well as religious doctrines on Muslim societies. The thought of Kant and Hegel, Feuerbach and Marx, Husserl and Wittgenstein, Heidegger and Ricoeur: they may be known and respected, but their views should not be adhered to as absolute truth.

Muslim discourses on the West's religious impact on Muslim societies, in particular through the missions, require separate study. There have been polemical writings against Christianity since the beginning of Islam, but since the nineteenth century a special genre developed. This consists of publications addressed specifically against Christian missions (Catholic and Protestant) that began to appear on the Muslim scene. Their educational activities, medical care, and charitable work in general was surely appreciated by the local people enjoying their benefits. It contrasted with the military and administrative rule imposed by Western governments, and with the economic interests pursued by Western colonists and traders. The Christian call to convert, however, has always been received with mixed feelings, and has sometimes caused friction; conversions implying apostasy from Islam could result in uproar.

Actual Muslim perceptions of and responses to Christian missions up to the 1920s deserve careful scholarly research. This must seek beyond the generally negative stereotypes that were later developed, in particular after World War One. Only by looking at the Muslim side will it be possible to arrive at a better insight into the ways in which Christian missions worked and were actually perceived and received in Muslim societies.[48]

At least in Egypt, public attacks on the work of Christian missionaries may have paralleled the rise of organized national and Islamic movements: incidents that disprove this hypothesis should be identified. The activities of missionaries from the West were generally seen as "Western" Christian activities: they were not perceived as possibly connected with the older, local "Eastern" Christian communities. In fact, the latter were

---

[48] Exemplary historical studies are POWELL, *Muslims and Missionaries in pre-Mutiny India*, and STEENBRINK, *Dutch Colonialism and Islam*. More such historical studies are needed.

also subjected to Western missionary work, especially when missions among Muslims did not bear fruit.

With independence, the work of existing Christian missions in Muslim countries was mostly limited to educational, medical, and social activities. It was carried out mainly by Christians from within the country concerned. In many respects, Christian missionaries and their communities were now freed from the burden of supposed complicity with foreign political and economic interests. Their communication with Muslim people may have become somewhat easier, and certainly less paternal and hegemonic. The Muslim discourse on Christian missions is thus slowly making way for a discourse on the possibilities of dialogue. In some Muslim countries, however, sectarian hard-line missions from North America continue to work.

10. A Discourse on Muslim Minorities in the West

The problem of relations between Islam and the West and thus of Muslim perceptions of the West has become more complex through the presence of minorities on both sides. In fact, all Muslim countries now have communities of Westerners and Christians of different origins. All Western countries today have Muslim minorities. The old rule that Muslims should not live under non-Muslim governments lost its sense when the right of religious freedom allowed them to practice their religion in Western countries.

Three different groups of Muslims living in Europe can be distinguished: (1) older communities that have been living for centuries in Southeastern and Eastern Europe; (2) immigrants from Muslim countries who settled in Western Europe and in North America; (3) indigenous converts to Islam. There are no reliable figures about the number of Muslims in Europe, but a rough estimate would be more than 30 million, including European Russia and the Caucasian republics.

The Bosnian War (1992–5) drew attention to the presence of Muslims in the former Yugoslavia, which may have had some four million Muslims by the end of the 1970s, or one-fifth of the total population at the time.[49] Muslims in Southeastern Europe had lived as quite traditional communities until World War Two. They were largely marginalized during the following half-century, in part under the pressure of communist regimes that sought to extirpate Islam along with other religions and in part due

---

[49]   Balić, *Der Islam – Europakonform?*, p. 281–2.

to economic development and social changes that took place in these societies after 1945.

Anti-Islamic campaigns arose in the nationalist anti-Turkish measures implemented in Bulgaria in the 1980s. Such campaigns assumed an extremely violent character in the nationalist radically anti-Albanian and anti-Bosnian measures adopted by Serbia and Bosnian Serbs since the late 1980s. Croatia, too, implemented anti-Bosnian measures.[50] The ensuing war between Orthodox Serbians (assisted for some time by Catholic Croatians) and Muslim Bosnians led to an "ethnic cleansing" and exodus from Bosnian territories, oppression with sexual violation and even genocide of Muslim groups, willful destruction of Islamic monuments, and an extended siege of Sarajevo. This was finally halted by Western military measures.

Bosnian Muslims have an intellectual history going back to fifteenth-century Sarajevo; since the end of the nineteenth century, its intelligentsia (living in Vienna and Sarajevo) was oriented toward an enlightened humanist culture. Sarajevo has continuously had important Muslim cultural institutions, including an Institute of Oriental studies, an Islamic theological faculty, and *madrasas* for the education of future *imāms*.

Looking at the situation of Muslims in both Western and Eastern Europe, the Bosnian scholar Dr. Smail Balić who worked at the State Library in Vienna and who knew Islam and Europe well, made the following observation. He suggested that Muslims in contemporary Europe cannot keep to those patriarchal and oriental ways of life that have found their way into Muslim communities, but are not an intrinsic part of Islam. In the non-Muslim European context today, he contends, Muslims are put to the test; they must give meaning to their religious practices and give shape to Muslim life in a non-Muslim context. They must adapt themselves to democratic structures of living together and be open to democratic processes.

Balić complains about the inadequate understanding so many Muslims have of their own religion, an understanding that does not correspond with the conditions of the new context in which they live. Under the general term "Islam", a number of antiquated models and structures of thinking that do not belong to the core of Islamic doctrine continue to exist. Looking at Islam in present-day Western Europe, he sees its fundamental weakness in its uncritical adherence to ancient authorities and the resulting alienation from reality. Islam for Balić is a continuous task that emerges from daily reality.[51]

---

[50] See below Chapter 14 on "Muslim Minorities: Politics and Religion in the Balkans".

[51] "Das islamische religiöse Leben muss sich neue Prioritäten zu eigen machen. Nur als ständige Aufgabe verstanden, die aus der alltäglichen Wirklichkeit erwächst, vermag sich der Islam im europäischen Westen dauernd anzusiedeln" (BALIĆ, *Der Islam – Europakonform?*, p. 286).

In Muslim publications, concerns about co-religionists in Europe have become greater over the last decades.[52] A number of reasons for this can be identified:

– the "ethnic cleansing" experienced by Muslim Bosnians and the oppression experienced by Muslim Albanians in Serbian Kosovo and by Muslim Chechens in Russian Chechnya;

– growing xenophobic trends in Europe over the last twenty years, which are directed against foreigners in general and Muslim foreigners in particular;

– the consequences of an existing Islamophobia that has been strengthened by Western fears of terrorism in the wake of the events of September 11, 2001;

– the repercussions of the Palestinian-Israeli conflict for Muslims as well as Jews, including those living in the West.

These concerns should be seen within the broader context of European countries' increasingly restrictive immigration policies and the European Union's attention to its new member countries in Central and Eastern Europe, rather than to the Arab Muslim countries around the Mediterranean. There is a manifest worry among Muslims that Europe will distance itself from the Muslim countries surrounding it and will prefer to receive needed immigrants from elsewhere.

As for what Muslim communities living in Europe themselves say about their situation and about European or Western culture in general: this must be left open. However, they do not necessarily share the ideal of an enlightened, liberal, European Islam.

11. Some Observations as a Conclusion

Our research has its place in the broader context of intercultural studies on Islam and the West and on the quest for authenticity.[53] It is concerned with human and cultural relations[54], relativizes confrontations[55], and is keen on communication[56].

The study of Muslim perceptions of the West, Muslim encounters with people from the West, and Muslim thinking about the West during the

---

[52] See, for example, NADWI, *Muslims in the West*. See also *Vivre et défendre l'islam à l'étranger.* Cf. *Reciprocity and Beyond: A Muslim Response to the European Churches' Document on Islam*, Markfield: The Islamic Foundation, 1997.

[53] Cf. VAN NIEUWENHUIJZE, *Cross-Cultural Studies*; ID., *Paradise Lost*.

[54] Cf. *Islam, Modernism and the West*.

[55] Cf. *Menschenbilder, Menschenrechte: Islam und Okzident*; HALLIDAY, *Islam and the Myth of Confrontation*; *Islam—Occident, la confrontation?*

[56] Cf. *Islamic Revival and the West: Common Values, Common Goals*.

twentieth century is a field of research in itself.[57] A number of studies have dealt with historical, social, and political relations between Western and Muslim countries. Attention has focused mostly on Western perceptions of these relations and actions following them. There is urgent need to bring to light how these relations were seen from the Muslim side, what kind of action Muslims took when they invoked Islam, and how they related to non-Muslims. Such a study of Muslim positions will by implication also reveal a lot about Western ones, about Western actors, and about the interaction between the two sides.[58]

Three arguments for this kind of research can be advanced:

1) In both Western and Muslim parts of the world, there is a lack of solid knowledge about their mutual relationships, current and historical. Most studies used by policy-makers and entrepreneurs are produced from a perspective of political and economic interests. These studies remain ethnocentric and often view Islam as a potential threat. There is an urgent need to disentangle scholarly research from ethnocentrism and to study the various aspects of these relationships, including their ideological expressions, in an impartial way.

2) Political, economic, and ideological pursuits on both sides need to be better known and illuminated. On both sides, political, ideological, and religious interests have been greatly mixed. Religious and moral aims have been pursued by socio-political means; likewise, political and economic strategies have been implemented with ideological as well as religious legitimations.

3) If Jews and Christians have their memories of suffering and persecution, Muslims also have theirs. Impartial study in search of historical truth is needed to overcome existing traumatizations. Scholarship can bring enlightenment and perhaps some relief.

This exploration of Muslim perceptions of the West during the twentieth century raises four major questions requiring further exploration:

1) In the twentieth century, Muslim societies had to respond to ever-new situations. A major challenge was the intrusion of the "foreign" into the Muslims' "own" society, culture, and religion. How did Muslims articulate Islam in their search for an adequate response to what was foreign to them?

2) New situations gave rise to new ways of thinking about Islam. What kinds of new interpretations have been developed in the twentieth century?

---

[57] Bernard Lewis was among the first to identify this as a task. See, for example, his "Muslim Perceptions of the West", in *As Others See Us*, pp. 3–22.

[58] There remains, of course, the problem of how to interpret the images that one party gives of the other. Cf. Jacques Waardenburg, *L'Islam dans le miroir de l'Occident*; Id., "L'Europe dans le miroir de l'Islam"; Id., *Islam et Occident face à face*.

3) If it is true that the West imposed itself on the Muslim part of the world during the twentieth century (if not earlier), what positive expectations did Muslims have of the West for their own future? When they went out to learn from the West, what exactly were they striving for?

4) With whom in the West did specific Muslim persons and groups communicate at that time? Can one distinguish particular networks? What did they ask from Westerners and what could they offer them in return? What kinds of structures of interaction and communication, temporary or enduring, existed between Muslims and Westerners in the course of the twentieth century?

It may very well be that during the twentieth century the West had at least as many stereotypes about Islam as Muslims had about the West. The latters' images and interpretations of the West do not show a particular Muslim aggressiveness toward the West except as a response to Western aggression.

Selected Literature

ABOU ZAYD, Nasr, *Critique du discours religieux*, trans. from the Arabic by Mohamed CHAIRET, Paris: Sindbad/Actes Sud, 1999.

ABU-LUGHOD, Ibrahim, *Arab Rediscovery of Europe*, Princeton: Princeton University Press, 1963.

ABUL-FADL, Mona, *Where East meets West: The West on the Agenda of Islamic Revival*, Herndon, Va.: International Institute of Islamic Thought, 1992.

The Academic Study of Religion during the Cold War: East and West, ed. by Iva DOLEŽALOVÁ, Luther H. MARTIN, and Dalibor PAPOUŠEK (Toronto Studies in Religion 27), New York, etc.: Peter Lang, 2001.

ĀL-I AHMAD, Jalāl, *Occidentosis: A Plague from the West*, trans. from the Persian by Hamid ALGAR (Contemporary Islamic Thought, Persian series), Berkeley, Cal.: Mizan Press, 1984.

Arabs and the West: Proceedings of a Three-day Seminar Organized by the University of Jordan (April 3–5, 1998), ed. by Jörgen S. NIELSEN and Sami A. KHASAWNIH, Amman: Jordan University Press, 1998.

ARKOUN, Mohammed, *Pour une critique de la raison islamique* (Islam d'hier et d'aujourd'hui 24), Paris: Maisonneuve et Larose, 1984.

As Others See Us: Mutual Perceptions, East and West, ed. by Bernard LEWIS. Special issue of *Comparative Civilizations Review* (New York), Nrs. 13–14, 1985–6.

BALIĆ, Smail, *Der Islam – Europakonform?* (Religionswissenschaftliche Studien 32), Würzburg: Echter, and Altenberge: Oros, 1994.

BOROUJERDI, Mehrzad, *Iranian Intellectuals and the West: The Tormented Triumph of Nativism*, Syracuse and New York: Syracuse University Press, 1996.

CHARLES (U.K.), Prince, "Islam and the West", *Islam and Christian-Muslim Relations*, 5/1 (1994), pp. 67–74.

CHARTIER, Marc, "La rencontre Orient-Occident dans la pensée de trois philosophes égyptiens contemporains: Hasan Hanafī, Fu'ād Zakariyya, Zakī Nagīb Mahmūd", *Oriente Moderno*, 53 (1973), pp. 605–42.

DJAÏT, Hichem, *Europe and Islam*, Berkeley and Los Angeles: University of California Press, 1985.

ENAYAT, Hamid, *Modern Islamic Political Thought*, London: Macmillan, and Austin: University of Texas Press, 1982.

ESACK, Farid, *On Being a Muslim Finding a Religious Path in the World Today*, Oxford: Oneworld, 1999.

Euro-Arab Dialogue: The Relations between the Two Cultures. Acts of the Hamburg Symposium, April 11–15, 1983, English version ed. by Derek HOPWOOD, London, etc.: Croom Helm, 1985.

FARŪQĪ, Ismā'īl Rāji al-, "Islamizing the Social Sciences", *Studies in Islam*, 16, Nr. 2 (April 1979), pp. 108–21.

—, *Islam and the Problem of Israel*, London: Islamic Council of Europe, 1980.

—, *Islamization of Knowledge*, Islamabad: National Hijra Centenary Committee of Pakistan, 1982.

Gegenseitige Wahrnehmungen—Orient und Okzident seit dem 18. Jahrhundert, ed. by Gerhard HÖPP and Thomas SCHEFFLER. Special issue of *Asien, Afrika, Lateinamerika*, 25 (1997), Nrs. 1–3.

GOLDAMMER, Kurt, *Der Mythus von Ost und West: Eine kultur- und religionsgeschichtliche Betrachtung*, Munich: Ernst Reinhardt, 1962.

HALLIDAY, Fred, *Islam and the Myth of Confrontation: Religion and Politics in the Middle East*, London and New York: I. B. Tauris, 1996.

HOURANI, Albert, *Europe and the Middle East*, Berkeley and Los Angeles: University of California Press, 1980.

HUNTINGTON, Samuel P., "The Clash of Civilizations?", *Foreign Affairs*, 72/3 (Summer 1993), pp. 22–49.

—, *The Clash of Civilizations and the Remaking of World Order*, New York: Simon and Schuster, 1996.

HUSSEIN, Taha, *The Future of Culture in Egypt*, trans. from the Arabic (1938) by Sidney GLAZER, Washington, D.C.: American Council of Learned Societies, 1954.

Islam, Modernism and the West: Cultural and Political Relations at the End of the Millennium, ed. by Gema Martín MUÑOZ, London and New York: I. B. Tauris, 1999.

L'Islam et l'Occident, Paris: Les Cahiers du Sud, 1947.

Islamic Revival and the West: Common Values, Common Goals. Final Report of a Conference held in Oegstgeest, the Netherlands, October 22–24, 1994, ed. by Ruud HOFF and Hanneke MULDER, The Hague: International Dialogues Foundation, 1995.

JOHANSEN, Baber, *Muhammad Husain Haikal: Europa und der Orient im Weltbild eines ägyptischen Liberalen* (Beiruter Texte und Studien 5), Wiesbaden: Franz Steiner, 1967.

KHOURY, Paul, *L'Islam critique de l'Occident dans la pensée arabe actuelle: Islam et sécularité* (Religionswissenschaftliche Studien 35), 2 Vols., Echter: Würzburg, and Oros: Altenberge, 1994 and 1995.

KORESHI, Samiullah M., *New World Order: Western Fundamentalism in Action*, Islamabad: Institute of Policy Studies & Islamabad Publications, 1995.

LAMCHICHI, Abderrahim, *Islam-Occident, Islam-Europe: Choc des civilisations ou coexistence des cultures?*, Paris: L'Harmattan, 1999.

LAROUI, Abdallah, *Islam et modernité*, Paris: La Découverte, 1987.

—, *Islamisme, modernisme, libéralisme*, Casablanca: Centre culturel arabe, 1997.

LEWIS, Bernard, *The Muslim Discovery of Europe*, New York and London: Norton, 1982.

—, *Islam and the West*, New York and London: Oxford University Press, 1993.

Menschenbilder, Menschenrechte. Islam und Okzident: Kulturen im Konflikt, ed. by Stefan BATZLI, Fridolin KISSLING, and Rudolf ZIHLMANN, Zurich: Unionsverlag, 1994.

MOUSSALLI, Ahmad S., *Radical Islamic Fundamentalism: The Ideological and Political Discourse of Sayyid Qutb*, Beirut: American University of Beirut, 1992.

MUSAWI LARI, Sayid Mujtaba Rukni, *Western Civilisation through Muslim Eyes*, trans. from the Persian by Francis John GOULDING, Guildford, U. K.: F. J. Goulding, 1977.

Muslims and the West: Encounter and Dialogue, ed. by Zafar Ishaq ANSARI and John L. ESPOSITO, Islamabad: Islamic Research Institute, International Islamic University, and Washington, D.C.: Georgetown University, Center for Muslim-Christian Understanding, 2001.

NADWI, Syed Abul Hasan Ali, *Muslims in the West: The Message and Mission*, ed. by Khurram MURAD, Leicester: The Islamic Foundation, 1983/1403.

NA'IM, Abdullahi Ahmed an-, *Toward an Islamic Reformation: Civil Liberties, Human Rights, and International Law*, Syracuse, N. Y.: Syracuse University Press, 1990.

NARAGHI, Ehsan, *L'Orient et la crise de l'Occident*, Paris: Entente, 1977.

NASR, Seyyed Hossein, *Islam and the Plight of Modern Man*, London: Longmans, 1975.

—, *Knowledge and the Sacred*, Edinburgh: Edinburgh University Press, 1981.

—, *Traditional Islam in the Modern World*, London: Kegan Paul, 1981, 1987[2].

NIEUWENHUIJZE, Christoffel Anthonie Olivier van, *Cross-Cultural Studies* (Publications of the Institute of Social Studies, Series Maior, Vol. 5), The Hague: Mouton, 1963.

—, *Paradise Lost: Reflections on the Struggle for Authenticity in the Middle East* (Social, Economic and Political Studies of the Middle East and Asia 56), Leiden, etc.: E. J. Brill, 1997.

Pioneers of Islamic Revival, ed. by Ali RAHNEMA, London: Zed Books, 1994.

POSTON, Larry, *Islamic Da'wah in the West: Muslim Missionary Activity and the Dynamics of Conversion to Islam*, New York: Oxford University Press, 1992.

POWELL, Avril Ann, *Muslims and Missionaries in pre-Mutiny India*, Richmond, U. K.: Curzon, 1993.

RAHIMIEH, Nasrin, *Oriental Responses to the West*, Leiden: E. J. Brill, 1990.

RAHMAN, Fazlur, *Islam and Modernity: Transformation of an Intellectual Tradition*, Chicago and London: University of Chicago Press, 1982.

RAMADAN, Tariq, *Islam: Le face à face des civilisations. Quel projet pour quelle modernité?*, Lyon: Tawhid, 1995.

—, *Les musulmans d'Occident et l'avenir de l'islam*, Paris: Sindbad/Actes Sud, 2003.

SHAHIN, Emad Eldin, *Through Muslim Eyes: M. Rashīd Ridā and the West*, Herndon, Va.: International Institute of Islamic Thought, 1993.

SHARĪʿATI, ʿAlī, *On the Sociology of Islam: Lectures*, trans. from the Persian by Hamid ALGAR, Berkeley, Cal.: Mizan Press, 1979.

—, *Marxism and Other Western Fallacies: An Islamic Critique* (Contemporary Islamic Thought, Persian series), trans. from the Persian by R. CAMPBELL, Berkeley, Cal.: Mizan Press, 1980.

SHAYEGAN, Daryush, *Cultural Schizophrenia: Islamic Societies Confronting the West*, Syracuse, N. Y.: Syracuse University Press, 1997.

—, *La lumière vient de l'Occident: Le réenchantement du monde et la pensée nomade*, Paris: Ed. de l'Aube, 2001.

STEENBRINK, Karel A., *Dutch Colonialism and Islam: Contacts and Conflicts 1596–1950*, Amsterdam and Atlanta: Rodopi, 1993.

STENBERG, Leif, *The Islamization of Science: Four Muslim Positions Developing an Islamic Modernity*, Stockholm: Almqvist & Wiksell International, 1996.

STÜMPEL-HATAMI, Isabel, *Das Christentum aus der Sicht zeitgenössischer iranischer Autoren: Eine Untersuchung religionskundlicher Publikationen in persischer Sprache* (Islamkundliche Untersuchungen 195), Berlin: Klaus Schwarz, 1996.

TALBI, Mohamed, "Possibilities and Conditions for a better Understanding between Islam and the West", *Journal of Ecumenical Studies*, 25 (1988), pp. 161–93.

TIBI, Bassam, *Krieg der Zivilisationen: Politik und Religion zwischen Vernunft und Fundamentalismus*, Hamburg: Hoffmann und Campe, 1995.

Vivre et défendre l'islam à l'étranger: Causeries et études recueillies par le Bureau de Paris, Ligue Islamique Mondiale, Madrid: Ligue Islamique Mondiale, 1981.

WAARDENBURG, Jacques, *Les universités dans le monde arabe actuel: Documentation et essai d'interprétation*, Vol. 1: *Texte*, Vol. 2: *Statistiques* (Recherches méditerranéennes, Etudes 8), Paris and The Hague: Mouton, 1966.

—, *L'Islam dans le miroir de l'Occident*, Paris and The Hague: Mouton, 1970[3].

—, *Islam et Occident face à face: Regards de l'histoire des religions*, Geneva: Labor et Fides, 1998.

—, "L'Europe dans le miroir de l'Islam", *Asiatische Studien/Etudes Asiatiques*, 53, Nr. 1 (1999), pp. 103–28.

Wessen Geschichte? Muslimische Erfahrungen historischer Zäsuren im 20. Jahrhundert, ed. by Henner FÜRTIG and Gerhard HÖPP (Zentrum Moderner Orient, Berlin, Arbeitshefte Nr. 16), Berlin: Das Arabische Buch, 1998.

YARED, Nazik Saba, *Arab Travellers and Western Civilization*, London: Saqi Books, 1996.

Chapter 10

Europe and its Muslim Neighbors: Glimpses of Dialogue[1]

Since the 1970s, dialogues have been underway between Europeans from various parts of the continent and representatives of Turkey and the Arab world. They have been conducted not only by individuals or private organizations, as had been customary, or by individual countries on a bilateral basis, but by groups of states such as the later European Union and the League of Arab States, with meetings taking place in the shadow of official international organizations.

This should encourage us to take stock of the history common to people living in present-day Europe and those living in the territories surrounding it. In the course of this history, both sides have made constant efforts to distinguish themselves from each other, stressing the differences in religious background, with the Jews present north and south of the Mediterranean as a kind of third party.

1. History: The Colonial Period

This history started in Southern Europe with the landing of Arab and Berber troops in Southern Spain in 711, pushing forward to the north, up to Poitiers in 732. For centuries, the larger part of Spain was under Moorish rule, and for a considerable time, southern France and southern Italy as well as Mediterranean islands were ruled by Arabs. A large part of Eastern Europe came under Mongol-Turkic rule in the mid-thirteenth century. The new rulers would be Islamized soon afterwards, being known as Tatars, and putting their stamp on Eastern Europe. On both fronts, a kind of "reconquest" took place that ended in the South with the taking of Granada in 1492 and in the East with the taking of Kazan in 1552. In the Southeast, the Turkish Ottomans crossed the Bosporus in the mid-

---

[1] Revised version of a text published under the title "Europe and its Muslim Neighbors: Recent Meetings of Intercultural Dialogue", in *Turkish Islam and Europe / Türkischer Islam und Europa* (see Selected Literature section 4.), pp. 107–39.

fourteenth century, defeated the Serbs near Kosovo in 1389, and took Constantinople in 1453. They occupied the Balkans and pushed forward toward Vienna in 1529 and 1683. Here the "reconquest" started with the peace of Karlowitz in 1698 and ended shortly before World War One, leaving a reduced European part to present-day Turkey.

Still today, monuments and collections in Spain, Sicily, Istanbul, and Moscow testify to the cultural heritage of Muslim civilization on European soil.

The common history continued with opposite military offensives. In the eighteenth century, Russia occupied Turkic Muslim regions at the Crimea, in the Caucasus, and eastward beyond the Volga as far as Kazakhstan. Starting with Napoleon's expedition to Egypt (1798–1801) and the capture of Algiers in 1830, European powers intervened in the Middle East and North Africa. By the end of the nineteenth century, the French and the British Empires stretched out over large Muslim and other African and Asian regions. As a consequence, Muslim peoples were drawn into European history, even Turkey and Iran, which had succeeded in keeping their independence. Certainly up to World War One and also afterwards, certain liberal Muslim elites showed great admiration for European culture and took the path of what later would be called "Westernization". For the broader masses, however, a certain fascination with Europe decreased parallel to the increasing struggle for independence of mostly newly-created states. The unavoidable decline and fall of the European empires and the rise of national Muslim states with a nationalist, left-wing, or Islamic orientation put an end to prevailing French, British, Russian, or American cultural models, as well as orientations promulgated in Dutch, Italian, or Spanish colonies.

For better insight into the history of Europe and its Muslim neighbors, we should pay attention to the impact of the colonial period. The then existing relationships rendered nearly all Arab countries utterly dependent and obliged Turkey and Iran to recognize and resist European hegemony. Unless this state of affairs is recognized and its consequences are kept in view, the common twentieth-century history of Europe and its neighbors remains obscure.

The following situation predominated around 1935, just before World War Two:

a) *North Africa.* Algeria, as a French *département*, and Tunisia and Morocco, as French protectorates, were under French rule. After the independence of Morocco and Tunisia in 1956, Algeria acquired independence following a bloody war in 1962. Libya's colonial relationship with Italy ended in the course of World War Two. The Western Sahara was a Spanish colony until 1976. Mauritania was a French protectorate and acquired independence in 1960.

b) *Northeast Africa*. Egypt was under British rule until 1923, acquired a large degree of independence in 1937, and full independence in 1956. British—and nominally Egyptian—rule over Sudan came to an end in 1956. Somalia was under Italian and British rule and became an independent state in 1960. Djibouti was under French rule and became independent in 1977. Ethiopia became an Italian colony in 1936 and acquired independence after World War Two.

c) *Levant*. After World War One, Palestine and Transjordan became Mandates of Britain. Transjordan became independent in 1946. Britain's Mandate of Palestine ended on May 14, 1948; part of it became then the state of Israel; the other parts came under Jordanian and Egyptian rule. Lebanon had a mandate relationship with France and became independent in 1943.

d) *Fertile Crescent*. After World War One, Syria became a Mandate of France and became independent in 1946. Iraq was a Mandate of Britain and became independent in 1934.

e) *Arabian Peninsula*. The Gulf Emirates and Aden with Hadramaut had particular relationships with Britain that came to an end in the 1960s and early 1970s. Kuwait became independent in 1961, South Yemen in 1967, Bahrain in 1970, Qatar and the United Arab Emirates in 1971. Britain's special relations with Najd and the Hejaz came to an end with the creation of independent Saudi Arabia in 1932. North Yemen had acquired independence from the Ottoman Empire in 1918.

f) *USSR*. The larger Muslim republics of the USSR, first under Tsarist Russian and then under USSR rule, became independent in 1991.

g) *Independent countries*. Turkey, Iran, Saudi Arabia, (North) Yemen, and Afghanistan retained their independence.

The weight of European power turned out to be a burden especially for the Arabs. The two world wars involved battles fought on Arab soil and Arab participation in battles in Europe. Plans for a larger Arab entity after World War One did not materialize. Zionist immigration and the establishment of Israel brought havoc to Palestine and misery to the Palestinians. They were a main factor in continuous tension in the Middle East and beyond. The Cold War incited rivalries, armament spending, and local conflicts in the region. The abundant revenues of the oil states did not benefit the broader population of the region. Notwithstanding political independence, economic dependence reigned. With Israel's annexation of East Jerusalem and colonization of the Occupied Territories, Sadat's peace treaty with Israel in 1979, the neglect of the Palestinian movement, the Gulf War of 1991, the failed "peace process" with Israel (1993–2000), the USA-declared war on international terrorism since 2001, and the Israeli reoccupation of the lands of the Palestine Authority, many Arabs feel they have been and are being cheated again. This time not by Britain as the winner of World War One, but by the USA as the winner of the Cold War. European domination made way for USA domination.

Looking back, a struggle for independence and authenticity was the hallmark of Arab responses to Europe and the West throughout the twentieth century. Three successive ideological responses can be distinguished.

In a first round, nationalist ideologies prevailed until independence was obtained, mostly between 1945 and 1971.

In a second round, a struggle for social justice was often motivated by left-wing ideologies. Various kinds of revolution took place in Arab countries. Once the enemy from outside (Europe) had been thrown out, the enemy inside (the ancient bourgeoisie) had to be put down in the hope of arriving at a more just society. Economic and social development was sought with the help of models of foreign origin.

In a third round, in contrast to foreign ideologies and after a failing economic development, more specific Islamic ideologies found broader acceptance. They could claim standing in the tradition of the countries concerned, maintaining Islamic norms and values and offering Islamic solutions to the serious problems of Arab and other Middle Eastern societies.

This led to a continuous appeal to Qur'anic texts and *hadīths*, a revitalization of Islamic discourse, and a political instrumentalization of Islam from various sides and with different aims. Islam could be used as a source of protest against prevailing misery, injustice, and corruption. Most states, however, took repressive measures against criticism.

2. New Relationships: Intercultural Dialogue

Europe's hegemonic role has been over since the 1960s. Yet, the cultural interaction between Europe and Muslim countries that started in the nineteenth century did not stop. Not only during their rule of Muslim lands but also afterwards European scholarly and broadly cultural efforts have been made to arrive at a better knowledge and understanding of the Muslim "others", with a more dialogical attitude than in imperial times. On the other hand, after European occupation, Arabs and others came to perceive and know Europe somewhat more humanly than before. A certain political decline seems to have opened relations between politically more independent partners. Perhaps a change of mental climate has taken place in the 1970s, with a need for communication.

Moreover, in the course of the last quarter of the twentieth century, some political changes have had an important impact on these relations. Particular examples are the Euro-Arab dialogue that started with the oil crisis of 1973, Turkey's coming closer to the European Economic Community in the 1980s, and the initiative of the European Union to arrive at broader Euro-Mediterranean cooperation and dialogue, as formulated at the Barcelona Conference of November 1996. After the demise of the USSR and communism, Western Europe came into contact with Muslim regions and peoples that had been practically closed off at the time of the Iron Curtain. They include the Balkans (Bosnia, Albania, Kosovo, Bulgaria), present-day Russia (with the Tatar people spread over the country and with Muslim regions like Tatarstan and Chechnya), and Muslim countries beyond Russia (Azerbaidjan, Iran, and the Central Asian republics with Kazakhstan).

European countries and their neighbors have been searching to define and develop new mutual relationships. This search has been most spectacular in the political and economic fields, but there have been considerable changes, too, in the field of cultural relations, which is our interest here. In the colonial era, Muslim countries had more or less exclusive cultural relations with the particular "mother" country to which they were subjected. Since independence, they have been able to develop bilateral relations with other countries as well. Cultural exchanges have taken place through bilateral cultural agreements but have also been furthered by private initiatives from cultural foundations and scholarly institutions. Some European countries conduct concerted cultural action abroad. France does this through the Alliance Française, research institutes and schools, the United Kingdom through the British Council, and Germany through the Goethe Institutes and research institutes.

I want to concentrate here, however, on those cultural relations that transcend the confines and interests of national states and that take place within a broader European or Mediterranean perspective. So I shall focus on four meetings of intercultural dialogue between Europe and Muslim countries surrounding it. I had the privilege of attending them, so that I can make some personal observations about them. "Culture" was at their center; in other words, we are not dealing here with strictly scholarly or religious meetings or with meetings concerned with the presence of Muslims in Europe. The conferences I will discuss are:

1. Strasbourg, November 14–15, 1991. Seminar organized by the Council of Europe on "Euro-Arab Understanding and Cultural Exchange";
2. Toledo, November 4–7, 1995. Conference organized by the European Union on "Mediterranean Society: A challenge for the three civilizations? Informal dialogue between Islam, Judaism and Christianity";
3. Amman, April 3–5, 1998. Conference organized at the University of Amman on "Arabs and the West";
4. Istanbul, March 6–8, 1998. Conference organized by the Municipality of Istanbul on "Interfaith/Intercultural Dialogue".

Of these four conferences, two were organized by European bodies and took place in Europe proper, and the two others took place in Muslim countries thanks to local initiatives.

3. Euro-Arab Dialogue: Strasbourg 1991

3.1. Historical Context

The so-called "Euro-Arab Dialogue" goes back to the October 1973 war between Egypt and Syria, on the one hand, and Israel, on the other. At the time, Iran and the oil-producing Arab countries increased the price of oil considerably and conducted an oil boycott against countries friendly to Israel. Following this, it was in Europe's interest to obtain guarantees for its oil imports from Arab countries in exchange for greater economic and political cooperation with the Arab world. On the Arab side, there was a need for development assistance but also the desire to arrive at a solution of the Palestine problem, for which pressure needed to be put on the Europeans. The misery of the Palestinians in general and the wretched situation in the territories that Israel had occupied in 1967 in particular, were known to the Europeans. They also knew that Israel had started to build Jewish settlements here against international conventions and that it had proclaimed the illegal annexation of East Jerusalem. These actions, however, had as yet not elicited from them any coherent response.

All of this led to the first phase of the Euro-Arab dialogue, for which France took the initiative and leadership.[2] This led to negotiations between the European Economic Community (EEC) and the League of Arab States (Arab League). It also opened up the area of cultural relations beyond political and economic relations. Its culmination may be considered the symposium organized by the Cultural Committee of the Euro-Arab Dialogue, in Hamburg (April 11–15, 1983).[3] Further relations in the 1980s were handicapped in particular through the exclusion of Egypt from the Arab League after the Camp David Agreement with Israel in 1978, the war between Iraq and Iran (1980–88), and the continuing war in Lebanon (1975–89) with various international involvements. Western countries had differing interests in all of this. The Palestine issue, however, increasingly became an international focus through the concerted action of various Palestine organizations and especially when the first *Intifāda* started in 1989 in the territories occupied by Israel. This would change with the first Oslo Agreement of 1993.

---

[2] BENCHENANE, *Pour un dialogue euro-arabe* (see Selected Literature section 6.).
[3] *Dialogue euro-arabe: Les relations entre les deux cultures. Actes du Symposium de Hambourg (11–15 avril 1983)*, Ligue arabe et Communauté européenne, Aix-en-Provence: Edisud, 1986; English ed.: *Euro-Arab Dialogue*, London 1985.

A second phase of the Euro-Arab dialogue started with the Gulf War of January and February 1991, after Iraq's occupation of Kuwait in August 1990. Just as the first phase was a response to the oil crisis of 1973, the second phase is to be seen as a response to the Gulf War and the turmoil in the Middle East in which Israel became involved. The two wars of 1973 and 1991 were consequently instrumental in the initiative and pursuit of Euro-Arab dialogue. Whereas the Americans after 1973 concentrated on achieving an Israeli-Egyptian settlement and after 1991 worked for a comprehensive "peace process" in the Near East, the Europeans since 1973 have been trying to protect their interests through a rapprochement with the Arab world under the title of "Euro-Arab dialogue".

3.2. Organization

The Strasbourg conference was a major event in intercultural relations during this second phase of the Euro-Arab dialogue. The initiative was taken by the Council of Ministers of the Council of Europe, which works in particular on cultural and humane issues. Its chairman at the time was the Swede Andersson, who developed the idea, which was followed up and energetically put into practice by Catherine Lalumière, at the time Secretary General of the Council of Europe.[4]

The seminar was further prepared by a committee chaired by C. Lalumière and consisting of two Arab intellectuals living in Europe, a professor from the University of Ankara, and seven Europeans. The main theme, "Euro-Arab Understanding and Cultural Exchange", was divided into three subthemes: "The historical dimension of the Euro-Arab cultural dialogue" (report by Bernard Lewis), "Contemporary Euro-Arab perceptions and communication" (report by Hussein Ahmad Amin), and "Comparing mutual ideas and values of coexistence: the notion of democracy" (report by Şerif Mardin).

The meeting took place in November 1991, that is to say nine months after the Gulf War of January-February of that year and one month after the Middle East Peace Conference held in Madrid in October 1991.[5] Of the 52 participants, 9 were Arabs from Cairo, Amman, and Tunis, 6 were Arabs living in Europe, 2 were from Turkey, 17 were European oriental-

---

[4]   In May 1991, the Parliamentary Assembly of the Council of Europe had already organized a Colloquium in Paris on *The Contribution of the Islamic Civilisation to European Culture*. Its proceedings were published as a Report of the Committee on Culture and Education (by Mr. Lluis Maria DE PUIG) with related documents by the Council of Europe in Strasbourg in 1992 (Document 6497).

[5]   The Acts of the Strasbourg seminar were published in three volumes under the general title *Euro-Arab Understanding and Cultural Exchange* (see Selected Literature section 6.). We refer here in particular to the second part of the *Proceedings* (Vol. 1) and to the *Contributions* (Vol. 2).

ists and 18 were Europeans with other specializations; 27 participants contributed texts that were published afterwards. Moreover, 20 diplomatic representatives and 35 other guests and observers were present. As far as time allowed, all those present could participate in the discussions.

3.3. Closing Speech

In her closing speech, Catherine Lalumière, who had presided over the seminar, highlighted some points that had arisen in the discussions and that she thought would be of interest for the Council of Europe's further political action.

1) In the course of the history of Euro-Arab relations there have been particularly favorable moments and periods in which positive initiatives were taken on both sides, especially in the Mediterranean area. Curiously enough, these favorable periods preceded the formation of states. As a consequence, it may be questioned whether the very existence of national states has furthered the cause of understanding.

2) Euro-Arab relations have not improved in the last centuries, but rather the reverse. This movement of regression has been caused by many factors. Among the economic ones is the economic upsurge in Europe since the seventeenth century, with an economic decline in the Arab lands at the same time. Among the political factors with negative effects on these relations is the colonization of Arab land by Europeans, the establishment of the state of Israel, and the issue of the rights of the Palestinians and of a Palestinian state. And among the cultural obstacles to good relations one should note the low level of information, knowledge, and understanding of each other, the existing problems of integrating Arab immigrants and their descendants in Europe, and a generally unsatisfactory presentation in the media.

3) Among the many factors creating a distance between the Arab and the European world or bringing them together, the first to be mentioned is how the state is organized and especially the question of democracy. How can the present-day absence of democratic governments in Arab countries be explained? One should first of all look for cultural explanations. To begin with, the political organization of society was everywhere based on religion, on religious texts. Later, first in Greece and Rome and then, several centuries later, in Western Europe, philosophical thought of a non-religious nature developed. In this way the doctrines of the separation of the three powers, of the secular organization of the state, and of the separation between state and religion took shape. A way of thinking that was religio-political in its origin developed into a purely political way of thinking that elaborated the concept of democracy. In this way European thought followed a unique path. The Arab countries, however, still find

themselves in a stage in which political thinking takes place within a religious framework.

Besides such cultural explanations for the relative absence of democratic governments in the Arab world, other explanations can be given as well, for instance economic ones. In the present-day struggle for economic survival in Arab countries, values other than that of democracy have priority. Political explanations can be given as well. The idea of democracy was brought by the colonial powers and compromised by that fact; democratic structures were sometimes imposed from outside or imitated from the West. On the whole, democratic experiments in Arab countries have not been very successful.

The chances of democracy in Arab countries, according to Lalumière, are difficult to estimate. In any case the simple acceptance of purely technical democratic institutions is not enough to democratize a society. Certain basic values such as freedom and justice, as well as the human rights should underpin the process. Human rights should be seen as reference values of democracy, as a foundation and orientation for it. If it is true that democracy cannot be imposed from the outside, it can at least be promoted through transitional measures. Lalumière gave the examples of the promotion of human rights and the support given to found and develop free associations, the growing recognition of the role of women and their work in Arab society, and acknowledging the rights of different kinds of minorities. Arab countries should promote new ideas through intellectual exchange and by means of the media.

4) The Secretary General of the Council of Europe expressed the opinion that certain political problems such as the Palestine problem have to be solved as a priority. Until this happens, the Arab side logically will continue to distrust European ideas which wait for implementation.

5) To give shape to democratic ideas, it will first be necessary to solve some major economic and demographic problems of the Arab countries.

6) On an intellectual and cultural level, the Council of Europe should take new initiatives to strengthen the Arab intelligentsia, for instance by means of exchange programs and by giving "Euro-Fellowships" allowing creative persons to write or do research in European countries of their choice.

3.4. Some Suggestions of Arab Participants to Bridge the Distance

Arab participants present at the seminar made various suggestions to bridge the existing distance between the Arab world and Europe. They focused less on concrete measures than on new cultural orientations.

1) Arabs expect from their European partners a basic respect for Islam. They gladly indicate that Muslims regard Christianity as being founded

on revelation and consequently value it positively. Certain contributions, such as those by Muhammad Saïd El-Ashmawy from Egypt and Ali Issa Othman from Jordan, referred to the spiritual values of Islam and noted that these are neglected both by Muslim "Islamists" who ideologically reduce Islam to a rational grid and by Western sociologists and political scientists, who apply their own models of explanation to Islam. In each Euro-Arab dialogue the moral and ethical as well as the religious and spiritual aspects of Islam should be fully recognized.

2) All Arab participants stressed forcefully the important role of intellectuals and authors in Arab societies, in particular as bearers of creativity, voices of freedom of thought, and defenders of human rights. Mohammed Arkoun from Paris classified these intellectuals in four categories of attitude toward the Arab political regimes:
a) Those who are attentive to what is said and what happens, but without responding to it;
b) Those who support and comment on the official statements and interpretations; they have access to the media and are allowed to participate in international meetings;
c) Those who carry out tactical opposition, who take a reformist attitude but who never express themselves on themes that are taboo;
d) Those who attack squarely what they judge to be wrong; these are only a minority, but they find themselves at a deeper level in the mainstream of contemporary history.

It is worthwhile to compare Arkoun's classification of the ways in which intellectuals respond to authoritarian regimes with that given by Ghayth N. Armanazi, from London, who distinguishes:
a) Those who are apologists for the regime and those in power;
b) Those who hardly deal with the situation in their own country, but who are more concerned with international problems, often living abroad;
c) Those who have the courage to accuse the regime concerned in a direct way and who do not avoid confrontation;
d) Those who constitute a "loyal opposition" and try through peaceful means to bring about changes for the better in the given situation.

The Arab participants clearly expected from their European colleagues and partners in the cultural field effective support for the cause of independent intellectuals and authors as well as of enlightened Muslim thinkers. Such a creative intelligentsia constitutes an alternative to those who have political power, to the established religious authorities, and to the oppositional "Islamist" ideologists.

3) Many Arab participants underlined the importance of the common history of Arab and European culture and of the common sources of these cultures. They advocated that this history in its complexity should be

studied and written anew. Tahar Guiga from Tunis underlined that, after the expansion of Islam, the Arabs had created a kind of Arab and Islamic cultural area that furthered exchanges with Christians and Christianity. In his own contribution he gave some historical examples of Euro-Arab cultural dialogue, for instance in Spain in the medieval period. In the course of history, however, there have also been examples of situations in which dialogue was impossible or even flatly refused. This was the case in Algeria during French rule, when the country was a *département*, or French province.

4) Several Arab participants, such as Mohammed Arkoun from Paris and Mohammed Sid-Ahmed from Egypt, stressed the importance of the Mediterranean as an area of communication between the Arab and European worlds. The participants clearly hoped that one day there would be peace in the present-day areas of tension in the Mediterranean, such as Israel, Palestine, Cyprus, and Algeria, and that the inland sea would then regain its rightful central place in Euro-Arab relations. The role of the large and wealthy parts of both Europe and the Arab world that happen not to border on the Mediterranean was not, alas, taken into consideration. Unfortunately, the contribution of Turkey and Greece to the Mediterranean dialogue and the role of Turkish-European and Turkish-Arabic relations fell outside the theme of the seminar, which was confined to Euro-Arab relations.

5) Many Arab participants referred to the much needed Euro-Arab dialogue that should take place inside Europe itself, given the new situation created by the presence of Arab immigrants and their descendants here. Although this topic fell outside the scope of the seminar, it was recognized that the problem of the "internal" dialogue inside Europe cannot be completely dissociated from that of the "external" dialogue between Europe and its neighbors if one wants to improve Euro-Arab relations.

6) Dialogue and understanding were not only aims of the seminar, they could also be seen as aims of Euro-Arab relations themselves. Hussein Ahmad Amin from Egypt, for instance, described these aims as part of a new world of fraternity in common humanity. Tahar Guiga from Tunis, however, warned that dialogue is not an easy matter. A cultural dialogue between peoples who equally honor their identity and love their culture is always difficult and ambiguous. He drew attention to the mostly outside factors that have had a negative effect on attempts at dialogue in the course of history. As examples he mentioned the effects of the instinct of domination, of religious extremism, and of intolerant ideologies. Dialogue implies that other people, too, have the right to express and practice their religious or philosophical convictions. Beyond simple tolerance, it requires attention on both sides for others as well as an open mind and an open heart.

3.5. Looking back at the Strasbourg Meeting

Looking back, I feel relieved that a seminar like the Strasbourg meeting was possible and that such a wide variety of people participated. The theme of "dialogue" was central and there were dialogues indeed, focusing on the cultural dimension of Euro-Arab relations. Economic, political, and demographic issues were implied but not explicitly treated. The abstract nature of the theme and the prevailing good will led to much generalization; the strong differences among different groups of Arab countries as well as among European countries including Eastern and Western, Southern and Northern Europe, were hardly touched upon. Hardly any mention was made of the many forces outside the Mediterranean whose impact is felt daily, such as the USA, or of unpleasant forces around the Mediterranean such as the right-wing movements on the Northern and the "Islamist" movements on the Southern side. On the other hand, many observations that were made about Euro-Arab relations are equally valid for Euro-Turkish relations, not only where Turkey is concerned but also with Turkic people elsewhere.

I cannot say, however, that—at least during the sessions—the European participants engaged themselves passionately in dialogue. There was a certain caution on their part, though not without a certain openness. What was lacking among the Europeans was any coherent vision of the future. This may be explained in part by the fact that people had been overwhelmed by events. The USSR and communism had just collapsed, the Gulf War had meant a surplus of Western power in the Arab world, and the Madrid Conference had not provided the breakthrough on the part of Israel that optimists had hoped for.

Unavoidably, some papers submitted had little to do with the official aims of the seminar. Unfortunately, some of the speakers were known to have no sympathy for Arab causes. Some old-timers with nostalgic feelings for history presented views of Arab affairs that dated from before the Suez War of 1956. More than once I was struck by antiquated views of religion and *laïcité*, history and society that were presented with aplomb and sometimes with spirit, but had rhetorical rather than scholarly foundations.

On the Arab side, there were some resourceful personalities, matured through experience and with clear intellectual positions, though expressed diplomatically. Some speeches—on the Arab side too—seemed to be ideologically colored, but they were always directed toward dialogue and so to speak waiting for an answer from their European partners. Whether the Arab participants received substantial answers from the European side remains an open question to me. For an answer, one should consult the three small published booklets of Proceedings of the seminar, which give an excellent and exhaustive overview of the meetings, speakers, and discussants.

In conclusion, many interesting ideas were expressed about Euro-Arab relations and their improvement, mostly with reference to the speaker's own experience. Unfortunately, neither on the Arab (mainly Egyptian) nor on the European (mainly British and French) side were clear statements made about factual realities. The words were not linked to the world of action. As a matter of fact, there were hardly any participants who themselves played an active role in one of the many existing Euro-Arab programs. Consequently, the discussions seemed to float, but since they were free, they were revealing and informative for the attentive listener who did not want to project his own concerns, wishes, or ideals on what was going on.

It seems to me that people on the European side had taken the subject of cultural relations and dialogue in order to manifest their will—but not their capacity—for a dialogue with the Arabs. Discussion prevailed, but only in the respective speaker's own language. There was hardly any treatment of any existing cultural expressions in literature, art, or scholarship or successful examples of intercultural relations between Europeans and Arabs. The Strasbourg seminar was in a way typical of the state of Euro-Arab dialogue on an "official" level, and precisely this made it interesting.

One aim of the seminar was to bring about an encounter of intellectuals and writers of both sides who did not necessarily create problems but who could identify certain problems and speak about them, either in the formal sessions or more informally outside the sessions. It seems to me that it was perhaps less important to find and propose a common solution for these problems. More important was whether and to what extent the two sides could enter into discussion and what ideas came out of that. If anything, a certain way of pursuing dialogue seems to be easier among authors, intellectuals, and artists than among other social groups. On the other hand, it has to be admitted that these creative individuals mostly occupy a rather marginal place in their societies and that their meetings have little immediate practical results. Whether living under more democratic or more oppressive regimes, in more open or more closed societies, such individuals often represent the deeper and less visible trends and orientations of societies. They sometimes suffer from their lack of visibility, and in quite a few cases others consider them to be an "asocial" group. However, their creative potential is recognized, and Strasbourg demonstrated a certain solidarity of European intellectuals with their Arab counterparts.

In this connection a few remarks are in place on the very organization of this meeting. It was set up by two organizations, the Council of Europe and the League of Arab States, which include practically all European and Arab states. The main purpose of these two organizations is of course not so much to cultivate Euro-Arab relations as to assure and strengthen the links that exist between states within Europe and the Arab world respectively. In other words, they concentrate on certain formal aspects of the European and the Arab world in the field of law, society, and social and cultural life.

The fact that the two organizations cooperate implies that the differences between the two worlds are taken into account but without being fixed or absolutized in terms of opposition. Cooperation between the organizations and interaction between the people invited by them opens a way to overcome the Euro-Arab antagonism that has lasted for centuries, if not for a millennium or more. Besides its immediate results, which seem to have been minimal, a seminar of intellectuals and authors consequently has a strong symbolic value. The Gulf War and the Peace Conference in Madrid of 1991, whatever their practical results, had again made the European and Arab worlds aware of the need for dialogue. The various interests and intentions existing in various countries on both sides deserve careful study. Something similar seems to hold true also for the relations between Europe and the Turkic world, at this stage primarily Europe and Turkey.

4. Mediterranean Cooperation and Dialogue: Toledo 1995

Among the preliminaries of the important European-Mediterranean Conference of Cooperation and Dialogue in the Mediterranean Region, organized by the European Union in Barcelona on November 27 and 28, 1995, was the holding of a small informal conference in Toledo from November 4 to 7, 1995. The theme of this conference was "Mediterranean Society: still a Challenge for the Three Civilizations?", with the subtitle "Informal dialogue meeting between Islam, Judaism and Christianity". It was a surprise to me that an organization that is devoted to European economics and politics took an initiative to call upon representatives of religious and humanistic traditions. They were invited to engage in dialogue, less about theological or religio-legal issues than about the construction of a future Mediterranean society.

4.1. Historical Context

The initiative of this meeting is less surprising if one recalls the historical context. Already in 1991, Jacques Delors, the President of the European Commission at the time, had invited representatives of the major European Churches to an informal meeting in Brussels, and from this developed regular informal meetings twice a year. Three years later, in December 1994, Mr. Delors organized a similar meeting but extended to a wider circle. In this way Catholic, Protestant, Orthodox, Jewish, Muslim, and

Humanist representatives met with the President of the European Commission, one of the topics of discussion being the possibility of holding joint conferences. Mr. Santer continued this initiative. He received the European Conference of Rabbis in March 1995, and it was apparently here that the idea emerged to organize a small conference for the major religions of the Mediterranean Basin, which resulted in the Toledo meeting.

Seen in a broader perspective, there can be no doubt that the Christian Churches were interested in the construction of a new, supranational Europe from the beginning. Before the three Scandinavian countries and Austria joined and Germany was reunified, the European Economic Community counted a Catholic majority. With John Paul II's proclamation of the program to re-Christianize a secularized Europe, the Vatican clearly had an interest in what happened in Brussels. The Protestant side made a similar effort; the Churches could not remain indifferent toward the place assigned to religion in the new Europe. On the other hand, the European Commission and its executive organs had to remain independent of religious interests. Islam was a new feature on the religious map of Europe; the presence of some eight million Muslims in European Union member states forced the European Union to take into account not only the Churches but also Islam and to listen to Muslim representatives. In a next step, Jewish and Humanist representatives, although numerically less significant, had to be heard too.

4.2. Orientation towards Dialogue

An important factor in the European Union's relations with Muslim countries has been the clear refusal of Samuel P. Huntington's idea of the probable clash between civilizations.[6] On several occasions, for instance in preparatory documents for the Toledo meeting, the European Union has offered intercultural exchange and dialogue as an alternative to the assumptions of the American political scientist. "European construction in the sense of Monnet and Adenauer is based on the opposite assumption, that there is a possibility for countries and cultures to sit around the same table on an equal footing in order to solve together their common problems"[7]. The Euro-Mediterranean initiative of the European Union breathes a spirit very different from that of Huntington.

---

[6]   Samuel P. HUNTINGTON, *The Clash of Civilizations and the Remaking of World Order*, New York: Simon & Schuster, 1996.

[7]   Document ML/fr (95) 929.1 of September 26, 1995.

4.3. Religious Leaders

It must still be explained, however, why specifically representatives of religions should be involved, however indirectly, in the dialogue aims of the Barcelona conference. Here the wider international context needs to be taken into consideration. In the 1992 elections, Israel received a Labor government, which turned out to be open to the "peace process" thought out by the USA. Especially after the "Oslo Agreement" of 1993, there were high hopes of a settlement of the Israel-Palestine conflict.

In the following mobilization of forces for peace, politicians saw religious leaders as men and women of reconciliation and asked for their cooperation. They could, for instance, oppose the tendency to bestow a religious legitimation on conflicts of a basically political, economic, or ethnic nature. Similar efforts had been made for instance by the World Council of Churches in the post-Yugoslavia conflicts. In the case of Euro-Mediterranean cooperation, it was hoped that a dialogue between the three monotheistic religions could not only contribute to the "peace process" in the Near East but also provide a cornerstone for building a future just and peaceful society around the Mediterranean.

4.4. Organization of the Toledo Meeting

This was also the mood of the Toledo meeting. I remember all the more vividly the shock caused by the news of the assassination of Yitzak Rabin on the very eve of the conference, November 4, 1995. Most of us realized that the meaning and significance not only of our meeting but also of the Barcelona conference itself, presupposing a peace process that would end in real peace, was at stake. The impulse toward real dialogue became stronger.

Participation in the conference was by invitation only and the sessions were held behind closed doors. There were 27 active participants: 7 Muslims (1 from Turkey, 1 from Tunisia, 1 from Algeria, 2 from Morocco, 1 from Egypt, 1 from Lebanon), 6 Catholics, 6 Protestants and Anglicans, 3 Orthodox Christians, 3 Jews (1 from Israel), and 2 Humanists. Officials of the European Union and observers from international organizations and national governments took part as listeners. At the end, the text of a press communiqué was agreed upon. A final report of the meeting, with a Preface by Jacques Santer, appeared as a *Cahier* in March 1997. A year later, a slightly modified version of this *Cahier* was published in English and French.[8]

---

[8]   *The Mediterranean Society: A Challenge for Islam, Judaism and Christianity.* Foreword by Jacques SANTER (European Commission Forward Studies Series). Office for official publications of the European Communities, London: Kogan Page, 1998. French version:

The meeting lasted for somewhat less than three days, with many opportunities for informal meetings and contacts. The program foresaw three Round Tables on the following three questions:
(1) Can the three monotheistic and humanist traditions develop a common vision of the future of Mediterranean society (*projet de société*)?
(2) How can these traditions contribute to reconciliation amongst the people in the region?
(3) How do the traditions view the role of women today?

For each Round Table two or three short papers had been prepared by participants; they were the starting point for a more general discussion. The final session had been planned for an evaluation and the formulation of the Press Communiqué.

4.5. Aims and Purposes

Here are the main points of the official letter that accompanies the final report of March 1997, signed by Mr. Jacques Santer, President of the European Commission. Mr. Santer reaffirms his view that the conference, for which he took the initiative, has a symbolic importance not only for the Euro-Mediterranean Conference held in Barcelona a few weeks later in November 1995, but also for the construction of Europe itself. This construction is based on the assumption that countries with different cultures can sit around the same table on an equal footing to construct peace by trying to solve common problems. Huntington's idea of an unavoidable "clash" is clearly rejected.

Mr. Santer then affirms that the European Commission wanted to offer the religions an open space for dialogue in Toledo, a "place of European memory". In this way it wanted to contribute to the inter-religious dialogue that is an essential condition for reconciliation between peoples. The Commission was keen to listen to what the religious and humanistic traditions originating around the Mediterranean have to say to the general public about the great problems that will face society in the future. In his view, the active participation of representatives of the European humanist traditions, too, is essential, because it shows the positive fruits of the pluralism of the European cultural heritage to which he himself is strongly attached.

Mr. Santer ends by expressing his joy that the conclusions of the Euro-Mediterranean Barcelona Conference explicitly defended intercultural and interreligious dialogue, in the line of the conferences held in Stock-

Les religions méditerranéennes: Islam, judaïsme, christianisme. Un dialogue en marche. Préface Jacques SANTER (Commission européenne, Les Cahiers de la Cellule de Prospective). Office des publications officielles des Communautés européennes, Rennes: Ed. Apogée, 1998.

holm (June 15–17, 1995) and in Toledo (November 4–7, 1995). In his opinion this dialogue is as important for the future as is the attention that the world of politics pays to religions at the present time.

4.6. Results

I refer here to some elements of the press communiqué agreed upon at the end of the Toledo meeting.[9] The conference underlined the tremendous importance of deepening interreligious dialogue around the Mediterranean. The monotheistic religions and the humanists show significant points of convergence such as:
– common points of reference to deal with changes in society, especially with regard to family life;
– agreement that economic forces should serve both the well-being of the individual and international justice;
– clarification of the question of the balance between rights and responsibilities in democracy;
– "... support for the renewal of religious reflection; confronted by on the one hand both the risks and opportunities characterizing secularization and on the other by the development of extremist movements within the religions themselves, dialogue can provide the religions with the courage to question their own traditions."

The participants recognized the difficulties of dialogue and outlined the conditions for its pursuit. Besides underlining the need for mutual respect and recognition and for a reassessment of history and images of each other's cultures, they proposed a specific project to support research on religion leading to better teaching about other religions and cooperation between them:

> "a concrete result would be the organization of a trans-Mediterranean network linking autonomous research centers either already in existence or yet to be created. This network should be provided with a means of documentation and translation enabling the distribution of texts, the creation of educational outlets for the teaching on other religions and a sort of intellectual hospitality between faithful professors and students of religious science throughout the Mediterranean Basin.

> The participants emphasized the responsibility of the political authorities, particularly in Europe, to support such a network and to ensure its financial independence."[10]

---

[9] For the French text of the press communiqué, see pp. 49–50 of the *Cahier* mentioned earlier.
[10] Translated from the French on pp. 49–50 of the *Cahier* mentioned earlier.

Regarding reconciliation between peoples, the participants called attention to the situations of alienation and the signals of distress that are so visible around the Mediterranean. They had a double message to those politicians who look to the religions to provide an example of reconciliation:

> "European societies have to question themselves concerning their responsibility in the promotion of justice, the improving of the welcome accorded to immigrants, the combat of poverty, the promotion of civil society, media treatment of Islam and religion in general.

> It is impossible to call upon the wisdom of the religions without recognizing the specificity of their spiritual dimension and their responses to questions of identity and otherness."

Finally, the dynamic evolution of civil society in the Mediterranean Basin and the central role played by women were stressed. These women, however, "whether veiled or not", remain largely invisible in society; "in the various religious traditions they are quite removed from any major roles of authority. Recognizing the full participation of women comes up not only against economic and social resistance, but also against certain perceptions on the part of the religious traditions".

The communiqué ends by mentioning several pressing causes whose implementation concerns both men and women, both political and religious authorities:

> "A more open dialogue between couples and in society in general; the judicial entering into force of equal opportunities; reflection in and between the various denominations and humanists, based on a deepening of the interpretation of fundamental texts, having in mind the change of society and that of the religious traditions."

As to the effect of the Toledo meeting on the large Barcelona conference of November 27–28, 1995, it is interesting to read in the Declaration of Barcelona, adopted at the end of that conference, regarding the dialogue between cultures and civilizations:

> "Given the importance of improving mutual understanding by promoting cultural exchanges and knowledge of languages, officials and experts will meet in order to make concrete proposals for action, *inter alia*, in the following fields: cultural and creative heritage, cultural and artistic events, co-productions (theatre and cinema), translations and other means of cultural dissemination, training.

> Greater understanding among the major religions in the Euro-Mediterranean region will facilitate greater mutual tolerance and cooperation. Support will be given to periodic meetings of representatives of religions and religious institutions as well as theologians, academics, and others concerned, with the

aim of breaking down prejudice, ignorance and fanaticism and fostering cooperation at grass-roots level. The Conferences held in Stockholm (15.–17.6.95) and Toledo (4.–7.11.95) may serve as examples in this context."[11]

4.7. Looking back at the Toledo Conference

In looking back at the meeting in Toledo, from which I have presented only official statements made at the beginning and at the end, I cannot but feel moved. I vividly remember encounters with participants of quite different religious traditions who were all intent on reflecting on the problems formulated by the European Commission. It is an extraordinary experience to exchange views on ethics and religion in a meeting organized by an essentially political body. We succeeded, however, in maintaining an open dialogue with each other and resisted the temptation to accept a draft declaration that had been prepared in advance. Instead, we prepared a final communiqué. Some elements of the discussion found their way into it, others did not.

Most of the invited participants were attached to universities; partly because of this, throughout the conference there was an "esprit de corps" and a practice of conscious dialogue that is rare in international encounters. It may also have been due to a common interest in the different kinds of meaning that religious and humanistic traditions can provide to their adherents in present-day situations.

5. The Arabs and the West: Amman 1998

From April 3–5, 1998 an international scholarly seminar took place in Amman on the theme "Arabs and the West". It was organized by the University of Jordan in cooperation with the Centre for the Study of Islam and Christian-Muslim Relations in Birmingham, England. Funding was provided by, among others, the European Union, the British Foreign Office, and the Ortega y Gasset Foundation in Madrid. The seminar took place under the patronage of Prince Hassan of Jordan.

5.1. Organization and Subjects Treated

Altogether, there were 29 active participants in the seminar, 15 from Arab countries (6 from Jordan, 5 from Lebanon, 2 from Morocco, 1 from Tunisia, 1 from Qatar) and 14 from Europe (8 of whom came from the United Kingdom). Of these, 21 presented papers, 10 of which were in

---

[11] P. 47 of the report.

Arabic and 11 in English. The papers were distributed to the participants on their arrival in Amman.

At the opening session, many guests from the university and official institutions in Jordan were present; later their number diminished so that the active participants developed into a more homogeneous group. University researchers read papers, nearly all of them of good quality, and a number of guests attended. They participated in the discussion, for which there was ample time and which moved from more scholarly subjects to the general theme of present-day Arab-European relations. The atmosphere was relaxed and there was plenty of opportunity to meet each other and discuss freely.

The papers dealt with a number of subjects concerning relations between Arabs (mainly from the Near East) and Europe, in imagination and reality, in recent history and at the present time. They included the European Union and the Arabs, the Arab-Western and the Euro-Arab dialogue, relations between particular European and particular Arab countries. There were several papers about attitudes, images, and stereotypes that exist in the West about Arabs. Others treated images about Europe and Europeans among Arabs and current reporting about the Muslim world in Western media. Two papers dealt with aspects of Muslim life in Britain and Denmark. Nearly all papers came from the humanities, sometimes moving to a broader cultural level. Economic, sociological, and political problems were hinted at but not explicitly treated. Although Arabic-English and English-Arabic translation was provided, the conference was most profitable to those European and Arab participants who had mastered both languages, who fortunately were the majority. All papers focused on the encounter between the European and the Arab world both in imagination and in actual fact. The papers—oh miracle—were published in the same year.[12]

5.2. Results

The final session was devoted to an evaluation and general discussion of the seminar itself, and suggestions were made for further Euro-Arab cooperation in the future. The general recommendations adopted included:[13]

- greater cooperation between universities in the study of the history, religion, and culture of both the Arab and the European world, for instance through shared research, the exchange of students and lecturers, and joint teaching posts;

---

[12] *Arabs and the West: Mutual Images* (see Selected Literature section 5.1.).
[13] See the report about the Amman seminar in *Campus News*, University of Jordan, Issue 96 (April–May 1998), pp. 3–7.

- the need to establish teaching positions and research posts for European Studies at centers and departments in Arab universities and other Arab scholarly institutions;
- cooperation in the development of good school curricula and textbooks on both sides in the fields of history, geography, culture, and religion;
- greater interaction between journalists working for European and Arabic newspapers and journals and between journalists and scholars in Europe and in the Arab world;
- greater exchange of literary, artistic, and media production, especially to increase awareness of Arabic writing, theatre, and film in Europe;
- more translations of the works of Arab authors representing various intellectual traditions into European languages to broaden the awareness in Europe of contemporary debates in the Arab world, and the other way around;
- a call for the European and Arab governments of the Barcelona conference of 1995 "... to increase their efforts in the dialogue of culture and civilization and to support initiatives seeking to establish long-term cooperation and continuity".

Besides these formal recommendations, a number of individual suggestions were made in the final session, including:
- to create a European Fulbright Program to provide Euro Fellowships to Arab intellectuals, writers, and artists who wish to stay up to a year in Europe in a country of their choice. This should enable them to carry on their research and writing and to learn what is going on at European scholarly, literary and artistic centers;
- to warn that a Euro-Mediterranean partnership should not eclipse the existing efforts for Euro-Arab dialogue;
- to admit more students, at least as auditors, to seminars like this one;
- to organize informative workshops on Euro-Arab relations for a broader interested public;
- to ensure better media coverage of seminars like this one without giving them a political color;
- to improve training in Euro-Arab relations for teachers at the elementary and secondary school level, both in the Arab world and in Europe;
- to translate the ideas from seminars like this into practical suggestions that are easy to realize;
- to bring the ideas developed at seminars like this to the attention of political and other decision-makers on both the Arab and the European side.

This was a highly successful conference, promising for the future. This was due not least to the good quality of the papers by some younger Arab scholars.

6. Intercultural Dialogue Symposium: Istanbul 1998

6.1. Organization and Subjects Treated

The fourth meeting was a dialogue symposium that took place in Istanbul, from March 6–8, 1998. Originally planned to take place on a large scale in October 1997, it was then postponed and realized on a somewhat smaller scale five months later. Although the original title "Interfaith Dialogue" was changed to "Intercultural Dialogue", the dialogue between religions remained the focus of interest. The Academic Advisor for the Symposium was Professor Bekir Karliga.

The dialogue symposium took place in the large Cemal Reşit Bey Concert Hall in Istanbul and was part of a broad cultural program launched by the Center for the Organization of Cultural Activities, which is under the authority of the Municipality of Istanbul. Other activities of the program included invitations extended to distinguished speakers from abroad, Muslims as well as non-Muslims, to present lectures for a broader Turkish audience. The program clearly aimed to inform a cultivated public in Istanbul about international trends of thought.

Altogether, 19 speakers contributed to the symposium, of whom 8 were Turkish. Of the non-Turkish participants, 2 were Muslims from Tunisia and Iran and 9 others from Belgium, France, Switzerland, the USA, and Italy. Among them was also a Zoroastrian speaker from Iran.

The program consisted of six sessions with panels devoted to the following subjects:

1) Interfaith Dialogue;
2) Religions and Living Together;
3) Religion, Peace and Tolerance;
4) Religion, Secularism and Human Rights;
5) The Place and Importance of Religions in the World of the Future;
6) Evaluation.

In conclusion, a final declaration, prepared by an ad hoc committee, was read aloud and applauded.

6.2. Looking back at the Istanbul Symposium

The meeting in Istanbul distinguished itself from the other three in several respects. The sessions were open to the public and had a large audience of hundreds of people who could also address questions to the speakers on the panels. More than in the other three meetings, the speakers here had an important role and task to give good information to the listening public about the subjects assigned to them. There was consequently a more immediate contact between the speakers and people interested in the subject; they could approach the individual speakers during the breaks between the sessions.

Given the sympathetic and open attitude of all who attended, I consider this meeting an important contribution to furthering the cause of information, exchange, and dialogue not only in academic, but also in broader circles. There was an evident interest not only in what the Turkish speakers, but also in what guests from abroad had to say about their religion and Islam. These guests were Catholic, Orthodox, and Protestant Christians from Europe, as well as a Shī'ī 'ālim and a Zoroastrian representative from Iran and a Muslim intellectual from Tunisia.

The Turkish historical context is well-known and should not retain us here. Since the 1980s, several dialogue meetings have taken place in Turkey, in particular with Christians from the West. Quite a few books have been published in Turkish about the relationship between Islam and Christianity. Christianity is taught at several Faculties of Theology at Turkish universities, and Christian theologians have been invited here to present informative lectures about Christianity. There is an obvious desire to become better informed about Christianity; the experience of Turkish immigrants in Europe may or may not have contributed to it. Turkish participants in international dialogue meetings have been inspired to organize in their turn similar meetings in Turkey itself.

Recent developments in the relations between Turkey and the European Union as well as within Turkey itself (democracy and human rights, Kurdish and "Islamist" movements) have made religion, Islam, and human rights sensitive subjects. Yet, in the last twenty years or so, religion in general and Islam in particular have become subjects of public discourse and a certain taboo on the subject of religion is being lifted. From the books that have been published in Turkey in recent years on Islam and Christianity as well as other religions, I cannot but deduce that people are keen on obtaining information about the existing religions. One way to acquire such information is through reading, study, and scholarship on the history of religions and the science of religions in general. Another way is through direct contact with living adherents of those religions.

Against this background, the interest of the Istanbul meeting is triple. First, it gave solid information about existing religions. Second, it showed how such dialogue actually proceeds between the panel speakers and the public. Third, it proved that such a public dialogue meeting can be organized in a city like Istanbul that has a cultural and scholarly life open to other cultures and civilizations. To me at least, it was clear that everyone attending the meeting was keenly interested in the event. Continuing such meetings would be a logical sequence to the Istanbul Dialogue Symposium of March 1998.

7. Looking back

If the last two meetings mentioned were of an open nature, with participants submitting papers on their own research and interests and entering into discussion about it, the Strasbourg and Toledo meetings were organized to obtain answers to specific problems formulated in advance. Here the organizers, after all, were international political organizations rather than academic or local cultural institutions.

The Council of Europe's concern was to take stock of present-day European and Arab views on Euro-Arab cooperation and discuss democracy in European and Arab and incidentally Turkish societies.

The European Union's concern was to see whether and how interreligious dialogue could be used to support cooperation and exchange between Mediterranean and other European societies and countries and whether changes in established religious positions could eventually be reached through interreligious dialogue in order to promote the aim of broader cooperation and dialogue.

The themes of the Amman and Istanbul meetings, "Arabs and the West" and "Intercultural Dialogue" respectively, allowed participants to formulate and treat problems as they saw them.

The selection of participants is crucial, since the resources of the persons present largely determine the extent but also the limits of the results that can be reached. My impression is that the participants of the Toledo meeting were the most promising in this respect. They were not only professional researchers, politicians, and administrators; there was some wisdom, too. The discussions between the participants themselves excelled perhaps not so much through their particular expert knowledge as through the exchange of insights into the common human problems of their communities and of society at large. There were flashes of the mind, and some intelligent proposals were made for weighty problems. Moreover, there was excellent leadership.

The resources of the Strasbourg meeting were larger and more varied, the perhaps 150 participants comprising "orientalists", researchers of different disciplines, political and diplomatic figures, journalists, and creative figures from literature and the arts. The Arab participants were mainly "liberal" figures from Egypt, Lebanon, and Tunisia, several of them living and working in Paris or London. One of the two Turkish participants was a professor from Ankara, the other a professor attached to an American university. The Western scholars were mostly of an older generation; fresh experience with new generations from the region and sensitivity to the shock waves set off by the 1991 Gulf War were largely lacking. Arab appeals for assistance found little positive response among them. Perhaps one had to be more or less "established" to be invited to the Strasbourg meeting. Europe made the impression of getting old. One person visibly rose head and shoulders above the others. This was the open-minded Secretary General of the Council of Europe, Madame Catherine Lalumière.

In Amman the papers and in particular the discussions breathed more scholarly research and freshness. The meeting took place in an Arab country, and the average age of the speakers was lower than in Strasbourg and Toledo. It was a definite advantage to be able to discuss relations between Arabs and the West on the other side of the Mediterranean.

The Istanbul meeting, between Europe and Asia, was above all a cultural event. The emphasis was more on providing good information and on clearly revealing one's standpoint than on giving complex disquisitions. Given the program and the large audience, the speakers had to be brief and clear in their presentations. This was the only meeting of the four where scholars met the general public.

Such international cultural dialogue meetings have certain common elements. One ingredient is the presence, besides official dignitaries and university professors, of younger open-minded and socially-committed researchers. Another is some typical pacemakers who stimulate the discussion without pretending to offer themselves anything substantially new. More controversial figures or people from what may be called "critical" countries or too extreme positions are conspicuous by their absence. But still there are surprising encounters. Who would have expected to discuss at the Istanbul meeting in March 1998 with both an *ālim* from Qum and a representative of Iran's Zoroastrian community?

One recurring question is what immediate and palpable results such meetings have. And the equally recurring answer is that the results are impossible to measure. Of course, more can be said. The results of the Strasbourg and Toledo meetings went to the political arena, and rumors about the results there are faint. The Council of Europe, as far as I know, did not take any of the concrete measures that had been recommended to strengthen European links with intellectuals on the Arab and Turkish sides of the Mediterranean. One reason is that the new members from Eastern Europe, including Russia, now demand not only much attention and organizational skill but also considerable amounts of money, so that little is left for activities further afield.

As for the European Union, it seems to have had difficulties implementing the recommendations of the Toledo meeting as well as the cultural part of the Barcelona conference. In fact, not much seems to have happened. This may have been partly due to the fact that the subject of "Islamic" matters within the European Union itself and that of relations between the European Union and the Mediterranean non-member countries are dealt with in two different departments of the EU in Brussels. It seems to me that politicians and administrators are hardly aware of the existence of serious scholarship that deals with religions such as Islam. Religion to them is linked largely to theology, churches, clergy, and religious orders. Their policies seem to be more conditioned by pressures from religious and political bodies than guided by sound knowledge about the meaning of faith or the changing role of changing religious traditions. In the background of the impasse after the Barcelona conference of November 1995 is also the changing Israeli policy toward the Palestinians.

My own impression is that both the European Union and the Council of Europe not only lack a coherent vision for the Mediterranean world and its relations with Western Europe. They also seem to lack the necessary know-how and fail to consult the proper expertise on the social, cultural, and religious dimensions of Mediterranean societies and of the migration movements to Europe. Perhaps such institutions are not equipped to recognize this as major European contemporary history. In this sense, the Amman and Istanbul meetings were certainly more appropriate in their modest set-up, arousing less sweeping expectations among the organizers and the participants and offering solid knowledge instead.

What strikes a relative newcomer in meetings such as these is the importance of communication. I do not mean here the psychological aspects, for instance the occurrence of a certain "conference fatigue" on the third or fourth day of such meetings. I am thinking of the challenge one continuously faces to grasp what other persons really want and have to say. One should somehow understand the message they want to convey and grasp both the precise problems for which they seek a solution and the kind of solution they propose themselves. No wonder there are so many monological discourses at dialogical meetings.

This difficulty is still greater if one has no immediate access to the languages used. I would suggest that all speakers and active participants in such meetings should be able to handle fluently both English and Arabic or Turkish. This certainly puts a burden on the Europeans. Speakers should also be pressed not to repeat current slogans or conventional ideologies; they should offer a new vision and suggest a new approach or solution to deeper-seated problems. In other words, the intellectual quality of such meetings can and should be enhanced.

But there is more. A certain arrogance that may be acceptable or appreciated in one's own little cultural circle should certainly not be demonstrated to people of another culture. I am always struck by the unfortunate fact that certain minds, brilliant in themselves, can be incapable or even averse to normal communication with people from the very culture they study.

8. Conclusion: Looking forward

The Europe that emerged in the late Middle Ages appropriated knowledge from Arab-Muslim civilization. While affirming itself in contrast to Islam, it was able to transcend its own borders. Through the development of paradigms of knowledge with greater general validity, it was able to discover and to enter into rational debate with what was foreign to it. The Renaissance, the Enlightenment, and the study of the history of Western culture as well as that of other cultures and religions implied that scholars and thinkers moved from what was familiar to what was foreign to them.

At present, Europe faces a similar alternative. Should it venture to move outward to other peoples or should it abandon this elan and work on its own problems in a self-centered way? And should an outward elan also envisage and include the Muslim regions that surround it? For centuries, these regions were considered antagonists of Europe. They were subdued and later became independent states.

8.1. A Suggestion

One can indeed imagine a kind of partnership relation of the European Union and its neighboring states, with the Mediterranean as a starting point. In a first round, this would comprise the regions that immediately surround Europe: North Africa, Egypt, the Arab East, Turkey, and the Caucasus. A second circle would contain regions like Tatarstan, the Central Asian republics, Turkmenistan, Azerbaijan, and Iran in Asia, and Ethiopia, Sudan, Chad, Niger, and further into West Africa. All these regions and countries have a majority Muslim population.

It will be a vital European interest not to close itself off from these countries, retreating into a fortress named Europe. It should rather promote exchange and relations with these countries, not only in oil and minerals but also in trade and social and cultural exchanges. These countries have considerable groups of intellectuals, authors, and researchers who would benefit from further exchange with Europe. If Europe closes itself off from these groups, this will further weaken their sometimes already precarious position. To carry out a judicious policy of good neighborhood, Europeans should become more familiar with these Muslim societies and their Islam and free themselves of the idea of dealing with a potential enemy.

The time has come to revisit and rewrite the history of the relations between Europe and the Muslim world. Until now, this history has been written mostly from an exclusively Western perspective. With a critically revised history that studies what happened, with virtues and vices on both sides, it will be easier to work together. Since Europe will no longer be seen as an immediate political and military threat, it may more readily find acceptance among Muslims in the sense of cooperation and dialogue.

The presence of Muslim immigrants in Europe is relevant here. They provide links with their countries of origin. It has been said repeatedly that their integration in the European countries is of the utmost importance. If long-term integration failed after say four or five generations, this would create serious problems for the coherence of the continent itself and for its relations with the surrounding countries. But if Europe can demonstrate that its societies are open to receive and integrate needed qualified Muslim immigrants, this can work out positively.

To be successful in this respect, however, we need open minds and a spirit of initiative. What is further needed, however, is a realistic and open view of Muslim people, Muslim societies, and relations between Europe and its Muslim neighbors.

8.2. Social and Cultural Cooperation

On the European side, high-level statements of a certain political weight have been made repeatedly about the need for cooperation and dialogue with the Arab countries and Turkey. On the Arab and the Turkish side, likewise, serious attempts have been made by public bodies as well as academic circles to arrive at cooperation and dialogue not only with institutions in individual European countries, but also with the Council of Europe and the European Union. The need for dialogue is especially emphasized after situations of conflict and in the cultural sector. In the economic and political fields, serious problems have arisen, not least because of the stagnation and finally the end of the Middle East "peace process". It is significant in this context that, while the Council of Europe has always been particularly active in the cultural field, the European Union has also started to extend its activities to this field.

Both in Europe and in the countries around it, there are what may be called "core people" who, as individuals or as groups, are genuinely interested in people of another culture, whether European, Turkish, Arab, or otherwise. They want to know more about another culture and establish contact with the people who belong to it. They also may commit themselves to the causes of these people. Beyond professional interests and the efforts of international organizations, the sheer presence of interested "core people" constitutes a basis and background for further contacts.

Further contact and cooperation between people from Europe, on the one hand, and from Turkey and the Arab countries, on the other hand, are urgently needed. This requires on all sides the expertise of persons who have done more than carried out their programs and fed the relevant data into their computer. They should also have a sensitivity for language and literature, an interest in social and cultural questions, an inclination for intercultural relations, a questioning mind, and that particular human gift, the ability to communicate. Better possibilities need to be created for young Europeans who want to engage in this, so that they can obtain the necessary education and instruction.

One should consider creating something like Euro-Fellowships for young Turks and Arabs, and others too, who have shown their worth in their own country and want to do research and write in Europe for a while. Such fellowships should be made available to creative intellectuals, researchers, writers, and artists from the countries concerned. They should be invited to come to Europe and become acquainted with what is going on here. They should be free to discover Europe themselves and to choose the countries and institutions they want to go to.

As a rule, people from the countries surrounding Europe should develop their own ideas on their own terms, Islamic or otherwise. Europeans should resist the lurking temptation to carry out a kind of "cultural colonization". A partnership for dialogue is essentially different from a relation of domination.

Such efforts toward cultural cooperation and dialogue are simplest in the case of students and researchers. Because of their interests in knowledge, they have their own way to get in touch with each other. If private and public institutions want to promote social and cultural relations between Europe and the Arab world or Turkey, they should facilitate exchanges between such individuals and groups in particular.

These people in turn can spread information about the countries concerned. They should be able not only to participate in international meetings. They should also be engaged in organizing workshops or informative courses for a broader interested public in their own countries. They may also gain access to the media, where they should do more than present factual data and repeat conventional opinions. They should also tell of their experience and show something of the needs of life as it is lived in other societies and countries. They can hint at the intricate nature and the broader connections of what may be called the "problems of the day", not as they are reported in our news bulletins but as they are seen from the other side of the Mediterranean.

What is needed are not monological experts or non-communicative maniacs or enthusiasts who only preach their own ideas about a better world and how to realize them. The need is for people who are able and ready to listen to each other, who look for knowledge and understanding and want to acquire experience. They should by nature be inclined toward communication, while training a capacity both to learn from others and to make people learn from others, whether they are Muslims or not. They would act not so much as missionaries of religious or political causes but rather as human explorers.[14]

---

[14] See also Jacques WAARDENBURG, *Islam et Occident face-à-face: Regards de l'Histoire des Religions*, Geneva: Labor et Fides, 1998.

One of the first conditions for success in European-Muslim relations is appropriate behavior on both sides. For instance, in Europe one should not express lightly one's ignorance about Islam, Islamism, and Muslims. In the Muslim countries one should support human rights and the rules of civil society and justice. We need a kind of general civic education, taking into account the lessons of history.

One of Europe's forces is its cultural diversity, and in intercultural cooperation this should be combined with the requirement of excellence. I am thinking of small, highly motivated groups that can awaken further interest. At a certain stage, similar workshops and encounters should be organized on a private level in Muslim countries.

European interest in Euro-Arab and Euro-Turkish relations is not necessarily an interest in Islam. But the absence of preconceived ideas about Islam as well as Christianity can certainly work positively for communication with Muslims. It would be one of the rules for the development of better Euro-Muslim relations.

Selected Literature

1. Meeting of Civilizations

DJAïT, Hichem, *L'Europe et l'Islam*, Paris: Seuil, 1978; English translation *Europe and Islam*, Berkeley, etc.: University of California Press, 1985.

HEGYI, Klára, and Vera ZIMÁNYI, *Muslime und Christen: Das osmanische Reich in Europa*, Budapest: Corvina, 1988.

Histoire et civilisation de l'Islam en Europe: Arabes et Turcs en Occident du VIIe au XXe siècle, ed. by Francesco GABRIELI, Paris: Bordas, 1983.

2. Political History

2.1. European Empires

CORM, Georges, *L'Europe et l'Orient: De la balkanisation à la libanisation. Histoire d'une modernité inaccomplie*, Paris: La Découverte, 1989.

DANIEL, Norman, *Islam, Europe and Empire*, Edinburgh: Edinburgh University Press, 1966.

DANISH, Ishtiyaque, *The English and the Arabs: The Making of an Image*, Delhi: Karakush, 1992.

L'expédition d'Egypte 1798–1801: Bonaparte et l'Islam. Le choc des cultures, ed. by Henry LAURENS, Paris: Armand Colin, 1989.

Franco-Arab Encounters, Rencontres Franco-Arabes: Studies in Memory of David C. Gordon, ed. by L. Carl BROWN and Matthew S. GORDON, Beirut: American University of Beirut, 1996.

FRAZEE, Charles A., *Catholics and Sultans: The Church and the Ottoman Empire 1453–1923*, Cambridge: Cambridge University Press, 1983.

FRÉMEAUX, Jacques, *La France et l'Islam depuis 1789*, Paris: Presses Universitaires de France, 1991.

HARRISON, Christopher, *France and Islam in West Africa, 1860–1960* (African Studies Series 60), Cambridge: Cambridge University Press, 1988.

KEDDIE, Nikki R., *An Islamic Response to Imperialism: Political and Religious Writings of Sayyid Jamāl ad-Dīn "al-Afghānī"*, Berkeley, etc.: University of California Press, 1968.

KEDOURIE, Elie, *Islam in the Modern World and Other Studies*, London: Mansell, 1980.

LOUIS, William Roger, *The British Empire in the Middle East 1945–1951: Arab Nationalism, the United States, and Postwar Imperialism*, Oxford: Clarendon Press, 1984.

MEULEN, Daniel van der, *Don't you hear the Thunder: A Dutchman's Life Story*, Leiden: E. J. Brill, 1981.

The Middle East and Europe: The Power Deficit, ed. by Barbara Allen ROBERSON, London and New York: Routledge, 1998.

RAYMOND, André, *Egyptiens et Français au Caire 1798–1801* (Bibliothèque Générale 18), Cairo: Institut Français d'Archéologie Orientale, 1998.

SEARIGHT, Sarah, *The British in the Middle East*, London: Weidenfeld and Nicolson, 1969; new, revised edition London and The Hague: East-West Publications, and Cairo: Livres de France, 1979.

2.2. Muslims under the Empires

BONDAREVSKY, Grogori, *Muslims and the West*, New Delhi, etc.: Sterling Publishers, 1985.

Fremdeinsätze: Afrikaner und Asiaten in europäischen Kriegen, 1914–1945, ed. by Gerhard HÖPP and Brigitte REINWALD (Zentrum Moderner Orient), Berlin: Das Arabische Buch, 2000.

Globale Prozesse und "Akteure des Wandels": Quellen und Methoden ihrer Untersuchung, ed. by Dietrich REETZ and Heike LIEBAU (Zentrum Moderner Orient, Arbeitshefte 14), Berlin: Das Arabische Buch, 1997.

MITCHELL, Timothy, *Colonising Egypt*, Cambridge: Cambridge University Press, 1988; paperback Berkeley, etc.: University of California Press, 1991.

Wessen Geschichte? Muslimische Erfahrungen historischer Zäsuren im 20. Jahrhundert, ed. by Henner FÜRTIG and Gerhard Höpp (Zentrum Moderner Orient, Arbeitshefte 16), Berlin: Das Arabische Buch, 1998.

3. Internal History of Christian-Muslim Societies

BENEDICTY, Robert, *Société civile et communauté religieuse: Expérience culturelle d'un village chrétien dans la société arabe contemporaine* (Series Hommes et Sociétés du Proche-Orient), Beirut: Dar el-Machreq, 1986.

CORM, Georges, *Contribution à l'étude des sociétés multi-confessionnelles: Effets socio-juridiques et politique du pluralisme religieux*, Paris: Librairie générale de Droit et de Jurisprudence, 1971.

GIBB, Hamilton Alexander Rosskeen, and Harold BOWEN, *Islamic Society and the West*, Vol. One: *Islamic Society in the Eighteenth Century*, Part II, London, etc.: Oxford University Press, 1957, etc.

MŪSĀ, Salāma, *The Education of Salāma Mūsā*, trans. by L. O. SCHUMAN, Leiden: E. J. Brill, 1961.

4. Cultural Interaction

GODDARD, Hugh, *A History of Christian-Muslim Relations* (Islamic Surveys), Edinburgh: Edinburgh University Press, 2000.

HERRMANN, Gottfried, "Die Karawane der Wissenschaft und des Fortschritts: Zur Auseinandersetzung iranischer Intellektueller mit der Europäisierung ihres Landes unter der Schah-Herrschaft", in *Asien blickt auf Europa: Begegnungen und Irritationen*, ed. by Tilman NAGEL (Beiruter Texte und Studien 39), Beirut and Stuttgart: Franz Steiner, 1990, pp. 89–117.

HOURANI, Albert, *Arabic Thought in the Liberal Age*, London and Oxford: Oxford University Press, 1962, 1970; new edition Cambridge: Cambridge University Press, 1963.

Islam und Abendland, ed. by Ary A. ROEST CROLLIUS, Düsseldorf: Patmos, 1982.

KURI, Sami, *Une histoire du Liban à travers les archives des jésuites*, 3 Vols., Vol. I: *1816–1845*, Vol. II: *1846–1862*, Vol. III: *1863–1873*, Beirut: Dar el-Machreq, 1985, 1991, and 1996.

NEILL, Stephen Charles, *Colonialism and Christian Missions*, London: Lutterworth, 1966.

D'un Orient l'autre: Les métamorphoses successives des perceptions et connaissances, 2 Vols., Vol. 1: *Configurations*, Vol. 2: *Identifications*, Paris: Ed. du Centre National de la Recherche Scientifique, 1991.

SCHIMMEL, Annemarie, *West-östliche Annäherungen: Europa in der Begegnung mit der islamischen Welt*, Stuttgart, etc.: Kohlhammer, 1995.

TLILI, Béchir, *Les rapports culturels et idéologiques entre l'Orient et l'Occident, en Tunisie, au XIXeme siècle (1830–1880)* (Faculté des Lettres et Sciences Humaines de Tunis, Quatrième Série: Histoire, Vol. XIV), Tunis: Université de Tunis, 1974.

Turkish Islam and Europe / Türkischer Islam und Europa: Europe and Christianity as Reflected in Turkish Muslim Discourse & Turkish Muslim Life in the Diaspora, ed. by Günter SEUFFERT and Jacques WAARDENBURG (Beiruter Texte und Studien 82; Türkische Welten 6), Istanbul and Stuttgart: Franz Steiner, 1999.

VANDER WERFF, Lyle L., *Christian Mission to Muslims: The Record*, Pasadena: William Carey Library, 1977.

ZAKZOUK, Mahmoud, "Die kulturellen Beziehungen zwischen dem Westen und der islamischen Welt: Begegnungspunkte und Möglichkeiten der Zusammenarbeit auf wissenschaftlicher Ebene", in *Gottes ist der Orient, Gottes ist der Okzident: Festschrift für Abdoljavad Falatori zum 65. Geburtstag*, ed. by Udo TWORUSCHKA (Kölner Veröffentlichungen zur Religionsgeschichte 21), Cologne and Vienna: Böhlau, 1991, pp. 509–21.

ZIADAT, Adel A., *Western Science in the Arab World: The Impact of Darwinism, 1860–1930*, Houndsmill and London: Macmillan, 1986.

5. Arab Views of Europe and Europeans

5.1. Descriptive or Appreciative Views

Arabs and the West: Mutual Images, ed. by Jörgen S. NIELSEN and Sami A. KHASAWNIH, Amman: The University of Jordan, 1998.

AYALON, Ami, *Middle Eastern Perceptions of the West: A Study in Arabic Political Terminology*, PhD Diss. Princeton University, October 1980.

—, *Language and Change in the Arab Middle East: The Evolution of Modern Political Discourse* (Studies in Middle Eastern History), New York: Oxford University Press, 1987.

Les Européens vus par les Libanais à l'époque ottomane, ed. by Bernard HEYBERGER and Carsten-Michael WALBINER (Beiruter Texte und Studien 74), Beirut and Würzburg: Ergon, 2002.

JOHANSEN, Baber, *Muhammad Husain Haikal: Europa und der Orient im Weltbild eines ägyptischen Liberalen* (Beiruter Texte und Studien 5), Beirut and Wiesbaden: Franz Steiner, 1967.

Marocains et Allemands: La perception de l'autre, ed. by A. BENDAOUD and M. BERRIANE (Publications de la Faculté des Lettres et des Sciences Humaines, Rabat, Série Colloques et Séminaires 44), Rabat: Université Mohammed V, 1995.

Les visions de l'Occident dans le monde arabe. Special issue *Egypte / Monde arabe*, Vols. 30–31 (1997), Cairo: CEDEJ, 1997.

WIELANDT, Rotraud, *Das Bild der Europäer in der modernen arabischen Erzähl- und Theaterliteratur* (Beiruter Texte und Studien 23), Beirut and Wiesbaden: Franz Steiner, 1980.

YARED, Nazik Saba, *Arab Travellers and Western Civilization*, trans. from the Arabic, London: Saqi Books, 1996.

5.2. Critical Views

ABDELMOULA, Mahmoud, *Islam et Occident: Affrontements culturels des idéologies*, Tunis: Ed. Tiers Monde, 1990.

KHOURY, Paul, *L'Islam critique de l'Occident dans la pensée arabe actuelle: Islam et sécularité*, 2 Vols. (Religionswissenschaftliche Studien 35/1–2), Vol. 1: *Chapitres I–IV*, Vol. 2: *Chapitres V–VI*, Würzburg: Echter, and Altenberge: Oros, 1994 and 1995.

RAOUF, Wafik, *L'Europe vue par l'Islam: Une perception ambivalente* (Histoire et perspectives méditerranéennes), Paris: L'Harmattan, 2000.

RUDOLPH, Ekkehard, *Westliche Islamwissenschaft im Spiegel muslimischer Kritik: Grundzüge und Merkmale einer innerislamischen Diskussion* (Islamkundliche Untersuchungen 137), Berlin: Klaus Schwarz, 1991.

SHAHIN, Emad Eldin, *Through Muslim Eyes: M. Rashīd Ridā and the West* (Issues in Contemporary Islamic Thought, Academic Dissertation Series 1), Herndon, Va.: International Institute of Islamic Thought & International Islamic Publishing House, 1993/1414.

6. Euro-Arab Dialogue

BENCHENANE, Mustapha, *Pour un dialogue euro-arabe*, Paris: Berger-Levrault, 1983.

Colloque international sur les relations euro-arabes, Mons-Hainaut 3–5 april 1984, ed. by Hayssam SAFAR, Mons: Université, 1986.

Coopération Euro-Arabe, Diagnostic et Prospective, Vol. III. *Actes du Colloque organisé à Louvain-la-Neuve 2–4 décembre 1982*, ed. by Bichara KHADER, Louvain-la-Neuve: Université, 1983.

Le dialogue euro-arabe, ed. by Jacques BOURRINET, Paris: Economica, 1979.

The Euro-Arab Dialogue, Le dialogue euro-arabe: Symposium Bonn June 1982, ed. by Hubert DOBERS and Ulrich HAARMANN (Institut für Internationale Solidarität), St. Augustin: Konrad-Adenauer-Stiftung, November 1983.

Euro-Arab Dialogue: The Relations between the Two Cultures. Acts of the Hamburg Symposium April 11th to 15th 1983, ed. by Derek HOPWOOD, London, etc.: Croom Helm, 1985.

Euro-Arab Understanding and Cultural Exchange: Euro-Arab Seminar organised by the Secretary General of the Council of Europe, Strasbourg, November 14–15, 1991, 3 Vols., Vol. I. *Proceedings* of the Seminar; Vol. II. *Contributions* of the Seminar, and Vol. III. *Summary* of the Seminar, Strasbourg: Council of Europe/Conseil de l'Europe, 1991.

JAWAD, Haifaa A., *Euro-Arab Relations: A Study in Collective Diplomacy*, Reading, U. K.: Ithaca, 1992.

MANI', Saleh al-, *The Euro-Arab Dialogue: A Study in Associative Diplomacy*, ed. by Salah al-SHAIKHLY, London: Pinter, 1983.

La Méditerranée réinventée: Réalités et espoirs de la coopération, ed. by Paul BALTA, Paris: La Découverte, 1992.

Chapter 11
Muslims and Their Islam in Europe: Initiatives and Responses[1]

Introduction

Since World War Two, an increasing number of migrants from outside Europe have established themselves on this continent, mainly in the Western part of it, where they now constitute important minorities. Among them are many people who identify themselves as Muslims, besides having national, ethnic, and other identities. Apart from some *imāms* and Sūfī *sheykhs*, they have not come for religious but mostly for economic reasons and later also as refugees. The majority of Muslim immigrants came from Turkey, North Africa, the Middle East, and South Asia.

There is an immense variety among the Muslims now living in Europe. On the one hand, in different Muslim countries and regions and among different groups, Islam has been articulated in different ways in national and social, communal, and individual life, even though all Muslims have some basic Islamic doctrines and prescriptions in common. On the other hand, Europe itself has a great variety of social and cultural, communal and individual patterns of life that have been historically and socio-politically conditioned. Today, Europe also has a diversity of Muslim groups that have been living in its southeastern and eastern regions for centuries, having various relationships with their non-Muslim neighbors. This double variety, both of Muslim ways of life and of living conditions in Europe, should warn any researcher from the outset against unreflected assumptions and quick generalizations about Islam on this continent.

There are other reasons, too, for such a warning. In the title of this chapter, I connect "Islam" with "Muslims". This suggests that Islam is something malleable and only vaguely defined. And "Europe" is no precise concept, either. Chechnya and Turkey west of the Bosporus also belong to it, but Azerbaijan and Tatarstan, for instance, do not. Europe

---

[1] This is an enlarged version of a text with the same title, published in *IMIS-Beiträge* of 2000, based on a lecture given at the *Institute for Migration Research and Intercultural Studies (IMIS)* in Osnabrück on 11 November 1999.

here simply designates a geographical, not a cultural or political entity; it is not even assumed to constitute a unity. I suggest that the notions of Islam and Europe should remain flexible also to avoid any suggestion that there might be some kind of opposition or even dualism between Islam as such, on the one hand, and Europe as such, on the other. There are more than these two worlds and there is no reason to idealize or demonize Europe or Islam. My interest is in what Muslim groups and persons mean when they appeal or refer to Islam and what Europeans mean when they refer to Europe or the West.

Here I am concerned with initiatives that Muslims have taken in European societies since they established themselves here. What did they do and make for themselves in order to live here? What did they do in terms of relations with indigenous people? Where did they create something radically new in Europe in recent decades?

   Some of these initiatives are of a general nature and could be taken by Muslims living in a non-Muslim context anywhere in the world. They have to do with basic human needs or with general features of the Islamic religion and way of life. Others are more specific. They have to do with particular contexts in which Muslims live in Europe at present or with particular features of social and cultural life in the Muslim societies from which they came.

1. Approach

Let me begin by clarifying my approach in the following five points.

1) I do not strictly separate what may be called the social, the cultural, and the religious expressions of Muslim communities and societies. These expressions are intimately linked to each other as different but inseparable aspects of Muslim communal and social life. But this does not dispense us from being attentive to the ways particular groups or individuals themselves distinguish between what they call "religious" and what they call "cultural", or between what they call "religious" and what they call "social".

2) From a scholarly point of view, I take for granted that "Islam" as it is lived by Muslims in individual and social life is something that is continuously socially constructed, primarily by Muslims who believe in Islam and identify themselves with it, but also by non-Muslims who develop their own discourses about Islam. Islam, of course, is a historical and social reality and should be studied as such. Yet it would not have existed without people who made or constructed it and who upheld and transmitted it the way they did.

3) I see believers as actors, not mere products of their religions. They not only undergo but also construct and reconstruct, interpret and reinterpret them. From a scholarly point of view, it is permissible to call articulations that refer to Islam and present a more or less coherent "Islamic" meaning, "constructions" of Islam. Beyond the temptation, among Muslims and non-Muslims alike, to reify Islam, this approach stresses the constant construction of Islam by Muslim groups and persons. The same should be said of Christianity and Judaism.

If we want to do justice to the original features of Muslims' initiatives, we have to pay due attention to their views and interpretations of Islam. That is to say, we have to be attentive to the "subjective" features of their references to Islam, not only in their ideas but also in their practices. Islam is not only the mass of age-old traditions of Muslim peoples and the huge corpus of prescriptions and doctrines, handed down via the scholarly and religious traditions of Islam. It is also the specific interpretation and practice that Muslims act out in particular contexts and situations and that they call "Islam".

As a consequence, we should first look for the ways in which particular Muslim groups and individuals in Europe select and articulate particular elements of the Qur'ān, the *Sunna*, and Islamic thought and practice as a whole. Then we should see how they link these Islamic elements with particular cultural and social elements of other origins, specifically those of the European societies where they established themselves. To explain the ways in which Islamic and other elements are brought together, the interaction of Muslim groups with the society in which they live and with each other, as well as the particular situations and contexts to which they respond, must, of course, be taken into consideration.

4) To carry out research on the ways Islam is constructed in Europe is more than a technical operation. It requires an interest in relationships between people of different cultures and an interest in interculturality and in social and cultural history. For a long time, this meant the relationships between particular cultures inside and outside Europe. Nowadays it also means relationships between different socio-cultural groups, including Muslims, within Europe itself. But since the Muslims in Europe remain in constant contact with the Muslim world outside Europe, both interests should be combined. Intercultural studies have become much more complex than in former times. For any correct understanding, a working knowledge of the languages used in this communication, mainly Arabic and Turkish, will of course be required.

5) An assumption of this approach is that Muslim initiatives taken in European contexts have their own reasons and that they make sense for the Muslim groups and individuals concerned. Sometimes it may be difficult for outsiders to grasp exactly what certain actions or discourses

mean to the Muslims concerned. Yet, fundamentally, we must assume that such initiatives have a particular meaning for the people concerned. Scholarship on Islam in present-day Europe has to do with social constructions of Islam as a provider of meaning.

2. Symbiotic Processes

In what follows, I shall concentrate on three large Western European countries where not only a considerable number of Muslim immigrants and their descendants are living, but where the majority of them also comes from a particular region of the Muslim world. These three countries have their own distinct social and cultural history and a sometimes far-reaching history of relations with particular Muslim regions. Muslims living in them tend to regard them as being representative of Europe and European culture itself.

The three countries are Britain, with Muslim immigrants from South Asia; France, with Muslim immigrants from North Africa; and Germany, with Muslim immigrants from Turkey. These immigrants and Europeans have a partly common history and were not completely foreign to each other. In two of the three cases, Britain and France, there were no major language difficulties, since many migrants knew English or French before their arrival. Yet in all three cases, the religious, cultural, and social patterns of the migrants' countries of origin differ considerably from those of the countries where they settled.

As a working hypothesis, I take it that in all three cases, whatever the problems of mutual adaptation of the immigrants and the local population, certain "symbiotic" processes have started between both parties. This has been possible because the legal provisions of the countries concerned enabled certain categories of immigrants to find a place in their societies. These provisions were based upon earlier migration experiences and allowed the admission of Muslim immigrants from outside Europe.

The occurrence of symbiotic processes should not obscure the fact that a number of factors can hamper such processes in European countries. Some of these negative factors are well-known:

1) Especially in Bulgaria, the former Yugoslavia, and the former Soviet Union, historical contrasts exist between mostly minority Muslim communities and the broader societies in which they live and which mostly consider themselves Christian. Ethnic and linguistic differences play a role, too. Political interests can effectively exploit such contrasts, as the history of the last three decades shows.

2) The strengthening of movements of the political right in several European countries, largely fed by the local population's insecurity and

fears, implies increasingly negative attitudes toward foreigners. Limitations are being put on immigration, including from Muslim countries.

3) Structural unemployment in Europe shows a lack of balance between the percentages of local and foreign unemployed people. This increases tensions between the local population and foreign workers, most of whom are Muslims.

4) Current geopolitical and economic interests have increased the distance between the richer and the poorer parts of the world, the "North" and the "South", with a growing domination of the former over the latter. Most Muslims happen to live in the South. The growing economic distance affects not only the relations between European and Muslim countries, but also relations between born Europeans and Muslim immigrants and their descendants in Europe.

5) The still current easy accusation that "Islamists" would be inclined to terrorism and the likewise still current simplistic association of Islam as such with violence have a negative effect on public opinion about Muslims. They negatively influence current efforts at bringing about symbiotic processes as sketched above. Although the immediate political effects have been most visible in Serbia in relation to Bosnian Muslims and Kosovo Albanians, and in Russia in relation to the Chechens, voices expressing similar ideas can also be heard in Islamophobic circles in Western Europe.

6) The events of September 11, 2001, with the following war against terrorism in general and also Israel's war against Palestinian terrorism, have created an atmosphere of anguish. In a number of cases, this has made cooperation and dialogue with Muslim immigrants in Europe more difficult.

On the other hand, there are also a number of factors that work in favor of symbiotic processes. These include:

1) During the last thirty years, initiatives have increased in Europe and elsewhere to bring Muslim and other people together for the sake of cooperation and dialogue. On both sides, groups have been formed that practice and promote cooperation for common causes, including human rights and the work of non-governmental organizations (NGOs) like Amnesty International.

2) The ways of life of Muslim immigrants and their descendants in European cities and regions have become better known to the local population. On their part, Muslim people have familiarized themselves more with their new countries. Moreover, migration processes have become better known and European states have acquired more experience with Muslim immigration.

3) New ideas have evolved about the contours of a civil society in which people of different backgrounds can participate. This offers an alternative to projects of society that stress growing homogeneity, con-

tinuing rationalization, and progressive secularization. In practice, such concepts imply a societal marginalization of Muslim and other religious communities.

4) European governments and the European Union have been insisting for some time on the need for qualified immigration from outside Europe and for further integration of Muslim and other immigrants with their descendants in European countries.

This short list should be supplemented by a number of initiatives on both sides explicitly meant to further positive interaction and communication between Muslim and non-Muslim Europeans. One example is the 1992 convention between the Spanish government and the Muslim and Jewish communities in Spain on equal treatment with the Churches in the country. Another is the strenuous effort made in Sweden to promote the integration of Muslim immigrants in society and their participation in the democratic process.

3. Muslim Initiatives in Europe

Let me briefly enumerate the main general initiatives involving Islam, taken by Muslim immigrants throughout Western Europe:

1) The establishment of various kinds of organizations on local, national, and international levels in support of religious, cultural, and social activities. These organizations are often meant for immigrants and their descendants from a particular country and of a particular Islamic orientation. They provide facilities like prayer halls or mosques and Qur'ān schools. Some of these organizations have a strong *da'wa* (missionary) character, calling on Muslims to practice their religion better. Other organizations, like sport clubs, are oriented toward non-religious activities. A number of Muslim organizations have both religious and cultural activities. Various organizations of migrants from a particular country (e.g. Turkey) or of a particular Islamic orientation (e.g. the Muslim Brotherhood and certain *turuq*) may be part of international networks centered in Muslim countries.

2) Within each European country, there is a multitude of Muslim organizations. Initiatives have been taken to establish a common representative body able to defend common Muslim interests in relation to the government of that country. Only exceptionally have complete representations been realized. More recently, Muslim women's organizations have also been founded.

3) The promotion of contacts with official agencies in the countries of origin or in countries able to give financial support, as well as with international Muslim organizations.

4) The establishment of prayer halls and mosques for communal religious and social life, in general around a local Muslim organization, sometimes as a prestigious mosque built with international support.

5) Support for religious activities prescribed by Islam, such as worship (ritual prayer), fasting during the month of Ramadān, collecting *zakāt* (alms tax), organizing the *hajj* (pilgrimage), assuring *halāl* food (ritually prepared meals), celebrating Muslim feasts, concluding Islamic marriages, taking care of the dead with Muslim facilities at the cemetery, etc.

6) The organization of religious education for children to give them a basic knowledge of Islam, varying from instruction at Qur'anic schools for smaller children to courses on Islam in primary and secondary schools; if possible the establishment of Islamic schools; sometimes the introduction of new teaching materials and new pedagogical methods.

7) Fundraising for current needs of the community, the mosque, etc., but also in support of Muslims elsewhere who are in need. The economic infrastructure of the acquisition and upkeep of the mosque, the payment of the *imām*, etc., need special care.

8) The promotion and defense of common causes, sometimes through public manifestations.

9) Increasingly, initiatives are taken to produce and spread religious informative materials about Islam to a broader public, in the form of journals and books, cassettes, videotapes, CD-ROMs. This is for education, preaching, and *da'wa* of Islam. On a more informative and communicative level, arrangements can be made for schoolchildren or interested visitors to visit a mosque.

10) At a certain point, initiatives are taken to create Islamic institutions meant to educate and instruct future *imāms* and teachers of Islam at secondary schools. Gradually, the legal status and work of *imāms* is being defined more clearly; at present, the payment is rather low, especially if the local community must pay the salary of the *imām*. Efforts are being made to create institutions for higher Islamic studies and research on Islam in an Islamic spirit, different from the Orientalist perspective. Important translation work is carried out on recognized Islamic texts from Arabic and Urdu, but also Turkish and Persian, into Western languages, especially English. As a consequence, the most important sources of Islamic studies are now accessible in English translations.

11) A number of Muslims in Europe ask for advice and guidance on matters that have to do with Islamic law (*Sharī'a*) and ethics. They can ask Muslim authorities to give a *fatwā* on a particular issue. They can also pose questions to authorities recognized in Muslim countries. A number of *fatwās* have already been issued on problems confronting practicing Muslims when living in the West.

12) Muslim conference centers organize lectures and conferences, but also socio-cultural activities including summer camps for youth. On certain occasions, non-Muslims may be invited, too.

13) Some private persons offer healing services to Muslims. This is meant as an alternative Muslim treatment of illnesses for which no Western medical treatment bears fruit.

14) A private initiative in the Sūfī tradition is the call to adhere to a particular master and follow his spiritual message. Often this comes down to adhering to a specific *tarīqa* and following its prescriptions. Various Sūfī orders have been active in Europe among both immigrants and born Europeans.

15) The last initiative to be mentioned here addresses non-Muslims. Muslim intellectuals in Europe increasingly participate in interreligious discussions and dialogues in the media. In most European countries, certain Muslims are invited to speak on radio and television. There is a growing number of properly "Islamic" channels as well as Internet sites. The information given by the media about Islam as a religion has improved considerably during the last twenty years or so. In contrast to this, media information about the links between Islam and terrorist activity, politics, and social issues remains prejudiced and often wrong, with constructions on all sides.

4. The United Kingdom

As the center of a colonial empire and later the Commonwealth, Britain has longstanding relations with a number of Muslim countries. Many of the immigrants living in Britain are Muslims, and the country meanwhile has a significant number of Muslim citizens. Its decentralized administration and its case law allow for local adjustments, and the communal life of Muslims in Britain is respected. The presence of a state Church and the tradition of teaching religion at schools gives religion a place in public life in Britain. The British notion of civility implies that foreigners are welcome, provided they respect the rules of British society. However, British society has been structured for a long time along class lines, with little upward social mobility, even for British citizens. Mixed marriages of whatever kind have been unusual and a degree of racism persists.

The Muslim immigrants who arrived from present-day India, Pakistan, and Bangladesh, sometimes after a prolonged or even multigenerational stay in East Africa, were accustomed to hierarchical social structures in their own societies. Many of them were conscious of belonging to an old and respected culture with its heyday in the Moghul empire from the sixteenth until the mid-nineteenth century. Islam in South Asia is known for its variety of legal, theological, and other religious orientations, each with its leadership, and also for a number of Sūfī orders in which holy men and women are highly respected.

Aside from South Asia, Muslim immigrants also arrived from the Middle East and English-speaking countries of Africa, such as Nigeria, Kenya, and Tanzania.

Several Muslim initiatives have gained influence in Britain.

1) Muslim immigrants and their descendants from South Asia, like Hindus and Sikhs, have a tendency to reproduce their traditional socio-religious communal structures in Britain. Their religion is by and large strongly dominated by the same Deobandī, Barelwī, and other Islamic orientations that traditionally exist in the countries of origin.

2) As British citizens, Muslim immigrants have developed a certain political consciousness and participate in British political life, with representatives acting in various political parties on various levels. In 1991, a group of Muslims established what was called an "Islamic Parliament", which took a critical stance toward British governmental and administrative practices. In 1998, the Muslim organizations in Britain started to form a common body to represent their interests, in particular in relation to the government and the Churches.

3) Although British common law applies to all residents of the country, some Muslim groups have repeatedly pleaded for the introduction and recognition of at least certain provisions of personal status in *Sharī'a* law to be applicable to Muslims in Britain. This was not possible. However, a kind of compromise solution has been found that encourages Muslim litigants to arrive at their own solution through Muslim arbitration, taking *Sharī'a* provisions into consideration, provided it does not violate British law.

4) Muslims have established important modern Islamic training and study centers in Britain, such as the Muslim College in London, the Markfield Institute of Higher Education near Leicester, the Islamic Study Centre in Oxford, and the Institute of Ismaili Studies in London. Several Muslim cultural foundations have been active in the realm of Muslim culture in Britain. In 1976, for instance, a large Muslim Festival was organized in London.

5) During the last twenty-five years or so, a number of books have been written by Muslim intellectuals living in Britain, reflecting on Islam and modernity or post-modernity as well as globalization and North-South relations. Numerous books appear on particular Muslim countries, issues in the Muslim world, and subjects of Islamic history and civilization. This testifies to a growing awareness and discussion of the place of Islam in the present-day world among new generations of English-speaking Muslims in the country or in contact with it.

6) As a cosmopolitan center, London provides numerous possibilities for certain elites from Muslim countries to meet. There are worldwide contacts, connections and cooperation among Muslims, including part-

ners from the Commonwealth and the U.S. These contacts and co-operations also concern a wide range of financial, economic, and political interests.

Traditional Islamic education, too, flourishes in Britain. The Islamic seminaries called *Dār al-'Ulūm* that South Asian immigrants founded in Bury (1975) and Dewsbury (1981) were modeled on the type that has been current in India and Pakistan. Teaching is in Urdu. In Britain, as in South Asia, the *'ulamā'* distinguish themselves through particular school orientations like the Barelwis and Deobandis, with distinctive approaches in the study of Qur'ān, *'ilm al-hadīth*, and the other Islamic religious sciences. At a later stage, the newer type of institutions mentioned under point 4 were founded, teaching also more modern disciplines that were not taught at the *Dār al-'Ulūm* institutions. Whereas *'ulamā'* play an important role at the *Dār al-'Ulūm* type, instruction at the newer type is provided by teachers who are fluent in both Urdu and English. The latter often come from new Muslim intellectual classes of society. The prestige of the *'ulamā'* declined, since they did not know English well enough and since they did not have the immediate contact with Muslim immigrants and their needs that emerging new groups of preachers had, even if the latter had not had the "classical" education in Islamic religious sciences. At the newer teaching institutions, Arabic, like Urdu, continues to be taught. However, interested students can rediscover here the broader Islamic intellectual tradition through the increasing number of English translations of classical Islamic texts. They are developing a more open eye for present-day Muslim debates, sometimes with new interpretations of the founding texts of Islam.

The links with South Asia are maintained. Muslim immigrants kept the communal kind of organization that exists there, in accordance with religious and other particular communal groupings. Certain textbooks are imported from India and Pakistan, and scholars from these countries can be invited to present lectures in Britain. However different the relationship between Britain and British India was from Britain's relationship to India, Pakistan, and Bangladesh nowadays, no conflict-ridden relationships developed after independence.

This seems to be the key to what Philip Lewis calls "the emergence of British Muslim identity" among the descendants of Muslim immigrants in the United Kingdom. This British Muslim identity is characterized by English language and education, by consciously identifying oneself as "Muslim", by a lively "South Asian" sense of discussion and debate, and by a certain predilection for Muslim and Islamic organization on a "national" British level. Among these people, there is an engagement with certain cultural and intellectual traditions of the West, as known in Britain, but they also contest aspects of Islamic tradition, though without leaving it. Maybe this is an amalgamation of a British style of life with a Muslim way of life.

An increasing number of Muslim women are now working with paid jobs outside the home. This is a needed addition to the family budget, but it also favors, in British tradition, a woman's independent personality. Muslim women associations, parallel to the existing Muslim men associations, attract members. Women are now playing a greater role in the public domain, also in representative functions for Muslim communities.

Muslim youth movements were organized in accordance with the orientations of the Muslim men and women associations.

5. France

After having been the center of a colonial empire stretching deep into Muslim Africa and with considerable influence in the Levant, France concluded this phase of its history with some bloody conflicts. The Algerian liberation war (1954–62), in particular, has impressed itself deeply in the Algerian and French collective memory. Immigration from North Africa to France already started before World War One. Since access to citizenship has traditionally been based on the place of birth (*ius soli*), France has a large number of Muslim citizens who are of North African origin and were born in France.

The country has a strongly centralized government and administration. As a heritage of the Revolution of 1789, it cherishes the ideal of a civil society in which all citizens enjoy complete equality in their rights and duties in public life and before the law, whatever their personal background or conviction. Since 1901, there has been a strict separation of Church and State. Public life in France is lived under a secular flag (*laïcité*, "secularism"), and religion is considered a private affair outside the domain of public life. The Constitution requires public life to be protected against the influence of religious organizations, including Churches and sects. The value of French culture has always been underlined and broadly respected. In colonial times, this provided the background for major efforts to spread the French language, education, and way of life throughout the Empire and beyond its boundaries.

The Muslim immigrants from North Africa were geographically close to France. Algeria was administered as a regular French province (except for particular rules on Islamic matters), whereas Tunisia and Morocco were protectorates under rather strict French control. North Africa is known for a certain cleavage between Arabs living in the coastal regions and Berbers with their own languages and customs living in the mountain areas. Rivalries between tribes or clans have been a common phenomenon, so that one of the tasks of *marabouts* and local branches of Sūfī orders (*turuq*) has always been to prevent the outbreak of conflicts. Around these *marabouts* and in the *turuq*, a rich popular religion has developed that the *'ulamā'* (religious scholars) frowned upon.

A certain individualism prevailing in North African societies found a parallel in certain equally individualistic orientations in French society. However, whereas throughout North Africa the political leadership has been accustomed to use religion as a political instrument, the separation of Church and State in France has been prohibitive for any close linkage here between religion and politics. Until very recently, Islam has not been allowed to manifest itself as a religion in public life in France.

Many North African workers, white-collar workers, writers, and intellectuals were familiar with the French language before arriving in France. This, as well as public acceptance of mixed marriages, has facilitated a certain insertion into French society. In practice, however, North African workers—socially often called "les musulmans"—have been looked down upon, not only by French colonists but also in French society at large, especially in the South.

Aside from North Africa, Muslim immigrants also arrived from the Middle East and from the French-speaking parts of Africa south of the Sahara, for instance Senegal. Most Muslims in France are Arabs.

Several important Muslim initiatives have gained influence in France.

1) Compared with other countries in Western Europe, Muslims in France have been able to establish their prayer halls and build mosques only relatively late, since the mid-1980s. There was much prejudice against this in the municipal councils, which continuously refused to give permissions. In certain cases, methods like strikes were needed to force employers and administrators to allow the opening and use of prayer halls.

2) Whereas in other countries in Western Europe discussions about wearing headscarves have mostly remained on a local level and led to local solutions, in France this issue has led to a national debate. In French society, wearing headscarves in public places has often been seen as a large-scale affirmation of the presence of Islam and Islamic identity, contradicting the ideology of *laïcité* (secularism) as the basis of French society.

3) Several large Arab Muslim organizations have been founded in France since the late 1970s, mostly centered on certain strong leaders. Notwithstanding various government efforts in the 1980s, there is not yet a single common representative body of all the Muslims in France.

4) During the 1990s, when the French government was no longer able to offer sufficient social and educational support, younger "Islamists" started to play an important social and educational role in the impoverished suburbs of French cities.

5) Because of the presence of a French-speaking Arab intelligentsia, Paris has become a center for the diffusion of Muslim Arabic literature and culture at large—in Arabic as well as in French—to the French-speaking world. Besides more secular views, there has been a growing output of religious literature.

6) In the 1980s and 1990s, some Muslim groups undertook terrorist activities on French soil, under Middle Eastern influence and under the impact of the Algerian civil war. They have had a negative impact not only on relations between the French population and Muslim immigrants, but also on the life of the latter when the French security agencies increased their control. In France, Algerians had already been discriminated against and victimized by the authorities since the beginning of the Algerian war in 1954. The Algerian and Tunisian governments' hunt for "Islamists" in the 1990s has also had negative consequences for Algerians and Tunisians living in France. The late Hasan II explicitly encouraged Moroccans living in France not to integrate in French society.

7) Important initiatives have been taken by Muslim women in France to improve their education and working conditions. Many of them have taken their lives in their own hand, intent to reconsider the traditional role of women in Arab Muslim societies.

Muslim initiatives to organize themselves in the French context of a strict separation of state and religion made use of a law on Associations dating from 1901. It allowed the organization of local associations that had social and educational aims in addition to specifically religious ones, although a permit was required. Muslims could organize such associations. This law and further legislation supports the individual integration of each person as a citizen in French society, if desired. As a consequence, it opposes a possible Islamic separatism or a particular communitarism around Islam. Muslim, Hindu, or Buddhist immigrants do not receive special treatment on the basis of their religion, but are treated as personal immigrants. For the state, Islam does not exist. This gives Muslims a certain freedom to take initiatives with their associations, but it restricts their forms of organization. It also implies that Islam or Christianity cannot be taught at state schools and that *imāms* in France have no juridical status.

In fact, however, there has been state interference in Islamic matters. On a local level, a municipality can refuse by majority vote the needed permission to create a prayer hall or build a mosque, for the sake of "public order". On a national level, in the 1980s and 1990s, the French government appointed rather arbitrarily certain Muslims to represent Islam or the Muslims of France. The government's wish to create a body representing the ca. four million Muslims living in France, without democratic legitimization, has not only led to wrong government decisions, but also contributed to the confusion existing in France about things Islamic, not to mention the quarrels between Muslim associations in the country.

In such a context, Muslim initiatives had to be self-defensive. Muslims had to argue and create space for Muslim life in a state and society proclaimed to be secular. They had to counter an anti-Islam mentality that was deeply rooted in French society, where Muslim culture was considered much lower than French civilization and where there was resentment that France had lost the Algerian war and that the French colonizers (*colons*) had left Algeria when it became independent in 1962. In the following decades, this mentality did not disappear. Ignorance about Islam prevailed and fears of it increased. This was not only a fear of Arabs and Algerians and worry about France's economic future. It concerned France itself as a nation and its identity in a time of decline and readjustment.

Debate and struggle, however, have been a feature of French society. It may very well be that something interesting will be born from it. Gilles Couvreur may not be entirely wrong when he speaks of a present-day "recomposition of Muslim religious identity" and "structuration of the Muslim community" in the country. Initiatives here are very much taken on an individual basis and often take unforeseen courses.

An important fact is the existence of authentic French-language Muslim thought and discourse about Islam, quite different from English-language discourses in the United Kingdom and the USA. Even the ways of conceptualizing Islam by French-speaking and by English-speaking scholars differ. All of this has led to the fact that, in the course of the last half-century, Muslims writing in French have developed their own ways of presenting Islam. Such presentations may differ in accordance with persons and groups, but their general approach is distinct from other approaches. I guess that their authors, too, are somewhat different from what most Westerners imagine Muslims to be.

French culture and society may be a special case in Europe, and so may be the four million Muslims living here, half of whom have French citizenship. But the situation leads, on the one hand, to new orientations and fresh thinking about what constitutes Muslim identity, especially among younger Muslims in France. On the other hand, the very refusal of the state to recognize Islam as a separate community on a religious basis forces Muslims to structure their communal life in an original way. Islam in France may become less tributary to the communal forms that were current in the past in the Muslim world. French-speaking Muslims may then also become a special case in Europe.

Several initiatives have been taken to guarantee the education and instruction of *imāms* in France, and a few institutions have been established. Efforts have also been made to create a university-based program of Islamic Studies in an Islamic perspective. Until now, however, plans to link such a program with existing French institutions of higher learning have not been successful.

A number of Muslims in France are open to cooperation and dialogue with Christians. The Roman Catholic Church, in particular, has given considerable support to Muslims in need, for instance, of a prayer hall. Such an outreaching hand in the land of *laïcité* has been appreciated, and valuable contacts have been established.

6. Germany

Apart from thirty-five odd years of colonization in some regions of Africa before World War One, Germany had no empire with Muslim inhabitants. Its history has mainly been played out in Europe. Germany's encounter with Islam arose largely through its cooperation with the Ottoman Empire, which became its ally in World War One. Republican Turkey maintained the links with Germany, and the migration of a large Turkish labor force as foreign workers (*Gastarbeiter*) to the Federal Republic took place within the framework of an official treaty between both countries in 1962. Yet until recently, Germany refused to be considered a country of immigration, and it was difficult to obtain German citizenship.

Most Muslim migrants to Germany arrived from Turkey, a state set up according to Western models. They hardly knew any German, and considerable efforts had to be made for their integration in German society. Cultural and religious affairs in the German Federal Republic are the responsibility of the various constituent provinces (*Länder*) that, for instance, also regulate the teaching of religion in school. Cases of violence against foreigners have occurred, especially in provinces of the former German Democratic Republic (East Germany), which had been practically closed to international communication.

In Turkey, forms of Islam that are not part of the official Turkish Islam as taught and practiced by the *Diyanet* (Presidium of Religious Affairs) are frowned upon. They may be marginalized as expressions of popular religion or forbidden if considered to be contrary to the official doctrine of the country as a secular state. Such unofficial Turkish Muslim organizations, however, could flourish among Turkish migrants in Germany and in their turn support Islamist and other movements in Turkey that call for an Islamization of the country and are opposed to the present-day state control of religion. Among the Turkish migrants in Germany there are also Alevis, Kurds, and other groups including Christians—in particular Syrian Orthodox Christians—that are not recognized in Turkey.

Germany also has a small number of Muslim immigrants from the former Yugoslavia and North Africa. These immigrants include a number of refugees.

Seen against this background, various Muslim initiatives in Germany deserve mention.

1) The most important, though unspectacular initiative with long-term consequences is the request several Muslim organizations in different provinces (*Länder*) have made to be recognized as a public body (*Körperschaft des Öffentlichen Rechts*), like the major Christian Churches and two Jewish communities. Until now, this request has not received a positive answer, which is a serious obstacle to Muslims participating as equal partners in the German religious scene.

2) The most spectacular Turkish-Muslim initiative in Germany has been the overt appearance of Islamic movements and organizations that were under pressure or forbidden in Turkey. Groups like the Suleymanli and the Milli Görüs, and even the "Grey Wolves" and the adherents of Kaplan, but also the Alevis, Nurculuk, and several dervish orders (*turuq*) have been able to express themselves freely in Germany, often to the dismay of Turkish officials. Ethnic groups like the Kurds, who are not fully recognized in Turkey, can speak out freely in Germany. A number of Turkish citizens have been accepted as refugees.

3) In the German school system, Protestant and Catholic Christianity is taught as a regular discipline during the school hours, under the responsibility of the Churches and provinces (*Länder*) concerned. Serious attempts have been made to introduce Islam for Muslim children on the same basis in Berlin, Hamburg, and Northrhine-Westphalia, with mixed success. Plans are in the making to establish a study program of Islamic Theology at the University of Hamburg and one of Islamic Religious Studies at the University of Bayreuth. They will distinguish themselves from existing programs in the framework of Oriental Studies and it can also serve for the education of future *imāms*.

4) Although many Turkish Muslims cling strongly to the Turkish language in a national and religious vein, there is a growing body of writing by Muslims on Islam in German. Second- and third-generation immigrants are familiar with German. This facilitates communication between the indigenous population and the immigrants. Especially when the teachings and practices of Muslim life in the country were conveyed only in Turkish, a certain distrust was aroused.

5) Noteworthy is the presence of an important Iranian Shī'ī community with a mosque and cultural center in Hamburg.

6) Several Sūfī dervish orders (*turuq*), often coming from Turkey, are active in Germany. They have their own networks, mostly with branches in Berlin.

The basic difference between the Muslim immigrants who came to Germany and those who came to Britain and France is that the great majority of the German immigrants came from one country only: Turkey. This happens to be an important nation with a strong nationalistic orientation and a rather rationally-oriented official Islam under the strict control of a state organization (*Diyanet*).

Turkish immigrants in Germany are probably identified more as "Turks" than as "Muslims", but they are known to be Muslims. Whereas "Islam" came to mean something more or less concrete in Britain and France in connection with their colonies, it has no such association in Germany. Seen from the outside, Turks in Germany seem to have their own world, as the Germans have theirs. There are no striking problems of coexistence between the two worlds; the problem seems rather to be how these two life worlds can get in touch with each other at school, at work, in sports, in the realm of culture, or in commitments to common causes.

In contrast to the first years of immigration, Turks in Germany—or wherever they could express themselves freely—are no longer seen as a homogeneous block. On the contrary, they have very different political views and parties. They take very different positions toward Islam and they have quite different orientations and forms of Muslim life. There are certain Turkish communities that are hardly considered "Muslims" in accordance with standard Sunnī idea and practice: certain Shīʿī and Sūfī groups, groups like the Nurculuk and the Alevis (Arabic: ʿAlawīs). Ethnically, there are non-Turkish groups, like the Kurds. Religiously, there are non-Muslim groups, like Christians and Jews. But all of them speak Turkish and possess Turkish passports.

Several initiatives have been taken to establish institutions for the education and instruction of future *imāms*. One Suleymanli initiative was the creation of an Academy for Islamic Culture, but it later closed.

A number of Germans have converted to Islam, as did a number of British and French people. Among German Muslims, voices critical of established Islamic traditions and institutions can be heard. In particular, criticism has been voiced of the increased politicization of Islam since the 1970s. Muhammad Salim Abdullah, for instance, unhesitatingly sees politicized Islam as a disaster (*Unheil*) for the Muslims in Europe. What is called the "Islamic Renaissance" is "... nothing more than a political-cultural counter-current that posits itself against the cultural imperialism that imposed itself from abroad"[2]. He forcefully argues that Islam "... in

---

[2]   "... eine rein politisch-kulturelle Gegenströmung, die sich dem fremden Kulturimperialismus entgegenstellt" (M. S. ABDULLAH, *Was will der Islam in Deutschland?*, Gütersloh: Gerd Mohn, 1993, p. 111).

its early history already became dependent on the state power"[3]. Voices like this one can hardly make themselves heard in the Muslim world itself. Europe offers a domain of free thought and expression that may be of benefit to Muslim societies.

7. Some European Responses to these Muslim Initiatives

Though this chapter is mainly on the initiatives taken by Muslim immigrants and their descendants in Britain, France, and Germany, it is worth noting some responses that these initiatives—affirming the presence, values, and proper character of Islam in European societies—have evoked.

Britain has been frightened by the explosion in Bradford in connection with Salman Rushdie's *Satanic Verses*, as well as by ethnic and other riots and manifestations elsewhere. Recent publications, such as the 1998 report on Islamophobia in the United Kingdom, show the existence of a widespread fear of Islam among the population and the presence of racist attitudes, for instance among the police. Consequently, some self-criticism and soul-searching is underway. But there are also positive responses, such as the World of Islam Festival of 1976, which attracted worldwide attention and led to a great number of publications in English dealing with various aspects of Islam and Muslim societies in the past and at present. The Church of England has taken a positive stand on dialogue with Muslims.

France has been frightened by terrorist attacks in the 1980s and 1990s, and was also disturbed by the ongoing controversies about Muslim girls wearing headscarves at state schools. Making Islam visible in the public sphere has planted a bomb under uncompromising secularism (*laïcité*) as the fundamental ideology of French society and state. It has also reopened old wounds in French society: the still-current deprecation of Islam as a culture and social order and bitter memories of the Algerian war that France lost so painfully. In France, Islam is a political issue that has resisted rational categorization. The number of publications from the Islamist as well as from the French Republican side arguing that Islam and *laïcité* are not necessarily in conflict actually suggest how deep the cleavage between French and Arab Muslim culture has been. Even certain French pro-Arab policies and the practice of mixed marriages do not preclude the conclusion that, for France, Islam still remains an ideological problem difficult to treat. The Roman Catholic Church has taken a positive stand on dialogue with Muslims.

---

[3]   "... ist der Islam bereits in seiner Frühgeschichte in die Abhängigkeit von staatlicher Macht geraten" (ABDULLAH, *Was will der Islam in Deutschland?*, p. 121).

Germany has been frightened by Turkish rivalries, Kurdish-Turkish tensions, and right-wing attacks on innocent asylum seekers. This country also seems to be involved in an ideological struggle about Islam. On the one hand, at the time of the Gulf War, there was a rather brutal demonizing of anything that has to do with Islam in the field of power and politics. On the other hand, one finds at the same time a sensitive but sometimes perhaps somewhat naive spiritualization of the Islam of mysticism and literature. Great efforts have been made in Germany to encourage dialogue and to work toward a civil and civic society. The Churches have taken a positive stand on dialogue with Muslims, but less so on an acceptance of Islam as a recognized public body.

8. Conclusion

In the preceding pages I discussed some initiatives that a number of Muslim immigrants to Europe have taken to make living according to the rules of Islam viable in the European context. It should be stated right at the beginning that these immigrants, because of their status here, simply were not able to take many initiatives at all. They were foreigners who did not know their new countries, they had not been prepared to do anything else than work, their work or refugee status brought them at most a low level of income, and their education was poor. So it is all the more remarkable that these people took any initiatives at all.

I concentrated here on the three major European countries in which Muslim immigrants settled: the United Kingdom, France, and the Federal Republic of Germany. The northern side of the Mediterranean, Scandinavia, the Netherlands and Belgium, Austria, and Switzerland fell outside this scope. It would be important to study in some detail initiatives that Muslims have taken in these four regions, especially those not found in the three countries considered here. This would illustrate once more the enormous variety of Muslims and their Islam recently established on this continent. This variety will probably increase to the extent that the models of the countries of origin will fade and symbiotic processes with European societies will increase, at least for a great many of the Muslims. Most important, new generations will make their way further into Europe, interacting with and participating in its societies. They will not easily lose their Muslim identity, though they probably will articulate it in new and more personalized ways. The current process of constructing Islam in a secularizing Europe testifies to an encounter between Muslims and European "others" that pushes Muslims to construct their Islam here.

Looking back, I would like to distinguish between the social and the intellectual level in this construction of Islam. This chapter concentrated on the first. So the Islam of the first generation of immigrants was basically constructed according to the models offered by the countries of origin. This generation had a conserving orientation.

The succeeding generations and especially Muslim women developed new needs in facing European societies, and they addressed Islam accordingly. Part of them remained simply "social" Muslims. Others looked for authoritative answers that Islam could give to their relatively new questions, mostly addressing texts of the Qur'ān and *Sunna*.

But there were others, too, in the later generations, who might be called the smart ones. They practiced techniques of reinterpretation and even of entirely new visions of the texts, freeing themselves from fixed traditions altogether, including those of text interpretation. They accepted reason and conscience as authoritative instances besides the literal textual meanings. And they often found their own singular way in society. They remained Muslims, but without carrying Islam as a well-defined authority or even as a burden.

In contrast to these exploratory and rather free attempts by immigrants' descendants, there have been and still are great pressures to adhere intellectually and accept socially one particular kind and form of Islam declared to be true or normative Islam and mostly identified with the *Sharī'a*. We can distinguish thereby a conservative and an ideological orientation, but in both cases all stress is put on Islam as something authoritative to which one has to submit. Islam enforces authority and discipline. In both orientations, this view of Islam has tremendous social consequences. The conservative orientation is based on a valorization of the traditions of Islam in addition to the founding texts. Whether these traditions are taken literally or seen in a perspective of reason is secondary: it is the very weight of text plus tradition that counts. This "fixed tradition" kind of Islam has been supported by many *'ulamā'* and *fuqahā'* all over the Muslim world at all times, and it is propagated by certain Islamic centers without much self-criticism. Though it is receding now in certain Muslim countries and in the diaspora, it weighs heavily on Muslim immigrants to Europe who, generally speaking, did not receive much critical education in religious matters.

The ideological orientation has been a revolt against this. It has a revolutionary character in that it appeals to the founding texts of Islam, the Qur'ān and early *Sunna*. Particular ideologies are derived from these, claiming to be true Islam. The so-called Islamists derived whole world views and ideological systems from Qur'ān texts and *hadīths*. Like the *'ulamā'*, the Islamists exercise enormous social, psychological, and if possible political pressures to impose their authoritative Islam on Muslim communities. Especially the support of conservative or ideological Islam by entire states has brought about a politicization of Islam in which religious and political pressures reinforce each other.

Among Muslims in Europe, both immigrants and converts, there has been resistance to such an authoritative and self-imposing view of Islam. Many younger Muslims, including those approaching Islam as a source of truth and meaning, have not been prepared to follow such a prescribed Islam from top to bottom. They may select from the existing texts and traditions the Islam that will be theirs. A number of educated women, familiar with the Qur'ān, question Islamic traditions, prescriptions, and doctrines on the place of women in the Muslim community. They may or may not debate these points with the men. But both younger Muslims and Muslim women who participate in European societies constitute a social yeast in the Muslim communities. This happens even if an older male generation tends to impose an authoritative version, either conservative or ideological, on those communities.

On an intellectual level, there is not much clarity. Most Muslim immigrants have other things than Islam to bother about in their struggle for survival. Moreover, the intellectual challenges are not restricted to the domain of religion.

Some circles cherish the idea of a radical reformation of Islam, which would make it compatible with modern civilization. The example of the sixteenth-century Protestant Reformation in Europe enjoys authority here. The idea is to go back to the Qur'ān and early *Sunna*, and to be directed by reason from there on, along the lines of Muhammad 'Abduh and Sayyid Ahmad Khan. Examples are M. S. Abdullah and Smail Balić.

Some figures who have been nourished by present-day intellectual currents in Europe also plead for a revitalization of Islam from its sources, in linkage with Western thought that enjoys authority. Examples are Mohammed Arkoun and Shabbir Akhtar.

Other figures who were educated in and well informed about the religious sciences of Islam attempt to reformulate the latter in terms of problems posed by modern society. Here the idea of a newly-conceived normative Islam beyond traditional views of the *Sharī'a* enjoys authority. Examples are Abdoldjavad Falaturi and Abdullahi Ahmed an-Na'im.

Finally, there are individual thinkers who, in a way, have detached themselves from Islam-claimed authorities and who follow their own creative course. They may not be well-versed in the intricacies of Islamic thought, but they consider themselves to be inspired by the Qur'ān. They may be primarily philosophical, literary, and artistic figures and may be called "personal" Muslims without representing any authority, Islamic or otherwise. My guess is that such individual thinkers can be found, for instance, among French-speaking Muslims.

On an intellectual level, until now there have been only rarely really new, not to say original, initiatives that pertain to Islam among Muslim immigrants. Nearly all Muslims who care about Islam seem to find themselves under pressure from a conservative or ideological interpretation of Islam, and socially under the pressure of Muslim communal traditions and opinions or of particular Muslim socio-religious authorities in Europe or abroad.

Maybe really new and original creative thought occurs precisely among those Muslims who do not like to speak of "Islam" as such as the highest norm or law. Paradoxically, they resist the temptation to absolutize Islam in a non-Muslim environment, while remaining Muslims. By not rallying themselves under "Islam" as such, they escape existing burdens and pressures connected with Islam on a social level.

In this connection, it may be relevant that Muslims, even of intellectual standing, hardly know through their own efforts other religions or cultures. If their intellectual horizon has been restricted by an Islam-oriented mind-set, that may be excusable in the Muslim world. But it becomes a handicap if one lives in a society outside the *dār al-islām*, causing additional distance and possibly some alienation.

The ways Muslim minorities experience their minority status should be a subject of further inquiry. Does relative powerlessness tend to paralyze them, or does it stimulate them to concentrate on activities in which visible power does not very much count?

Appendix: Studying Islam in Europe

I would like to add some remarks about how to study Islam and Muslims in Europe. Let me try to draw some conclusions going beyond the three countries we discussed.

First of all, our research should take into account how Muslim individuals and groups living in Europe live, act, and speak themselves and how in this way they are constructing their Islam or their Islams. As scholars, we should keep aloof from participating in Muslim discourses about what Islam is in itself or what its true interpretation is. And, equally, we should be careful about using generalizing terms and concepts like "fundamentalism" that are current in political and social discourses about Islam in Europe. Instead of trying to account for all kinds of things related to Islam in general terms, we should pay attention to specific cases to obtain concrete knowledge and deeper insight into the issues involved. In such research, we should study and analyze the various ways in which Muslims themselves speak and write about their experience in Europe. We should note how they formulate and stress certain norms and values in their descriptions. We should appreciate the ways they give expression to their often rich imagination, including what may seem at first glance utopian hopes and projects. And most of all, we should learn to observe correctly.

Second, as scholars, we should be careful in choosing the terms we use. Muslims often speak with terms like *Sharī'a, dīn wa-dunya* (religion and politics) or *dīyānāt sanawīya* (heavenly religions) and feel attracted by them. Christians are pleased to speak about "faith", "religion" and "separation of Church and State" and feel at home with them. Both Muslims and Christians are delighted to speak of "the monotheistic religions", "Christianity", "Islam", "Europe", "the West", and "European Islam". In fact, however, these have often become hollow words that receive a meaning largely through the spiritual ends and ideological purposes for which they are used. As a consequence, we should pay attention to the ways such terms are used in present-day discourse and try to detect the political or other aims behind that use.

Third, we should be on our guard against scholarly naiveté. Our task is not to guide Muslims in their constructions of Islam in Europe or to denounce such constructions. As scholars, we have no business supporting or obstructing the presence of Islam as such on this continent. We are not in the service of politicians or governments. Our task is a scholarly one. We have to find out what is really going on, which references to Islam are made and why, which expressions and forms of Islam occur and why, which initiatives Muslims take, and how they view and practice their Islam. All of this should be studied in context.

Research in the sensitive area of Islam in Europe is a critical operation. It uses rational procedures and checks its results not only with the help of reason and empirical facts, but also with a critical assessment of the researcher's own starting points. After all, when observing the other, Muslim side more or less sympathetically, we also have to look at our own, European side more or less critically.

In these encounters taking place between non-Muslim Europeans and Muslims becoming Europeans, both sides may feel some kind of astonishment. On one side, there is surprise about a new kind of religion turning up in a secularizing Europe. On the other side, there is astonishment about a society in which religion hardly plays a visible role.

To study such encounters impartially demands an independent position from the scholar. After all, as scholars we are not working to please the media, or publishers, or politicians, or religious leaders. We simply have to acquire and to communicate sound scholarly—that is verifiable—knowledge. During the process, we may obtain some insight into what is going on in Europe nowadays, among old-time Europeans and among those who have joined them recently.

Selected Literature

1. The West: North America and Western Europe

KEPEL, Gilles, *Allah in the West: Islamic Movements in America and Europe*, Stanford, Cal.: Stanford University Press, 1997.

LEBOR, Adam, *A Heart turned East: Among the Muslims of Europe and America*, New York: St. Martin's Press, 1997.

Making Muslim Space in North America and Europe, ed. by Barbara Daly METCALF, Berkeley, etc.: University of California Press, 1996.

Muslim Minorities in the West, ed. by Syed Z. ABEDI and Ziauddin SARDAR, London: Grey Seal, 1995.

Muslims in the West: From Sojourners to Citizens, ed. by Yvonne Yazbeck HADDAD, New York, etc.: Oxford University Press, 2002.

RASMADAN, Tariq, *Les musulmans d'Occident et l'avenir de l'islam*, Paris: Sindbad/Actes Sud, 2003.

2. North America

BASSIRI, Kambiz Ghanea, *Competing Visions of Islam in the United States: A Study of Los Angeles* (Contributions to the Study of Religion 50), Westport, Conn., and London: Greenwood Press, 1997.

ELKHOLY, Abdo A., *The Arab Moslems in the United States: Religion and Assimilation*, New Haven, Conn.: College and University Press, 1966.

HADDAD, Yvonne Yazbeck, and Adair T. LUMMIS, *Islamic Values in the United States: A Comparative Study*, New York and Oxford: Oxford University Press, 1987.

Indian Muslims in North America, ed. by Omar KHALIDI, Watertown, Mass.: South Asia Press, n.d. (1991?).

MCCLOUD, Aminah Beverly, *African American Islam*, New York and London: Routledge, 1995.

The Muslim Community in North America, ed. by Earle H. WAUGH, Baha ABU-LABAN, and Regula B. QURESHI, Edmonton, Alb.: University of Alberta Press, 1983.

Muslims on the Americanization Path?, ed. by Yvonne Yazbeck HADDAD and John L. ESPOSITO, New York, etc.: Oxford University Press, 2000.

3. Europe in General

DASSETTO, Félice, *La construction de l'islam européen: Approche socio-anthropologique*, Paris: L'Harmattan, 1996.

L'islam et les musulmans dans le monde. Vol. 1: *L'Europe occidentale*, ed. by Mohammed ARKOUN, Rémy LEVEAU, and Bassem EL-JISR, Beirut: Centre culturel Hariri, 1993.

Islam in Europe: The Politics of Religion and Community, ed. by Steven VERTOVEC and Ceri PEACH, Houndsmill, U. K.: Macmillan, and New York: St. Martin's Press, 1997.

Islams d'Europe: Intégration ou insertion communautaire?, ed. by Robert BISTOLFI and François ZABBAL, Paris: L'Aube, 1995.

LATHION, Stéphane, *De Cordoue à Vaulx-en-Velin: Les musulmans en Europe et les défis de la coexistence* (series Europe), Chêne-Bourg: Georg, 1999.

Muslim Communities in the New Europe, ed. by Gerd NONNEMAN, Tim NIBLOCK, and Bogdan SZAJKOWSKI, Reading: Ithaca Press, 1996.

Muslime in Europa – ein Ländervergleich (Grossbritannien, Frankreich, Niederlande, Belgien, Deutschland). Fachtagung der Katholischen Akademie in Berlin und der Friedrich-Ebert-Stiftung, Berlin am 9./10. Februar 2001, Berlin: Friedrich Ebert Stiftung, 2002.

Muslims in Western Europe: An Annotated Bibliography—Musulmans en Europe occidentale: Bibliographie commentée, ed. by Felice DASSETTO and Yves CONRAD (Musulmans d'Europe), Paris: L'Harmattan, 1996.

The New Islamic Presence in Western Europe, ed. by Tomas GERHOLM and Yngve Georg LITHMAN, London: Mansell, 1987, etc.

NIELSEN, Jörgen, *Muslims in Western Europe*, Edinburgh: Edinburgh University Press, 1992, 1995[2].

Paroles d'Islam: Individus, sociétés et discours dans l'islam européen contemporain / Islamic World: Individuals, Societies and Discourse in Contemporary European Islam, ed. by Felice DASSETTO, Paris: Maisonneuve et Larose, and European Science Foundation, 2000.

WEIBEL, Nadine B., *Par-delà le voile: Femmes d'islam en Europe* (Les Dieux dans la Cité), Paris: Ed. Complexe, 2000.

4. Balkans and Eastern Europe

BALIĆ, Smail, *Das unbekannte Bosnien: Europas Brücke zur islamischen Welt*, Cologne and Weimar: Böhlau, 1992.

Balkans: A Mirror of the New International Order, ed. by Günay Göksu ÖZDOĞAN and Kemāli SAYBAŞILI (Marmara University, Dept. of International Relations), Istanbul: Eren, 1995.

HANDZIC, Adem, *Population of Bosnia in the Ottoman Period: A Historical Overview* (Organisation of the Islamic Conference; Research Centre for Islamic History, Art and Culture [IRCICA]; Studies on the History and Culture of Bosnia and Hercegovina 1), Istanbul: IRCICA, 1994.

—, *A Survey of Islamic Cultural Monuments until the End of the 19th Century in Bosnia* (Studies on the History and Culture of Bosnia and Hercegovina 5), Istanbul: IRCICA, 1996.

Muslim Communities Reemerge: Historical Perspectives on Nationality, Politics and Opposition in the Former Soviet Union and Yugoslavia, ed. by Andreas KAPPELER et al., Durham and London: Duke University Press, 1994.

The Muslims of Bosnia-Herzegovina: Their Historic Development from the Middle Ages to the Dissolution of Yugoslavia, ed. by Mark PINSON (Harvard Middle Eastern Monographs 28), Cambridge, Mass.: Harvard University Press, 1993.

Le Nouvel Islam balkanique: Les musulmans, acteurs du post-communisme 1990–2000, ed. by Xavier BOUGAREL and Nathalie CLAYER, Paris: Maisonneuve et Larose, 2001.

POPOVIC, Alexandre, *L'Islam balkanique: Les musulmans du sud-est européen dans la période post-ottomane*, Wiesbaden: O. Harrassowitz, 1986.

Relations of Compatibility and Incompatibility between Christians and Muslims in Bulgaria. Research Project of the Foundation "International Centre for Minority Studies and Intercultural Relations", Sofia, n.d. (ca. 1994/95).

5. Britain

BARTON, Stephen William, *The Bengali Muslims of Bradford: A Study of their Observance of Islam with Special Reference to the Function of the Mosque and the Work of the Imam* (Monograph Series, Community Religions Project), Leeds: University of Leeds, Department of Theology and Religious Studies, 1986.

Desh Pardesh: The South Asian Presence in Britain, ed. by Roger BALLARD, London: Hurst, 1994.

Faith and Power: Christianity and Islam in "Secular" Britain, ed. by Lesslie NEWBIGIN, Lamin SANNEH, and Jenny TAYLOR, London: SPCK, 1998.

JOLY, Danièle, *Britannia's Crescent: Making a Place for Muslims in British Society*, Aldershot, etc.: Avebury, 1995.

LEWIS, Philip, *Islamic Britain: Religion, Politics and Identity among British Muslims. Bradford in the 1990s*, London and New York: I. B. Tauris, 1994.

MCDERMOTT, Mustafa Yusuf, and Muhammad Manazir AHSAN, *The Muslim Guide: For Teachers, Employees, Community and Social Administrators in Britain*, Markfield, U. K.: The Islamic Foundation, 1980/1400; second revised ed. 1993/1413.

POOLE, Elizabeth, *Reporting Islam: Media Representations of British Muslims*, London and New York: I. B. Tauris, 2002.

RAZA, Mohammad S., *Islam in Britain: Past, Present and Future*, Leicester: Volcano Press, 1991, 1993[2].

SHAW, Alison, *A Pakistani Community in Britain*, Oxford: Blackwell, 1988.

VERTOVEC, Steve, *Annotated Bibliography of Academic Publications regarding Islam and Muslims in the United Kingdom, 1985–1992*, Coventry: CRER, University of Warwick, 1993.

6. France

BABÈS, Leïla, *L'islam positif: La religion des jeunes musulmans de France*, Paris: Ed. de l'Atelier & Ed. Ouvrières, 1997.

BENCHEIKH, Soheib, *Marianne et le Prophète: L'Islam dans la France laïque*, Paris: Grasset, 1998.

BOUBAKEUR, Dalil, *Charte du culte musulman en France*, Paris: Ed. du Rocher, 1995.

BOYER, Alain, *L'islam en France*, Paris: Presses Universitaires de France, 1998.

CESARI, Jocelyne, *Être musulman en France: Associations, militants et mosquées*, Paris: Karthala, and Aix-en-Provence: IREMAM, 1994.

—, *Musulmans et républicains: Les jeunes, l'islam et la France*, Paris: Ed. Complexe, 1998.

ETIENNE, Bruno, *La France et l'islam*, Paris: Hachette, 1989.

La formation des cadres religieux musulmans en France: Approches socio-juridiques, ed. by Franck FRÉGOSI (Musulmans d'Europe), Paris: L'Harmattan, 1998.

JOINVILLE-ENNEZAT, Maxime, *Islamité et laïcité: Pour un contrat d'alliance* (Religion et sciences humaines), Paris: L'Harmattan, 1998.

KEPEL, Gilles, *Les banlieues de l'islam: Naissance d'une religion en France*, Paris: Ed. du Seuil, 1987, 1991[2].

Les musulmans dans la société française, ed. by Rémy LEVEAU and Gilles KEPEL, Paris: Presses de la Fondation Nationale des Sciences Politiques, 1988.

RAMADAN, Tariq, *Muslims in France: The Way towards Coexistence*, Markfield, U. K.: The Islamic Foundation, 1999/1420.

SAÏBI, A., *Guide pratique du musulman en France*, Paris: Ed. du Dauphin, 1984.

SELLAM, Sadek, *L'islam et les musulmans en France: Perceptions, craintes et réalités*, Paris: Ed. Tourgui, 1987.

7. Germany

BECKER, A., and R. MÜLLER, *Wir und die anderen Religionsgemeinschaften* (Unterrichtsmappe). Unterrichtsreihe "Wir und die Anderen" (Materialien für den Unterricht mit muslimischen Kindern; IPD-Schriftenreihe 03), Cologne: Institut für Internationale Pädagogik und Didaktik, 1998[2].

ELSAS, Christoph, *Identität: Veränderungen kultureller Eigenarten im Zusammenleben von Türken und Deutschen*, Hamburg: Rissen, 1983.

Grenzfall Europa: Deutsch-türkisches Symposium 1998, Hamburg: Körber Stiftung, 1999.

HEINE, Peter, *Halbmond über deutschen Dächern: Muslimisches Leben in unserem Land*, Munich and Leipzig: List Verlag, 1997.

—, *Konflikt der Kulturen oder Feindbild Islam: Alte Vorurteile, neue Klischees, reale Gefahren*, Freiburg, etc.: Herder, 1996.

—, *Kulturknigge für Nichtmuslime: Ein Ratgeber für alle Bereiche des Alltags*, Freiburg, etc.: Herder, 1994, 1996[2].

In fremder Erde: Zur Geschichte und Gegenwart der islamischen Bestattung in Deutschland, ed. by Gerhard HÖPP and Gerdien JONKER (Zentrum Moderner Orient, Arbeitshefte 11), Berlin: Das Arabische Buch, 1996.

Islam in Deutschland: Dokumentation einer Anhörung der CDU/CSU-Bundestagsfraktion (15.06.1999) (series Zeitthemen), Berlin 1999.

Islamische Theologie: Internationale Beiträge zur Hamburger Debatte, ed. by Ursula NEUMANN, Hamburg: Körber-Stiftung, 2002.

Kern und Rand: Religiöse Minderheiten aus der Türkei in Deutschland, ed. by Gerdien JONKER (Zentrum Moderner Orient, Studien 11), Berlin: Das Arabische Buch, 1999.

KLINKHAMMER, Gritt, *Moderne Formen islamischer Lebensführung: Eine qualitativ-empirische Untersuchung zur Religiosität sunnitisch geprägter Türkinnen in Deutschland* (Religionswissenschaftliche Reihe 14), Marburg: Diagonal-Verlag, 2000.

LEMMEN, Thomas, *Islamische Organisationen in Deutschland* (Friedrich-Ebert-Stiftung, Abteilung Arbeit und Sozialpolitik), Bonn: Friedrich-Ebert-Stiftung, Juli 2000.

MIHÇIYAZGAN, Ursula, *Wir haben uns vergessen: Ein intrakultureller Vergleich türkischer Lebensgeschichten* (Pädagogische Beiträge zur Kulturbegegnung 4), Hamburg: Rissen, 1986.

Moscheen und islamisches Leben in Berlin, ed. by Gerdien JONKER and Andreas KAPPHAN (Miteinander leben in Berlin), Berlin: Die Ausländerbeauftragte des Senats, 1999.

Religion – Ein deutsch-türkisches Tabu?, ed. Körber-Stiftung, Hamburg: Körber-Stiftung, 1997.

RIEMANN, Wolfgang, *Über das Leben in Bitterland: Bibliographie zur türkischen Deutschland-Literatur und zur türkischen Literatur in Deutschland*, Wiesbaden: O. Harrassowitz, 1990.

ROHE, Mathias, *Der Islam – Alltagskonflikte und Lösungen: Rechtliche Perspektiven*, Freiburg, etc.: Herder, 2001.

SCHIFFAUER, Werner, *Fremde in der Stadt: Zehn Essays über Kultur und Differenz*, Frankfurt on Main: Suhrkamp, 1997.

—, *Die Gottesmänner: Türkische Islamisten in Deutschland*, Frankfurt on Main: Suhrkamp, 2000.

SEN, Frauk, and Andreas GOLDBERG, *Türken in Deutschland: Leben zwischen zwei Kulturen*, Munich: C. H. Beck, 1994.

SPULER-STEGEMANN, Ursula, *Muslime in Deutschland: Informationen und Klärungen*, Freiburg, etc.: Herder, 1998, 2002[3].

Turkish Islam and Europe/Türkischer Islam und Europa: Europe and Christianity as Reflected in Turkish Muslim Discourse & Turkish Muslim Life in the Diaspora. Papers of the Istanbul Workshop October 1996, ed. by Günter SEUFFERT and Jacques WAARDENBURG (Beiruter Texte und Studien 82; Türkische Welten 6), Istanbul and Stuttgart: Franz Steiner, 1999.

8. Some European Countries with Smaller Numbers of Muslims

8.1. Belgium

DASSETTO, Felice, and Albert BASTENIER, *L'Islam transplanté: Vie et organisation des minorités musulmanes de Belgique*, Berchem: Ed. EVO, 1984.

Facettes de l'islam belge, ed. by Felice DASSETTO, Louvain-la-Neuve: Academia Bruylant, 1997.

FOBLETS, Marie-Claire, *Les familles maghrébines et la justice en Belgique: Anthropologie juridique et immigration* (Hommes et Sociétés), Paris: Karthala, 1994.

Voix et voies musulmanes de Belgique, ed. by Ural MANÇO, Brussels: Publications des Facultés universitaires Saint-Louis, 2000.

8.2. Netherlands

Islam in Dutch Society: Current Developments and Future Prospects, ed. by Wasif A.R. SHADID and Pieter Sjoerd van KONINGSVELD, Kampen: Kok Pharos, 1992.

8.3. Norway

AHLBERG, Nora, *New Challenges, Old Strategies: Themes of Variation and Conflict among Pakistani Muslims in Norway* (Transactions of the Finnish Anthropological Society 25), Helsinki: Finnish Anthropological Society, 1990.

8.4. Switzerland

ASHMAWI, Fawzia al-, *La condition des musulmans en Suisse*, Geneva: Ed. Cera, 2001.

Muslime in der Schweiz / Musulmans en Suisse / Musulmani in Svizzera (Tangram. Bulletin der Eidgenössischen Kommission gegen Rassismus, Nr. 7), October 1999.

Les musulmans de Suisse / Muslime in der Schweiz, ed. by the Swiss Academy of Humanities and Social Sciences, Bern 2003.

WINDISCH, Uli, *Immigration: Quelle intégration? Quels droits politiques?*, Lausanne: L'Age d'Homme, 2000.

Chapter 12
Diversity and Unity of Islam in Europe: Islamic Constructs

Throughout history, the Muslim world has known a great diversity of ethnic, social, and political as well as cultural and religious life and expressions. Discovering beyond the obvious variety of people a unity of ritual and faith is said to be one of the deeper emotions Muslims feel during the *hajj* in and around Mecca. Something similar must be true for Muslim immigrants in Europe, even if their diversity is striking on first sight. How then can one grasp in scholarly research the unity beyond the obvious empirical diversity of Muslims in Europe?

1. Factual Diversity

Let me summarize some well-known differences among immigrant Muslims and their descendants, apart from their personal choices and life stories.

1. Differences due to the regions and countries of origin and to influences from the Muslim world:

(a) Different languages, ethnic differences, and social-cultural differences of the regions and countries of origin;

(b) Different orientations toward Islam due to traditions existing in the regions of origin and to various Islamic communities, groupings, and movements that are active in these countries;

(c) Different political systems in the countries of origin and in countries giving support to Muslim immigrants in Europe;

(d) Different social classes from which immigrants came;

(e) The impact of different Muslim discourses and practices from the Muslim world in general, including transnational Islamic movements and organizations, through private or public channels, including media.

2. Differences due to the host countries and the host societies:

(a) Different practices, in the various European countries and societies, of norms and values that are generally accepted here, such as democratic institutions, human rights, separation of state and religion, various forms and degrees of the emancipation of women, varying forms and degrees of the secularization of public life;

(b) Different juridical and social provisions in the various European countries;

(c) Different attitudes toward Islam as a religion and a way of life and different mentalities toward the presence of Muslims and contact with them;

(d) Different political, social, and cultural climates in the host societies;

(e) Different policies applied by the host countries toward immigration from outside Europe and toward the integration of immigrants.

3. Differences in responses of Muslim immigrants to their situation in Europe:

(a) Different ways of organizing;

(b) Different responses to the call to participation and further integration in European societies;

(c) Different responses to the situation of economic dependence—with the risk of unemployment—of most immigrants and their descendants in European societies;

(d) Different responses to Islamophobia and hostile attitudes among the European populations toward immigrants as foreigners in general and Muslim immigrants in particular;

(e) Different strategies of survival and improving the situation of one's group or oneself;

(f) Cooperation, rivalries, and conflicts between various organizations and interest groups of immigrants in general and Muslim immigrants in particular.

Diversity within the Muslim community in each European country is increased by the absence of an authoritative Islamic institution. Muslim individuals and groups are in principle free to constitute their own identity and to follow what they accept or consider to be normative Islam.

Most Muslims in Europe are of Turkish, North African, or South Asian background. These are the majorities in the Muslim communities in Germany, France, and the United Kingdom respectively. A great number of these people are not formal members of a Muslim organization. They may or may not go to mosques and participate in the major Islamic celebrations. In fact, little is known about them.

Since the 1960s, numerous Muslim organizations have emerged in Europe on the basis of the region or country of origin and of the orientation of Muslims, often using their particular language. These organizations are a subject in itself. A useful division is between state-linked and non-state-linked organizations. Among the Turks, for instance, a sharp distinction exists between the state (*Diyanet*)-linked and other Muslim organizations. South Asians often remain linked to private South Asian religious schools (Brelvi, Deobandi) and groupings (*Tablīgh, Jamā'at-i Islāmī*) and their leaders (*'ulamā'* and Sūfī *pīrs*) in the countries of origin, rather than with government institutions.

We should also make a division according to the European countries in which Muslim immigrants settled. Muslim communities in Britain, which has an official state Church and which privileges decentralization and communal self-organization, are in a fundamentally different situation than in France, for instance, with its centralized administration addressing individual citizens and residents and which has an official doctrine of secularism (*laïcité*). Germany recognized only recently the status of immigrant for foreign workers. German nationality has been difficult to obtain and, unlike Christianity and Judaism, Islam has not been recognized as a body under public law.

For succeeding generations, many additional factors influence their general attitude, including their ideas about Islam and possibly their practice and interpretation of it. Class distinctions are important. Whether Muslim immigrants were admitted as, and their descendants are working as, unskilled labor, office workers, commercial agents, religious leaders, professionals, or refugees, and whether they risk or do not risk losing their job makes a lot of difference also for their ideas about Islam. Under such conditions, the search for "normative" Islam and the construction of a more "personalized" Islam will vary considerably or may be absent altogether. All of this leads to an individualization and diversification of Muslim immigrants in Western Europe, with an increasing variety of practice and interpretation of Islam among those outside the control of specifically Islamic groups.

2. Unity on a Factual Level

On the level of empirical verifiable facts, we have a common testimony (*shahāda*) of faith in one common God (*tawhīd* as the Islamic concept of monotheism) and in a common prophet considered to be final (Muhammad). We also find a common act of surrender (*islām*) to God, which expresses itself visibly in common acts of worship, a common recognition of the Qur'ān as the authoritative source of religion (considered to be revealed), and the acceptance of a common Muslim way of life (in the framework of an Islamic social order).

Added to these are the common recognition of prophetic tradition (early *sunna*) as a second source of religious knowledge, of religious law (*sharī'a*) containing prescripts considered valid for the whole of human-kind, and of Islam as the true and absolute religion (*dīn al-haqq*).

Apart from these common empirical elements given with religion, Muslims are aware of a common history, with its religious and cultural traditions. It starts with the prophetic era of Muhammad, passes through the medieval period with its great Islamic civilization, and finally arrives at the contemporary modern and post-modern era. The call and search for common "Islamic" answers to given problems and questions indicates an awareness of Islam, however defined and understood, as a common cause and framework of reference.

There are, of course, many empirical factors that have little to do with Islam that reinforce the awareness of unity among Muslims on a world scale. Certain political and military pressures imposed from outside, including Israeli policies, stress the unity of Muslims. Certain ideological challenges, including Christian missions and secularism, call for taking a common stand. Problems of demographic growth, economic hardship, and unforeseeable catastrophes demand mutual assistance. Situations of danger, conflicts, and discrimination imposed from outside reinforce the feeling of solidarity. Anger about the control of Muslim territory by foreign powers and forces and about the victimization of Muslim peoples strengthens the awareness, including among Muslims in Europe, of Islam as a common cause. For Muslim immigrants and their descendants, Islam as such remains a possible common recourse. This is especially true for people living in two cultures: one to which they keep an attachment in their mind and the other in which they are in fact living, with the multiple identities modern society confers upon people.

For a better understanding of the socialization of Muslim people in Europe, it is useful to distinguish between "societies" in the broader sense and "communities" in a narrower one. Muslim *communities*—often consisting of several associations that may, for instance, take care of prayer halls—offer an explicit common articulation of Islam. They want to be "Islamic" in a particular sense and strive consciously toward realizing Islam as they understand it, in society and the world at large. Muslim *societies*, on the other hand, consist of Muslims who happen to live and come together, for instance in a town quarter. They are utterly diverse and hardly demanding about the kind and form of Islam to which people adhere. The Muslim identity of the members of such societies is just taken for granted, and Islam is implicitly accepted as being normative without further elaboration.

3. Sociological Theory and Analysis

Sociological theory allows a social science approach to the problem of diversity and unity of Islam. I refer here to Felice Dassetto's study on the construction of European Islam as a social given (1996). It focuses on how "Muslimness" (*muslimité*) is socially constructed and how it functions. The author is intent on studying "new" social constructs, and Islam in

Europe is one of them. Like post-modernity, Islam in Europe presents new constructs that Dassetto discusses in his book. He analyzes the strategies and interactions between the various Muslim groups, as well as between these groups and the socio-political context in which they live.

At the end of the study, the author summarizes some models or "ideal types" of the various ways in which Muslims in Europe construct their "Muslimness" and Islam. He makes a distinction between two basic alternatives represented by two axes:

One alternative is whether the construct of such a "Muslimness" and Islam was initiated outside Europe or among Muslims in Europe itself. What was the nature of such initiatives? Did they create something new?

The other alternative is whether the Muslim groups concerned perceive themselves as being fully part of European society or if they draw a distinction between this society and themselves. Where can we speak of participation in society, for instance in the work sphere, and where is there an obvious distance from society, for instance in the family sphere?

As a result, Dassetto presents the following models or "ideal types" of social orientation of present-day Muslims in Europe:

A. *Orientations of participation in Europe*
1. Clear de-Islamization: "Islam" as a reference is lost;
2. Assimilation in European society: "Islam" is restricted to the private sphere;
3. Institutional integration: institutionalization of Islam takes place;
4. Muslim minority self-definition in contrast to the non-Muslim majority: "Islam" as an alternative to "Europe".

B. *Orientations that distance themselves from Europe*
5. Muslims in Europe perceive themselves as living on the periphery of the Muslim world;
6. Muslims in Europe perceive themselves as a diaspora community.

C. *Intermediary orientations between A and B*
7. External integration in Europe but inner loyalty to Islamic causes or authorities outside Europe;
8. Desire to live in Europe in a fully Islamic way as a ghetto community.

D. *Missionary orientations in Europe*
9. Muslim groups that see it as their task to work to convert Europeans to Islam.

In this sociological perspective, there is a basic social unity among all those Muslims who choose, among the nine possibilities, the same social orientation toward Europe.

4. Muslim Views of Diversity and Unity

How do different groups of Muslims in Europe see each other and in what ways do they consider Islam a binding element between them? Do they indeed see unity among themselves, and if so, how? Four points deserve attention in further research.

1. Muslim perceptions of fellow Muslims are very much conditioned by the outlook of their own group, especially if the weight of that group is stressed. Turkish groups, for instance, are very much concerned with what may be called typically "Turkish" questions, with Islam, and with themselves. On these subjects, they have engaged in much discussion about the principles of Turkish identity and Islam. I have often wondered if and to what extent they are interested in other Muslim groups at all. What do they think about Arab or other Muslim nationalities? What do they actually know about South Asian Muslims living in Britain or about North Africans living in France? And the other way around, how do South Asian Muslims living in Britain perceive North Africans or Turks living on the continent? Ethnic feelings are and remain strong, especially if they are linked to language groups. And countries like Turkey and Morocco have a conscious policy of stimulating national feelings among expatriates working in Europe. To what extent do Muslim communities in Europe perceive each other at all in their respective particularities? What do they know in fact about each other?`

2. Muslims living in Europe share the condition of being minorities in at least two respects. They are minorities among non-Muslim Europeans who constitute the large majority, and they are also a religious minority within Christianity, which is the majority religion in Europe. They may also be conscious of being ethnic, cultural, and other minorities. To what extent are Muslims in Europe aware of this persistent, common minority condition? To what extent does this common condition enhance feelings of solidarity among the various groups of Muslims, as expressed in assistance to Bosnians, Chechens, and Kosovo Albanians? Is this a solidarity of compassion in suffering or also of resistance against oppression?

3. One may point to the differentiation among people caused by the formation of states. Muslim immigrants in Europe have been divided according to states in two different ways: first by the Muslim states in which they or their forebears were born, and second by the various European states where they settled. To what extent will they identify at all with European states that do not impose themselves by external force or nationalist ideologies? Do they identify with Europe? Perhaps immigrant people are more or less sympathetic to a Europe that is slowly overcoming the old separations erected between its nation-states. Are

there perhaps immigrants who would not like to see a united Europe? To what extent does living in Europe help to overcome the often narrow nationalisms of the immigrants' countries of origin?

4. Let me point to the fact of ordinary Muslim life. When meeting in daily life, whatever their backgrounds and orientations, Muslims will quickly identify each other as Muslims. Such a natural recognition in ordinary life in Europe is intensified on special occasions, for instance when various people meet for Islamic celebrations or when they commit themselves to causes that have to do with Islam. Without being necessarily articulated as a faith, a religion, an ideology, or a social structure, Islam remains simply a common way of life. As such, it is a medium creating and facilitating communication among people who identify themselves through Islam.

Given the great variety among Muslims in Western Europe, it is only natural that, often encouraged from outside, they have made attempts to create unifying structures. Already in the early 1970s, the Islamic Council for Europe was established, in which Muslim organizations are represented according to their countries of residence. Prestigious mosques have been established in cities like Brussels, Geneva, and Rome, under the patronage of Muslim countries through their embassies. Important international cultural foundations and institutions like the *Institut du Monde Arabe* in Paris have been founded to bring Muslims together and make Muslim culture better known to the European public. Most important Muslim organizations in Europe have branches in several countries, and networks have developed across national borders. Most Turkish organizations have direct links with a base in the "motherland". There are numerous informal international contacts between groups working in the spirit of the Muslim Brotherhood or a particular *tarīqa* or dervish order. European converts to Islam tend to develop their own organizations and networks. The Centre of Islamic Studies in Oxford and the Institute of Ismaili Studies in London are known for their research activities.

5. The Quest for Normative Islam

In the present-day Muslim discourse on Islam, two features of the demands of Islam are particularly striking. First, among consciously practicing Muslims, there is a continuous search for norms and rules for living, acting, and believing in accordance with Islam. Second, in this quest for correct behavior and thought, the individual Muslim reaches out to his or her community, and the communities and their leaders address the individual members to make them live as good Muslims. There is a process of interaction between the individual and the community. In both cases, Islam is presented as a source of norms, as something that is thought to be normative in itself. The quest for normative Islam is another rallying point, another point of unity of Muslims.

To better understand present-day Muslim discourses on Islam, also in Europe, one should take into account the normative character of Islam for Muslims as a social fact. Besides the social reality of "practiced" Islam, Islam has a "normative" dimension for its adherents. Each Muslim is conscious of this, even if he or she does not live up to it. Many discussions on religious issues in Muslim communities are about what true Islam prescribes in matters of behavior and belief.

This quest takes on new forms in the diaspora situation. Many Muslims living in the secular context of Western societies stress that they have a religion that implies a faith and a way of life. It commands them to lead a moral life, observing duties and prohibitions according to norms and rules referred to as "Islam".

What Muslims consider to be the norms imposed upon them by Islam has been studied in the West for a long time, mostly on the basis of *fiqh* literature. In the colonial period, the subject was relevant to Western administrators of Muslim societies, who were particularly concerned with the juridical implications of Islam. The colonial administration recognized the validity of Islamic law for its Muslim subjects on matters of personal status.

At the present time, the subject has obtained a new relevance for Muslims living in Western societies. They are the first who should know the demands their religion makes upon them. Western scholars, too, should know Islamic norms when they study Muslim communities and their role in Western societies and in the Muslim commonwealth (*umma*) at large, not only in Europe but also worldwide. And for Western politicians dealing with the place of Muslim minorities in Western societies or with relations between Western and Muslim countries, neglecting normative Islam may lead to political errors.

Within Muslim communities in Europe, as elsewhere, normative Islam is taught through education at home, in Qur'ān schools, or in regular schools through children's educational books on Islam. It is transmitted through sermons (*khutbas*) in the mosques, literature about Islam circulating among Muslims, Islamic broadcasting and television, and more recently cassettes, videotapes, and also the Internet. Questions are asked to clarify what Islam prescribes in particular cases. Books have appeared about how Muslims should live in the context of European secular societies. Questions have been posed to religious authorities about how to live correctly according to Islam; authoritative answers (*fatwās*) to such questions have been given; and collections of such *fatwās* have been published. Discussions on this matter vary according to the authors, the nature of the

Muslim communities concerned, and the contexts in which they live. Such discussions show, however, that many problems are common to conscientious Muslims in Europe.

I consider this quest for guidance in present-day Muslim discussions in Europe as of utmost importance. It has a practical relevance, even urgency for religious Muslim communities. Besides numerous detailed practical questions, at least three major issues occur again and again in the European context:
(1) What norms of behavior should be upheld at all costs in different situations to guarantee the Islamic character of Muslim communal and personal life?
(2) What orientations, norms, and values should one follow in particularly critical situations in which one should act as a responsible Muslim?
(3) What are the essential beliefs in Islam that may not be abandoned under any circumstance?

Normative Islam is assumed to offer Muslims guarantees and benefits:
(1) an orientation of the soul to be maintained for the sake of the believer's own eternal destiny and for the well-being of the Muslim community at large;
(2) a monotheistic faith and ethic that are opposed to any form of idolatry;
(3) a definitive legal and moral order of society;
(4) a legal and moral order of individual life;
(5) essential solutions for life problems.

The practical religious question is what a Muslim should do and believe in order to lead the life for which he or she is destined.

In the foregoing, I focused on the ways Muslims, of whatever origin, living in Europe and the West in general, in a quest for norms and values given with Islam, establish rules of behavior and general social order and doctrines of belief and general human orientation. The main sources used in this quest are the Qur'ān and early *sunna*.

Qur'anic texts, for instance, are often invoked and used as arguments in disputes to support a particular point of view or to legitimate a particular way of acting. They then function as symbols more or less at the mercy of the practical interests of users, who hardly ask what these texts really mean. Qur'anic texts can also be used for typically religious purposes, such as personal prayer and meditation or Sūfī rituals (*dhikr*). They may also be simply enjoyed because of their wordings and style. Persons known as knowledgeable in Qur'anic matters may be consulted in times of crisis or when important decisions have to be made. They can then give private authoritative advice, drawing on Qur'anic texts.

As Muslim discourses on normative Islam, that is to say what is authoritative for Muslims, have multiplied in the European context, so too have more general discourses about Islam as a religion and ideology. The question of the validity of Muslim statements has become urgent, especially since Islam has no central religious authority, let alone religious hierarchy, able to give a final verdict. There is freedom of judgment in religious matters, with basically two options to arrive at a decision. The first is the option of "learned authority", that is, to consult the judgment of a recognized authority on normative Islam.

The second is to go ahead according to the consensus within the community to which one belongs. Indeed, what is considered normative and binding in a number of Muslim communities in Europe is not only deduced from what the Qur'ān and certain *hadīths* say. It can also be derived from what may be called "living tradition", that is, what people transmit as wisdom under the heading of "Islam". In this sense, Islam in a living community is primarily "transmission" in a communicative process. It is this transmission, in a process of continuous discussion and debate, that creates authoritative living tradition.

I submit that normative Islam, especially in the Western context, is something constantly searched for. Rather than consisting of factual texts and specific practices derived from a bygone past, it is constantly constructed by successive generations of Muslims appealing to "true" Islam. They choose particular elements from Scripture and *Sunna* and they add other elements to it, such as local tradition, prevailing ideology, reason, or spiritual insight, depending on situation and context, place and time. As a consequence, it is difficult for relative outsiders to grasp the contents of this normative Islam, to dominate it intellectually, or to control it politically. It does not exist apart from the people who draw meanings from it.

6. Recognized Authorities on Islam

Whether Muslim communities seek norms and values through a recourse to scripture, living tradition, ideology, reason, or spiritual orientations, there are always certain figures of authority involved who are recognized as mediating these sources. We must distinguish between established, traditionally accepted authorities, on the one hand, and new bearers of authority on Islam, on the other.

6.1. Traditional Authorities

6.1.1. Authorities on the basis of knowledge. Those who search for knowledge, especially in religious matters, have always enjoyed prestige and authority among Muslims. The first level of such knowledge, for children at the Qur'anic school (*kuttāb*), entails learning the elementary rules of Islam and some Qur'anic texts. At elementary schools in most European countries, Muslim children can take classes on Islamic religion outside the normal school hours; in several European countries, private Islamic elementary schools have been established.

On a second level of religious learning, we find in Muslim countries programs preparing students for a career of teaching religion and preaching as *imāms* (the *imam-hatip* schools in Turkey). On a third level, state universities in Muslim countries and the more recently established International Islamic Universities in, for instance, Kuala Lumpur and Islamabad all have Faculties of *Sharī'a* and/or Theology where one can study the "religious sciences" (*'ulūm al-dīn*) of Islam. At traditional *madrasas* (a kind of college) in Muslim countries, Islam is taught at the second and part of the third level. Some established Islamic universities such as al-Azhar in Cairo have great prestige. Someone who has finished his studies here enjoys religious authority as an *'ālim* (literally someone who "knows" Islam). Some Muslim countries have specialized Islamic research institutes and academies.

In Europe, there are at present only a few Islamic institutions on the post-secondary level for the training of *imāms* and higher teachers of Islam. They are inadequate to supply sufficient Muslim religious personnel for the continent. At present, those Muslim religious scholars in Europe who have studied the "religious sciences" (*'ulūm al-dīn*) of Islam have nearly always studied them in Muslim countries or India. Many of them are only temporary residents here; very few *'ulamā'* or *fuqahā'* are permanent residents in Western Europe. This implies that there are few recognized Muslim authorities here with a complete "traditional" training in and knowledge of the religious sciences of Islam.

6.1.2. Authorities on the basis of personal gifts. Persons with religious charisma, often of Sūfī background, have always enjoyed great authority in Muslim communities, even if they never studied the religious sciences of Islam. Some of them distinguish themselves through their spiritual insight or their aura. Some dispense the gift of healing. Others are connected with Sūfī brotherhoods (*turuq, tarīqas*), for instance as local leaders of particular *tarīqa* branches. Others again are deemed to possess special qualities because they are descendants of Muhammad or of particular illustrious religious families. Such persons can play an important social and also political role.

People belonging to all these categories can be found among Muslims in Europe. Most important on a practical level are people whose authority is recognized because of their gifts, for instance for giving psychological advice, healing, or finding solutions to intricate human problems. They may play a role in *tarīqa* networks and their authority may be spread throughout Europe and beyond.

There are also some tightly organized religious communities with a strong *tarīqa* discipline or with a supreme religious authority, such as the Aga Khan among the Khoja Ismāʿīlīs. Research is needed about such more informal Islamic religious networks that are active in Europe at the present time, often aside from politics.

6.1.3. Religious authority enhanced through traditional social structures. In traditional Muslim communities, religious authority has often had the support of traditional social structures that, taken in themselves, have little to do with religion. A strict separation between the men's and the women's worlds, patriarchal structures, extended kinship relations, and social hierarchies of different kinds are omnipresent in such communities. While in the traditional Muslim women's world attention to natural processes, gifts of healing, and experiences of ecstasy, for instance through spirit possession, have always been important, in the men's world, it is especially leadership qualities in the public sphere, learning, genealogy, and age that count.

Second- and third-generation descendants of Muslim immigrants in Europe often do not recognize such traditional authority structures any more. New bearers of Islamic authority have been emerging among Muslims living in the West where there are few *ʿulamāʾ*, where help to others is professionalized, and where traditional structures are weakening.

6.2. New Bearers of Authority

Especially since the mid-twentieth century, new kinds of Muslim authority on Islam have emerged besides the traditional authorities mentioned. Most important are the following ones.

6.2.1. Leaders of Islamic movements. Persons with responsible positions in present-day national and international Islamic movements enjoy considerable socio-religious authority, not only within but often also outside of such movements. They may be good speakers, active in *daʿwa* ("call") activities, engaged in social work and mutual help, and responsible for the management of the movement or for keeping up relations with other movements. They may also be active politically, maintaining relations with various authorities and representatives in the country of immigration, in the country of origin, or in international organizations. They are also able to ideologically mobilize Muslim groups for particular causes, as happened in the Salman Rushdie and headscarf affairs in Europe around 1990. They can be opposed to the regimes of particular Muslim countries. If an Islamic movement takes on a militant character, its leadership becomes politicized. Only exceptionally is violence used.

6.2.2. Islamic officials. A new group of persons enjoying authority in Muslim communities in the West are the officials of government or international Muslim bodies in charge of Islamic religious matters. Quite a few Muslim countries have officials for Islamic religious affairs, both in ministries at home and posted to embassies in Western countries. Turkey, for instance, has civil servants of the *Diyanet* attached as officials to Turkish embassies in several European countries. They bear responsibility, for instance, for the *Diyanet*-linked Turkish Islamic foundations and their mosques and *imāms* in Europe. The Secretariat of the "Organization of the Islamic Conference" in Jedda has officials who are in contact with the leaders of Muslim organizations in Europe. Needless to say, such officialdom often leads to a bureaucratization of Islam.

6.2.3. Islamic media. A growing number of Muslim religious scholars and preachers have become known through the media not only in the Muslim world, but also among Muslims in European countries, including on a local level. They address in the first place Muslim audiences about their religion. However, along with Muslim journalists, they may also mediate between the general public, which is often poorly informed about Islam and matters related to it, and adherents of Islam in the country. Muslim media give a new coherence to Muslim communities spread over the world that constitute a kind of commonwealth (*umma*) but have no formal organization.

6.2.4. Alternative forms of religious authority. A number of non-political Muslim organizations enjoy a moral prestige because of their commitment to human causes. Examples are the Muslim women's organizations, Muslim human rights organizations, as well as branches of Amnesty International in Muslim countries. Relief has been organized for victimized Muslim communities, such as in Bosnia and Kosovo in the 1990s. There are often special organizations of Europeans who have converted to Islam, often called European Muslims. Last but not least, associative networks have developed around prominent Muslim personalities working in the socio-religious, Sūfī-minded, or intellectual sphere. The leadership of such voluntary associations and organizations enjoys authority and has an impact on Muslims in Europe and beyond.

7. The Ideal Unity

In addition to the four kinds of mutual perception and communication among Muslim immigrants in Europe just mentioned, I would like to touch upon Muslim views of each other on an ideal level, where the binding element is Islam as a religion. It is here that the religious aspects of Islam and Islam itself as a religion are most articulated.

A first step in cementing a more palpable kind of religious unity among Muslims is the common acceptance, especially in situations of disorientation, that Islam contains the fundamental norms for good human behavior. The various answers given to the question of what exactly this common "normative" Islam prescribes in a given situation or context may differ, but the question itself is standard. In Europe, the answer mostly has moral rather than legal consequences. Important for our subject is that Islam as such is recognized fundamentally as providing the true and absolute norms to which Muslims should refer. As is well-known, the quest for normative Islam is pursued systematically in the discipline of *fiqh*. It has already resulted in a number of *fatwās* concerning a Muslim's proper way of life in a secular society, as found in Europe.

The ideal character of Islamic unity takes on still clearer religious features in view of Islamic signs, symbols, and their meanings. Indeed, Islam as a religion functions as a signification system, the center of which, of course, is the Qur'ān. The Qur'anic verses (*āyāt*) are the signs or symbols par excellence to which Muslims refer and which constitute the fundamental religious unity of Muslims. It is through meditation on and the understanding of Qur'anic passages as signs or symbols that a universe of meanings opens up to people sensitive to them. Muslims who know a number of Qur'anic verses or *hadīths* by heart possess a common symbolic reservoir at important moments in the course of life. This reservoir provides a religious universe of meaning, discourse, and action. Sharing in this symbolic universe provides unity on an ideal level.

We should, however, make a distinction between poetic symbolism and the symbolism of religious vision that is largely accessible only to believing Muslims. Both can bring about a sense of unity, but the direction seems to be different. Poetic symbolism seems to remain linked to individual momentary experiences and what may be called esthetic views of unity. A religious experience of symbolism, on the other hand, may lead to public testimony and positive action for the sake of Muslim unity. This may lead to a call for common efforts for the sake of Islam or to puritanical reforms going back to the sources of Islam. But it may also lead to a mystical deepening where the unity of Muslims in common adoration of the one God is perceived as something given "from beyond". In such a religious view, the unity of Muslims is greater than their diversity, simply because it is more profound.

The study of Islam as a religion of unity (*tawhīd*) or as a religion at all is not an easy matter. It seems to me that our proclaimed modern and post-modern societies are losing particular notions of religion and in a number of cases the notion itself. As a result, it seems to have become increasingly difficult in Islamic studies to grasp Islam as a religion with its religious problems in a scholarly way. Maybe such a task should fall to *Religionswissenschaft*, the scholarly study of religions and religious signification systems such as Islam.

8. Scholarly Realism

From a scholarly point of view, any religion, including Islam, can be used for good and bad. It can be instrumentalized for political use or interiorized for spiritual elevation. Islam in itself is not more problematic than other religions; as a matter of fact, they all are. Islam as seen from the West, however, is surrounded by ambiguity.

A current opinion still considers Islam a religion of foreigners, which suggests that people wanting to integrate in Western society should change their religion. This is a wrong view not only of Islam but also of Western and in particular European societies. At present, in most European societies Islam is judged rather negatively, especially in its application in Europe. The criteria according to which the judgment is passed are not trivial. There are moral criteria, judging for instance the treatment of Muslim women and the status of women in Islamic religious law or the sad record of human rights in Muslim countries. There are legal criteria, judging for instance the fact that there is no strict separation of state and religion and no strict separation of functions of the state in Muslim countries and that corruption is widespread. There are political criteria, judging for instance authoritarian rule in most Muslim countries or the dilapidated state of democracy. There are also religious criteria, judging the way in which non-Muslims are treated in Islamic states and in most Muslim states generally. The criteria applied are valid and should be applied in Europe and Western states in general, but they should be applied not only to Islam but also to other religions, including certain varieties of Judaism and Christianity.

The problem in Europe is that judgments that are correct in themselves are mixed up with judgments that have less justification but are current, too. Muslims complain about the prevailing ignorance of Islam in Europe and the West in general. Many judgments are based on certain experiences reported from Muslim countries (such as intolerance and violence) or certain experiences with Muslims in the West (high claims attributed to Islam but poor actual practice, stubbornness and unwillingness to learn, and lately of course terrorism). Muslims seem not to understand why the media present certain ugly aspects of Islam that are in fact deformations and have nothing to do with true Islam. They have difficulty with the scholarly study of Islam as an empirical reality, and they protest against a scholarly study that applies critical analysis to religious texts and religious reports of historical events. Last but not least, Muslims may be surprised if not confused by the different appreciations of Islam given by Christians who hardly know a word of Arabic, varying from proposing dialogue on an equal footing to flatly condemning to hell Islam as a socio-religious system. Most of this goes back to misunderstandings and plain ignorance of each other on both sides. The problem, however, is that so few people want to learn and know the truth, not *from* a European or an Islamic point of view but *about* these European and Islamic points of view.

As I see it, it is not only European ignorance of true Islam that has led to current negative images of Islam. At bottom, there is ambiguity in Islam itself, and European intellectuals do not like ambiguity in speaking about one's religion. Let me give a few examples.

1. Muslims for whom Islam is religious truth are confronted with the fact that, during the last thirty years, this same Islam has become so politicized that in practice it has become a political instrument. Instead of being able to condemn the misuse or abuse of power, Islam shows itself to be helpless when confronted with the power of Muslims themselves.

2. Muslim communities in Europe stand under considerable pressures from outside that aim to prescribe or impose the kind of Islam they want to see realized in Europe, rather than letting European Muslims themselves decide what kind of Islam they want and need. Pressures are exerted not only by international Islamic organizations and Islamic movements, but also by governments of immigrants' countries of origin and of money-giving Muslim countries. That is to say, not much freedom is left to Muslim organizations in Europe to articulate Islam as they see fit. Their leaders lack the capacity to articulate Islam in fresh ways and this is one of the reasons that Muslim organizations within a particular country cannot arrive at a common representation.

3. Muslim communities in Europe suffer from a lack of sound discussion and debate on essential issues. Often intellectual options are confused with social solidarity. The integration of younger Muslims in European societies is hindered by a heavy burden of Islamic traditions. The burden of the assumed authority of religious leaders and of collective tradition and representation in the community stands in the way of the free development of the persons concerned, both women and men. What are in the last analysis personal views and practices are covered by the formula: "Islam says!"

In the European perception, Islam does not correspond with what is considered "religion" in Europe. Islam seems an ambiguous entity showing religious, social, and political aspects, depending on circumstances.

This ambiguity leads to what Muslims consider a misunderstanding, ignorance, or willful deformation of Islam.

On closer consideration, each religion turns out to have its own interpretation of itself and of others. This is only now becoming clear, since people of different religious traditions are now encountering each other on European soil. But these people have to live together and, from this perspective, we can subscribe to the scenario of a growing civil society in Europe that allows different religious communities to live together.

9. Scholarly Research on New Readings of Islam

From a scholarly point of view, Islam is not only a set of authoritative texts contained in the Qur'ān and *Sunna*. Nor is it only an established religious tradition or a set of historical traditions accumulated in the course of history. It is not only a social structure to be realized in society. Nor is it only a faith expressed in doctrinal formulas or a way of life with particular prescriptions and prohibitions. From the perspective of empirical scholarly research, Islam as a religion is first and foremost something of the mind, a particular view and reading of the meaning of certain religious data. Or to put it in abstract terms, Islam is something that has been and continues to be constructed by successive generations of Muslims at different times and places. Of the many constructions that have been made of Islam in the course of time, a number did not gain a following and were lost or went their own way, but others found enough following to survive until the present day.

In the course of the twentieth century, a number of new constructions of Islam developed. A first classification led to categories like Reformist Islam, Modernist Islam, Fundamentalist Islam, Liberal Islam. They have been studied in great detail and have a place of honor in handbooks about present-day Islam. But others do not fit into these categories, for instance Ahmadi Islam, the Sūfi Movement of Inayat Khan, and the Black Muslims in the USA. It is noteworthy that such new constructions of Islam that are difficult to classify originated by and among Muslims who were living in or were more or less familiar with the West, be it Europe or North America.

From the point of view of the study of religions or science of religions, there is great need for further research on new, twentieth-century readings of Islam that elude the abovementioned categories. Such research should be carried out without prejudice or preference for particular readings, whether based on Europeans' ideas about a suitable "European" Islam or more traditional Muslims' ideas about truly "Sunnī" or "Shī'ī" Islam. It is precisely the variety of readings and constructions of Islam that is the subject of the present inquiry. Special attention should be given to what must be considered to be new and in a sense "original" constructions or readings of Islam.

For practical purposes, such study should be carried out separately for Europe and for North America. Regarding Europe, a useful distinction would be that of constructions in the French cultural area (M. Arkoun, T. Ramadan, etc.), the German cultural area (S. Balić, and others), the English-speaking cultural area (London-based thinkers), and of course the Spanish and Italian cultural areas (with which I am less familiar).

Further research on the roots of such new constructions and readings will undoubtedly show the hybrid character of many of them. Here, texts from the sources (Qur'ān, *Sunna*) are combined with certain present-day spiritual and intellectual trends. Other constructions and readings will show more or less direct links with present-day ideological trends existing in and coming from Muslim countries ("official" Islam of the *Diyanet* in Turkey; the Islam furthered by particular Islamic movements such as the Muslim Brotherhood). A third possibility is that Islam is read and constructed in connection with social and political trends in Europe itself, as a kind of Islam "applied" to the European situation or European contexts. Yet, such links do not deny that there are quite original and constructive versions of Islam developed in Europe.

The same sort of inquiry should be carried out in North America.

10. The European Framework

In actual fact, however, things are not that simple with religions. The interpretations, applications, and uses of Islam in Europe—as of any religion—depend not only on the views of the people concerned, but also on the economic, social, and political realities in which these people are involved. These realities must be taken into account in an adequate study of Muslims and their Islam in European contexts. The diversity and unity of Islam in Europe must not be seen as a problem of European Muslims among themselves, but within a European framework, both social and cultural.

The European social framework makes itself palpable, for instance, in the following cases.

1. Social tensions experienced in European societies in which Muslims perceive themselves as victims can give them cause to articulate Islam as an alternative to Europe. Especially if their knowledge of the language and society is defective, misunderstandings are unavoidable. This in turn may strengthen interpretations of Islam that insist on the superiority of Islam and stress the distance between normative Islam and experienced European society. The theme of the distance or nearness that immigrants

feel to European society, as well as the reasons given for it, would be an important subject for ongoing research.

2. There are very different views and judgments of Islam and very different attitudes toward Muslims depending on the various social and legal settings in European countries. Social classes and cultural milieus play an important role in this. Fundamentally, the treatment of Muslim immigrants and their descendants and the appreciation of Islam in European societies is in debate everywhere. There are situations of Islamophobia, discrimination, and exclusion of Muslims, but also of human contact, participation, and cooperation. One of the consequences of this situation is that it is always possible to say that Islam is discriminated against, somehow and somewhere, and that Muslims in Europe can always feel somehow victimized at present. But one should work for the future. Arriving at mutual recognition and understanding demands time, continuing education, and unceasing efforts among European people, who tend to have their prejudices, just as immigrants have theirs. It also demands much information, education, and willingness to learn on the part of Muslims, who have a different cultural background. Better communication between both groups is a condition for improvement of the situation.

3. For a viable future in Europe, there is a great need to think about society. If in the past the idea of an "open" society was held as a virtue of Western democracies in contrast to communist societies, Europe can hold the idea of a "civil" society against many societies in the Muslim world. Yet, the ideal of a true civil society is still far from being fully realized in Europe itself. Democratic institutions have been created and the rights of minority groups have been strengthened and guaranteed. Some countries are further ahead than others. Yet, at the moment, full equality is still true primarily for born Europeans; immigrants from outside Europe and their descendants still tend to be felt and considered to be groups distinct from "us". For Muslims, in particular during a war against terrorism, the situation has become difficult. There are, moreover, political dangers. Besides the tasks of bringing about a civil society and of providing the necessary information and education to the new and the old Europeans, there is a problem of popular feelings against too many "foreigners" and of political abuse of such feelings by ruthless politicians. Islam is an important issue in this European debate, and there are ever more reasons to strive for a true civil society in Europe.

Fortunately, the diversity and unity of Islam in Europe can also be seen in a cultural framework. In this perspective, there are indeed signs of a hopeful future on a European scale. Among the descendants of the Muslim immigrants of the 1960s and 1970s there is a growing interest in acquiring a more adequate knowledge about Islam. Since studying Arabic and Urdu, Turkish and Persian is not given to everyone, people have to address the founding and following classical texts in translation. Since good translations of a number of these texts have appeared, those interested have access to them at least in English. This opens to the more inquisitive minds the possibility of establishing new and creative links with these texts and of reconnecting with the intellectual traditions of Islam. This in turn gives a more solid base to arrive at a contemporary reinterpretation that does justice to the problems and needs of our time.

Muslims who are staying in Europe also badly need a better knowledge of the continent where they have established themselves and of its history. Most immigrants and their descendants are hardly aware of the history of the particular country where they have settled and of the broad lines of the social and cultural history of Europe, beyond imperialism and colonization. This would be an incentive for engagement with certain cultural and intellectual achievements in Europe at the present time. For Europeans, too, a better knowledge of Europe and its history, beyond the histories of individual countries, is badly needed.

The ideal, however, would be to combine new knowledge of and reflection on Islam with the acquisition of a better knowledge of European cultural and intellectual traditions. This implies for the Muslim side, besides knowing their own past, a constructive learning from those "others" who are inheritors of the European past, to broaden their own outlook of the Muslim cultural heritage. This can and should lead to a growing awareness among students of future generations of new and old Europeans that a good part of Europe and of at least the Arab and Turkish world can be recognized and should be studied as part of one common history. The present-day "rediscovery" of each other, induced through the immigration and its ensuing contacts, can then be seen as a more or less logical sequence to an earlier common history in which the Mediterranean and then also the Balkans played a pivotal role.

This may lead, logically, to the common study by New and Old Europeans not only of past, but also of present-day features of the European and the Arab-Turkish worlds, actualized by the presence of the Arab and Turkish immigration in Europe. Then we will have a common study not only of the past, but also of the present and its weighty construction of new identities on the European-Muslim "green line". The presence of Muslim immigrants will then help put Europe and its immigrants in the broader social and cultural history and framework within which it has its place.

Selected Literature

1. Diversity of Islam in Europe (See also "Selected Literature" of Chapter 11)

ANSARI, Humayun, 'The Infidel Within': The History of Muslims in Britain, from 1800 to the Present, London: Hurst, 2003.

CESARI, Jocelyne, *Etre musulman en France: Associations, militants et mosquées*, Paris: Karthala, and Aix-en-Provence: IREMAM, 1994.

LEMMEN, Thomas, *Islamische Organisationen in Deutschland*, Bonn: Friedrich-Ebert-Stiftung, Juli 2000.

NIELSEN, Jörgen, *Muslims in Western Europe* (Islamic Surveys), Edinburgh: Edinburgh University Press, 1992, 1995^2.

2. Constructions and Visions of Islam in the West

BALIĆ, Smail, *Der Islam – Europakonform?* (Religionswissenschaftliche Studien 32), Würzburg: Echter, and Altenberge: Oros, 1994.

BOUBAKEUR, Dalil, *Charte du culte musulman en France: Présentation et commentaires*, Paris: Ed. du Rocher, 1995.

DASSETTO, Felice, *La construction de l'islam européen: Approche socio-anthropologique* (Musulmans d'Europe), Paris: L'Harmattan, 1996.

RAMADAN, Tariq, *Les musulmans dans la laïcité, responsabilités et droits des musulmans dans les sociétés occidentales*, Lyon: Tawhid, 1994, 1998^2.

—, *Islam, le face à face des civilisations: Quel projet pour quelle modernité?*, Lyon: Les deux Rives, 1995, 1998^2.

—, *Aux sources du renouveau musulman: Un siècle de réformisme islamique*, Paris: Bayard-Centurion, 1998.

—, *Muslims in France: The Way towards Coexistence*, Markfield, U. K.: The Islamic Foundation, 1999.

—, *To be a European Muslim: A Study of Islamic Sources in the European Context*, Markfield, U. K.: The Islamic Foundation, 1999/1420.

—, *Les musulmans d'Occident et l'avenir de l'Islam*, Paris: Sindbad/Actes Sud, 2003.

ROY, Olivier, *Vers un islam européen*, Paris: Esprit, 1999.

SARDAR, Ziauddin, *Islamic Futures: The Shape of Ideas to Come*, London and New York: Mansell, 1985.

Turkish Islam and Europe / Türkischer Islam und Europa: Europe and Christianity as Reflected in Turkish Muslim Discourse. Turkish Muslim Life in the Diaspora. Istanbul Workshop October 1996, ed. by Günter SEUFERT and Jacques WAARDENBURG (Beiruter Texte und Studien 82, Türkische Welten 6), Istanbul and Stuttgart: Franz Steiner, 1999.

Chapter 13

Muslims and Others in Europe: Cultural and Intercultural Contacts[1]

Speaking about Muslims and Islam at present in general and in Europe in particular presents a challenge. There has been and is a kind of mystification of Islam that must be clarified. Unfortunately, the concept of Islam itself, including the ways it is used by Muslims, has a broad spectrum of meanings. Moreover, nearly all present-day users of the term Islam take a position toward it. Nearly always, they want to express a particular conviction or convey a particular message—political, religious, or otherwise—associated with Islam. There has also been confusion about what Muslims are religiously and politically, what they are doing here, and their identity and deepest intentions. The conflicts and wars that have taken place between various European and Muslim peoples and the often complex situations in which Europeans have met Muslims unfortunately have lent themselves to ambiguities in their relationships. All of this needs to be clarified and the present text is meant to make a contribution to this.

1. Western Europe and Islam

What distinguishes Muslims in Western Europe from Muslims in other parts of the world?

The first and main characteristic is that the Muslims here come from various ethnic and national groups outside Europe. That is to say, nearly all Muslims in this part of Europe are immigrants or descendants of immigrants. As a consequence, these people can be visibly recognized as having come from abroad. Yet they cannot always be immediately identified as Muslims: Near Eastern Christians, for instance, have sometimes been treated as if they were Muslims.

---

[1]   This text is the elaboration of a paper read at a Symposium held at the Johann Wolfgang von Goethe University, Frankfurt on Main, June 15, 2002. The style of the oral presentation has been maintained and only a few footnotes have been added. See also Chapters 11 on "Muslims and Their Islam in Europe: Initiatives and Responses" and 12 on "Diversity and Unity of Islam in Europe: Islamic Constructs", with bibliographies.

A second significant feature is that the vast majority of these people belong here to socially deprived classes. Especially on the continent, nearly all of them arrived here as unskilled and sometimes illiterate workers and later as refugees and asylum seekers. When they were joined by wives and families, these came from the same social groups, economically dependent on the European labor market.

A third feature, at least on the European continent, is that nearly all of them have come from countries neighboring Europe, mostly the Mediterranean region: Turkey and North Africa. Even if Europeans feel themselves to be distant and tend to put forward the unique character of their part of the world, for the people concerned, the Muslim world and even the heartlands of Islam are not really too far away. Contacts with their countries of origin are relatively easy and family visits remain possible. No doubt these links guarantee a certain continuity of identity and certainly of Muslim identity.

A comparison with the United States is useful. Leaving aside the special situation of black Americans who were brought there as slaves, the USA also has an Islam based on largely post-World War Two immigration. But compared with the USA, Europe has not been very selective in its admission of Muslim or other immigrant workers. The USA has put much higher demands on its immigration, so that Muslim immigrants have only rarely come from unskilled backgrounds. They have actually included a considerable number of middle-class people, including a number of technicians. Moreover, whereas immigrants in Europe have very much had to find their place in the existing structures of society, in the USA, from the day of arrival, their independence and self-help abilities have been stressed. They could hardly count on social welfare measures. They have had to assimilate as quickly as possible. Becoming Americans, mostly belonging to the middle classes, and living at a greater distance from the countries of origin has encouraged them to develop a stronger sense of personal identity. They have not been treated as slaves or as a reservoir of cheap labor. It is only the follow-up of the events of September 11, 2001 that has led to suspicion at least of immigrants who came from certain Muslim countries. It meant insecurity for Muslims who could be suspected of terrorism.

Europe, however, is not a paradise for Muslims, either. European societies tend to stress their own identity, to which immigrants are expected to adapt themselves. Existing cultural and religious resistance to Islam has been increased by ethnic, social, and also political confrontations with Muslim groupings. This has had visible political consequences since the 1990s.

Once communism was no longer the enemy of the West, the idea arose in certain quarters that Islam could be considered—or should be used—

as such. The new Israeli-Palestine confrontation after the Oslo agreements has done a lot of harm, and the Western public has been confused by it. But already since the 1970s, the attitudes taken by most Western countries in nearly all conflicts in which Muslims have been involved have increasingly tended to identify Islam as such as a security risk. And there were arguments for it:

1) Muslims were involved in crucial conflicts: Palestine-Israel, Pakistan-India, Lebanon, Bosnia, Chechnya, Sudan, and elsewhere.

2) Muslim *jihād* fighters, and most recently al-Qā'ida, were active in Afghanistan, Northern Nigeria, the Philippines, and Indonesia.

3) Muslims in Europe itself could be recruited for terrorist activities, for instance in France.

4) Muslims questioning Christianity and rational secularism as the foundations of European civilization and attacking the West for its aggressive policies toward Muslim countries are ideologically subversive.

5) Muslim movements aiming at the establishment of Islamic states, following the example of Iran, proclaimed themselves a revolutionary force threatening existing balances of power, both nationally and internationally.

Whatever the immediate reasons, deeper causes, and existing ideological strategies, the image of Islam for Westerners became more negative.

Yet, to a number of better informed Europeans, Islam at the same time represents a positive value as a civilization and spirituality or simply as a human way of life. A number of native Europeans have become Muslims. This may have been mostly in connection with marriage, but sometimes also out of a need and desire to belong to a religion with clear communal rules and values. This could appeal to people living in a secular society governed by the laws of the market, not only in economic terms but also in terms of accepted values.

The extent to which Islam will change from a "foreign" to a "European" religion—though with a wide range of varieties—will largely depend on the degree of social and economic integration of Muslim immigrants and their descendants in European societies. Many factors are conditioning whether or not they will be socially marginalized or become an economic subproletariat. Islam as such has little to do with this. If a large part of them succeeds in integrating in society here—which should be a policy priority—their religion will reflect the fact.

But it is not only the economy that counts. As long as indigenous Europeans identify "Islam" as totally foreign, and as long as Muslims here identify "Europe" as being fundamentally opposed to Islam, serious problems will remain with the integration of Muslims in European societies. "Cultural" and "intercultural" communication, consequently, even simply understood as ways in which Muslim and non-Muslim people deal with each other, is a core problem of the integration of Muslim immigrants in Europe, with important consequences.

Something that adds to the existing confusion on this matter is the complex discourse that Europeans and Westerners generally articulate on Islam. In many cases, the decisive elements of ideological debates in European countries have little to do with Muslims and Islam as they are. The various images or views of Islam existing in Europe should actually be made a subject of research revealing the various political and other interests at the bottom of various Western interpretations of Islam that overemphasize its political aspects.

In contrast to this politicization of the image of Islam in the West, much more attention should be paid to its less politicized aspects as they occur in popular Muslim culture and religion or in the social history of Muslim societies, especially on a local level, as distinct from the broader, more schematized political history. There is a definite need to de-politicize Islam at the present time after the political views, just as there was a need to de-theologize Islam some decades ago after the missionary views. Unfortunately, the interest in impartial knowledge is limited at the present time. Yet, there is great need to obtain this to end an existing confusion.

On closer consideration, we can distinguish five types of current discourse on Islam, implying five different kinds of conceptualization:

1) Islam is seen as something definable; attention is focused on its facts and phenomena and on the contexts in which they appear. The aim here is to study and to arrive at a maximum of objective scholarly knowledge based on empirical data, rational deduction, and intellectual clarity. Islam is studied in terms of a clearly defined category in the Western sense of the word: for instance as a religion, as a social system, as a civilization, or as a regional or local culture.

2) Islam is seen as definable, but it is the speaker's ideas about Islam and the speaker's attitude toward Islam that are the center of attention. Here we have to do with fundamentally subjective views, appreciations, and judgments. They are based, however, on knowledge of the data and they are coherent. Here we are dealing with views of Islam from a particular standpoint, religious, moral, political, or otherwise.

3) Islam is not considered something clearly definable. On the contrary, it is seen as a largely unknown and even not quite knowable entity with religious, cultural, social, political, and other aspects. It is evaluated according to the perspective from which one looks at it (as a non-Muslim) or from which one bears witness to it (as a Muslim). In the end, however, it is admitted that Islam itself cannot be fully known. Still, attention is directed toward Islam as such, which remains the "intentional object" of the discourse. In a way, Islam is constructed here with the help of factual knowledge.

4) Islam is perceived as something basically diffuse, consisting of masses of items not necessarily related to each other. Such items are taken from different kinds of news reports, articles, speeches, and conversations, mostly communicated through the media. People have difficulty seeing coherence among the various items they "undergo" more or less passively. Yet, Islam is a subject of conversation and discussion without claims to offer new knowledge.

5) Islam itself is not really the focus of interest, but it serves to attract attention. The concept of Islam is used instead to create a movement of sympathy or antipathy, or to bring about a particular orientation, or to suggest a certain idea. The reasons for this use of Islam have hardly anything to do with "real" Islam or "real" Muslims. In the worst case, Islam is taken simply as a scapegoat onto which people can project their own negative ideas, feelings, or emotions. Here we have to do with constructions of Islam made in the service of other—mostly ideological—aims and purposes. Such strategic manipulations of the concept of Islam may be temporarily effective, but they can be unmasked by factual knowledge.

The use of the word "Muslims" in European discourse is not very clear either. In some cases, Muslim people are identified primarily by their country of origin, for instance as Turks, Moroccans, Pakistanis, etc. It is their country of origin, not their religious adherence, and their competence, job, social grouping, personality, etc., that are the focus of attention. This facilitates distinctions and promotes clarity.

In other cases, however, people are identified explicitly as "Muslims", especially if they do it themselves. If Europeans do this, it may imply stressing the difference between these people as a group in contrast, for instance, to Christians, secular people, progressive groups, and enlightened minds (*Aufgeklärte Geister*). This may imply a conscious or unconscious setting apart of the category of people called "Muslims"—as happens with the categorization of people as Jews. This is not without danger if the term "Islam" itself already evokes a negative echo. It also neglects the many differences that exist among individual Muslims or between so many groups of Muslim people. As in the case of Jews, speaking about Muslims in general leads to generalizations that can easily become stereotypes.

The study of the social history of concrete Muslim communities may be the best remedy against an over-accentuation of the "special" character of Muslims and of Islam.

2. Encounter with Muslims

If at one time Muslims and Islam were a faraway object of administration, study, and research, they have come now in direct relation with the European life-worlds, and Muslims have become residents and citizens here.

Looking back, one can see that intercultural communication with Muslims has taken very different forms in the course of the twentieth century.

It started as a communication between Europeans and mostly overseas countries at a geographical distance. These countries were discovered and evoked curiosity. They awakened interest and trade relations were established. Then they were ruled and Europeans developed a keen interest in peoples and mentalities, societies and cultures. Numerous encounters took place in the colonial settings, traces of which we have in documents and literature of the time. What were first directly or indirectly governed colonies (apart from Turkey, Iran, and Afghanistan) with Muslim populations then turned into newly independent Muslim nation states. Compared with the Europeans, the Muslim peoples concerned had a variety of very different cultural and religious backgrounds, though with Islam as a common framework. It was the differences from Europe that first struck the Europeans, and they responded in various ways to this fact. Most notably, it stimulated their interest in and their further study of the history of these other cultures and religions.

In a second stage, with the growing travel of Muslims to Western Europe, Europeans and Muslim newcomers met in the context of European countries. The first Muslims came with diplomatic missions, as honored visiting observers, and as traders. Already before World War One, students and other "learners" spent some years here. A number of Muslims did war service in the two World Wars, on both sides. Between the two World Wars, a certain number of distinguished Muslims spent time in Europe on invitation, as diplomats, establishing their own socio-cultural societies and clubs. In some European cities there were also mixed societies promoting cultural and social encounters between prominent Europeans and Muslims.

The third stage, mostly starting in the 1950s, was that of an increasing migration to Europe. Now the encounters by and large were not between intellectuals or representatives of what may be called high culture. They primarily involved mostly unskilled workers at the workplace and also people living in the same neighborhoods. It is certainly not true that the first generation of migrants had no culture. They brought with them elements of a living culture from their regions of origin. Strangely enough, most Europeans at the time, even from the middle and somewhat higher classes, hardly perceived this as culture, but brought it under a religious denominator: Islam.

For migrants, most of life in the new country consists by definition of inter-cultural communication. But in this case, it was at a rather low level, conditioned by the need for material and instinctive survival. There are few written reports by the migrants themselves, but it was here that the encounter between "Muslims and their Islam" and "Europeans and their Europe" started as a social story.

On reflection, however, the intercultural communication that Muslims experienced in Europe after World War Two has been very complex. There were not only numerous forms and degrees of communication of a more social or personal nature. There also arose communication with others than the established Europeans.

First, in Europe, Muslims have met on a broad scale fellow Muslims coming from different regions with very different cultures, for instance from Turkey, North Africa, and South Asia. There were great differences between them, but as Muslims they had their own "intercultural communication".

Second, many Southeastern European Muslims, like the Bosnians, and many Eastern European Muslims, like the Tatars, stayed after the conquest of their countries. Their destiny was different from that of the Spanish Muslims, who had to go. They can claim to be Europeans and to be themselves part of European culture in their "intercultural communication".

Third, a number of born Europeans have decided to become Muslims by their own choice. This reverses the sequence: here it is not Muslims who became Europeans, but Europeans who became Muslims. They can claim to belong to Western European culture while adhering to Islam as their religion.

Fourth, last but not least, among the immigrants there have not only been various orientations of members of the same first generation. Changes of orientation took place during the lifetime of individual or group immigrants after arrival and throughout the history of immigrant families. Important gaps have also arisen between the generations, depending largely on the extent to which younger people have participated in life in the new environment. There arose more conscious choices and possibilities of orientation. Within the families themselves, we can speak of "intercultural communication" between successive generations.

I shall limit myself here, however, to relations between Muslim immigrants and their descendants, on the one hand, and the native European populations, on the other hand. My point of departure here is the fundamental fact of distance and difference. Precisely in the more narrow field of culture, differences and distances express themselves more clearly to the extent that the people concerned are more themselves and more original. This is what makes intercultural communication interesting and relevant.

In this approach, we take Islam as a self-evident "universe of discourse" or "sign and signification system" in which Muslims find themselves and through which they communicate with each other. In given contexts, specific elements of this discourse or sign system will be chosen and emphasized. The basic research question then is how Muslims in particular contexts accentuate particular elements of their discourse or system and how they interpret and apply them.

3. Some Factual Data: The Variety of Muslims in Europe

For a first orientation, let me provide some factual data on Muslims in three major European countries: Britain, France, and Germany. Britain must have some 1.5 million Muslims, for the most part originally from South Asia. France has some 4.5 million Muslims, most of them originally from North Africa, but nowadays about half of them are French citizens. Germany has some 3 million Muslims, the majority of whom are from Turkey.

Muslims on the continent already show great ethnic and national, but also numerous cultural differences, depending on their countries, regions, and even towns and villages of origin. But also the various European states and societies where they have settled, the particular ideological, spiritual, and religious currents with which they identify, and the organizational Muslim frameworks in which they are part make for an astonishing variety of Muslims in Europe that prohibits easy generalizations. And I am still leaving aside their place on the social ladder, their economic status, and their possible political involvement. As I suggested earlier, there also is an ongoing differentiation among the second, third, and following generation of descendants of immigrants, in terms of subjective choices, individualization, and personalization. There are many reasons for this differentiation. Although much sociological research on immigrants has been carried out, many Muslim immigrants' underlying attitudes and ideas are still unknown. As a consequence, from a scholarly point of view, any attempt to forecast their practice, ideas, and attitudes toward Islam is risky.

There certainly is not one "European" Islam, unless if one wants to make a clear distinction between all those forms of Islam that can be found in the Middle East, Asia, Africa, and North America and forms of Islam that occur in Europe. It would be more precise to say that existing orientations and forms of Islam may acquire here a European style and that there are a few orientations and forms that cannot be found elsewhere. The expression "European Islam" often presupposes a certain model of what Europe is and what kind of Islam is most suitable to it. Whatever the social, political, or religious interests at work in generalizing a European Islam, it goes very much against the findings of concrete empirical research on the ways in which quite different Muslim groupings in quite different European countries give shape to their Islam.

It is precisely when Muslims themselves have hardly been studied and heard or listened to in their nearly infinite variety that general patterns and rules are constructed on a theoretical basis. I think that, from a scholarly point of view, too little is known yet about Muslim communities and individuals and about the ways they are articulating their Islam to allow such generalizations. At the moment, we need careful research on

Muslims and Muslim communities in their immense diversity, taken as actors in their own right in very different contexts and responding to very different forces.

4. Interaction and Communication

My starting point is the experience of both indigenous Europeans and Muslim immigrants with their descendants of encountering people who are clearly "other". For the first time, ordinary Europeans could experience the presence of "other", not quite white and sometimes rather black people, with other ways of life and other kinds of community building, based on other traditions. And also for the first time, ordinary people from countries south and east of the Mediterranean found themselves being dropped into towns and cities with "other", white or pinkish-grey people with their own individual way of life, in other kinds of societies based on rationalized rules of behavior, living in comfort and much concerned with material security and gain.

This experience was a confrontation of cultures on a very elementary level, of traditions of life that both parties had considered self-evident. In the past, such confrontations had taken place mostly in the colonies, and they have continued in what have been called the "Third World" countries. Now, however, they started to take place on an increasing scale on European soil, at "home".

The differences often drew more attention than the common elements and they demanded an explanation. On both sides, people tried to explain and rationalize the differences between Muslim immigrants and the European-born population. On both sides, a first attempt toward such a rationalization was made by a simple schematization reducing differences simply to the presence of Islam as the religion of the Muslims and to the social impact of that Islam on Muslim people and society. On the one hand there were the Muslims with Islam, on the other hand there were those without Islam: Christians, agnostics, secularists, and the rest.

This way of looking should be seen in a broader context. For centuries, not only Christians but also Europeans at large have been accustomed to identify other peoples by means of their religions, and the early descriptions of newly discovered peoples give large scope to their respective religions. In other words, the European view of other cultures tended to overestimate the place of religion in those cultures.[2] Muslim cultures could then all be subsumed under the common denominator "Islam".

---

[2]   Prof. Bert FRAGNER stressed this point in the general discussion. For a long time, Europe's view on the world outside has shown a holistic religious interest; in European views of other cultures, the religious moment has been too much stressed.

The use of Islam to "explain" differences between Muslim and Western societies or between the Christian or Western and another way of life is, however, a fallacy from a scholarly point of view. This is because, first, the concept of "Islam" itself is in fact an unknown entity for nearly everyone, even though many people think they know what it is. And one cannot explain one unknown thing by another unknown. Second, there are many factors other than Islam that condition Muslim ways of life and thought. One needs to know social life, cultural rules, and economic and political realities as they exist among other people and in other societies. Third, after the first chaotic experiences of people of different backgrounds meeting each other—or in fact being exposed to each other—reason claimed its place. One needs to study their interaction.

Interaction, however, is a complex matter. Earlier I said that we cannot know the attitudes Muslim immigrants in Europe may take in the near future. One of the main reasons is simply that we cannot foresee the complex kinds of interaction that can take place between the indigenous populations and the descendants of the immigrants. Whatever the ideals one may have of integration, empirically we have to do with a number of processes of negative and positive interaction that may vary from utter rejection to constructive cooperation. Many factors are at play.

Human communication in general is something unforeseeable.

First, paradoxically, human communication presupposes that the people concerned possess some kind of culture with human values, norms, etc. Communication between people without any culture or even any notion of culture is not human, as I see it, but comes down to biological interaction, like that of animals, or the technological interaction of robots.

Second, it is not so much the cultures to which people belong that determine what kind of communication can take place, but the people involved in that communication. Cultures only offer frameworks that give shape to communication and make communication more or less possible. One might say that they condition the way and the forms in which communication can take place. But the decisive element is whether or not the concrete people themselves intend to communicate with each other and how they use their culture for that purpose.

Third, in interaction between people, even within the same culture, communication may very well not take place. People may refuse it for one reason or another. There may also be particular external factors, beyond the will of those involved, that make communication difficult or impossible. Or individuals may simply be unable to sustain ordinary human communication with particular other people, or in a particular situation in which they find themselves, or through a more general indifference to other people beyond their own group or even simply beyond themselves as solitary beings.

It is not primarily a difference in culture (for instance Muslim or non-Muslim), as we have learned to think, but the very absence of interest in communicating altogether that fundamentally stands in the way of communication between, say, Europeans and Muslim immigrants. Lack of communication as well as a reduction of cultural diversity are features of modern societies.

Intercultural communication presents its own problems. As long as there is some culture at all and as long as there is a will to communicate, problems of intercultural communication are not insurmountable. The basic question that always returns is: do you want or don't you want to communicate? Problems then should not be impossible to solve, at least on the level of behavior.

The main problem then remains: how to handle obvious differences. This is foremost a practical problem. Another problem is the experience of difference. This requires some kind of reflection.

5. Some Examples

Let us examine some elementary practical cases of communication between Muslims and others. The simplest case is probably what takes place between and around young children of different cultural backgrounds. One may think of mothers or fathers bringing small children to a playground or making a common effort to establish one for Muslim and other children. Or of Muslim and other children in a school class, playing or not playing with each other, with technicalities for Muslim girls involving swimming, gymnastic lessons, or wearing headscarves. Since all children have to go to school anyway, interaction takes place and is natural.

Another case is that of lodging and housing. Can Muslim families find housing in non-Muslim town quarters if they are able to pay the rents there, or is there discrimination consisting in not offering housing or renting apartments to Muslim immigrants? Do Muslim inhabitants participate in the social life of the street, the town quarter, or the village, and if not: why not? Are there quarters that are inhabited in practice by "foreigners" only, so that cultural communication with the native inhabitants can hardly take place in daily life?

The third case concerns the work situation in the private or public sphere. Muslims may ask for facilities to perform their prayers, especially the *salāt* on Fridays, or for a day off on religious holidays. Muslim women may expect to wear a certain attire and a headscarf. But there may be farther-reaching problems: whether Muslims are accepted for a particular job like others, how relations develop between Muslims and other staff or workers, or cases of discrimination or straightforward avoidance.

The fourth case is social life. Do Muslims and others participate in activities meant for particular social aims and purposes, for instance to solve a problem in the town quarter, to improve the life situation of a particular group of people, or to solve a specific common problem? Are there contacts in leisure time for sports, certain hobbies, even travel?

The fifth and last case is that of relations between the sexes and of family life. To what extent are people here open to people from another culture if these people have remarkable qualities? One extreme is when a future bride is simply chosen for a young man she does not know and brought to him from the country of origin. In this case, families remain irrevocably bound to the local culture of the country of origin. Or there may be a prohibition against meetings with men and women who are not all Muslims, which makes intercultural communication impossible. The other extreme is when youngsters' adventures or escapes in intercultural communication end in marriages—and perhaps conversions—that may finally end in disillusionment and divorce. Between both, the possibility may exist of friendship, and marriage with prudence may be accepted. In practice, especially practicing Muslim families in Europe are less open to intercultural communication than secular ones are. They may have many reasons for this, including a fear of possible non-Muslim suitors. It should not be forgotten, however, that Orthodox Jewish, Hindu, and until well into the twentieth century, Catholic, Protestant, and Orthodox families were closed to this as well. And it is not only daughters but also sons who are victims of a lack of intercultural communication in present-day urban life.

On a social level, indeed, such intercultural communication is often needed simply to make life possible or bearable at all. Consider issues such as permissions to establish a mosque or even a prayer hall in the neighborhood, the acceptance of celebrations in the evenings during Ramadān and at Islamic feasts, some official release from work during Ramadān, provisions for places for Muslims at public cemeteries, for Islamic slaughtering, etc. All this needs negotiation, one of the most down-to-earth forms of intercultural communication.

Often, however, there are obstructions and problems. Already in daily life, intercultural communication is not always evident or even admitted. Certain factors or attitudes can make it difficult or even impossible. The former *pieds noirs*'s contempt for Arabs in Southern France or racist attitudes toward non-white communities in British towns may be extreme cases, but they lend themselves to destructive political exploitation. In most cases, social pressure exists on the part of both indigenous and immigrant people to cling to separation or at least distance and to keep interaction within strict limits. It then requires energetic youngsters or resolute public figures to break through the "*Wurst* curtain".

Women may be the breaking point in intercultural communication when they are forbidden to participate in it, which they often are, including in Europe. European women who converted to Islam can play an important role here. Muslim women of immigrant origin are much less equipped to play such an "intercultural communicative" role. Most of them are very much bound to the Muslim community and family and stand under social control in their relations with men in general and non-Muslim men in particular.

A chronic disadvantage for Muslim immigrants in their communication with native Europeans is the fact of social inequality, specifically inequality in social status. Apart from existing prejudices and awkwardness, this is often due to unequal education opportunities and consequently a less advantageous position in the competition for jobs or for promotion.

The media play a role in promoting or hindering intercultural communication. Programs differ. In general, however, whatever their intentions, like political and religious quarters, they tend to construct and maintain the idea of an "Islam" that is as such opposed to modernity, Western values, and Western forms of modernity. Ordinary Muslim men and women, their lives, cares, and small joys are still rarely seen on the TV screen. It would be good to present them in a natural form of "intercultural communication" with non-Muslim Europeans.

European societies, however, present their problems too. When people distance themselves from immigrants by moving to the political right, this implies in practice the demise of intercultural communication, not only individually but also socially. This can take many forms. Here we are not necessarily dealing with real animosity, like that expressed in the molestation of colored foreigners, skinheads' violent behavior, or a revival of national socialist symbolism and ideology. Often we rather have to do with forms of avoidance. Where are those distinct circles that hate foreigners in general or just Muslim immigrants and their descendants in particular?

My guess is that in many cases of anti-immigrant behavior there is a diffuse kind of alienation, a loss of certain elementary feelings of human life, largely due to a decrease in the feeling of security and a decline in what may be called the human livability of modern and post-modern society. Is this not a kind of negative attitude that may be directed toward anything that is felt to be "other" and threatening? It emerges when the warmth goes out of people's relations with their fellow beings. It hints at a certain disintegration—if not collapse—of the substance of modern society itself and a corresponding atomization and feeling of solitude of individuals. Immigrants who arrive in such a society have bad luck.

As always, the best remedy seems to be to return to lived realities and the daily practice of human relations. There is a new Dutch weekly *Contrast* on intercultural communication in the Netherlands. It gives lots of information and openly discusses happenings of all kinds between indigenous Dutch people and descendants of migrants. Instead of announcing conflicts and insoluble problems, the media should rather report on issues of daily life. They could discuss solutions to ordinary difficulties emerging between indigenous and non-indigenous groups of people, without romanticizing the ones or demonizing the others and without applying established schemes. People should be encouraged to face up to the critical reality of human relationships in general and their own relations in particular and to learn to distinguish between what is possible, what may become possible, and what is impossible.

A primary demand for intercultural relations in daily practice is to be or sit together and to discover the reactions and responses of the other side. There should be occasion for open discussion between non-Muslims and Muslims who develop their own solidarities and develop their own ideas. And such discussion should be between equals, on a personal, social, and organizational level. What the *Körber Stiftung* in Hamburg does for exchanges between younger German and Turkish intellectuals should inspire other groups, institutions, and foundations to take similar initiatives.[3]

Intercultural communication is one of the possibilities of interaction between old and new Europeans. It can take place on various levels: on an individual level between persons of different cultural backgrounds, on a social level within given collectivities and between various groups, and on an organizational level in the framework of existing or newly created institutions. Things cultural are a subtle instrument of communication.

6. Some Conditions for Integration

For some twenty years we have heard the call for migrants to be integrated into European societies. The subject has given rise to much discussion and a rich literature, especially in Western Europe. I must leave this for what it is and restrict myself to some practical and other conditions for an economic, social, and to some extent cultural integration of Muslims who settled down in European societies. It is not meant as a list of pious wishes, but as a list of things that I see as absolute preconditions for a "normal" integration of immigrants once they have been admitted under whatever title in West European societies.

---

[3]   See the interesting texts of the important German-Turkish Symposia organized by the *Körber Foundation* in Hamburg, published in both German and Turkish. Some of the titles are *Religion – ein deutsch-türkisches Tabu?* (1997), *Was ist ein Deutscher? Was ist ein Türke?* (1998), *Grenzfall Europa* (1999), *Perspektiven der Zivilgesellschaft* (2001). Cf. Chapter 19 on "Muslims and Westerners: Changing Attitudes" (see below pp. 497, note 3). Similar initiatives should be taken elsewhere too.

1) *Work*. It should be properly paid, there should be proper working conditions, and proper social security should also be assured in case of loss of work.

2) *Legal status*. It should be clear under which title people have been admitted and what the conditions were for admission. Improvement of legal status ought to be possible. People who were not regularly admitted should not indiscriminately be sent back and they should be properly treated.

3) *Naturalization*. This is more than the acquisition of citizenship of one particular European state; it also implies obtaining the status of a European.

4) *Language*. Obtaining sufficient knowledge of the language should be a condition for receiving a certain legal status.

5) *Civil society*. Basic instruction should be given about the organization of society and the state and about the ways in which society and state function in practice. The laws and rules valid for residents in the country and the civil behavior expected from them should be clarified.

6) *Education*. People should be encouraged to obtain as much education as is possible for them, with special encouragement of further studies for the more intellectually gifted.

7) *Social participation*. Active participation in social institutions should be encouraged, thus developing a sense of responsibility toward society at large. Forms of discrimination, apartheid, and the formation of ghettos should be fought against in civil society and by legislation.

8) *Interaction*. Private and other efforts should be made to promote interaction between native people and immigrants through meeting groups, common courses, commitment to human causes, etc.

9) *Religion*. The religions of immigrants as well as native people should be respected and any aggressive politicization of these religions should be resisted.

10) *Indigenous Europeans*. People should be informed about the arrival of immigrants and their culture, so that mentalities can change. The ideas of constituting a homogeneous society and of a certain self-satisfaction or purity should be relativized. It is precisely these ideas that lead to feelings of being threatened by foreigners and corresponding fears and anguish. Attitudes of distance and superiority toward Muslim immigrants and Islam in general should be combated. People should come to accept others and be called to action, communication, and responsible initiatives. Courses of continued education, working groups, and meeting places can be created. People should be made attentive to Muslims' sensitive issues, their religion and culture, and their kinship and family and they may come to see themselves as being in charge of guests from abroad. The presence of Muslim Europeans should be accepted, in the first place by Christian leadership. On both sides, there is a need for communicative capabilities, acceptance, and appreciation of the others.

Beyond daily life practice, there are also conditions for integration and intercultural communication that go deeper. On the European side, for instance, I see the following five points:

1) Acceptance of the fact that Europe is now no longer as Europeans once learned and thought it was. Europe itself is going through profound transformations that would still be taking place if there were no immigrants from outside. Western Europeans must accustom themselves to the idea that Eastern Europeans as well as immigrants admitted from outside Europe have become intrinsically part of Europe.

2) Revision of certain idealized images of European culture modeled on the past of specific European nations or of Europe as a whole. It is true that certain human values now held to be universal were formulated in Europe. However, the values that are to be lived now need to be discovered and discussed anew by each generation. They should be made clear at school and in the media and be clarified to new generations of both old and new Europeans.

3) The various socio-political views and possible options concerning life in European societies should be discussed by born Europeans, and immigrants should be invited to pose questions and participate. They should be sure that they can stay in Europe. Native Europeans should be familiarized with the prospect of Muslim Europeans. All of this will enhance common deliberation on the future of societies and social and political life in Europe.

4) The "Neo-Europeans" can be asked to contribute here their human experience and to articulate human values on the basis of their own traditions, so that life in Europe can be enriched. Asian, African, and Middle Eastern societies' and cultures' values concerning human relations, warmth, and imagination as well as spiritual orientations should be welcomed.

5) The key term for relations between Europeans and others living inside or outside Europe is dialogue. Though being part of what is commonly called "the West", Europe distinguishes itself from other components of the Western part of the world by opting for a constructive cooperation and dialogue with the non-Western including the Muslim part of the world.

Integration of people in new societies and communities is closely linked to a capacity for changing one's self-identification and of distinguishing one's self-identification in a given social context and one's deeper identity. Only after having identified oneself, that is delimiting oneself, do possibilities of dialogue and intercultural communication open up. Numerous instances in and outside the immigrant community are at work to orient and polish a migrant's identity. European societies tend to appreciate self-identification as a positive choice and personal act.

7. Wider Perspectives

Apart from the "reconquests" against the Moors in Spain, the Tatars in Russia, and the Turks in the Balkans, until the mid-twentieth century major cultural encounters and clashes took place outside Europe with the expansion of Western civilization. The arrival of Muslim workers in Europe implies a rather new and large-scale cultural encounter in the continent, in a peaceful way this time. It would be a nightmare if the arrival of some ten million people from outside had been accompanied by the same superior military force with which Europe established its colonies.

In any case, the impact of the newcomers has been tangible in quite a few nervous reactions in certain European groups. The reasons are different, such as the confrontation with foreigners with a different way of life, collective memories of invading Arab or Turkish armies or revolts in the colonies, the association of Islam with violence, or half-conscious feelings of insecurity in a continent emerging from the Cold War. Or on a deeper level, the very presence of Muslims and Islam brings to light certain social and cultural assumptions of existing European culture itself. In some cases there is even a certain feeling of helplessness in view of the religious dimension of the Muslim immigration. If I read the signs correctly, we are dealing with a case of intercultural encounter in Europe as a result of one of the large worldwide migration processes that have been going on in the last decades.

When we look at it in this way, the notion of intercultural communication, for instance between born Europeans and Muslim immigrants, appears in a wider perspective. Such communication is more than a matter of more or less haphazard encounters between persons or groups of different cultural backgrounds. It implies encounters between groups, peoples, collectivities involving deeper issues. Some intellectuals, artists, and writers who have gone beyond the confines of the lifestyles of their own local Western or other cultures are more conscious of this.

One thing we need is a wider and much more critical awareness of history to situate the present situation properly. In Europe, the radical ruptures of the two World Wars and the subsequent Cold War, with their confrontation of ideological extremisms, still weigh heavily. Somewhat earlier, we had a period of European domination of a large part of the world, which is still alive in the Muslim collective memory.

There are, however, surprising examples of positive intercultural communication in history. The early humanists still recognized their indebtedness to Arab thought and science, but in the fifteenth century Europe cut the umbilical cord with Arab culture and concentrated on its Greek and Roman cultural roots. At the beginning of the sixteenth century, the Ottoman Turks occupied most of the Arab world, which increased its distance from Europe.

Since the mid-nineteenth century and up to World War Two, however, a number of Muslim intellectuals in the Middle East and South Asia were open to contemporary European culture and wanted to learn from it. However, such a dependence could hardly be reconciled with the rise of nationalist and Islamist ideologies of resolute independence. The two sides seemed to be aware that they owed much to each other, but they refused to further accept the other's domination, Spain and Western Europe from 1492 on, the Balkans in the nineteenth century, and most of the Muslim world roughly since 1945.

We need more comprehensive studies and presentations of so much common history—including cultural history—of the European and Muslim worlds extending to India and Indonesia, Central Asia and Central Africa. This broader perspective is particularly necessary concerning the Mediterranean region, at the crossroads of Europe, Asia, and Africa. Whereas Scandinavia and Iran, Germany and the Arabian Peninsula may have little history in common, the three sides of the Mediterranean have had tangible trade relations. They have certain social patterns, cultural features, and particular sensitivities in common up to the present time. Here first European domination and then the Israeli-Arab conflict have caused ruptures from which all sides suffer at present.

We should also see the so-called Euro-Arab dialogue initiatives in this same wider perspective. They witness to a growing need and desire for intercultural communication, including in umbrella bodies such as the Council of Europe, the Arab League, and the European Union. The German President at the time, Roman Herzog, even organized a meeting between cultural representatives of European and Muslim countries, including such faraway ones as Malaysia, in Berlin in April 1999. Whatever their further political and economic aims may have been, these dialogues wanted to foster durable intercultural communication between creative and motivated cultural elites on both sides. Initiatives of this kind had already been taken by several European countries individually.

Initiatives for Christian-Muslim dialogue on a local or an international, a personal or an institutional level can be seen from the same perspective. Whatever their further religious and ethical aims may have been, they have contributed to intercultural communication. However, more than "intercultural" communication, the "interreligious" one addresses more permanent norms, values and ideals, so that it only can bear fruit mostly over an even longer period.

No need to say that, besides these organized efforts of top-level dialogue, many other intercultural dialogue situations have arisen as a result of increased large-scale migrations. We can speak there of a "dialogue of life" between Muslims and non-Muslim Westerners.

The very fact that both parties are reaching out beyond the all too fixed boundaries of a given culture or given religion and are searching for communication with "other" people is significant. It unlocks resources of thought and feeling on one side that encourage the other party to rise in its turn above the self-sufficiency of closed cultural borders or the defense of its own righteousness. It also mitigates the distrust, if not worse, of a party that tended to be seen as a potential enemy.

8. Forces Standing in the Way of Intercultural Communication

Besides the concrete factors that I indicated earlier and that hamper open communication between Muslim immigrants and native Europeans, there are also broader forces that stand in the way and that can block personal initiatives. I would like to mention two of them here.

First, the immigrants continue to have links with their countries of origin. These provide not only family and other personal relations but also a lifestyle and social orientation. Modern means of communication keep such links alive more easily than was formerly possible. Migrants find themselves culturally in a limbo between the society where they live, on the one hand, and the culture from which they stem, on the other. The links with the countries of origin are not only on a personal or family level. Collective experiences and memories with religious connotations can have a tremendous impact, maintaining solidarities and mobilizing people for particular causes. Well-organized official directives and appeals from Ankara have their impact on Turkish emigrants abroad.

Second, tension is growing between the poorer Southern and the richer Northern countries. Although basically of an economic nature, it has increasingly become a political tension as well, especially since the Iranian revolution, the Gulf War, and the events since September 11, 2001. Not only is the economic contrast developing into political opposition with ideological aspects in the Islam-and-the-West debate. Also the idea of a confrontation with Islam, as is alive in certain American circles, and of using violence indiscriminately to solve problems cannot but increase tension. Europe has nothing to gain by sustaining tensions with its immigrants or with the rest of the world. Willingness to engage in dialogue and using the bridge of intercultural communication with Muslims and others on a world scale are more reliable than the use of power, certainly in the long run.

An illustration in recent history is what has happened since 1990. After the Cold War—as at the end of any large war—expectations for a European-Muslim rapprochement were high, at least on the Muslim side. Yet they have not been fulfilled. I would like to mention only three possible reasons for this, taking the ascent of the USA for granted.

First, on an ideological level, Islamist ideologies that see a secular West as a danger to Islam and European rightist movements that reject further immigration both claim to defend the deeper identity of the respective sides. Such rightist movements reject Islam as an outdated religion, whereas leftist movements reject it as an outdated socio-religious system. Both tend to be closed to open intercultural communication with Muslims.

Second, on a socio-political level, Europe finds itself in a process of far-reaching transformations of society, with an open market economy and a reorganization and extension of the European Union. The continent has become very much concerned with itself and is hesitant to engage in intercultural communication that could intellectually question its foundations.

Third, on an economic level, to the extent that Europe is afraid of the possible consequences of the demographic vitality and poverty of the countries surrounding it, the process of its self-enclosure tends to reinforce itself. The Muslim minorities living in Europe may be viewed largely as a kind of reserve labor force. Intercultural communication with the Muslim world will then be seen as a necessary by-product of the needed political and economic relations, but not as an aim valid in itself. It might even lead to a criticism of the way Europe was constructed in the past and is being constructed at present.

9. The Future of Europe

The future of the European Union implies the incorporation of a large part of Eastern Europe, the need for qualified immigrants from outside Europe, and the presence of a significant percentage of Muslims from different countries among its citizens. Our vision of present-day Europe depends to a large extent on our vision of the future. This future will of course be conditioned by a great number of factors. Among them is the presence of Muslims inside and around Europe.

The integration and place of Muslim minorities in Europe, consequently, needs to be seen in connection with Europe's relationships with the Muslim countries surrounding it, in particular with Turkey and the Arab countries around the Mediterranean. In principle, of course, the situation of Muslim minorities in Europe largely depends on the attitudes these people themselves take toward Europe.

Europe needs more than oil from the Middle East, for example the contributions of individuals in the domain of technology, of experts and intellectuals doing research and teaching at scholarly institutions, of businessmen and craftsmen. I also think of the workers in the exotic restaurants, some offering Muslim cuisine, that have emerged in Western Europe during the last half a century. Many people coming from Muslim cultures evoke a different style of life: of people who take time, spread conviviality, and orient themselves through friendships and affectionate relationships. In brief, a lifestyle characterized by warmth.

The pivotal question, then, is the direction in which we have to go to reach a future of more intercultural communication. I do not mean this in the political sense of a more liberal or a more welfare type of state, or in the economic sense of a free market or a planned economy, but rather in the social sense: the kind of society we are striving for, a civil society respecting human rights.

Such a society can be realized on the basis of norms and values that were born and developed from within European experiences. It can be held up to societies surrounding Europe, including the Muslim ones, without being linked politically to any religion in particular.

Open to intercultural communication, such a society could also condition a European response to the present world situation that has an increasingly negative impact on intercultural communication. Muslims are involved in this.

If I understand correctly, the situation changed some ten years ago with the Gulf War and its sequence. The attack of September 11, 2001 can well be seen as an extremist response to growing arrogance. The USA considered itself under attack and declared war, without repositioning itself, however, in the world of nations as it did when Iraq occupied Kuwait in August 1990. Declaring war against an undefined crime of "terrorism" and using brute force as an anti-terror device becomes, however, itself a form of terror. The resulting atmosphere of fears is perhaps the greatest threat to normal human communication, including intercultural communication. In contrast to this, Europe has nothing to gain in constructing a conflict with "Islam"; on the contrary. Relations between the richer North and the poorer South, between Western and Muslim countries, and of course between Christians and Muslims are long-term problems and it is of the utmost importance for Europe to face them squarely. But economic domination would be as poor a solution at the present time as political domination was in colonial times. We need deliberation, dialogue, and common decisions instead.

As I see it, intercultural communication, whether with Muslim and other people in Europe or with Muslim and other people outside Europe, goes beyond the exchange of museum pieces or diplomatic speeches. It implies a willingness to learn from others, which by the way is also an underlying intention in Islamic studies.

Being prepared to learn from the other makes intercultural communication a form of culture itself. It distinguishes itself by an attitude of respect for the other rather than by the will to control or dominate him or her, which is in the end itself a form of barbarism.

So I make a plea for interaction, communication, and intercultural communication in the case of Muslims too, whether they are living in or outside Europe. Maybe Muslim Neo-Europeans will contribute to culture in a future Europe; there is no reason to deny this possibility. But then they will have to study Europe and to know it. If we in turn are prepared to learn from Muslims and their culture—past and present, outside Europe and in Europe—we may arrive not only at an *inter*cultural but at an even more mutually enriching *cultural* communication.

Selected Literature

1. Interaction, Communication

GRAF, Peter, and Peter ANTES, *Strukturen des Dialogs mit Muslimen in Europa* (Europäische Bildung im Dialog: Region – Sprache – Identität 6), Frankfurt on Main: Peter Lang, 1998.

HEINE, Peter, *Kulturknigge für Nichtmuslime: Ein Ratgeber für alle Bereiche des Alltags*, Freiburg, etc.: Herder, 1994, 1996[2].

ROHE, Mathias, *Der Islam – Alltagskonflikte und Lösungen: Rechtliche Perspektiven*, Freiburg, etc.: Herder, 2001.

SCHOEN, Ulrich, *Bi-Identität: Zweisprachigkeit, Bi-Religiosität, doppelte Staatsbürgerschaft*. Vorwort Annemarie Schimmel, Zurich and Düsseldorf: Walter, 1996.

2. Problems of Organization and Participation in European Societies

The Integration of Islam and Hinduism in Western Europe, ed. by Wasif A. R. SHADID and Pieter Sjoerd van KONINGSVELD, Kampen: Kok Pharos, 1991.

Muslims in the Margin: Political Responses to the Presence of Islam in Western Europe, ed. by Wasif A. R. SHADID and Pieter Sjoerd van KONINGSVELD, Kampen: Kok Pharos, 1996.

Political Participation and Identities of Muslims in non-Muslim States, ed. by Wasif A. R. SHADID and Pieter Sjoerd van KONINGSVELD, Kampen: Kok Pharos, 1996.

Religious Freedom and the Position of Islam in Western Europe: Opportunities and Obstacles in the Acquisition of Equal Rights, ed. by Wasif A. R. SHADID and Pieter Sjoerd van KONINGSVELD, Kampen: Kok Pharos, 1995.

Section 5

Muslim-Christian Relations and Minority Problems

Chapter 14
Muslim Minorities:
Politics and Religion in the Balkans[1]

Introduction

The Balkans have had a turbulent history, with peoples invading from outside and various peoples inside struggling for survival. But they have also witnessed several civilizations with a variety of cultural and religious expressions, from Romania to Albania, from Neolithic times up to the present day. Alexander the Great (356–323 B.C.) was a Macedonian king. For the Greeks, however, and later the Romans and the Byzantines, the Balkans were primarily a region from whence barbarian invaders could rise and which therefore had to be kept under control as much as possible. The Slavs, for instance, who now constitute the majority of the population, arrived from the sixth century on, pushing aside older peoples living there, like the Albanians. Most of the region was converted to Christianity by the Orthodox Church from Constantinople and in the northwest and along the Adriatic coast by the Catholic Church from

---

[1] This text is a somewhat extended version of the article "Politics and Religion in the Balkans" which appeared in *Islamic Studies* (Islamabad), 36, Nrs. 2/3 (Summer/Autumn 1997/1418), pp. 383–402.
   Literature in English on Islam in the Balkans in general is rather limited. The following publications may be mentioned here. Zacharin T. IRVIN, "The Fate of Islam in the Balkans: A Comparison of Four New State Policies", in *Religion and Nationalism in Soviet and East European Politics*, ed. by Pedro RAMET (Durham, N. C.: Duke University Press, 1984), pp. 207–25; *Islam in the Balkans: Symposium on Islam*, ed. by Jennifer SCARCE, Edinburgh: Royal Scottish Museum, 1979; *Muslim Communities in the New Europe*, especially pp. 1–163; Harry Thirlwall NORRIS, *Islam in the Balkans: Religion and Society between Europe and the Arab World*, London: Hurst, 1993; Hugh POULTON, *Minorities in the Balkans* (The Minority Rights Group Report 82), London: Minority Rights Groups, October 1989; 1993[2] under the title *The Balkans: Minorities and States in Conflict*; Wayne S. VUCINICH, "Islam in the Balkans", in *Religion in the Middle East*, ed. by Arthur John ARBERRY, Vol. 2: *Islam* (Cambridge: Cambridge University Press, 1969), pp. 236–52. A valuable reference work in French is Alexandre POPOVIC, *L'Islam balkanique: Les musulmans du sud-est européen dans la période post-ottomane*, Wiesbaden: O. Harrassowitz, 1986. See by the same author *Les musulmans yougoslaves (1945–1989): Médiateurs et métaphores*, Lausanne: L'Age d'Homme, 1990.

Rome. Bosnia acquired a political status under Ban Kulin (1180–1204). Under his reign and later, groups like the "dualist" Bogomils, who were persecuted elsewhere, found refuge in the Bosnian mountain area, which was almost impenetrable to regular armies. Here they established their own "Bosnian Church", which existed until the Ottoman conquest in the fifteenth century.

It was only the later Ottoman Turkish conquest that brought a complete pacification of the Balkans. Bosnia came under Ottoman rule in 1463, after which it was largely islamicized, starting with Eastern Bosnia; Hercegovina was conquered in 1482. The glorious time of Muslim Bosnia was the sixteenth and seventeenth centuries, which saw important economic activity and a high culture; most Bosnian towns date from this period. The majority of the Albanians, too, converted to Islam, as did groups of other indigenous people, such as the Pomaks in present-day Bulgaria.

After the withdrawal of the Ottoman Turks, the Balkans again became a conflict-ridden area of independent states. Austria with Hungary occupied Croatia, Hercegovina, and Bosnia until their defeat in World War One. In the nineteenth century, Western European travelers considered Balkan territory, even after the independence of certain Christian nations, already as part of "the Orient".

In the twentieth century, the Balkans experienced frightful times. World War One started with the events in Sarajevo in 1914 and plunged the region into battle. In 1918, Austria and Hungary had to withdraw from Croatia, Hercegovina, and Bosnia. Yugoslavia was created, consisting of peoples with different ethnic and religious identities. World War Two witnessed fighting and massacres, even of civilians, in Yugoslavia. The Balkans were temporarily disciplined by the iron hands of the Communist regimes between 1944 and 1989. Between 1991 and 1995, again ferocious killings, violations, and "ethnic cleansings" of innocent peoples were committed in Bosnia and elsewhere. Kosovo followed.

1. From Ottoman Times to the End of World War Two

On the whole, Turkish Ottoman rule from the fourteenth century on did not impose Islam on Orthodox and Catholic Christians. They were taxed, however, with the *jizya* and until the eighteenth century were required to hand over young boys as *devshirme* to the state; these boys converted to Islam and served the state later as Janissaries or in other capacities. As mentioned before, a number of local Christians converted for various reasons, partly to improve their social and economic status, partly because they were attracted by the spirituality of the dervish orders. The situation of the non-Muslims was regulated by the *millet* system. It grew worse, however, when this system no longer applied correctly as the state declined from the end of the sixteenth century on and state officials and especially tax farmers became increasingly corrupt—and also because of the continuous wars.

Since the middle of the seventeenth century, and in particular after their defeat before the walls of Vienna in 1683, the Ottomans were slowly driven back by the Austrians and later by the Russians. One can speak of a gradual "reconquista" of the Balkans from the end of the seventeenth century until the beginning of World War One, comparable to the reconquista of Spain from the middle of the eleventh to the end of the fifteenth century and a similar "reconquista" of Russia from the fifteenth to the middle of the eighteenth century. In general, the majority of Slavic and other Muslims left the lost territories together with the Turks; those who remained were converted to Christianity, with the exception of the groups mentioned earlier.

The Balkan Christians used to call all Muslims "Turks", which already shows the close relation between politics and religion in the perceptions of the time. Bosnia was conquered together with Croatia and Hercegovina by the Austro-Hungarians in 1878 and annexed to the Habsburg Empire in 1908. The first Austro-Hungarian census, of 1879, showed a presence of 39 % Muslims, 42 % Orthodox Christians, and 18.5 % Catholic Christians within the borders at the time.[2] According to a previous Ottoman census (1287 H.), there had been nearly 50 % Muslims in Bosnia in 1870. Many Muslims left after the Austro-Hungarian occupation in 1878.[3]

The wars against the Ottoman Turks were waged not only by the Austrians, Hungarians, and Russians, but also by the Balkan peoples themselves in what they called their wars of independence. Significantly, the Bosnians did not conduct such a war, for their country was simply occupied by Austria. As in the reconquista of Spain, these wars of independence were conducted on a popular level through an ideological offensive in which the Churches played an important role. The Roman Catholic Church played its part in the wars in Slovenia and Croatia, and the Orthodox Church in the wars in Greece, Serbia, and Bulgaria. Especially in Greece and Serbia, Orthodox Christianity became a focus for political nationalist assertion in the first half of the nineteenth century.

---

[2] Alexander LOPASIC, "The Muslims of Bosnia", in *Muslim Communities in the New Europe*, pp. 99–114 (= chapter 5), here p. 102. This article gives a useful summary of the history of the Muslims in Bosnia. On Islam in Bosnia, see also the following books in English: Robert J. DONIA, *Islam under the Double Eagle: The Muslims of Bosnia and Herzegovina, 1878–1914*, New York: Columbia University Press, 1981; FRIEDMAN, *The Bosnian Muslims*; and *The Muslims of Bosnia-Herzegovina*. A standard work in German is BALIĆ, *Das unbekannte Bosnien*.

[3] See Justin MCCARTHY, "Ottoman Bosnia, 1800 to 1878", in *The Muslims of Bosnia-Herzegovina*, pp. 54–83.

Two and a half centuries of warfare by Balkan peoples against the Ottoman Empire have resulted not only in hatred of the Turks as military and administrative oppressors, but also in a deep aversion to Islam, which is considered evil. This aversion to Islam has found expression in mythological terms. The Orthodox past of pre-Ottoman times has been hailed as a period of purity, and the struggle against the Turks has been depicted as a struggle between Orthodoxy and Islam, viewed as the forces of good and evil respectively. Besides this mythical representation of struggle, ideas have also developed of the blessed election of the Christian peoples and their glorious superiority to the Turks and Muslims in general.

No doubt such representations are, to a large extent, a reaction to the frustrations of what are felt to have been centuries of oppression and persecution. We have here a clear example of how religion has played an important political role and has been inextricably bound up with nationalist feelings and ideology. This was the case on the Christian, but probably also on the Turkish Muslim side, certainly in the Greek-Turkish war of 1821–33 and in the Cyprus conflict. But nationalist ideologies and conflicts between Christian peoples themselves, in particular between Orthodox and Catholics, could also be supported by the absolutization of denominational differences. This has played an important role in the conflicts between Orthodox Serbs and Catholic Croats, which people are prone to ascribe to denominational difference to the present day. These conflicts, however, have profound historical, ethnic, and economic roots in addition to their religious dimension.

In any case, in the consciousness of all the Balkan peoples, their own real history, apart from prehistoric beginnings and a medieval religious period, starts with the demise of the Ottoman Turks, different peoples reckoning from different dates. The rough historical order in which independence was obtained is as follows:

Hungary 1683–97
Dalmatia 1683–1718
Slovenia 1686–1718
Montenegro around 1707–9
Romania (Banat) 1716
Greece 1821–33
Serbia 1804–42 and 1858–67
Hercegovina 1875–8 (independent from the Ottoman Empire)
Bosnia-Hercegovina 1918 (independent from the Austrian Empire)
Bulgaria 1876–8
Albania 1912

After these regions were conquered by Austria-Hungaria or attained independence, they generally became new political units where the Christian religion was closely linked to the state. An important exception was

Bosnia, which had been receiving Muslim refugees from different parts of the Balkans and even from southern Russia. The Muslims in Bosnia stayed after the Austrian conquest of 1878 and were fairly well treated by the Austrians, who did not want to alienate them, in view of the nearby Serbian enemy. It was under Austrian occupation, and perhaps through Austrian initiative, that the idea of a "Bosniak" nation consisting of three equal religious communities (Muslims, Orthodox, Catholics) arose. In this period, Bosnia developed close relations with Europe, via Austria, not only politically but also economically. Another exception was Albania, where the majority of the population, in particular in the north, was Muslim. Those Bulgarians who had converted to Islam stayed, too. In these three countries, the Muslim peoples survived, at least partly, thanks to the inaccessible mountainous areas in which they lived.

A political map of the Balkans was drawn at the Congress of Berlin in July 1878, but changes were again brought about by the wars of 1912 (Albania) and 1913 (Bulgaria), in which the Russians supported Balkan nations against the Turks. World War One meant an outbreak of the conflict between the new states, since Serbia and Greece were on the winning side with Britain and Italy, while Bulgaria was on the losing one with Austria-Hungary. After the war, in 1918, Yugoslavia was created as a union of the southern Slavic peoples under Serbian leadership, but with inherent tensions between Serbs and Croats. In 1929, it became a kingdom. During the period between the two world wars, nearly all the Balkan states had strongly centralized mostly right-wing governments.

This came to an end with World War Two. Hungary, Romania, and Bulgaria allied with Germany. After German invasion and victory, Yugoslavia was dissolved. Croatia, also comprising Bosnia and Hercegovina, was created as a vassal state of Germany. Other parts of Yugoslavia were occupied or annexed by Germany, Italy, and their allies, Hungary, Bulgaria, and Albania, the latter occupied by Italy. A new "war of independence" by guerrilla forces started, now directed against the German and other (Italian, Hungarian, and Bulgarian) occupation forces, as well as against the fascist Croatian regime. On the one hand, this enflamed the old antagonism between Croats and Serbs, for many Serb civilians were massacred by the Croatian Ustasha. The latter tried to win Bosnians to their side and to put them in their service. On the other hand, it also led to bitter rivalry between two guerrilla armies fighting the Germans. On one side were the Serbian-led Chetniks, who wanted to reestablish the pre-war monarchy with Serbian hegemony; on the other were the leftist partisans led by Tito, who had received his training in Moscow in the thirties. Tragically, these liberation armies began fighting with each other, with many civilian casualties. The USSR and the Western allies had an interest in keeping German and Italian troops engaged against the two guerrilla armies in Yugoslavia.

2. The Communist Period (1944–89)

At the end of World War Two, the political situation in all countries in the Balkans except Greece changed completely with the establishment of Communist regimes under the auspices of the Soviet Union. Greece escaped when the civil war of 1946–49, fought chiefly in the north, was finally won by the Athens government, supported by the USA and NATO. The latter was established in 1948 in response to the Communist takeover in Czechoslovakia in that year.

Yugoslavia was the most important Balkan state in several respects. Tito, who had reconstituted pre-war Yugoslavia as a federal socialist republic, succeeded in taking a rather independent position toward the Soviet Union while governing the country on Marxist lines. This was possible because he carried out a huge military buildup to protect Yugoslavia against any outside intervention from East or West and because he received economic and other assistance from the USA and Western Europe. Inside the country, cooperative initiatives by the workers under general Party control were encouraged; they even attracted attention in some Western European countries as a possible model. In the seventies, a degree of intellectual freedom was allowed and Western ideas could be discussed; some prominent intellectuals entered into dialogue with Western counterparts.[4]

Bosnia's aspirations for autonomy increased after the experience of World War Two and ultimately achieved its aim. In 1964, Bosnia received the right of self-determination, and in 1971 it was recognized as a separate nationality on the same footing as Serbia, Croatia, and the others. After Tito's death in 1980, however, the Party prescribed a rigorous suppression of all pan-Islamic or Muslim nationalist tendencies.

Throughout the Balkans, the authoritarian Communist system exerted control and domination, eliminating all opposition by force. The all-pervading Communist ideology intended to eliminate—or at least to suppress—existing ethno-religious differences by categorizing people in nationalities according to cultures. Neither religion nor ethnicity but only "nationality" was considered a valid category of classification. In the end, this approach did not solve the problem of ethno-religious differences. They were to manifest themselves again, once they were no longer politically suppressed.

After 1989, a number of Communist leaders in all Balkan countries—and especially Romania and Yugoslavia—succeeded in maintaining their

---

[4]   In Dubrovnik, annual summer sessions were organized with participants from Western countries as well as Yugoslavia. Similar dialogue efforts with Yugoslav intellectuals were pursued elsewhere, too.

positions of power. They used the ruthless strategies they had learned in the Communist period for their own personal or national ends.

Religion

The Communist period had an immense effect on the situation of religion, both Christian and Muslim, in the various Balkan countries.

1) Religion could not be expressed in the public sphere anywhere; any political expression was precluded. It was confined to the private sphere and the domain of cult and liturgy. Officially and in public, religion was decried as intellectually backward and politically reactionary. Since the late 1960s, newborn Albanians of any religion had to receive non-religious names, and Muslims here had to change their names to properly Albanian names.

2) Religious organizations, to the degree that they were allowed, could operate only inside church or mosque and for strictly religious purposes only. No religious organizations were allowed to engage in education, health service, or social work. As a rule, religious property was confiscated or nationalized.

3) All religious leaders were strictly controlled and could be questioned and imprisoned on the slightest suspicion.

4) People known to be religious were excluded from careers in the public sphere. Spiritual quests and expressions were judged to be damaging to society. On the other hand, members of the Party had to declare themselves convinced atheists.

5) The authoritarian structure and sanctions of the state, with its secret police and ideological indoctrination, prevented any open discussion and real dialogue. On the contrary, it promoted monologue, individual solitude, and the development of strategies to obtain power or to escape from other people's power.

6) As a result, younger generations of Christians and Muslims could not learn their own religion well. To the degree that they considered themselves Christians or Muslims, they did so primarily in a social sense. For the state, they were secular citizens of equal status with the others.

7) If Christians could still be identified by their membership in Churches, the official identification of Muslims was more problematic. It was not carried out according to religious criteria, since these were not recognized; only social and cultural criteria counted. This is clear from the different categories according to which Muslims were identified in the various censuses held in Bosnia. In 1948, Bosnian Muslims could still declare their identity as "Muslims", but in 1953 they had to register as "Yugoslavs ethnically undetermined", in 1961 as "Muslims in the ethnic sense", and in 1971 as "Muslims in the national sense". The last two identifications could not be used by the Albanian and Turkish Muslims in

Yugoslavia. The stress on the "social" nature of Muslim identity has undoubtedly contributed to a growing political "social consciousness"—or social "political consciousness"—of Muslims in these countries.[5]

8) Communist regimes tended to play down Islam and Muslim communities even more than they did Christianity and Churches.

Nationalism

Notwithstanding the official Communist ideology, there were still nationalist movements in the Balkans that were linked with ethnic rivalries and especially with minority problems. Such movements could arise either from above, that is to say from the state, or from below, that is to say from opposition to the state. A case of the first kind is Bulgaria.[6]

According to the census of December 1992, Bulgaria had about 8.4 million inhabitants, most of whom were ethnic Bulgarian members of the Bulgarian Orthodox Church. The total number of Muslims was estimated at 1.2 million, that is to say about 16 % of the total population. Among these Muslims, three groups can be distinguished.

1. The *Bulgarian Turks* or ethnic Turks identify themselves as ethnic Turks (with Turkish language and culture) and Bulgarian citizens at the same time. They are descendants of the Turks who stayed after 1881 when independence was achieved, although more than two million Turks emigrated between 1881 and 1978. The Bulgarian government did its best to instill a Bulgarian national consciousness in these people, and various campaigns of assimilation were carried out to reduce existing tensions between ethnic Bulgarians, who are Slavs and Christian Orthodox, and ethnic Turks, who are Muslims. There are also differences between the two groups in education as well as in social and economic status.

A typical nationalist assimilation and "purification" movement took place between 1984 and 1990, known as the "revival process". This was a government initiative primarily directed against the Bulgarian ethnic Turks. It can be called an "ethnic cleansing" operation, though without the use of physical violence. There may have been some 750,000 ethnic Turks around 1984, that is to say 9 % of the population, compared with

---

[5]   Besides other factors, such conceptual problems influenced of course the data obtained and interpreted about the Muslim presence in Balkan countries. See Chapter 2 of *Muslim Communities in the New Europe* under the title "Islam and Ethnicity in Eastern Europe" (pp. 27–51). This chapter was written by the three editors and treats problems of conceptualization and statistics. The total number of Muslims in the Balkans is here estimated to be 7 to 8.3 million (p. 34).

[6]   Ivan ILCHEV and Duncan PERRY, "The Muslims of Bulgaria", in *Muslim Communities in the New Europe*, pp. 115–37 (= chapter 6).

86 % ethnic Bulgarians. They had to take Bulgarian names; Turkish literature was no longer taught at schools; Turkish-language media were forbidden; so were the wearing of Turkish dress and the observance of Turkish holidays. As a result, some 350,000 ethnic Turks left Bulgaria for Turkey in 1989, some of whom later returned after intense international and Bulgarian protests had been aroused. It goes without saying that this Bulgarian nationalist "revival process" was completely at odds with Communist state doctrine.

For the sake of clarity, the other two groups of Muslims in Bulgaria must be mentioned as well.

2. A great number of the gypsies (*Roma*) who arrived in Bulgaria around the thirteenth and fourteenth centuries were Muslims. Their number today is not known, but some estimates are that there may be between 600,000 and 800,000 Roma in Bulgaria. They are the poorest of the poor, despised by the population, and scapegoats in any misfortune. Of the Roma, 39 % are supposed to be Muslim and 44 % Christian.

3. The *Pomaks* are descendants of Bulgarians who converted to Islam between 1650 and 1800. They constitute a religious rather than an ethnic minority, since ethnically they are Bulgarians. On several occasions, the Bulgarian government tried to suppress their Muslim religious identity, since ethnic Bulgarians are supposed to be Orthodox Christians. In dire need, they have been seeking a rapprochement with the ethnic Turks.

In Bulgaria, the culture of Muslims is distinct from that of Christians, at least in part. The "revival process" between 1984 and 1990 increased polarization between Muslims and Christians; it contributed to the overthrow of the Communist Zhivkov regime in 1990.

Nationalist movements, however, can also arise from below, among minorities who feel threatened. The movement of Muslim Bosnians to acquire autonomy and the status of a nationality is a good example. It was crowned with success in 1971. Another example is the Albanian Muslims in Kosovo, at the time an autonomous region in Serbia, who rose up in rebellion in April 1981 because of discrimination by the Serbs. The Serbian leader Slobodan Milošević responded with ruthless suppression, less for reasons of Marxist doctrine than because Serbian national pride had been hurt.

The repressive measures that were taken against the Bosnian leader Alija Izetbegović because of his *Islamska deklaracija* (Islamic Manifest) of 1980 are significant. They show, on the one hand, the fears of Yugoslavia's leaders at the time of a growing Muslim Bosnian nationalism. On the other hand, they bring to light the old anti-Muslim attitude prevailing in Serbia. It goes back to the Serbian-Turkish wars of the nineteenth century and—in mythical imagination—to the battle of Kosovo, which the Serbs lost against the invading Ottomans in 1389.

The Communist period came to an end in the Balkans in 1989 and 1990, when in most states multi-party systems were established and free elections held. In Bosnia and Albania this happened later. It is striking to see how in some cases the losing parties refused to recognize results that went against their immediate interests. Totalitarian rule had made democratic procedures unwanted and much of the political turmoil here during the following years has to do with the relative novelty of democracy.

In August 1991, Bosnia declared itself a democratic, independent state of three nationalities (Muslims, Serbs, and Croats) who lived largely mixed throughout Bosnia-Hercegovina. At that time, the Muslims constituted 43.7 % of the total population, the (Orthodox) Serbs 31.3 %, the (Catholic) Croats 17.3 %, and other groups 7.7 %.[7] Muslims were then strongly represented in eastern and northeastern Bosnia, whereas western Bosnia was the main area of the Serb population. The northwestern part of Bosnia (the Bihać region) was and still is predominantly Muslim nowadays. Elsewhere, however, the situation changed in the following years through "ethnic cleansing" operations.

3. Balkan Politics and Religion after 1989

3.1. New Political Problems

In the political changes that have occurred in the Balkan countries since the demise of Communism and that have had important consequences for the place of religion, it is difficult to find initiatives from religious bodies or organizations themselves that have had any relevance for political life. The thorough politicization of public life itself may be seen as an effect of the Communist period. Where religion has reawakened after this, it seems to have been either as a legitimization of political orientations or as a spiritual renewal without political consequences. The key to the changes, as I see it, has been in the political sphere.

Of the region's great political dreams and ambitions of the twentieth century—Greater Serbia, Greater Croatia, Greater Bulgaria, Greater Albania—the latter three were achieved for a short time, and that during the war years. The Serbian dream led to territorial expansions in 1878, 1912–13, and 1918. It was also relevant in the period between the two World Wars. It exploded, however, after the demise of Communism and contrib-

---

[7]   LOPASIC, "The Muslims in Bosnia" (see above note 2), p. 108.

uted to the ending of Yugoslavia. Though political in character, this Serbian dream has been closely linked to religion and a collective memory that goes back to the medieval Christian Serbian kingdom and its defeat at Kosovo by the Muslim Turks in 1389. The sufferings of the Christian Serbs under Ottoman rule, the Serbian war of independence ending with the expulsion of practically all Muslims, the antagonism between Orthodoxy and Islam in the collective consciousness: all of this has played an enormous role in Serbian mythological thinking, as have the massacres of Orthodox Serbians perpetrated by Roman Catholic Ustasha Croats. None of this could ever be discussed in Communist Yugoslavia. Tito had to make continuous efforts to keep the Serbs, Croats, Bosnian Muslims, and Albanians in check, and he succeeded.

It needed a strategic mind trained in the Communist party and the passion for power of a Slobodan Milošević to bring all this psychological material to action in the context of an increasingly authoritarian and totalitarian regime excluding other voices. His plans ultimately failed, but at a terrible price. Milošević was the mastermind of the Bosnian war, with his dispossessing of Bosnians adhering to the religion he despises and hates most, Islam, and with his ambition to create a Greater Serbia, opposing the dreams of Greater Croatia or Greater Albania. He was ruthless toward rebellious minorities and political opponents, aggressive against seceding Slovenes and Croats, perverse in setting Serbian Bosnians to fight and ethnically "cleanse" Muslim Bosnians, and to destroy any possible reminder of Muslim culture. For the final solution, he used a general Ratko Mladić and an unscrupulous Montenegrin, Radovan Karadjić, as his acolytes sent on duty in Bosnia.

For a short while, Serbia then tried to enforce its stronghold on Kosovo. As in Bosnia, it was thanks to American military intervention that this could be halted. As a result, a certain democratization of Serbia started to take place.

3.2. New Ideological Problems

The attack on Bosnia, which actually was a Serbian initiative after the fighting between Serbs and Croats, was not only a political aggression but also the latest outburst of a long-lived antagonism between Christianity and Islam in the Balkan area. We have already seen the negative image of Turks and (Turkish) Islam that was cultivated here in the nineteenth century. This image had deeper dimensions. Since most Orthodox Churches are nation- or people-bound, Orthodox and ethnic-nationalist assertions go hand in hand, both institutionally and in the minds of the people, the more so if directed against Muslim nations or communities. What happened in Bosnia was an Orthodox version of what the Catholic kings did in Spain. Ethnic conflict took the place of the Inquisition, both used as a terrible weapon against that fantasized enemy called Islam.

In Western Europe we heard the myth of "endangered Orthodoxy" and the "Muslim conspiracy".[8] We heard from Christians about the heroic role of Christian Greece, Bulgaria, and Serbia in preventing the Islamic threat from penetrating into Europe via the Turkish, Albanian, and Bosnian corridor. And how often were we not told in Switzerland or elsewhere that it was impossible to allow an "Islamic state" to exist on European soil. In fact, however, in 1991 Bosnia had all the features of a secular state with a slight Muslim majority, more enlightened than its Serbian and Croatian Christian neighbors, and certainly less aggressive.

Medieval as such stories sound, they had a certain effect on uncritical Western European minds, and for a number of Balkan Christian minds they just represented truth. In a region that has known neither the Reformation and Counterreformation, nor the Enlightenment or a science of religions, religious dreams can be turned into political myths that provide mythical instead of realistically human solutions. Worse still, religious myths lend themselves to political manipulation, especially in the sensitive domain of communal interfaith relations. And socialist thinking was too linked to the political terror of the Communist regimes of the region to bring confused minds to reason and instill the need for peace.

On the one hand, the Bosnian war showed the incapacity of the Communist ideology to provide a solution for the problem of the Serbian-Croat-Bosnian triangle. On the other hand, the complete submission of almost all Serbian media to the war effort, the thorough mobilization of Serbian Bosnians against Muslim Bosnians, and the use of the resources of the powerful Yugoslav army were strategies that excluded in advance any dialogue, discussion, or debate. The Bosnian Serbs deluded the Western powers in meetings of purely verbal effect in Geneva and elsewhere while Sarajevo was under siege. I have been told that the leading Western representatives hardly knew the region or the issues involved. In any case, the Europeans were unable to come to a common action.

The role of the clergy during these years was more than ambiguous. There certainly were honest Christians who tried to prevent war. But research should be done on the subservience of the Serbian Orthodox Church and the Roman Catholic Church in Croatia to their respective states. Research should equally focus on the support the Vatican gave to Croatia in these years and earlier; the Pope's sympathies are known. If the highest Catholic and Orthodox echelons on the scene could at least in some way be interrogated by delegations from Rome to Zaghreb or from

---

[8]   Mirjana NAJCEVSKA, Emilija SIMOSKA and Natasha GABER, "Muslims, State and Society in the Republic of Macedonia: The View from Within", in *Muslim Communities in the New Europe*, pp. 75–97 (= chapter 4), here pp. 85–90.

Geneva to Belgrade, subservience to Croatian and Serbian political inter-ests resumed once the delegations had left. The lower clergy, at any rate, did not have the education to think in critical terms and shared, sup-ported, and encouraged ideological bellicism. The Christian Churches of the former Yugoslavia have been severely compromised. In the Balkans, Christianity stupidly limped in the shadow of political forces along the lines of political interests.

3.3. New Minority Problems

An old problem that has reappeared in full force since the Communist period is that of relations between majorities and minorities, especially ethnic and cultural—including religious—minorities. Marxism offered a certain solution by considering such minorities "nationalities" that de-served recognition, playing down cultural and religious differences within the general context of socialist society. Tito had treated Yugoslavia's minority problems along these lines, not without success. This was due in part to his own prestige and a certain sense of justice, although he has always kept silent on the World War Two massacres. He knew how to "rank" the different existing groups within the overall federal state as he understood it, and he was able to create various balances between the interest groups involved. He tried to avoid obvious discrimination of smaller groups and made Kosovo, where the majority consisted of Muslim Albanians, an autonomous region in 1974.

In 1974, Yugoslavia consisted of six *nations*, recognized as the con-stituent elements of the federation. These were the Serbs, the Croats, the Slovenes, the Bosnians, the Montenegrins, and the Macedonians. Other ethnic communities like the ethnic Albanians and Hungarians had the status of *nationalities*, with educational and cultural rights. In part, Tito's success was due to the iron discipline he imposed upon the Party and to the strong state apparatus and army he had been able to build up.

After Tito's death in 1980, however, and the following weakening of the Party and state apparatus, the Serbian and also the Croatian Commu-nist leadership could not restrain their lust for domination. Unfortunately, there were not sufficient safeguards for non-Serbian or non-Croatian minorities or even for the Serbian minority in Croatia, whose status was not satisfactorily guaranteed. The same was the case with the Muslim minorities in Bulgaria or, for that matter, the Hungarian minority in Romania. Both Marxist ideology and the authoritarian nature of the regimes had prevented constructive dialogue between the various interest groups within the Balkan states. They had also prevented any airing of the resentments they felt toward each other for past ill-treatment, real or perceived. Worst off were the gypsies (*Roma*) in this region, who still are exceedingly poor and hardly organized.

The status of the ethnic Muslim minorities was nowhere sufficiently guaranteed, even not in Albania where they were in fact an oppressed majority. The Communist ideology and political system simply were not able to provide such guarantees.

It has been observed that ethnic Muslim minorities themselves on the whole favor an ethnically-organized state with proportional representation as a guarantee of participation in decision-making. Yet, the leadership of such minorities, being more familiar with the West, may prefer a civil state in which all citizens enjoy equal rights as individuals, and where Muslim citizens are not classified as a separate group or community. Only in exceptional cases would Muslim minorities favor what is called a national state, since such a state tends to be ruled according to what the majority considers to be "the nation". As Robert W. Mickey observes, Muslim minorities in the Balkans probably wish the state to be ethnically organized and take into account the communal interests of the Muslims.[9]

An example is Macedonia[10], some 1.5 million of whose roughly 2.1 million inhabitants were ethnic Macedonians adhering to the Macedonian Orthodox Church around 1995. There were three groups of Muslims in Macedonia. First, there were around 400,000 ethnic Albanians, representing 23 % of the total population and mostly speaking Macedonian. Second, there were around 80,000 ethnic Turks, mostly speaking Turkish. And third, there were a small number of Muslim Macedonians who are ethnically Macedonians and religiously Muslims. Moreover, there are some other smaller minority groups of *Roma* (gypsies), Serbs, and Vlachs. The Albanians are not Slavs as most Balkan peoples are. The ethnic Albanians live in the west and the northwest of Macedonia along the Albanian and Kosovo borders. Given their large numbers, they demanded a "partner nation" status in Macedonia, which would imply joint decision-making by the ethnic Macedonians and Albanians.

Evidently, this concept goes against current views of state organization as conceived in the Western European and North American tradition. It is resisted by the local Muslim elite, who were educated in the same more or less secular tradition, as it is by Bosnian intellectuals, who see Bosnia as one state with three ethnic-religious communities. But the idea is worth consideration, since a communally organized state is forced, at least, to recognize the status and to take into account the interests of Muslims as a group.

---

9   Robert W. MICKEY, "Citizenship, Status and Minority Political Participation: The Evidence from the Republic of Macedonia", in *Muslim Communities in the New Europe*, pp. 53–74 (= chapter 3), here pp. 69–70.

10 NAJCEVSKA, SIMOSKA, and GABER, "Muslims, State and Society in the Republic of Macedonia" (see above note 8).

Recent research in minority-majority relationships has shown the importance of mutual perceptions and the role of fear in them. Majorities, for instance, feel threatened by minorities who can be used as possible levers by other states. It may very well be that the treatment of minorities in a state is a function of threats from outside as perceived by the majority. The Serbian crackdown on minorities, which started in Kosovo in 1981 and intensified since 1989, provoked reactions of fear among minorities. As a result, the Yugoslav system became unbalanced not only politically, but also psychologically, through what must be called a strategy of terror. Radical activists within threatened minorities will respond with a call to arms in order to ensure survival.

3.4. New Expressions and Functions of Religion

Visitors to Yugoslavia and other Balkan countries in the 1970s and 1980s often reported the tolerance that existed between adherents of different religions and denominations sometimes living side by side. In Yugoslavia, religious communities were then apparently more recognized than twenty years earlier. Such visitors could hardly believe stories of religious-ethnic conflicts in the Balkans; the immediate impression they had was one of forced but peaceful coexistence. The people themselves declared that they wanted to live together peacefully, affirming that this was also the message of the religions themselves.[11]

The same is reported of Albania[12] after the old Communist regime was overthrown. Even changes of religious identity, that is to say conversions, could be found here, especially among young people, for instance to Catholicism or the Bahā'ī faith. Unlike during the preceding decades, religion was now described in the "Western" sense as a question of a personal choice of faith and morality, much more linked to the family than to economic activities and political constitutions. Muslims in Albania are reported as being most tolerant, followed by the Orthodox. Religious organizations that stimulate the spirit of religious divisions are negatively branded, as are particular links between aid given to a (Muslim) community from outside and obligations imposed on it, specifically if such obligations are imposed on women. After many years in which religion was suppressed, its present recognition is thoroughly enjoyed.

---

[11] An interesting book published at the time, difficult to find nowadays, is *Religions in Yugoslavia*, ed. by Zlatko FRID, Zagreb: Binoza, 1971. It describes the main religious communities at the time with attention to a historical survey, the legal status, the Church in socialism, ecumenicalism, dialogue between Marxists and Christians, etc.

[12] Elira CELA, "Albanian Muslims, Human Rights, and Relations with the Islamic World", in *Muslim Communities in the New Europe*, pp. 139–52 (= chapter 7).

When reading such reports one cannot help but wonder. Did the relations between adherents of different religions and confessions indeed improve thanks to the official suppression of the power of religious institutions and organizations? Did ordinary people really discover their common "religious" humanity when organized religion was generally oppressed? Did this oppression somehow indeed shield human relationships from negative interference from outside, including the interference of established religious authorities and institutions? And, once the Communist straitjacket was removed, were these same peaceful people not exposed to certain existing divisive competitive religious forces they had not the slightest idea about and against which they had not built up the least resistance? An attentive observer cannot but ponder what has really happened to religious people beyond the institutional level of religious authority according to denominations.

There are opposite reports about the present-day situation of religion in the Balkans as well, even in great abundance.[13] Religion is said to have been "released" with the demise of Communism and to play an increasingly important role, first of all in private orientations, commitments, and spirituality. Individual religious expressions are free now, whatever their intrinsic value. Participation in religious feasts and festivals is open to anyone, across denominational boundaries. Religion now also plays an important role in the relations between citizens, individually and as groups. Religious identification has become socially acceptable again and can help individuals confront hardships through communal participation. Whereas in the Communist period religion could not play any social and political role whatsoever, it can play such a role nowadays. This implies obedience to the rules of religious authorities and institutions, but also a stronger identification with the community, mostly an ethnic group that considers this religion a natural sign of adherence. After a time in which people were disciplined to pay obedience to the Party and the State, new obediences apparently crystallize around new authorities, ethnic, religious, or ethnic-religious.

Politically, religion now can and does serve again to legitimate sociopolitical projects, including one's own community's or nationality's domination of others. In the Balkan context, in Communist times and afterward, in both Orthodox or Catholic Christian and Muslim circles, religion was expected not to criticize the policies of the government in public. This rule was of course strengthened under Communist regimes, under which any criticism of those in power was forbidden. We are still waiting for a

---

[13] Gerd NONNEMAN, "Muslim Communities in the New Europe: Themes and Puzzles", in *Muslim Communities in the New Europe*, pp. 3–24 (= chapter 1), here pp. 14–5 and 18.

White Book about the actions taken by Serbian clergy to promote warfare against Slovenes, Croatians, and in particular Bosnians. Television showed a pious Karadjić taking the sacrament in liturgical service. One never heard that his Church reprimanded personally a man after all who was utterly compromised by organized crimes against humanity.

Orthodox or Catholic Christians and Muslims have all turned out to be rather naive when confronted with evil. With some exceptions, they were incapable of taking a moral stand apart from their collectivities. All those groups were also ill prepared to resist political manipulations, including conscious efforts to politicize religious differences and to negatively influence relations between religious-ethnic communities. The Bosnian Muslims had to fight bitterly to survive as a community.

Apparently, most of the Balkan states show a return to Christian Orthodoxy closely linked to national and ethnic causes. The expressions of other religions and religious denominations may also lead to further denominational fragmentation of Christianity. This may be in part a reaction against Communist egalitarianism and homogeneity and in part a return to age-old structures of pre-Communist times. But are there not lessons to be drawn from history?

Until now, we have looked briefly at the history of the Balkan states, in particular after the Ottoman Turks departed from the various regions of the peninsula. We have paid special attention to the Communist period of some forty years in the Balkan states, in particular Bosnia, and its implications for the situation of the religions at the time. This concerned Christianity as well as Islam.

Following this historical survey, we indicated four important problems that arose after the demise of Communism. They are (1) new political problems given with some states' current strategies of domination; (2) new ideological problems arising out of the mythicized antagonism between Christian Orthodoxy and Islam; (3) new articulations of minority-majority relations between different ethno-religious groups in which Muslims are involved; and (4) new expressions and functions of religion, both Christianity and Islam, in Balkan societies after the absence of these two from the public sphere for some forty years.

At a time in which Balkan and other countries experience a growing nationalism among the majority populations and a growing ethnic awareness among minority groups, a more critical reflection is needed on what is going on in politics and religion. Considering some major failures by Western Europe countries to respond to events of the 1990s in the Balkans, we should draw some conclusions from these events for the situation of Muslim communities in Europe generally. Finally, we have to look afresh at future interfaith relations between Christians and Muslims in Europe.

4. Conclusion

4.1. The Study of the Religion and Culture of Muslim Minorities

The many issues involved in religion and politics among Muslim minorities in the Balkans and elsewhere gain clarity if we focus on the different interpretations that people on both sides, the majority as well as the minority, give of their situations and of these issues. If it is the subjective elements that convey and indicate meaning to human beings, it is these same subjective elements that contain the key for the study of relations between people. Consequently, to do adequate research on a specific ethnic group in relation to others, knowing factual data such as kinship, anthropological characteristics, language, and cultural features is a necessary but not a sufficient condition. We should also examine the representations that a group has of itself and others, the way in which it constructs boundaries between itself and outsiders, the more or less universal notions it has of the human being and society, and how all of this applies in practice.

Parallel to this, for adequate research on a specific religion, it is necessary to know the factual data of its history, the various orientations and traditions that have developed in the course of that history, and the forms that the religion has taken in different contexts. But we should also look at the ways these "religious facts" have been handled, interpreted, and applied in particular contexts. We may even inquire about fundamental notions of truth and justice underlying these interpretations.

A religion can be many things. It can be a foundation for the feeling of togetherness that is constitutive of community, through rituals, common memories, mutual help, and distinguishing marks. A religion is also a way of orienting oneself in the world and the universe, by means of revelations and truths, through laws and rules governing behavior, and by proposing a new order transcending the material world. But a religion can also mean an authority to be followed or an institution to be obeyed; this can be, for instance, a charismatic personality, a hierarchically organized religious institution, a more egalitarian way of deliberating and deciding, or a model of life exemplified by particular people. And a religion can also be a transforming experience, on the personal or communal plane, a communication with a dimension of reality that escapes empirical verification. If we study the ethnic, national, and religious characterizations that people give of themselves, the corresponding identities turn out to be not completely different things, but rather linked to each other.

I contend that such an approach can also be followed in the study of Muslim majorities and minorities. Instead of studying things like "Muslim revival", "Muslim fundamentalism", and whatever (often wrong) names have been given to the phenomena, we should examine the names that the particular Muslims themselves give to matters of concern. There is then a clear distinction to be made between Muslim self-affirmation in social and political terms, and Muslim appeals to Islam in religious and ideological terms. In the first case, the Muslims' primary concern, especially in minority situations, is how to survive, live, act, view themselves, keep their identity, and build up communal life. This is their empirical, lived reality. It includes their frustrations, their feelings of unequal treatment and discrimination, but also their efforts for emancipation and liberation. It involves the place they assign themselves in the broader society and nation in which they live and how they see themselves in relation to the broader Muslim community.

In this case, we have to do with Islam as something to which people appeal as a normative entity. This is Islam as a religion and ideology, a way of life and value recognized by Muslims, which ultimately indicates the meaning of life and the way it should be conducted. More than life and reality as it is lived in actual practice, it is this normative Islam and its contents that are here the subject of research and discussion. The concern for normative Islam is the so-called "Islamic factor" that has made itself palpable throughout the Muslim world in recent decades and in the Balkans in recent years. As I see it, it is this concern for normative Islam that gives Muslims—and Muslim minorities in particular—their specific identity and distinguishes them from other, non-Muslim cultures and societies. The way they realize and can give shape to this normative Islam depends, of course, largely on the political and economic frameworks and the social, cultural, and religious contexts in which they live, and the degree to which these frameworks and contexts allow them to articulate their Muslim identity.[14]

   Consequently, taking into account this distinction between lived and normative Islam, Muslims should be defined and studied not only in social, cultural, and economic terms, as was done in Eastern Europe by Marxist ideology and within the Communist political system. Nor should they be defined and studied exclusively in spiritual terms, since anything Islamic has human social and political implications. Islam itself is not only, or even primarily, a religious experience or a spiritual reality, although it can be and has been interpreted as such. A failure of so many Western studies of Islam and Muslim societies is that they have concentrated either on empirical social realities or on normative religious realities. Any real understanding of what is going on in Islamic social life, politics, and religion should take into account the continuous tension and interaction between both levels, that is to say between what is lived and what is considered normative.

---

[14] See for instance SZAJKOWSKI, NIBLOCK, and NONNEMAN, "Islam and Ethnicity in Eastern Europe" (see above note 5), pp. 38–9.

4.2. Muslim Minorities in Europe

The Bosnian war had its roots in Serbian dreams, ambitions, and strategies, but it would not have been possible if the Western European states had really wanted to put an end to it. Through Western Europe's silence both to Bosnian demands and to American pressures, it implicitly accepted, though without legitimizing, the Serbian attempt to destroy multi-ethnic Bosnia with its Muslim majority, which is part of Europe. If the USA through NATO had not intervened in a direct way for whatever reasons, still more of Bosnia would have been destroyed than was already the case during four years of fighting. Of course, some Serbian war criminals still have to be brought to court, which is also a European responsibility.

As a consequence, Europe has been severely compromised by the Bosnian war, not only on a political but also on a moral and social level. The general European public, strangely enough, has hardly been really moved by the fact that some two million people were expelled, imprisoned in camps, raped, or massacred. Apart from some humanitarian action, including the temporary acceptance of refugees, no real initiatives were taken to help the Bosnians defend themselves.

This time—contrary to traditional European religious mythology—the forces of evil were on the Christian side, but unfortunately European Christianity has not been able to see it that way. As a consequence, Christianity itself, and in particular the Churches involved in the Yugoslav drama—the Roman Catholics principally in Croatia and the Orthodox principally in Serbia—have been seriously compromised. One is tempted to draw parallels to the fate of both Jews and Muslims in Spain, where Christianity was equally compromised without being aware of it.

The implications of what happened in the Balkans to the Bulgarian Turks, the Muslims of Bosnia, and the Albanians in Kosovo for the position of Muslim minorities in Western Europe are not immediately clear. Yet, in the light of these events and the responses to them in European societies, one can no longer afford to be overly optimistic about the well-being of the Muslim communities in Europe as ethnic, cultural, and religious minorities. Certainly, Western Europe is not the same as Eastern Europe during the Cold War. It has not been under Communist rule and it has developed a form of civil society in which the individual rights of citizens and permanent residents are legally guaranteed. Although in cultural decline, in periodic economic recessions, and politically divided and morally crippled, Europe still has resources of respect for human life and dignity that spring from a rich tradition.

But as is well-known, here too there is still an ancient religious and historical mythology about, or rather against, Islam, which expresses itself politically and socially. There are racist attitudes toward non-European immigrants. Here too, as in the Balkans, the larger Churches, including Roman Catholics and Anglicans, Lutherans and Calvinists, and also secular ideologists from right to left, have fundamentalist currents and quarters for whom Islam is, if not the Antichrist, at least a nightmare. It can be perceived as a danger and often enough it is seen as an enemy people are supposed to be afraid of. Here too, powerful interests are at work, with politicians speaking of an imagined purity to be preserved, a sacred past to be restored, a glorious culture to be defended, a terrorism against which one has to go to war. Nor should the all-too-human fears of certain Europeans for any loss of their well-being, security, and riches be ignored. Faced with the masses of Asian and African poor, who, nearest to Europe, happen to be Muslims in their great majority, they tend to feel outnumbered and threatened.

After centuries of common history, the question may well be raised how the relations between peoples from Europe and the broader Muslim world have developed in the course of time. Who has gained most from these relations and whose domination would have been preferable? What has the Muslim civilization brought to Europe, and what has European civilization brought to the Muslim world? If the European Union opted for dialogue instead of confrontation with Islam, why did it and what kind of dialogue did it have in mind? The accounts should be drawn up on both sides some day.

4.3. Interfaith Relations

It would be preposterous to prescribe to Christians or Muslims how they, adherents of the two largest world religions, ought to behave toward each other. This is their own responsibility. It is necessary, however, to stress the need for cooperation and dialogue between representatives of these two religions for the sake of the well-being of the world. Mixed contact groups, working groups, and associations of people committed to common study and social action exist in various places. Among the subjects they address are: what kind of society should we strive for (liberal, civic, communal, religiously based, socialist)? What kind of separation between Church and State (including Christianity and Islam) do we want? What kind of individual and communal rights and duties do we see as absolutely necessary and even prescribed (a fundamental respect for human dignity, a code of behavior between adherents of different religions, a global ethics)?

It is said that the Bosnian war has led to more frequent and intense contacts between the religious leaders concerned; before, such contacts did not really exist in Yugoslavia. It seems to me that, precisely after the Bosnian experience, Muslim-Christian dialogues should become more politically conscious than was possible in the first decades, when each side still had to become acquainted with the other. Since real political and religious problems between Muslim and Christian communities have now arisen in the Balkans—as also in southern Russia, in the southern Caucasus, and somewhat earlier in Lebanon—, there is no reason to assume that such problems will not arise elsewhere as well. In these cases, the number of nonpartisan experts was extremely limited, and this certainly added to the West's incapacity to act appropriately.

In Western Europe, with its humanist and Enlightenment tradition, more scholarly knowledge is available about Islam and Muslims in Europe and more impartial information is available on the subject. This is less the case, however, for relations between Muslims and Christians in the Middle East and Southeast Asia, and still less for those relations in Africa. We badly need impartial observers to trace the relations between the two religions, as they develop in different parts of the world, and to make suggestions to diminish tensions in critical situations.

4.4. The Bosnian War as Shock Therapy?

In one respect, at least, the Bosnian catastrophe may have a therapeutic effect. In traditional European imagery, Muslims were depicted as aggressive, violent, and more or less stupid, and Islam was viewed as a backward religion of people without much personal conscience. The story of the Bosnian Muslims offers a much-needed corrective to this caricature. Here it is Muslims, not Christians or Jews, who are victims; here it is Islam and not Christianity that has been able to live self-critically in a secularized society. Here it is a region that has known the Enlightenment and considers itself fully a part of Europe.

This may result in the awakening of a certain intelligence, if not a moral conscience, in unmasking the traditional antagonisms that have been constructed between Europe and Islam, Christianity and Islam, and that continue to haunt us. People are becoming aware of the evil consequences that such social, religious, and cultural ideas have had in the Balkans and to what they might lead elsewhere in the future. This reinforces my plea for cooperation and dialogue between Christians and Muslims to resist current forms of anti-Islamism. There seems to be more evil here than most of us have been aware of.

A few years ago, a learned Bosnian colleague who was a Muslim said to me: "The Bosnian experience is the end of talking Muslim-Christian dialogue". I could not answer at the time. At present I would say: "There is no other way than reconciliation, cooperation, and dialogue out of this mess made between Christians and Muslims." What we need is intellectual honesty to each other, moral concern for the future, communication, and adequate action.

Selected Literature

Balić, Smail, *Das unbekannte Bosnien: Europas Brücke zur islamischen Welt*, Cologne and Weimar: Böhlau, 1992.

Friedman, Francine, *The Bosnian Muslims: Denial of a Nation*, Boulder, Col., and Oxford: Westview Press, 1996.

Funke, Hajo, and Alexander Rhotert, *Unter unseren Augen. Ethnische Reinheit: Die Politik des Regime Milosevic und die Rolle des Westens* (Schriftenreihe Politik und Kultur am Fachbereich Politische Wissenschaft der Freien Universität Berlin), Berlin: Das Arabische Buch, 1999.

Muslim Communities in the New Europe, ed. by Gerd Nonneman, Tim Niblock, and Bogdan Szajkowski, Reading, U. K.: Ithaca Press, 1996.

The Muslims of Bosnia-Herzegovina: Their Historic Development from the Middle Ages to the Dissolution of Yugoslavia, ed. by Mark Pinson (Harvard Middle Eastern Monographs 28), Cambridge, Mass.: Harvard University Press, 1993.

Chapter 15
Muslim-Christian Minority Problems in Europe and the Middle East

If it is true that societies and cultures can be judged according to the way they treat their minorities, the same can be said about religions. They too can be judged according to the way they treat religious minorities, both on the level of prescriptions and doctrine and on the level of social and individual practice. In this connection, it is interesting to compare present-day situations of Muslims in Western Europe with those of Christians in the Middle East. Such a comparison demands that the researcher compare only what is comparable, and it may lead to a reconsideration of current notions of minority and majority in religions like Christianity and Islam.

On a level of common sense, and mostly with good intentions, Europeans tend to compare the social situation of Muslim immigrants in Europe and that of indigenous Christians in the Middle East. They then easily conclude that the situation of the latter—both in Muslim countries and in Israel, Jerusalem, and the Occupied Territories, but with the exception of Lebanon—is worse than that of the former. Whereas during the last thirty years hundreds of prayer halls have emerged and a number of new mosques have been built in Western European countries, the total number of church buildings in the Middle East has hardly increased. And whereas the number of Muslims in Western Europe has grown rapidly through immigration and birth, the number of Christians in the Middle East has been on the decline. A considerable number of Christians have migrated during the last thirty years from Egypt, Israel, and the Occupied Territories, Lebanon, and Iraq to countries like Canada, the United States, or Australia. And whereas a number of Westerners see the future of Christianity in the Middle East in rather bleak and even sometimes gloomy terms, Muslims tend to assess the future of Islam in Europe as rather bright, at least in terms of numbers of immigrants from Muslim countries and various ethnic groups. Apparently, it requires much more effort for local Christians for Christianity to survive physically in a Muslim and Jewish Middle East than it does for local Muslims for Islam to survive physically in a secular and Christian Europe.

The subject stirs emotions on all sides. Two observations should be made right at the beginning. First, the acquisition of foreign labor in

Europe in the 1960s and 1970s did not intentionally engage Muslims: it just so happened that most of the workers engaged—Turks, Algerians, Moroccans—were Muslims. They were not admitted as Muslims, but as cheap labor. Second, the Christians and Jews living in Middle Eastern societies were a subject of concern to the Muslim leadership, not primarily because they adhered to this or that religion, but because they constituted pockets of non-Muslims in an overwhelmingly Muslim society. They stood "apart" as an exception to the dream of one homogeneous Muslim society and were comparable in this respect to certain Muslim sects. In studying the available facts of minority-majority relations as impartially as possible, however, one must take a scholarly attitude detached from the feelings and emotions perceptible in both current Western and Muslim discourse on the subject.

1. Muslims in Western Europe and Christians in the Middle East

When we speak about Muslim minorities in Western Europe and Christian minorities in the Middle East, we are dealing with groups of people from the Middle East and North Africa who identify themselves not only by their religion, but also by their language, ethnicity, nationality, and way of life. Consider, for instance, Turks and Kurds, Arabs and Berbers, Sunnīs, Shīʿīs, and Turkish or Syrian Alevis (ʿAlawī) on the Muslim side, and Copts and Maronites, Greek Orthodox and Syrian Orthodox, Armenians and Assyrians on the Christian side. All these groups have their own history and social structures and they want to maintain their own identity. It would be preposterous to explain their differences only by the fact that they call themselves Muslim or Christian or by the context and conditions in which they live. We are dealing with complex identities. For purposes of comparison, however, let me put the two kinds of minorities under the three broad headings of history, security of existence, and communal life.

1.1. History

The Muslims living in Western Europe have a short history here, which is essentially the history of individual migration for work, family reunion, or obtaining asylum. Nearly all of them come from Muslim countries, mostly one or two generations ago, but sometimes more. Once arrived, their main problem has been to survive economically, socially, and humanly in their countries of residence that have ways of life profoundly different from those in their regions of origin. This meant a struggle to retain certain basic values and identity from the past in industrialized and largely secular Western societies, also for the next generation. Different

European states have adopted different policies, but they all have an interest in promoting the new immigrant integration—and to some extent assimilation—within the economic, social, and cultural life of their societies and to avoid their marginalization. In this complex situation, most immigrants want to preserve their Muslim identity and consider radical secularism as a greater danger than Christianity.

The Christians living in the Middle East[1], on the other hand, have a long history that, for the major towns of the region, goes back to the second or even first century of our era, that is, some five centuries before the Arab conquests of the region between 630 and 650 C.E. The various Churches had been established by that time. While maintaining their own languages as liturgical languages, they underwent the subsequent process of Arabization, starting in the towns and cities. They witnessed the process of Islamization of the region which led to the decrease of the number of Christians. By the tenth or eleventh century, the majority of the population were Muslims. Christian communities continued to exist in special quarters of the towns and in less accessible rural and mountainous areas. For some twelve centuries, these Christian communities have been living as *dhimmīs* under sometimes trying social and economic circumstances under different kinds of Muslim regimes. They had to make great efforts to survive as *dhimmī* communities. Their situation improved during the colonial period, but met with new challenges in the national states and the political turbulences of the last fifty years. This has meant not only a struggle for economic and social survival, but also conscious efforts to preserve their Christian identity and find their place in Muslim societies, which underwent considerable changes, especially in the second half of the twentieth century. Christians of the region had to resist temptations to convert to Islam.

1.2. Security of Existence

Although situations have differed according to countries and regions, I submit that, generally speaking, the oil crisis of 1973–4 and the subsequent rise in unemployment in European societies has struck the immigrants in Europe hard, since the new situation made their lives increasingly insecure and hindered the process of integration. In this situation and with the arrival of spouses and families, a number of Muslims in Europe have started to build their own religious and cultural institutions since the 1970s, and they developed communicative networks with Muslims in other European countries as well as with their countries of origin

---

[1] See section 3 of Chapter 17 on "Between Baghdad and Birmingham: Opportunities of Minorities" for more details.

and the Muslim world at large. This led to a growing institutionalization of Islam in Europe since the 1970s.

Apart from its religious aspects, this has been at least in part a social and moral response to the growing material and social insecurity caused by the worsening economic situation. Unfriendly attitudes among the local population towards foreigners including Muslims started to manifest themselves in the 1980s, heightening their feeling of insecurity. This, as well as the rise of "Islamist" ideologies among Muslims and the incidental occurrence of violence have put a further brake on the hoped-for rapid integration of immigrants in European societies. Such an integration, at any rate, would require several generations.

The Christians in the Middle East, whose situation has varied from country to country with different regimes succeeding each other, have also had to cope with the problem of security of existence. They suffered under the status of *dhimmī*—in Lebanon and Egypt until the second half of the nineteenth century, elsewhere in practice still longer—and their recognition as ordinary citizens during the colonial period and in the newly established states furthered their emancipation. On the whole, however, their economic and social security has decreased during the last fifty years or so. This is not necessarily the result of planned action. Most countries of the region where Christians live underwent profound political, economic, and social changes that have strongly affected the privileged classes of society, which included a relatively high proportion of Christians. The armaments race and wars have placed a heavy burden on the entire population of these countries, including the Christians.

The departure, first of non-Arab—often Greek and Italian—Christians, then also of a number of Copts and Arab Christians from Egypt, has many causes. Aside from the growing economic and social insecurity, they also suffered from the region's growing political insecurity. Most regimes of the region have developed non-democratic systems of government and have exercised increasing control over the population, restricting democratic rights and human rights in general. The efforts of "Islamist" movements to bring about an Islamization of society, and in some cases to destabilize the existing social order altogether, have led to increasing insecurity for Christians, in particular in Egypt. The civil war in Lebanon, which also included Maronite as well as Shī'ī factions fighting among themselves, shattered the claims of security maintained for decades by Christians in that country. During the last thirty years, many Christians also left the Occupied Territories and East Jerusalem, as well as Turkey, in search of a viable life and future. Many indigenous Christian Churches of the Middle East now have flourishing communities in Europe and North America, where a number of adherents of non-Sunnī Muslim communities also found refuge.

1.3. Communal Life and Freedom of Expression

Among the immigrant Muslims in Europe, communal life has been largely articulated according to ethnic and national origin. Given the need to organize oneself in Western societies and the existing freedom of organization, ethnic and language divisions existing in the countries of origin are often reflected in distinct organizations among the Turks, Moroccans, Algerians, Pakistanis, and other Muslim communities in Europe. In Britain, such ethnic communities were encouraged. On the continent, personal identities were stressed much more.

Within Islam, differences in religious orientation in connection with interpretations of religion and socio-religious loyalties to different authorities and leaders also express themselves in great organizational variety, in part competitive. In most countries it has not been possible to constitute one body representing all existing Muslim organizations. Differences are too great, and this is not restricted to countries but extending to international networks. Muslim religious and cultural organizations have their own networks extending throughout Europe. On the other hand, such organizational differences and divisions, unlike those between Sunnī and Shī'ī or Sunnī and Ahmadī, rarely claim to be of a religiously absolute nature. Islam as a religion, an ideal, and a social structure bridges the differences spiritually and makes for one *umma* (Muslim community).

The *umma* constitutes a kind of Muslim commonwealth and provides a fundamental solidarity that manifests itself when critical issues are at stake. Examples are the Salman Rushdie affair in England, with tensions between an Islamic religious and a worldly secular universe, and the issue of wearing headscarves at school in France, which marks the tensions implicit in Muslim minorities living in secular societies that do not allow public religious activities. In such cases, activists of Islam resort to symbolic action for the Muslim commonwealth. They defend what they hold to be basic Islamic norms and values, and their deeds find an echo in broader Muslim circles.

In most Western countries, as long as violence is avoided, Muslims can publicly express themselves in word and action on the basis of the fundamental freedoms of Western societies, although they need permission from local authorities for larger public manifestations. There are, however, structural limitations to their possibilities of action in Western societies. Their political leverage in Western countries is small. They are often in competition with contesting Muslim groups. They can be harassed by anti-foreigner campaigners and persecuted by racist skinheads or right-wingers. Most importantly, except if the media are cooperative, their interaction with the majority population is limited and their views and statements risk being distorted.

Among Christians in the Middle East, communal life is largely articulated within the existing Church communities that have strictly religious as well as social activities. Such activities are not always free. A country like Iraq, for instance, only allows religious, not social Church activities. Saudi Arabia does not allow any Church activity at all, not even behind closed doors. Most Churches of the region transcend national borders and have their own networks throughout the region and also with Western Churches. Most of them belong to the Middle East Council of Churches.

The Christian religious institutions, by their very nature, are in principle distinct from the given social and political order, and this is quite visible in Muslim countries. The indigenous Christian religious institutions in the Middle East date from a distant past and are surrounded by ancient traditions, their guardians being endowed with an aura of authority that is not restricted to the religious sphere, but also extends to matters of personal and social life.

The Churches must continuously defend their rights against possible interventions by the state or by Muslim activist and possibly even extremist groups. However, where democratic institutions are weak or absent, the Churches have to be careful in word and action. They are not allowed to carry out what is construed to be political action. Only in rare cases, the tensions inherent in Christian-Muslim relations in Muslim majority countries come into the open, and it is difficult to know what is going on, not only within each side, but also between both sides.

1.4. Parallels and Common Features

There are of course innumerable differences between the situation of the new Muslim immigrant communities in Europe and that of the long-existing Christian communities in the Middle East. These differences are largely due to the differences between the European and Middle Eastern societies and states in which these minorities live, to the history and social organization of the minorities concerned, and to differences between the respective religions.

We should, however, notice some striking *parallels* due to facts like the following:
1) both are a religious minority among a majority with a different religion or without religion;
2) both have ways of life distinct from the secular Western one;
3) both stress their religious identity as the ultimate cause of their difference from the majority;
4) both tend to ascribe possible discriminations by the majority to the latter's lack of respect for the religion of the minority.

Some *concrete common features* are the following:

1) In both cases, social and individual life has some typical features that distinguish both Muslim and Christian communities from current (post)modern Western lifestyles: strong family ties, firm rules governing relations between the sexes, particular social traditions of social behavior, hygienic traditions related to food and care of the body, and cultural traditions in the domain of arts, oral and written literature, proverbs, and so on. Often these features are considered as being linked to religion or at least to the religious traditions of the particular communities.

2) In both cases, religion, even if it is not practiced actively by each person, plays a key role in maintaining a social identity that is recognizable, not only to the people themselves but also to the wider society of which they are in varying degrees part.

3) In both cases, the communities concerned include movements that want to keep to existing traditions, and other movements that insist on going back to the very sources of the religion that the community adheres to, that is to say, the Revelation that gives basic rules and truths, mediated by recognized Scriptures. These latter movements are far too varied to be subsumed under such general headings as "fundamentalism" or "integrism". Both movements—the desire to keep to tradition and the will to go back to the sources—can be found abundantly among Muslims in Europe as well as among Christians in the Middle East. These movements should be seen not only as a defense of communal identity and life, but also as a moral and spiritual response to problems these groups encounter in society.

4) In both cases, too, there is a striking tendency to renew and strengthen the links with the broader religious community: for Muslims, the Muslim commonwealth, for instance through their countries of origin, and for Christians, the World Council of Churches, the Roman Catholic Church, or other specific Churches in the West. Muslims in Western Europe, just like Christians in the Middle East, combine forces to ensure their continued presence with the help of a country or organization backing them. There is a growing "ecumenical" concern, notwithstanding all the differences within the broader religious community, both among Muslim groups in Europe and among Christian communities in the Middle East.

5) In both cases, finally, in some countries a certain *rapprochement* between religious leaders takes place. The leadership of certain Muslim groups in Europe is in dialogue with that of certain European Churches; the leadership of certain Christian groups in the Middle East is in dialogue with certain Muslim leaders in the region; the Netherlands and Lebanon provide examples here. This *rapprochement* serves mostly practical interests: defense against common dangers, action for common causes, and strengthening common resources. It entails a positive kind of interaction between minority and majority communities and specifically between individual members of these communities.

2. Comparing the Comparable

To be strict in comparing minority communities that are indeed comparable, we should make a clear distinction between recently formed communities of immigrants, on the one hand, and older established communities that have developed their own traditions, on the other hand. Following this distinction, I shall first make some comparative remarks about the established Muslim communities in Europe and the established Christian communities in the Middle East. I shall then make similar comparative remarks about some Christian immigrant communities in the Middle East and Muslim immigrant communities in Europe. It should be noted that immigrant communities bring with them traditions from their countries of origin. There are, moreover, also Muslim immigrant communities in the Middle East and Christian immigrant communities in Europe, but I shall not deal with them here.

2.1. Established Communities

The Muslim presence in medieval Spain and Italy is well-known; it has left its traces in Western European culture. We should note, however, that Muslim communities are still present as minorities in Eastern and Southeastern Europe. The Mongol-Turkic Golden Horde, for instance, converted to Islam in the 1260s and dominated the Eastern European scene for some two and a half centuries. Their descendants, the Tatars, were defeated by the Russians in the mid-sixteenth century. They underwent harsh treatment, and Orthodox Christian missions were imposed on them. The same must be said about Russian policies toward the Crimean Tatars after the mid-eighteenth century and toward the Muslim peoples in the Caucasus, who were conquered shortly afterward. It was only with Catherine II's edict of tolerance (1782) that Islam became a recognized religion in Russia, which extended its empire to Muslim Central Asia in the mid-nineteenth century.

The situation was different in the Austrian Empire. With the reconquest of territories that had been occupied by the Ottomans up to the 1530s, the majority of the Muslims, mainly Turks, left the areas conquered by the Austrians. Still a number of them came to live under Austrian rule. Here it was Maria Theresia (1740–80) who promulgated an edict of tolerance making Islam a recognized religion. When Austria occupied Bosnia-Herzegovina in 1878, Islam received the same status here as in Austria.

In the Muslim communities living in the Russian and the Austrian empires, ethnicity and religion were closely linked. They lived under strict political and military control, as did the Christian communities in the Ottoman Empire. In the independent Christian states that arose in and around the Balkans in the course of the nineteenth century, those Muslims who had stayed were tolerated, but in Serbia, for instance, their departure was encouraged.

On the other side of the border, from the fifteenth to the nineteenth century, beginning with the Ottoman conquests, the Christian communities living in different parts of the Ottoman empire had a recognized juridical status that, among other things, protected them from open attempts to convert them to Islam. Though the harsh *devshirme* (the periodical levy of Christian boys by the Ottoman state) in the Balkans was abolished practically from the eighteenth century on, they could suffer hard times due to heavy taxation, demands from the army, and corrupt officials.

Indeed, from the middle of the eighteenth century on, when the situation of the Muslim minorities in the two European empires improved, the situation of the Christian minorities deteriorated in the Ottoman Empire, including its European and Arab provinces. This was due to a decline of the correct functioning of the state institutions, but also to the Ottoman authorities' growing distrust of the Christian minorities, especially in the Balkans. On the one hand, the rise of movements for political independence among the Balkan peoples during the nineteenth century meant a disintegration of the European part of the empire. On the other hand, the European powers at the time made political use of the deteriorating situation of the Christian minorities as an argument to intervene, first in Greece, then in the Balkans proper, and finally in the Arab provinces. In the Russian-Turkish wars, the Russians presented themselves as liberators of Christian populations oppressed by Islam. The massacres of Christian Armenians in the Ottoman Empire in 1896 and 1915–6 were a "final solution" for the Armenians that Hitler referred to when he proclaimed his *Endlösung* (final solution) of the Jews.

In the course of the twentieth century, from World War One on, the situation of the established Muslim communities in Europe deteriorated in an unforeseeable way. The persecutions of all religious leaderships and their followers and the dismantling of all religious institutions in the Soviet Union since the twenties—with an interruption during World War Two—are well known. After World War Two, similar hardships befell the Muslims in Albania, Bulgaria, and Yugoslavia. The tragic events that happened to the Muslim communities in Bulgaria in the 1980s and in Bosnia and Kosovo in the 1990s are still on our minds. On a popular level, Islam is still seen as the enemy of Orthodox Christianity. Quite a few Turks ascribe European hesitations to let Turkey join the European Union to the fact that Turkey is a Muslim country.

There is a need for cooperative scholarly research on the history of Muslim minorities in Eastern and Southeastern Europe.

In the Middle East, the position of the established Christian minorities improved when some of them were no longer under the direct authority of Istanbul, specifically after the middle of the nineteenth century. This is true for the Copts in Egypt, a country that attracted numerous Christian immigrants from Syria and Lebanon, and for the Maronites and Orthodox of "Mount Lebanon", which in fact became an autonomous "Christian" region in the Ottoman Empire in the 1860s. Elsewhere in the region, Christians and Jews were further emancipated in the mandate territories administered by Great Britain and France between the two World Wars. Since World War One, except on the Arabian Peninsula, Christians and Jews enjoyed equal status with Muslims as citizens in the countries of the Middle East. After independence, in nearly all these countries a number of privileges enjoyed by the wealthier classes, including many Christians, came to an end. The creation of Israel and the emigration of nearly all the Jews from the Arab countries brought new attention to the minorities in the Middle East.

During the second half of the twentieth century, Christians in Middle Eastern countries have been able to improve older Church structures, thanks to a better-educated clergy and the support given to the Uniate Churches by the Roman Catholic Church and to other Middle Eastern Churches by the World Council of Churches. They have been obliged to reflect on their identity, playing a more active role in their societies, to the extent the political situation allowed. In some countries—like Iraq—the state has intervened and forbidden Christian social activities; in other countries—like Jordan—the state has taken a more liberal attitude. Thanks to their education and connections with the West, Christians have been at times in a somewhat better position than their Muslim compatriots. The rise of undemocratic regimes throughout the region has been a burden on the population as a whole, and restrictions on freedom of expression have also affected the relations between Muslims and Christians. The more recent rise of "Islamist" movements and their work to establish an Islamic state has also affected these relations. Christian citizens want to remain recognized as full citizens with equal rights and duties.

The old Christian minorities in republican Turkey are special cases. Even apart from what happened to the Armenians in 1915–6, the actual situation of the Christians in Turkey has been and remains puzzling. Most Christians simply left a state that is officially secular and where the state and the religion are legally separate. In fact, the state controls Islam, and a close link has developed between secular nationalist Turkish and a specifically Turkish ideology of Islam. As a result, the Turkish-Muslim identity of Turkish citizens is officially taken for granted. As a consequence, there has been no real place in the country for non-Turks like the Kurds, or for non-Muslims who were not officially recognized by the Treaty of Lausanne of 1923. I am thinking of the Syrian Orthodox,

Christians from the southeastern part of the country, who have no legal place in the republic, and also of the Protestants. But also those Turkish Christians whose Church is recognized are living under various pressures, though they do not talk about it. On a popular level there is bitterness about the presence of Christianity, and the "Islamist" movements have increased this.

Another special case is the situation of the old Christian communities living in Israel and the Occupied Territories and East Jerusalem. The Palestinian Christian communities have suffered from Israeli Jewish nationalism just as the Turkish Christian communities have suffered from Turkish Islamic nationalism. Both nationalisms have received indigenous religious blessings. In both cases, the Christian minority is on the decline. As in Turkey, a number of Christians have simply left.

Whereas there are no old established Christian communities in Arabia, there are in Syria, Iraq, and Jordan. They enjoy a certain favorable position under the Syrian regime, which itself has its roots in a Muslim minority group. Like other Iraqi citizens, they are under heavy pressure from the Iraqi regime, which traditionally distrusts non-Sunnī citizens. In Jordan, Christian citizens enjoy equal rights with Muslim citizens. Since the revolution of 1979, Iran has become an Islamic state in which the Christian communities of the Armenians and the Nestorian "Assyrians"—like the Zoroastrians—have the legal status of *dhimmīs*, protected minorities, but without paying special taxes (*jizya*).

2.2. Immigrant Communities

A fair treatment requires that the situation of Muslim immigrants be compared not so much with the old established Christian communities in the Middle East, but rather with that of Christian immigrants to Muslim countries of the Middle East. Here I mean specifically Arab and Asian Christian migrant workers who moved to find work along the Gulf and in Saudi Arabia. As far as I know, there is no immigration of migrant workers to other Muslim countries in the Middle East.

For Arab migrants, in particular Palestinians, Egyptians, and Jordanians, certainly if they are Christians, the Arabian Peninsula may be very different from their own country. They nevertheless share a common Arabic language with the indigenous people, and Christian and Muslim Arabs have many common features of family and social life. Incentives may be offered to convert to Islam, but a polite refusal will be accepted. For Asian migrants, however, the situation is different. Especially Christian women, coming for instance from the Philippines or Sri Lanka, the transition is infinitely greater, since they are women and treated accordingly, often nearly as slaves. Throughout the Gulf region, with the exception of Kuwait, Bahrain, and Oman, no visible sign of the Christian religion is permitted in public life. This is also the case in Saudi Arabia, but here not only churches but also religious gatherings of non-Muslims are straightforwardly forbidden. Throughout the region, the treatment of migrant workers, whether Muslim or Christian, is particularly harsh. They cannot be organized in unions, they can always be sent back within twenty-four hours, and they have to leave the country once their contract is finished. Christians cannot do missionary work and they cannot marry local Muslim women. The legal position of migrant workers is extremely weak and they are not considered potential immigrants.

In the case of Muslim migrant workers moving to Europe and of Christian migrant workers going to the Gulf area, economic reasons explain the willingness to expose oneself to adversities. If the Gulf region and Saudi Arabia are known for their strict religion, their harsh climate, and the haughtiness of the men in power, Europe is experienced as a secular society where Muslim and other immigrants find themselves under pressure to work as much as possible and to abandon traditional ways of life, cultural and religious. In Europe, the risk of unemployment and other kinds of insecurity make migration a bittersweet adventure. Once admitted and having found work, however, the immigrants and their families can stay. They can establish prayer halls, mosques, and Islamic schools when they know the right procedures. They can display their religion in public and, if they want, work for the expansion of Islam. They can marry European women. All of this means that Muslim migrants in Europe, once they have taken the step of moving and have succeeded in settling down, enjoy a degree of freedom, including religious freedom, that is unknown to Christian migrants to the Gulf area. Health, unemployment, and social security schemes are provided by law to legal immigrants, so that they can stay. As a consequence, continuity of the Muslim presence in Europe is guaranteed. Certain categories of refugees and asylum seekers are accepted.

Now, of course, there are stricter immigration laws and societal structures and forces in European societies that stand in the way of immigrant workers' social mobility, political participation, and emancipation in general. The practice of life in secular societies here may be disappointing when measured against the humane standards of traditional societies, the ideal norms of Islam, or the aspirations of civil society. But at least there is a normative legal framework and political power is democratically controlled.

Only by comparing comparable communities do we get a better insight into the real situation of older established Christian communities in the Middle East compared to the real situation of older established Muslim societies in Europe. And if a comparison of the situation of Muslim and

Christian immigrant communities in Europe and the Gulf region, including Saudi Arabia, favors Europe, a fair comparison of the situation of the more established Muslim and Christian communities may very well turn out to the advantage of the Muslim Middle East, at least in its Arab parts.

3. Muslims in Europe and Christians in the Middle East

If Muslim immigrants in Europe and Christian communities in the Middle East are so different that they can hardly be compared, how can we summarize their main differences?

The Muslims in Western Europe are busy building up an existence in countries and states that are very different from those they come from. They have to adapt their behavior to survive. They suffer the pressure of living in largely secular societies that have a market economy and where unemployment and lack of schooling are major obstacles to any integration. They have to create their own networks of companions and of cultural and religious institutions. They find themselves subject to laws and regulations whose meaning often escapes them, but that are enforced equally on all people. They have to learn constantly and to find their place. The Christians in the Middle East, on the other hand, have a long history of maintaining themselves in a rather complex equilibrium of social structures and forces. This equilibrium has now been disrupted to a large extent through transformations of society and the state, economic problems, and threats of war. This means that the Christians with the Muslims and their societies have now come under pressure, all the more so because of the actions of Islamic activists and their goal of further Islamizing society.

In both cases it seems that religion, family, and kinship play an important role in providing an identity to the people concerned, who in turn respond by giving their loyalty. In the case of the Muslim immigrants in Europe, Islam provides a solidarity beyond linguistic, ethnic, and national differences. There are traditions, but there is also a great variety of organizations, institutions, and leaderships. Muslims can rediscover their Islam in Europe. In the case of the Christian communities in the Middle East, religion provides them with various ecclesiastical institutions that are distinct from each other, each having its own hierarchically organized leadership, structures, and rather firm traditions largely off limits to society. Since the mid-twentieth century, Christian youth movements have emerged that have given a new elan to their communities.

Both groups suffer a degree of uncertainty at present. Muslim immigrants are confronted with economic adversity, Eurocentric and Islamophobic attitudes, and here and there social and political obstruction. They are uncertain not only about whether they and their descendants will be able to establish themselves satisfactorily in European societies, but also about whether these societies themselves will accept them as they are. As a last resort, there remains the option of returning to their country of origin, but this will be difficult for the second and later generations. Christians in the Middle East, on the whole, are uncertain about whether not only economic and social conditions, but also political adversity and obstruction carried out in the name of Islam—on a popular level or by organized groups—will prevent them from participating in society and leading a life of dignity. It seems to be especially the political unpredictability of the region and the weak legal and sometimes even simply physical protection given to them that feeds uncertainty about their future. As a last resort, there is the possibility of emigration, but this—apart from being a painful measure—would further weaken the Christian presence in the region.

The differences between the two groups and their respective prospects, consequently, are considerable. Muslim immigrants in Europe and Christians in the Middle East, though both living as minorities and—with the exception of Lebanon—possessing little political power, are in fact very different cases in very different contexts. The economic and social position of the Christians in the Middle East is better than that of Muslim workers in Europe. The legal protection and social insurances for Muslims in Western Europe is better than that of Christians in the Middle East. However, considerable support, moral and practical, is forthcoming to the Muslims or Christians in question from countries where Islam or Christianity, respectively, constitutes the majority religion. Muslim immigrants receive support from their countries of origin; Christians in the Middle East receive support from Churches in the West. Such support, however, implies a degree of dependency. It also implies the possibility of direct or indirect ideological and political control and even manipulation from abroad. European and Middle Eastern governments are conscious of this.

This leads to the awkward question of the possible future of the religions of these two minority groups. Islam in Western Europe has a short history, but enjoys various forms of loyalty; on various levels, Islam is being rediscovered by descendants of immigrants from Muslim countries. Islam is still largely seen as a religion of immigrants and an indicator of ethnic differences.

For the future, much depends on whether European societies are able to accept the existence and presence of Islam as a religion with its own values. This, in turn, will depend partly on whether a politicization of Islam, as has taken place in a number of Muslim countries, can be avoided in Europe and whether any appeal to violence in connection with Islam, from whatever side, can be contained. It will partly depend on attitudes taken by the Christian Churches. Whether Christians will stress an opposition between Christianity and Islam or will be able to enter into cooperation and even dialogue with Muslims while discerning certain values in the Muslim way of life and in Islam as a religion will influence future relationships.

An important negative factor is the lack of communication and of adequate information. There is still much ignorance on both sides. Most Muslims in Europe have little or no knowledge of what different groups of Christians really believe and do. Most Christians in Europe or even in the Middle East have little feeling for what different groups of Muslims believe and do and how in Islam religious belief and social action are closely related.

Too much has been speculated about the future of Christianity in the Middle East. Traditionally, its spirituality has led a life separate from society. It then runs the risk of being incapable of responding adequately to the further changes and unforeseeable new forms that Middle Eastern societies will take in the years to come. Cooperation and dialogue with responsible Muslims for the sake of the societies in which they live seems to be vital for the future of the Christians themselves. Both Christians and Muslims should see it as a privilege to make their contribution to the construction of civil societies in which justice will prevail and people of various backgrounds can live and construct their future together.

Selected Literature

1. The Muslim World and its Minorities

AMJAD ALI, S., *The Muslim World Today*, Islamabad: National Hijra Council, 1985/1405.

IQBAL, Afzal, *Contemporary Muslim World*, Islamabad: Institute of Islamic Culture, 1985, 1992[2].

Islam Outside the Arab World, ed. by David WESTERLUND and Ingvar SVANBERG, Richmond, U. K.: Curzon, 1999.

MANDAVILLE, Peter, *Transnational Muslim Politics: Reimagining the umma* (Series Transnationalism), London and New York: Routledge, 2001.

PLANHOL, Xavier de, *Minorités en Islam: Géographie politique et sociale*, Paris: Flammarion, 1997.

2. Arab World

2.1. Christian Minorities in General

BETTS, Robert Brenton, *Christians in the Arab East: A Political Study*, Athens: Lycabettus Press, 1975.

Christian Communities in the Arab Middle East: The Challenge of the Future, ed. by Andrea PACINI, Oxford: Clarendon Press, 1998.

CORM, Georges, *Contribution à l'étude des sociétés multi-confessionnelles; effets socio-juridiques et politique du pluralisme religieux*, Paris: Librairie générale de Droit et de Jurisprudence, 1971.

HAJJAR, Joseph, *Les chrétiens uniates du Proche-Orient*, Paris: Seuil, 1962.

—, *Le christianisme en Orient: Etudes d'histoire contemporaine, 1684–1968*, Beirut: Librairie du Liban, 1971.

HARTMANN, Klaus-Peter, *Untersuchungen zur Sozialgeographie christlicher Minderheiten im Vorderen Orient*, Wiesbaden: Reichert, 1980.

HASSAN BIN TALAL, El, *Christianity in the Arab World*, Amman: Royal Institute for Inter-Faith Studies, 1994.

HOURANI, Albert H., *Minorities in the Arab World*, Oxford, etc.: Oxford University Press, 1947, etc.

MASTERS, Bruce, *Christians and Jews in the Ottoman Arab World: The Roots of Sectarianism* (Cambridge Studies in Islamic Civilization), Cambridge, U. K.: Cambridge University Press, 2001.

Minorities and the State in the Arab World, ed. by Ofra BENGIO and Gabriel BEN-DOR, Boulder and London: Lynne Rienner, 1999.

PANZER, Regina, *Identität und Geschichtsbewusstsein: Griechisch-orthodoxe Christen im Vorderen Orient zwischen Byzanz und Arabertum* (Studien zur Zeitgeschichte des Nahen Ostens und Nordafrikas 3), Hamburg, etc.: Lit Verlag, 1997.

VALOGNE, Jean-Pierre (ps.), *Vie et mort des chrétiens d'Orient: Des origines à nos jours*, Paris: Fayard, 1994.

YE'OR, Bat (ps.), *Les chrétientés d'Orient entre jihād et dhimmitude VIIᵉ–XXᵉ siècle*, Paris: Cerf, 1991; English edition: *The Decline of Eastern Christianity under Islam: From Jihad to Dhimmitude. Seventh – Twentieth Century*, Madison, etc.: Fairleigh Dickinson, 1996.

—, *Juifs et chrétiens sous l'Islam: Les dhimmis face au défi intégriste*, Paris: Berg International, 1994.

2.2. Lebanon

AZAR, Fabiola, *Construction identitaire et appartenance confessionnelle au Liban: Approche pluridisciplinaire* (Comprendre le Moyen-Orient), Paris: L'Harmattan, 1999.

HANF, Theodor, *Koexistenz im Krieg: Staatszerfall und Entstehen einer Nation im Libanon* (Schriften des Forschungsinstituts der Deutschen Gesellschaft für Auswärtige Politik), Baden-Baden: Nomos, 1990.

Lumières sur Saïda: Quand chrétiens et musulmans bâtissent la paix au Sud-Liban, by Georges BAGUET, Boutros HALLAQ and Michel JONDOT, Paris: Desclée de Brouwer, 1994.

MAKDISI, Ussama, *The Culture of Sectarianism: Community, History, and Violence in Nineteenth-Century Ottoman Lebanon*, Berkeley and Los Angeles: University of California Press, 2000.

SEMAAN, Wanis A., *Aliens at Home: A Socio-Religious Analysis of the Protestant Church in Lebanon and its Backgrounds*, Beirut: Librairie du Liban, 1986.

2.3. Egypt

ALDEEB ABU-SAHLIEH, Sami Awad, *Non-musulmans en pays d'Islam: Cas de l'Egypte*, Fribourg: Ed. Universitaires, 1979.

BEHRENS-ABOUSEIF, Doris, *Die Kopten in der ägyptischen Gesellschaft, von der Mitte des 19. Jahrhunderts bis 1923* (Islamkundliche Untersuchungen 18), Freiburg: Klaus Schwarz, 1972.

FÔDA, Farag, *Minorities and Human Rights in Egypt* (CSIC Papers, Africa Nr. 16), Birmingham: Centre for the Study of Islam and Christian-Muslim Relations, Selly Oak Colleges, December 1994.

MOTZKI, Harald, *Dimma und Egalité: Die nicht-muslimischen Minderheiten Ägyptens in der zweiten Hälfte des 18. Jahrhunderts und die Expedition Bonapartes (1798–1801)* (Studien zum Minderheitenproblem im Islam 5), Bonn: Selbstverlag des Orientalischen Seminars der Universität, 1979.

2.4. Other Arab Countries

ANSCHÜTZ, Helga, *Die syrischen Christen vom Tur ʿAbdin: Eine altchristliche Bevölkerungsgruppe zwischen Beharrung, Stagnation und Auflösung*, Würzburg: Augustinus-Verlag, 1985.

Christians in the Holy Land, ed. by Michael PRIOR and William TAYLOR, London: World of Islam Festival Trust, 1994, 1995².

HADDAD, Mohanna Yousuf, *Christians in Jordan: A Split Identity* (Gitelson Peace Publication 17), Jerusalem: Harry S. Truman Research Institute for the Advancement of Peace, May 2001.

HADDAD, Robert M., *Syrian Christians in Muslim Society: An Interpretation* (Princeton Studies on the Near East), Princeton: Princeton University Press, 1970.

Histoire des chrétiens d'Afrique du Nord (Mémoire chrétienne), ed. by Henri TEISSIER, Paris: Desclée, 1991.

SHALIT, Yoram, *Nicht-Muslime und Fremde in Aleppo und Damaskus im 18. und in der ersten Hälfte des 19. Jahrhunderts* (Islamkundliche Untersuchungen 197), Berlin: Klaus Schwarz, 1996.

3. Turkey, Iran, Pakistan

3.1. Turkey

SONYEL, Salâhi R., *Minorities and the Destruction of the Ottoman Empire* (Publications of Turkish Historical Society, Serial. VII-No. 129), Ankara: Turkish Historical Society Printing House, 1993.

3.2. Iran

The Armenians of Iran: The Paradoxical Role of a Minority in a Dominant Culture: Articles and Documents, ed. by Cosroe CHAQUERI (Harvard Middle Eastern Monographs 30), Cambridge, Mass.: Harvard University Press, 1998.

FRANZ, Erhard, *Minderheiten in Iran: Dokumentation zur Ethnographie und Politik* (Aktueller Informationsdienst Moderner Orient, Sondernummer, Nr. 8), Hamburg: Deutsches Orient-Institut and Dokumentations-Leitstelle Moderner Orient, 1981.

LYKO, Dieter, *Gründung, Wachstum und Leben der Evangelischen Christlichen Kirchen in Iran* (Oekumenische Studien V), Leiden: E. J. Brill, 1964.

SANASARIAN, Eliz, *Religious Minorities in Iran* (Cambridge Middle East Studies), Cambridge, U. K., etc.: Cambridge University Press, 2000.

WATERFIELD, Robin E., *Christians in Persia: Assyrians, Armenians, Roman Catholics and Protestants*, London: Allen & Unwin, 1973.

3.3. Pakistan

AMJAD-ALI, Christine and Charles, *The Legislative History of the Shariah Acts* (CSC Monograph 29), Rawalpindi: Christian Study Centre, 1992.

Human Rights Monitor, Reports on the Situation of Religious Minorities in Pakistan, Lahore: National Commission for Justice and Peace, Catholic Bishops' Conference of Pakistan, 1998–2001.

JOHN JOSEPH, Bishop, *A Peaceful Struggle: A Collection of Bishop John Joseph's Writings against Black Laws and Discrimination*, ed. by Fr. Khalid Rashid ASI, Faisalabad: National Commission for Justice and Peace, Catholic Bishops' Conference of Pakistan, May 1999.

News from the Country: Pakistan 1980–84, by Editorial Staff of Christian Study Centre (CSC Series 21), Rawalpindi: Christian Study Centre, 1985.

Religious Minorities in Pakistan: Struggle for Identity, ed. by Domnic MOGHAL and Jennifer JIVAN (CSC Publication 33), Rawalpindi: Christian Study Centre, 1996.

VEMMELUND, Laurits, *The Christian Minority in the North West Frontier Province of Pakistan* (CSC Series Nr. 6), Rawalpindi: Christian Study Centre, 1973, pp. 92–202.

Why are we Afraid of Secularism in Pakistan?, ed. by Dominic MOGHAL and Jennifer Jag JIVAN (CSC Publication 39), Rawalpindi: Christian Study Centre, 1999.

4. Southeast Asia

4.1. Malaysia

ACKERMAN, Susan E., and Raymond L. M. LEE, *Heaven in Transition: Non-Muslim Religious Innovation and Ethnic Identity in Malaysia*, Kuala Lumpur: Forum, 1990.

CHEW, Maureen K. C., *The Journey of the Catholic Church in Malaysia: 1511–1996*, Kuala Lumpur: Catholic Research Centre, 2000.

Christianity in Malaysia: A Denominational History, ed. by Robert HUNT, Lee KAM HING, and John ROXBOROGH, Petaling Jaya: Pelanduk Publications, 1992.

METZGER, Laurent, *Stratégie islamique en Malaisie (1975–1995)* (Series Points sur l'Asie), Paris: L'Harmattan, 1996.

4.2. Indonesia

BOLAND, Bernard Johan, *The Struggle of Islam in Modern Indonesia*, The Hague: M. Nijhoff, 1971, 1982[2].

—, and I. FARJON, *Islam in Indonesia: A Bibliographical Survey 1600–1942 with post–1945 Addenda* (Koninklijk Instituut voor Taal-, Land- en Volkenkunde, Bibliographical Series 14), Dordrecht: Foris, 1983.

HEFNER, Robert W., *Civil Islam: Muslims and Democratization in Indonesia* (Princeton Studies in Muslim Politics), Princeton and Oxford: Princeton University Press, 2000.

Ministry of Religious Affairs: Tasks and Functions, Jakarta: Ministry of Religious Affairs, 1996.

STEENBRINK, Karel, *Dutch Colonialism and Indonesian Islam: Contacts and Conflicts, 1596–1950* (Currents of Encounter 7), Amsterdam and Atlanta: Rodopi, 1993.

TAHER, H. Tarmizi, *Aspiring for the Middle Path: Religious Harmony in Indonesia*, Jakarta: Center for the Study of Islam and Society (CENSIS), 1997.

WAWER, Wendelin, *Muslime und Christen in der Republik Indonesien* (Beiträge zur Südasien-Forschung 7), Wiesbaden: Franz Steiner, 1974.

5. Africa outside the Arab World

5.1. Islam in Africa

African Islam and Islam in Africa: Encounters between Sufis and Islamists, ed. by David WESTERLUND and Eva Evers ROSANDER, Athens, Oh.: Ohio University Press.

CUOQ, Joseph M., *Les musulmans en Afrique*, Paris: Maisonneuve et Larose, 1975.

Faces of Islam in African Literature, ed. by Kenneth W. HARROW (Studies in African Literature, New Series), Portsmouth, N. H.: Heinemann, and London: James Currey, 1991.

The History of Islam in Africa, ed. by Nehemia LEVTZION and Randall L. POUWELS, Athens, Oh.: Ohio University Press, and Oxford: James Currey, 2000.

TAYOB, Abdulkader, *Islam in South Africa: Mosques, Imams, and Sermons*, Gainesville, Fla., etc.: University Press of Florida, 1999.

—, *Islamic Resurgence in South Africa: The Muslim Youth Movement*, Cape Town: University of Cape Town Press, 1995.

TRIMINGHAM, J. Spencer, *Islam in West Africa*, Oxford: Clarendon Press, 1959, etc.

—, *Islam in East Africa*, Oxford: Clarendon Press, 1964.

—, *The Influence of Islam upon Africa* (Arab Background Series), London: Longmans Green, and Beirut: Librairie du Liban, 1968.

5.2. Christian Minorities in African Muslim Countries

CHUKWULOZIE, Victor, *Muslim-Christian Dialogue in Nigeria*, Ibadan: Daystar Press, 1986.

DENIEL, Raymond, *Croyances religieuses et vie quotidienne: Islam et christianisme à Ouagadougou* (Recherches Voltaïques 14), Paris: Ed. du CNRS, 1970.

Islam in Africa: Perspectives for Christian-Muslim Relations. Consultation of the World Alliance of Reformed Churches, 6–10 June 1994 in Malawi, ed. Henry S. WILSON, Geneva: World Alliance of Reformed Churches, 1995.

MAINA, Kahumbi N., *Christian-Muslim Relations in Kenya: An Examination of Issues of Conflicts* (CSIC Papers, Africa Nr. 17), Birmingham: Centre for the Study of Islam and Christian-Muslim Relations, January 1995.

NYANG, Sulayman S., *Islam, Christianity, and African Identity*, Brattleboro, Vt.: Amana Books, 1984.

SANNEH, Lamin, *Piety and Power: Muslims and Christians in West Africa* (Faith meets Faith), Maryknoll, N. Y.: Orbis Books, 1996.

—, *The Crown and the Turban: Muslims and West African Pluralism*, Boulder, Col.: Westview Press, 1997.

TRIMINGHAM, J. Spencer, *Islam in West Africa: The Report of a Survey Undertaken in 1952 at the Request of the Church Missionary Society and the Methodist Missionary Society*, London: Church Missionary Society and the Methodist Missionary Society, 1953.

—, *The Christian Church and Islam in West Africa* (I.M.C. Research Pamphlets Nr. 3), London: SCM Press, 1955.

YOH, John Gay, *Christianity in the Sudan: Overview and Bibliography*, Amman: Royal Institute for Inter-Faith Studies, 1996.

6. Muslim Minorities outside the West

Journal for Islamic Minority Affairs (*JIMA*), Jeddah and London (since 1979, twice yearly).

KETTANI, M. Ali, *Muslim Minorities in the World Today*, London and New York: Mansell, 1986.

Chapter 16
Issues in Muslim-Christian Relations[1]

I would like to say something about Muslim-Christian relations on the basis of "critical realism", on the one hand, and "constructive partnership", on the other. My purpose is to identify some issues we have to cope with if we want to improve relations between Muslims and Christians.

1. The Study of Muslim-Christian Relations

The historical study of the relationships between Muslim and Christian communities, between Islam and Christianity, is still in its beginnings. It cannot be otherwise, since Islamic history itself as well as the history of Christian communities that have been in contact with Islam in different times and places is still being written. One could even call it premature to start studying relations between entities that are themselves not yet fully known. Much research needs to be done, for instance, on the cultural, social, and economic history of the Christian communities living within Muslim territories. The same holds true for the study of the life of Muslim communities after their territories were conquered, for instance in Russia, the Balkans, nineteenth-century Africa and Asia, and of course the twentieth-century Middle East. And what happened after these people regained independence?

One privileged field of research on Muslim-Christian relations, because of the richness of these relations and the existence of various kinds of sources, is that of medieval Spain. Recent studies have shown that certain generalizing ideas about these relations ought to be abandoned to do justice to the historical facts. Another field of research that has proved to be rewarding is the Crusade period, whose historical reality, again, does

---

[1] Revised version of a paper read at the Center for Muslim-Christian Understanding, at Georgetown University, Washington, D.C., in April 1995. A first version of this paper was published under the title "Critical Issues in Muslim-Christian Relations: Theoretical, Practical, Dialogical, Scholarly", *Islam and Christian-Muslim Relations*, 8, Nr. 1 (1997), pp. 9–26.

not at all conform to the general ideas current about it in either the Western or the Muslim world. There are still many blank spots in the history of the encounters of Europeans with Tatars and Turks in Europe from the thirteenth and fourteenth century respectively on.

Poorly known, too, is the nature of the intricate relationships that developed between European and Muslim peoples outside Europe. This holds particularly true for the period of European colonial expansion, roughly speaking between 1800 and 1950. This history has mostly been described as a confrontation between religions or civilizations: on one side to build empires and to dominate, on the other side to develop and use various strategies to survive under foreign domination. Here too, I surmise, the historical reality, when it becomes better known, may very well contradict current general ideas. Within both the colonizing and the colonized countries, different orientations and interests were at play at the same time, and ignorance was rampant on both sides. In any case, there is an urgent need for continuous historical research on situations in which Muslims and Christians, or Europeans and Westerners in general, have encountered each other or lived together as people.

Research on more personal initiatives and interactions between Christians and Muslims, on their perceptions and judgments, discussions and debates, and the various cultural and religious interests involved is a fascinating part of the broader study of the history of Muslim-Christian relations. Such interactions have of course been largely ruled by power relations, political and economic interests, legal prescriptions, and rules of etiquette. Partly, however, they have also depended on choices of the persons meeting each other. The more personal quality of meetings that took place since World War Two, when the participants could respond more directly to each other and when more information had become available, makes accounts of them all the more fascinating to read. Some of these meetings have been occasions of committed debates and discussions.

An especially interesting part of the study of Muslim-Christian relations in the past concerns the ways the parties perceived each other in situations of encounter or developed ideas about each other in their own reflection and imagination. The ways in which they then perceived and judged each other's religions are an especially rewarding subject. There were many more nuances and variations in these perceptions than is commonly known, given the stereotypes both parties cherished about Islam and Christianity.

2. Dialogue Efforts

Not until the 1950s was the term "dialogue" applied to meetings of rapprochement between Christians and Muslims as adherents of two different religions and the idea of organized dialogues and dialogue programs launched. These started with the meetings of the Continuing Committee for Muslim Christian Cooperation (CCMCC) in Bhamdoun, Lebanon, in 1954 and 1956. They continued through meetings arranged by the Vatican and the World Council of Churches since the end of the 1960s. Initiatives were taken on the Muslim side through conferences and symposia organized by Qadhdhāfī in 1976, by the Centre d'Etudes et de Recherches Economiques et Sociales (CERES) in Tunis between 1974 and 1991, and by the Āl al-Bayt Foundation in Amman between 1985 and 2000. We can speak here of a unique kind of summit meetings of Muslim and Christian leaders keen on rapprochement.

However, the civil war and further armed conflicts in Lebanon (1975–89), the Gulf War (1991), the Bosnian War (1992–5), the wars in Chechnya, and of course those in Afghanistan (1979–2001) have put an end to what may be called an exploratory and somehow more innocent phase of Muslim-Christian dialogues. To these critical contexts should be added the problems of the integration of Muslim immigrants in Western societies, campaigns in the West defaming Islam and the other way around, and fears of Islamist violence against Western people.

In such a context, dialogue can no longer be pursued apart from socio-political and economic realities, restricted to a sphere of personal ethics, ideals, and spirituality. Indeed, both religions risk being seriously compromised if their leaders make common statements during their summits about the need for peace, while at the same time ordinary people are exposed to the realities of discrimination, hatred, and violence. Radical movements want to mobilize people ideologically, at least partly in the name of their religions, against others. This degradation of relationships seems to be a more general process in which both Muslims and Christians have their share.

Looking back, it would seem that the top-level Muslim-Christian encounters in the sixties, the seventies, and still the eighties took place in a context that was favorable to such encounters. The broader public was relieved when it saw reports in the media of Muslim and Christian dignitaries speaking with each other. Later it became clear, however, that the religious leaders, including even the Pope, could not significantly influence the political leadership in either Western or Muslim countries. One might even surmise that it would be better not to speak of religion at all if pragmatic solutions are sought.

Consequently, in a somewhat unexpected way, the official Muslim-Christian dialogue has shown certain limits after the first successful decades. It has brought to light not only the strengths, but also the weaknesses of existing religious institutions and of the current leadership. This brings us to the question of what the fruits of this dialogue have been for societies in Western and in Muslim countries, where so many ordinary people who happen to be Muslims or Christians are desperately longing for a life in peace and justice?

2.1. Kinds and Levels of Dialogue

In the light of this, it is all the more significant that there have also been kinds of dialogue other than what may be called the officially organized ones that attracted public attention. These have worked on various levels.

1) On the level of *thought*, a good example is the Muslim-Christian Research Group (GRIC), which has existed since 1977, with Catholic, Protestant, and Muslim participants. It consists of four working groups in Brussels, Paris, Tunis, and Rabat that work on a common theme; once a year representatives of these groups gather to evaluate the work done. So far the group has published four books.[2] On this level there are also regular publications. On the Catholic side, the yearbook *Islamochristiana*, a publication of the Pontifical Institute for Arabic and Islamic Studies (PISAI) in Rome, has appeared annually since 1975. The PISAI is organized by the White Fathers, who also publish the monthlies *Encounter* in Italy and *Se Comprendre* in France, both dealing with Christian-Muslim relations. The PISAI also publishes the series *Studi arabo-islamici del PISAI*, with publications in French and English.

Among Protestant publications, I recall the quarterly *The Muslim World*, founded in 1910 and now published by the Duncan Black Macdonald Center for the Study of Islam and Christian-Muslim Relations at Hartford, Connecticut. *Islam and Muslim-Christian Understanding*, founded in 1989, now appears four times yearly, edited in a joint venture by the Centre for the Study of Islam and Christianity at the University of Birmingham, U.K. and the Center for Muslim-Christian Understanding at Georgetown University, Washington, D. C.

---

[2] The first is a study of the way in which the Bible and Qur'ān ought to be approached (*The Challenge of the Scriptures: The Bible and the Qur'ān*, Maryknoll, N. Y.: Orbis, 1989). The second deals with Faith and Justice (*Foi et Justice: Un défi pour le christianisme et pour l'islam*, Paris: Centurion, 1993). The third discusses plurality and secularity (*Pluralisme et laïcité: Chrétiens et musulmans proposent*, Paris: Bayard/ Centurion, 1996), and the fourth evil and ethical responsibility (*Péché et responsabilité éthique dans le monde contemporain: Chrétiens et musulmans s'interrogent*, Paris: Bayard, 2000).

These four institutions in Rome, Hartford, Birmingham, and Washington, D. C.—and some others as well—offer courses and degrees on Islam and Christian-Muslim relations. A number of Catholic and Protestant institutions in Muslim countries have opened libraries on Christianity and Islam; a number of Muslim institutions in both Muslim and Western countries have libraries with books on Islam and Christianity in its various denominations.

2) On a *practical* level, broader cooperation is being developed by Muslims and Christians in Western and Muslim countries who have committed themselves to causes such as human rights, the conditions of minorities, and efforts toward conflict solution, justice, and peace, through Amnesty International and other organizations. This may broaden out to political action in favor of oppressed peoples and against various forms of economic exploitation.

Other efforts concentrate on *intercultural information and exchanges*. Persons with special qualifications from a wide variety of Muslim countries are now being invited to speak or write about their society and culture in Europe or North America. They address training courses, colloquia, and workshops on Muslim societies, Islam, and Muslim-Christian relations.

3) On the level of scholarly *research*, cooperation is increasing. Muslim researchers and scholars contribute to international encyclopedias and handbooks and are attached to international scholarly institutions concerned with Islam. Muslim staff is increasingly appointed at Western universities to teach "Islamic" languages and literatures, history and anthropology, religion and culture. More and more scholarly books on Islamic subjects have Muslim authors. The Muslim contribution to scholarship on Islam in the broad sense has increased greatly during the last half century, and not only in the USA. Since research facilities are better in the West, it is in Western countries that common research projects have taken off. International scholarly meetings on Islamic culture and societies now take place in Muslim countries as well.

It is time now to address some issues in the relations between Muslims and Christians that will continue to demand attention in the foreseeable future. I have divided these issues into four groups: theoretical, practical, dialogical, and scholarly.

3. Theoretical Issues

At first sight, the following issues seem to be of a rather abstract, philosophical nature. Yet, on a theoretical level they have and will continue to have a decisive impact on relations between thoughtful Muslims and Christians in the future.

3.1. Identity

Who are the Christians and the Muslims about whose relations we speak? What makes the Christians Christians and the Muslims Muslims, and what constitutes the identity of the parties involved in Muslim-Christian dialogues? Is it the creed, the fact of being baptized or men being circumcised, the fact of belonging to a community considering itself Muslim or Christian, or simply having by birth and education a Muslim or Christian background?

The question is far from being academic. Throughout history, in different times and contexts, the words "Christian" and "Muslim" have had different kinds of meanings, and it may very well be that the more specifically "religious" reading of the words is of rather recent date. Muslims have traditionally considered all "Franks" to be automatically "Christians", and many of them are shocked that Europe has become secularized and that an increasing number of Europeans have no clear Christian affiliation. The other way around, Europeans have mostly considered all Turks, Iranians, and Arabs to be Muslims and are surprised to discover that there are Christian Arabs whose roots go back to pre-Islamic times, just as there are Christian Turks, Iranians, and Pakistanis. In French discourse, North Africans have often been called "the Muslims" (*les musulmans*), without a specific religious connotation. Marxist-oriented states like China and the former Soviet Union and Yugoslavia speak of their Muslim minorities not as a religious but as a socio-ethnic group. And the other way around, Muslims tend to see Christians primarily as a social group or a particular church community, rather than as people of a personal faith or a specific religiosity. What in all of this indicates a "religious" identity?

In ordinary usage in the Middle East, including Israel, people have been and still are identified and defined according to the socio-religious communities to which they belong, without considering whether some have a more personalized identity than others. A Christian Arab may call him- or herself in the same breath a Christian and an agnostic.

Especially in situations of conflict and in minority situations, the social meaning tends to predominate over the religious one. The Azeris are Muslims and the Armenians Christians, and there is little point in asking what kind of Muslim a particular Azeri is or what kind of Christian a particular Armenian is. But also in regions where Christians and Muslims live peacefully in proximity, the identity "Christian" or "Muslim" has fundamentally been a social, even a collective identity. It indicates membership in a local Muslim or Christian group, a broader community of Muslims or Christians in the country concerned, or the worldwide community of all Muslims or all Christians. Varieties are practically neglected.

In such a context, an expression like "Muslim-Christian dialogue" suggests a situation of negotiating between two communities rather than a meeting of two or more individuals who expose to each other a conscious and strictly personal faith. People from the Middle East who participate in Western Muslim-Christian dialogues actually risk not being able to express in what precise sense they are Muslims or Christians, even though they identify themselves as such. What would they think of a more personal Muslim-Christian dialogue in which the Muslim may have sympathies for the Christian religion, or the Christian perhaps sympathies for the Islamic religion?

The problem of identity, however, arises in dialogues not between adherents but between conscious persons. Organizers of official Muslim-Christian dialogues may wish to have straightforward Muslims and straightforward Christians who are willing and prepared to enter into dialogue from their respective positions. In fact, however, such persons representing "the" Muslim or Christian religious position are not that easy to find. Their identity may have either too many social and collective aspects for them to engage in a more personal dialogue, or their position may be too personal to be recognized as being "representative". In fact, people sensitive to the difference between social and personal identity or who are themselves searching in the broad area of faith tend to be more "dialogically" minded than people who identify themselves straightforwardly in contrast to others. This is one of the paradoxes of any organized dialogue.

The issue of identity is critical indeed and will probably become even more so in the future. It makes a great difference whether we speak of relations between Muslims and Christians for whom religious and social identity is basically the same thing or if we have in mind people who take a personal stand. In the first case, people tend to identify themselves through a particular way of life or set of doctrines held by others, too. In the latter case, they distinguish themselves apparently through a more personal kind of identity.

As a consequence, one should distinguish relations between "socially religious" Muslims and Christians who stress their socio-cultural identity, on the one hand, from relations between "personally religious" Muslims and Christians who stress their personal stand, on the other. In the first case, the Muslims and Christians concerned may see themselves as in harmony with or in opposition to others practically beyond their own will. In the second case, they may present a quite personal view of the difference between Islam and Christianity, between Muslims and Christians. It largely depends on the degree to which the believer has personalized a given religion or faith in his or her life.

3.2. *Opposition or Complementarity*

Throughout history, Muslims and Christians have tended to see each other not only as inevitably different but also as opposed to each other. Much depended on the context. An opposition arises clearly in direct military or political conflicts in which two parties take a stand against each other while identifying themselves with Islam or Christianity (the Church) respectively. In the many conflicts of this kind that have occurred in history between "social" Muslims and Christians and in which Christianity and Islam were presented as social or political causes to fight for, it made sense to construct such an opposition. It also made sense to stress the element of opposition in situations of majority-minority relations in which the minority had to distinguish itself clearly from the majority if it wanted to survive. These two special cases of conflict and minority situations do not allow us, however, to predicate a general and more or less absolute opposition between Muslims and Christians as such. It largely depends on who these Muslims and Christians are.

The really interesting question is when and where the idea of an absolute opposition between Muslims and Christians developed, generalizing what had occurred in specific historical and political situations. When and where did it become a scheme imposed by both parties on all their relationships? Who made an ideology of it and with what aims and purposes? What responsibility did theologians, whether Muslim or Christian, bear here? And when did the scheme of a general opposition between Christians and Muslims come to prevail in the West?

I am inclined to think of specific historical situations, such as the Arab and Turkish conquests, the period of the Crusades in the Middle East, the period of the Reconquista in Spain and its equivalent in sixteenth century Russia, the period of the Turkish wars in the Balkans, and of course the colonial period. It must have been in the practical interests of various parties on the Western side to establish this scheme of opposition. I am thinking of the military, the Church and its ideological centers, the Christian minorities in Muslim countries—who tended to ascribe their sufferings to an oppressive Islam—but also of imperialists and nationalists, and all those ideological centers in the West that have seen Islam as the great political enemy and that could advocate a crusade against it. The result is that, on the Western side, Islam came to be constructed as the opposite of Christianity, Europe, civilization, and progress.

A similar absolute opposition has been worked out on the Muslim side, though for different reasons. Up to the mid-twentieth century, there and here very few people have dared to speak of a possible complementarity between Muslims and Christians.

3.3. Constructs of Islam and Christianity

Especially when normal direct interaction was nearly impossible, Muslims and Christians perceived each other largely through the representations of their own and the other's religion. This may of course take innocent forms, fastening on certain visible idiosyncracies of the other religion, for instance that Muslims do not eat pork or that Christians can choose celibacy.

But such representations of another religion are no longer innocent and come to have wider implications when they are consciously elaborated and when they claim and are believed to grasp the essence of that other religion. In this case we speak of a "construct", that is to say a way of representing the other religion, not on the basis of empirical facts and of direct contacts with its adherents, but by making a thing of it. Muslims, for instance, have a particular construct of Christianity, based on certain Qur'anic verses. Though they permit certain variations of interpretation of these *āyāt*, Muslims have difficulty in recognizing experienced Christianity as a primary source and in seeing Christianity as a human religion that can take many different forms.

Similarly, Christians have developed their own construct of Islam in the course of history. The Christian construct of Islam, however, seems to me less fixed than the construct that most Muslims have of Christianity. In fact, there has been a variety of Christian and Western constructs of Islam, and in the course of time important changes have taken place in them. A good example is the vision of Islam that the Catholic Church formulated officially during the Council of Vatican II (1962–5) and that was clearly different from earlier official views. The very fact of studying Islam from all available sources and through what Muslims themselves have said about it implies a continuous scholarly revision of existing constructs of Islam. Similar revisions of prevailing Muslim constructs of Christianity may be expected from Muslim scholars when they study all available sources and what Christians themselves have said about it.

To the extent that Muslims and Christians have become accustomed to looking at each other largely through the lenses of the constructs they made of each other's religion, these constructs turn out to have a negative impact on their relationships. Fortunately, individual persons and groups can discover that their own mental construct of someone else's religion does not correspond to the reality of the other person or group and to what their religion means to them. The logical consequence is that such a construct should be abandoned and current general ideas be revised. Where Muslims and Christians are in daily contact, they may become aware of the subtle difference that exists between the idea they have of each other's religion and the experience they have of each other as persons.

3.4. *Changing Relationships*

The relationships between Muslim and Christian communities depend in part on what these communities have made of their religions and thus on the religious leadership. But there are many other factors that play a role. When Muslims and Christians share a certain way of life in society and participate in a common culture and when there are common economic and social interests, there will be certain orientations, norms, and ideals in common. Common rules may result in friendly relationships. Arab Muslim and Arab Christian peasants, for instance, may very well live in peace together in a given region; Muslim and Christian traders or bankers may do profitable business together. Things will change, however, when one community is mobilized against the other, specifically if an appeal is made to one religion against another and when both religions are taken up in a conflict and are absolutized. This happens, for instance, when ideological activists stir up conflict with the other community or other factions of their own community. In such a case, the religion of that community is ideologized and may take aggressive forms. As a result, more or less balanced relationships deteriorate.

It is not Islam or Christianity as such or the Muslim or Christian character of communities as such that determines relationships. It is always specific interpretations and forms of Islam and of Christianity, articulated by particular Muslim and Christian groups, added to practical interests on both sides that condition possible relationships in particular situations. Relationships between Muslims and Christians in traditional societies change when existing balances are shattered by new political regimes, new technologies, new economic forces, or new social structures—against the background of influences from outside. Such changes may bring about an ideologization, an absolutization, and fanatical support for one particular form of a religion at the expense of all others. In the long run, however, practical as well as religious considerations may prevail over ideological ones.

4. Practical Issues

4.1. *Geopolitical Context*

The geopolitical context is one of the overriding factors that condition Muslim-Christian relations worldwide at present. Two examples may suffice. During the colonial period, relations of domination between the "Christian" West and the Muslim world as a whole called forth defensive interpretations and attitudes among Muslims. And during the Cold War, cooperation with Muslim countries was a Western political interest. The end of the colonial period and later the end of the Cold War brought about new worldwide contexts for new kinds of relations between Muslims and Christians on a global scale, for better or for worse. Events since 1990 and especially 2000 confirm this.

Regional contexts, too, can become important within the geopolitical context. The Middle Eastern situation with the conflicts around Israel has influenced Muslim-Christian as well as Muslim-Jewish relations and even Christian-Jewish relations worldwide. Political interests, religious readings, and current ideologies are inextricably mixed, while everyone thinks they are right.

4.2. Political and Religious Leadership

The history of the Middle East during the last half century has shown the important role of leadership for the heightening or reducing of tensions that have been to the detriment of Muslim-Christian relations too. The political leadership has great power in the countries of this region. However, civil society, democratic procedures, and the implementation of justice appear here, as elsewhere, to be conditions sine qua non for any constructive rapprochement, cooperation, and dialogue to take place between religious communities and for any balanced relationships to develop between religious majority and minority groups.

The critical question is then how a civil society, democratization, and justice can be promoted and prevail in countries that have been living under authoritarian regimes and injustice for a long time. Political structures in the region have been built on maintaining tensions and conflicts; political leaders have had vested interests in presenting "the other" as a potential enemy; people are enslaved in fears both of state power and of potential terrorists. Not only Muslim and Christian civilians but also Muslim-Christian relations can only benefit from a change in this predicament. The promotion of open dialogue, democratic procedures, and justice should be on the political agenda, but it is not.

Unfortunately, the traditional religious leadership in the region, both Christian and Muslim, has seldom been well educated and informed about other religions or about other possible relationships than the existing one between state, society, and religions. Traditionally, these leaders' main task has been to guide their own religious community and they have always tended to preserve the existing religious institutions and to guard the traditions as they found them. Their conservative role in society and on the political scene should be analyzed.

Significant changes in the religious institutions themselves could in practice only be brought about from outside, by imposition through the state or through Islamic movements, in the case of Islam, or through interaction with Western Churches in the case of Christianity. The traditional religious leadership in both religions in the Middle East around 1950 would certainly have had great difficulty in even imagining religious plurality and interaction between equal partners. It would probably have rejected any serious dialogue between Christians and Muslims, seeing it as a betrayal of the communal faith, whose defense has always been its first duty.

Since the very beginnings, however, in both Christianity and Islam, alternative religious spokesmen have emerged in addition to the established traditional religious leadership. A number of socio-religious and religious-political movements have arisen in both religions, and charismatic figures who had a distinct religious experience have enjoyed spiritual authority in both of them.

Since the late nineteenth century, however, besides the *'ulamā'* and *fuqahā'*, a new, non-professional kind of expertise on Islam started to arise in the Middle East and elsewhere, with a more rational outlook and concerned that Muslim education and moral values keep pace with the demands of a modernizing society. Also, more secularly oriented intellectuals started to play a role. These more liberal intellectuals, willing to learn from the West, formulated severe criticism of the traditional religious leadership that was in fact ignorant of modernity and of other religions.

During the last decades, yet new groups of religious spokesmen have arisen claiming to speak religiously directly from the sources of religion, Qur'ān and *Sunna* ("fundamentalists"), and to act politically accordingly ("activists"). This has contributed to the widespread ideologization and politicization of Islam since the 1970s, and not only in the Middle East. The new constructs of Islam that have seen the light in this vein were mostly too self-centered to show interest in or concern for other religious communities living next door. Muslim-Christian relations tended to take on a pragmatic character.

4.3. Education of Young People and Adults

For the future of Muslim-Christian relations, the attitudes inculcated in young people on both sides are of major importance. How can respect for people of other faiths be instilled in children, so that they will not speak later in a derogatory way about those not belonging to their own religious group? How can youngsters be given at least some basic knowledge about other faiths present in the country and the world? How can current social attitudes toward those not belonging to one's own community be revised for the better? In traditional communities, such a change of attitude means a kind of revolution. Especially for established majority groups, introducing the notion of alterity on a basis of equality is a painful operation. On the individual level, however, recognizing differences may strengthen the sense of dignity and individual responsibility in the person growing up, in contrast to collective emotions and the authorities behind them.

This means a change in religious education. It implies revising school-books, not only those about religion, but also those about history and geography, altering derogatory remarks about Muslims in European books and derogatory remarks about Christians in Muslim books. Revisions of schoolbooks have already been carried out, partly at the request of Muslims, in a number of European countries. In Muslim countries, how-ever, with the exception of Indonesia, Jordan, Tunisia, and Turkey[3], hardly any revisions have yet been made. By and large, schoolbooks still depict Christianity and Christians according to mistaken ideas and judg-ments from the past. This leaves Muslim children, youngsters, and also adults in a state of ignorance about who Christians really are, which is a handicap for any constructive Muslim-Christian relations.

Traditionally, both Christians and Muslims have been taught and admonished to keep to their faith and to contribute to the life and spread of the community they belong to. The various reform movements in Christianity and Islam have encouraged people to learn more about their own religion and to apply it better. As a result, however, religious people have been accustomed to viewing the world from the perspective of their own specific religion. Typical forms of Christianocentrism and Islamo-centrism have arisen and have been promoted. The same, by the way, is true for the teaching of Judaism at Jewish schools.

In concentrating on their own religion, adherents have hardly ever been made aware of what people of other faiths believe and do, and this is not as irrational as it seems at first sight. Just as the education of children should draw their attention to the existence of people with other religions, adults should be informed about these people and learn how to relate to them.

The acceptance of pluralistic societies with different communities in interaction and with a plurality of religions and world views may be one of the most critical issues for Muslim-Christian relations in times to come. People should be educated to it.

---

[3]   Monika Tworuschka, "Das Bild des Christentums in türkischen Religionsschulbüchern mit Ausblick auf einige iranische Schulbücher: Erste Eindrücke eines umfangreichen Forschungsfeldes", in *Gottes ist der Orient, Gottes ist der Okzident: Festschrift für Abdoldjavad Falaturi zum 65. Geburtstag*, ed. by Udo Tworuschka (Kölner Veröffent-lichungen zur Religionsgeschichte 21), Cologne and Vienna: Böhlau, 1991, pp. 563–74.

4.4. Minority Situations

What has been said about pluralistic societies has an immediate bearing on the subject of religious and other minorities. Measured against present-day standards, minorities professing a different faith have been subject to various forms of social discrimination if not worse in Christian and in Muslim societies, though in different ways. One of the most urgent practical issues in present-day societies is the need for equal treatment of religions. This implies recognition of minority communities professing another religion as well as of "deviant" communities of the same religion.

From the beginning, there has been a nearly irresistible urge in both Christian and Muslim societies to turn the others into "Christians" or "Muslims", too. It is the urge to make others as we are ourselves and not to accept existing differences. It leads to the dream or the desire to make society homogeneous. As a consequence, majorities hardly perceive minorities and minorities tend to keep to themselves. It is apparently only the experience of belonging to a minority oneself that can open one's eyes to the existence and situation of others as minorities. The *Journal of the Institute of Muslim Minority Affairs* has been drawing attention since 1979 to the fact that, in contrast to the past, at present a growing number of Muslims live as minorities in non-Muslim, including Western, countries. Similarly, a great number of Christians live as minorities in non-Western, including Muslim, countries. The question of what may happen to Muslim minorities living in Western countries is somehow linked to the question of what will happen to Christian and other minorities living in Muslim countries. This will no doubt remain a critical issue in Muslim-Christian relations for many years to come.

4.5. Conversions

A subject that stands high on the list of practical issues in Muslim-Christian relations is that of efforts made to spread one's faith. Christianity and Islam have been missionary religions since their beginnings and as such they have been in mutual competition to win adherents not only from elsewhere, but also from each other. However, just as Muslims have been quite sensitive to the efforts of Christian missionaries to bring Muslims to the Christian faith, Christians and Westerners generally have been very sensitive to the crude rulings against apostasy in Islam in current practice, which goes against the freedom of religion and of changing one's religion, as stipulated in the Universal Declaration of Human Rights. And when some Muslims reproach Christians for evangelizing and carrying out good works among those who suffer, Christians may accuse Muslims of putting often unacceptable social and psychological pressure on non-Muslims to accept Islam. Moreover, they do not give them in advance proper instruction in this religion and they do not tell them that, once one has accepted Islam, one can never leave it.

As I see it, the issue of conversions will become one of the most urgent issues, with a growing interaction between Muslims and Christians, implying an increasing number of mixed marriages. Some code of behavior for Christian mission and Islamic *da'wa* will have to be devised to guarantee respect for each other's faith. People of both religions should be protected from falling victim to doubtful practices used by zealots on either side.

5. Issues of Dialogue

5.1. Freedom of Expression

We mentioned already the need for a civil society, justice, and democratic procedures in Muslim as well as in Western societies, for equitable Muslim-Christian relations. For dialogue, on whatever subject, the right to freedom of expression, too, is urgent. Dialogue implies the possibility to discuss matters in an open and direct way and to address questions of truth to each other.

The problem is that nearly all Muslim societies and their countries stand under social controls and political pressures that make free expression difficult and in certain countries impossible. Whereas I remember that around 1960 religion could be freely and critically discussed among students in Muslim societies, at present religion has in fact become a taboo subject. This is the case not only in Islamic states like Saudi Arabia, but also in a number of other Muslim states, like Algeria and Tunisia.

People under pressure tend to become monological, less disposed to listen, and in the end even unable to understand other points of view. Such a situation prevents any true dialogue, including that between Muslims and Christians. If in the past a Muslim could be suspected of not being a good Muslim, he or she may now be suspected of being an Islamist Muslim(a). An attempt to arrive at an open Muslim-Christian dialogue may endanger at least one of the parties involved. If conditions worsen, true Muslim-Christian dialogues will only be possible in what may be termed the freer parts of the world.

One of the topics of Muslim-Christian dialogue is justice. Although Muslims and local or Western Christians may have different ideas and traditions of justice, they mostly hold common views about what injustice is. In this way, a dialogue for defending justice can be established and one can well imagine the rise and development of solidarity groups for justice, formed by both Muslims and Christians. To some extent this idea already functions in Human Rights committees and in organizations like Amnesty International.

5.2. Institutions for Dialogue

There is a need, then, to sustain, safeguard, and if possible create cultural institutions, in which people can meet and exchange opinions on matters related to culture, including Islam and Christianity. At the present time, besides universities and academic research centers, it is often foreign institutions that provide occasions for such exchanges. Yet, Muslim societies have a long tradition of free exchange of opinions between persons. This tradition should be preserved and developed to enable and encourage exchanges in new ways, including cultural exchange programs and information about and studies of each other's culture. A new kind of institution that functions well in this respect is the Internet.

5.3. Cultural Exchange Programs

It seems to me that there is an urgent need to invite creative figures from Muslim and other African and Asian countries to spend some time in Europe as well as North America. I am thinking of intellectuals, scholars, researchers, writers, and artists who are at important stages in their creative work. Such a stay should preferably be for about one year, but even a couple of months would give them time to establish contacts and orient themselves in the aspects of Western artistic, literary, and scholarly productions they want to become familiar with. This would enable them to present their own work and to let it be discussed or published. They should be invited to colloquia and workshops in specific fields of research and on broader cultural subjects. This may then also lead to further cooperation in the future. The USA has its Fulbright exchange program; the European Union should start a parallel kind of program of Euro-Fellowships. In this way, Europeans will be challenged to show what they have to contribute and what is innovating in what they do. In the same spirit, scholars as well as artists and writers from European countries could be invited to visit Muslim countries in similar exchange programs, facilitating a "dialogue of cultures".

5.4. Common Studies of Muslims and Christians

One of the most important post-World War Two initiatives in the field of Muslim-Christian relations has been that of Muslim and Christian staff and students carrying out Islamic studies in common. The late Professor Wilfred Cantwell Smith first put this idea into practice on a graduate level at the Institute of Islamic Studies, which he founded at McGill University, Montreal, at the beginning of the 1950s. Similar ideas were later developed and applied for the study of Christian-Muslim relations at two private religious institutions that were established for this purpose in the

1970s in Hartford, Connecticut, and in Birmingham, U.K. The latter became part of the University of Birmingham in 1999.[4] Both institutions also publish journals devoted to the same aim. Initiatives in this direction have also been taken elsewhere in the USA, for example at Temple University in Philadelphia and at Georgetown University in Washington, D.C. All these places also employ Muslim staff for research and teaching.

It may become a critical issue in the future to decide which particular versions of Islam and Christianity may best serve as the point of departure for such studies, apart from the Scriptures. The present-day differentiation of both religions and their multiplication of orientations, trends, communities, Churches, and ideologies makes it more difficult to speak of Christianity and Islam as two entities in themselves. There are of course the Scriptures and fundamental beliefs of both religions that should be studied, but throughout history there has been increasing diversity. Scholarship itself has also evolved. Whereas in the 1950s certain constructs of Islam and Christianity were still widely current, research of the last decades has brought about a variety of perspectives on both religions. This enriches the field, but it also complicates the study of the two religions.

5.5. The Non-dialoguers

A new problem in matters of dialogue between Muslims and Christians is the difference between those who opt for an open dialogue without preliminary conditions and those others who want to restrict themselves to scholarly or practical cooperation only. In practice there may be forms of human communication that may lead to further contact and exchanges. Here I am not considering those Muslims and Christians for whom there is no problem of Muslim-Christian relations or those who simply do not identify themselves as Muslims or Christians.

Another problem is those religious-ideological movements, Muslim or Christian, that simply want to keep to the foundations and integrity of their religion and impose themselves forcefully on others. They close themselves off from what others do or have to say. Their ideas may testify to a certain self-sufficiency, so that they do not see any need for contact with "others". On the contrary, other religions may represent a danger for them. They may call themselves Defenders of the Faith, or defenders of God in a metaphorical sense, but this self-defense may go hand in hand with militant attitudes toward others. They may resort to dialogue for tactical reasons, pursuing their own well-defined aims.

Among Christians, I am thinking not only of the so-called fundamentalists and Evangelicals, but also of those missionary diehards for whom

---

4   See below Chapter 17 "Between Baghdad and Birmingham: Opportunities of Minorities".

all Muslims must become Christians, and of those conservatives who see their tradition as eternal and for whom other options simply do not exist. Among Muslims, I am thinking especially of those "Islamist" movements that tend to identify Islam with their own particular version or that in fact only want to pursue their own political interests. They may think that they know what Christianity is and why they reject it. Here too, of course, there are the same ultra-conservatives that can be found in any religion.

Non-dialoguers present a challenge inasmuch as they close themselves off from communication with others. Their problem may not be religious dialogue, but dialogue or communication as such, and specifically between Muslims and Christians. Dialogue cannot be imposed, and in certain contexts Christians and Muslims may have valid reasons not to engage in dialogue.

There are also those groups with whom some kind of communication remains possible if one only knows and uses their way of thinking. Among both Muslims and Christians, there are the literalists and traditionalists for whom religion consists of following sacred texts and established tradition. And on both sides there are the rationalists who submit their religion to reason as they see and want to apply it. There are also the spiritual universalists who may emerge from either the Christian or the Muslim tradition but who will gladly say that they are not Christians or Muslims anymore—which is their solution to the problems of Muslim-Christian dialogue.

6. Scholarship

6.1. Research on the Two Religions

For a long time, studies of Christianity and Islam have been distinct fields of research, requiring different kinds of specialization, training for which is provided in separate institutions or university faculties. More recently, the relationships between both religions have become a subject of research.

Detailed textual and historical research has been carried out on influences that the two civilizations and their religions have exercised on each other in the course of history, and on interactions and underlying structures between them.

Scholarly comparative studies of the two religions have shown similarities and differences, common elements as well as unique features of Islam and Christianity as historical and societal religions.

Anthropological and sociological research has contributed to explain certain relationships between particular Muslim and Christian groups or communities at given times and places, also at the present time. Such relationships have developed sometimes on an equal level, with various kinds of exchanges taking place, but more often in majority-minority relationships, with various kinds of domination, coexistence, and confrontation. They could be part of tensions and conflicts, but also of peaceful coexistence.

Such research is evidence of the fact that unprejudiced scholarly study of forms of Christianity and Islam is possible if due attention is paid to similarities, differences, and common structures.

6.2. Interest in Muslim-Christian Relationships

Several scholarly initiatives have been taken over the last forty years to broaden the scope of the study of Islam and Christianity as two separate religions and to focus on their relationships. Thus, for instance:

1) the nature and presuppositions of current scholarly approaches in Islamic studies have come under discussion;
2) a range of symposia has been organized on the historical relationships between the two religions and civilizations, especially during the medieval period;
3) bibliographical work has been initiated on Christian texts concerning Islam and on Muslim texts concerning Christianity, including polemical and apologetic texts, a number of which have already been edited and studied;
4) growing attention has been paid to mutual perceptions, including Christian and Western images of Islam as well as Muslim images of Christianity;
5) several specialized journals publish scholarly articles, based on historical texts and direct observation, about specific cases of relationships between Muslims and Christians in the past and at present.

These scholarly initiatives and studies cannot be seen independently of efforts that started after World War Two to improve cooperation and dialogue between Muslims and Christians as well as between Islam and the West. They distinguish themselves, however, by their impartial scholarly character and by their self-critical orientation to arrive at scholarly truth.

6.3. A Distinctive Field of Specialization

The time has come to constitute the study of Muslim-Christian relationships as a distinct field of specialization that is more than the sum of Christian and Islamic Studies. Such a field is justified on scholarly grounds:

1) Muslims and Christians have a common history since the beginnings of Islam, expanding with increasing encounters in various parts of the world; this history should be known;
2) both religions have certain fundamental views and trends in common, such as a universalistic outlook on the history of humankind and on the nature and responsibility of the human person; other fundamental views and trends differ; these fundamental views and trends should be studied;
3) the historical, social, cultural, and religious interactions between the Muslim and Christian worlds demand, besides specialist expertise, more comprehensive scholarly approaches; attention should be given to Islamic and Christian varieties;
4) the science of religion can contribute to this field of research specifically by focusing on the various roles that the two religions have played as normative systems in various relationships between Muslims and Christians.

The impulse to pursue this research as a distinct field is of a scholarly nature; its aim is to further scholarly knowledge and understanding. There should be no question of propagating particular Christian or Muslim points of view.

6.4. Special Subjects of Research

In this field, the following subjects of research deserve particular attention:

1) the kind of Islam or Christianity with which Christians and Muslims were in contact during their encounters and the perception they had of the other party's religion;
2) important texts of Christian authors about Islam and Muslims and analogous texts of Muslim authors about Christianity and Christians;
3) the precise historical and social contexts in which these texts were written;
4) specific situations or regions in which Muslims and Christians have met or have lived side by side, such as the relations between Slavic peoples (often with Orthodox Christianity) and Muslims, various confrontations between Christians and Muslims in the colonial period, mutual perceptions in the course of the second half of the twentieth century; the imaginary dimension of Muslim-Christian meetings in written and popular literature;
5) the growing worldwide expansion of the two religions, leading to increasing encounters of their adherents;
6) the sources of tensions and conflicts that have existed between Muslim and Christian communities in various situations.

6.5. A Practical Suggestion

Given the need for research in this area, I suggest organizing from time to time scholarly workshops around a particular theme. Moreover, to meet the need for further expanding research on Muslim-Christian relations as a field of studies, there is a need for at least two academic research centers concentrating on Muslim-Christian relations in Asia and in Africa respectively. The research centers should be of an academic quality, possibly attached to an academy or a university, and independent from political or other strings. They should encourage research on relevant subjects that have been neglected until now.

Selected Literature

1. Islam and Christianity in General

ADAMS, Charles J., "Islam and Christianity: The Opposition of Similarities", in *Logos Islamikos: Studia Islamica in Honorem Georgii Michaelis Wickens*, ed. Roger M. SAVORY and Dionisius A. AGIUS (Papers in Mediaeval Studies 6), Toronto: Pontifical Institute of Mediaeval Studies, 1984, pp. 287–306.

ASAD, Talal, *Genealogies of Religion: Discipline and Reasons of Power in Christianity and Islam*, Baltimore and London: The Johns Hopkins University Press, 1993.

WAARDENBURG, Jacques, "Selected Bibliography", in *Muslim-Christian Perceptions of Dialogue Today: Experiences and Expectations*, ed. by Jacques WAARDENBURG, Leuven, etc.: Peeters, 2000, pp. 305–23.

WATT, William Montgomery, *Islam and Christianity Today: A Contribution to Dialogue*, London, etc.: Routledge & Kegan Paul, 1983.

—, *Muslim-Christian Encounters: Perceptions and Misperceptions*, London and New York: Routledge, 1991.

2. Encounters in History

2.1. In General

Christian-Muslim Encounters, ed. by Yvonne Yazbeck HADDAD and Wadi Z. HADDAD, Gainesville, etc.: University Press of Florida, 1995.

GAUDEUL, Jean-Marie, *Encounter and Clashes: Islam and Christianity in History*, 2 Vols., Vol. I: *A Survey*; Vol. II: *Texts*, Rome: Pontificio Istituto di Studi Arabi e d'Islamistica, 1984.

GODDARD, Hugh, *A History of Christian-Muslim Relations* (Islamic Surveys), Edinburgh: Edinburgh University Press, 2000.

WAARDENBURG, Jacques, art. "Religionsgespräche II. Muslimisch-christlich", *Theologische Realenzyklopädie*, Vol. 28 (Berlin-New York: Walter de Gruyter, 1997), pp. 640–8.

2.2. From Crusades to Renaissance

Actes du IIe Congrès International sur: Chrétiens et musulmans à l'époque de la Renaissance, ed. by Abdeljelil TEMIMI, Zaghouan: Fondation Temimi pour la Recherche Scientifique et l'Information, 1997.

Arab Historians of the Crusades. Selected and translated from the Arabic sources, ed. by Francesco GABRIELI, London: Routledge and Kegan Paul, 1969.

ATIYA, Aziz S., *Crusades, Commerce and Culture,* Bloomington, Ind.: Indiana University Press, 1962.

BEN-AMI, Aharon, *Social Change in a Hostile Environment: The Crusaders' Kingdom of Jerusalem* (Princeton Studies on the Near East), Princeton: Princeton University Press, 1969.

CAHEN, Claude, *Orient et Occident au temps des Croisades,* Paris: Aubier Montaigne, 1983.

Chrétiens et musulmans à la Renaissance. Actes du 37e colloque international du Centre d'Etudes Supérieures de la Renaissance à Tours, ed. by Bartolomé BENNASSAR and Robert SAUZET, Paris: Honoré Champion, 1998.

Crusaders and Muslims in Twelfth-Century Syria, ed. by Maya SHATZMILLER (The Medieval Mediterranean 1), Leiden, etc.: E. J. Brill, 1993.

DANIEL, Norman, *Islam and the West: The Making of an Image,* Edinburgh: Edinburgh University Press, 1960, etc.; revised edition Oxford: Oneworld, 1993 (paperback edition 1997).

East and West in the Crusader States: Context—Contacts—Confrontations, ed. by Krijnie CIGGAAR, Adelbert DAVIDS, Herman G. B. TEULE (Orientalia Lovaniensia Analecta 75), Leuven: Peeters, 1996.

GLICK, Thomas F., *Islamic and Christian Spain in the Early Middle Ages: Comparative Perspectives on Social and Cultural Formation,* Princeton: Princeton University Press, 1979.

HILLENBRAND, Carole, *The Crusades: Islamic Perspectives,* Edinburgh: Edinburgh University Press, 1999.

MAALOUF, Amin, *Les croisades vues par les Arabes,* Paris: Ed. J'ai lu, 1998.

L'Occident musulman et l'Occident chrétien au Moyen Age, ed. by Mohammed HAMMAM (Publications de la Faculté des Lettres et des Sciences Humaines, Série Colloques et Séminaires 48), Rabat: Université de Rabat, 1995.

RICHARD, Jean, *Orient et Occident au Moyen Age: Contacts et relations (XIIe–XVe s.)* (Collected Studies Series 49), London: Variorum, 1976 (repr. Aldershot: Variorum, 1997).

SCHAUER, Alexander, *Muslime und Franken: Ethnische, soziale und religiöse Gruppen im Kitāb al-I'tibār des Usāma ibn Munqid* (Islamkundliche Untersuchungen 230), Berlin: Klaus Schwarz, 2000.

SOUTHERN, Richard William, *Western Views of Islam in the Middle Ages,* Cambridge: Harvard University Press, 1962 (repr. 1978).

VERNET GINÉS, Juan, *La cultura hispanoarabe en Oriente y Occidente,* Barcelona: Editorial Ariel, 1978; French edition: *Ce que la culture doit aux Arabes d'Espagne,* traduit de l'espagnol par Gabriel Martinez GROS, Paris: Sindbad, 1985, 2000²; German edition: *Die spanisch-arabische Kultur in Orient und Okzident,* Zurich: Artemis, 1984.

2.3. From Christian Missions to Islamic da'wa

ALLIEVI, Stefano, *Les convertis à l'islam: Les nouveaux musulmans d'Europe* (Musulmans d'Europe), Paris: L'Harmattan, 1998.

CAMPS, Arnulf, *Jerome Xavier S.J. and the Muslims of the Mogul Empire: Controversial Works and Missionary Activity* (Supplementa NZR, 6), Fribourg: St. Paul's Press, 1957.

DANIEL, Norman, *Islam, Europe and Empire*, Edinburgh: Edinburgh University Press, 1966.

JESSUP, Henry H., *Fifty-three Years in Syria*, 2 Vols., Reading, U. K.: Garnet, 2003.

POWELL, Avril Ann, *Muslims and Missionaries in Pre-Mutiny India*, Richmond, U. K.: Curzon, 1993.

ROCHER, Lisbeth, and Fatima CHERQAOUI, *D'une foi l'autre: Les conversions à l'islam en Occident*. Paris: Seuil, 1986.

WOHLRAB-SAHR, Monika, *Konversion zum Islam in Deutschland und den USA*, Frankfurt and New York: Campus Verlag, 1998.

2.4. Encounters under Tension

CRAGG, Kenneth, *Palestine: The Prize and Price of Zion*, London and Washington: Cassell, 1997.

The Christian-Muslim Frontier: Chaos, Clash or Dialogue?, ed. by Jörgen S. NIELSEN, London and New York: I. B. Tauris, 1998.

Muslim-Christian Conflicts: Economic, Political, and Social Origins, ed. by Suad JOSEPH and Barbara L. K. PILLSBURY, Boulder, Colo.: Westview Press, and Folkestone, U. K.: Dawson, 1978.

Palestine, Palestiniens: Territoire national, espaces communautaires, ed. by Riccardo BOCCO, Blandine DESTREMAU, Jean HANNOYER (Les Cahiers du CERMOC Nr. 17), Beirut: Centre d'Etudes et de Recherches sur le Moyen-Orient Contemporain, 1997.

RABINOWITZ, Dan, *Overlooking Nazareth: The Ethnography of Exclusion in Galilee* (Cambridge Studies in Social and Cultural Anthropology), Cambridge: Cambridge University Press, 1997.

REINKOWSKI, Maurus, *Filastin, Filistin und Eretz Israel: Die späte osmanische Herrschaft über Palästina in der arabischen, türkischen und israelischen Historiographie* (Islamkundliche Untersuchungen 186), Berlin: Klaus Schwarz, 1995.

The Role of Religion in Conflict Situations: A consultation by the Middle East Council of Churches, Limassol: Middle East Council of Churches, 1991.

The Vatican, Islam, and the Middle East, ed. by Kail C. ELLIS, Syracuse, N. Y.: Syracuse University Press, 1987.

3. Efforts toward Dialogue between Christians and Muslims

3.1. Centers

LEVRAT, Jacques, *Une Expérience de Dialogue: Les Centres d'Etude chrétiens en monde musulman* (Studien 9), Altenberge: Christlich-Islamisches Schrifttum, 1987.

Le PISAI: Cinquante ans au service du dialogue ("Studi arabo-islamici del PISAI" 14), Rome: PISAI, 2000.

3.2. Meetings

Déclarations Communes Islamo-Chrétiennes 1954c.–1995c., 1373h.–1415h. Choix de textes présentés par Juliette Nasri HADDAD. Sous la direction de Augustin DUPRÉ LA TOUR, S.J., et Dr. Hisham NASHABÉ (Université Saint-Joseph, Beyrouth: Institut d'Etudes Islamo-Chrétiennes), Beirut: Dar el-Machreq, 1997.

Documents and Researches of (the) Seminar of the Islamic-Christian Dialogue. Tripoli 2–6 Safar, 1396; 1–5 February 1976, Tripoli: Office of Foreign Relations, Congress General of People, Arab Libyan Popular Socialist Jamahirya, 1981/1390.

Gerechtigkeit in den internationalen und interreligiösen Beziehungen in islamischer und christlicher Perspektive, ed. by Andreas BSTEH and Seyed A. MIRDAMADI (Teheran, February 1996), Mödling: Verlag St. Gabriel, 1997.

GRIC (Groupe de recherches islamo-chrétien; Muslim-Christian Research Group), *Ces Ecritures qui nous questionnent: La Bible et le Coran,* Paris: Centurion, 1987; English translation: *The Challenge of the Scriptures: The Bible and the Qur'ān,* Maryknoll, N. Y.: Orbis, 1989.

– *Foi et justice: Un défi pour le christianisme et pour l'islam,* Paris: Centurion, 1993.

– *Pluralisme et laïcité: Chrétiens et musulmans proposent,* Paris: Bayard/ Centurion, 1996.

– *Péché et responsabilité éthique dans le monde contemporain: Chrétiens et musulmans s'interrogent,* Paris: Bayard, 2000.

RUDOLPH, Ekkehard, *Dialogues islamo-chrétiens 1950–1993: Introduction historique suivie d'une bibliographie étendue des sources arabes* (Cahiers du Département Interfacultaire d'Histoire et de Sciences des Religions 1), Université de Lausanne, 1993.

3.3. Mutual Perceptions

GODDARD, Hugh, *Muslim Perceptions of Christianity,* London: Grey Seal, 1996.

Islam and Christianity: Mutual Perceptions since the Mid–20th Century, ed. by Jacques WAARDENBURG, Leuven and Paris: Peeters, 1998.

Islamic Interpretations of Christianity, ed. by Lloyd RIDGEON, Richmond, U. K.: Curzon, 2001.

Muslim-Christian Perceptions of Dialogue Today: Experiences and Expectations, ed. by Jacques WAARDENBURG, Leuven and Paris: Peeters, 2000.

ZEBIRI, Kate, *Muslims and Christians Face to Face,* Oxford: Oneworld, 1997.

3.4. Interreligious Dialogue

BASSET, Jean-Claude, *Le dialogue interreligieux: Chance ou déchéance de la foi,* Paris: Cerf, 1996.

3.5. Muslim Views on Dialogue with Christians

AYOUB, Mahmoud, "Roots of Muslim-Christian Conflict", *The Muslim World,* 79 (1989), pp. 25–45.

CHARFI, Abdelmajid, "Pour une nouvelle approche du christianisme par la penséee musulmane", *Islamochristiana* 13 (1987), pp. 61–77.

DENFFER, Ahmad von, *Dialogue between Christians and Muslims,* 3 Vols., Leicester: The Islamic Foundation, 1980–4.

Le dialogue vu par les musulmans, in *Etudes Arabes,* Dossiers No 88–89, 1995/ 1–2, Rome: PISAI, 1995.

FARŪQĪ, Ismāʿīl Rāji al-, *Islam and Other Faiths,* ed. by Ataullah SIDDIQI, Markfield, Leicester: The Islamic Foundation, 1998/1419.

—, "Islam and Christianity: Diatribe or Dialogue?", *Journal of Ecumenical Studies,* 5 (1968), pp. 45–77.

JOHNSTONE, Penelope, "Articles from Islamic Journals: An Islamic Perspective on Dialogue", *Islamochristiana*, 13 (1987), pp. 131–71.

KIMBALL, Charles Anthony, *Striving together in the Way of God: Muslim Participation in Christian-Muslim Dialogue*, ThD Dissertation, Harvard University, March 1987.

Muslim-Christian Perceptions of Dialogue Today: Experiences and Expectations, ed. by Jacques WAARDENBURG, Leuven, Paris and Sterling: Peeters, 2000.

Muslims in Dialogue: The Evolution of a Dialogue, ed. by Leonard SWIDLER, Lewiston, etc.: Edwin Mellen, 1992.

NASR, Seyyed Hossein, "Comments on a Few Theological Issues in Islamic-Christian Dialogue", in *Christian-Muslim Encounters*, ed. by Yvonne Yazbeck HADDAD and Wadi Z. HADDAD, Gainesville, etc.: University Press of Florida, 1995, pp. 457–67.

OSMAN, Fathi, et al., "Jesus in Jewish-Christian-Muslim Dialogue", *Journal of Ecumenical Studies*, 14 (1977), pp. 448–65.

RENAUD, Etienne, "Le dialogue islamo-chrétien vu par les musulmans", *Islamochristiana*, 23 (1997), pp. 111–38.

RUDOLPH, Ekkehard, "Muslim Approaches towards Islamic-Christian Dialogue: Three Decades in Retrospect", in *Encounters of Words and Texts: Intercultural Studies in Honor of Stefan Wild*, ed. by Lutz EDZARD and Christian SZYSKA (Arabistische Texte und Studien 10), Hildesheim, etc.: Georg Olms, 1997, pp. 149–58.

SA'AB, Hasan, "Zum islamisch-christlichen Dialog", *Kairos*, N.F. 10 (1968), pp. 29–52.

SIDDIQUI, Ataullah, *Christian-Muslim Dialogue in the Twentieth Century*, Houndsmill and London: Macmillan, and New York: St. Martin's Press, 1997.

TALBI, Mohamed, *Islam et dialogue: Réflexions sur un thème d'actualité*, Tunis: Maison Tunisienne de l'Edition, 1972; English translation by L. MARCHANT: "Islam and Dialogue: Some Reflections on a Current Topic", *Encounter* (Rome), Nrs. 11–12 (1975), repr. in *Christianity and Islam: The Struggling Dialogue*, ed. by Richard W. ROUSSEAU (Scranton, Pa.: Ridge Row Press, 1985), pp. 53–73.

3.6. Christian Views on Dialogue with Muslims

BIJLEFELD, Willem A., "Christian-Muslim Studies, Islamic Studies, and the Future of Christian-Muslim Encounter", in *Christian-Muslim Encounters*, ed. by Yvonne Yazbeck HADDAD and Wadi Z. HADDAD (Gainesville, etc.: University Press of Florida, 1995), pp. 13–40.

BORRMANS, Maurice, *Guidelines for Dialogue between Christians and Muslims* (Interreligious Documents I, Pontifical Council for Interreligious Dialogue), New York and Mahwah, N. J.: Paulist Press, 1990.

—, *Dialogue islamo-chrétien à temps et contretemps*, Versailles: Ed. Saint-Paul, 2002.

Christian-Muslim Dialogue: Theological and Practical Issues, ed. by Roland E. MILLER and Hance A.O. MWAKABANA, Geneva: The Lutheran World Federation, Department for Theology and Studies, 1998.

Christians meeting Muslims: WCC Papers on 10 Years of Christian-Muslim Dialogue, Geneva: World Council of Churches, 1977.

HOCK, Klaus, *Der Islam im Spiegel westlicher Theologie: Aspekte christlich-theologischer Beurteilung des Islams im 20. Jahrhundert*, Cologne and Vienna: Böhlau, 1986.

Islam in Asia: Perspectives for Christian-Muslim Encounter. Consultation Bangkok, June 11–15, 1991, ed. by J. Paul RAJASHEKAR and H.S. WILSON, Geneva: Lutheran World Federation, Department for Theology and Studies & World Alliance of Reformed Churches, 1992.

Meeting in Faith: Twenty Years of Christian-Muslim Conversations Sponsored by the World Council of Churches, ed. by Stuart E. BROWN, Geneva: WCC Publications, 1989.

MOUBARAC, Youakim, *Recherches sur la pensée chrétienne et l'islam dans les temps modernes et à l'époque contemporaine* (Publications de l'Université Libanaise, Section des Etudes historiques, XXII), Beirut: Université Libanaise, 1977.

Recognize the Spiritual Bonds which Unite us: 16 Years of Christian-Muslim Dialogue, Vatican City: Pontifical Council for Interreligious Dialogue, 1994.

SPERBER, Jutta, *Christians and Muslims: The Dialogue Activities of the World Council of Churches and their Theological Foundation* (Theologische Bibliothek Töpelmann 107), Berlin and New York: Walter de Gruyter, 2000.

3.7. Regional and Local Christian-Muslim Dialogue

BAGUET, Georges, Boutros HALLAQ and Michel JONDOT, *Lumières sur Saïda: Quand chrétiens et musulmans bâtissent la paix au Sud-Liban*, Paris: Desclée de Brouwer, 1994.

FITZGERALD, Michael L., and Robert CASPAR, *Signs of Dialogue: Christian Encounter with Muslims*, Zamboanga City, Philippines: Silsilah Publications, 1992.

GRAF, Peter, and Peter ANTES, *Strukturen des Dialogs mit Muslimen in Europa* (Europäische Bildung im Dialog: Region-Sprache-Identität, 6), Frankfurt on Main: Peter Lang, 1998.

MÉTÉNIER, Edouard, *Le dialogue islamo-chrétien vu d'Egypte 1962–1992: Thèmes, problèmes et enjeux.* Mémoire de Maîtrise en Histoire, Centre d'Histoire de l'Islam contemporain (juin 1994), Paris, 1994.

3.8. Reflections about Christian-Muslim Dialogue

Christianity and Islam: The Struggling Dialogue, ed. by Richard W. ROUSSEAU, S.J., Montrose, Pa.: Ridge Row Press, 1985.

CRISLAM, *La foi en marche: Les problèmes de fond du dialogue islamo-chrétien.* Premier congrès international à distance organisé par CRISLAM (Studi arabo-islamici del PISAI, no 4), Rome: PISAI, 1990.

GODDARD, Hugh, *Christians and Muslims: From Double Standards to Mutual Understanding*, Richmond, U. K.: Curzon, 1995.

MOHAMMED, Ovey N., *Muslim-Christian Relations: Past—Present—Future* (Faith meets Faith series), Maryknoll, N. Y.: Orbis, 1999.

Muslim-Christian Dialogue: Promise and Problems, ed. by M. Darrol BRYANT and S.A. ALI, St. Paul, Minn.: Paragon House, 1998.

TALBI, Mohamed, and Olivier CLÉMENT, *Un respect têtu* (Series Rencontres), Paris: Nouvelle Cité, 1989.

4. Islam in Discussion

4.1. Islam as a Religion

ABUL-FADL, Mona, *Introducing Islam from within: Alternative Perspectives*, Markfield, U. K.: The Islamic Foundation, 1991 (contains W.A. BIJLEFELD, "On being Muslim: The Faith Dimension of Muslim Identity", pp. 95–118).

CARRÉ, Olivier, *L'islam laïque ou le retour à la Grande Tradition*, Paris: Armand Colin, 1993.

ESACK, Farid, *On Being a Muslim Finding a Religious Path in the World Today*, Oxford: Oneworld, 1999.

IZETBEGOVIC, ʿAlija ʿAli, *Islam between East and West*, Plainfield, Ind.: American Trust Publications, 1984, 1993³.

—, *Le manifeste islamique*, traduit, présenté, et commenté par Ahmed ABIDI (L'Islam autrement), Beirut: Ed. Al-Bouraq, 1999/1420.

LAWRENCE, Bruce B., *Shattering the Myth: Islam beyond Violence* (Princeton Studies in Muslim Politics), Princeton, N. J.: Princeton University Press, 1998.

NEIRYNCK, Jacques, and Tariq RAMADAN, *Peut-on vivre avec l'islam? Le choc de la religion musulmane et des sociétés laïques et chrétiennes*, Lausanne: Favre, 1999.

Sacrilege versus Civility: Muslim Perspectives on The Satanic Verses Affair, ed. by Muhammad Manazir AHSAN and Abdur Raheem KIDWAI, Markfield, U. K.: The Islamic Foundation, 1991/1412; revised and enlarged edition 1993/1414.

TAHA, Mahmoud Mohamed, *The Second Message of Islam*, Translation and Introduction by Abdullahi Ahmed AN-NAʿIM, Syracuse, N. Y.: Syracuse University Press, 1987.

4.2. Human Rights and Religious Freedom

Human Rights and Religious Values, ed. by Abdullahi Ahmed AN-NAʿIM, Grand Rapids: W. B. Eerdmans, 1995.

Religious Freedom in the World: A Global Report on Freedom and Persecution, ed. by Paul MARSHALL, Nashville, Tenn.: Broadman & Holman, 2000.

Religious Liberty and Human Rights in Nations and in Religions, ed. by Leonard SWIDLER, Philadelphia: Ecumenical Press, and New York: Hippocrene Press, 1986.

YE'OR, Bath (ps.), *Islam and Dhimmitude: Where Civilizations Collide*, Madison, N. J.: Fairleigh Dickinson University Press, and Lancaster, U. K.: Gazelle Books, 2002.

4.3. Fundamentalisms

ALI, Tariq, *The Clash of Fundamentalisms: Crusades, Jihad and Modernity*, London and New York: Verso, 2002.

Fundamentalisms Comprehended, ed. by Martin E. MARTY and R. Scott APPLEBY (The Fundamentalism Project 5), Chicago and London: University of Chicago Press, 1995.

LAWRENCE, Bruce B., *Defenders of God: The Fundamentalist Revolt against the Modern Age*, San Francisco, etc.: Harper & Row, 1989.

Religious Fundamentalisms and the Human Rights of Women, ed. by Courtney W. HOWLAND, New York: St. Martin's Press, 1999.

TIBI, Bassam, *The Challenge of Fundamentalism: Political Islam and the New World Disorder*, Berkeley, etc.: University of California Press, 1998.

4.4. Role of the Media

KARIM, Karim H., *Islamic Peril: Media and Global Violence*, Montreal, etc.: Black Rose Books, 2000.

New Media in the Muslim World: The Emerging Public Sphere, ed. by Dale F. EICKELMAN and Jon W. ANDERSON, Bloomington and Indianapolis: Indiana University Press, 1999.

POOLE, Elizabeth, *Reporting Islam: Media Representations of British Muslims*, London and New York: I. B. Tauris, 2002.

SIDDIQUI, Mohammed Ahmadullah, *Islam, Muslims and Media: Myths and Realities*, Chicago, etc.: Naamps Publications, 1997.

5. Christianity in Discussion

Der Islam als Anfrage an christliche Theologie und Philosophie: Erste religionstheologische Akademie St. Gabriel, ed. Andreas BSTEH (Studien zur Religionstheologie 1), Mödling: St. Gabriel, 1994.

Christlicher Glaube in der Begegnung mit dem Islam, ed. by Andreas BSTEH (Studien zur Religionstheologie 2), Mödling: St. Gabriel, 1995.

Chapter 17

Between Baghdad and Birmingham:
Opportunities of Minorities[1]

1. Introduction

Baghdad, at the beginning of the ninth century, was an astonishing city—
and it still is. The site was well situated in relation to the north-south and
east-west trade routes. The city itself was well planned and constructed
from 762 on at the order of the Caliph. It became one of the largest cities
of the medieval world, with more than a million of inhabitants. Since the
city was newly constructed, all its residents were in a way immigrants
from all parts of the immense empire, especially Iraq and Iran. Baghdad
businessmen, administrators, and policy-makers conducted commercial,
administrative, and diplomatic relations with the whole world known at
the time, including China.

The center of town was the palace area, the residence of the Caliph and
his court, inaccessible to the common people. Around it were rings of
streets with *sūq*s (markets), residences, and of course mosques. For this
was to be an Islamic city, a symbol of Islam and of the prestige of the
empire. Islam had indeed implanted itself in the Middle East, especially
through existing and newly-built cities, of which Baghdad and Cairo in
the center, Cordoba in the West, and Nishapur in the East were famous
examples. These cities not only had splendid mosques and other religious
monuments, they were also places of scholarship and culture, centers of
an impressive civilization.

As I have implied, the inhabitants of Baghdad were for the most part
Muslims, Shīʿīs as well as Sunnīs. Various communities had their own
traditions and particular orientations in matters of religion and otherwise, and if need be they could demonstrate in the streets for the causes
they defended. Yet, pressure was exerted on those Muslims who tended

---

[1]   Lecture given in Birmingham on September 12, 2001 on the occasion of the 25th
anniversary of the Centre for the Study of Islam and Christian-Muslim Relations, which
is now part of the University of Birmingham. A nearly identical text has been published
in *Islam and Christian-Muslim Relations*, 14, Nr. 1 (January 2003), pp. 3–22.

toward dualist thinking, who were accused of *zandaqa,* identified with Manichean leanings. But the city also made room for Christians who enjoyed autonomy within the established order. They were of various denominations: from the great (Nestorian) Church of the Orient and the important (Syrian) Orthodox Church, as well as the mainline (Melkite) Orthodox Church. The latter was the only one that followed the decisions of all Ecumenical Councils held by the Byzantine and Western parts of the Church situated outside the Muslim empire. The Catholicos (Patriarch) of the Church of the Orient represented all Christians before the Caliph. There were also Jews, Zoroastrians, and those from the northern or southern part of Iraq who called themselves Sabians.

All these people were *dhimmīs.* They could be put under considerable pressure, but they were not persecuted, as could the Manicheans, who had an intellectual elite of their own. From time to time, debates Baghdad could be proud of were organized by government officials or even the Caliph himself between representatives of the various recognized religions.

Birmingham, at the beginning of the twenty-first century, is an industrial and commercial city in the process of complete renovation, as any visitor arriving at the City Centre can see. The diversity of people who have established themselves here is fascinating. There is not only ethnic, linguistic, regional, and of course professional variety, but there is also a great religious diversity, with Christians, Muslims, Jews, Hindus, Sikhs, Buddhists, and others living in the city. Let me point out the recognized variety among the Christians here since more than three centuries. The Church of England, succeeding the Church of Rome, was there from the beginning. Quakers (Friends) have had their own place of worship here since 1663, Baptists since 1737, Congregationalists since 1747, Methodists since 1782, Roman Catholics since 1786, not to forget the Unitarians. Already in the nineteenth century, the role of nonconformist ministers was formulated as "… stressing responsibility for improving the lives of all the people of Birmingham", as quoted in a tourist guide book.

As far as the Muslims are concerned, the new Central Mosque, used by Deobandis as well as Barelwis, was opened in the southeastern part of the Center, in 1974. The Sunnī Dar-ul-Ulloom Islamic Mosque, established in 1983 and known for its educational work, and the Shī'ī mosque, Khoja Shia Ithna-Asheri Muslim Jamā'at, are both in the southeast of the city. A number of prayer halls are spread over the city for local use.

The municipality sees it as its task to deal adequately with the religious variety of the Birmingham population. Since the 1960s, a core task of the authorities has been to provide work, housing, health services, and educational facilities for the immigrants in particular. Private initiatives brought people more into contact with each other. One such initiative paid special attention to the encounter between British Christians and

Muslims who had arrived from abroad, mostly from Pakistan and India, and had settled in Birmingham.

It must have been in June 1975 that, with funding largely from the Birmingham Quaker family Cadbury, a conference for invited partici- pants took place at Selly Oak with Christians from Britain—and some from overseas—together with Muslims from the Birmingham area. It was organized and presided over by David Kerr, then Lecturer in Islam at Selly Oak Colleges, following illustrious predecessors such as Alphonse Mingana and J. Windrow Sweetman, and in the 1960s Sheila McDonough and John B. Taylor. The purpose of the conference was to discuss relations between Christians and Muslims and to see what could be done to improve such relationships through teaching and research, cooperation and dialogue. As a result of this cooperative Christian-Muslim effort, the Centre for the Study of Islam and Christian-Muslim Relations (CSIC) was founded in 1976 as a unique place in Europe with both Christian and Muslim staff, students, and, as far as possible, funding.

The Centre was to extend the existing lectureship in Islam to these broader activities:

1) teaching and research not only on Islam but also on the relations between Christianity and Islam and relations between Christians and Muslims in the past and present;
2) promoting encounter, cooperation, and dialogue between Christians and Muslims;
3) publishing regular reports about such relations at present; and
4) establishing a documentation unit on Muslims in Britain and Western Europe in general.

To realize these aims, scholars—Muslims and Christians, that is to say Anglicans, Protestants, and Catholics—were attracted from Britain and abroad. Their task was to teach, do research, write, and participate in national and international Christian-Muslim gatherings. Summer schools were held that also attracted overseas Christian and Muslim students. A number of publication series appeared dealing with present-day Chris- tian-Muslim relations in Europe and Africa, as well as with Christians and Muslims as minorities. In 1990, a scholarly journal *Islam and Christian- Muslim Relations* was created, first with three, then four issues a year, which enjoys an international reputation. It is now published under the auspices of the Birmingham Centre and the Center for Christian-Muslim Understanding in Washington, D.C. Ever more students from Muslim countries have enrolled at the Centre, whose library and documentation resources have been further extended.

Such was the Birmingham Anglican-Protestant-Muslim-Quaker initia- tive, unique not only for Britain but also for Europe at the time. This is not the place to trace the twenty-five odd years of the Centre's history, through its various stages from the heroic phase of the Founding Fathers to its institutionalization as part of the University of Birmingham in 1998. It will not be easy to write that history, but it should be done one day. It may unveil something not only about scholarly minds and human souls, but also about the intellectual and spiritual orientation as well as the practical funding of all these activities.

The history of the Centre should also be seen in the broader context of the British Empire and the Commonwealth, leading to migration to Britain. Its very creation throws some light on forms of Christian-Muslim rapprochement at the time when Britain was clearly ahead of continental Europe in intercultural relations. The principal Muslim partner in the creation of the Centre, the Islamic Foundation, which was founded around the same time as a *Da'wa* Center in Birmingham in the spirit of al-Mawdūdī, has gone its own way since then, first to Leicester and then to nearby Markfield.

Between the foundation of Baghdad and the initiative of Birmingham (762 and 1976), some twelve centuries elapsed. In the course of this time and in the space between the two places, we have not only the great history of Muslim and Christian majorities with their glorious empires and nations. We also have the social history of Muslim and Christian minorities living in each other's territories, with their continuing struggle for life if not survival. This has always been true for Christians, and for Muslims especially since their twentieth-century migrations to the West.

Part I: Some Factual Data

2. Muslims in Europe

Substantial numbers of Muslims in Western Europe live in France, Germany, and the United Kingdom, in very different legal and social frameworks. The contexts of these countries largely condition the ways their Muslim communities have organized themselves and in which they have institutionalized their Islam. A quick glance shows the differences.

France[2] has had links with North Africa, and the great majority of its Muslim immigrants come from this region. Secularism (*laïcité*) is the official ideology of the country; religion is not to appear in the public sphere, and there is no religious instruction at state schools. As a consequence, Muslims in France were not able to establish prayer halls and mosques until the mid-1980s. This has also to do with the fact that Arab

---

[2] See Chapter 11 on "Muslims and Their Islam in Europe: Initiatives and Responses", section 5.

Muslim organizations could not be founded freely until the early 1980s, when legal regulations on associations in general became more flexible. Yet, an issue like wearing headscarves led to a national debate, since it was seen as a large-scale public affirmation of the presence of Islam and Islamic identity, contrary to the ideology of secularism as the basis of society. The debate on the relationship between Islam and secularism has been dominating the socio-political discussion on Islam in France, but not only "religion" was involved here.

On the one hand, during the 1990s, younger "Islamist" groups have shown themselves capable of playing a constructive social role in the impoverished suburbs of French cities. For instance, they helped young-sters when the local government no longer had the means to offer suffi-cient social support and education to the second and third immigrant generation of Muslim youth. On the other hand, the presence of a French-speaking and -writing intelligentsia has made Paris a center for the diffu-sion of Muslim Arabic as well as French literature and culture, with a great diversity in social and cultural orientations. Muslim women in France have taken a number of initiatives to improve the traditional role of women in Muslim societies through better education and working conditions. There are a number of mixed marriages. There are an esti-mated four million Muslims in France, of whom a large proportion have acquired French nationality.

Germany[3] has old links with Turkey and the migration of a large Turkish labor force to the Federal Republic took place within the framework of an official agreement between both countries in 1962, when the Wall built in 1961 prevented people from the German Democratic Republic from going to work in West Germany. The great majority of Muslims in Germany are of Turkish origin. Until the end of the 1990s, Germany refused to be considered a country of immigration and made it difficult to acquire German citizenship. As a result, the legal situation of the "guest workers" remained precarious. Cultural and religious affairs are the responsibility of the various constituent *Länder* ("provinces"), which also regulate the obligatory offer of religious instruction in schools. Several Muslim organizations have requested recognition as a *Körperschaft des Öffentlichen Rechts*, or public body, like the major Churches and even two different Jewish communities. Many Muslims consider this refusal of juridical recognition of Islam on an equal basis with Christianity and Judaism as a form of religious discrimination, and not without reason.

Most interesting for research on minorities has been the public appear-ance in Germany of Islamic movements and organizations that were

---

[3]   See Chapter 11 on "Muslims and Their Islam in Europe: Initiatives and Responses", section 6.

under pressure or even forbidden in Turkey, such as the Suleymanli, the Milli Görüs, and the Nurculuk. Kurdish groups that were not recognized in Turkey could speak out freely here; the non-Sunnī Alevis, who had barely subsisted in Turkey, could organize themselves in Germany. The Turkish authorities had never recognized the existence of these "nonconformist" Muslim minorities alongside the official government body for Islam in Turkey, the *Diyanet*. This body also controls a number of Turkish mosque organizations outside the country and is really a political instrument of the Turkish government rather than a religious organization in its own right. There may be some one and a half million Muslims in Germany.

The *United Kingdom*[4], needless to say, has a state Church and religious instruction is obligatory in schools. Under Commonwealth rules, many Muslim immigrants and their descendants—especially those originating from South Asia, who constitute the majority—are British citizens. Mixed marriages are unusual here, and a certain racism has continued to exist notwithstanding the Anti-Discrimination Act. Immigrants from South Asia were accustomed to hierarchical social structures in their own societies, supported by age-old traditions. Muslim as well as Hindu immigrants from South Asia tend to reproduce their traditional communal structures in Britain, so that they constitute their own communities without much interaction with British society. For a long time this has been welcomed by British authorities. This implies, however, that among these immigrants Islam is mostly still dominated by attitudes, orientations, and schools of thought from the countries of origin. The same holds true for kinship relations, family life, and marriage arrangements.

Muslim immigrants in Britain have developed a certain political consciousness, and, as British citizens, they can participate actively in political life here. On the municipal level, they have considerable influence in various constituencies. In the cultural sphere, Muslims have established several important study centers and cultural foundations. Especially since the 1970s, a number of studies and other books dealing with aspects of Muslim societies and Islam and written by Muslim scholars and intellectuals living in Britain have seen the light. Added to this, London provides numerous possibilities for certain elite groups from Muslim countries and elsewhere to meet and establish contacts in a variety of spheres, economic and political, social and cultural. There may be altogether some two million Muslims in the United Kingdom.

The present-day economic situation of most Muslims in these three and also the other countries of the European Union is weak. This is particu-

---

[4]   See Chapter 11 on "Muslims and Their Islam in Europe: Initiatives and Responses", section 4.

larly so when they have no work, since the search for work has mostly been the reason for migrating, and since work constitutes one of the keys to integration. Socially, participation in social life demands a good knowledge of the language and a kind of familiarity with particular groups in society that can usually only be acquired after the first or even the first two generations. Tensions grow when the native population distance themselves from "foreigners" and when there is no real positive interaction between them. Conflicts arise when extremist groups start committing crimes against these "foreigners" without being adequately corrected. Only after naturalization and through political action can immigrants have a voice in the political arena of their new country.

Culturally speaking, there are many negative stereotypes about Islam and Muslims in European societies that need to be corrected and to be replaced by knowledge and direct experience. If the fact of being an immigrant in itself implies limits in society, that of being a Muslim adds an extra burden. Many Muslims in Europe live in fact without any personal communication with the non-Muslim majority. This has been seriously aggravated by apprehensions and fears since September 11, 2001. I see their situation as potentially threatened.

What happened to the older Muslim communities settled in the Balkans and further eastward should be a serious warning. The Muslim Bosniacs have suffered a devastating war with "Christian" Croatians and "Christian" Serbs who carried out intentional "ethnic cleansing" and genocide. The fact of this war (1992–5), which Europe was not able to end by itself, still weighs heavily in present-day Muslim views of Europe and of European tolerance of Islam. The Albanians have no particular ideology of Islam but have suffered nevertheless for years under "Christian" Serbian claims to Kosovo and repression of the Muslim inhabitants. In Bulgaria, the Muslim communities suffered expulsion to Turkey in the 1980s, that is to say during the Cold War; only some of them returned later when the government changed policy and life conditions improved. All of this shows that Muslim communities in the Balkans live in a region where feelings run high. They remain exposed to various pressures that have many causes but that they themselves and the non-Muslim majorities often put down to the fact that they are Muslims. The situation of Muslims in present-day Russia has not really improved since the end of the Soviet Union. In fact, it deteriorated when that end was accompanied by legitimate aspirations to political freedom, for example when Muslim Chechens, including civilians, were massacred by Russian armies.

3. Christians in the Middle East

If most Muslims in Europe are in a situation Europeans do not envy, most Christians in the Middle East are in a situation not all Muslims in the region would find enviable. One complaint is the basic lack of a secure existence. The recognition of Christians as ordinary citizens—during the colonial period and in the newly established independent states—furthered their emancipation. However, on the whole, their economic and social security decreased considerably. This is not necessarily the result of planned action against the Christians specifically. With the exception of a small political and financial elite, the social and economic situation of the whole population in Middle Eastern countries has deteriorated.

Most countries of the region have undergone, with or without revolutions, fundamental political, economic, and social changes that have strongly affected the old privileged classes of society, which included a relatively high proportion of Christians. The arms race in the Middle East and actual wars have placed a heavy burden on the entire population of these countries, including the Christians. Even aside from the growing economic and social insecurity, the populations in general and especially the intellectual elites suffer from the growing political insecurity in the region. Peace and war, promising and oppressive political situations, and even the political and economic leadership turn out to be unpredictable. All regimes have undemocratic systems of government, exercise increasing control over the population, and assign privileges and favors to the happy few. The population of East Jerusalem and the territories occupied by Israel in 1967 has lived and still lives under a largely arbitrary military rule, with an Israeli colonization of the occupied territories. And this was before the willful Israeli destruction of the Palestinian infrastructure and terrorization of the population since October 2001. To the indigenous factors of the region, a number of influences and interferences from outside should be added, especially since September 11, 2001.

The efforts of "Islamist" movements to bring about an Islamization of society—and in some cases to destabilize the existing social order altogether—have led to increased insecurity for Christians. The West, with which a number of Christians have close links, is decried by Islamists. The civil war in Lebanon—which also included Maronite or Shīʿī factions fighting among themselves—shattered the security enjoyed for decades by Lebanese Christians and of which they had been so proud. Since the 1970s, Christians have increasingly left the occupied territories and East Jerusalem, as well as Turkey, Egypt, Iraq, and Lebanon, hoping to exchange the past bitter experience of life there for a more viable future elsewhere.

Many indigenous Christian Churches of the Middle East now have flourishing communities in Europe and North America. We should also note that a number of Muslim people who were able to leave have found refuge here.

If the communal life of Muslims in Western Europe is largely in the private sphere and separate from Western society, among Christians in the Middle East, communal life is articulated to a large extent within the various Church communities. These not only have strictly religious but also social activities that, however, are never completely free. Iraq only allows religious, not social Church activities. Saudi Arabia does not even allow any Church activity at all. Most Churches in the Middle East transcend national borders, have their networks throughout the region and with Western Churches, and are at present members of the Middle East Council of Churches.

Christian religious institutions are linked to Churches and consequently in principle distinct from the given social and political order. This is quite visible in Muslim countries. Moreover, the indigenous Christian religious institutions in the Middle East are older than Islam. They are surrounded by ancient traditions and "mysteries" and their guardians are endowed with an aura of authority that is not restricted to the religious sphere but extends to matters of personal and social life as well. Although in Middle Eastern Christianity, as well as in Islam, the religious sphere is distinct from the social and political sphere, in practice it is not considered to be completely separate from them.

Following centuries of historical experience, nowadays the Churches have to defend their rights ferociously against interventions by the state, on the one hand, and by Muslim activists on the other. Where they constitute a small minority and where democratic institutions are weak or absent altogether, the Churches have little recourse to law or outside protection and have to be careful in word and action. Nowhere are they allowed to carry out what is considered to be "political" action. Although both parties are past masters at covering tensions in Christian-Muslim relations, the cracks do sometimes show. These cases are significant and need to be analyzed in their contexts. In general, however, it is difficult to know exactly what is going on, not only on each side, but also between them.

Let us now make a quick survey of the state of affairs of ancient Christian communities living in Muslim-majority countries in the Middle East, as we did for Muslims living in Europe.

In present-day republican *Turkey*, with its official ideology of Turkish-Islamic synthesis, little to nothing is left of the once flourishing Greek and Armenian Churches that existed up to World War One. They suffered persecution and most of their members left. The Syrian Orthodox Church in the southeastern part of the country has never been recognized. This region was ravaged during the Turkish-Kurdish war, and most Syrian

Orthodox Christians left for Istanbul and abroad, where they were received as refugees. The Ecumenical (Orthodox) Patriarch of Constantinople and his staff have to work under extremely difficult conditions in Turkey, whether or not this is intended. Not less than in other Muslim countries, Turkish public opinion is ill-informed about Christianity and has generally been opposed to dialogue between Muslims and Christians.

Christian communities everywhere in Muslim countries must prove their social value. In the *Arab countries*, situations vary.

Saudi Arabia, still a kind of nomocratic absolute monarchy, does not recognize the right of Christians—that is to say, foreign workers—to practise their religion; officially there are no Christians in the country. The two Ba'th countries have contrasting policies: the Christian minority in Iraq is under heavy pressure from the regime and in fact not allowed to leave the country, whereas it has enjoyed recognition and certain privileges in Syria. In Egypt, the Copts are mostly not considered a "minority" at all, and they align themselves with the Muslims as children of "our Mother Egypt". Lebanon suffered a most serious civil and further war (1975–89) and is now a Muslim-majority country, consisting in fact of minorities of all sorts. In the Occupied Territories and East Jerusalem, both Christians and Muslims have been at the mercy of short-sighted aggressive and greedy Israeli state policies. Jordan has made an effort to pursue a balanced policy, in which Christians are neither discriminated against nor privileged above Muslims.

Eastward, *Iran*—a clerical state—has an ancient Armenian Christian community centered in Isfahan, which continues to be recognized. The Christian communities in Iran that resulted from Western missionary work in the nineteenth and twentieth centuries—for instance the Anglican Church—passed through a difficult period when the Islamic Revolution took place in 1979. At present, Christians in Iran have in practice a somewhat modernized *dhimmī* status.

Further eastward again, *Pakistan*—a military state—has no ancient indigenous Churches, but only Christian communities arising from Western missions. The official Islamization policies that Zia ul-Haqq started in 1977 led to the end of democracy and increased discrimination against Christians and other non-Muslims. The Anti-Blasphemy Law, for instance, has led to false accusations and much injustice to Christians.

Beyond the strictly Middle Eastern region, I should at least mention in passing the plight of Christian communities that resulted from the work of Christian missions in the nineteenth and twentieth centuries. They are now under persecution in an Islamic war state such as Sudan. There have been waves of persecution of Christians in Northern Nigeria and in parts of Indonesia. Their situation in other Muslim countries is not improving but worsening. Reports exist on cases of aggression, violence, and terror exercised against Christians in the name of Islam. Mutual relations between Christians and Muslims have suffered from the "war on terrorism", which itself has "terrorizing" effects on Muslim-Christian relations.

4. Some Parallel Features of Muslim and Christian Minority Groups

There are some interesting common *features* of both minority groups, that have to do with Middle Eastern cultures and societies.

1) In both cases, social and individual life has typical features that, though different among Muslims here and Christians there, distinguish these communities from current (post)modern Western lifestyles: strong family ties, patriarchal authority structures, firm rules governing relations between the sexes, particular traditions concerning social behavior, food, and drink, ways of taking care of the body (cleanliness), and particular cultural traditions about, for example, oral literature and the arts. Often these features are considered to be religiously prescribed or at least linked to the tradition of a particular religious community.

2) In both cases, religion, even if it is not practiced actively by each person, plays a key role in legitimizing certain rules with authority and maintaining a social identity that is recognizable, not only to the people themselves but also to other people and to the broader society of which they are a part. Its religious aspects contribute to the integration of the members in the group.

3) The Christian and Muslim minority communities concerned nowadays have in common at least three different kinds of movements among their members. First, those that want to open up and modernize; second, those that, on the contrary, want to keep to the traditions they know (for self-defense); and third, movements that insist on going back to the very sources of the religion of the community.

All movements in Christianity and Islam that want to go back to the sources are confronted with two basic questions. The first is fundamental: what exactly in these sources is to be considered "Revelation" and consequently must be recognized unconditionally by the believer? The second question is more concrete: what are the rules of living, the views of the human being, and the statements about God's relation to human beings that we can deduce from these sources? This third kind of movements— "back to the sources"—is far too varied for all of its forms to be included under such general headings as "fundamentalism" or "integrism", as is often done nowadays.

All three movements mentioned—the impulse to open up and accept modernity, the desire to keep to tradition, and the search to go back to the sources—can be found among Muslims in Europe as well as among

Christians in the Middle East. These movements should be seen not only as defense mechanisms, but also as practical, moral, and also spiritual views and practices to overcome negative situations and problems.

4) In both minorities there is a striking trend to renew and strengthen the links with one's own broader religious community: for Muslims, the Muslim commonwealth—often through their countries of origin—and for Christians the World Council of Churches, the Roman Catholic Church, or specific Churches in the West or elsewhere. Muslims in Western Europe, just like Christians in the Middle East, tend to ensure their continued life, existence, and presence with the help of some *Hinterland*. This may be a particular country, but there is also a certain "ecumenical" concern growing, both among Muslim groups in Europe and among Christian communities in the Middle East.

5) In both cases, finally, at least in some countries, there is a certain *rapprochement* between the leaderships. The leadership of certain Muslim organizations in European countries is in contact with that of certain Churches in those countries; the leadership of certain Christian communities in the Middle East is in contact with certain Muslim leaders in the region. The Netherlands and Lebanon provide examples here. This *rapprochement* serves in the first place practical interests: defense against common dangers, such as extremism or secularism; action for common causes, such as relief in catastrophes or defense of human rights; and strengthening common resources on humanitarian and broader human issues, such as family life or religious education. It entails a mutual acceptance and sometimes a further-reaching kind of interaction between minority and majority communities, at least between certain individual members of these communities.

Part II: Some Fresh Questions
about "Minorities" and "Majorities"

Until now we have simply taken the terms "minority" and "majority" as they are used in ordinary speech. This served to take an initial inventory of the groups and communities concerned. It is time now, however, to question this terminology and to look for a more adequate way to describe the social and human realities underlying the supposed opposition between a quantitative majority and minority. When we speak about "Christian" and "Muslim" minorities as opposed to "Muslim" and "Christian" majorities, is this not in fact a political terminology indicating and stressing a power relationship? And when we describe social and human realities in terms of numerical differences and power relationships, do we not in fact neglect the substance of social and human relationships?

5. Diversity within Majorities and Minorities

As long as relationships between a given minority and a given majority were conceived in terms of an opposition between two separated communities, the diversity that exists within both the majority and the minority group was necessarily obscured. Until the mid-twentieth century at least, for instance, Muslims and Christians mostly must have seen and identified themselves as well as each other as two easily recognizable social entities, more or less as two distinct blocs. They did this not only in the external relations between Muslim and European countries or states. They did it also in the internal relations within the state, such as between one Muslim majority and several Christian minorities, or—more rarely—the reverse: between one Christian majority and several Muslim minorities.

Such a dualistic scheme of thinking is especially useful for political purposes—such as hiding differences in one's own ranks—, for administrative purposes—such as levying taxes—, and in situations of plain confrontation—such as in war or in resistance to military and political oppression. Such a dualism may also boost the prestige and further the influence of the religious leadership on both sides of the religious divide. But it is mostly a simplistic scheme imposed on reality. Whether consciously or by implication, it obscures the diversity that always exists within both the majority and the minorities. It implies a political perception of relations in terms of power. It can easily be used for political ends to defend one group as a whole and to attack the other group as such. It encourages tension and conflict.

For our purpose, however, which is to obtain more knowledge and better insight into what has really been happening in relations between Muslims and Christians, this model is not very helpful. Speaking of "Muslim majority versus Christian minorities" or "Christian majority versus Muslim minorities" obscures rather than elucidates the nature and substance of relationships. It provides a glimpse and gives a first explanation of the utterly distorted views that Christians and Muslims often had and have of each other and of relationships between them. Christians and Muslims, be they majorities or minorities, behave as monolithic blocs only in situations of confrontation, that is to say in crisis situations. In more normal situations, various political and religious currents are always present on both sides, even if these currents cannot always express themselves openly and even if in some cases opposing trends are simply suppressed.

For research purposes, the true question in my view is not: "Who are the adherents of Christianity and Islam as two given entities?" but: "Who are the persons or groups who identify themselves as 'Christians' and 'Muslims', what do they mean by this self-identification, and how do they in fact behave when they call themselves 'Christians' and 'Muslims'?"

Other questions follow from this. What are the aims of those who identify themselves as Christians and Muslims, what do they want to stress? What orientations, currents of thought, and programs of action do we find among them? Are there parallels? What kinds of orientation, thinking, and acting can we find in only one of the two groups, or even in only one particular section of one group? This is what I call an empirical approach concerned with specific data and the particular significance that specific people attribute to them.

6. The Concept of Minority

I contend that the concept of "minority", with its connotation of numerical weakness and lack of visible force, is problematical for a religious community. The concept may be useful if we want to stress a difference and opposition between those who have numerical power and those who have not. But if we are not primarily concerned with numbers and visible force, as in the case of our study of religions, the picture is different.

In religions, perhaps more than in many other fields, differences are natural. The history of Christianity and Islam is full of examples of differences: the constant rise of new orientations, new religious movements, and the splitting off of sectarian movements—linked to new authorities, new personal projects, interpretations, and applications. It also shows the existence of a variety of more established religious institutions and recognized authorities claiming to offer needed and satisfying rules, a fruitful way of life, perhaps even a kind of salvation. This diversity implies that, precisely in the field of religion, majority and minority groups are natural, well known, and accepted, although we may not use the term. Often we speak rather of larger and smaller communities. The relations between these groups are not necessarily measured in terms of numerical or political power. Moreover, they can always change, depending on the claims of the groups concerned and their enforcement, their desire for communication, their communal and possibly organizational structure within a certain hierarchy, their participation in society, and their affinity with other social groups. Relations between religious communities, moreover, are very dependent on the political, economic, and social contexts and situations in which people find themselves and encounter each other. It is especially the alliances that specific religious groups willingly or unwillingly entertain with particular social forces or political and economic interests, and vice versa, that seem to be at the root of problems in the relations between the groups. And it is especially those religious minorities that enjoy no particular social, political, or economic protection and that cannot well defend themselves that risk becoming victims in societies where power counts.

In all societies with "given" ethnic or cultural minorities, these minorities tend to develop their own specific resources to make themselves indispensable to society so that they can survive. Conversely, those individuals and groups who have special kinds of non-economic interests and non-political competences that are absolutely needed in society constitute what I would like to call "voluntary" minorities with qualitative resources. They may survive successfully although they lack economic or political power. Artistic, intellectual, and broad cultural creativity—as well as deep social concerns, high moral standards, or an elevating spirituality—can radiate and bear fruit.

From this point of view, the integration and dynamics of a society are strengthened by the contribution of minorities with relevant qualitative resources. The life of people may indeed be hampered or simply blocked by the design of a more or less "homogenized" society often consciously or implicitly promoted by ideological or religious majorities trying to realize their dreams of an all-Islamic, all-Jewish, all-Hindu, or all-Catholic unified society. In a long-term perspective, so-called "minority" religious or other communities, provided they have qualitative resources and bear fruit, can be an asset rather than a burden to a society. Unfortunately, most "majority" communities enjoying power seem to have difficulty in recognizing this. They do not like exceptions.

7. The Self-articulations of Minorities

Let us use here the concepts of "minority" and "majority" as purely social or political concepts without any specific religious reference. And let us then plead for the study (1) of minorities, (2) of the behavior of a particular minority and a given majority toward each other, and (3) of relationships between a given majority and existing minorities and vice versa.

In a first stage, such a general study can throw light on different kinds of social interaction and power relations between these groups. This includes groups that identify themselves as "Muslims" and groups that identify themselves in other ways. In this way, we should be able to explain in general terms the relationships between Muslim minority communities and a different kind of majority in Western countries, or between a given Muslim majority and different kinds of minority communities in Muslim countries. There are certain general rules in the behavior of people who find themselves in a majority or minority situation. On this general level, we apply these general rules to relations between Christians and Muslims without taking into account what they mean exactly when they call themselves Christians or Muslims. On this level it is the general structure that counts.

But above this level of general rules, there is the more specific level of meanings and contents. In a second stage, we have to do with the specific ways in which Christians and Muslims identify themselves by means of their religions. They articulate their relationship by means of the articulation—that is to say interpretations—of their own and the other's religion.

Two questions seem to be particularly relevant here:

1) In which situations and in what ways do minority Christians and minority Muslims express their Christian or Muslim identity? They may do this for instance by stressing and following the traditions, doctrines, and practices by which their community has always considered itself distinct from others. They may also express their identity—through their own experience, thought, and action—in new ways. In identifying themselves, they may present new interpretations of their religion.

2) When and how in the course of history did Christians and Muslims live in minority situations? Do Christianity and Islam as religions still bear the mark of this? Or, to be more precise, do certain religious doctrines and practices of particular Muslim and Christian groups reflect an outlook and sensitivity that is connected with a minority situation? How were these two religions articulated when their adherents had no visible power in relation to a majority consisting of adherents of the other religion or in relation to a majority that gave a different interpretation of their own religion?

At first sight, such questions seem to be rather abstract and, as far as I know, they have rarely been posed by historians of religion. Yet they are scholarly important and they are relevant today. Minorities have their own experiences that are hardly known to majorities. "Minority people" may propose more or less ingenious solutions for certain problems that would hardly have occurred to people living in a majority situation. Different from "majority people", they articulate their identity less in terms of power. They are not in a position to "impose" themselves or their particular views on others. "Minority people" instead tend to present themselves by posing certain questions and looking for an answer without recourse to power in the quantitative sense. They have to resort to other kinds of power, in a qualitative sense.

8. Is the Model of "Social Separateness" Adequate?

The common usage of the terms "minority" and "majority", certainly in the context of religious communities, suggests a separation between a religious minority and a religious majority, both conceived as being as autonomous as possible. I would like to speak here of the model of "social separateness" of religious communities and thus of their religions. This model was current in the Middle East, for instance, up to the formation of nation-states that superseded religious communities.

This model presupposes, however, that religious communities can be autonomous or even nearly autarchic. Such communities may entertain necessary practical contacts, but certainly not relations that extend into private life or into the heart of religious matters. This model of social separateness was not only a practical necessity for survival under the threat of oppression and persecution. It was also legitimated doctrinally by the religious authorities' insistence on the presence of incommensurable—cultural, doctrinal, juridical, etc.—differences between the religions concerned. This could be extended to the idea of a mutual exclusion of—and even an absolute opposition between—the religions concerned, with its logical consequences.

Jews in the societies of medieval Europe were forced to minimize relations with the Christians, who were here in the absolute majority and held power in both Church and state. In a similar way, in Muslim societies basing themselves on the *Sharī'a*, Christians and Jews had restricted relations with the Muslims, who were there in the absolute majority and held power in state and society. Yet, unlike Christian territories, the Muslim ones gave to Christian and Jewish minorities at least a certain legal recognition. On a popular level, Christians and Jews could sometimes share certain local celebrations with Muslims.

In most cases, however, on both sides the self-conscious and even arrogant behavior of the dominating majority wanting to show off power required the dominated minority to adopt a pattern of servile behavior. Any ostentatious action of the minority was perceived by the majority as provocative arrogance. It is not without reason that, whenever possible, religious minorities such as the Maronites or the Druzes in Lebanon withdrew to inaccessible places in the mountains to be as independent as possible.

People coming from the Middle East and living at present in the West still tend not only to define religions in terms of separate socio-religious communities, but also to put clear boundaries between them. Those who belonged to certain Jewish or Christian communities in the Middle East continue to speak of what they call oppression from "Islam" and tend to warn the West against it. The absolutization of the differences between the religions of these communities in fact hampered "normal" relationships between them. This occurred especially in times of war, crisis, or decline, when economic and political interests—mostly of the majority or the stronger party—pressed toward exploiting and oppressing minorities. Existing differences were then overstressed. We have historical reports about the sad conditions under which Christian and Jewish *dhimmīs* had to live in various Muslim regions in the eighteenth and nineteenth centuries, often humiliated and treated as scapegoats. The application of the well-known Qur'anic idea of "humiliating" subdued Christians and Jews in wars that Muhammad conducted at the end of his life has done a lot of harm to at least Muslim-Christian relationships.

With modern state formation, economic and social development, urbanization and industrialization, and the ideas accompanying them, the model of social separateness could be maintained only at a high price. And it was not only the minority that had to pay the price. The majority, too, could suffer under the situation. Examples are the South African policy of apartheid, the ethnic-religious cleansing in ex-Yugoslavia, and the separation between Jewish Israelis on the one hand and Arab Israelis and Palestinians on the other hand.

It seems to me that, for their survival on a planetary scale, modern states have to admit that minority groups—including religious communities—can in principle constitute positive assets for the well-being and growth of society and the state as a whole. Economic interests and the need for survival force a shift from the older model of social separateness to a new one of social participation, implying a certain division of tasks. The power of the majority need not be exercised to the detriment of the minorities, as could be held in former times. In Western countries, carrying out political action, including opposition, has become a recognized right of minorities that have the country's nationality.

Other rules were developed in different contexts. In the Middle East, for instance, social minority groups are often still linked to specific religious communities or to specific religious positions. In this way, religions continue to play a political role; in some cases, state power can even be exercised by religious minorities against a religious majority.

It has rightly been said that in the Middle East all groups are minorities in one respect or another, all of them being involved in a constant struggle for survival. In such a context, consequently, the situation of Christian communities is more complex than the still-popular scheme of an oppressed "Christian minority versus a tyrannical Muslim majority" suggests. The states of the region are quite different from each other, the Muslim majority is nowhere one coherent political bloc, and the various Christian minority communities live under very different political regimes. The consequences are clear.

It seems that a similar situation has come about nowadays in Europe, where the political reality of secular states has broken the scheme of an oppressed "Muslim minority versus a dominating Christian majority". Nowadays there are not only many more—and more important—minorities and majorities than only religious ones; and the latter are no longer one bloc, but have differentiated into various kinds of social and political as well as religious orientations. The situation varies according to countries and ideologies, and it is difficult to generalize.

It is safe to say, however, that the well-known scheme of a permanent structural antagonism between a religious majority and one or more religious minorities is not adequate and should be rejected. Such a scheme veils rather than reveals what is in fact going on between Muslims and Christians in specific contexts.

I contend that modern states, both in Europe and in the Middle East, have a long-term interest in encouraging and following the model of participation and possible integration, rather than that of separation leading to opposition, unless they want to create or continue conflicts.

Integration may lead to increased assimilation and even to the gradual disappearance of certain minorities, or at least certain of their traditional characteristic features. However, the opposite may happen, too. In contrast to integration, centrifugal forces may arise, supported by regional minority interests that define themselves as minorities seeking recognition. If this is the case, the state should resist the temptation to identify itself with the majority. As I see it, the state needs to distinguish itself clearly from both the majority and the minorities. In principle, with further differentiations, new kinds of interaction between religious minorities and majorities can develop.

In this view, there is much more scope for and variety in minority activities than the older schemes imposed on minority-majority relations between Christians and Muslims suggest. These schemes were developed on the basis of a traditional Middle East. In contrast to that past, I tend to think that, in certain ways, the future may well depend on certain highly qualified minorities, rather than on a majority that is sinking under its own weight or strangled by the obsession to extend its power at any price.

9. Majority-Minority Breakthroughs

Precisely in situations of majority-minority relations, we should look and see when and where people have taken action to break through social separateness and religiously justified antagonism. When and where did Christians or Muslims pursue positive interaction and when and where did they arrive at some form of cooperation and dialogue?

This seems to have happened much less than we would hope. This is certainly so in the Middle East, with its contrasting political interests and its fixed religious traditions, but also in Africa, where so many Christians and Muslims are living in fear, tension, and even armed conflict. Up to the end of the nineteenth century, Christians in a minority situation in fact simply could not take initiatives for dialogue; legally or socially, they were just *dhimmīs* within the framework of traditional Islamic states. In an analogous way, Muslims could not take such an initiative, either, when most of them lived in the colonial setting under Western rule.

Conversely, those who are in a majority position or simply have power have only rarely been interested in taking initiatives for dialogue, except for the sake of law and order or for diplomatic reasons. In other words, the very search for power and the interest in maintaining prevailing power structures—including those of the religious institutions existing on both sides—have made breakthroughs between religious majorities and minorities extremely difficult. After all, from a majority point of view, minorities might become a threat to the existing order. As always, influences from outside—Saudi Arabia, Pakistan, or Iran; Europe or North America—also play a role in a possible breakthrough in majority-minority relations. Perhaps it would be like interreligious dialogue in situations of real crisis, when the best results are reached if religious differences are hardly mentioned or discussed.

After the colonial era, the establishment of nation-states that recognized the rights and duties of all their citizens seems to have opened the way, at least in principle and from a theoretical point of view, to more communication between religious minorities and the religious majority. Once the equality of the citizens before the law is recognized, initiatives for cooperation and dialogue are possible, certainly as private initiatives. This assumes, of course, that the human reality of plurality and the social reality of differences be accepted and that the false dream of a "homogenized" society—following one of the existing Christian or Muslim ideologies, or similar future ideologies in which everyone would have the same ideology or religion—be halted.

The intriguing question is then: when, where, and in what circumstances has not only the state but also any religious majority been able to recognize the intrinsic value of the participation of a religious minority in the activities of society? And vice versa: when, where, and in what circumstances has any religious minority been able to make itself heard not only by the state but also by the religious majority? My honest guess is that this has hardly ever happened, alas.

Nearly all cases of interaction between religious minorities and majorities suggest that serious interaction started with practical cooperation out of sheer need. This could be, for instance, under the pressure of a common danger, the pressures of political and economic interests including those of the state, or some pressure from outside the country itself. It seems that whenever positive interaction between religious majority and minority groups has occurred, it was due either to the fact that a third party, nonreligious itself, simply imposed it, or to the fact that the parties concerned recognized mutual consultation in a given situation or context as a condition for survival. In the latter case, they could fall back on three sources that had been available for a long time but that had not always been put into effect for this particular purpose. Besides material resources and good scholarship with insight and a broad horizon, people of faith and good will are needed who are ready to put their hands to the plough.

But where is the plough? And where are the hands?

10. Conclusion

Whatever the cultural splendor of ʿAbbāsid Baghdad or the terrorizing forces of present-day Baghdad, reports say that the situation of the Christians was and is not good and was and is even worsening, with their number decreasing, and with social, economic, and political pressures increasing. I guess that the situation of the Muslim people there was and is not much better.

And whatever the view one may have about the fruits of interreligious tolerance and dialogue in present-day Birmingham, a quiet walk around the Digbeth Coach station shows Pakistani business at its lowest and Birmingham residences in bad shape and even falling down. The situation of Muslims is not good and that of ordinary other people is not much better.

The difference between my view of Christian and Muslim minorities and earlier views is largely one of perspective. In former times, Christians in the West used to be worried about the situation of Christian minorities in the Muslim East. Nowadays—if I may say so—Muslims in the East worry about the situation of Muslim minorities in the West. My concern here is to see the situation of both Muslims and Christians as a common condition in a shared context, be it Baghdad or Jerusalem, be it Birmingham or Bradford. If there is oppression, both parties suffer, certainly in Baghdad and Jerusalem. And if life is under pressure, both parties feel it, in Birmingham as in Baghdad.

The problems that Muslim and Christian minority communities confront in states that are themselves in transition are gigantic: misunderstandings in intercultural encounters, the need for a more civil society and for upholding human rights and doing our utmost to be and keep in communication. Islam and Christianity are also involved in these problems. Theologians give thought to it; philosophers of religion develop audacious theories; social scientists carry out empirical investigations; educators work for the future of today's children; governments ask for expert advice; the communities concerned are taken up by their own views and interests; and politicians look for what might still be possible in situations where most things are impossible. There is a lack of means, qualified people, and also of common "human" sense. As I see it, the well-being of Muslim and Christian minorities is in the utmost interest of the Western and the Muslim world together.

There is not much light that I see in these and other critical situations. As a student of religions, I mention two needs. On the level of socio-political realities, there is an urgent need to create conditions for developments—in both Western and Muslim countries—toward more civil and civic societies, different according to cultures. On the level of the mind, there is need for further study of the actual reality of Muslim and Christian minorities and what can be done about it.

In such study, we need impartial insight with equal concern for both sides, as far as this is humanly possible. We need a new kind of enlightenment, after the earlier Scottish, French, and German versions. That is, an enlightenment not only of one's own mind but also of persons and minds in a kind of enlightened communication. I hope our travel from Baghdad to Birmingham has contributed to this.

11. Appendix: Muslim-Christian Relations in Terms of Minority-Majority Situations

It may be useful to present a rough scheme of different minority-majority situations underlying Muslim-Christian relations. My purpose is not to present a country-by-country survey, which would require reliable statistics, but a more general scheme with a few fitting examples. In view of the problem as defined in the text, we are in any case more concerned with the qualitative than with the quantitative aspects of the relations. I suggest the following division of countries where Christians and Muslims live together.

11.1. Asian and African Countries with Large Muslim Majorities

1. *Sharī'a*-based states without indigenous Christians. Example: the Arabian Peninsula. Christians are foreigners coming mostly from particular Asian countries. They are present as temporary workers but not as immigrants.
2. *Sharī'a*-based states with small indigenous Christian communities. Examples: Iran since the revolution of 1979 (with the ancient Armenian Church), Pakistan since the Islamization program started in 1977 (Christian communities since the nineteenth century).
3. Muslim states with indigenous Christian communities dating from before Islam. Examples: Syria, Egypt, Jordan, Iraq, Palestine.
4. Muslim states with indigenous Christian communities established since the nineteenth century. Examples: Senegal and various other West and East African countries; Indonesia and some other Asian countries.
5. Muslim states with small numbers of Christian immigrants. Examples: Tunisia, Morocco, and Algeria with immigrants mainly from France; the

Caucasian and Central Asian Republics with immigrants mainly from Russia.

11.2. Asian and African Countries with Considerable Numbers of Muslims

1. Sharī'a-based states with a certain balance between Muslims, on the one hand, and Christians plus adherents of other religions, on the other hand. Example: Sudan.
2. States with a certain balance between Muslims and Christians. Examples: Lebanon, Nigeria.
3. States with other major religions besides Islam and Christianity. Examples: India (large Hindu majority), Malaysia (Chinese, Buddhist, and Hindu minorities), South Africa (Hindu and other small minorities).

11.3. Asian and African Countries with a Small Percentage of Muslims

1. States with both Muslim and Christian minorities. Examples: People's Republic of China, Japan.
2. States with a Christian majority and a Muslim minority. Example: Philippines.

11.4. European Countries

1. European countries with ancient Muslim majorities. Examples: Albania, Bosnia-Herzegovina.
2. European countries with ancient Muslim minorities. Examples: Bulgaria, Russia.
3. EU countries with Muslim immigrants also from former colonial territories. Examples: France, United Kingdom.
4. Other EU countries with Muslim immigrants. Example: Germany.
5. European non-EU countries with Muslim immigrants. Example: Switzerland.

11.5. Other Countries with Muslim Immigrant Minorities

1. North American countries. Examples: USA, Canada.
2. Latin American countries. Examples: Mexico, Argentina.
3. Australia.

Selected Literature

1. General Questions

YACOUB, Joseph, *Les minorités: Quelle protection?*, Paris: Desclée de Brouwer, 1995.

2. Socio-Political Aspects

BETTS, Robert Brenton, *Christians in the Arab East: A Political Study*, Athens: Lycabettus Press, 1975.

CHABRY, Laurent and Annie, *Politique et minorités au Proche-Orient: Les raisons d'une explosion*, Paris: Maisonneuve et Larose, 1987.

Middle Eastern Minorities and Diaspora, ed. by Moshe MA'OZ and Gabriel SHEFFER, Brighton and Portland: Sussex Academic Press, 2002.

3. Christian Minorities in the Muslim World

The Christian Heritage in the Holy Land, ed. by Anthony O'MAHONY, Göran GUNNER, and Kevork HINTLIAN, London: Scorpion Cavendish, 1995.

COURBAGE, Youssef, and Philippe FARGUES, *Chrétiens et juifs dans l'islam arabe et turc*, Paris: Fayard, 1992; English ed.: *Christians and Jews under Islam*, London and New York: I. B. Tauris, 1997.

HAJJAR, Joseph, *Le christianisme en Orient: Etudes d'histoire contemporaine, 1684–1968*, Beirut: Librairie du Liban, 1971.

HASSAN BIN TALAL, El, *Christianity in the Arab World*, Amman: Royal Institute for Inter-Faith Studies, 1994.

HARTMANN, Klaus-Peter, *Untersuchungen zur Sozialgeographie christlicher Minderheiten im Vorderen Orient*, Wiesbaden: Reichert, 1980.

HEYBERGER, Bernard, *Les chrétiens du Proche-Orient au Temps de la Réforme catholique*, Rome: Ecole Française de Rome, 1994.

Histoire des chrétiens d'Afrique du Nord: Libye, Tunisie, Algérie, Maroc, ed. by Henri TEISSIER, Paris: Desclée, 1991.

MASTERS, Bruce, *Christians and Jews in the Ottoman Arab World: The Roots of Sectarianism* (Cambridge Studies in Islamic Civilization), Cambridge: Cambridge University Press, 2001.

Religious Minorities in Pakistan: Struggle for Identity. The Presentations of the National Seminar held at the Christian Study Centre, Rawalpindi, Pakistan, July 18–20, 1996, ed. by Dominic MOGHAL and Jennifer JIVAN (CSC Publication Nr. 33), Rawalpindi: Christian Study Centre, 1996.

SEMAAN, Wanis A., *Aliens at Home: A Socio-Religious Analysis of the Protestant Church in Lebanon and its Backgrounds*, Beirut: Librairie du Liban, 1986.

VALOGNES, Jean-Pierre (ps.), *Vie et mort des chrétiens d'Orient: Des origines à nos jours*, Paris: Fayard, 1994.

YOH, John Gay, *Christianity in the Sudan: Overview and Bibliography*, Amman: Royal Institute for Inter-Faith Studies, 1996.

4. Muslim Minorities in the Western World

BALIĆ, Smail, *Das unbekannte Bosnien: Europas Brücke zur islamischen Welt*, Cologne and Weimar: Böhlau, 1992.

BASSIRI, Kambiz Ghanea, *Competing Visions of Islam in the United States: A Study of Los Angeles*, Westport, Conn.: Greenwood Press, 1997.

Être musulman en France: Associations, militants et mosquées, ed. by Jocelyne Cesari, Paris: Karthala, and Aix-en-Provence: IREMAM, 1994.

Graf, Peter, and Peter Antes, *Strukturen des Dialogs mit Muslimen in Europa* (Europäische Bildung im Dialog 6), Frankfurt on Main, etc.: Peter Lang, 1998.

The Integration of Islam and Hinduism in Western Europe, by Wasif A. R. Shadid and Pieter S. van Koningsveld, Kampen: Kok Pharos, 1991.

L'Islam et les musulmans dans le monde. Vol. 1: *L'Europe Occidentale*, ed. by Mohammed Arkoun, Rémy Leveau and Bassem al-Jisr, Beirut: Centre culturel Hariri, 1993.

Islams d'Europe: Intégration ou insertion communautaire?, ed. by Robert Bistolfi and François Zabbal, La Tour d'Augues: Ed. de l'Aube, 1995.

Journal of the Institute of Muslim Minority Affairs (JIMMA). Published twice a year, Djeddah and London, since 1979.

Kepel, Gilles, *Les banlieues de l'islam: Naissance d'une religion en France*, Paris: Ed. du Seuil, 1987.

Kettani, M. Ali, *Muslim Minorities in the World Today*, London and New York: Mansell, 1986.

Kim, Young-Kyung, *Die Identitätsfrage der Muslime in der Diaspora*, Hildesheim and Zurich: Georg Olms, 1994.

Lebor, Adam, *A Heart Turned East: Among the Muslims of Europe and America*, New York: St. Martin's Press, 1998.

Lewis, Philip, *Islamic Britain: Religion, Politics and Identity among British Muslims*, London and New York: I. B. Tauris, 1994.

McCloud, Aminah Beverly, *African American Islam*, New York and London: Routledge, 1995.

Muslim Minorities in the West, ed. by Syed Z. Abedin and Ziauddin Sardar, London: Grey Seal, 1995.

The Muslims of Bosnia-Herzegovina: Their Historic Development from the Middle Ages to the Dissolution of Yugoslavia, ed. by Mark Pinson, Cambridge, Mass.: Harvard University Press, 1993.

The New Islamic Presence in Western Europe, ed. by Tomas Gerholm and Yngve Georg Lithman, London and New York: Mansell, 1988.

Nielsen, Jörgen S., *Muslims in Western Europe*, Edinburgh: Edinburgh University Press, 1992, 1995[2].

Ramadan, Tariq, *Les musulmans dans la laïcité: Responsabilités et droits des musulmans dans les sociétés occidentales*, Lyon: Tawhid, 1994.

—, *Les musulmans d'Occident et l'avenir de l'Islam*, Paris: Sindbad/Actes Sud, 2003.

Sellam, Sadek, *L'islam et les musulmans en France: Perceptions, craintes et réalités*, Paris: Tougui, 1987.

Section 6

Muslims and Others in Processes of Change

Chapter 18
Muslims and Christians: Changing Identities

I would like to start by stressing three empirical points about human identity. The first one is that people are always in processes of change and that changes affect the way one identifies oneself. These changes are due to organic processes including aging, to human including family relations, to changes in living including working conditions, and to unexpected experiences including catastrophes of various kinds. They have also to do with broader changes, for instance in the environment due to urbanization, or in society due to industrialization and technological development. People change on a psychological, a mental, and a spiritual level.

The second point is that the ways people identify themselves as Christians or as Muslims have varied. This is due not only to different versions of the two religions and different interpretations given by individuals and communities. They have also changed in the course of history of the same communities and in the course of individual lives. This is given with the human condition.

The third point follows from the two preceding ones. Whatever the deepest roots of human identity may be, empirically speaking, this identity is not a fixed thing but part of a movement of life. People themselves tend of course to fix once and for all how a Christian or a Muslim should be, and they will resist "losing identity", as they will call it. In situations of conflict or oppression, such a "stiffening" of identity is understandable. Its result, however, will be that normal interaction with others, called "outsiders", decreases even if there is need for it.

Dialogues between Christians and Muslims

These observations have a relevance for present-day efforts toward Christian-Muslim dialogue. There may have been times in which ready-made Christians met ready-made Muslims in dialogue. At present, however, and not only in the West, the terms "Christian" and "Muslim" cover a broad spectrum of meanings. Christian and Muslim identities have become more personalized, so that people can call themselves Christians and Muslims in many ways. And to the extent that identities on both sides are in change, relations between them are naturally changing, too.

I submit that relations have come about between a great number of Christians and Muslims and that they are different from those in, say, colonial times. Furthermore, there is no reason to assume that there will be no further changes in these relations in times to come, for better or for worse. The fact that Christians and Muslims meet each other more in ordinary life situations will bring about further changes and an increasing variety of relationships, unless we want to become fundamentalists on both sides. Needless to stress that change does not imply lack of continuity. On the Muslim side, both in majority and minority situations, much care is given to maintain the continuity of the Muslim identity, even when personal interpretations of being a Muslim change. On the other side, the Churches are putting much effort into maintaining and strengthening the Christian identity of their members, precisely in a world that apparently is less Christian than in past decades.

In the context of changing identities and changing Christian-Muslim relations, the chances for dialogue would be enhanced if one could have a better perception or idea of what someone else who happens to identify himself or herself as a Christian or a Muslim in fact means by that. One may of course ask that person what his or her religion means to him or her. Still, the question remains how to "read" the other person's identity even when he or she is willing to talk freely about it. How should one interpret such expressions, facts, meanings, dreams, and aspirations? The rule of attentive listening may be simple, but it is already difficult to apply it to people of one's own society. It is especially difficult with regard to people who have religious, ethnic, social, and cultural identities that are and perhaps want to be clearly different from one's own. Misunderstandings seem to be the rule here.

But there are other problems in the study of identity and dialogue too.

Construction of Identities

The views that Christians and Muslims tend to hold of themselves and of each other have a long history. After the first communities had gathered around Jesus and Muhammad during their lifetimes, they retained certain practices and statements about life and the world, the human being and God. They established certain rules and doctrines for communal life that were sanctioned and handed on to later generations. They fixed the texts of their Scriptures. Both religions were constructed in distinction to existing ones. Once the identity of the adherents had been shaped, non-adherents were identified as different from the new community's point of view. From the beginnings of Islam, Muslims defined what Christians are as distinct from Muslims; Christians identified later what Muslims are and how they are different from Christians. The normative views that Muslims and Christians held about the others and their identity strengthened the normative views they had of their own unique identity. Seen in this light, the history of Muslim-Christian relations contains a recognition, but also a mutual construction of not only one's own but also the other's identities. These views of identity have been handed down through tradition and have found acceptance in the respective communities until the present day. I submit that in current Christian-Muslim dialogues, the views that Christians and Muslims hold of themselves and each other are, at least in part, "constructions" of identity: of oneself as different from the other and of the other as different from oneself.

Besides these religious views, more general social views developed of what Christians and Muslims are. They correspond neither with the precise factual reality of these people nor with the way in which Christians and Muslims identify themselves. In part, such social views date back from a past with its particular traditions, authorities, and ideologies that were carried on through time. In part they are simply stereotypes or the product of imagination.

Developments in Christian-Muslim Dialogue

Initiatives to dialogue between Christians and Muslims were taken in the mid-twentieth century, on the assumption that those participating in it possessed firm Christian or Muslim identities and were open-minded to others. It seems to me that the situation nowadays has altered for those people who identify themselves now in less firm and fixed ways than was the case in the 1950s.

Perhaps more than in the beginnings, in present-day situations of encounter, personal identities tend to play an important role. Christians have to speak as people who are personally responsible not only for the way in which they interpret and live Christianity but also for the views they have of Muslims and Islam. And Muslims are expected to speak nowadays as persons held responsible both for the way in which they interpret and apply Islam and for the views they have of Christians and Christianity. As I see it, at least in the West, people from the two sides have to meet primarily as persons, rather than as representatives of their religion or community. And persons are per definition in a constant process of acquiring and further shaping their identity.

After a first phase of reconciliation and opening up for encounter and of a certain institutionalization of more or less official and formal dialogues between Christians and Muslims, a further personalization of encounters and dialogue is needed. And in times to come, more attention has to be given to common causes to which particular groups of Christians and Muslims commit themselves.

Complexity of Christian-Muslim Dialogue

Awareness has grown of the complexities of dialogue. One should not hold overly simple views of Christian-Muslim dialogue, lofty as the ideal may be for people of good will.

In regard to identity, current discourses about and views of Muslim-Christian dialogues are unsatisfactory. They not only make generalizations that stand in the way of perceiving specific individuals, their needs, and their expressions. They also tend to view Christians and Muslims as more or less fixed entities without change, instead of accepting the realities of change and development proper to human life. There is always a risk of subsuming encounters between particular individuals and groups in specific situations and contexts under useless or dangerous generalizations and fixations.

In regard to context, one should be aware that, in situations of pressure, Islam and Christianity both tend to assume rigid forms and fundamentalist versions that are not conducive to dialogue. One particular identity is imposed with a discipline that does not allow for compromise, leading for instance to particular puritan or fundamentalist versions of these religions, often combined with rigid political ideas and practices. In such situations, persons who are keen on personal integrity may tend to defend such views and practices to the bitter end. In their religious zeal or through uncritical obedience, they may take an aggressive attitude toward whomever they perceive as their fundamental enemies. In fact, the very perception of others is at stake here.

Perceptions of Others

There are several questions about mutual perceptions of Christians and Muslims and the extent to which they are aware of each other. A first question is how Muslims and Christians are at all identifiable in social life and recognizable in Muslim-Christian encounters and dialogues. Are they seen as such if they do not proclaim themselves as such? A second question is that of the perception of religious meanings. When and how did the terms "Muslim" and "Christian", applied to people, have a specifically religious meaning? When and how is there a specifically religious dimension or identity perceived in current discourses about Muslims and Christians? A third question is that of the personal character of Christians and Muslims. When dealing with Muslim-Christian dialogues, how do we know what kind of Muslim or what kind of Christian a particular person is, beyond what others say or report about him or her, with whatever intentions they may have?

Last but not least, there is a fourth question, about the role of situations in the mutual perceptions of Muslims and Christians. In certain situations there is a striking neglect of what may be called the religious commitment and the personal identity of "the others". In conflict situations, they are simply enemies; in minority situations, they are simply exceptions, in migrant situations, they are simply foreigners. And in ordinary social life, notably in the Middle East but elsewhere as well, people are largely defined in accordance with the social entities or communities to which they belong. It is interesting to pay attention to the situations in which certain people manifest themselves as "personal believers". This may be the case, for instance, when they know how to deal with a crisis precisely on the basis of their religious commitment and personalized identity.

Different Sorts of Christian-Muslim Dialogue

Organized dialogues between Christians and Muslims can be of different sorts.

One alternative is between a kind of negotiation between representative leaders of various communities and what may be called an encounter between Christians and Muslims dealing with each other as persons.

Another alternative is between what may be called "socially religious" Christians and Muslims, for whom their religious identity is not in tension with their social identity, and what may be called "personally religious" Christians and Muslims able to take a personal religious stand that is different from their social identity and may imply protest and even rebellion.

A third alternative is between dialogue among more or less ready-made, straightforward, and conscious Christians and Muslims and what may be called searching people. In the first case, we are dealing with an exchange of convictions between persons who tend to define themselves in terms of contrast and who try to convince each other. In the case of what may be called searching people, there is a particular form of dialogue to find one's way or to find a solution for a problem.

Human Identities

In this connection, it is appropriate to put Christian and Muslim identities in the broader context of human identity in general. Human identities arise and grow in interaction with other human beings. Of special importance hereby are the common concerns held by the participants and the recourse to sources conveying meanings. This appears to be especially true for what are considered to be fundamental attitudes to life, including religious views and practices.

In contrast to empirical differences between human identities, one may ascertain the growth of a more fundamental communicative level among human beings, where what may be called the roots are laid bare. Here reigns a fundamental openness to questions basic to human life and that can be and are shared with others. Such a basic openness is opposed to the more or less forced construction of one's own or a group's own, private and more or less closed universes. This is particularly relevant for any communication between Muslims and Christians, where the construction of such universes has been customary.

The interaction between convinced people adhering to different established worldviews poses its own problems.

The "Golden Rule" for Christians and Muslims

What seems to be new at the present time, especially in the West but not only here, is that, more than in former times, the conditions of life oblige individuals, and certainly younger people, to make an effort to acquire, construct, and live their own personal identities. This is particularly intensified by the increasing need for people to settle in large urban conglomerations, which tends to bring about a crisis in traditional social structures. More than before, individuals have become responsible for their own thoughts and doings. This implies rejecting possible false identities and distancing oneself from what may be called non-identities. It also entails conscious interaction with other persons who have their particular other identities. Identities become more personalized and may be called self-identifications by the people themselves. People who do not succeed in developing their personal identity freely and who are not able to take a personal stand are liable, in critical situations, to surrender more or less blindly to a given authority, tradition, or ideology that imposes itself, sacrificing in this way their own identity. The occurrence of encounters, cooperation, and dialogue between Christians and Muslims, possibly at a younger age, involves additional change and development in the self-identification of the persons concerned.

The "Golden Rule" of Christian and Muslim identity follows from the foregoing. On the one hand, changes of identity of Muslims and Christians will bring about changes in their interpretation of their religion. On the other hand, changes in the interpretation of one's religion imply changes of identity and occur in given contexts and situations. And last, if there is no change in the interpretation that a Christian or Muslim gives of his or her religion, nothing can be said about his or her personal concern with religion. If a person, Christian or Muslim, experiences a vocation in his or her religion, changes his or her religion for another religion, or abandons religion altogether, this implies changes of identity. Such changes should be seen both in relation to the person's process of development and in connection with specific situations and contexts.

Where societies are in processes of rapid change, the identities of the people concerned are affected and, voluntarily or not, they will undergo changes too. Certain social situations encourage people to accept a mobility of identity. In other cases, individuals develop a conscious desire to escape from the closure and the fixed identity that certain religious communities impose on their members through tradition or discipline.

The place and role of religion in human identity is a matter of concern in religious communities. At present, in particular in the West, people tend to participate in several identities that are horizontally juxtaposed without a clear hierarchical order. Here, religious identity is one identity alongside others. Yet, for some persons there is what may be called a "religious level": for them, their religion will underly their other identities. In certain cases, this may help a person integrate his or her various identities and strengthen the unity of his or her personality. In particular in situations in which the identity of people is put to the test, as in migrant or minority situations, religion may play an important role in reaffirming and integrating identity on a communal level.

The Concept of Human Identity

Although we can take human identifications and specific identities as an object of scholarly empirical study, human identity itself is not a "thing" like other things. In the experience of actual life, human identity presents itself rather as a project, something potential to be realized. It gives an orientation that the person or group concerned has to express and further develop on their own.

Seen in this light, religions like Christianity and Islam function as open potentialities that give distinct orientations to life. Persons and groups can develop them and even choose to realize a more "religious" life. Christians will draw on the sources offered by their Christian religion and acquire their Christian identity, Muslims will draw on the sources offered by their Islamic religion and acquire their Muslim identity. How are both identities related?

A handicap in treating this question adequately is that, for a long time, Christianity and Islam have been seen not only as different from each other, but also as in opposition to each other and in fact as two antagonistic religions. In the course of history, Western institutions tended to identify Muslims negatively: as enemies (by the Church in the Crusades and later), as adversaries (by colonizing states), as people to be converted (by missionary societies), or as people of lower cultures (by spokesmen of Western civilization).

For a long time, the identity of Christians has been considered to be squarely opposed to that of Muslims, and vice versa. For the ideal-typical

Muslim and Christian with either a straight Muslim or a straight Christian vocation, this could not but be true. At the time, religions were seen as more or less ready-made systems to which people adhered or to which they submitted. Until the mid-twentieth century, moreover, direct contacts between Muslims and Christians on an equal level were difficult, certainly as far as religion was concerned.

Since that time, however, such contacts have been realized. Yet in public life, much still needs to be done. We need a code of respect for the identity of Muslim migrants and minorities in the West. Public manifestations of anti-Islamic sentiment should be treated on a par with public manifestations of anti-Semitism.

Revision of the Concept of Christian and Muslim Identity

At present, contacts between Muslims and Christians have become easier, and the identity of Christians and Muslims can be seen now more as a personal and communal existential orientation than as a subservience to a given system. At a time when modern and modernizing societies simply force people to construct their identities themselves, persons have to make their own efforts. Identity has become an existential project indicating what persons or groups want to be or to become, rather than what they are at a given moment. They may want to be, for instance, Christian or Muslim. The religions offer the resources for it.

In this view, tradition, authority, and ideology are only pedagogical instruments. Beyond a certain point, people have the freedom to learn, acquire knowledge, and find their own way. They can then communicate, cooperate, and engage in dialogue with whoever crosses their path. Persons can make now their own choices, at least in the West.

If we accept that human identity is basically open, the relevant question is how so much rigidification of identity has been possible. History is full of it. I would look for an explanation in the rigidification of a given system, either because power was exerted on it or because it wanted to exert power itself. Islam, for instance, has been much involved in struggles for power, but religious groups of believers have always tended to reject a political use of Islam, holding that Islam should be religious.

In contexts of pressure, religions, too, can become rigidified systems imposing a particular tradition, authority, and ideology as a kind of pseudo-absolute. When religions are deformed, they become rigidified; they then tend to rigidify human identities in turn. At worst, they stand in the way of people acquiring a personal identity. At best, people acquire their identity through them. No tradition is absolute and no authority infallible; no religion is inflexible and no identity without change.

Selected Literature

BASSET, Jean-Claude, *Le dialogue interreligieux: Chance ou déchéance de la foi*, Paris: Cerf, 1996.

CRAGG, Kenneth, *The Privilege of Man: A Theme in Judaism, Islam and Christianity*, London: Athlone Press, 1968.

ELSAS, Christoph, *Identität: Veränderungen kultureller Eigenarten im Zusammenleben von Türken und Deutschen*, Hamburg: Rissen, 1983.

KIM, Young-Kyung, *Die Identitätsfrage der Muslime in der Diaspora*, Hildesheim and Zurich: Georg Olms, 1994.

SACKS, Jonathan, *The Dignity of Difference: How to Avoid the Clash of Civilizations*, London and New York: Continuum, 2002.

WAARDENBURG, Jacques, "L'Islam et l'articulation d'identités musulmanes", *Social Compass*, 41, Nr. 1 (1994), pp. 21–33.

—, "Migrants and Minorities: Religion as a Factor in Identity", in Driss DADSI, *Specificities and Universality: Problems of Identities. Report of the Seminar held in Klingenthal (France), June 23–25, 1994*, Strasbourg: Council of Europe Press, 1995, pp. 47–56.

—, *Islam et Occident face à face: Regards de l'histoire des religions*, Geneva: Labor et Fides, 1998.

—, "Muslims and Christians: Changing Identities", *Islam and Christian-Muslim Relations*, 11, Nr. 2 (July 2000), pp. 149–62.

Chapter 19

Muslims and Westerners: Changing Attitudes

I would like to conclude this book with a final note on present-day Muslim orientations and attitudes toward the West and Westerners. Most of us, including politicians and journalists are used to thinking of events in terms of short-term causes and effects. I plead for thinking in a long-term perspective. It is not only the immediate effects of present-day decisions but especially their consequences in the long run that are important in the relations between groups of people. From this perspective, what counts is fundamental orientations and attitudes toward others and the level on which they are articulated.

This brief note draws attention to three different ways in which Muslims have dealt with the West in recent times: through a clarification of their own minds on an intellectual level, through an ideological struggle against what hurts them in the West, and through attempts at a cultural rapprochement in the broader sense of the word. In the following pages, some examples will be given. Although the political context has in a way provoked these responses, I want to see them as orientations that have a particular relevance for intercultural communication. In their turn, they may lead to some fresh reflection about long-term problems that occur when people of different backgrounds—and their political leaders—have to live together.

1. Intellectual Debate on the West

For a number of reflecting Muslim intellectuals, especially in countries that have had longer ties with the West, the latter has become an intellectual problem. How is the West defined? How did the West become what it is now, in its European and North American varieties? What have been the forces at work in Western civilization, strengthening or weakening it? Are the individualism, a certain social disintegration, and a certain secularization that are visible in the present-day West, a particular case, or are they part of general processes that occur in all modernizing human societies?

But the relationship between Islam and the West has also become an intellectual problem. How are these two terms defined? Are these two constructs really each other's antipodes? Is there a framework within which the Western and the Muslim worlds can interact positively? What could be the practical value of the Muslim model of Christianity and Islam as two "revealed religions" at the heart of two civilizations?

Each Muslim country has had its own historical relations with the West. Given this history and current needs and interests as well as plans for the future, such countries will take different attitudes to the West. This is all the more so if they mean by "the" West in fact the American, British, French or another Western variety. Here I concentrate on debates among Iranian intellectuals.[1]

Since the overthrow of Mosaddeq and his democratization program in 1953, and even earlier than that, Iranian intellectuals were opposed to a regime they perceived as selling out the country to foreign interests. For them, "the West" stood not only for the geographical area of Western Europe and North America, but also for a much despised barbarian way of life. What were the foundations of what was called "Western civilization"? For its philosophically-minded Iranian critics, Western civilization was constructed on a set of ontological doctrines that directly opposed the metaphysical postulates of Iran's own cultural and religious tradition, which was identified to a large extent with Islam. This self-awareness that a particular Iranian cultural elite had of its cultural roots contributed to the intellectual reaction against Western influences.

Paradigmatic is the case of the book *Gharbzadegī* ("Westoxication") by the Iranian author Jalāl Āl-e Ahmad (1923–69), published in 1962. The impact of the West on Iranian culture is described and analyzed here as an illness, a kind of disease whose symptoms should be analyzed to arrive at a treatment. Not only the Shīʿī clergy, but also secular-oriented intellectuals felt that resistance was needed against the West's overriding impact on Iran. Although democracy and scholarship in the West were approved and respected, the weakness of morality and ethical values was castigated. The blatant hypocrisy of the West's words versus the West's dealings with Muslim countries in general and Iran in particular was severely attacked.

Most Iranian intellectuals at the time felt that one should appropriate the good aspects of Western civilization but not everything Western.

---

[1] I refer here especially to Mahrzad Boroudjerdi, *Iranian Intellectuals and the West: The Tormented Triumph of Nativism*, Syracuse and New York: Syracuse University Press, 1996.

    See also Gottfried Herrmann, "Die Karawane der Wissenschaft und des Fortschritts: Zur Auseinandersetzung iranischer Intellektueller mit der Europäisierung ihres Landes unter der Schah-Herrschaft", in *Asien blickt auf Europa: Begegnungen und Irritationen*, ed. by Tilman Nagel (Beiruter Texte und Studien 39), Beirut and Stuttgart: Franz Steiner, 1990, pp. 89–117.

Iranians in particular, they felt, should have recourse to their own resources, including the Persian language, "Eastern" philosophy based on
metaphysics and ontology, and of course the norms and values of the
Iranian cultural tradition. To resist the intellectual and spiritual seduction
of the West, they wanted Iranian intellectuals to be aware of their responsibility in society and to study the ontological presuppositions of Western
thought and the very foundations of Western civilization, to be able to
resist this particular enemy. Āl-e Ahmad gave a particular turn to the
discussion by taking the stand that the intellectuals should cooperate with
the Shī'ī clergy if the latter abandoned its conservative stance.

Āl-e Ahmad called for a more socially-minded and activist Islam. He
developed an instrumentalist view of Shī'ism as a political ideology that
could mobilize the people.

Among the lay religious intellectuals of the 1970s, 'Alī Sharī'atī (1933–
77) was most prominent. For him, Orient and Occident differed in what
he called their cultural archetypes. Whereas the first is intent on realizing
a truth that gives meaning and direction to reality, the Occident is keen
to know reality as it is empirically.

Sharī'atī was devoted to the cause of a reformed Islam, socially and
politically conscious and ideologically elaborated, which he saw as a
parallel to the Protestant Reformation. Such a reformed Islam was to be
promoted by committed Muslim intellectuals, rather than by the tradition-bound Shī'ī clergy. Such Muslim intellectuals, however, had to distinguish themselves both from their European counterparts and from those
Third World intellectuals who were assimilated to and sided with the
West. Muslim intellectuals should return to the "self": that is, to their
Islamic roots, which is a quest for authenticity.

Several scholars held that a conscious analysis of Western civilization
could lead to a better self-awareness of the East. They were in favor of
"occidentalism" (gharbshenasi), the critical study of the West.[2] Noteworthy among these scholars were the philosopher Abolhasan Jalili, the social
scientist Ehsan Naraghi in his Ghorbat-e Gharb ("The Alienation of the
West", 1974), and the political scientist Hamid Enayat (1932–82).

The Iranian "Orientalist" Daryush Shayegan, who studied Sanskrit
and Indian religions as well as Arabic, Turkish, and several Western
languages, takes a special place. His book Āsiyā dar barābar-e Gharb

---

[2]   BOROUDJERDI draws attention to "… the extent to which a systematic critique of the West
      was viewed by Iranian intellectuals as a prerequisite to their own process of identity
      formation" (Iranian Intellectuals and the West [see above note 1], p. 133). Boroudjerdi
      adds that twentieth-century Iranian intellectuals took Western civilization as their
      culture of reference in the process of identity formation and that this led to a certain
      dichotomization between the West and Iranian Islam. We may see here one of the roots
      of the construct "Islam" versus "the West".

("Asia facing the West", 1977) and other writings contrast the spirituality of Asian civilizations and ontological philosophies against the secular nature of science and philosophy as these developed in the West. He formulated a severe criticism of technical thought, which he saw as leading to nihilism. In his *Cultural Schizophrenia: Islamic Societies Confronting the West* (English translation of 1992), he analyzes the "schizophrenia" of intellectuals from the East who have been further educated in the West. They participate in two civilizations at the same time and are living dangerously, like tightrope walkers. Daryush Shayegan, who studied both Eastern and Western religious thought, may be considered one of the most eminent Iranian scholars of religions and equally eminent among critical as well as self-critical intellectuals in Iran of the late twentieth century.

In the 1980s an important controversy arose in Iran between Reza Davari-Ardakani (penname Davari) and Hoseyn Faraj-Dabagh (penname Abdolkarim Sorush).

Davari maintained that the West should be seen as the absolute other against which an Islamic identity must be constructed. The West is a totality, a unified whole, a kind of "essence". On the one hand, it is characterized by modernity that has also been imported into and also imposed upon Muslim countries. On the other hand, it rests on an individualistic humanism that considers the human being the center of the universe, disregarding God. This West abandoned metaphysical philosophy and subordinated philosophy to a narrow rationalism that took "method" and "science" as its guides, with a strong leaning toward materialism and ignoring religion. In this way, the West developed technology as a way of thinking that subjugates the world to humankind. In fact, however, the humankind thus imprisons itself and the world. The result of this development is an alienation, solitude, and solipsism of the human being in the West. This implies that Western civilization is coming to an end. In this view, there is no remedy available to the West except a radical detachment from humanism and a total submission to God. Davari contends that non-Western societies like Iran are not facing individual Westerners, but a unified West. He therefore maintains that Iranian intellectuals should not be concerned with individual Western thinkers, but with the destiny of the West itself.

Sorush entered into debate with Davari on several points. He contended that philosophy is a cosmopolitan and even a universal enterprise. Constructing the West as one unified and totalizing entity and then pressing people to accept or to reject the West as such simply excludes dialogue and intellectual exchange. Moreover, the West does not constitute one unified whole with well-defined cultural and intellectual boundaries. Non-Western societies do not face "the West", but always individual

Westerners. The issue is not whether one submits to the West or denounces it, but how one can analyze it and nourish oneself by it. One can
very well adopt certain parts of Western thought, politics, or technology
without necessarily incurring evil consequences.

In contrast to Davari, Sorush believes in cultural exchange and in
promoting thought, including thinking about religion. Iranian civilization
has several historical roots, including pre-Islamic Persian culture and
Islamic culture as well as the Western heritage. As a consequence, Sorush
says Iranians should become more tolerant of these roots. Last but not
least, the Iranian intelligentsia should address their own problems, instead
of constantly blaming the West for what it has done.

2. Ideological Struggle against the West

Here I try to sketch the basic structure of a broader Islamist ideology of
Islam that has developed especially in the Middle East since the 1970s and
that has found acceptance among Muslim activists. I shall not examine the
many varieties, but try to identify a basic common structure. The West is
perceived here as a power with many aspects, as an intruding force
coming from elsewhere that has an impact on people. In the end it
represents a danger, in particular for Muslims and the Muslim way of life.
What is needed is an ideological defense against the West—and Islam
plays a role in this resistance.

In any analysis of the ideological role of Islam, we should distinguish two
levels, depending on the way Islam is articulated and used.

On a *first level*, the concept of Islam is not so intensely articulated.
Muslim people are mobilized primarily by appealing to their being Muslims, that is to say on a human level, in accordance with their Muslim
identity. They are warned against the dangers coming from the West.
They are told they should unite and defend themselves as Muslims and
citizens, in order not to be trampled under foot by forces from the West.
The struggle is primarily a matter of self-defense. It has a social and moral
character, but it may extend further to imply the use of economic resources and if necessary and possible military action. Such a collective
self-defense of Muslims was already the program of al-Afghānī some 125
years ago and of the Pan-Islamic movement at the beginning of the
twentieth century.

On a *second level*, the concept of Islam is emphasized much more. It
is elaborated, absolutized, and contrasted to the West. Here we have
ideology in the proper sense, for political purposes but with a religious
aura. It is a mobilization of Muslims by means of ideologizing Islam
against the West. Here I would like to distinguish three stages in such an
ideological mobilization.

First, Islam is stressed as the Muslims' true alternative to the West, which constitutes a danger from outside. Comparisons are made between practices and experiences in Western societies and the norms and values that are valid in Muslim societies. The foreign and aggressive West is demonized and Islam is presented as the known good order of society and for the world at large.

Second, Islam is hailed as being the absolute good. It contains all the norms, values, and rules needed by humankind to live properly. Compared with Islam, all other social systems, ideologies and religions are considered defective, a number of them being squarely false. Muslims are exhorted to live according to this absolute Islam.

Third, Islam *can* be held to imply and demand a struggle of Muslims against the West and its collaborators representing a kind of modern *jāhilīya*. This struggle is to be carried out in the name of Islam. As a result of this struggle for Islam, Islam itself tends to be ever more absolutized, possibly to the point of becoming an object of idolatry. It should be noted that similar unconscious processes can also take place in other religions and with other religious institutions.

One may wonder how Islam can be made such a tool—and an efficient one—in Muslim resistance to a certain West and in an ideological struggle against such a West, possibly ending in violence and war. Two questions arise. Is Islam intrinsically a warlike religion? Is Islam an inhuman religion?

I do not want to make an apology for such a use of Islam, but I must make a small theoretical digression.

In contrast to thoroughly organized and systematized religions, like Roman Catholicism for instance, Islam bases itself on particular verses from the Qur'ān and texts from *hadīths*. Depending on one's selection and interpretation of these verses and texts, one can read Islam in various ways. Completely different groups—varying from puritanical Tālibān to mystical Sūfis—can appeal to Islam and adduce texts supporting their particular point of view or practice. And since texts on the conduct of war can be found in Qur'ān and *Sunna*, fighters can present Islam in wartime as supporting the Muslim side. This does not happen because Islam impels certain warlike groups to undertake *jihād*. It is rather a natural response of people to aggression or oppression imposed from outside. Muslims certainly do not have a different human nature than others. They defend themselves, too, and like other believers they can mobilize religion for an overall defense—if needed, for a total war. This with regard to the first question.

In connection with the second issue, the question can also be reversed. One can hear or read in circles that are critical of the West that the West has somehow taken on an inhuman character: not only for the people living in the West itself, who can be working and living like slaves, but also in the way the West treats people elsewhere, outside the West. They say the West can somehow have a dehumanizing influence. One reason that Muslims nowadays give for this is the secularization of the West, which they see as bringing about a weakening and even loss of religion and morality. Another reason given is that Western society is dominated by political and economic conflict and struggle and by forces beyond the control of individual human beings. Western society is seen as a jungle ruled by the survival of the fittest. Consequently, the West is aggressive toward the outside world, and the only adequate response of the non-Western world is: self-defense against the West.

Muslim societies and states may have little reason to trust the economic and political forces coming from the West. In case of concrete tensions and conflicts between certain Western forces and certain defenses by Muslims, a researcher should look attentively at both sides. And when judging, he or she should be an apologist neither of the West nor of Islam.

3. Orientations toward Communication

There are also orientations other than intellectual disputes and ideological struggles. One can find searches for communication, not only of a spiritual or "idealistic" kind, but also a realistic one based on human necessity.

Four varieties of such communication between Muslims and others can be distinguished.

First of all, there is a constant need for *knowledge* and thus a search for it to survive. From the nineteenth century on, if not earlier, Muslim elites have regarded the West as superior to the Muslim world, largely because of its science and technology. Continuous efforts have been made in Muslim countries to learn from the West, to spread education, and to carry out research. This thirst for knowledge would allow Muslim societies to develop toward a viable future. Increasing numbers of Muslim students have been studying at Western universities. The desire to discover the "secrets" of the success of Western civilization and the reasons for its power led to taking the West as an object of study, in particular such "positive" aspects as the Reformation and Enlightenment. The search for education and knowledge, in itself, is communicative. Moreover, it can contribute to a higher level of communication between minds through the exercise of independent thought and judgment.

Second, serious efforts have been made toward *dialogue* with Westerners, largely after the colonial period. At the beginning, the initiatives came from Westerners, after a period of largely Western monologue. In the following decades, much attention has been paid, for example, to Muslim-Christian and Euro-Arab forms of dialogue. In this context, however, the very phenomenon of "dialogue" itself is important, since it implies a new kind of orientation toward the West. Not without caution, a number of Muslim responses to Western dialogue openings were positive. Such interest in dialogue allowed Muslims to speak out, to deliver a message to the West, and to be heard by a West that became more "listening". It also opened an opportunity to enter into debate with the West instead of being submissive. It allows for negotiations and deliberation whenever the West tends to assume a hegemonic role.

Third, *other parties* than Muslims and Westerners appeared on the scene and mobility increased. There were other Europeans who did not come from the former colonizing countries. There were Americans, too. There also came people from Asia, Africa, and Latin America. Moreover, the number of situations of encounter increased tremendously. Muslim migration to Europe, North America, and elsewhere enabled Muslims to leave their own societies and to live in other ones. An impressive number of Muslims learned to associate with others through the school of international life. On both sides, Muslims and others could overcome the boundaries of their own societies and cultures.

Fourth, communication increased through new *common struggles and commitments* of Muslims and others in view of particular social, economic and political causes, including what may be called ethical causes, like human rights, including those of women, liberation, justice, and peace. Muslims and others are moved by a common sense of personal responsibility in a world that presents problems to human dignity and life.

These four varieties of communication are still a bleak scheme when measured against the immense variety of real interactions that can take place between Muslims and Westerners or "others" in general. Such interactions, when successfully started in concrete contexts and situations, can have a snowball effect and even bypass intellectual or ideological discourses.

4. Is there a Dualism between the West and Islam?

I have often wondered why so many theories have been developed in the West that claim and explain an antagonism existing between Islam and the West. If Muslims formulated such an antagonism, it would be understandable. After all, most of their societies have stood under Western pressure. So Muslim countries and Islamic movements had to defend themselves and it is logical that they would develop an antagonism against the dominating West. But why should the West have posited from time to time a kind of dualism of the West and Islam, as if no other civilizations were at stake?

My guess is that serious Western interests have been and are at stake in this construction of an Islamic-Western dualism. The current view that Islam is so different from the West is rather arbitrary and reveals both a rather simple ethnocentric point of view and an unreflected sense of superiority. According to what norms should Islam be declared inferior?

All of this reinforces my suspicion that in the construction of an Islam-West opposition, a political element is involved. In colonial times, such a construct tended to legitimate Western domination of Muslim territories. Governments claimed that there was a need to control Islam, since it was a potential danger for the European empires that extended over Muslim territories at the time. The formula of an Islam-West antagonism suggested a common interest of the West in controlling the Muslim part of the world to prevent infractions against the then-established colonial world order. Politically, the formula imposed a dualism, as if, in Islamic matters, there were no third way. A Westerner's loyalty should be either to the West or to Islam. Such a dualistic formula was typical for the colonial period, with its dominating Western party and its dominated Muslim party. The West had to legitimate its dominating role. At that time, there were hardly any Muslims living in the West itself.

At present, a good century later, the terms "Islam" and "the West" have not become much clearer than they were in the colonial period. They lack precision and, despite suggestions to this effect, they do not at all represent what may be called united fronts. The contemporary West displays considerable differences. If there is a certain common front against "international terrorism", hardly defined, there is certainly no common front against Islam, as there was in public opinion a hundred years ago. Moreover, several million Western citizens happen to be Muslims nowadays.

Islam, too, does not represent one tangible reality. It exhibits differences that are highly significant. There may be a few Islamic states now, as well as Islamist movements. But militant Islamists waging war à la al-Qā'ida constitute a minute extremist faction outside the more than one billion ordinary Muslims. Moreover, different Muslim countries have different institutional and other forms of Islam: not only very different Muslim groupings and movements, but also quite different forms of "official" Islam. Most Muslim countries in fact do their utmost to suppress Islamist tendencies, which threaten the regimes that are in place.

5. Conclusion

Notwithstanding its lack of clarity and the dualism it suggests, the formula "Islam and the West" or "the West and Islam" is again enjoying a boom. Like a century ago, there is much ignorance and there are again certain ideological interests at play. As in former times, the formula does not suggest that Islam is a lofty spiritual reality or a religious faith in contrast to a materialist West, but that it is a base earthly power constituting a potential threat to the civilized West.

Once given formulas like "the clash of civilizations" and "war on international terrorism", the broader Muslim public can sense behind these terms a militancy that may very well end in a fundamental conflict in which they will be the real victims. Such terms, like "Islam versus the West" may strengthen their Muslim solidarity and resolution, but they may have other consequences as well, for the West itself.

Speaking insistently about "Islamic" violence and terrorism as an imminent danger to the Western world at large has already resulted in strange forms of nervousness based on an anxiety one would not have thought possible before September 11, 2001. Such anxiety has a paralyzing effect on people's sense of reality and their critical rationality, as if there were no third way except being "for" or "against" a given policy. Political parties and governments, even in Western countries, may very well be tempted to exploit hidden anxieties of this kind to mobilize people for activities and actions that are in fact beyond moral and rational control. They only need to be presented as a fight against an invisible enemy proclaimed to be a threat. Ordinary people, Muslims and others living in Western and Muslim societies, would be and sometimes have been in fact victims of an atmosphere poisoned by distrust arising from anxieties and a lack of justice. This is an ethical problem.

In this book, I wanted to plead for impartial research on past and present Muslim perceptions of others, including Westerners. This can lead to a better understanding of relations between Muslims and others. In this short final note, I broadly distinguished three kinds of orientations that people can have toward others: intellectual, ideological, and communicative. I argued that these orientations appear in an analysis of Muslim attitudes toward the West.

It should be noted, however, that such attitudes do not emerge from a vacuum. When held by Muslims, especially in the heartlands of Islam but also elsewhere, they reflect certain pressures from the West. They show a need for intellectual clarity, for an elementary self-defense, and for fundamental communication. In this way, attitudes can be led to change for the better.[3]

---

[3]   In this connection, the work of the *Körber Stiftung* in Hamburg may be mentioned and suggested as an example. Since 1995 it has organized yearly symposia of German and Turkish intellectuals, the results of which have been published by the Foundation both in German and in Turkish. The following German-Turkish Symposia have been published until now:

1. *Kulturkontakte* (1995), published in 1996.
2. *Religion – ein deutsch-türkisches Tabu?* (1996), published in 1997.
3. *Was ist ein Deutscher? Was ist ein Türke?* (1997), published in 1998.
4. *Grenzfall Europa* (1998), published in 1999.
5. *Ehre und Würde* (1999), published in 2000.
6. *Perspektiven der Zivilgesellschaft* (2000), published in 2001.
7. *Chance Bildung* (2001), published in 2002.

Looking at the materials at hand and at the responses given to the West, I submit that we are not dealing with an entity called "Islam" that is aggressive and blind to others. We have a certain West that constitutes a danger for others. As a result, constructive relations between Westerners and others, including Muslims, are in danger, especially if the West wants to impose power. Just as in colonial days, but a little more acute nowadays.

Selected Literature

A Global Ethic: The Declaration of the Parliament of the World's Religions, ed. by Hans KÜNG and Karl-Josef KUSCHEL, New York: Continuum, 1993.

Human Rights Today: UN Briefing Papers, New York: United Nations, Department of Public Information, 1998.

Islamic Political Ethics: Civil Society, Pluralism, and Conflict, ed. by Sohail H. HASHMI (Ethikon Series in Comparative Ethics), Princeton and Oxford: Princeton University Press, 2002.

Muslims and the West: Encounter and Dialogue, ed. by Zafar Ishaq ANSARI and John L. ESPOSITO, Islamabad: Islamic Research Institute, International Islamic University, and Washington, D.C.: Center for Muslim-Christian Understanding, Georgetown University, 2001.

Bibliographical List

The following list refers to the "Selected Literature" sections given at the end of the chapters. The subjects listed correspond with those of the "Selected Literature" sections. The numbers refer to the pages where literature about specific subjects can be found. The "Selected Literature" is meant for those who want to read further on a given subject.

1. Index of Persons

2. Index of Subjects

3. Index of Concepts